Comprehensive Multicultural Education:

Theory and Practice

SEVENTH EDITION

Christine I. Bennett

Indiana University at Bloomington

PEARSON

Boston ■ Columbus ■ Indianapolis ■ New York ■ San Francisco ■ Upper Saddle River
Amsterdam ■ Cape Town ■ Dubai ■ London ■ Madrid ■ Milan ■ Munich ■ Paris ■ Montreal ■ Toronto
Delhi ■ Mexico City ■ Sao Paulo ■ Sydney ■ Hong Kong ■ Seoul ■ Singapore ■ Taipei ■ Tokyo

Acquisitions Editor: Kelly Villella Canton
Editorial Assistant: Annalea Manalili
Senior Marketing Manager: Darcy Betts Prybella
Marketing Assistant: Robin Holtsberry
Production Editor: Mary Beth Finch
Manufacturing Buyer: Megan Cochran
Cover Administrator: Elena Sidorova
Editorial Production Service: Modern Graphics, Inc.

Library of Congress Cataloging-in-Publication Data
Bennett, Christine I.
    Comprehensive multicultural education : theory and practice / Christine I. Bennett. — 7th ed.
      p. cm.
    Includes bibliographical references and index.
    ISBN-13: 978-0-13-704261-6
    ISBN-10: 0-13-704261-2
  1. Multicultural education—United States. 2. International education—United States. 3. Global method of teaching. I. Title.
    LC1099.3.B46 2010
    370.117—dc22
      2009045837

10 9 8 7 6 5 4 3 2 1 RRDVA 13 12 11 10

www.pearsonhighered.com

ISBN 10: 0-13-704261-2
ISBN 13: 978-0-13-704261-6

Contents

Part III. ***Individual Differences and Societal Inequities That Affect Teaching and Learning   209***

Preface

Today, more than ever before, we are in urgent need of national and global citizens who possess multicultural competence, and who are committed to the achievement of worldwide social justice and economic equity as a foundation for lasting peace on the planet. As we face horrific terrorism; warfare in Afghanistan, Iraq, and Pakistan; and the aftermath of natural disasters such as the Asian tsunami and hurricane Katrina; we can see conflicts and decisions that could have been enlightened by greater multicultural knowledge and competence. As we seek wise and compassionate decisions in the future, the ideals, knowledge base, and practices of multicultural education are essential. Classroom teachers as well as educators in college, community, and religious settings across the globe can make a difference in meeting this need. We can start small with the young children and youth in our own classrooms, making sure each one reaches his or her potential for academic achievement as well as fair minded thought, compassion, and concern for fellow humans everywhere. In addition to developing a strong sense of self, including ethnic, national, and religious or spiritual identities, our children and youth need to gain the ability to view people and events from multiple perspectives. To some readers this may sound overly optimistic or unrealistic, given the many demands teachers face every day. Indeed, since the 1960s, multicultural education scholars and advocates have been idealistic and hopeful for educational reform that can make a difference in our society and world. Current world events have only intensified these hopes and ideals.

New to this Edition

In response to extensive reviewer feedback and new research and information since writing the last edition, this Seventh Edition reflects the following changes and additions:

- **Expansion** of Part II, "Roots of Ethnic Diversity in the United States: The Conflicting Themes of Assimilation and Pluralism," **from two to four chapters,** and it has been updated and almost totally rewritten throughout.
- **New sections in Chapters 8 and 9** tie into contemporary immigration issues in schools (e.g., culture in teaching and learning, culturally competent teaching, and the needs of students and parents who are immigrants, including refugees).
- **New case study research by ethnogeographers** provides representative examples of the immigrant experiences in the heartland (e.g., Latinos and Asians) as well as on the West Coast (e.g., Ukrainians) and Southwest (e.g., Mexicans and Cubans).

- **Additions to the section on American Indians** includes "how the land was lost," conflicting federal policies regarding Indian rights, and self-determination efforts today, including the preservation of native languages and cultures.
- **Chapter 10, "Teaching and Learning in Linguistically Diverse Classrooms," replaces the previous Chapter 8** that had included only a small section on this topic.
- **Expansion of and greater emphasis on subjects** such as the "achievement gap," poverty, and the needs of LGBT youth in Chapter 9, and white privilege, difficulties with the U.S. Census racial categories of race, multiracial identities, and how race and culture are conceptually different in Chapter 2.
- **Substantial updates** to **Selected Sources for Further Study** for each chapter.
- **Revised supplementary materials and teaching tools,** including chapter objectives and end-of chapter components (i.e., compare & contrast pairs, follow-up questions and activities) are now conveniently located in the Instructor Manual, along with test items, transparencies, and sample teaching activities and syllabi.
- **MyEducationLab integration** provides reference to specific, relevant assignments on this brand new online resource developed for Multicultural Education courses. Set in the context of real classrooms and real stories, these assignments and learning units built around ABC News footage, case scenarios, and classroom video afford opportunities for reflection and practice in an easy to assign format.

Comprehensive Multicultural Education: Theory and Practice was first written for my students and others new to the field of multicultural education. My goal in the early 1980s was to create a framework that would help them make sense out of a complex, ambiguous, multidisciplinary field that asks teachers to take risks and deal with controversial topics such as prejudice, racism, social justice, and cultural pluralism. I wanted to provide some of the historical background, basic terminology, and social science concepts that many students have not yet encountered when they enter the field. I hoped to engage readers on an emotional level, move them to take action in their classrooms, and encourage them to pursue academic inquiry and self-reflection after the book had been read. While the book's basic philosophy and approach remain the same, changes in later editions have grown out of more than thirty years of conversations with my own students as well as other students and instructors who are engaged in multicultural teacher education. These conversations have provided a steady barometer of the book's strengths and limitations, and they indicate that the book stimulates thinking and dialogue about critical issues in multicultural education in ways that I had only hoped would be possible.

The book deals with questions students continually ask that too often are left hanging. Doesn't multicultural education lead to lower academic standards? Won't cultural pluralism lead to the Balkanization of our society? Aren't we really stereotyping when we talk about cultural differences? Isn't it racist? Are you saying I can't set up my own standards for acceptable behavior in my classroom? How can I add multicultural content when I don't have time to cover the basic curriculum? What does multicultural education have to do with math and science, or with physical education? Doesn't multicultural education really boil down to indoctrination?

My approach to multicultural education focuses on ethnic diversity and community in the United States, diversity rooted in racial, cultural, and individual differences; it also emphasizes basic human similarities and global connections. Given that we live in a multicultural world, multicultural education is for everyone. Few of our nation's schools, however, have become multicultural in their vision or practice. They are hampered by societal policies and practices, often beyond their control, that impede reform of formal and hidden curricula. Shortage of funds and lack of understanding, for example, make it difficult for schools to replace or supplement biased or outdated books and films, to hire new personnel who can provide positive role models from a variety of ethnic groups, or to study alternatives to discriminatory school practices in areas such as co-curricular activities or student discipline. Teachers and administrators who are uninformed about cultural diversity, whose knowledge of history and current events is mono-cultural in scope, and who are unaware of their own prejudices are likely to hinder the academic success and personal development of many students, however unintentional this may be. And curriculum standards usually provide little help in the development of content that includes diverse ethnic, gender, socioeconomic, or global perspectives. How we might meet challenges such as these through multicultural education is what *Comprehensive Multicultural Education* is about.

The book's approach is unique in several ways. First, its content is comprehensive and interdisciplinary in scope and practical in focus. Key concepts from education and the social sciences are often explained with primary source material, and the implications for teaching and learning are developed through vignettes of teachers and students I have known over the years. A primary goal is to assist practicing and prospective teachers to bridge the gap between multicultural concepts or theories and practices in our schools, such as classroom management, instructional strategies, and curriculum development.

Second, the book develops an interaction between cultural and individual differences. Teachers often fear that tuning into students' cultural differences is an indication of being prejudiced or racist. This fear is related to the misconception that equates color consciousness with racism. It also stems from feelings that differences are bad or inferior, and from the mistaken notion that recognition of differences means we must imitate or adopt these differences. Many cultural awareness and human relations workshops have failed because these basic concerns of the participants were not dealt with. On the other hand, most teachers do believe in differentiating or personalizing their instruction. Most would agree that our ultimate goal as teachers is to foster the intellectual, social, and personal development of all students to each one's fullest potential. This book shows that the ability to reach this goal can be strengthened by an understanding of cultural and individual differences, as well as societal contexts.

Our population has changed dramatically since the first edition of this text was written (nearly three decades ago) due to changes in immigration policies and the influx of newcomers from Asia, Latin America, and Africa. Immigration engenders ethnicity and today our school-age population is more diverse than ever before in terms of languages spoken at home, race, religion, and national origin. Over 20 percent of our school-age population is either an immigrant or the child of immigrants, and more and more of these newcomers are moving into the heartland of America. Therefore, a major aspect of this revision is to provide readers with an accessible overview of contemporary immigration, how it impacts our schools and society, and how teachers can be successful in linguistically and ethno/racially diverse classrooms.

Part II, "Roots of Ethnic Diversity in the United States: The Conflicting Themes of Assimilation and Pluralism," has been expanded from two to four chapters. The content has been is updated and almost totally rewritten. It also introduces a new theme—"Immigration and the American Dream" and a new analytic framework, the classic (1880–1924) and contemporary (post-1965) immigration eras. Differences within the Asian and Latino pan-ethnic groups are examined in terms of socioeconomic status, educational attainment, and assimilation issues associated with people from different nations of origin (e.g., Filipinos, Chinese, South Asian Indians, Koreans, Japanese, Vietnamese, and Hmong among Asian Americans and Latinos from the Caribbean and Mexico). Chapters 4 through 7 develop classic and contemporary immigration perspectives in light of immigration and the American dream among European and Jewish Americans (Chapter 4); involuntary immigration and the American dream among American Indians and African Americans (Chapter 5); immigration and the American dream among Latinos (Chapter 6); and contemporary immigration and the American dream among Asian, Muslim, and Arab Americans (Chapter 7). New case study research by ethnogeographers provides representative examples of immigrant experiences in the heartland (e.g., Latinos and Asians) as well as on the West Coast (e.g., Ukrainians) and in the Southwest (e.g., Mexicans and Cubans). The updated section on American Indians adds themes of "how the land was lost," conflicting federal policies regarding Indian rights, and current self-determination efforts, including the preservation of native languages and cultures.

Part III has also been revised extensively. Chapter 8, "Learning Styles and Culturally Competent Teaching," and Chapter 9, "Reaching All Learners: Perspectives on Gender, Class, and Special Needs" have new sections that tie into contemporary immigration issues in schools (e.g., culture in teaching and learning and the needs of students and parents who are immigrants, including refugees). Chapter 10, "Teaching and Learning in Linguistically Diverse Classrooms," written by James Damico, replaced a chapter from the previous edition that had included only a small section on this topic. (Content from the previous edition on differentiated instruction and multiple intelligence theory has been included in the supplements for this edition.) Professor Damico develops examples from African American Vernacular English (AAVE), Spanish, and indigenous languages in his discussion of theory, research, and teaching.

This edition also has expanded content on the "achievement gap," poverty, and the needs of LGBT youth. It also examines difficulties with the U.S. Census racial categories, multiracial identities, and how race and culture are conceptually different in Chapter 2. White privilege and antiracist teaching are examined in Chapter 3.

The book's conceptual framework (see Figure 1.1) integrates four dimensions that are developed throughout the chapters: (1) equity pedagogy (a focus on *classroom instruction* and an end to the achievement gap); (2) curriculum reform (focus on *content* inquiry and transformation guided by four core values: acceptance and appreciation of cultural diversity, respect for human dignity and universal human rights, respect for the earth, and responsibility to a world community); (3) multicultural competence (focus on the *individual*'s ethnic identity development and reduction of all forms of prejudice and discrimination), and (4) social justice (a focus on *society*; becoming agents of change, however small the steps; and the eventual eradication of racism and other forms of oppression locally, nationally and globally). Overall, the approach is critical multicultural education focused on social justice in schools and society.

The seventh edition also maintains the book's four-part structural organization that gives readers and instructors flexibility as to the order in which chapters are read or assigned in various course syllabi. Some instructors prefer to start with Chapter 9 (the achievement gap, demographics, etc.), some with Chapter 11 (multicultural curriculum decision making and sample lessons), and some with Chapter 2 (culture and the contexts of multicultural teaching), whereas many others use the book's structure as the basic outline for their course. However, this revision makes a major change by moving all chapter-end instructional tools (i.e., compare and contrast, questions, and follow-up activities) to the Instructor Manual (IM). Selected Sources for Further Study are updated from previous editions and remain at the end of each chapter; all chapter endnotes are moved to the end of the text.

"Teacher educators who are developing pedagogies for the analysis of teaching and learning contend that analyzing teaching artifacts has three advantages: it enables new teachers time for reflection while still using the real materials of practice; it provides new teachers with experience thinking about and approaching the complexity of the classroom; and in some cases, it can help new teachers and teacher educators develop a shared understanding and common language about teaching. . . . "[1]

As Linda Darling-Hammond and her colleagues point out, grounding teacher education in real classrooms—among real teachers and students and among actual examples of students' and teachers' work—is an important, and perhaps even an essential, part of training teachers for the complexities of teaching in today's classrooms. For this reason, we have created a valuable, time-saving website—MyEducationLab—that provides you with the context of real classrooms and artifacts that research on teacher education tells us is so important. The authentic in-class video footage, interactive skill-building exercises and other resources available on MyEducationLab offer you a uniquely valuable teacher education tool.

MyEducationLab is easy to use and integrate into both your assignments and your courses. Wherever you see the MyEducationLab logo in the margins or elsewhere in the text, follow the simple instructions to access the videos, strategies,

---

[1]Darling-Hammond, l., & Bransford, J., Eds. (2005). *Preparing Teachers for a Changing World.* San Francisco: John Wiley & Sons

cases, and artifacts associated with these assignments, activities, and learning units on MyEducationLab. MyEducationLab is organized topically to enhance the coverage of the core concepts discussed in the chapters of your book. For each topic on the course you will find most or all of the following resources:

Connection to National Standards

Now it is easier than ever to see how your coursework is connected to national standards. In each topic of MyEducationLab you will find intended learning outcomes connected to the appropriate national standards for your course. All of the Assignments and Activities and all of the Building Teaching Skills and Dispositions in MyEducationLab are mapped to the appropriate national standards and learning outcomes as well.

Assignments and Activities

Designed to save instructors preparation time, these assignable exercises show concepts in action (through video, cases, or student and teacher artifacts) and then offer thought-provoking questions that probe your understanding of theses concepts or strategies. (Feedback for these assignments is available to the instructor.)

Building Teaching Skills and Dispositions

These learning units help you practice and strengthen skills that are essential to quality teaching. First you are presented with the core skill or concept and then given an opportunity to practice your understanding of this concept multiple times by watching video footage (or interacting with other media) and then critically analyzing the strategy or skill presented.

General Resources on Your MyEducationLab Course

The *Resources* section on your MyEducationLab course is designed to help you pass your licensure exam, put together an effective portfolio and lesson plan, prepare for and navigate the first year of your teaching career, and understand key educational standards, policies, and laws. This section includes:

- **Licensure Exams:** Access guidelines for passing the Praxis exam. The *Practice Test Exam* includes practice questions, *Case Histories*, and *Video Case Studies*.
- **Portfolio Builder and Lesson Plan Builder:** Create, update, and share portfolios and lesson plans.
- **Preparing a Portfolio:** Access guidelines for creating a high-quality teaching portfolio that will allow you to practice effective lesson planning.
- **Licensure and Standards:** Link to state licensure standards and national standards.
- **Beginning Your Career:** Educate yourself—access tips, advice, and valuable information on how to write impressive résumés and prepare for job interviews;

setting up your first classroom, managing student behavior, and learning to more easily organize for instruction and assessment; Law and Public Policies, including specific directives and requirements you need to understand under the No Child Left Behind Act and the Individuals with Disabilities Education Improvement Act of 2004.

Visit www.myeducationlab.com for a demonstration of this exciting new online teaching resource.

Supplements for the Instructor

The following ancillary materials have been developed to support instructors using this text. These instructor supplements are located on the Instructor Resource Center (IRC) at www.pearsonhighered.com. Please contact your Pearson representative if you need assistance downloading them from the IRC.

Instructor's Resource Manual and Test Bank

An expanded Instructor Manual/Test Bank includes (1) chapter objectives; (2) compare and contrast items, with one fully developed "example answer" for students who need extra guidance; (3) chapter questions for thought and discussion; (4) chapter follow-up activities; and (5) chapter short-answer test items and (6) selected film discussions.

PowerPoint™ Presentations

Ideal for lecture presentations or student handouts, the PowerPoint™ Presentation for each chapter include key concept summaries.

Acknowledgments

For this seventh edition, I am especially grateful to James Damico, a colleague in the Department of Literacy, Culture, and Language Education at Indiana University, who authored the new chapter, "Teaching and Learning in Linguistically Diverse Classrooms" (Chapter 10) and developed the Chapter 10 supplements. I am also deeply grateful to the former students and colleagues who over the years have contributed to the lesson plans in Chapter 11 and to George McDermott for his continued assistance in interpretation of the NAEP results. I also want to thank Kelly Canton Villella for her extraordinary guidance and support during this revision process, as well as Annalea Manalili for her prompt and professional assistance. The reviewers for this edition were also especially helpful, even though they sometimes provided very different recommendations! Warm thanks to the reviewers Henry M. Codjoe, Dalton State College; Rick Gay, Davidson College; Richard Orem, Northern Illinois University; Ann Krell Petersen, Buena Vista University, and Anita Jones Thomas; Loyola College Chicago. Special thanks to Jennifer Coker, my copyeditor, for her outstanding attention to detail, and Marty Tenney at Modern Graphics, for her calm and competent management. As ever, my deepest appreciation goes to David Blair, my soul mate and fellow educator who provides love, energy, and boundless support. Over the two years of this revision process Dave was a great listener, critic, and technology assistant whose patience never flagged during the tedious process of researching statistical data and producing the instructor manual and Power Point presentations. This book is dedicated to our grandsons, Max and Ty, and the children of their generation, with the hope that worldwide justice and peace will become a reality in the twenty-first century.

Part I
The Case for Multicultural Education

Chapter 1

Multicultural Schools: What, Why, and How

Envision a society where *all* the nation's schoolchildren are provided the educational opportunities and support needed to reach their fullest potential; a society where all teachers are caring and culturally competent advocates for students from all ethnic, linguistic, socioeconomic, family, and personal backgrounds; a society where teachers are fully supported in material and nonmaterial ways as they engage in this important work for the nation. Envision, also, an interconnected world where local, national, and global societies are working toward equity, environmental sustainability, wise innovation, economic security, and affirmation of the common good on a global scale.

Can we ever attain this vision? Whatever the answer, it is imperative that we try; the alternative is too grim to imagine. Because teachers play a crucial role in this vision, their work can be extraordinarily rewarding. However, classroom teaching in the twenty-first century is demanding and difficult work, especially given the intense national climate of educational standards, high-stakes testing, growing racial and cultural diversity within the school-age population, inadequate resources in many schools, and the ever-increasing expectations for schools to address special needs and community concerns. While recognizing the challenges teachers face, this book takes a hopeful approach that teachers *can* make a difference. It provides a foundation for multicultural teaching in any school context, a foundation developed from theory, research, and practice in multicultural education that spans nearly four decades. Advocates of multicultural education believe teachers can make a difference—locally, nationally, and globally—by preparing future world citizens who understand that without social justice there cannot be lasting peace.

 ## What Is Multicultural Education?[1]

Multicultural education is a complex approach to teaching and learning that includes the movement toward equity in schools and classrooms, the transformation of the curriculum, the process of becoming multiculturally competent, and the commitment to address societal injustices. Multicultural education originated in the United States as a hopeful and idealistic response to the civil rights movement of the 1950s and 1960s; its primary purpose was reformation of the nation's schools. The *Brown vs. Board of Education of Topeka* decision in 1954 reversed the legality of "separate but equal schools" and triggered rising expectations and aspirations for equal opportunity and social justice, especially in public education. Instead, disproportionately high numbers of the nation's African American, American Indian, and Latino children and youth were placed in "special" education for the handicapped or "culturally disadvantaged." Others were suspended or expelled for reasons of "teacher discretion," or attended schools where teachers and the curriculum reflected primarily Anglo-European American perspectives. In reaction, the multicultural education movement emerged quickly and passionately, drawing upon a long history of multidisciplinary inquiry, artistic and literary achievement, social action, and scholarly writing. By the early 1970s, the movement had embraced a set of core values and ideals that stand in contrast to the old "culturally disadvantaged" and assimilationist Anglo-Eurocentric perspectives that pervaded the nation's school systems. It rests upon four broad principles: (1) the theory of cultural pluralism; (2) the ideals of social justice, which would bring an end to racism, sexism, and other forms of oppression; (3) affirmations of culture in the teaching and learning process; and, (4) visions of educational equity and excellence leading to high levels of academic learning and personal development for all children and youth.

In particular, the ideal of cultural pluralism is a foundational principle of multicultural education in the United States. Developed early in the twentieth century by democratic philosopher Horace Kallen at the time of the "great deluge" of immigrants from Europe, the concept of cultural pluralism affirms the democratic right of each ethnic group to retain its own heritage as the newcomers become acculturated and are integrated into society.[2] It envisions a society based upon core values of equity and social justice; respect for human dignity and universal human rights; and the freedom to maintain one's language and culture, provided the human dignity and rights of others are not violated. It stands as a compromise between cultural assimilation on the one hand, whereby ethnic minority groups are expected to give up their language and culture to blend into mainstream Anglo-European culture, and segregation or suppression of ethnic minorities on the other hand.[3] Although ethnic minorities may be expected to compromise in some areas in order to maintain societal harmony and national identity, implicit are the assumptions that every child's home culture must be affirmed and respected and opportunities must be provided for *all* children to reach their fullest potential. Although cultural pluralism was not widely accepted during Kallen's lifetime and most immigrants from past eras did assimilate, as we shall see in Part II of this book, it was revived in the 1960s and 1970s, and today this ideal is widely accepted.

A second foundational principle of multicultural education is antiracism and the elimination of structural inequities related to identity groups beyond ethnic groups, such as race, class, and gender. In particular, the redress of *racial* inequities in a society built upon and maintained by White privilege is a primary focus of multicultural education, especially societal structures rooted in deep-seated structural injustices and systematic patterns of dominance and suppression that denied people of color economic and political equality. The end of institutional and cultural racism is at the heart of multicultural education, even when conceptions of diversity are expanded to include gender, class, disabilities, and sexual preference.

A third foundational principle is the importance of culture in teaching and learning. The concept of culture has been described as anthropology's "seminal contribution" and a "welcome palliative to existing notions of inherited, and therefore immutable, racial differences."[4] *Culture* refers to a people's shared knowledge, beliefs, social values, worldviews, and preferred standards of behaving, as well as the material products they create. In a culturally diverse society such as the United States, it is not possible to "individualize" or personalize instruction, an idea most teachers embrace, without considering culture.

Finally, the need for academic excellence and equity is also a foundational principle of multicultural education. *Equity* in education means equal opportunities for all students to reach their fullest potential. It must not be confused with *equality* or sameness of result or even identical experiences. Student potentials may be diverse, and at times equity requires different treatment according to relevant differences, such as instruction in a language the child can understand. Achieving educational excellence requires an impartial, just education system where all students are perceived to be capable of learning at high levels and are provided opportunities to be academically successful.

These principles of cultural pluralism—eradication of racism and other forms of oppression, the importance of culture in teaching and learning, and high equitable expectations for student learning—provide the basic premises and philosophy that underlie the conceptual framework proposed in Figure 1.1. The framework depicts four interactive dimensions of multicultural teaching that are developed throughout this book.

Dimension One: Equity Pedagogy

Equity pedagogy envisions teachers who create positive classroom climates, use culturally responsive teaching to foster student achievement, and consider cultural styles and culturally based child socialization, as well as the conditions of poverty or wealth, in their approach to teaching and learning. Equity pedagogy aims at achieving fair and equal educational opportunities for all of the nation's children and youth, particularly ethnic minorities and the economically disadvantaged. It attempts to transform the total school environment, especially the hidden curriculum expressed in teacher expectations for student learning, as well as the grouping of students and instructional strategies, school disciplinary policies and practices, school and community relations, and classroom climates. Greater equity would help reverse the problems many ethnic minorities and low-income students face in our schools and ensure that they attain the highest standards of academic excellence.

Millions of children enter our schools each year with little or no proficiency in the English language. The story of Jesús Martinez, a highly intelligent Puerto Rican child, is echoed in the school experiences of many language minority children in schools across the country. His case shows the need for equity pedagogy.

Dimension Two: Curriculum Reform

Curriculum reform envisions teachers who conduct inquiry to rethink and transform the traditional curriculum, which (in the United States) is primarily

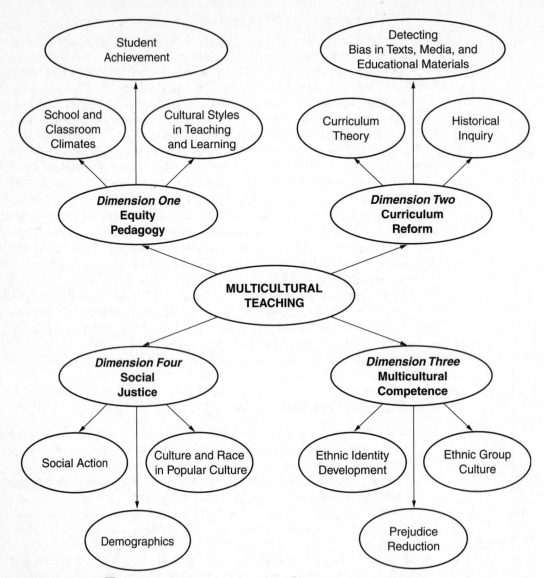

Figure 1.1 ▒ A Conceptual Framework of Multicultural Teaching

Source: Adapted from C. I. Bennett (2001). "Genres of Research in Multicultural Education," *Review of Education Research,* 72(2), 171–217.

Anglo-European in scope. Curriculum reform expands traditional course content through inclusion of multiethnic and global perspectives. For most of us, this revision requires active inquiry and the development of new knowledge and understanding about cultural differences and the history and contributions of contemporary ethnic groups and nations, as well as of various civilizations in the past. This aspect of multicultural education focuses on both minority and nonminority

The Example of Jesús Martinez

Jesús Martinez was a bright, fine-looking six-year-old when he migrated with his family from Puerto Rico to New York City. At a time when he was ready to learn to read and write his mother tongue, Jesús was instead suddenly thrust into an English-only classroom where the only tool he possessed for oral communication (the Spanish language) was completely useless to him. Jesús and his teacher could not communicate with each other because each spoke a different language, and neither spoke the language of the other. Jesús felt stupid, or retarded; his teacher perceived him to be culturally disadvantaged and beyond her help. However, she and the school officials agreed to allow him to "sit there" because the law required that he be in school.

For the next two years Jesús "vegetated" in classes he did not understand—praying that the teacher would not call on him. She rarely did and seldom collected his papers, since she felt Jesús was not capable of what "more fortunate" children could do. Jesús' self-concept began to deteriorate.

Another Puerto Rican boy in the classroom who spoke English was asked to teach Jesús English and help him in the process of adjustment. They were not permitted, however, to speak Spanish to each other because the teacher believed it would "confuse Jesús and prolong the period of transition" into English; also, it annoyed other people who could not understand what they were saying. The other boy, then, could not translate academic subject matter for Jesús. Jesús was expected to "break the code," to learn English before learning his other subjects. By the time he began to understand English, he was so far behind in all his coursework that it was impossible to catch up. He was labeled "handicapped" by his teachers and taunted by his schoolmates. In fact, each time he would attempt to use his English, some of the other children would ridicule him for his imperfect grasp of the language. The teacher thought the teasing was all right because it would force Jesús to check his mistakes and provide him an incentive to learn proper English. School had become a battlefield for Jesús, and he began to find excuses to skip his classes. The situation became unbearable when, as a result of a test administered in English, Jesús was found to be academically retarded and was put in a class for the mentally retarded.

When Jesús finally dropped out of school, he had not learned English well. Today, although he is fluent in Spanish, he has never learned how to read and write his mother tongue. He is functionally illiterate in both languages.

Source: Based on F. Cordasco and D. Castellanos, "Teaching the Puerto Rican Experience." In J. A. Banks (Ed.), *Teaching Ethnic Studies: Concepts and Strategies* (pp. 227–228). Washington, DC: National Council for Social Studies.

students, in contrast to equity pedagogy, which targets primarily ethnic minorities and the poor. The importance of curriculum reform is evident in the classroom of Sam Johnson, a middle school science teacher.

The case of Johnson's science class illustrates the importance of a multicultural curriculum for students in mainstream schools and classrooms, in this case White, middle-income students from a small town that is ethnically encapsulated. Students

The Example of Sam Johnson's General Science Class

Sam Johnson, general science teacher in Oak Grove Middle School, leaned back in his chair and sighed. The student reports had been a disaster. It's true that technically they were terrific. The students had dutifully done extensive research, and the classroom was decorated with the results of their labor: an elaborate bulletin board on world hunger; large poster displays on nuclear weapons; the expense of toxic waste control, American technological superiority, and biological differences among races; a pictorial essay of famous scientists; an audiovisual show of how the U.S. government disposes of nuclear wastes; and another bulletin board on the AIDS epidemic throughout the world.

What bothered Johnson were the subtle (and not so subtle) expressions of attitudes, values, and beliefs that permeated the student reports. It was clear that the students felt culturally, and even biologically, superior to people from other nations, especially those from the Third World, the "undeveloped countries," as Stacey had referred to them, or the "primitive people," according to John. Sam Johnson had been chilled by Steve's remark that AIDS had originated among African Negroes, showing "a weakness among these people that makes it dangerous for us to associate with them." Margaret and Mark were concerned that nuclear wastes are indeed damaging to human health, as evident by the high rate of leukemia, sterility, and birth defects found in people who drink water from rivers that flow near the deposit sites; they were relieved that these deposits are located on barren lands where few people, mainly Indians, live. One of the bulletin board panels on world hunger explained how the infant death rate climbed in "undeveloped countries" after the United States sent huge supplies of canned formula, because the sanitary conditions were inadequate to keep the baby bottles clean. One would also conclude from this display that all the world's starving people are dark skinned and have naked children; there was no indication that millions of North

from monocultural backgrounds must learn about multiple perspectives and worldviews in order to live harmoniously in a multicultural world. Whether a school's student population is multi-ethnic or mono-ethnic, it is essential that students become knowledgeable about increasing global interdependence and the worldviews associated with different nations, as well as attaining an awareness of the state of the planet.[5] In Chapter 11, we will revisit Sam Johnson's classroom and witness the transformation in his students' presentations as a result of the changes Sam made in his curriculum.

Dimension Three: Multicultural Competence

Multicultural competence envisions teachers who are comfortable with and can interact well with students, families, and other teachers who are racially and culturally different from themselves. The process of becoming multicultural is one whereby a person develops competencies in multiple ways of perceiving, evaluating, believing, and doing.[6] The focus is on understanding and learning to negotiate cultural diversity among nations as well as within a single nation and a single classroom. In their book *Communicating with Strangers*, for example, Gudykunst and Kim describe the multicultural person as

American children suffer from malnutrition and poverty. Rachael's research on famous scientists showed the "superiority of modern Western Civilization"; all of her selections were White and male (with the exception of Madame Curie), and there was no recognition of the scientific developments in earlier civilizations across the globe.

Johnson was appalled, and actually a bit scared, by Steve and Peter's brilliant but uncompassionate report on nuclear weapons. The boys had glowed over the fact that "today nuclear weapons are over one million times more destructive than the bombs that were dropped on Hiroshima and Nagasaki," and they went on with statistics about the nuclear weapons various nations have stockpiled. Without questioning, they accepted the assumptions that these stockpiles are necessary to prevent a future nuclear holocaust.

What happened to these kids? Sam wondered. How had he failed them? Could anything be done? As he thought back over the school year, he remembered the students' reactions when the Japanese plant for Honda parts was set up in the county. The students reflected their parents' outrage and concern that this was unfair competition for the General Motors factory that provided a major source of employment for the townspeople. Sammy Nakamura, Johnson's only non-White student and one of a handful of Japanese Americans in a town that is over 99 percent White, was beaten on the way home from school, and his family received hate mail and taunts of "Japs go home." Then there was the time Vicki Miller was struck by a car and killed. Joshua had remarked, "That's one less mouth for the government to feed. That whole family has been on welfare for years."

Sam had let these occasions (and others) slip by without any class discussion. So much had to be covered in the eighth-grade curriculum, but he wondered, isn't there a way to do both? Couldn't he teach science in a way that would lessen his students' ethnocentrism and prejudices and deepen their awareness of human similarities and the increasing global interdependence?

. . . one who has achieved an advanced level in the process of becoming intercultural and whose cognitive, affective, and behavioral characteristics are not limited but are open to growth beyond the psychological parameters of any one culture. . . . The intercultural person possesses an intellectual and emotional commitment to the fundamental unity of all humans and, at the same time, accepts and appreciates the differences that lie between people of different cultures.[7]

According to the authors, *intercultural people*:

- Have encountered experiences that challenge their own cultural assumptions (e.g., culture shock or "dynamic disequilibrium") and that provide insight into how their view of the world has been shaped by their culture
- Can serve as facilitators and catalysts for contacts between cultures
- Come to terms with the roots of their own ethnocentrism and achieve an objectivity in viewing other cultures
- Develop a Third World perspective that "enables them to interpret and evaluate intercultural encounters more accurately and thus to act as a communication link between two cultures"[8]

■ Show cultural empathy and "imaginatively participate in the other's world-view."[9]

This process of developing multicultural competence is a major goal of multicultural education. It enables students to retain their own cultural identity while functioning in a different cultural milieu; for example, the school. Furthermore, this dimension avoids divisive dichotomies between native and mainstream culture, and brings about an increased awareness of multiculturalism as "the normal human experience."[10]

Dimension Four: Social Justice

Social justice envisions teachers who are concerned about (and encourage student inquiry about) inequitable social structures; images of race, culture, class, and gender in popular culture; and social action to bring about greater societal equity, both locally and globally. Teaching toward social justice affirms the commitment to combat racism, sexism, and classism (as well as other *isms* that degrade an individual's basic human rights and dignity) through the development of appropriate understanding, attitudes, and social action skills. This essential ingredient of multicultural education addresses the fact that when people acquire knowledge and appreciation of cultural diversity, they will not necessarily be moved to help put an end to prejudice and discrimination or to solve basic problems of inequity.

The social justice dimension might begin with clearing up myths and stereotypes associated with race, culture, and gender, as well as other identity groups. It also brings out basic human similarities, as well as the historical roots and current evidence of individual, institutional, and cultural racism, sexism, and classism in the United States and elsewhere in the world. The ultimate goal is to develop an anti-oppression orientation and antiracist, antisexist, anticlassist behavior in basic everyday life.

The Core Values in Multicultural Education

Multicultural education has ideological overtones based on democratic ideals that are lacking in less controversial content areas of the curriculum, such as mathematics, reading, or spelling. Arguments may take place over what methods are most appropriate in these other areas, but there is little disagreement about what knowledge is true. In multicultural education, however, where there are no hard and fast rules about truth, there is disagreement about not only what the curriculum entails, but also whether it should exist at all.

Four core values provide a philosophical framework for the multicultural curriculum model described briefly at the end of this chapter and developed more fully in Chapter 11: (1) acceptance and appreciation of cultural diversity, (2) respect for human dignity and universal human rights, (3) responsibility to the world community, and (4) respect for the earth.[11] These core values are ideals that are yet to become a reality, or even widely accepted, as seen in controversies over environmental issues, national and global inequities between the rich and the poor, terrorism, the death penalty and criminal justice system, and public support for children living in poverty. They are rooted in democratic theory and American Indian philosophy; together they illustrate the strong ethical foundations of multicultural education.

Although democratic principles are set forth in such documents as the Declaration of Independence, the Bill of Rights, and the U.S. Constitution, democracy in the United States falls short of democracy as an ideal. Still, the ideal provides an inspiration for change and reform, as was evident in the civil-rights movement of the 1960s, when nonviolent civil disobedience was a tactic used to change unjust discriminatory laws and practices. As a form of government, a way of life, and a goal or ideal, democracy is based on principles of justice and the recognition of the equality and dignity of all persons regardless of race, religion, gender, or lifestyle. It is also based on procedural justice that assures all citizens equal protection under the law and establishes the principle of majority rule with minority rights. Democratic society protects basic liberties such as freedom of speech, conscience, expression, and association, provided that the human dignity and liberty of others are not violated. A democratic society fosters a "free marketplace of ideas" and depends on an informed, participatory citizenry. Thus it is opposed to indoctrination and censorship and encourages dissent, a free press, free elections, and diverse political parties. Democratic societies attempt to provide equal educational opportunities to help all citizens develop their full potential.

The fourth value, respect for the earth, originates in the belief that "all things in the universe are interdependent." This philosophy develops an understanding of "the balances that exist in all natural systems, or ecology. . . . All beings are related and therefore human beings must be constantly aware of how our actions will affect other beings, whether these are plants, animals, people, or streams."[12] It requires a caring and compassionate populace, an ethical community where people do not seek the best for themselves and their families at the expense of others.

The possibility that these core values might someday become widely acceptable is evident in the Universal Declaration of Human Rights that was adopted by the United Nations General Assembly in 1948 and reaffirmed in 1993 at the International Human Rights Conference in Vienna. The declaration, which is designed to serve "as a common standard of achievement for all peoples and all nations," states that all persons are born free and equal in dignity and expresses basic civil, economic, political, and social rights of all humans.

These values are brought to life in the following Human Manifesto, a document prepared by the Planetary Citizens Registry in Ottawa, Canada:

Human life on our planet is in jeopardy.
It is in jeopardy from war that could pulverize the human habitat. It is in jeopardy from preparations for war that destroy or diminish the prospects of decent existence.
It is in jeopardy because of the denial of human rights.
It is in jeopardy because the air is being fouled and the waters and soil are being poisoned.

If these dangers are to be removed and if human development is to be assured, we the peoples of this planet must accept obligations to each other and to the generations of human beings to come.

We have the obligation to free our world of war by creating an enduring basis for world-wide peace.

We have the obligation to safeguard the delicate balance of the natural environment and to develop the world's resources for the human good.

We have the obligation to make human rights the primary concern of society.

We have the obligation to create a world order in which man neither has to kill or be killed.

In order to carry out these obligations, we the people of this world assert our primary allegiance to each other in the family of man. We declare our individual citizenship in the world community and our support for a United Nations capable of governing our planet in the common human interest.

Life in the universe is unimaginably rare. It must be protected, respected, cherished.

We pledge our energies and resources of spirit to the preservation of the human habitat and to the infinite possibilities of human betterment in our time.[13]

The core values enable teachers to clarify basic goals about teaching and learning that is multicultural. This clarification is essential in protecting, improving, and building the case for multicultural education, and points the way to needed changes should currently held goals be found inappropriate in the future. The core values can also enable teachers to deal more effectively with controversial issues that are an integral part of multicultural education, such as violations of human rights and destruction of the environment.

Why Is Multicultural Education Essential?

The Need for Academic Excellence and Equity

Demand for the reform of schooling in the United States was a persistent theme throughout the twentieth century and it continues today. The educational reform movement gained momentum in the mid-1980s, beginning with the Reagan administration report "A Nation at Risk." Nearly a dozen additional major reports on U.S. schools appeared in 1983 alone. In January 2002, the No Child Left Behind Act (NCLB) of 2001 was passed with overwhelming bipartisan support. The goal of this legislation was to close the academic achievement gap between White middle-class students and low-income students, as well as students of color and English language learners. On one level, NCLB is consistent with principles of multicultural education in its emphasis on academic success for *all* schoolchildren and the elimination of racial, linguistic, and socioeconomic disparities. But the narrow emphasis on high-stakes standardized tests, a shrinking of the curriculum to line up with the tests rather than curriculum reform and transformation, inconsistencies in how states and school corporations define "success," inadequate funding, and inequitable school resources, especially in urban areas and high-poverty regions have made it impossible to reach the NCLB's goal.

The common thread throughout all these reports and initiatives is the demand for a national commitment to true excellence in education. What these reports and initiatives do not acknowledge, however, is that educational excellence in our schools cannot be achieved without educational equity. Equity in education means equal opportunities for all students to develop to their fullest potential. Equity in education must not be confused with equality or sameness of result or even identical experiences. The potential of students may differ, and at times equity requires different treatment according to relevant differences. For example, the example of Jesús Martinez on page 7 shows how the exclusive use of English in the classroom provided equal treatment without equity. The common language of instruction was unfair for Jesús, because he could not understand English as well as his classmates and was at a disadvantage because all the subjects, including mathematics, science, and social studies, were taught only in English.

Additional evidence of inequity in education exists in the nation's high school dropout rates, which are disproportionately high among African American, American Indian, and Hispanic youth and the poor. In many schools across the nation, racial and language minority students are overrepresented in special education and experience disproportionately high rates of suspension and expulsion. The majority of African American and Latino students attend schools that have large concentrations of economically disadvantaged and/or lower-achieving students. The latter may be attributed to outdated texts, poor facilities, and underprepared teachers.[14] These are schools where teachers often de-emphasize higher-order thinking skills because of the misconception that low-achieving students must master the basic skills before they can develop higher-level skills.[15] Other studies suggest that there is differential treatment and lower teacher expectations of racial and language minority students, compared with their nonminority peers.[16] If these trends are to be reversed, drastic steps are needed to enhance the achievement and academic success of students labeled "at risk." Achieving educational excellence requires an impartial and just educational system. Consider the recent high school graduation rates by ethnicity and gender shown in Table 1.1. These figures come from researchers at the Civil Rights Project at Harvard University (now located at UCLA) who examined the graduation rates for students who complete high school in four years. They make the valid point that most other dropout reports are seriously flawed in that they underreport school dropout rates and inflate graduation rates by looking only at how many members of a senior class graduate and ignore those who did not make it to the twelfth grade. Copies of the entire report may be obtained from their website: www.civilrightsproject.harvard.edu.

Several major trends are evident within and across these broad categories of race/ethnic groups. (Some additional *within group* differences based on region and national origin will be noted in Chapters 5, 6, 7, and 9. For example, some Asian groups, such as Japanese Americans, have the highest national graduation rates and others, such as Cambodian, Hmong, or Laotian, have the lowest; the same variation is true among Latino groups.) First of all, we see that the graduation rate for females is higher than males in all five major ethnic groups, with the largest gender differences among Black high school graduates, with 56.2 percent of the females

Table 1.1 High School Graduation Rates by Race/Ethnicity and Gender

Race/Ethnicity	% of Student Population	Nationwide Graduation Rate	Female Graduation Rate	Male Graduation Rate	% Difference Compared to 74.9% White
American Indian/ AK Native	1.2	51.1	51.4	47.0	−23.8
Asian/Pacific Islander	4.2	76.8	50.0	72.6	1.9
Hispanic	16.6	53.2	58.5	48.0	−21.7
Black	17.0	50.2	56.2	42.8	−24.7
White	61.0	74.9	77.0	70.8	NA
All Students	99.0	68.0	72.0	64.1	NA

Source: Orfield, G., Losen, D., & Swanson, C. (2004). *Losing Our Future: How Minority Youth Are Being Left Behind by the Graduation Rate Crisis*. Cambridge, MA: The Civil Rights Project at Harvard University/UCLA.

graduating in four years compared to 42.8 percent of the males. Second, we see an overall graduation gap compared to White four-year high school graduates of −24.7 percent for Black students, −23.8 percent for American Indian/Alaskan Native students, and −21.7 percent for Latino students. The percentage of Asian/Pacific Islander students who graduate "on time" is slightly higher than White students, at 1.9 percent. Third, the overall high school graduation rates reported here are notably lower than the figures culled from census data, which report graduation rates of over 90 percent for some groups.[17]

Given that the major goal of multicultural education is the development of the intellectual, social, and personal growth of all students to their highest potential, it is no different than the goal of educational excellence. However, it depends on the teacher's knowledge, attitudes, and behavior and whether he or she provides equitable opportunities for learning, changes the monocultural curriculum, and helps all students become more multicultural (i.e., helps them understand different systems of perceiving, evaluating, believing, and doing). This goal includes students in relatively monocultural classes and schools. Although one's ethnic group is just one of a number of identity sources available, ethnicity and social class are at the heart of the equity problem in U.S. society. Therefore, discussions about achieving educational excellence require concern about those ethnic groups that are consistently cut off from equal access to a good education.

There is a lot of rhetoric in education about the human potential and the need for equality of opportunity. Multicultural education moves beyond the rhetoric and recognizes that the potential for brilliance is sprinkled evenly across all ethnic groups. When social conditions and school practices hinder the development of this brilliance among students outside the predominant culture, as is the case within our society, the waste of human potential affects us all. The cumulative loss of talented scientists, artists, writers, doctors, teachers, spiritual leaders, and financial and business experts is staggering. The concern for developing human potential goes beyond individuals with special talents and gifts, however. High levels of development and achievement are believed possible for nearly everyone. Only those who are known to have limited mental capacity or to have severe psychological problems might be considered to be beyond the reach of most schools. (And this is only because most teachers must work with large groups of students and often lack the resources or skills required for learners with special needs.)

Multicultural education contributes to excellence in a second important way: It builds knowledge about various ethnic groups and national perspectives into the curriculum. The traditional curriculum is filled with inaccuracies and omissions concerning the contributions and life conditions of major ethnic groups within our society and for nations across the globe.[18] Obviously, the attainment of any degree of excellence is stunted by curriculum content that is untrue or incomplete. Given that we live in an interdependent world that is rapidly shrinking, ignorance of global issues and national perspectives is foolish and even dangerous.

The Existence of a Multiethnic Society

Today, over 40 percent of this society's school-age children are ethnic minorities.[19] Current patterns of immigration, particularly with the influx of people from Southeast Asia, Latin America, and the Caribbean, ensure that ethnic pluralism will continue to be the American way in the foreseeable future. It is estimated that nearly 40 percent of this nation's school-age children live in low-income families, with 19 percent at or below the poverty level.[20] Given the extensive research indicating that disproportionately high numbers of ethnic minority and low-income students are dropping out of school or are being suspended or expelled, and that disproportionately high numbers of those who do remain in school are achieving far below their potential, teachers today face a tremendous challenge. If these patterns are to be reversed, schools must affirm cultural diversity. Multicultural schools would obviously be better equipped to deal with the complexities of a pluralistic society than are the traditional monocultural schools. Schools based on the ideal of cultural pluralism, as in culturally competent teaching discussed in Chapter 8, represent a compromise between cultural assimilation on the one hand and cultural separatism or segregation on the other.

Those who believe that cultural pluralism will heighten ethnic group identity and lead to separatism, intergroup antagonism, and fragmentation consider it to be dangerous to society. However, cultural pluralism seems possible in a nation such as the United States, because it is, from a non-Native-American perspective, a nation of (voluntary and involuntary) immigrants.[21] With the exception of American Indians and certain segments of the Latino population, land is not an issue in ethnic identity for most groups. In contrast to those areas of the world where cultural pluralism has resulted in fragmentation—for example, portions of Europe and the former Soviet Union—many ethnic groups in the United States have contributed to the development of the predominant culture or were immersed in an already existing dominant culture when they arrived.[22]

By the year 2020, children of color will exceed forty-five percent of the school-age population in the United States.

Clearly, our schools are faced with educating a culturally pluralistic population. Pluralistic schools can identify baseline expectations for learning and behavior that are expected of all students. Every attempt must be made to lessen the cultural conflict that may result from cultural bias at this baseline. Some groups may perceive certain rules as culturally biased, such as the prohibition of hats (a yarmulke) in a school serving Orthodox Jews or unexcused absences during religious holidays. The scheduling of extracurricular activities after school discourages students who travel to school by bus, and certain school traditions, such as team names and colors, school emblems, and yearbook titles, may also symbolize the preeminence of a particular group.

The Existence of an Interconnected World

It is urgent that we foster global awareness among today's children and youth. The human race faces a number of critical concerns that if left unresolved are likely to result in the destruction of life as we know it: destruction of the ozone layer, environmental pollution, poverty, overpopulation, nuclear arms, drought and famine and world hunger, and the spread of AIDS and other diseases. The resolution of these problems, as well as participation in global trade and economic development, require global cooperation. This cooperation requires human beings who possess some degree of cross-cultural understanding.

The urgency of teaching about the state of the planet and of developing responsible world citizens was expressed over three decades ago by Robert Muller, Assistant Secretary General of the United Nations, on the occasion of the fortieth anniversary of the United Nations and International Youth Year (1985):

> *A child born today will be faced as an adult, almost daily, with problems of a global interdependent nature, be it peace, food, the quality of life, inflation, or scarcity of resources. He will be both an actor and a beneficiary or a victim in the total world fabric, and he may rightly ask: "Why was I not warned? Why was I not better educated? Why did my teachers not tell me about these problems and indicate my behavior as a member of an interdependent human race?" It is, therefore, the duty and the self-enlightened interest of governments to educate their children properly about the type of world in which they are going to live.*[23]

All of us are participants in the global arena. It is unavoidable. The question is the degree to which this participation is informed and enlightened.

Equity, Democratic Values, and "Every Day" Social Justice

Finally, equity is not only a matter of bettering our country's educational system. It is required if we value this nation's democratic ideals: basic human rights, social justice, respect for alternative life choices, and equal opportunity for all. Making reality fit these ideals, however, is not always easy. Reconciling the differences between these democratic ideals and the realities of social injustices in our society has been a concern for decades and in the 1940s was aptly described as the "American dilemma" by the famous Swedish social scientist Gunnar Myrdal. Recently, I was shocked and dismayed to discover that few of my university students, undergraduate and graduate students alike, had ever heard of the American Creed or the American dilemma, even though they were familiar with famous words from the Declaration of Independence and the Preamble of the Constitution. Thus, I want to quote briefly from this description of Myrdal's thoughts on the American Creed, because it provides moral support for our work in multicultural education.

> *. . . America is a land of great differences and rapid changes. Still there is great unity in this nation. Americans of all national origins, classes, regions, creeds, and colors have something in common: a set of beliefs, a political creed. This "American Creed" is the cement in the diversified structure of this great nation.*
>
> *America, compared to every other country in western civilization, large or small, has the most definitely and clearly expressed system of ideals in reference to human relations. This body of ideals is more widely understood and appreciated than similar ideals anywhere else. To be sure, the political creed of America is frequently not put into effect; but as a principle, which ought to rule, the Creed has been made conscious to everyone in American society. . . . These ideals of essential dignity of the individual, of basic equality of all men and of certain inalienable rights to freedom, justice, and fair opportunity, represent to the American people the meaning of the nation's early struggle for independence. These principles were written into the Declaration of Independence, the Preamble of the Constitution, the Bill of Rights, and into the constitutions of the states. The ideals of the American Creed have become the highest Law of the land.*[24]

It is ideally un-American to be racist or sexist, for example, but because many teachers fear teaching about values or changing attitudes, they ignore the issues of prejudice and discrimination. Multicultural education, in contrast, confronts the fact that this is a racist society with a history of White supremacy and privilege. An effective curriculum would point out that White racism has greatly influenced how people perceive, evaluate, believe, and act—and that this legacy persists. Because its aim is to reduce the ignorance that breeds racism and to develop the understanding and actions people need to become antiracist, multicultural education can help overcome barriers to achieving our ideals.

Democratic principles are at the heart of many issues addressed by multicultural education, such as the struggle for minority rights in a society based on majority rule, the right to dissent, and the limits of free speech. Multicultural classrooms nurture freedom of expression, the search for truth, and fair-minded critical thinking, but they are not value free. For example, multicultural advocates affirm fairness in the allocation of scarce positions and national resources and the elimination of economic exploitation, as well as the end of cultural exploitation and "assimilationist models of citizenship."[25]

 ## Conditions for Multicultural Schools: What Are They?

Under what conditions do students benefit from desegregated schooling? Most desegregated schools were forced to do so before this question was answered. The assumption over the past quarter century seems to have been that segregated schools are inherently bad and desegregated schools inherently good.

To the degree that segregated schools foster unwarranted fears, misconceptions, and negative stereotypes between isolated groups, in addition to unequal educational opportunities, this assumption is correct. It is false, however, to assume that simply desegregating a school will eliminate these inherent problems. Both research and casual observation in the vast majority of desegregated schools document the existence of resegregation through formal practices such as tracking, grouping, and scheduling of extracurricular activities, and through informal practices such as student seating preferences in classrooms and cafeterias. Many desegregated schools face the problems of racial tension, apathy, and absenteeism as a reaction to forced busing and desegregation. All these conditions mitigate against personal growth and achievement among students.

Unfortunately, there has rarely been time for thoughtful consideration of the question, under what conditions do students benefit from desegregated schooling? In most U.S. schools, teachers, students, and administrators have been forced to desegregate without the help of guidelines to establish good race relations and academic achievement among minority and majority students alike. Nevertheless, answers to the question do exist. The purpose of this section of the chapter is to provide a synthesis of important, but not widely used, concepts and theories that hold promise for school desegregation, and to suggest guidelines for effective desegregation in a variety of settings.

The focus will be on the urban setting, which typically has involved racial desegregation. Urban desegregation highlights the process that occurs unrecognized in many other school settings where race may not be a factor. Numerous possibilities come to mind: rural versus urban, labor versus management, wealthy versus poor, military versus civilian, Christian versus non-Christian, Polish American versus Italian American, and town versus gown.

Integration: Not Resegregation

There are at least four possible ways schools can respond to school desegregation: business-as-usual, assimilation, pluralistic coexistence, and integrated pluralism. These possible responses have been identified and described by H. A. Sagar and J. W. Schofield, as a result of their research in desegregated schools.[26]
Business-as-usual may be characterized as follows:

> *Insofar as possible, these interracial schools tried to maintain the same basic curriculum, the same academic standards, and the same teaching methods that prevailed under segregation. . . . Furthermore, they strove to enforce the same behavioral standards, to espouse the same values, and to apply the same sanctions to student offenses. In short, the schools did not perceive themselves as having to adjust their traditional practices in order to handle the new student body. Rather, the students were expected to adjust to the school.*[27]

This type of response does not consider whether old rules or procedures are desirable when the nature of the student population has changed.
Compatible with the business-as-usual approach to desegregation is the assimilationist response.

> *The assimilationist ideology holds that integration will have been achieved when the minority group can no longer be differentiated from the white majority in terms of economic status, education, or access to social institutions and their benefits. This will be accomplished by fostering a "color-blind" attitude where prejudice once reigned . . . and by imparting to minority persons the skills and value orientations which will enable them to take their place in the currently white-dominated social structure. . . . No significant change is anticipated since the newly assimilated minority individuals will be attitudinally and behaviorally indistinguishable from the majority. Stated in its boldest form, the assimilationist charge to the schools is to make minority children more like white children.*[28]

Those who do not assimilate are resegregated, drop out, or are suspended or expelled. The fact that students' race and culture may make a difference in students' and teachers' perceptions of each other and expectations about appropriate classroom behavior, is not considered. The assimilationist response is often based on an erroneous assumption that to recognize race is to be racist.
Schools that desegregate with the business-as-usual or assimilation response appear similar. The subtle difference is that under the assimilation response a conscious decision is made by the host school about expectations for new students. Business-as-usual schools proceed as they have in the past and, perhaps unconsciously, expect all new students to fit in.
Like the business-as-usual and assimilation response, the pluralistic coexistence response also involves resegregation. But in contrast to the assimilation response,

where only those students who do not fit in are resegregated, pluralistic coexistence is based on separation of different racial or ethnic groups. Students are allowed to maintain different styles and values, but within a school environment consisting of separate turfs for different racial groups. Typically, there are different schools within a school, and little or no attempt is made to encourage students to mix. Describing one such school, Sagar and Schofield wrote,

> *The principal tolerated almost complete informal resegregation of the students, to the point where there were considered to be "two schools within a school." The school's annex, for example, became known as a black area, or the "recreational study hall," while the library served as a white area, or "non-recreational study hall."*[29]

In this formerly all-White school, the African American principal tried to appease White parents by maintaining advanced academic programs to prevent them from withdrawing their children, who had become the minority. In this school situation, separate was clearly unequal.

In contrast with these three responses to school desegregation, integrated pluralism, or integration, actively seeks to avoid resegregation of students.

> *[It] is pluralistic in the sense that it recognizes the diverse racial and ethnic groups in our society and does not denigrate them just because they deviate from the white middle class patterns of behavior. Integrated pluralism affirms the equal value of the school's various ethnic groups, encouraging their participation, not on majority-defined terms, but in an evolving system which reflects the contributions of all groups. However, integrated pluralism goes beyond mere support for the side-by-side coexistence of different group values and styles. It is integrationist in the sense that it affirms the educational value inherent in exposing all students to a diversity of perspectives and behavioral repertoires and the social value of structuring the school so that students from previously isolated and even hostile groups can come to know each other under conditions conducive to the development of positive intergroup relations. . . .*
>
> *Integrated pluralism takes an activist stance in trying to foster interaction between different groups of students rather than accepting resegregation as either desirable or inevitable.*[30]

The first three responses are obviously unacceptable. Integrated pluralism, the last response, is the goal to strive for. Desegregation per se, or merely mixing formerly isolated ethnic groups in the same school, does not go far enough. Integration, however, recognizes and accommodates all the groups that were formerly segregated—in other words, it creates the conditions for cultural pluralism.

More than half a century ago, noted Black sociologist W. E. B. DuBois wrote about the issues of segregated versus desegregated schools:

> *A mixed school with poor and unsympathetic teachers, with hostile public opinion, and no teaching of truth concerning black folk, is bad. A segregated school with ignorant placeholders, inadequate equipment, poor salaries, and wretched housing, is equally bad. Other things being equal, the mixed school is the broader, more natural basis for the education of all youth. It gives wider contacts; it inspires greater self-confidence; and sup-*

presses the inferiority complex. But other things seldom are equal, and in that case, Sympathy, Knowledge, and Truth, outweigh all that the mixed school can offer.[31]

The philosophy of DuBois lends powerful support to the case for multicultural schools. Teachers must be free of racial prejudice and ethnocentrism (the belief that one's own culture is superior to all others) if they are to be effective with students of diverse cultural, racial, and socioeconomic backgrounds. Although prejudice and ethnocentrism seem to be part of the human condition, teachers should be less prejudiced and ethnocentric than the average person.

Research on the characteristics of effectively integrated schools shows that a policy consistent with integrated pluralism has the best potential for encouraging good race relations, academic achievement, and personal development among students. Three necessary conditions underlie the integrated pluralism response: positive teacher expectations, a learning environment that encourages positive intergroup contact, and a multicultural curriculum.[32]

Positive Teacher Expectations

Teachers often make snap judgments, based on their perceptions, about students and go on to treat them differently. Many teachers interact with students differently according to the student's race and socioeconomic status. Sara Lawrence Lightfoot has aptly referred to teachers as "judges of deviance."

Much has been written about the power of teacher expectations. Research also supports the basic assumption that teacher attitudes influence student achievement. One of the first studies, and probably best known, is the controversial study by Rosenthal and Jacobson, who reported their success in influencing student achievement by giving teachers phony data about their students.[33] Approximately 20 percent of the student population, selected at random, were identified as "bloomers" on an intelligence test. Teachers were given the names of these supposedly high-potential students, to be held in confidence, and these students did indeed achieve at significantly higher levels than their classmates. Although some scholars question the methodology used in this study, even its critics accept the notion that teacher expectations often affect student achievement.

Decades of research since this study "leads to a consensus that teachers' expectations can and sometimes do affect teacher-student interaction and student outcomes; however, the processes are much more complex than originally believed."[34] One conclusion, for example, is that teacher beliefs and expectations interact with student beliefs and behaviors. To the extent that ethnicity influences behaviors and beliefs, it is a factor in teacher expectations. Only a few recent studies have focused on ethnicity, however, although several researchers in the 1970s and early 1980s did so.

In one follow-up to Rosenthal and Jacobson's "Pygmalion" study, social studies student teachers were asked by their university supervisors to rank their students from high to low in terms of academic ability after two days in the classroom.[35] The student teachers did so without expressing uncertainty or difficulty. During the semester, their university supervisors coded their interactions with the high and low students. Results showed that lows were less frequently encouraged to participate in class discussion or to interact with the teacher, either directly by being called on or indirectly by receiving extended teacher feedback when they volunteered. Teachers tended to neglect the students they rated low.

In another study involving student teachers, all White females, the women were asked to teach a comparable current events lesson to a biracial group of students.[36] Each was given a class roster that contained phony IQ data for each student. High and low IQs were distributed at random, but evenly for Black and White students. Classroom observers recorded no significant difference in student behavior during the lesson, but the student teachers perceived the bright African American students as more hostile and disruptive. A likely explanation is that these student teachers felt threatened by students who did not fit their expectations (that is, they were not expecting a group of African American students who were also bright).

A growing body of evidence indicates that many White teachers have lower expectations for their non-White students. In one Midwestern study of high school student discipline in two large urban school corporations, for example, teachers who responded to an anonymous questionnaire felt Black students had less innate potential than White students on every variable, except basketball (where Blacks were perceived as having equal potential). Other variables included band, orchestra, drama, and scholastics.[37]

Another study of classroom interaction in forty-one middle school classrooms showed that when teachers have equal achievement expectations for Black and White students there is more interracial friendship and interaction among the students. A classroom climate of acceptance among students was more likely to exist when teachers did not distinguish between the learning potential of Black and White students.[38] Other studies have shown that a classroom climate of acceptance is related to increased student achievement, especially among minorities in the classroom.

Studies by Gay, Rist, and the U.S. Civil Rights Commission have shown that many teachers have lower expectations for African American and Mexican American students.[39] In the Rist study, which involved Black teachers and students, the teacher had lower expectations for the darker-skinned children. All three studies showed that teachers interacted with low-expectation students in intellectually limiting ways and were more supportive and stimulating with their White or light-skinned students.

Given the fact that teacher expectations can and do influence student achievement, and given the fact that many teachers hold lower expectations for African American and Latino students, is integrated education possible? I believe it is. Not all administrators, teachers, and students are racially prejudiced and not all have low expectations. Therefore, racial prejudice is not necessary to the human condition. Many teachers, administrators, and students who are racially prejudiced can develop the kinds of understanding required to become less so. This is a major goal of multicultural education among adults.

Lower teacher expectations for particular racial or ethnic groups are based on negative racial or ethnic prejudice. Teachers, like all people, often are not aware of their prejudices; thus they may not be aware of their lower expectations for some students.

A major theme in this book is the belief that if teachers are to have equally positive expectations for students of all ethnic backgrounds, they must understand the cultural differences that often exist in the desegregated classroom. The fact that cultural differences frequently are associated with racial differences often confirms myths and stereotypes associated with race. Teachers need guidelines, such as the Aspects of Ethnicity discussed in Chapter 2, to help them observe and interpret culturally different behavior. Such guidelines can help prevent blanket assumptions that certain behaviors and values go with certain racial groups.

A Learning Environment That Supports Positive Interracial Contact

Too often, we simply bring together groups of students who share different histories and hope for the best. The best rarely happens. Casual contact between different ethnic groups may reinforce existing negative stereotypes or generate new ones. I observed this phenomenon in a kindergarten classroom in a Florida school district during its initial attempts at desegregation. As the school year began, White students, most of whom had already had several years of nursery school, could be found busily working in one of the higher ability achievement groups. Their African American classmates, who had been bused from across town and had not had preparatory nursery school experience, ran wildly around the room until they could be settled into one of the remedial or lower achievement groups. White parents who advocated school desegregation were dismayed by their children's negative reports. For many of these White kindergartners, initial contact with Black children appeared to be creating negative racial prejudices. For most of the African American kindergartners, the vicious cycle of low expectations and low academic achievement was beginning.

Scenes like this can be avoided when school policies and practices are guided by social contact theory. In 1954, the year of the landmark school desegregation decision, Gordon Allport first published his theory of positive intergroup contact. He summarized his theory as follows:

> Given a population of ordinary people, with a normal degree of prejudice, we are safe in making the following general prediction: Prejudice (unless deeply rooted in the character structure of the individual) may be reduced by equal status contact between majority and minority groups in the pursuit of common goals. The effect is greatly enhanced if this contact is sanctioned by institutional supports (i.e., by law, custom or local atmosphere), and if it is of a sort that leads to the perception of common interests and common humanity between members of the two groups.[40]

It is unlikely that the young children described in this scene harbored deep-seated racial prejudice. If this is also true for the teacher, classroom practices can be implemented to encourage academic achievement and good race relations. Social contact theory provides a framework that can help educators identify policy guidelines for effective school desegregation, as well as promising practices that have been uncovered by recent research in desegregated schools.

According to contact theorists, at least four basic conditions are necessary if social contact between groups is to lessen negative prejudice and lead to friendly attitudes and behaviors:

1. Contact should be sufficiently intimate to produce reciprocal knowledge and understanding between groups.
2. Members of various groups must share equal status.
3. The contact situation should lead people to do things together. It should require intergroup cooperation to achieve a common goal.
4. There must be institutional support—an authority and/or social climate that encourages intergroup contact.[41]

These four conditions of positive social contact can be used as guidelines for observing desegregated schools and for detecting problem areas. One of the most difficult conditions for most schools to establish is an equal status environment for the different racial groups within the student body. Often there are sharp socioeconomic differences, as well as differences in the initial achievement levels of Black and White classmates. Tracking and grouping practices may be viewed as necessary, but they may also lead to resegregation. A history of racial discrimination in education and hiring practices means schools often face a limited pool of available Black and Latino administrators and teachers who can serve as high-status role models.

Other potential violations of the conditions of positive intergroup contact stem from school rules, discipline practices, extracurricular activities, and symbols and traditions. Some rules are perceived as inequitable (for example, prohibition of "bad language" and hats). Scheduling extracurricular activities after school excludes students who travel by bus and limits opportunities for intergroup contact in cocurric-

How a school responds to court-ordered desegregation is critical in the development of equitable, effective learning environments.

ular activities. School traditions often become a problem during initial stages of desegregation and act as symbolic indicators of where the school's authority stands on integrated pluralism.

> *If "new" students come to an "old" school, there is a frequent tendency for both racial groups to perceive the school as "belonging" to the "old" group. The school name, team nicknames, school songs, and titles of school publications are a few of the many symbols that may symbolize preeminence of a particular racial group. There are other, more subtle, customs that may symbolize segregation in ways not anticipated. If editors have always been college preparatory students, and there are few college preparatory students in the "new" group, continuation of the tradition will symbolize unequal status.... "Preserving traditions" can be a euphemism for "putting minorities in their place." Opposition to integration may focus on defense of symbols. When this happens, school personnel need to realize what is happening and deal with reality.*[42]

Underlying these relatively visible concerns is a hidden problem: a mutual lack of knowledge about communication modes, values, and perceptions among culturally different students and teachers, which often leads to misunderstanding and conflict. For example, many White teachers and students are unknowingly ignorant about the structures and meanings of Ebonics, African American vernacular. The double negative "ain't got no" may signify a "low-class," uneducated person, while use of the term "nigger" among Blacks may be viewed by Whites as insulting or threatening. Black students, on the other hand, might regard all Whites as racist and interpret the behaviors of White teachers and classmates from that perspective. As long as students and teachers are left to their own devices, there is little opportunity for the kind of intimate contact between culturally different students that could foster mutual understanding. Informal segregation is typically the rule throughout the school.

Let's look at two examples of desegregation in action. Although they took place several decades ago, they ring true today, as shown in the 2005 book by Stephen J. Caldas and Carl L. Bankston, *Forced to Fail: The Paradox of School Desegregation*.

The case of Isaac Washington portrays the unfair burden African American schoolchildren and their families have borne in the struggle to desegregate U.S. schools. Typically, though not always, it is the Black children who are bused farthest from home into areas that are unfamiliar and sometimes hostile: it is the Black children who have to adjust to new school expectations, sometimes numerous times in a single school career; it is the Black community that is forced to give up its schools, and all of the history, symbols, and traditions these schools represent.

White children from middle- and upper-income backgrounds can also find it difficult to adjust to new schools. Thrust into a desegregated setting, they often misinterpret and are misunderstood, and they are sometimes fearful and vulnerable.

Marcia's situation, that of being one of a few White students in a predominantly African American urban school, is a reversal of what many Black, Hispanic, Asian, and Native American children often face. Marcia's situation is complicated by the fact that her parents are using her to act in accordance with their belief in school desegregation. Liberal White parents are frequently criticized for not sending their children to inner-city schools.

The Example of Isaac Washington

Isaac Washington is a junior at Jefferson Davis High School, a school known for its academic excellence and located near a burgeoning metropolis in Texas. Having entered Davis High as a freshman, Isaac is among the first group of Black students to attend the school in response to a school desegregation court order.

Isaac had attended elementary and junior high schools in the African American community. He and his friends had expected to enroll in George Washington High School, an outstanding all-Black educational facility with a national reputation. For decades, Washington High School had provided a nurturing learning environment that encouraged academic excellence and fostered personal ambition and self-confidence among the student population, many of whom became successful in business, the arts, and the professions. The school was shut down three years ago, despite pleading and protest from the African American community, and its student body was distributed throughout the previously all-White schools. This was done so that the incoming Black students would not exceed 10 to 15 percent of the host school student population. Most of these students face a lengthy bus ride at the beginning and end of each school day, and most can remember the anger and resentment expressed by members of the White community who opposed their presence in the school. Sports and other extracurricular activities scheduled after school have become impossible because of the long bus ride home.

In contrast to most of his former classmates from Washington High School, who were placed in the low-ability tracks, Isaac's classes are in the advanced placement and honors sections. Although he excels in all of his classes, his new school experience weighs heavily on him. Most of his close friends have dropped out of school, even the ones who had thrived in elementary and junior high school, and he is experiencing tensions with old friends in the neighborhood.

At school he is uncomfortable being the only African American in most of his classes. The phenomenon of all-eyes-upon-him whenever a Black writer is studied, for example, or a civil rights issue is discussed is a daily occurrence that he feels he will never get used to. And then there are the insults and racial slurs that constantly occur and seem incurable.

Students in this school situation may require a good deal of emotional support. Marcia is afraid of disappointing her parents; she confuses her fears and anxieties about her classmates with being racist and thus is unable to confide in her parents.

Although most of the African American students are willing to accept Marcia and try to make her feel welcome, there are some students who will take out their anger and frustration on her. Because she is a symbol of what they believe to be White oppression, her safety is threatened.

Social contact theory can be used as a guide to alleviate obstacles experienced by students like Isaac Washington and Marcia Patton. Although visions of integrated schools may differ, there are at least two necessary observable characteristics. First, there is a relaxed interracial mixing among the majority of students and

The Example of Marcia Patton

Marcia Patton is the 12-year-old daughter of Mavis and Lew Patton, two politically active lawyers who practice law in a large midwestern city. Marcia is in the first group of White children to attend Jefferson Junior High School, traditionally a school for inner-city Blacks. Although most of the children in her neighborhood attend a high-powered prep school, Marcia's parents are sending her to Jefferson on principle.

On her second day at Jefferson, Marcia clutched her books tightly to her chest as she entered Ms. Samson's language arts class. The teacher smiled as she greeted Marcia. She stepped into the hall to speak with several noisy students who were scrambling around the drinking fountain.

At that moment five classmates burst into the room. They slammed their books down on the desk and crowded around Marcia.

Most of the students were very friendly to her. Several offered to take her to the cafeteria at lunch. Marcia became uncomfortable with the attention when one classmate handled her braids and another swatted them out of the offending student's hands shouting, "Let her hair alone!"

That evening Marcia wrote a letter to Ms. Bryant, her teacher last year, in the secrecy of her bedroom.

"When I first walked in, I saw all these dark faces and for the first time I felt so White. There was nothing but laughing, noisy, dark-skinned faces. My heart was beating so fast I thought I would drop dead for sure. I guess a lot of them won't like me. Still, most of the kids are real nice to me. But even so, I'm scared. Everyone is so loud and sometimes they get so close I can hardly breathe.

"The teachers are real nice to me but I wish Ms. Samson wouldn't call on me so much. We use the book we used in your class last year, and lots of the kids in the class can't read it.

"I've been there over a week now and was feeling better until today. A horrible thing happened and I can't tell anybody but you.

"I went to the bathroom after lunch, and two girls I don't know told me to give them all my money or they would hurt me. I gave them twelve dollars, all I had. They said they'd slash my face if I told anybody. I'm afraid to go back."

teachers in casual and informal settings at school. Second, there is real academic achievement and personal growth among all students, as seen in formal course work and extracurricular activities. These two characteristics appear to be interactive. Where good race relations exist, student achievement is higher, and the reverse is also true.

There is no standard recipe for integrating the desegregated school. Neither are there specific requisite practices. There are, however, necessary conditions for positive intergroup contact (equal status, knowledge, cooperation, and institutional support) that schools can use as a guide in making decisions about specific desegregation practices. For example, some form of ability grouping might be appropriate in creating an equal-status environment in one school but not in another.

What is important is that ability groups do not produce racially visible differences and do not limit the opportunities for low-income students.

Research by scholars such as the late Elizabeth Cohen suggests ways of creating equal status among racially different students who bring differing entry-level skills to the classroom.[43] In one study, Cohen provided special instruction to lower achievers before their participation in small-group cooperative learning. The lower achievers could then make unique contributions to their group, which helped equalize their classroom status. Furthermore, achievement and interracial friendship were enhanced.

A study conducted by Garlie Forehand and Marjorie Ragosta focused on school characteristics of effectively desegregated schools.[44] They defined effectiveness in terms of student achievement and race relations. Data were collected from tests, questionnaires, and interviews in nearly 200 schools. All the schools were racially mixed and represented a wide range of socioeconomic, demographic, and geographic conditions.

The results identified school conditions under which benefits in integrated education were maximized in a wide variety of settings, sometimes even where large socioeconomic differences existed within the student population. In their *Handbook for Integrated Schooling*, which developed from their findings, the researchers have presented a number of practices that characterize effectively desegregated schools. Table 1.2 presents an overview of these and other research findings and shows their relationship with the conditions of positive intergroup contact.

Other research shows that biracial work and play teams among students are one of the most powerful ways to improve race relations. As seen in Table 1.2, this practice meets the four conditions of positive intergroup contact. One promising strategy that builds on this fact is team learning, an approach developed by Robert Slavin and his associates at the Center for Social Organization of Schools at the Johns Hopkins University. Team learning can help establish an equal-status environment among students who bring different entry skills to the classroom, because the tasks can be designed to fit student strengths. (Team learning is examined in Chapter 9.)

Culturally Competent Teaching

Given the cultural and racial complexities of contemporary society in the United States, as well as the disproportionate number of students of color and low income students who are being left behind in our schools, we need teachers who are both culturally competent and antiracist. Equity pedagogy, a major dimension of multicultural education, as defined on page 5, is needed in schools across the heartland as much as in our inner cities. Culturally incompetent teachers, especially those unable to work with English Language Learners, or teachers who are unable to counter institutional racism in both its hidden and overt forms, cannot implement it.

The need for culturally competent teachers was recently addressed by one of the writing teams working with the Educator Standards Board in the State of Ohio.[45] The team defined cultural competence as the teacher's ability to

Table 1.2 ▨ Strategies for School Integration: Summary of Research Findings

School Practice	*Shows Conditions of Positive Intergroup Contact that*			
	Create Equal Status	*Lead to Interpersonal Acquaintance*	*Are Based on Common Goal*	*Show Institutional Support*
Multiethnic curriculum	✓	✓		✓
Extracurricular activities scheduled during school day	✓	✓	✓	✓
Open discussion of race and racial issues in classroom		✓		✓
Biracial work and play teams among students	✓	✓	✓	✓
Biracial seating patterns		✓		✓
Rules and discipline: equal punishment for equal offense	✓			✓
Equitable rules (If punishment for the infraction of a rule appears to be associated with race, determine whether the rule is equitable.)	✓			✓
Academic achievement and good race relations established as explicit goals				✓
Biracial staffing that reflects school's racial composition	✓			✓
Biracial staffing in high-status positions				✓
Student-focused human relations activities	✓	✓	✓	✓
Class and program assignments that do not result in racially identifiable groups	✓	✓		✓
Individualized instruction that rewards improvement as well as academic absolutes	✓			✓

. . . (s)ee differences as assets. They create caring learning communities where individual and cultural heritages, including languages, are expressed and valued. They use cultural and individual knowledge about their students, their families, and their communities to design instructional strategies that build upon and link home and school experiences. They challenge stereotypes and intolerance. They serve as change agents by thinking and acting critically to address inequities distinguished by (but not limited to) race, language, culture, socioeconomics, family structure, and gender.

Beyond using images, literature, and other forms of expression that represent students' diverse cultures and backgrounds, teachers understand, affirm, and use students' home and primary languages, communication styles, and family structures for learning and discipline.[46]

Although this definition was not included in the final document adopted by the Ohio Board of Education in 2005, it has inspired others who are writing about racial and cultural competence in the classroom.[47] It also captures a central message within the three chapters in Part III that focus on individual learning styles and the promise of culturally competent teaching; reaching all learners, with perspectives on gender, class and special needs; and teaching in linguistically diverse classrooms.

A Multicultural Curriculum

Curriculum can be viewed as the experiences, both official and unofficial, that learners have under the auspices of the school. Following this definition, a multicultural curriculum is one that attends to the school's hidden curriculum—for example, teachers' values and expectations, student cliques and peer groupings, and school regulations. It also attends to the values, cultural styles, knowledge, and perceptions that all students bring to the school. A multicultural curriculum, in its broadest sense, influences the total school environment.

Here, however, the focus will be limited to those planned experiences in school that are intended to develop student understandings, values, attitudes, and behaviors related to the goals of multicultural education shown in Figure 1.2.

Understanding Multiple Historical Perspectives

Most of us tend to be ahistorical when it comes to knowledge about Third World nations as well as ethnic minorities within our own society. It is difficult to be otherwise, given the nature of the traditional curriculum that emphasizes the political development of Anglo-American civilization. An important goal of a multicultural curriculum, therefore, is the development of multiple historical perspectives that will correct this Anglo–Western European bias. Past and current world events must be understood from multiple national perspectives, and both minority and nonminority points of view must be considered in interpreting local and national events.

Developing Cultural Consciousness

Cultural consciousness is the recognition or awareness on the part of an individual that she or he has a view of the world that is not universally shared and differs profoundly from that held by many members of different nations and ethnic groups. It includes an awareness of the diversity of ideas and practices found in human societies around the world and some recognition of how one's own thoughts and behaviors might be perceived by members of differing nations and ethnic groups.[48]

Developing Intercultural Competence

Intercultural competence is the ability to interpret intentional communications (language, signs, gestures), some unconscious cues (such as body language), and customs in cultural styles different from one's own. Emphasis is on empathy and

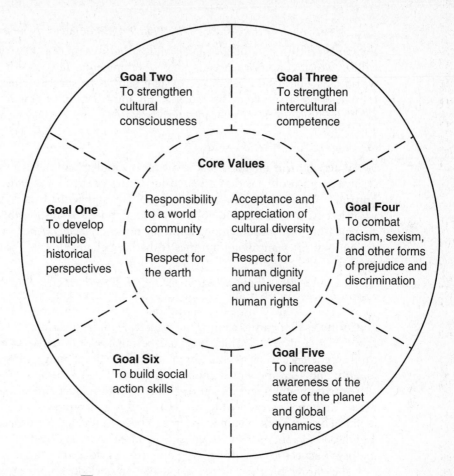

Figure 1.2 ✖ Conceptual Model of a Comprehensive Multicultural Curriculum

communication. The goal is to develop self-awareness of the culturally conditioned assumptions people of different cultural backgrounds make about each others' behaviors and cognitions.

Combating Racism, Sexism, and All Forms of Prejudice and Discrimination

Combating racism, sexism, prejudice, and discrimination means lessening negative attitudes and behaviors based on gender bias and misconceptions about the inferiority of races and cultures different from one's own. Emphasis is on clearing up myths and stereotypes associated with gender, different races, and ethnic groups. Basic human similarities are stressed. The goal is to develop antiracist, antisexist behavior based on awareness of historical and contemporary evidence of individual, institutional, and cultural racism and sexism in the United States and elsewhere in the world.

Raising Awareness of the State of the Planet and Global Dynamics

Awareness of the state of the planet and global dynamics is knowledge about prevailing world conditions, trends, and developments. It is also knowledge of the world as a hugely interrelated ecosystem subject to surprise effects and dramatic ramifications of simple events, such as the introduction of new technologies or of health and nutrition practices into a society.[49]

Developing Social Action Skills

Social action skills include the knowledge, attitudes, and behaviors needed to help resolve major problems that threaten the future of the planet and the well-being of humanity. One emphasis is on thinking globally and acting locally; the goal is to develop a sense of personal and political efficacy and global responsibility resulting in a participatory orientation among adult members of society. Another emphasis is enabling minorities and nonminorities to become change agents through democratic processes.

The six goals contained in the curriculum model overlap; each individually represents a necessary but insufficient focus for multicultural education. For example, to increase cultural consciousness without also developing the understanding, skills, and attitudes that cluster around intercultural competence might lead to greater ethnocentrism and polarization. It would be impossible to develop people's intercultural competence (such as empathy) without also developing their senses of personal identity and security, which come with cultural consciousness. Furthermore, both these goals should foster an appreciation of both human similarities and ethnic diversity and an awareness of how racism and negative prejudices originate and subjugate. The sixth goal, enabling people to become change agents, goes beyond study and discussion and deals with the skills and behaviors needed to eradicate discriminatory practices as well as to bring about other desired changes.

The cluster of goals in the curriculum model does not require that teachers stress each goal equally. Rather, these six goals should be woven into an overall curriculum design that allows separate subject areas and courses to emphasize those goals that are most compatible with the subject matter boundaries and age groupings of a particular school system. In some school settings, for example, historical perspectives and cultural consciousness might be emphasized in literature and the arts; intercultural competence in language and communications; reduction of racial/ethnic prejudice and discrimination in biology and world and U.S. history; and social action skills in government, business, or economics.

Furthermore, a careful sequence of learning experiences designed to foster social action skills could begin in kindergarten with simple decision-making activities and culminate in the final year of high school with a community action project. Ideally, teams of teachers within a school, school system, college, or university would collaborate on the sequencing and articulation of multicultural perspectives in curriculum objectives, strategies, and materials. Multicultural content could extend, enrich, and perhaps even transform state and national content standards across the curriculum. With clarification of multicultural goals, it becomes possible to connect them with curriculum standards, as is illustrated in Chapter 11.

A multicultural curriculum cannot come to life unless fair-minded critical thinking is at the heart of teaching and learning. Both teachers and their students must become critical thinkers who can "gather, analyze, synthesize, and assess information, enter sympathetically into the thinking of others, . . . [and] deal rationally with conflicting points of view."[50] Furthermore, a multicultural curriculum requires that teachers and students genuinely care about human welfare beyond themselves, their family, and their friends. And, finally, it requires a focus on community action so that teachers and students can become agents of change. But without critical thinking and teaching at the center, multicultural education is likely to result in indoctrination rather than ethical insights based on core values.

 ## The Critics of Multicultural Education

Multicultural education is a loaded term. It conjures up images of ethnic divisiveness and conflict, biased revisionism in history lessons, accusations about White racism, attacks on Christianity, disrespect for our nation's democratic ideals, fluffy lessons about other cultures, reinforced stereotypes, and an endless array of diverse groups and identities that need to be considered. Many teachers and administrators are turned off by the mere mention of the phrase, as are some academic scholars, even in history and the social sciences, where one could argue multicultural education has a natural home. Why does multicultural education have a bad name in some circles? Misconceptions about what multicultural education looks like, *at its best*, is part of the reason. Let's consider some of the main areas of criticism.[51]

Potential for Conflict and Divisiveness

Critics worry that an emphasis on race and culture will be harmful to our national unity. They argue that the United States has developed a common culture that unifies its people by allowing everyone to shed their past and ethnic membership in order to think and speak as an individual American. Furthermore, they believe the attention contemporary minority group members are giving to ethnic origin also promotes White guilt and national self-hatred. Western thought must be emphasized because it is the source of thought that allows individuals to rise above their origins. Other critics argue for only English to be taught in schools, and they perceive the maintenance of other first languages to be a threat to national unity.

Liberal Bias and Cultural Relativism

Some conservative critics see multicultural education as a movement led by college professors, formerly radical protesters of the 1960s, who are on the political fringe with ideas such as affirmative action, gay rights, and a woman's right to choose in matters of health and reproduction. Some liberal critics argue that multiculturalism means excessive cultural relativism—the idea that all cultural practices are equally good, including torture, genocide, and the suppression of women's rights—and will lead to "moral anarchy" because there are no guiding principles or values to organize society. Other critics see a conflict between multicultural education and their religious beliefs. Still others criticize what they regard to be "politically correct trivia and dogma that replaces sound intellectual scholarship with shoddiness," especially in university-level diversity courses and K–12 Afrocentric curricula.[52]

Superficial Conception of Culture

Some critics note that many teachers (preschool through college) focus on surface culture, such as food, dress, crafts, literature, language, and festivals. They argue that students are not encouraged to get into the unspoken and unconscious rules of deep culture, such as concepts of courtesy, time, beauty, cleanliness, past and future, and so forth when studying about other cultures at home and around the world. Some comment that images of the melting pot (or sometimes of a soup or stew) to represent assimilation of ethnic groups, versus the salad bowl to represent a culturally pluralistic society, are trivial metaphors for complex social conditions. Still others criticize the false self-esteem building associated with feel-good lessons that focus on ethnic leaders and contributions but mask societal inequities. Others are critical when culture is viewed as static and essentialized, which leads to ethnic stereotypes and lists of cultural attributes associated with a specific ethnic group or nationality.

Co-option of Minorities

Many critics of multicultural education believe that it emphasizes cross-cultural understanding and celebration but overlooks inequities in education and society. In their view, multicultural education ignores racism and rarely addresses issues of poverty in the United States, such as why people of color are overrepresented in poverty and what kinds of actions could be taken to bring about change. They believe that superficial attention to culture and ethnic heroes lulls parents and students of color into thinking significant changes in educational equity are taking place. Furthermore, these critics argue that this infusion of ethnic heroes and culture often works to drive a wedge between students and families of color and lower-income Whites, who also experience societal inequities and often feel alienated at school.

What Do You Think?

As you read over these criticisms, some may resonate with you. Which ones do you agree with most? And why? You may also be wondering, given all these criticisms of multicultural education, why read on? In the rest of this book, I will provide answers that I hope you will find encouraging.

Conclusions

The case for multicultural education presented in this chapter takes a position that may not be widely accepted. It could be viewed as overly idealistic and based on unrealistic assumptions about the possibilities for human altruism.

It would be possible to develop an alternative, perhaps more negative, approach, one based on fear of human annihilation and concerns about the survival, health, and future of one's grandchildren. People become concerned about multicultural and global issues when the focus is on economic competition in the world arena, unsafe storage of nuclear wastes, the greenhouse effect, and futile military or diplomatic efforts based on ignorance of history and culture. Even the goal of combating racism, which has never been a national policy, could be viewed positively by perpetrators of racism once it is realized that economic and political gains in (or in cooperation with) Third World nations cannot be taken seriously as long as we practice racism at home and abroad.

The fact is, however, that the multicultural education movement *is* idealistic. It means learning to think through a "language of hope and possibility."[53] Multicultural education is based on visions of humans living in greater harmony with each other and with the earth. It asks that we develop citizens who are able to consider alternative viewpoints, are able to examine values and assumptions (one's own as well as those of others), and are willing to learn to think critically. It requires a degree of open-mindedness that may be impossible to develop in people with a highly rigid belief structure. This does not mean that the visions of multicultural education should be abandoned.

By clearly stating the goals and core values of multicultural education, it becomes possible to articulate reasons for disagreement. This can lead to a healthy dialogue, even among strong supporters, that can move us beyond theory and rhetoric into practice.

The concept of radical cultural relativism, or the notion that anything goes, is a frequently voiced concern. Many adults who have school-age children, for example, see multicultural education as requiring students to accept abhorrent sociopolitical practices. These objectionable practices may include news-making events such as the stifling of political dissenters within ethnic communities, and physical violence such as female infanticide, or the mutilation of the genitalia of young women. The goals and core values proposed in this chapter can help us deal with cultural relativism in at least three ways. First, if we accept respect for human dignity and universal human rights as a basic value, then we cannot be neutral about injury to or destruction of human life. Ultimately, the goal is for these practices to end. Second, if we consider multiple historical perspectives we can at least understand why such practices do occur. And third, if we develop cultural consciousness and intercultural competence we may be able to understand that we might very well accept and even participate in such behaviors had we been born and raised in that society.

Another important concern is that many nations, ethnic minorities, and economically disadvantaged people will not participate in multicultural education efforts. We know, for example, that Third World people who fear a continuation of Western racism and imperialism view multicultural and global education with suspicion. This is a sobering limitation. If we were to take seriously our own national creed of justice and equality for all and if combating racism were to become a national policy, this suspicion might be lessened.

Selected Sources for Further Study

Abdi, A. A., & Shultz, L. (2008). *Educating for Human Rights and Global Citizenship*. Albany, NY: SUNY Press.

Adams, M., Blumenfeld, W. J., Castaneda, R., Hackman, H. W., Peters, M. L., & Zuniga, X., Editors. (2000). *Readings for Diversity and Social Justice: An Anthology on Racism, Antisemitism, Sexism, Hetersexism, Ableism, and Classism*. New York: Routledge.

Andrzejewski, J., Baltodano, M., & Symcox, L. (Eds.). (2009). *Social Justice, Peace, and Environmental Education: Transformative Standards*. New York: Routledge.

Ayres, W., Quinn, T., & Stovall, D. (2009). *Handbook of Social Justice in Education*. New York: Routledge.

Banks, J. A. (2004). Multicultural Education: Historical Development, Dimensions, and Practice, in *Handbook of Research on Multicultural Education, Second Edition*, J. A. Banks & C. M. Banks, eds. (San Francisco: Jossey-Bass) pp. 3–29.

Banks, J. A. (2006). *Race, Culture, and Education: The Selected Works of James A. Banks*, New York: Routledge.

Bell, D. (2004). *Silent Covenants: Brown v. Board of Education and the Unfulfilled Hopes for Racial Reform*. Oxford: Oxford University Press.

Bennett, C., (2001). "Genres of Research in Multicultural Education." *Review of Educational Research, 72*(2), 171–217.

Champagne, D. (2007). *Social Change and Cultural Continuity among Native Nations*. Lanham, NY: Altamira Press.

Cohen, E. G., & Lotan, R. A. (2004). Equity in Heterogeneous Classrooms, in *Handbook of Research on Multicultural Education, Second Edition*, J. A. Banks & C. M. Banks, eds. (San Francisco: Jossey-Bass) pp. 736–750.

Darling-Hammond, L. (2004). What Happens to a Dream Deferred? The Continuing Quest for Equal Educational Opportunity, in *Handbook of Research on Multicultural Education, Second Edition*, J. A. Banks & C. M. Banks, eds. (San Francisco: Jossey-Bass) pp. 736–630.

Gay, G. (2004). Curriculum Theory and Multicultural Education, in *Handbook of Research on Multicultural Education, Second Edition*, J. A. Banks & C. M. Banks, eds. (San Francisco: Jossey-Bass) pp. 30–49.

Ladson-Billings, G. (2004). New Directions in Multicultural Education: Complexities, Boundaries, and Critical Race Theory, in *Handbook of Research on Multicultural Education, Second Edition*, J. A. Banks & C. M. Banks, eds. (San Francisco: Jossey-Bass) pp. 50–65.

Multicultural Pavilion, www.edchange.org/multicultural.

Pettigrew, T. P. (2004). Intergroup Contact: Theory, Research, and New Perspectives, in *Handbook of Research on Multicultural Education, Second Edition*, J. A. Banks & C. M. Banks, eds. (San Francisco: Jossey-Bass) pp. 770–781.

School Colors. (1996). PBS Film. (The story of race relations and academics at Berkeley High School in the 1990s. 2½ hours.)

Now go to Topics #12 and 13: **Strategies** and **School-Wide Diversity Issues** in the MyEducationLab (www.myeducationlab.com) for your course, where you can:

- Find learning outcomes for these topics along with the national standards that connect to these outcomes.

- Complete Assignments and Activities that can help you more deeply understand the chapter content.

- Apply and practice your understanding of the core teaching skills identified in the chapter with the Building Teaching Skills and Dispositions learning units.

Chapter 2

Culture, Race, and the Contexts for Multicultural Teaching

Over the past several decades many of my students have questioned why we need to study the concept of culture in an education class. One student's journal comments, written some time ago, capture the initial thoughts of many of my students early in the semester, minority and nonminority alike. Here is what the student ("Tom") wrote:

> *Why be concerned about culture? After all, we all live in the same country. Most of us speak the same language, and those who don't have the chance to learn English in school. Most of us dress the same, bathe every day, and enjoy the same foods and entertainment and comforts. If you don't think so, just spend some time in a really foreign country. Then you'll see just how American you are.... Sure, I plan to be a teacher ... and I see it as my responsibility to help everyone learn to the best of their ability and to fit into the American society. When we start to look at differences between the races and other groups, we tend to develop stronger stereotypes.... Besides, I think it's prejudiced to look at a person's race or cultural differences, especially in the classroom where we're supposed to treat everyone equally.*

We can see that Tom agrees with the assumption that our main goal as teachers is to strive for the intellectual, social, and personal development of our students to their highest potential. He wants to provide each student with an equal opportunity to learn. However, he expresses some serious misconceptions that are common among teachers from preschool through college. First, there is no awareness that the cultural expectations of students' families and school may differ, causing academic difficulties related to transitional trauma in the classroom (sometimes called *cultural discontinuity*). Second, there is confusion between *equal* and *equitable* learning conditions. Third, there are misconceptions about racism. And fourth, there is a false idea of what it means to be an American. One can also detect in Tom's statement an ethnocentrism that is strikingly similar to the students' science reports in Sam Johnson's classroom (see Chapter 1). In short, Tom lacks a multicultural perspective.

A primary purpose of this chapter is to show how teachers' knowledge and understanding of culture can help all students reach their potential. If we are going to equalize the opportunities we provide, we must consider culture. We must be aware of our own cultural assumptions and the assumptions of our students, which may be different from our own.

Many classrooms provide an opportunity for students from various ethnic backgrounds to meet for the first time.

Multicultural teachers seek intercultural competence—the knowledge and understanding of their students' cultural styles. They feel comfortable and at ease with their students. Interculturally competent teachers are aware of the diversity within racial, cultural, and socioeconomic groups, they know that culture is ever changing, and they are aware of the dangers of stereotyping. At the same time, they know that if they ignore their students' cultural attributes they are likely to be guided by their own cultural lenses, unaware of how their culturally conditioned expectations and assumptions might cause learning difficulties for some children and youth.

 ## What Is Culture?

Culture is a complex concept that anthropologists and sociologists have defined in a variety of ways. Prior to the late 1950s, it was typically defined in terms of patterns of behavior and customs. As early as 1871, for example, the great E. B. Tylor defined culture as "that complex whole which includes knowledge, belief, art, morals, law, custom, and any other capabilities and habits acquired by man as a member of society."[1]

This definition contrasts with more recent definitions of culture that focus on shared knowledge and belief systems, or symbols and meanings, rather than on habits and behavior. Geertz defines culture as "an historically transmitted pattern of meanings employed in symbols, a system of inherited conceptions expressed in symbolic form by means of which men communicate, perpetuate and develop their knowledge about and attitudes towards life."[2] Spradley and McCurdy define culture as "the acquired knowledge that people use to interpret experience and to generate social behavior."[3] They also assert that *cultural knowledge* "is like a recipe for producing behavior and artifacts." Goodenough explains further:

> *A society's culture consists of whatever it is one has to know or believe in order to operate in a manner acceptable to its members, and do so in any role that they accept for any one of themselves. Culture, being what people have to learn as distinct from their biological heritage, must consist of the end product of learned knowledge, in a most general, if relative, sense of the term. By this definition, we should note that culture is not a material phenomenon—it does not consist of things, people, behavior, or emotions. It is rather an organization of these things. It is the forms of things that people have in mind, their models for perceiving, relating and otherwise interpreting them. As such, the things people say and do, their social arrangements and events, are products or by-products of their culture as they apply it to the task of perceiving and dealing with their circumstances.*[4]

According to LeVine, culture is "a shared organization of ideas that includes the intellectual, moral, and aesthetic standards prevalent in a community and the meanings of communicative actions."[5] Triandis makes a distinction between subjective culture, the "worldview or the way a cultural group perceives its environment, including stereotypes, role perceptions, norms, attitudes, values, ideals, and perceived relationships between events and behaviors, and . . . material or concrete culture which includes the objects and artifacts of a culture."[6]

There exists a great deal of cultural diversity within any society, since few individuals know or have access to all of the cultural heritage of their group. Some individuals have access to multiple cultures and may develop multiple standards for perceiving, believing, doing, and evaluating.[7] Where we happen to be born and when, may influence the culture, or cultures, we acquire. The family, the neighborhood, the region, the nation, and the era or decade can all make a difference. Initially, we have little control over the language we learn to speak, the concepts and stereotypes we acquire, the religion we accept, the gestures and expressions that amuse or reassure us, or the behavior that offends or pleases us. Furthermore, if we have been exposed to just one culture, we tend to assume that our way is the best way, the only way, and are likely to be unaware that we even have a culture. One way to develop cultural consciousness is to see how someone from another culture perceives or *mis*perceives us. The views of international visitors and students in the United States can trigger deeper insights into our own culture. For example, some regard dating and romantic love as a source of severe psychological strain and are thankful that their families select their mate. Some are offended by the chemical odor of antiperspirants and soaps or the body odor associated with eating beef. Many become sick after eating food to which they are unaccustomed. Many perceive the nursing home phenomenon as evidence that older family members are not loved or valued. Some are appalled by the material comforts we lavish on our pets. And some are uncomfortable in the typical American classroom where students are encouraged to question and challenge the teacher.

Understanding our own and other cultures clarifies why we behave in certain ways, how we perceive reality, what we believe to be true, what we build and create, what we accept as good and desirable, and so on. In a complex society that combines peoples of diverse national and indigenous origins, such as the United States, a variety of cultures coexist, along with the Anglo–Western European predominant culture. Avoiding ethnocentric explanations of students' behavior—that is, not interpreting their behavior from our own culturally biased viewpoint—requires awareness of our own cultural expectations.

The Importance of a Worldview

Worldview refers to "the way people characteristically look out on the universe."[8] It consists of values, beliefs, and assumptions, or the way a cultural group perceives people and events. Individual idiosyncrasies do exist, but it is also true that people who share a culture develop similar styles of cognition; similar processes of perceiving, recognizing, conceiving, judging, and reasoning; and similar values, assumptions, ideas, beliefs, and modes of thought.[9] What we see as good or bad depends on whether or not it supports our view of reality. Saral points out that

> . . . it is thus apparent that there is no absolute reality, nor is there a universally valid way of perceiving, cognizing, and/or thinking. Each world-view has different underlying assumptions. Our normal state of consciousness is not something natural or given, nor is it universal across cultures. It is simply a specialized tool, a complex structure for coping with our environment.[10]

Because schools are patterned after the predominant culture, it is essential to understand the dominant worldview that originated primarily in Britain and Western Europe. This is not an easy task for those who happen to share this view of the world and take it for granted. Lessening the transitional trauma many students face in our classrooms, however, requires awareness of our expectations or of our worldview.

How can we gain insights into our unconsciously held assumptions and worldview? Kluckhohn writes that "studying [other cultures] enables us to see ourselves better. Ordinarily we are unaware of the specialized lens through which we look at life."[11] The comparison in Box 2.1 is an example of how we can understand the macrocultural worldview by learning about a microculture.

It is easy to identify ways in which our schools are consistent with the non-Indian way. School days are organized into strict time schedules punctuated by the bell. The competitive learning environment rewards individual excellence. Students learn ways to control disease, and they dissect frogs in the science lab. They debate the rightness or wrongness of public policies such as nuclear arms control, school prayers, and school desegregation. Many questions are asked; quick answers are associated with intelligence, slow ones with dullness. The list could go on.

Different worldviews often lead to mutual misperceptions, hostility, or conflict. For example, an American professor and his wife visiting Thailand for the first time were greeted with inquiries about their weights and salaries. A Japanese businessman terminated dealings with an American because the latter, not wishing to waste time or pry, initiated business discussions without the customary inquiries about family and other personal matters.

Evidence indicates that the same process of misperception that operates between members of different nations who are unaware of each other's worldview also operates in many schools and classrooms. The Panther Prowl, an annual homecoming celebration at a high school in central Florida, illustrates this misperception and cultural conflict. The Black and White students experienced little interracial contact outside of school. Two different musical groups, one Black and one White, had been hired to perform at the assembly. When the Black musicians began to perform, Blacks in the audience responded by clapping, stomping, singing, and dancing. The Black performers kept cool, interacted with the Black audience, and were clearly enjoying it. A group of White students became very upset, demanded quiet, and finally walked out. Black students, in turn, felt the Whites were being purposefully rude and unresponsive to the Black performers. Later that evening, several interracial fights broke out on campus.

According to anthropologist Roger Abrahams, what happened at the Panther Prowl is an example of the different performance traditions in Black and White cultures. The Anglo-European tradition places a virtuoso performer on a pedestal. The audience is but a passive recipient, and appreciation is expressed with applause at acceptable times only. For many Black Americans, however, the essence of the performance is an active interchange between performer and audience. Great performers, including public speakers and ministers, are those who keep their "cool" while getting their audience "hot."[12] Many Blacks and Whites have, of course, learned to appreciate and enjoy each other's music and performance traditions. Where this mutual understanding has not occurred, however, conflicts such as at the Panther Prowl can be expected.

Recent research on the educational needs and barriers for refugee and immigrant students in the United States provides valuable insights into the mutual misperceptions, hostility, and cultural conflict students and their families experience in our schools.[13] Given that over 20 percent of our schoolchildren are themselves immigrants or refugees or are from immigrant or refugee families, most teachers will have the opportunity to work with them and will need to be culturally competent, as discussed in Chapter 8.

Both parents and teachers often misinterpret cultural cues, especially when English language fluency is required and no interpreters are available. For example, in one study of Hmong children in American society, during parent–teacher conferences the parents did not understand what the teachers were asking of them. Meanwhile, the teachers misinterpreted "the Asian custom of nodding and shaking one's head up and down as understanding and agreement, when, in fact, it was the parents' way of being polite."[14] Many Asian parents and students are confused by U.S. school practices because they expect strict control and an emphasis on memorization as an indication of learning.[15] Some students have responded to unexpected freedoms at school by "acting out" or becoming "discipline" problems; some have difficulty understanding how memorizing and even copying scholarly work is con-

Box 2.1
The Navajo Way

To a Navajo, time is ever flowing; can't be broken. Exactness of time is of little importance.

To a non-Indian, time is of the utmost importance and must be used to its fullest extent.

To a Navajo, the future is uncertain. Nature, which is more important than man, may change anything. This life is what counts—there is no sense that life on earth is a preparation for another life.

Non-Indians prepare for the future. Such items as insurance, savings, and plans for trips and vacations show to what extent non-Indians hold this value.

Patience: Navajo. To have patience and to wait is considered a good quality.

Non-Indian. The man who is admired is the one who is quick to act.

Age: Navajo. Respect is for the elders. Experience is felt to bring knowledge. Age has priority though increasing power is going to those who speak English well. Knowledge is power.

Non-Indian. The great desire to look younger and live longer. Much money is spent to pursue these efforts.

Family: Navajo. The Indian cultures consider many more individuals to be relatives than do non-Indians. Clan relationships are strong. The Navajo is wary of nonrelatives and foreigners.

Non-Indian. Biological family is of utmost importance, and relationships are limited within this group.

Wealth: Navajo. Wealth is to be consumed and used as security—always to be shared. Many Indians are suspicious of individuals who collect material possessions. Some tribes give love gifts and enjoy this practice.

Non-Indian. Non-Indian cultures have measured wealth in terms of material things. Many such possessions often constitute status symbols and are considered highly desirable.

Nature: Navajo. Humanity lives in perfect balance with nature. The earth is here to enjoy. Heed signals from nature—learn from animals. People are an integral part of this universe and must do their part to maintain harmony and balance among the parts of the cosmos.

sidered plagiarism in the United States. Other studies have found that both Mexican-origin immigrant parents and Hmong parents view teachers as experts in their children's education, are not accustomed to participating in school events, and do not expect or desire to be involved in this aspect of their children's education, although they value it highly and want their children to be successful. For parents who work long hours, travel long distances to job sites, have no reliable access to transportation, or feel inadequate speaking English, coming to school is a hardship. Most of the teachers interpreted this as a lack of parental interest and concern for their children and complained about the absence of parental involvement.[16] A study of Cambodian refugee families who fled during the Pol Pot regime revealed that the lack of parental involvement in their children's education was rooted in the spiritual beliefs of Khmer people:

Non-Indian. Culture here is a constant search for new ways for control and mastery of the elements around. Artificial lakes are made; natural waters are controlled; electricity is generated and controlled. Such accomplishments are looked upon with pride.

Cultural premises among the Navajos may be summarized as follows:

1. The Universe is orderly.
2. There is a basic quest for harmony.
3. The universe, though personalized, is full of dangers.
4. Evil and good are complementary and both are present in all things, thus human nature is neither basically good nor evil.
5. Everything exists in two parts, male and female, which belong together and complete each other.
6. The future is uncertain—nature (which is more powerful than people) might change anything.
7. This life is what counts—there is no sense that life on earth is a preparation for another existence.
8. Time and place are symbols of recapitulation.
9. Events, not actors or quality, are primary.
10. Time is ever flowing, can't be broken.
11. Concept of life as one whole—Navajos have a hard time thinking in terms of social, economic, and political distinctions.
12. Like produces like . . . the part stands for the whole.

Source: "Teacher-Aide Guide for Navajo Area," product of a conference at the Dzilth-na-o-dith-hle Community School, Bloomfield, NM, June 8–12, 1970. Reprinted by permission of the Bureau of Indian Affairs, Eastern Navajo Agency—OIEP.

Khmer parents believed that an individual's identity and personal qualities emerge from within the child, and it is the parents' job to discover, rather than direct, these qualities. They feared loss of face by pushing a child who subsequently failed. They also believed that through reincarnation, one's present position was determined by a life lived previously . . . (and, as one example of impact of these beliefs) parents tended not to push their children to attend bilingual classes . . . even though they favored bilingual education.[17]

Post–9/11 studies of Muslim families in the United States found that parents were eager to be involved in their children's education but they feared they would be misunderstood due to language barriers and their culture. Their children were often teased by U.S. born students for their Arab names, taunted or bullied for wearing hijab and fasting during Ramadan, viewed as fanatics, and feared as terrorists, even though the vast majority of Muslims abhor terrorism. In a study of Somali youth in Maryland, the girls revealed how their religious practices, such as "clothing, daily prayer, and refusal to date" led to discrimination at school, and they felt disrespected when "school personnel expected them to remove their scarves for school ID photos."[18]

Overall, many of the teachers and administrators in these studies viewed students' cultural differences as evidence of deficient cultures, low intelligence, or learning disabilities they were unable to diagnose, especially if the children were not fluent in English. However, researchers have also identified exemplary school programs for immigrant and refugee students. Such schools can become a major source of hope and security for these newcomers when teachers are prepared to understand their needs and are willing to work toward culturally competent teaching.[19] A first step is to understand one's own cultural assumptions and worldview.

High- and Low-Context Cultures

One promising way to conceptualize culture and avoid cross-cultural misunderstanding has been developed by Edward T. Hall. *Beyond Culture*, *The Silent Language*, and *The Hidden Dimension* are classics in the area of intercultural study and vividly describe how humans can be unknowingly influenced by their culture. People from different cultures may perceive the world differently, often unaware that there are alternative ways of perceiving, believing, behaving, and judging. Hall argues that most of us hold unconscious assumptions about what is appropriate in terms of personal space, time, interpersonal relations, and ways of seeking truth (e.g., scientific inquiry, meditation, revelation, etc.). These cultural differences exist to varying degrees among Anglo-Europeans and ethnic minorities within our society as well as among different nations.

Cultural differences and misunderstandings often become evident when people from different cultures try to communicate. Often they assume erroneously that they are communicating. This is why Hall's simple but elegant theory of culture can be helpful to us, provided that it is used as a framework for observing and understanding behaviors, while avoiding stereotypes and guarding against a reified and static view of culture.

Hall envisions a continuum of *sociocultural tightness* to distinguish between high-context cultures at one end and low-context cultures at the other; specific cultures may be described according to where they lie on the continuum.[20] Hall focuses on interpersonal communication styles as a key for illuminating basic cultural differences and similarities. In low-context cultures, such as much of the United States, Germany, and Scandinavia, meaning is gleaned from the verbal message itself, for example, a spoken explanation, a memo, or computer program. What is said is more important than who said it, and often we don't even know the author. Members of the university community, for example, often communicate by phone or email over a period of years or decades without ever meeting each other in person. High-context cultures, such as East Asian, Arab, southern European, Native American, Mexican, and portions of the rural United States, are generally the opposite. Meaning must be understood in terms of the situation or setting in which communication takes place. A classic example is the Chinese language, in which many words may be pronounced in several different ways, depending on the context within which they are used. Thus

Table 2.1 ⬛ Summary of Hall's Conception of Culture According to Context

	High Context	*Low Context*
Time	*Polychronic* Loose schedules, flux, multiple simultaneous activities. Last-minute changes of important plans. Time is less tangible.	*Monochronic* Tight schedules, one event at a time, linear. Importance of being on time. Time is more tangible (e.g., is spent, wasted, is "money").
Space & tempo	*High-Sync* Synchrony, moving in harmony with others and with nature, is consciously valued. Social rhythm has meaning.	*Low-Sync* Synchrony is less noticeable. Social rhythm is underdeveloped.
Reasoning	*Comprehensive Logic* Knowledge is gained through intuition, spiral logic, and contemplation. Importance of feelings.	*Linear Logic* Knowledge is gained through analytical reasoning (e.g., the Socratic method). Importance of words.
Verbal messages	*Restricted Codes* "Shorthand speech," reliance on nonverbal and contextual clues. Overall emotional quality more important than meaning of particular words. Economical, fast, efficient communication that is satisfying, slow to change; fosters interpersonal cohesiveness and provides for human need for social stability. Stress on social integration and harmony; being polite.	*Elaborate Codes* Verbal amplification through extended talk or writing. Little reliance on nonverbal or contextual cues. Doesn't foster cohesiveness but can change rapidly. Provides for human need to adapt and change. Stress on argument and persuasion; being direct.
Social roles	*Tight Social Structure* Individual's behavior is predictable; conformity to role expectations.	*Loose Social Structure* Behavior is unpredictable; role behavior expectations are less clear.
Interpersonal relations	*Group Is Paramount* Clear status distinctions (e.g., age, rank, position), strong distinctions between insiders and outsiders.	*Individual Is Paramount* Status is more subtle, distinctions between insiders and outsiders less important.

(continued)

Table 2.1 ▨ (continued)

	High Context	Low Context
Interpersonal relations *(cont.)*	Human interactions are emotionally based, person oriented. Stronger personal bonds, bending of individual interests for sake of relationships. Cohesive, highly interrelated human relationships, completed action chains. Members of group are first and foremost.	Human interactions are functionally based, approach is specialized. Fragile interpersonal bonds due to geographic mobility. Fragmented, short-term human relationships, broken action chains when relationship is not satisfying. Individuals are first, groups come second.
Social organization	**Personalized Law and Authority** Customary procedures and whom one knows are important. Oral agreements are binding. In face of unresponsive bureaucracies, must be an insider or have a "friend" to make things happen (e.g., going through the "back door"). People in authority are personally and truly responsible for actions of every subordinate.	**Procedural Law and Authority** Procedures, laws, and policies are more important than whom one knows. Written contracts are binding. Policy rules, unresponsive bureaucracy. People in authority try to pass the buck. Impersonal Legal procedures

it is necessary to avoid reification of the categories that will be discussed below, and to keep in mind the diversity within nations and ethnic groups that is related to regional, gender, and socioeconomic differences.

With these limitations in mind, consider the overview of key characteristics of high- and low-context cultures in Table 2.1.[21] In theory, high- and low-context cultures differ according to orientations toward time and space, reasoning, verbal messages, social roles, interpersonal relations, and law and authority in social organizations. Initially, it might appear that high-context cultures are more humanistic and low-context cultures more mechanistic. This interpretation is too simplistic. It is true that members of high-context cultures tend to live in tune with nature and with other humans who are part of their social network, and that people in low-context cultures are often at odds with nature and tend to have more fragmented social relationships. It is also true that individuals in high-context cultures tend to gain their identity through group associations (e.g., place of work, neighborhood organizations, family or lineage), while individuals in low-context cultures usually develop an identity based on their personal efforts and achievements. However, members of high-context cultures are less open to strangers (although they are often known for their warm hospitality toward foreigners who are "guests"), make

Cultural immersion experiences in China provide Westerners with insight into their own worldview.

stronger distinctions between insiders and outsiders, and are more likely to follow rigid role expectations and bureaucratic traditions that have become outdated and inefficient. In comparison, the greater personal freedom, openness, and individual choice found in low-context cultures might be seen as more humanistic than mechanistic. It is important to realize that both high- and low-context cultures possess positive ingredients that are necessary for human survival. For example, high-context cultures provide a strong human support network that helps guard against the alienation of a technological society; and low-context cultures provide ways of adapting, changing, and using new knowledge that can help resolve human problems such as starvation and disease.

What does this theory have to do with schools in the United States: Consider the case of Fred Young.

In contrast to the low-context culture at school, many students like Fred Young have grown up in high-context microcultures. Without an understanding of the different assumptions and expectations of their home and classroom culture, they are likely to experience some degree of psychological discomfort, or transitional trauma, as they attempt to adjust to school.

The vast majority of schools in this society are modeled after the low-context, dominant culture. Academic and social events operate according to tight schedules, often printed months in advance. Competition, individual excellence, and personal responsibility are stressed. Interpersonal relations, nonverbal communication, and cooperation are de-emphasized. Consider again the Navajo and non-Indian cultural premises in Box 2.1. These can be understood in terms of high- and low-context

Box 2.1
The Example of Fred Young, or Clever Fox, Navajo Physicist

Fred Young grew up in the traditional world of the Navajo. Today, after having earned a doctorate in nuclear physics, Fred works at the Los Alamos scientific labs, where the United States' best scientists seek to understand the universe.

As a child, Fred lived in desperate poverty. He helped support his family at a very young age by hunting game, and sometimes he dug for food in the garbage cans outside homes in Gallup, New Mexico. During these early years, Fred also developed a deep curiosity about the world of nature, wondering what it was made of.

Fred's parents sent him to a boarding school at Ignacio, Colorado, so that he could eat regularly. His curiosity and love of nature continued, and he wondered whether clocks could tell the time of day because they were controlled by the sun. His years at the boarding school were filled with hurt and resentment. "In the White world the basic assumptions are so different that something that would be taken for granted by all my classmates wasn't obvious to me at all," Fred says. "So they thought I was scared or dumb or both. It was embarrassing at times, and it made me angry." The daily insults and arrogance Fred experienced in school built up feelings of resentment and hostility, and he sometimes ran off from school and returned to his family in Monument Valley. His intense curiosity and desire to know always brought him back to school, where he put up with the hurt in order to satisfy his quest for knowledge. When Fred attended the University of New Mexico on a tribal scholarship, a textbook explanation of how the rainbow works so excited him that he decided to become a physicist.

Today, despite his accomplishments in the world of White America, Fred is still bewildered about how Anglo society works. And there is still hurt. "Even now strangers will sometimes treat me like a dumb Indian," Fred says.

Source: Based on "The Long Walk of Fred Young." *NOVA*. Reproduced by permission of the British Broadcasting Corporation.

culture in that time orientations tend to be polychronic, harmony with nature is highly valued, clan relationships are strong, and there is a wariness of nonrelatives and foreigners.

Moreover, Hall's theory of high- and low-context culture can be included in the school curriculum as a means of helping students become more multicultural. Students can learn to use Hall's theory as a tool for understanding human conflicts that are rooted in deep culture.

What Is Race and How Does It Differ From Culture?

In the United States, race is a widely accepted myth that the human species can be divided into scientifically valid categories based on biological traits such as skin color, hair texture, eye shape, and other facial features.[22] European scientists created the idea of different "races" during the "Age of Enlightenment" as a means to classify or categorize humans according to observable physical differences, much as they classified other animals and plants. Chapter 3, on page 83, provides an overview of the racial categories that were created in the eighteenth century and became part of the flawed and damaging cultural knowledge that prevailed until recently, and still lingers in the minds of some people.

The authors of an outstanding new book, *How Real Is Race?*, explain how the idea of race became a part of the predominant worldview in the United States. They write,

> *Most long-term residents in the United States have been raised to see race, to notice the physical characteristics such as skin color, hair texture, and nose and eye shape. This is not surprising, given the history of the United States. For nearly 200 years, U.S. religious, legal, political, and educational institutions promoted a belief that physical traits were markers of fundamental biological divisions of humanity. . . . And U.S. racial ideology, especially racial science, tried unsuccessfully to link visible traits, like skin color, to more profound biological differences in capacities, especially the capacity for civilization and intellectual achievement.*[23]

In contrast to culture, which is learned and can be modified (even rejected) over time, *race* refers to immutable physical traits that we are born with. In the United States, we have learned to tune into a few visible biological traits, "whereas much of the human genetic variation is invisible and often more significant medically."[24]

Darwin attacked the scientific use of race, and many social scientists have abandoned the concept because it has not provided useful knowledge in understanding human nature and cannot be easily defined.[25] Anthropologist Ashley Montagu called race "man's most dangerous myth."[26] The myth of race is at the root of racism (a topic we will explore in Chapter 3) and has led to tragic atrocities such as slavery in the United States and Latin America, the Holocaust in Europe, and the internment of Japanese Americans during World War II. He warns, "It is not possible to make the sort of racial classifications which anthropologists and others have attempted. The fact is that all human beings are so mixed with regard to origin that between different groups of individuals . . . 'overlapping' of physical traits is the rule."[27] Typically there are greater physical differences among individuals within a given race than there are between people of different races. Today, most scientists discount the utility of "race" as a biological concept, and they estimate that only a tiny fraction of our genetic makeup is associated with racial features. More important is the fact that all humans share a common ancestry, believed to have originated in Africa, and belong to a single species, *Homo sapiens* (Latin for "human being" and "wise"). As surgeons and pathologists know, under the skin we all look the same. We all belong to one race, the human race.

Despite the irrelevancy of race as a concept for defining humanity, the United States is a race-conscious society, as are some other nations and regions, such as South Africa, Brazil, Japan, Puerto Rico, and most of South and Central America. So, how can we explain the physical traits we have learned to see as "race"? These physical attributes developed over the eons in response to geographic differences humans encountered as they migrated out of Africa. Many scientists argue that only the fittest survived extreme climatic conditions, high altitudes, intensity of the sun, and life-threatening pests such as the mosquito that carries malaria. Where people were relatively isolated due to geographic barriers like mountains and the oceans, breeding in isolation led to more distinct phenotypes. The commonly identified but misconstrued racial types today are remnants of the eighteenth century racial classification categories: Mongoloid, Negroid, and Caucasoid, and sometimes Malayan and Native American.[28]

It should be clear that culture is in no way determined by skin color or other physical attributes associated with race. Individuals from any so-called racial group can become multicultural, or competent in any cultural milieu they have access to, if they so choose. For example, there are Whites who act "Black" and vice versa; many Latino communities contain tremendous racial diversity (e.g., Puerto Ricans include people who are Black, Indian, Latino, or White), and there are Black Africans in Ethiopia who are Orthodox Jews, as well as African Americans who identify with Judaism. It is also true, however, that racial isolation and segregation are a fact of history for large segments of the population; as a result, cultural differences that can be associated with race have survived. The fact that cultural differences are sometimes linked with racial differences confirms myths and stereotypes associated with race. African Americans, for example, are often perceived as having more rhythm and as being natural athletes. Jews are often perceived as being miserly and more intelligent. Asians are regarded as the "model minority." These perceptions are usually based on the erroneous belief that genetic biological factors, rather than cultural factors and societal treatment explain what is perceived. Nevertheless, the concept of race persists and remains a primary basis for categorizing self and others within U.S. society.[29]

What Do We Mean by Ethnic Groups?

An *ethnic group* is a community of people within a larger society that is socially distinguished or set apart, by others and/or by itself, primarily on the basis of racial and/or cultural characteristics, such as religion, language, and tradition. An ethnic group may be distinguished "by race, religion, or national origin."[30] The central factor is the notion of being set apart from the larger society; the distinctiveness may be based on either physical or cultural attributes, or both. As is explained on pages 54–55, an ethnic group may also be an ethnic minority, but not always.

The U.S. Census Categories

The U.S. Census Bureau's Department of Racial Statistics' approach to classification and counting the American population lists the nation's numerous ethnic groups, as shown in Table 2.2, according to five "races": White or Caucasian; Black or African American; American Indian or Alaska Native; Asian; and Native Hawaiian and other Pacific Islander. The Bureau also includes Latinos, "the officially designated pan-ethnic category of Hispanic Americans," adding that "Hispanics can be of any

Table 2.2 ☒ Estimated Population of Ethnic Groups in the United States

Race	2007 Total	2007 Percentage
All Persons	**301,621,159**	**100.0%**
White (one race and multiple races)[a]	228,569,609	75.8%
White (one race)[b]	223,005,483	73.9%
White (alone)[c]	198,553,437	65.8%
Black or African American (one race and multiple races)[d]	39,663,004	13.1%
Black or African American (one race)[e]	37,334,570	12.4%
Black or African American (alone)[f]	36,657,280	12.2%
American Indian and Alaskan Native alone	2,365,347	0.8%
Cherokee tribal grouping	279,123	—
Chippewa tribal grouping	105,028	—
Navajo tribal grouping	289,135	—
Sioux tribal grouping	109,213	—
Asian alone (100%)	13,233,287	4.5%
Asian Indian (19.4%)	2,570,166	0.9%
Chinese (23.0%)	3,045,592	1.0%
Filipino (18.2%)	2,412,446	0.8%
Japanese (6.1%)	803,092	0.3%
Korean (10.2%)	1,344,171	0.4%
Vietnamese (11.4%)	1,508,489	0.5%
Other Asian (11.7%)	1,549,331	0.5%
Native Hawaiian and Other Pacific Islander (100%)	434,675	0.1%
Native Hawaiian (32.9%)	142,919	—
Guamanian or Chamorro (17.2%)	74,947	—
Samoan (16%)	69,615	—
Other Pacific Islander (33.9%)	147,194	—
Some other race	18,738,784	6.21%
Hispanic or Latino (100%)	45,427,437	15.1%
Mexican (64.2%)	29,166,981	9.7%
Puerto Rican (9.1%)	4,120,205	1.4%
Cuban (3.5%)	1,611,478	0.5%
Other Hispanic or Latino (23.2%)	10,528,773	3.5%

[a]People who checked White race alone or in combination with one or more other races.
[b]People who checked White race alone.
[c]Non-Hispanic or Latino people who checked White race alone.
[d]People who checked Black or African American race alone or in combination with one or more other races.
[e]People who checked Black or African American race alone.
[f]Non-Hispanic or Latino people who checked Black or African American race alone.

Source: U.S. Census Bureau, 2007 American Community Survey.

racial group."[31] Harvard sociologist Orlando Patterson questions the Department's insistence that Asian Americans are a "race" (although they come from many culturally different ancestry groups), whereas "Hispanics," who also represent many diverse ancestry groups, can be of any racial group. He speculates that the reason is the presence of Blacks in Latin America, and their absence in "the Asian mix."[32] Patterson also disagrees with the popular view that the non-Hispanic White population is declining; he argues that the White population in the United States will actually *increase* in coming decades due to "the massive infusion of white-identified people from the Hispanic cluster . . . the high intermarriage rates of whites from the Hispanic cluster with non-Hispanic whites, and the strong tendency of the progeny of such unions to shed any Hispanic identity that leaders of their parents' generation attempt to impose on them."[33]

As we will see in Chapters 4 through 7, this classification system does not capture the complexities of ethnicity or how people grouped into these huge categories affiliate with one or more ethnic groups based on nations of origin, geographical region in the United States and/or religion. In addition, many Americans have parents and/or more distant relatives from a number of ethnic groups or nations of origin; they may reject the Census Bureau's broad categorization scheme and prefer the mixed-race category that was added in 2000 (see next section). Others who also have a multiracial background may choose just one race. For example, although the vast majority of African Americans have a "mixed heritage," approximately 95 percent identify themselves as Black or African American.[34] Because there are very few in the Black community who are of fully African descent, many fear the mixed-race option could diminish the political influence of African Americans and their ability to address Black community concerns. Indeed, and perhaps because many citizens of color vote Democratic, some Republicans would like to eliminate racial or ethnic data from the Census. However, despite the limitations of the system, a critical advantage of the Census Bureau's ethno/racial categorization is that it keeps track of racial inequalities in our population demographics, such as educational attainment, health care, employment, and other important indicators of well-being. Although race is not a valid concept, biologically speaking, racial inequalities in U.S. society have not disappeared.

Diversity within Ethnic Groups

It is important to think of ethnic groups as imprecise and arbitrary social constructions, not absolute categories of people. Even within relatively well-defined ethnic groups, such as African Americans or Jewish Americans, there exists tremendous heterogeneity. When we consider factors such as income, level of education, geographical region, generation of immigration or entry (and whether it was voluntary, forced, or a product of colonialism), family structure, size and composition of the ethnic community, and biological features, such as skin color, we see greater variation within ethnic groups than between them. We will pursue this diversity among Anglo-European and Jewish Americans in Chapter 4, American Indians and African Americans in Chapter 5, Latinos in Chapter 6, and Asian, Muslim, and Arab Americans in Chapter 7.

Ethnic Identity Adds to the Complexity

Ethnic identity, or *ethnicity*, refers to the degree to which a person feels connected with a racial or cultural group, one's familial ethnic group while growing up. It is a complex cluster of factors "including self-labeling, a sense of belonging, positive evaluation, preference for the group, ethnic interest and knowledge, and involvement in activities associated with the group."[35] The strength or degree of one's ethnic identity is significantly influenced by factors such as language spoken at home, ethnic composition of the neighborhood, and percentage of friends who are of the same ethnic group. There are developmental differences within an individual over the span of a lifetime, as well as tremendous variability within any one ethnic group in terms of the strength of ethnic identification, the adherence to familial cultural values and norms, and experiences in the predominantly White society.[36] A person's sense of identity may be strong even when there is little involvement in the traditional culture, such as language use and dress. For example, some third- or fourth-generation Irish or Italian Americans might retain little of their traditional culture of origin but still maintain a symbolic ethnicity, or strong sense of loyalty to their ethnic group. Sometimes individuals who are perceived and labeled by others as members of an ethnic group (often based on surname and/or skin color) reject or do not identify with their ethnic group and feel totally assimilated into mainstream society, as is the case for some middle- and upper-income Latinos whose families have lived in the United States for several generations.

Multiracial Identities

In 2000, for the first time in our history, the U.S. Census allowed people to identify themselves by more than one race. As a result, 7.3 million Americans, or about 3 percent of the population identified themselves as being two or more races.[37] As aptly stated by Maria P. P. Root, a clinical psychologist who specializes in America's racially mixed people, "This change in the racial classification scheme fundamentally challenges a race system wedded to notions of racial purity and one-drop rules to enforce a mono-racial reality (meaning you could only be one race)."[38] She notes that nearly 7 percent of youths under age 18 were identified as biracial or multiracial and describes the challenges many of them face in developing a sense of personal and social identity and finding acceptance in our schools and society.

The challenges of growing up as a multiracial person in America are vividly described by the actor and film director Teja Arboleda in his recent autobiography, *In the Shadow of Race: Growing Up As a Multiethnic, Multicultural, and "Multiracial" American*. He writes, "My father's father was Filipino-Chinese. . . . My father's mother was African American-Native American. . . . My mother's father was German-Danish. . . . My mother's mother was German. . . . I was born in Brooklyn, New York, but grew up in Japan. . . ."[39] He tells the story of his search for identity in a world where he was called *Nigger, Spic, Jap, Nazi, Turk, Stupid Yankee, Afghanistani,* and *Iraqi.* Furthermore, he adds,

> *I've been called* mulatto, criollo, mestizo, simarron, Hapahaoli, masama, exotic, alternative, mixed-up, messed-up, half-breed, *and in between. . . .*

I've been ordered to get glasses of water for neighboring restaurant patrons. I've been told to be careful mopping the floors at the television station where I was directing a show. Even with my U.S. passport, I've been escorted to the "aliens only" line at Kennedy International Airport. I've been told I am not dark enough. I've been told I'm not White enough. I've been told I could talk American real good. I've been told, "Take your humus and your pita bread and go back to Mexico!" I've been ordered to "Go back to where you belong, we don't want your kind here!"[40]

These experiences are nothing new for the millions of multiracial people in the United States, and yet they have been largely overlooked in our schools and multicultural education initiatives. However, this neglect is beginning to change. With the 2008 Presidential Campaign and the election of Barack Obama, conversations about what it means to be mixed-race in America have become more prevalent. For example, some mixed-race individuals now talk openly to the news media about not being accepted by either or any of their racial identity groups, about "getting a lot of flak for not being 100 percent Black," about being Asian mothers who are perceived as the "nanny" for their own children, or about being multiracial individuals who are suspected of trying to escape racism, or being perceived as the oppressor.[41] By now virtually all Americans, from elementary school on up, are aware of Barack Obama's family history as the son of a White American mother from Kansas and a Black African father from Kenya whom he met only once. His powerful autobiography and search for self-identity, *Dreams from My Father: A Story of Race and Inheritance*, reveals how he finds his identity as an African American while maintaining lasting love and connections with his mother and White grandparents who raised him. His book is an inspiration for everyone who hopes for racial reconciliation and the end of racial injustice in America, as well as hope for multiracial Americans who seek ways to reconcile their divided ancestry. Moreover, for teachers and administrators, Obama's school experiences in Indonesia and Hawaii provide wisdom and content that can help shape equitable school policies as well as curriculum revisions that would better serve *all* of our students, but especially those who are multiracial.

When Is an Ethnic Group a Minority Group?

The label *minority group* is confusing; today, many individuals prefer not to be labeled a *minority*, because the term connotes inferior or lesser status vis-à-vis the majority. Furthermore, *minority* is often confused with numerical minority, when in fact a numerical minority may control a numerical majority. White slave owners, for example, were a numerical minority on the large Southern plantations, and today in many small towns throughout the South and Southwest White minorities hold political and economic control despite the larger numbers of African American or Mexican American citizens. A numerical minority of White South Africans controlled the South African government and society from 1910 until the end of apartheid in the 1990s.

From a sociological perspective, whether an ethnic group is also a minority group depends on the degree to which it holds a subordinate status in the society.

Wirth defines minority group in terms of subordinate position as "a group of people who, because of their physical or cultural characteristics, are singled out from others in the society in which they live for differential and unequal treatment and who therefore regard themselves as objects of collective discrimination."[42] Most social scientists view ethnic groups as minority groups when they:

- Suffer discrimination and subordination within a society
- Are set apart in terms of physical or cultural traits disapproved of by the dominant group
- Share a sense of collective identity and common burdens
- Inherit their group membership at birth
- Marry primarily within their groups[43]

A review of U.S. history reveals that most, if not all, ethnic groups have experienced minority group status, usually during the early stages of immigration or colonization. From the above definition, it is clear that some ethnic groups have remained minority groups for many generations and others have not. It has been easier for White ethnics to shed their minority status because discrimination against them has not been based on racial classification.

The degree to which an ethnic group retains minority group status depends on how it is received by and/or receives the predominant society. Does it experience long-term segregation? Is it quickly absorbed into the mainstream? Does it wish to retain its own cultural traditions? It is important to realize, however, that individuals in the same ethnic group differ in their experiences associated with minority status, including prejudice, discrimination, and feelings of powerlessness.

What Works Best in Twenty-First-Century America: Cultural Assimilation, Pluralism, or Something Else?

Cultural assimilation, sometimes referred to as the result of the American "melting pot," is often mistakenly equated with multicultural education. *Cultural assimilation* is "a process in which people of diverse ethnic and racial backgrounds come to interact, free of constraints, in the life of the larger community. It is a one-way process through which members of an ethnic group give up their original culture and are absorbed into the core culture, which predominates in the host society."[44] Cultural assimilation has been a strong theme throughout the history of the United States.

Between 1820 and 1970, more than 45 million immigrants, mostly from European nations, entered the United States. The prevalent view was that the newly arrived ethnic groups would give up their unique cultural attributes and accept the Anglo-American way of life. The schools were expected to play the major role in this forced assimilation. Education historian Cubberly vividly describes the process:

Everywhere these people (immigrants) tend to settle in groups or settlements and to set up their own national manners, customs, and observances. Our task is to break up their groups and settlements, to assimilate or amalgamate these people as part of the American race, and to implant in their children, so far as can be done, the Anglo-Saxon conception of righteousness, law, order, and popular government, and to awaken in them reverence for our democratic institutions and for those things which we as a people hold to be of abiding worth.[45]

The melting-pot theory is still widely accepted, especially by classroom teachers. In an attempt to educate students in "the American way," many teachers view cultural differences as deficits and disadvantages. They are blind to their students' personal and cultural strengths. As an example, many Spanish-speaking students, like Jesús Martinez (see page 7), who could not read English, were placed in classes for the mentally retarded after scoring low on IQ tests that were written in English. Students like Fred Young were perceived as "dumb."

In recent years, the theory of cultural pluralism has emerged as an alternative to the melting pot. Cultural pluralism, in its ideal form, is a process of compromise characterized by mutual appreciation and respect between two or more cultural groups.[46] In a culturally pluralistic society, members of different ethnic groups are permitted to retain many of their cultural traditions, such as language, religion, and food preferences, so long as they conform to those practices deemed necessary for social harmony and the survival of society as a whole. The symphony orchestra is an appropriate metaphor for cultural pluralism. Each section retains some of its uniqueness while contributing to the beauty and strength of the whole composition.

The concept of cultural pluralism fits well with the democratic ideals of the United States, such as majority rule with minority rights and the national motto *e pluribus Unum* (out of many, one). As noted in Chapter 1, this societal ideal was developed in the early twentieth century by democratic philosopher Horace Kallen, who wrote that each ethnic group had the democratic right to retain its own heritage.[47] Kallen was a Jewish immigrant from Poland, and he argued vehemently against forced Americanization of immigrants. His views, however, were not given much credence until after the civil rights movement in the United States during the 1960s and 1970s.

Gay described the psychological and political effects of this civil rights movement in our society:

Newly formed student activist organizations, as well as the older established civil rights groups, began to demand restitution for generations of oppression, racism, and cultural imperialism. The shifting ideological focus of the movement was captured in such slogans as "Black is beautiful," "Yellow is mellow," "Black power," and "Power to the people." Moreover, as the slogans suggest, the civil rights movement for Afro-Americans gradually became a movement for recognition of all minority groups, including Mexican-Americans, Native Americans, Asian Americans and Puerto Ricans.[48]

What began as a Black Power movement spread to include many other minority groups and women. It also helped inspire and rekindle ethnic consciousness among numerous White ethnic groups, particularly among the third and fourth generations of Southern and Eastern European immigrants. As a result, today's society is much more aware, and even appreciative, of its cultural diversity.

A common misconception is that cultural pluralism is dangerous to society because it heightens ethnic group identity and leads to separatism, polarization, and intergroup antagonism. This view overlooks a critical ingredient of cultural pluralism: All groups must conform to certain rules that are necessary for the survival of the society as a whole. The question of what is good and necessary for the survival of a society is a difficult one, and the processes maintaining social boundaries between different ethnic groups are complex. The Amish provide a good example of the struggle for cultural pluralism in this society. In some regions, they are allowed to maintain their own communities, schools, and traditions, but are expected to abide by the rules of the larger society. Orthodox Jews provide another example: They maintain their religious traditions in a society that is highly secular and primarily Christian in religious outlook. Other examples include the Cherokee, Navajo, and Chippewa Nations, as well as other Indian tribes that have treaty rights to land, fishing rights, and other special relationships with the federal government.

Cultural pluralism is an ideal state of societal conditions characterized by equity and mutual respect among existing culture groups. How we can envision and work toward cultural pluralism in multicultural classrooms is the focus of the last section of this chapter.

Symbolic Ethnicity, Segmented Assimilation, and Racialized Ethnicity

Today's social scientists have developed new conceptual frameworks to predict the extent to which contemporary immigrants are assimilating into U.S. society. Three of the most promising are *symbolic ethnicity*, the theory of *segmented assimilation*, and *racialized ethnicity*.[49] Symbolic ethnicity refers to second- and third-generation children who are structurally assimilated into mainstream society in terms of where they live, the schools they attend, and their occupations. They retain a token sense of their heritage and celebrate their ethnic roots "when and where they choose to do so in multicultural America."[50] The theory of segmented assimilation argues that the children and grandchildren of immigrants will follow one of three paths as they adapt to American society, depending on their race, their parents' income and occupational status, where they live, and other aspects of family and community support. Some are highly successful educationally, find high-status occupations, and enter into the White middle class; others identify with ethnic minority youth cultures where there is little chance to escape societal inequities; and still others find support and social mobility within their ethnic communities.[51] The theory of racialized ethnicity identifies the social boundaries that exist for non-White ethnic groups, no matter how successful they are academically and economically. Encounters with racial prejudice and discrimination among middle-class adolescents of color generate a heightened sense of ethnicity that can take different forms.[52] These new theories of assimilation and pluralism will come to life in the brief histories of ethnic groups in Chapters 4 through 7.

Guidelines for the Classroom: Aspects of Ethnicity

Longstreet has developed a clear and useful scheme (based in part on Hall's theory) for understanding differences in culturally pluralistic classrooms.[53] Originally conceived for desegregated classrooms, it can be used as a guideline for observing and interpreting human behavior in any setting.

Longstreet defines ethnicity as "that portion of cultural development that occurs before the individual is in complete command of his or her abstract intellectual powers and that is formed primarily through the individual's early contacts with family, neighbors, friends, teachers, and others, as well as with his or her immediate environment of the home and neighborhood."[54] Most older students will have gained some intellectual control over these learned behaviors and are to some degree bicultural, but even among bicultural adults that control is likely to remain incomplete.

Longstreet goes on to identify five aspects of ethnicity that provide teachers with guidelines for pinpointing potential sources of misunderstanding in multicultural classrooms. These aspects of ethnicity can be used to illuminate cultural differences among nations as well as among ethnic groups within a society. The outline in Box 2.2 is based on Longstreet's aspects of ethnicity.[55]

Longstreet distinguishes between an individual's ethnic heritage and the culture of the school. She regards *scholastic ethnicity* (i.e., school culture) as a national phenomenon because the public school bureaucracy and traditions are similar throughout the nation and across several generations. The form and uses of grading, the content of study, the "uniform number of periods per day, bells, hall monitors, and even required notes for absences" are all examples of century-old school practices that still predominate.[56] The greater the distinction between scholastic ethnicity and the student's ethnic heritage or home culture, the greater the alienation that student is likely to experience. Let's consider these aspects of ethnicity in greater depth.

Verbal Communication

The almost exclusive use of standard American English in U.S. schools is a striking example of the macrocultural orientation. Whether or not all schoolchildren should develop enough skill in standard English to make its use a functional option is not being debated. (All students should be expected to attain proficiency in standard American English.) What should be examined, however, is the cultural conflict many children experience in schools that ignore or repress the language they have known since birth. According to Mario Benitez,

> . . . all the pre-primers available on the market assume a level of development in oral languages that the Mexican American child has not reached at the beginning of first grade. Phonologically speaking he neither hears nor discriminates certain sounds. Accustomed as he is to hearing Spanish mostly at home, he hears Spanish in the classroom instead of English and tries to decode accordingly. The result is frustration and awareness that he is failing at something [while] the other children are succeeding.[57]

Box 2.2
Guidelines for Understanding Cultural Differences

Verbal Communication

- Grammar
- Semantics—meanings of words
- Phonology—sound, pitch, rhythm, and tempo of words
- Discussion modes—patterns of participating and listening

Nonverbal Communication

- Kinesics—body language
- Proxemics—personal space
- Haptics—frequency, quality, and location of touch
- Signs and symbols—meanings associated with artifacts, such as clothing, jewelry, emblems, flags, and traffic lights

Orientation Modes

- Body positions—unconscious movements and relaxation
- Spatial architectural patterns
- Attention modes
- Time modes

Social Values

- Ideal behaviors (beliefs about how one ought or ought not to behave, such as seeking truth and beauty, being sincere, fair, compassionate, rational, loyal, and orderly.)[a]
- Ideal goals (beliefs about some end-state of existence that is worth or not worth attaining, such as "security, happiness, freedom, equality, ecstasy, fame, power, and states of grace and salvation.")[b]

Intellectual Modes

- Preferred ways of learning
- Knowledge most valued
- Skills emphasized

[a, b]M. Rokeach, *Beliefs, Attitudes, and Values* (San Francisco: Jossey-Bass, 1969), 124.

The truth of Benitez's remarks is usually accepted when referring to Latino, American Indian, and East Asian American children—those whose first language often is not English. It is recognized as well that standard American English may create similar learning problems for African American children. Recently, a group of elementary teachers in a rural school in central Florida noted that, as early as first grade, White students surpassed Blacks in reading. Until they listened to tapes of Black students speaking, they were oblivious to the distinct Black dialect. They then realized that asking many of these children to learn to read available materials was like asking Whites to begin reading Old English.

Areas of potential conflict related to verbal communication are dialect differences, especially grammar and semantics, and discussion modes. Students who speak "country," African American vernacular, or any nonstandard dialect are often perceived as uneducated or less intelligent. Many White students and some upper- and middle-income Black students who have grown up in ethnically encapsulated environments cannot understand their Black or Latino peers, or incorrectly assume they do understand. Use of the term "nigger" among some African Americans, for example, is distressing to some teachers even when students use the term with affection.

Abrahams and Gay have clearly identified some important classroom implications of language differences.

> To understand the relationship that exists between [the teacher and] students, and the students' classroom behavior, the middle-class teacher needs to realize that older Black students use a variety of verbal techniques, and that they use these techniques to discover [the teacher's] strengths and weaknesses, to find out where [the teachers] stand on issues ranging from how "hip" [they are] to racial attitudes, and to locate [their] breaking point. Once these are discovered they help the student to exert some control over the situation.
>
> Because [Black] street culture is an oral culture, and is dependent largely upon the spoken word for its perpetuation and transmission, its language is very colorful, creative, and adaptive. It is in a constant state of flux and new words are always being invented. Further, new slang words are constantly created as a way of maintaining an in-group relationship and of excluding outsiders. Thus, there emerges something of a secret code that only in-group members completely understand. It is used by students and others in street culture to convey messages to each other about the "enemy," even in his presence. Of course, some of these terms have been picked up by White "hipsters," but often the meaning is changed because of the different cultural perspective.[58]

Discussion modes, or the way members of the same ethnic group "engage in discussion when they are among themselves, at parties, at home with their families, or at meetings of committees,"[59] are also a frequent source of intercultural misunderstanding. Longstreet offers a vivid illustration:

> I had invited five black students in an economic opportunity program to my graduate workshop [Inner Detroit, Michigan]. The ostensible purpose was to discuss the inadequacies of university programs for diverse ethnic minorities. The discussion was, to begin with, quite orderly, that is, first one person spoke, then another, and so forth. However, as the discussion turned to more heated topics, the black Americans literally took it over. The whites in the group (more than half) sat as though they were an audience invited to observe an extraordinary event. The blacks seemed to all talk at once, becoming progressively louder and more shrill in pitch. Even as teacher, I did not feel there was any opportunity for me to interject an opinion or comment. There was a lull, and most unexpectedly one of the black girls turned to the whites who were gathered on one side of the circle: "And you," she asked pointing her finger at them, "why aren't you joining in? Do you think you're too good to tell us how you feel?" The whites seemed to find no

way to respond to her accusation, and I, myself, was stunned. Vaguely in my mind I had decided that the black group was determined to take over the discussion and make those "whiteys" listen. There really had been, as far as I could remember, no pause that would have let any of the whites enter the animated discussion. Furthermore, so many people seemed to be talking at once that I had trouble following what was being said.[60]

Longstreet and the White students in her seminar obviously assumed that the best way to conduct a discussion was to follow the "you-take-a-turn-then another-takes-a-turn" model. This is, in fact, the accepted mode in most classrooms. While some African American students might find this mode too restrictive, many Asian American students, even those considered to be culturally assimilated, are also uncomfortable with the mode but for different reasons. Accustomed to thinking through a position and verbalizing only after careful reflection, they are often frustrated by not having an opportunity to express their thoughts in the midst of a spontaneous, heated, seemingly loud discussion. And non-Asian classmates perceive them negatively, as the Whites were perceived negatively in Longstreet's seminar.

The typical mainstream mode is for the teacher to talk and students to listen. Students are passive recipients. Indeed, research indicates that teachers do over 75 percent of the talking in classrooms. The cardinal rule is that students must raise their hands and may not speak until given permission. One must never interrupt another who is speaking, especially the teacher.

This may sound like good classroom management, and often it is, especially for middle-class children. In mainstream society, adult questioning of children is common practice. Parents enjoy that kind of interaction and often use it to develop the child's ability to speak; thus the child is not confused when adults in school continue the process. For many inner-city African American children, however, question-and-answer elicitation may be wrongly interpreted as hostile because it occurs most frequently in their homes when the adult is angry at the child. And among language minority students, the strategy may trigger feelings of embarrassment and inadequacy.

Several scholars note that the "passive" and "indirect" language many White middle-class teachers use creates confusion and misunderstanding between themselves and many low-income children and children of color.[61] Based upon their view of politeness and showing respect, these teachers often speak in soft tones, offer choices, and use questions rather than commands. For example, they may say "Johnny, don't you want to sit down?" Or, "Tishanna, what did I ask you to do?" rather than telling the students to behave or get to work. The students often misinterpret this style as indications that the teacher is incompetent and uncaring.

What about students who learn best in a more informal setting that encourages an active interchange between the speaker and the audience? Think back to the Panther Prowl and the different participation styles of the Blacks and Whites in that audience. Daniels and colleagues show how, for many Blacks, communication and participation involve the whole self in a simultaneous interaction of intellect, intuition, and physicality.[62] Because communication and participation are central to learning, students with an African American worldview may learn best in settings that encourage a simultaneous response of thought, feeling, and movement. Silence and sitting still are often signs that the Black child is bored.[63]

In the low-context dominant culture, in contrast intellectual, emotional, and physical responses are easily separated. Messages in the form of memos become distinct from people, and ideas are analyzed in their written form, without the benefit of nonverbal cues. Society assumes that individuals, such as lawyers, sometimes argue viewpoints they do not believe, and in school, teachers often ask students to sharpen their thinking by arguing a position they cannot accept. In some cultures, these are impossibilities.[64] Children from White middle-class families are often comfortable in the classroom role of passive recipient. They can learn to be rational and to remove emotions and feelings from decisions. Many are unable to concentrate in a more active, noisy environment. These generalizations are supported by the extensive ethnographic research of Kochman in Chicago. Kochman, who is White, writes that "Black culture has given me a powerful appreciation of qualities and concerns that my own middle-class culture tends to downgrade: individual self-assertion and self-expression, spiritual well-being, spontaneity and emotional expressiveness, personal (as opposed to status) orientation, individual distinctiveness, forthrightness, camaraderie, and community."[65]

Nonverbal Communication

It is estimated that 50 to 90 percent of what humans communicate is nonverbal. That is, most of the messages we send are manifested through unconscious body movements, facial expressions, and gestures (kinesics); our unconscious use and organization of personal space (proxemics); and when, where, and how often we unconsciously physically touch others (haptics).

The literature is filled with fascinating examples of cultural differences in nonverbal communication. Much of this research was conducted over two decades ago. If misunderstood, it could foster racial stereotypes. It is included in this chapter because it illuminates cultural differences that sometimes do exist among members of a culturally pluralistic society. Ignorance of cultural differences allows us to mistakenly assume that everyone is operating according to the same verbal and nonverbal speech patterns and cultural norms. Acknowledging differences within foreign cultures can alert us to more subtle differences at home. Greetings are one example and illustrate how the accepted behaviors of one culture may be seriously misunderstood in another.

The Copper Eskimo welcome strangers with a buffet on the head or shoulders with the fist, while the northwest Amazonians slap one another on the back in greeting. Polynesian men greet one another by embracing and rubbing each others' back; Spanish-American males greet one another by a stereotyped embrace, head over the right shoulder of the partner, three pats on the back, head over reciprocal left shoulder, three more pats. In the Torres Straits, the old form of greeting was to bend the right hand into a hook, then mutually scratching palms by drawing away the right hand, repeating this several times. An Ainu, meeting his sister, grasped her hands in his for a few seconds, suddenly released his hold, grasped her by both ears and gave the peculiar Ainu greeting cry; then they stroked one another down the face and shoulders. Kayan males in Borneo grasp each other by the forearm, while a host throws his arm over the shoulder of a guest and strokes him endearingly with the palm of his hand. When two Kurd males meet, they grasp one another's right hand, raise them both, and alternately kiss the other's hand.

Andamanese greet one another by one sitting down in the lap of the other, arms around each other's necks and weeping for a while; two brothers, father and son, mother and daughter, and husband and wife, or even two friends may do this; the husband sits in the lap of the wife. Friends' "good-bye" consists in raising the hand of the other to the mouth and gently blowing on it, reciprocally. At Matavai a full-dress greeting after long absence requires scratching the head and temples with a shark's tooth, violently and with much bleeding. This brief list could be easily enlarged by other anthropologists.[66]

Imagine how public hugging and kissing, customary behaviors during greetings and departures among many Westerners, is often perceived by non-Westerners. "Kissing is in the Orient an act of private lovemaking, and arouses only disgust when performed publicly: thus, in Japan, it is necessary to censor out the major portion of love scenes in American-made movies."[67]

Eye aversion (looking down or away) is another potential source of intercultural misunderstanding. Within the dominant culture, "good"—that is, direct—eye contact signifies that one is listening to the speaker, is honest, and is telling the truth. Within some African American communities (particularly when survival often depends on showing deference to Whites), as well as among the Navajo and many Asian nations, eye aversion is a sign of deference and respect accorded to another. Imagine how a teacher raised within the White dominant culture is likely to perceive a student who looks down or away when questioned about some stolen lunch money or cheating on an exam. On the other hand, many students are bicultural and may give mixed messages.

In general, it appears that people from high-context cultures require less personal space and do more touching. Americans in the United States attempt to preserve a layer of personal space around themselves even in crowded conditions and are careful to ask for pardon should personal belongings touch another person. Libraries are perfect places to observe proxemics in the United States. Most library patrons set up their own territory at the study table and feel irritated or uncomfortable when someone else's pencil, paper, books, or foot invades the space. In China, a relatively high-context culture, bumping or stepping on another's foot seems to pass unrecognized and certainly requires no apology.

Variations in proxemics within a high- or low-context culture do exist, however. In China, for example, gender makes a difference. It is common to see males walking hand in hand (or even intertwined) with males, and females with females. This does not signify being gay or lesbian, as it would in some cultures. Traditionally, heterosexual touching was strictly private in China, although today this is changing in most urban areas. Despite these changes, deeply rooted cultural expectations related to dating and courtship are likely to cause misunderstandings between Chinese and Americans.

Orientation Modes

Differences between *Black time* and *White time* in this society are common knowledge. White time is monochronic time during which things are accomplished one at a time in a linear fashion familiar to low-context Anglo-Western Europeans. Events occur "on time" according to a clearly stated schedule. Black time, polychronic time, is the opposite. The notion of Black time should be expanded to include people from polychronic cultures more generally, for example, southern Europeans and American Indians. In high-context cultures, time is polychronic. Many activities take place simultaneously, and schedules are invisible. In fact, these activities each seem to operate on a schedule of their own. A party or powwow takes place when people get there and ends when people leave. Business deals are closed only after preliminary exchanges concerning family, friends, and personal niceties that may take days or weeks. Hall states that "polychronic cultures are by their very nature oriented to people. Any human being who is naturally drawn to other human beings and who lives in a world dominated by human relationships will be either pushed or pulled toward the polychronic end of the time spectrum. If you value people, you must hear them out and cannot cut them off simply because of a schedule."[68]

School life operates according to monochronic time. Schedules and procedures "take on a life of their own without reference to either logic or human needs." Classes end at a specified time, it does not matter if an exciting discussion is still going on. Such attitudes as the following are implicit: People who know how to organize their time do not "waste" time. People who can meet deadlines are more successful than those who do not.[69]

Architectural arrangements in schools and classrooms are another important consideration in orientation modes. Room arrangements may range from very formal—students' desks arranged in straight rows and the teacher located behind a desk or lectern—to very informal—pupils roam freely or read lying on carpet scraps or comfortable furniture. Some students will associate serious learning with a formal environment and be confused or feel discomfited by an open-concept classroom, but other students will feel stifled in a formal setting. Central to Hall's cross-cultural research is the way humans use and organize space:

> My own interest in space as a cultural phenomenon stemmed from the observation that Americans overseas were confronted with a variety of difficulties because of cultural differences in the handling of space. People stood "too close" during conversations, and when the Americans backed away to a comfortable conversational distance, this was taken to mean that Americans were cold, aloof, withdrawn and disinterested in the people of the country. U.S. housewives muttered about wasted space in houses in the Middle East. In England, Americans, who were used to neighborliness, were hurt when they discovered that their neighbors were no more accessible or friendly than other people, and in Latin America, ex-suburbanites, accustomed to unfenced yards, found that the high walls there made them feel "shut out." Even in Germany, where so many of our countrymen felt at home, radically different patterns in the use of space led to unexpected tensions.[70]

Social Values

Social values are an important aspect of worldview. Values are beliefs about how one ought or ought not to behave or about some end state of existence worth or not worth attaining. Values are abstract ideas, positive or negative, that represent a person's beliefs about ideal modes of conduct and ideal terminal goals.[71] Core values refer to the most general beliefs about desirable and undesirable goals and behaviors and are especially important for the selection of cultural behavior from among alternatives.[72] Values are like a yardstick used to judge and compare the attitudes and behaviors of ourselves and others.

Consider some of the mainstream values that are predominant in U.S. society, although they vary tremendously by region and social class: cleanliness, hard work, material comforts and material wealth, private property, health and youth, promptness, problem solving and progress, formal education, being direct, and the right to dissent.

These values are reflected in many of our folk expressions:

Cleanliness is next to godliness.
It's better to have tried and failed than never to have tried at all.
Time is money.
Never put off until tomorrow what you can do today.
Early to bed and early to rise make a man healthy, wealthy, and wise.
If at first you don't succeed, try, try again.

Anthropologist Francis Hsu describes a series of postulates about U.S. society, based on his experience in both the United States and China. His observations may provide insight into mainstream values in the United States. Hsu's Blueprint (see Box 2.3) can also guide reflections about our own personal social values that may or may not be consistent with the dominant culture. To what extent do you agree with Hsu's perceptions?

Although cooperation ("team player") may be highly valued in certain sports, most academic activities are based on competition and individual achievement. Many "mainstream" children, therefore, learn best when working on their own, sometimes with the help of an adult. Most learn to expect and accept this competitive structure, and some need and thrive on it. Tests in school are nearly always individual rather than group exercises. Whole systems of instruction are individualized (programmed texts, learning labs, computer-assisted instruction, and independent study projects). Educators motivate students with classroom games modeled after competitive sports and quiz shows (for example, baseball and Jeopardy). They reward individual achievement with gold stars, "happy face" stamps, and privileges.

Within high-context cultures, these preferences are often reversed: competition and individual excellence in play and cooperation in work situations. Gay and Abrahams focus on inner-city African American youth and suggest that the preference for cooperation in work may develop "because so much of the transmission of knowledge and the customs of street culture takes place within peer groups (and thus) the Black student is prone to seek the aid and assistance of his classmates at least as frequently as he does the teacher's."[73] We also find this among most Mexican schoolchildren.[74] What is nearly always interpreted by teachers as cheating, copying, or frivolous socializing may in fact be the child's natural inclination to seek help from a peer (borrowing a pencil or talking after a test has begun).

Box 2.3
A Blueprint of United States Culture

Postulate I. An individual's most important concern is his self-interest: self-expression, self-development, self-gratification, and independence. This takes precedence over all group interests.

Postulate II. The privacy of the individual is the individual's inalienable right. Intrusion into it by others is permitted only by his invitation.

Postulate III. Because the government exists for the benefit of the individual and not vice versa, all forms of authority, including government, are suspect. But the government and its symbols should be respected. Patriotism is good.

Postulate IV. An individual's success in life depends upon his acceptance among his peers.

Postulate V. An individual should believe or acknowledge God and should belong to an organized church or other religious institution. Religion is good. Any religion is better than no religion.

Postulate VI. Men and women are equal.

Postulate VII. All human beings are equal.

Postulate VIII. Progress is good and inevitable. An individual must improve himself (minimize his efforts and maximize his returns); the government must be more efficient to tackle new problems; institutions such as churches must modernize to make themselves more attractive.

Postulate IX. Being American is synonymous with being progressive, and America is the utmost symbol of progress.

Source: Francis L. K. Hsu, *The Study of Literate Civilizations* (New York: Holt, Rinehart and Winston, 1969), pp. 78–82. Reprinted by permission of author and copyright holder.

In a powerful ethnographic study of ten Mexican-origin families living in border communities, Guadalupe Valdes uncovers cultural conflicts and misunderstandings between the parents and teachers that are based upon differing values and assumptions.[75] For example, what appears to be a lack of interest in education by Mexican-origin parents is in fact a strong commitment to family values. Valdes is critical of school interventions that are designed to promote school success without consideration and respect for these familial values. In Chapter 8, we will examine some promising approaches that address this concern: culturally relevant teaching and teaching that makes strategic connections between household cultures (funds of knowledge) and classroom culture.

Intellectual Modes

Intellectual modes refer both to what type of knowledge is valued most, and to learning styles, or how learning takes place within an individual. Students who value spiritual or religious knowledge may experience transitional trauma when religious beliefs are challenged or when courses seem to overemphasize science and technology. Students who seek knowledge related to practical living may feel frustrated when their coursework seems too theoretical. As important as the types of knowledge offered is the way students are expected to learn. In the average classroom those students learn best who are competitive, work well independently, use linear logic rather than intuition, emphasize rational thought over feeling (and can separate these), prefer abstract thinking over the senses, and require little physical mobility.

The dominant culture emphasizes visual learning through the written word. In Euro-American tradition, seeing is believing, and it is commonly accepted that the highest levels of thinking are possible only for humans who can reflect on thoughts recorded on the written page. No equivalent to the West African *griots*, musicians who served as living/singing encyclopedias, exists in the Euro-American core culture (although they are often compared to the bards of yore). Griots serve as professional oral historians who continue the "ancient traditions of praise-singing, story-telling, and genealogy in contemporary African culture."[76]

Many African Americans have grown up in an oral tradition, which, Herskovitz claims, is a carryover from Africa. Traditional African societies, for example, had elaborate communication systems using drums, singing, and dance rituals. From the time African Americans first arrived in the United States, music and the spoken word have been at the heart of the Black experience.[77] African oral/aural traditions thrive in the Americas. Classroom examples of the oral/aural tradition are easily illustrated. My students, mostly Black or Latino males labeled remedial, scored considerably higher on tests when I *read* the questions to them. Working with Black and Mexican American eighth graders in Texas, I found that their comprehension of a U.S. history text was better if they listened to a tape of the text while reading it. Many of my Anglo pupils preferred to read without hearing the tape. Similar examples are abundant, and helpful, provided that they do not lead to racial stereotypes and assumptions that all Blacks learn aurally and all Whites learn visually.

Current research suggests that certain learning styles are associated with specific ethnic groups in this society. For example, Shade, in her article "African American Cognitive Style: A Variable in School Success?" makes a strong case that many African Americans have learning styles that conflict with our low-context schools.[78] And, according to the late Asa Hilliard, who wrote widely on race and intelligence, African Americans who have grown up outside the dominant culture process information differently from what is expected in our schools.[79] Other research suggests that many Latinos and Native Americans, indeed anyone from a high-context culture, face comparable cultural conflicts related to intellectual modes. (This research is examined more closely in Chapter 8.)

The notion that certain learning styles are associated with different ethnic groups is both promising and dangerous. Promise lies in the realization that low academic achievement among some ethnic minorities may sometimes be attributed to conflicts between styles of teaching and learning, not low intelligence. This leads to the possibility that teachers will alter their own instructional styles to be more responsive to the learning needs of students. Danger lies in the possibility that new ethnic stereotypes will develop while old ones are reinforced, such as "Blacks learn aurally," "Asians excel in math," "Mexican American males can't learn from female peer tutors," and "Navajos won't ask a question or participate in a discussion."

In summary, Longstreet's aspects of ethnicity provide useful guidelines for observing and understanding human behavior. Although it is impossible to fully understand the cultural orientations of all students, the five aspects of ethnicity discussed above are common components of any cultural orientation that teachers can cue into: verbal communication, nonverbal communication, orientation modes, social values, and intellectual modes. The greater the differences between the deep culture of teachers and students, the more likely it is that students' and teachers' preferred ways of communicating and participating are different. Those teachers who are unaware of their pupils' needs and preferences force the learner to do most of the adjusting. Those pupils, like Jesús Martinez (see page 7), who cannot make the adjustment cannot learn much in the classroom. Unless the teacher is knowledgeable about students' cultural identity, pupils whose ethnic group differs from the teacher's and/or classmates' are more likely to experience cultural conflict in the classroom than pupils who share the same ethnicity as the teacher.

 ## Conclusions

This chapter has emphasized understanding human diversity as it relates to culture. However, if we limit our focus to culture, we run the risk of stereotyping. If, however, we ignore students' cultural attributes and rely totally on our own culturally biased lenses, we are likely to limit the chances for successful learning to those who are most "like us."

Differences in modes of communication, participation, and worldview enter the classroom when students and teachers represent different ethnic groups and/or different nationalities. Equalizing the learning opportunities for students becomes more difficult to achieve when teachers and students have alternative worldviews. It is a challenge to find out how learners can be taught when we do not understand their language, when we misinterpret their behavior, when our tried-and-true methods of diagnosing and motivating fail. Most of us expect cultural differences when meeting recent immigrants or visitors from another country, such as Vietnam, Saudi Arabia, or France. Fewer of us are aware that cultural differences can also occur between ethnic groups in our own society, as well as among individuals within these groups.

Even as we enter the twenty-first century, despite the fact that we live in a polycultural society, most of our schools remain monocultural. Students from different ethnic groups often bring with them cultures that are to some degree distinct from the schools of the predominant culture. To teach effectively in pluralistic classrooms, which characterize most schools in the United States, teachers must recognize the validity of the cultures present.

Selected Sources for Further Study

Building Bridges: A Peace Corps Classroom Guide to Cross-Cultural Understanding, www.peacecorps.gov/wws/bridges.

Cornelius, C. (1999). *Iroquois Corn in a Culture-Based Curriculum: A Framework for Respectively Teaching about Cultures.* Albany: SUNY Press.

Gonzalez, N., Moll, L. C., & Amanti, C. (2005). *Funds of Knowledge: Theorizing Practices in Households, Communities, and Classrooms.* Mahwah, NJ: Lawrence Erlbaum.

Hofstede, G. (2001). *Culture's Consequences: Comparing Values, Behaviors, Institutions, and Organizations Across Nations.* Thousand Oaks, CA: Sage.

Igoa, C. (1995). *The Inner World of the Immigrant Child.* Mahwah, NJ: Lawrence Erlbaum.

Intercultural Communication Institute, www.intercultural.org.

Lee, C. D. (2007). *Culture, Literacy, and Learning: Taking Bloom in the Midst of the Whirlwind.* New York: Teachers College Press.

McBrien, L. (2005). "Educational Needs and Barriers for Refugee Students in the United States: A Review of the Literature." *Review of Educational Research, 75*(3), 329–364.

Moya, P. M. L. (2002). *Learning from Experience: Minority Identities, Multicultural Struggles.* Berkeley, CA: University of California Press.

Mukhopadhyhy, C. C., Henze, R., & Moses, Y. T. (2007). *How Real Is Race? A Sourcebook on Race, Culture, and Biology.* Lanham, MD: Rowman & Littlefield.

Obama, B. (2004). *Dreams from My Father: A Story of Race and Inheritance,* Rev. ed. New York: Three Rivers Press.

Portes, A., & Rumbaut, R. G. (2006). *Immigrant America: A Portrait,* 3rd ed. Berkeley, CA: University of California Press. See Chapter 9, "Religion: The Enduring Presence."

Purkayastha, B. (2005). *Negotiating Ethnicity: Second-Generation South Asian Americans Traverse a Transnational World.* Rutgers, NJ: Rutgers University Press.

Root, M. P. P. (2004). "Multiracial Families and Children: Implication for Educational Research and Practice" in J. A. Banks & C. M. Banks (Eds.), *Handbook of Research on Multicultural Education,* 2nd ed. (pp. 110–124). San Francisco: Jossey-Bass.

Sue, D. W. (2004). "Multicultural Counseling and Therapy (MCT) Theory" in J. A. Banks & C. M. Banks (Eds.), *Handbook of Research on Multicultural Education,* 2nd ed. (pp. 813–827). San Francisco: Jossey-Bass.

Valdes, G. (2001). *Learning and Not Learning English.* New York: Teaschers College Press.

Zuberi, T., & Bonilla-Silva, E. (Eds.). (2008). *White Logic, White Methods: Racism and Methodology.* Lanham, NJ: Rowman & Littlefield.

Now go to Topics #1 and 2: **Ethnicity/Cultural Diversity** and **Race** in the MyEducationLab (www.myeducationlab.com) for your course, where you can:

■ Find learning outcomes for these topics along with the national standards that connect to these outcomes.

■ Complete Assignments and Activities that can help you more deeply understand the chapter content.

■ Apply and practice your understanding of the core teaching skills identified in the chapter with the Building Teaching Skills and Dispositions learning units.

Chapter 3

Race Relations and the Nature of Prejudice

The improvement of race relations through the reduction of prejudice and racism is a central goal of multicultural education. Teachers, along with parents and other important family members, can make a significant difference in how children and youth perceive themselves and others. In my work with beginning and experienced teachers over the years, I have seen many examples of teachers working through the hidden curriculum as well as the formal curriculum to reduce prejudice. There is the physical education teacher who uses interracial teams and peer coaching to develop technical skills; mathematics and science teachers who use partner learning and cooperative learning teams to teach concepts within a classroom climate of acceptance; and English teachers who use multicultural literature and peer editing in cooperative teams to enhance writing skills, as well as positive intergroup relationships. In my own teaching in a newly desegregated high school serving Black, Latino, and White students, I remember the positive impact on virtually all the students when they discovered the distinctions between individual and institutional racism, and developed insights into their own socialization concerning racial attitudes and beliefs. There are teachers like Sam Johnson (on pages 8–9) who work to reduce racial prejudice in schools where most of the students are White.

Teaching aimed at reducing prejudice and discrimination can be difficult as well as rewarding. It requires an understanding of the prevalence and nature of prejudice, as well as clarity about key concepts such as prejudice, stereotype, discrimination, racism, and sense of racial or ethnic identity. This chapter provides an introduction to these concepts and contemporary race relations as a context for multicultural teaching.

 ## How Prevalent Are Prejudice and Racism?

With the election of President Barack Obama, some people argue that race no longer matters in America and that at last we have been cleansed of our racist past. Some European leaders view the election as evidence that Americans have chosen not only a president, but also an identity that shows we have "regained the torch of a moral revolution."[1] While the 2008 election has filled Americans with hope for the future, it has also made us more aware of our racial legacy and the persistent racial injustices that are central to our future agenda. Teachers will play a crucial role in how well we address this agenda, through the content they select for their lessons, the climates they create in their classrooms, and the connections they make with their communities.

Contemporary Indicators of Our Racial Climate

In March 1968, the Kerner Commission released its report on civil disorders and warned that the United States was becoming dangerously divided into two societies, unequal and separated by race. At the turn of the twenty-first century, some social scientists believed that racial tensions had worsened. For example, sociologists Feagin and Vera wrote, "At some time in the not-too-distant future a racial war between the haves and have-nots in the United States is not inconceivable. The hour is already late to take action to prevent such a racial war."[2]

Yet other scholars and government officials argued that race relations had improved dramatically. For example, according to a Gallup poll in 1997, the number of surveyed White Americans who would vote for a Black presidential candidate increased from 35 percent in 1972 to 93 percent in 1997, surpassing the 91 percent of African Americans who would vote for a Black presidential candidate.[3] According to another Gallup poll, conducted in November 2003, 70 percent of Whites said they approved of interracial marriages, compared to just 4 percent in a 1958 Gallup poll, as did 77 percent of Latinos and 80 percent of African Americans.[4] And although the preference to live in a mostly mixed neighborhood was high (61 percent of Latinos, 57 percent of Whites, and 72 percent of African Americans preferred an integrated neighborhood), most believed that race relations will always be a problem in the United States (i.e., 60 percent of Latinos, 62 percent of Whites, and 72 percent of African Americans felt this way).[5] Moreover, 19 percent of Latinos and 24 percent of African Americans had been denied a rental or an opportunity to buy a home, compared with 2 percent of Whites; and nearly half of the African Americans and Latinos surveyed had experienced discrimination in the previous 30 days, including incidents in stores (26 percent), public transportation (10 percent), restaurants and theaters (18 percent), and interactions with the police (22 percent of African Americans and 24 percent of Latinos).[6]

A *New York Times*/CBS poll taken in the summer of 2008 indicated that presidential candidate Obama, although generating tremendous enthusiasm among Black voters and some Whites, was not closing the divide on race.[7] Black and White Americans agreed that the nation was ready to elect a Black president, but they disagreed on every other question in the survey:

> Nearly 60 percent of black respondents said race relations were generally bad, compared with 34 percent of whites. Four in ten blacks say that there has been no progress in recent years in eliminating racial discrimination; fewer than two in ten whites say the same thing. And about one-quarter of white respondents said they thought that too much had been made of racial barriers facing black people, while one-half of black respondents said not enough had been made of racial impediments faced by blacks. . . .
>
> As it was eight years ago (when a previous poll was taken), few Americans have regular contact with people of other races, and few say their own workplaces or their own

neighborhoods are integrated. In this latest poll, over 40 percent of blacks said they believed they had been stopped by police because of their race, the same figure as eight years ago; 7 percent of whites said the same thing.

Nearly 70 percent of blacks said they had encountered a specific instance of discrimination based on their race, compared with 62 percent in 2000; 26 percent of whites said they had been the victim of racial discrimination. (Over 50 percent of Hispanics said they had been the victims of racial discrimination.)[8]

Although Asian Americans were not included in this poll, a recent report from the Associated Press highlighted a persistent pattern of discrimination and physical attacks around the country.[9] The violence is especially disturbing because it often occurs in our public schools.

Nationwide, Asian students say they're often beaten, threatened, and called ethnic slurs by other young people, and school safety data suggest that the problem may be worsening. Youth advocates say these Asian teens, stereotyped as high-achieving students who rarely fight back, have borne the brunt of ethnic tension as Asian communities expand and neighborhoods become more racially diverse. . . .

Stories of Asian youth being bullied are worse and common. In recent years: a Chinese middle schooler in San Francisco was mercilessly taunted until his teacher hid him in her classroom at lunchtime; three Korean-American students were beaten so badly near their Queens high school that they skipped school for weeks and begged to be transferred; a 16-year-old from Vietnam was killed last year in a massive brawl in Boston. . . .

Increasingly, some victims are fighting back.[10]

How do Asian American students respond to the taunting and abuse that goes on at school? About 14 percent say they join gangs for protection, increasing numbers are carrying weapons, and more are "being brought to juvenile court for assault and battery."[11]

Some argue that although there are still racial tensions in the United States, they are not as bad as in other countries. Others point out the numbers of refugees seeking asylum in the United States, such as Haitians in the 1990s and Chinese college students and professionals after Tiananmen Square in 1989, and the new immigrants (approximately one million) who come every year, as evidence of freedoms and the higher quality of life here.

Let us consider a sample of recent indicators of the nation's racial climate over the past two decades or so. Think of other examples you could add to the list.

- In April 1992, the acquittal of four White Los Angeles police officers in the beating of an African American motorist, Rodney King, triggered violent riots in South Central Los Angeles. Approximately fifty people were killed, 1,600 businesses (primarily Korean-owned) were destroyed or severely damaged, and financial losses were nearly $800 million.[12]
- A Harvard University study of the nation's schools found that desegregation is being dismantled, with schools becoming more isolated by race, poverty, and lack of connection to the outside world. It reported that Hispanic students are even more likely than African Americans to "be isolated in schools that are largely minority and poor.[13]

- The O. J. Simpson case fueled discussions and disagreements within families, communities, college classrooms, and the workplace. Reactions to the not-guilty verdict were deeply divided along racial lines. Differing racial perceptions of our criminal justice system and of the trustworthiness of local law enforcement became visible, but the roots of these different views often remain misunderstood.

- Incidents of ethno-violence on college campuses and elsewhere in society have increased, with more than a hundred incidents reported each year. These "hate crimes" are directed primarily at people of color, Jews, and gays and lesbians. The Southern Poverty Law Center alone reported a "sampling" of 90 violent acts during the summer of 1994, just a portion of the year's total incidents.[14]

- The number of "hate sites" on the Internet increased dramatically in the 1990s, with over 250 hate sites available in 1997. From a website on the Internet called Nazism Now, it is only a mouse click to reach I Hate Jews—The Anti-Semitic Homepage, Knights of the Ku Klux Klan, and the White Nationalism Resource Page. These sites "celebrate white supremacy, anti-Semitism, anti-Government fervor and denial of the Holocaust.[15]

- In 1998, in a vicious hate crime in Texas, two white males driving a pickup truck dragged African American James Byrd Jr. to his death and left him at the side of the road, still tied to the rope.

- On July 4, 1999, World Church follower Benjamin Smith, an upper-income White Indiana University student, shot and killed Won-Joon Yoon, a Korean doctoral student, as he entered his church in Bloomington, Indiana. The previous Friday, Smith also killed Northwestern University basketball coach Ricky Birdsong, an African American, as he walked with his children in Skokie, Illinois. Smith wounded nine others, targeting Jews who were on their way home after Friday evening services, as well as additional African Americans and Asian Americans in several Chicago suburbs during the three-day killing spree.

- During the spring of 2001, several weeks of racial violence broke out in Cincinnati, Ohio, after an unarmed African American youth was shot and killed by police.

- In 2004, over 1,500 cases of harassment and anti-Muslim violence were reported, an increase of 50 percent from the previous year.[16]

- The killing of an unidentified White woman in 2007 did not make news until the burial of her corpse revealed racial conflict over the desegregation of the cemeteries in a rural Texas county.[17]

- The March 2008 shooting of Jamiel Shaw, Jr. (an African American star high school athlete who was not known to be a gang member, and whose mother was a soldier fighting in Iraq at the time) by a man police say was a gang member and illegal immigrant "inflamed tensions between many blacks and Hispanic immigrants, groups long resentful of each other as shifting demographics and a smattering of racially motivated killings have racked South Los Angeles."[18]

In addition, the number of White Americans who perceive "reversed racism" in affirmative action programs is increasing. Feelings of alienation are especially strong among White males. One White college student expressed this view as follows:

As a white male, I feel like I'm the only subsection of the population that hasn't jumped on the victim bandwagon. And I feel from a racial perspective, as a white man, I have been targeted as the oppressor, and frankly I'm getting a little tired of it, because I haven't done a whole lot of oppressing in my life. . . . I feel like I'm branded with this bad guy label. . . . Supposedly, as we study gender and race, as white men we run the world; I never knew that . . . I haven't oppressed anybody, but I've experienced feeling oppressed.[19]

Racial and ethnic tensions are also widespread across the world. Some examples include: Indians in Brazil who are estranged from their land and suffer an epidemic of suicide; "ethnic cleansing" in Bosnia-Herzegovina and elsewhere; the persistent Arab–Israeli conflict and violence in the Middle East; neo-Nazi attacks on Turkish immigrants in German cities; genocide massacres in Rwanda of Tutsi by Hutu, followed by Tutsi reprisals in Congo (formerly Zaire); cruel treatment of Mbutu, commonly named Pygmies, by Bantu throughout central Africa; ongoing violent conflict in Britain between Anglos and Pakistanis; and discrimination against the Ainu in Japan. In late summer of 2001, the United Nations sponsored the World Conference against Racism, Racial Discrimination, Xenophobia, and Related Intolerances. The agenda included discussions of the North–South hemispheric divide as a color line, treatment of immigrants and asylum-seekers in industrialized countries, "the caste system in India, contemporary slavery in Africa as well as discrimination in Latin America and parts of the Caribbean against people of African descent."[20] And on September 11, 2001, an international network of terrorists attacked the World Trade Center in New York and the Pentagon in Washington, D.C., killing thousands of innocent civilians from the United States and many other nations from around the world.

Our focus in this chapter, however, is on prejudice and race relations in the United States. Although it is unlikely that prejudice can ever be completely eradicated, "the situation is not without hopeful features. Chief among these is the simple fact that human nature seems, on the whole, to prefer the sight of kindness and friendliness to the sight of cruelty."[21]

Most race-relation experts have studied racism in terms of the costs of racism to the victims, especially the denial of equal access to educational, economic, and political power. Other deleterious effects include loss of role models and knowledge of the past, physical and mental suffering, and even loss of life. Scholars have begun to recognize that racism victimizes Whites as well. Jack Forbes, for example, in his studies of Native American and Chicano peoples, wrote, "Anglo American young people grow up in a never-never land of mythology as regards non-whites, and it is crucial for our society's future that damaging myths be exposed and eliminated."[22]

Rutledge Dennis is a sociologist who studies the effects of racism on White children. In a discussion of these effects, Dennis stresses ignorance of other people, development of a double social-psychological consciousness, group conformity, and moral confusion and social ambivalence.[23] A dual consciousness develops within White children who are taught to hate and fear others and to conform to racial etiquette on the one hand, while being taught Christian love on the other. Because racism deprives Whites of getting to know Blacks (and other people of color), it fosters "their ignorance of the many-sidedness of the Black population" and thus reinforces stereotypes.[24] Given the interdependency of the human race and the great variety of cultures on earth, this ignorance is not only senseless but also dangerous.

Among White adults, Dennis sees three effects of racism: irrationality, inhibition of intellectual growth, and negation of democracy. He argues that feelings of White superiority contribute to the basic immaturity of many Whites and their inability "to grow up, to accept the judgments of civilization."[25] Dennis also reminds us of the words Booker T. Washington spoke in 1911:

> It is a grave mistake for the vast majority of Whites to assume that they can remain free and enjoy democracy while they are denying it to Blacks. The antidemocratic not only wants to ensure that Blacks do not enjoy certain rights, he also wants to ensure that no White is free to question or challenge this denial.[26]

What Is Prejudice?

Prejudice is an attitude based on preconceived judgments or beliefs (usually negative) that develops from unsubstantiated or faulty information. These attitudes are learned from people who have significant influence in our lives, such as parents and peers; experiences in school; and societal messages in films, television, and the news media. Prejudice can be directed toward an entire group or an individual because he or she is a member of the group. It can be race-based, gender-based, age-based, ethnicity-based, class-based, etc. It can also be based on religion. For example, prejudice against Jews is called anti-Semitism.

An attitude is a relatively enduring organization of interrelated beliefs centered on an object or situation that includes a predisposition to take action.[27] Thus, because prejudice is an attitude, it is likely that action will result. A common expression of prejudice is telling ethnic jokes or "talking about" certain groups, among like-minded people and sometimes with strangers. Some prejudiced individuals make a conscious effort to avoid people from the group, such as taking a longer route home to avoid certain neighborhoods, or frequenting restaurants and taking vacations where members of the group are unlikely to be present. Prejudice becomes *discrimination* when the individual actively excludes members of the group, or denies them participation in a desired activity. In its most extreme form discrimination causes physical harm, or even death, to members of the group.[28] Thus, discrimination is the overt expression of prejudice in behavior that does harm to members of the group, ranging from exclusion to violent action. While discrimination usually stems from prejudice, sometimes nonprejudiced people discriminate unintentionally because they are unaware of unfair societal practices and policies.

Gordon Allport, a national authority on prejudice and the personality, visualizes social relationships among groups along a continuum from most friendly (cooperation) to hostile (scapegoating), with respect, tolerance, predilection, prejudice, and discrimination in between (see Figure 3.1). Mildly hostile relationships begin with predilections, the most normal form of group exclusion, where people prefer to associate with those with whom they feel most comfortable and familiar. Allport

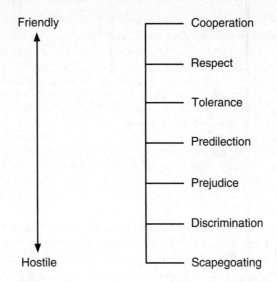

Figure 3.1 ▨ A Continuum of Social Relationship among Human Groups

From Gordon Allport, *ABC's of Scapegoating* (New York: Anti-Defamation League of B'nai B'rith, 1979). Reprinted by permission of the Anti-Defamation League of B'nai B'rith.

argues that humans prefer the familiar because of "the principles of ease, least effort, congeniality, and pride in one's own culture," not prejudice.[29] Many of my students say they become aware of their predilections when they attend churches or places of worship different from their own. They also sense their predilections when entering a crowded cafeteria filled with strangers; there is a strong desire to sit with friends. It is natural to prefer one's own family, religion, or ethnic group. But if a person *exaggerates* the virtues of one's own group and also develops a dislike for another group (as often happens when there is no opportunity to get to know members of the group), then it is easy to develop prejudices.

Although prejudice takes many forms, *racial* prejudice is our emphasis in this chapter. Racial prejudice often leads to racial discrimination, but not necessarily. Since the Holocaust of World War II and the civil rights movement of the 1960s, most people now believe that discrimination is unfair and many acts of discrimination are now illegal. Thus racial prejudice takes much more subtle forms than in the past.

We cannot assume that it is mainly White people who are racially prejudiced. There are racially prejudiced people in every ethnic group, and many people of color are quick to point out that feelings of racial prejudice exist within their communities. African American anthropologist John Gwaltney's study of African Americans in the Northeast, *Drylongso, A Portrait of Black America*, illustrates racial prejudice held by Blacks in interviews such as the following:

My uncle is a preacher and he says that white people are born evil. He'll tell you in a minute that the Bible says that the wicked are estranged from the womb. Now, as far as he is concerned, when you say "the wicked," you have said "the white race." He cannot stand white people, and although he is a man with good common sense most of the time, you cannot make him see reason about this race thing. He looks as white as any white person, but you'd better not tell him that unless you are ready to go to war. He won't even call them men. He says, "The beni did this" or "The beni have said so-and-so."

His daughter married a white boy about five years ago. They have two nice kids and are getting along fine, but Uncle Joshua acts like they're dead. She was—I mean she is—his only girl and they were very close, so it's hard for everybody. It's been five years now, and you could count the weeks on the fingers of your hands that Felicity has come to see him. He just won't have anything to do with her. She said that she'd keep coming to see him, and I guess she will because she's just as stubborn as he is.[30]

African Americans, American Indians, Asian Americans, Latinos, and other minorities may hold racial prejudices, and may act upon them by discriminating against Whites or other minorities. Such forms of prejudice among oppressed groups often develop *in response* to their condition in society, in an attempt to recover a sense of dignity. Thus efforts to end the nation's racial tensions and to work toward the eradication of racial prejudice require the involvement of everyone, minority and nonminority alike, if we are to succeed.

What Is Racism?

Racism involves systematic oppression through persistent behavior that is the result of personal racial prejudice and racial discrimination within societal structures. Racism is a complex concept that includes attitudes of racial superiority, institutional power that suppresses members of the supposedly inferior race, and a broadly based ideology of ethnocentrism or cultural superiority. Racism is an action or policy that harms or suppresses members of a racial group. It "results from the transformation of race prejudice and/or ethnocentrism through the exercise of power against a racial group defined as inferior, by individuals and institutions with the intentional or unintentional support of the entire culture."[31] However, most social scientists argue that ethnic minorities do not hold sufficient power to be actively racist on a broad societal scale. It is *not* possible for minority groups in the United States to systematically deny Whites access to opportunities and privileges, or to maintain privileges for themselves at the expense of nonminorities. According to this argument, while anyone can be racially prejudiced and can discriminate on the basis of race, in the United States only White people can benefit from a racist system based on White privilege. They can also become antiracist. For example, many Whites actively support affirmative action programs because they believe these programs are needed to counteract centuries of racial inequities in education, health care, nutrition, political participation, job opportunities, etc. They envision the best education, health care, nutrition, etc., for *all* children, not only their own at the expense of other people's children. However, many people (minority and nonminority alike) view affirmative action programs as reversed discrimination against Whites, rather than as antiracism needed to address persistent societal inequities based on White privilege. Many believe that with talent and hard work, anyone can make it in this society.

Distinguishing Individual, Institutional, and Cultural Racism

Racism operates on three interrelated levels: individual, institutional, and cultural. It is important to understand the distinctions and similarities among these types of racism if it is to be eradicated on all levels.

Individual Racism

This is the belief that one's own race is superior to another (racial prejudice) and behavior that suppresses members of the so-called inferior race (racial discrimination). The racist believes that members of another race are inferior, and assumes that the physical attributes of a racial group determine the social behavior of its members, as well as their psychological and intellectual characteristics. These racist beliefs might remain submerged as hidden racial prejudice, but usually the racist believes this inferiority is a legitimate basis for inferior social treatment.

Let's consider some examples and nonexamples of individual racism.[32] Alice is a White elementary school teacher who believes minority students are less motivated than her White students and, therefore, she intentionally assigns them to the less desirable and less challenging classroom activities. Gregg is a White high school assistant principal who assigns a majority of the African American and Mexican American students to unchallenging classes taught by the most disliked or inexperienced teachers because he believes these students cannot be taught, anyway. Kevin, the newly hired mathematics teacher, who is also White, finds that most of his students in his basic math classes are African Americans and Latinos, many more than a random selection of the student population should produce. Raised in a racially diverse neighborhood, he feels comfortable with his students, but he has had no experience or preparation for the basic math curriculum. Sue is a middle school teacher who misinterprets a minority student's nonassertiveness and lack of eye contact as an indication that the student is not interested in school. She devotes her attention to the students who are active participants or who show their interest with direct eye contact.

Both Alice and Gregg depict individual racism that is intentional. Alice's behavior is overt and easily observable, but Gregg's covert behavior may go unnoticed. Kevin and the other teachers who are assigned most of the African American and Mexican American students may not question or even wonder about the silent resegregation of the student population by Gregg. While Kevin is not acting in a racist manner per se, unless he questions the system that places most minority students in an unchallenging class with inexperienced teachers, he is (however unwittingly) participating in a system that perpetuates inequities in education (institutional racism). Like Alice and Gregg, Sue conveys individual racism even though it is unintentional. Her lack of understanding of the student's background leads her to misjudge the student through her own cultural lens; as a result, the student does poorly in her class.

Institutional Racism

Institutional racism consists of "those established laws, customs, and practices that systematically reflect and produce racial inequalities in American society . . . whether or not the individuals maintaining those practices have racist intentions."[33] In contrast to individual racism, where perpetrators can be identified, institutional racism is embedded in policies and practices that have generally become accepted as natural or normal over time. When racism is not challenged by oppressed groups or by non-minorities who are antiracist, people may be unaware of the impact of discriminatory policies and how they benefit from or are hurt by them, while others are aware that a change in policy would result in a loss of power and prestige.

Consider some examples of institutional racism from the past. Article 1, section 2, of the U.S. Constitution provided that three-fifths of the slave population would be counted for purposes of representation, and slavery was not abolished until the 13th Amendment was passed in 1865. White abolitionists who may not have been individually racist, that is, they may not have believed in the racial inferiority of African Americans in slavery, were nonetheless part of a society whose institutions were racist. They benefited from the national wealth generated by enslaved African Americans. Until passage of the voting rights act in 1965 that was renewed for

Taking a stand against racism: a middle school poster.

25 years in 1982, and again in 2006, there were laws on the books in many states that prevented African Americans from voting. For example, anyone whose father or grandfather had not voted in a given year (say 1866) was denied the right to vote. Interracial marriages were illegal in many states, and in Louisiana until late in the twentieth century citizens with any African American ancestry could be denied passports. Even the Supreme Court has, at times, upheld racial segregation laws, the most famous case being *Plessy v. Ferguson* in 1896, which ruled that separate facilities were legal as long as they were equal.

After the Civil War and up until World War II, lynching became a major means of keeping Blacks in their place. Between 1892 and 1921, nearly 2,400 African Americans were lynched. Most of the perpetrators were never punished for their actions; in some cases local police officers were involved in these crimes.[34] (Many Whites, particularly Jews and Italians, were also lynched, but Blacks made up the greatest proportion.)

Mexican American citizens have been the victims of racism as well. The outrageous Sleepy Lagoon incident and the zootsuit riots in Los Angeles during World War II are just two egregious examples. Disproportionately higher numbers of Black and Latino soldiers were given the most dangerous combat duties in Vietnam. Today Blacks and Latino are overrepresented in prisons and on death row, as they are among students who are suspended, expelled, or placed in classes for the retarded. Inequitable access to highly skilled lawyers is another prevalent example of institutional bias, as were many of the draft deferments in the past.

Other examples of institutional racism include formal and informal real estate practices that prohibit some races from buying or renting in particular sections of town, and policies that deny certain races access to clubs and organizations such as fraternities and sororities. Textbooks and educational materials that present erroneous information about certain racial groups or omit their contributions are other examples of institutional racism in our schools, although they could also result from "personal" racial prejudice of the author.

Carmichael and Hamilton were among the first to distinguish between individual and institutional racism:

> *Racism is both overt and covert. It takes two, closely related forms: individual whites acting against individual blacks, and acts by the total white community against the black community. We call these individual racism and institutional racism. The first consists of overt acts by individuals, which cause death, injury or the violent destruction of property. This type can be recorded by television cameras; it can frequently be observed in the process of commission. The second type is less overt, far more subtle, less identifiable in terms of specific individuals committing the acts. But it is no less destructive of human life. The second type originates in the operation of established and respected forces in the society, and thus receives far less public condemnation than the first. When white terrorists bomb a black church and kill five black children, that is an act of individual racism, widely deplored by most segments of society. But when in that same city—Birmingham, Alabama—five hundred black babies die each year because of the lack of proper food, clothing, shelter and proper medical facilities, and thousands more are destroyed or maimed physically, emotionally, and intellectually because of conditions of poverty and discrimination in the black community, that is a function of institutional racism.*[35]

In another pioneering book that distinguishes between individual and institutional racism, Knowles and Prewitt wrote that individual acts of racism as well as racist institutional policies can

> *occur without the presence of conscious bigotry, and both may be masked intentionally or innocently. . . . Institutions have great power to reward and penalize. They reward by providing career opportunities for some people and foreclosing them for others. They reward as well by the way social goods are distributed—by deciding who receives training and skills, medical care, formal education, political influence, moral support and self-respect, productive employment, fair treatment by the law, decent housing, self-confidence and the promise of a secure future for self and children.*[36]

Feagin extends these early works in his writings about institutionalized racism and sexism in terms of direct discrimination and indirect discrimination.[37] Examples of direct and indirect institutional racism in education illustrate the difference. Direct institutional racism includes laws and informal practices that segregate ethnic minority children into inferior public schools, or resegregate them into inferior classrooms. Direct institutional discrimination leads to indirect institutional discrimination when these poorly educated minorities cannot compete with nonminorities and do not qualify for advanced education and/or employment even though school officials and employers may be eager to recruit ethnic minorities. As a result of unemployment or low-paying jobs, most cannot afford adequate health care, nutrition, or housing.

The doctrine of White racism was also institutionalized in national immigration legislation. In 1793, George Washington proclaimed that the "bosom of America is open to receive not only the Opulent and respectable Stranger, but the oppressed and persecuted of all Nations and Religions whom we shall welcome to a participation of all our rights and privileges."[38] Obviously, slaves and free people of color were not to be included in this policy, nor were native peoples or Mexicans of the Southwest. In 1882, Chinese people were excluded, and in 1908 the exclusion was extended to Japanese immigrants. The National Origins Acts passed in 1924 and 1929 restricted the number of immigrants to 150,000 annually and set up quotas that favored people from Northern and Western Europe. About 70 percent of those allowed to enter were from Britain, Ireland, Scandinavia, and Germany. The remaining 30 percent came from Southern and Eastern Europe. The Walter-McCarran Act, passed in 1952, did little to change these discriminatory quotas. And, in fact, this law was aimed at keeping so-called undesirables out of the United States.

In 1965, the quota system was abolished, with results we will explore in Chapters 4 through 7.

Cultural Racism

Cultural racism includes both individual and institutional expressions of racial superiority and suppression. It refers to the subtle and pervasive uses of power by Whites "to perpetuate their cultural heritage and impose it upon others, while at the same time destroying the culture of ethnic minorities."[39] Cultural racism combines ethnocentrism, the view that other cultures are inferior to the Anglo-European, and the power to suppress or eradicate manifestations of non-Anglo-European cultures. The legacy of cultural racism can be found in the formal curriculum—in tests, media, and course offerings. It can also be detected in the hidden, informal curriculum, as in low expectations for minority student achievement held by nonminority teachers, ethnic/racial myths and stereotypes held by students and teachers, and an unfamiliar, nonsupportive, unfriendly, or hostile school environment.

Cultural racism within the United States is the belief in the inferiority of the implements, handicrafts, agriculture, economics, music, art, religious beliefs, traditions, language, and story of non-Anglo-European peoples and the belief that these people have *no distinctive culture* apart from that of mainstream White America.[40] An early example of cultural racism that still pervades Western society is the following racial classification of humankind developed by Carl von Linné (Carolus Linnaeus), the eminent eighteenth-century Swedish biologist.

1. HOMO. Sapiens. Diurnal; varying by education and situation.
2. Four-footed, mute, hairy. WILD MAN
3. Copper-coloured, choleric, erect. AMERICAN
   Hair black, straight, thick; nostrils wide, face harsh; beard scanty; obstinate, content, free. Paints himself with fine red lines. Regulated by customs.
4. Fair, sanguine, brawny. EUROPEAN
   Hair yellow, brown, flowing; eyes blue, gentle, acute; inventive. Covered with close vestments. Governed by law.
5. Sooty, melancholy, rigid. ASIATIC
   Hair black, eyes dark; severe, haughty, covetous. Covered with loose garments. Governed by opinions.
6. Black, phlegmatic, relaxed. AFRICAN
   Hair black, frizzled; skin silky; nose flat, lips tumid; crafty; indolent, negligent. Anoints himself with grease. Governed by caprice.[41]

Linné's list has three major problems that fuel misconceptions about humanity. First, he links physical attributes such as skin color, hair texture, and facial features to personality, mental abilities, and behavior. Second, he classifies large segments of humanity into categories according to a few visible traits. And, third, he makes value judgments based on his own ethnocentric view of the world. Native Americans have wide nostrils and harsh faces and are "obstinate, content, free . . . [and] regulated by customs." Europeans are "gentle, acute, inventive . . . [and] governed by law"; Asiatics have black hair and dark eyes, and are "severe, haughty, covetous . . . [and] governed by opinions"; and Africans have black, frizzled hair and are "crafty, indolent, negligent . . . [and] governed by caprice." Western society has tended to accept the logic behind this classification of *Homo sapiens*, along with the erroneous assumption that mental, behavioral, and sociocultural tendencies are determined by a few visible biological traits and the belief that Western Europeans are superior to all others.

Linné's classification of human races is no longer accepted. Nevertheless, his early misconceptions that racially identifiable physical characteristics determine character, behavior, and intellect are still alive: Scholars still argue about the intellectual and moral superiority or inferiority of different racial groups.[42]

As noted in Chapter 2, social scientists like Montagu have called race man's most dangerous myth. They warn that it is impossible to categorize people according to their physical traits.[43] Nevertheless, the concept of race persists and remains a primary basis for categorizing self and others within U.S. society.[44] The eighteenth-century conception of race has had a powerful influence on our cognition, and we find that in this society race is often an important basis for ethnic identity.

Some people mistakenly believe that simply recognizing a person's race is racist. Sometimes teachers say, "I love all of my children. I don't even know what color they are." Given the social reality, to be unaware of a student's race is being dishonest. Don't we notice whether a student is male or female, has blue eyes or brown? Granted, we cannot always know if a student is ethnically Black or White or Native American, but where race is obvious, why not recognize the fact? It is only when we lower our expectations, accept stereotypes, or discriminate that racial identity can conjure up negative attitudes and behaviors. The recognition of physical racial differences does not mean racial prejudice or racism. Many people of color regard race as an essential aspect of their personal identity and may be offended by teachers and others who claim to be color-blind.

White Privilege and Becoming Antiracist

Each one of us "is to some degree privileged or targeted" according to categories of human similarities and differences that are important in our society: race or skin color, culture (especially language and religion), gender and sexual orientation, abilities, socioeconomic status, and geographic area. We are systematically advantaged or disadvantaged according to our social identities (how we see ourselves and how others see us in these various groups); some identity groups are "dominant or *agent* (such as male, white, heterosexual, able-bodied, or upper class)" and some are "subordinate or *target* (such as female; black, or Latino/a; gay, lesbian or bisexual; physically disabled; working poor or unemployed.)"[45] In this section, we will look at privilege attached to "Whiteness," a social identity that characterizes about 90 percent of our nation's teachers at a time when children of color are nearly 50 percent of our school-age population.

White privilege is the other side of racism.[46] Whereas racism means systematic inequalities that put people of color at a disadvantage at birth, White privilege means systematic advantages that give White people a head start in life, whether or not they realize it and even if they believe it is unfair. White privilege refers to the unearned advantages provided to people who are perceived to be White; in the United States anyone born "White" automatically inherits benefits that people of color do not inherit, such as being seen as "the real Americans" and not foreigners (as is the case for may Asian Americans and dark-skinned Latinos), feeling comfortable in a new neighborhood, finding appropriate greeting cards with ease, shopping without arousing suspicions, learning about your history in school (in a language you can understand), and not having to worry about being perceived as an "affirmative action" hire. White privilege also means not having to see or deal with racism on a regular basis, such as paying higher rates for loans, being questioned by police in White neighborhoods, being by-passed by taxi drivers everywhere, or being perceived as the nanny of one's own children, the gardener in one's own yard, or the doorman at an exclusive hotel. White privilege also includes "the privilege of voice," as noted by Gary Howard in his book, *We Can't Teach What We Don't Know: White Teachers, Multiracial Schools*. He writes,

> *Dominant groups have the power to control public discourse. Whites in Western nations have written the official history, established the systems of education, owned the media, directed the flow of funding, disproportionately influenced the political climate, and occupied the seats of power in most social institutions. Because of our (White people's) social position, we have had the power to silence or interpret other people's voices and cultures. For example, groups attending the World Indigenous People's Conference continually speak out against the "commodification of culture," which is the process whereby White anthropologists, explorers, missionaries, writers, scientists, and entrepreneurs have for centuries appropriated Indigenous culture for their own purposes and profit.[47]*

White privilege is a concept many of my White students have difficulty understanding; some totally reject the idea and many argue that they do not think of themselves as "White." Some say they don't *feel* privileged, especially if they are first-generation college students or come from a low-income background and are struggling to put themselves through school. Others believe they have nothing to do with racism because their ancestors came to America in the twentieth century, long after the days of slavery. And still others point out that in addition to the many "poor Whites" that are "by definition" not privileged, there are many privileged people of color with money and a good education. These beliefs are not surprising, given the invisibility of White privilege. However, I find the writings of Dr. Beverly Tatum are extraordinarily helpful to my students as they develop self-knowledge and begin to see the importance of becoming antiracist teachers. (Dr. Tatum is a psychologist, former college professor who taught courses on the psychology of racism, and, at the time of this writing, President of Spellman College). She writes:

> *While there may be countless ways one may be defined as exceptional, there are at least seven categories of "otherness" commonly experienced in U.S. society. People are commonly defined as other on the basis of race or ethnicity, gender, religion, sexual orientation, socioeconomic status, age, and physical or mental ability. Each of these categories has a form of oppression associated with it: racism, sexism, religious oppression/anti-Semitism, heterosexism, classism, ageism, and ableism, respectively. In each case, there is a group considered dominant (systematically advantaged by society because of group membership) and a group considered subordinate or targeted (systematically disadvantages). When we think about our multiple identities, most of us will find that we are both dominant and targeted at the same time. But it is the targeted identities that hold our attention and the dominant identities that often go unexamined.[48]*

The diagram in Figure 3.2 provides a springboard for self-study and discussion. It can help initiate and support courageous conversations about "diversity" topics many of us need to become more comfortable talking about. Each category is associated with dominance or oppression, the systematic advantage or disadvantage one receives in society because of group membership. Most of us are both dominant and

RACE or ETHNICITY

(Racism or Ethnocentrism)

GENDER

(Sexism)

RELIGION

(Religious Oppression/Antisemitism)

SEXUAL ORIENTATION

(Heterosexism)

SOCIOECONOMIC STATUS

(Classism)

AGE

(Ageism)

PHYSICAL OR MENTAL ABILITY

(Ableism)

Figure 3.2 ▨ Who Am I? Multiple Identity Categories

Adapted from Beverly Daniel Tatum (2000), "The Complexity of Identity: 'Who Am I?'" pp. 9–14 in Maurianne Adams (et al.), Eds., *Readings for Diversity and Social Justice: An Anthology on Racism, Antisemitism, Sexism, Heterosexism, Ableism, and Classism.* New York: Routledge.)

targeted at the same time, but we tend to focus on our targeted identities while our dominant identities go unexamined.

White people have *the* critical role to play in dismantling White privilege, and many have devoted their lives to this end.[49] One example is John Howard Griffin who published the book *Black Like Me* in 1959, just before the civil rights movement gained national momentum. The book documents the power of skin color in America as Griffin, a White investigative journalist, worked with a dermatologist to darken his skin and pass for Black. Griffin describes his six weeks as a Black man traveling through the segregated South, how he was denied basic rights and freedoms simply because of his dark skin color (aspects of life he had taken for granted), and the psychological impact he felt. White friends no longer recognized him, and they as well as strangers judged him solely by the color of his skin. At the end of his experience, Griffin's skin color was reversed and he became a "first-class citizen" again, a fact that haunted him and led to his becoming a civil rights advocate for the rest of his life.

Advocates of multicultural education know that White Americans who understand the insidious effects of White privilege can choose to become antiracist by taking a stand against racial injustice, everyday types of injustice as well as institutionalized forms. In his essay "How White People Can Serve as Allies to People of Color to End Racism," Paul Kivel's first tactic in a list of twelve is to "Assume racism is everywhere, everyday."

Just as economics influences everything we do, just as our gender and gender politics influence everything we do, assume that racism is affecting whatever is going on. We assume this because it is true, and because one of the privileges of being white is not having to see or deal with racism all the time. We have to learn to see the effect that racism has. Notice who speaks, what is said, how things are done and described. Notice who isn't present. Notice code words for race, and the implications of the policies, patterns and comments that are being expressed. You already notice the skin color of everyone you meet and interact with—now notice what difference it makes.[50]

Theories of Ethnic Identity: How Can Teachers Benefit?

Counselors and psychologists who are working to improve race relations and reduce prejudice agree that "race appreciation is a lifelong developmental process that begins with a healthy sense of one's own racial/ethnic identity."[51] People must feel good about themselves before they can respect and feel good about others.

Ethnic identity refers to the degree to which a person feels connected with a racial and/or culture group that is important to one's family. This group may be linked to national origins, such as Polish or Irish societies, or to an ethnic group created within the context of generations of segregation from the dominant society, as with African Americans. All people belong to an ethnic group, but we may differ from other members of our group in terms of how closely we affirm the core lan-

Mapping one's sense of cultural identity.

guage, including body language, social values, and traditions. Thus, ethnic identity is a complex cluster of factors "including self-labeling, a sense of belonging, positive evaluation, preference for the group, ethnic interest and knowledge, and involvement in activities associated with the group."[52] The strength or degree of one's ethnic identity is significantly influenced by factors such as language spoken at home, ethnic composition of the neighborhood, and percentage of friends who are in the same ethnic group. There are developmental differences within an individual over the span of a lifetime, as well as tremendous variability within any one ethnic group in terms of the strength of ethnic identification, the adherence to familial cultural values and norms, and experiences in the predominantly White society.

Several theories of ethnic identity have recently been developed to help understand this developmental process. Beginning in the 1960s, the original focus was on ethnic identity development among African Americans. The sense of ethnic identity often developed in response to racism or oppression. Since the early 1980s theories have also been developed for Latinos, Asian Americans, and Whites.[53] These theories can help us understand increasing racial tensions in the United States (see Table 3.1).

"The Negro-to-Black Conversion Experience"

William Cross, an African American psychologist at Cornell University, developed one of the earliest theories of ethnic identity and has continued to develop and refine his work over three decades.[54] Cross originally focused on the "Negro to Black conversion experience," which occurred as African Americans lived through the civil rights movement of the 1960s. Although his theory focuses on Nigrescence, the "process of becoming Black," it is applicable to any group that has experienced oppression and is moving toward liberation, for example other ethnic minority groups

Table 3.1 ◪ Three Frameworks of Ethnic Identity Development

Stage	Janet Helms: Stages of White Identity Development	James Banks: The Emerging Stages of Ethnicity	William Cross: Theory of Nigrescence (Negro-to-Black Conversion Experience)
Six	Autonomy	Globalism and Global Competency	
Five	Immersion-Emersion	Multiethnicity and Reflective Nationalism	Internalization and Commitment
Four	Pseudo-Independence	Biethnicity	Internalization
Three	Reintegration	Ethnic Identity Clarification	Immersion-Emersion
Two	Disintegration	Ethnic Encapsulation	Encounter
One	Contact	Ethnic Psychological Captivity	Pre-encounter

and women. Cross describes five developmental stages: Pre-encounter, Encounter, Immersion-Emersion, Internalization, and Internalization and Commitment.

Black people who are in stage one, or *pre-encounter*, accept the dominant worldview. They seek to be assimilated into White mainstream society and could be described as anti-Black and anti-African. The second stage, *encounter*, is triggered by a shattering experience that destroys the person's previous ethnic self-image and changes his or her interpretation of the conditions of Black people in the United States. For many Black Americans the murder of Martin Luther King Jr. was such an experience. White violence and outrage over the busing of Black school children to historically White schools is another *encounter* experience for African Americans.

A person who enters stage three, *immersion-emersion*, desires to live totally in the world of Blackness. The individual feels Black rage and Black pride and may engage in a "kill Whitey" fantasy. Cross describes the stage-three person as having a pseudo-Black identity because it is based on hatred and negation of Whites rather than on the affirmation of a pro-Black perspective. Stage-three Blacks often engage in "Blacker than thou" antics and view those Blacks who are accepting of Whites as Uncle Toms. In stage four, *internalization*, the individual internalizes his or her ethnic identity and achieves greater inner security and self-satisfaction and may be characterized as the "nice Black person" with an Afro hair style and an attachment to Black things. There is a healthy sense of Black identity and pride and less hostility toward Whites.

The individual who moves into stage five, *internalization and commitment*, differs from the one who remains in stage four by becoming actively involved in plans to bring about social changes. The uncontrolled rage toward Whites is transformed into a conscious anger toward oppressive and racist institutions, from symbolic rhetoric to dedicated long-term commitment. Stage-five individuals feel compassion toward those who have not completed the process. They watch over new recruits, helping them conquer hatred of Whites and the "pitfalls of Black pride" without understanding/knowledge of Black cultural styles. The super-Black revolutionary of stage three gives way to the Black humanist in stage five.[55]

More recently, Cross has made distinctions between the development of *personal identity* (PI) and the development of a *reference group orientation* (RGO). Personal identity refers to "variables, traits, or dynamics that are in evidence, to one degree or another, in all human beings, regardless of social class, gender, race or culture."[56] These are "universal components of behavior" such as "high or low anxiety, self-esteem, introversion-extroversion, depression-happiness, concern for others, and so on."[57] Reference group orientation, on the other hand, refers to "those aspects of 'self' that are culture, class, and gender specific"[58] and focuses on "values, perspective taking, group identity, life styles, and world views" that are associated with these various groups.[59] Cross points out that, to date, most of the research and discussion of ethnic identity development among people of color living in the United States has focused on African Americans. However, he believes that the important distinctions between personal identity and reference group identity are generic to the analysis of identity development in most minority groups. It is possible, therefore, for members of ethnic minorities who have a healthy sense of personal identity and a sense of well-being to range along a continuum of strong-to-weak identification with their ethnic group. In other words, two individuals from the same ethnic group (for example, Black, Mexican American, or Chinese American) might have very similar personality types but hold extremely different worldviews. The opposite is also possible. Black people in the United States, for example, have created a strong sense of community among a group of individuals who represent a broad range of personalities.[60]

The Banks Typology of Ethnic Identity Development

Another theory of ethnic identity, developed by James A. Banks, is particularly helpful because of its well-developed implications for the classroom and its applicability to all ethnic groups, including Whites. Banks's six-stage typology is based on "existing and emerging theory and research" and on his own "observations and study of ethnic behaviors."[61]

In stage one, *ethnic psychological captivity*, "the individual has internalized the negative ideologies and beliefs about his or her ethnic group that are institutionalized within the society."[62] The stage-one person feels ethnic self-rejection and low self-esteem and is ashamed of his or her ethnic group identity. Typically, such a person tries to avoid situations that lead to contact with other ethnic groups or strives aggressively to become highly culturally assimilated. Examples would be the Black person who passes for White, the guilt-ridden White liberal who tries too hard to be accepted in the Black community, the Mexican American who is afraid to leave the barrio, or the Polish American who anglicizes his or her name out of embarrassment.

Stage two, *ethnic encapsulation*, is characterized by ethnic exclusiveness and separatism.

> *The individual participates primarily within his or her own ethnic community and believes that his or her ethnic group is superior to that of others. Many stage-two individuals, such as many Anglo-Saxon Protestants, have internalized the dominant societal myths about the superiority of their ethnic or racial group and the innate inferiority of other ethnic groups and races. Many individuals who are socialized within all-White suburban communities and who live highly ethnocentric and encapsulated lives may be described as stage-two individuals.[63]*

Members of the Ku Klux Klan are ethnically encapsulated, as were Black Muslim followers of Elijah Muhammad. Both groups appealed to stage-one individuals who feel the pain of low self-esteem and are thus susceptible to groups that preach the supremacy of their special group.

In stage three, *ethnic identity clarification*, the individual is able to clarify personal attitudes and develops a healthy sense of self and ethnic identity. Once the individual learns to accept self, it is possible to accept and respond more positively to outside ethnic groups. According to theories of human development, such as Abraham Maslow's hierarchy of needs, until a person has met basic human needs (i.e., physiological, safety, love, and esteem) and is becoming self-actualized, ethnic identity clarification is not likely. The individual in stage three feels ethnic pride, but at the same time feels respect for different ethnic groups.

Stage four is *biethnicity*. "Individuals within this stage have a healthy sense of ethnic identity and the psychological characteristics and skills needed to participate in their own ethnic culture, as well as in another ethnic culture. The individual also has a strong desire to function effectively in two ethnic cultures," and may thus be described as biethnic.[64] According to Banks, levels of biethnicity vary greatly. Many African Americans, for example, "learn to function effectively in Anglo-American culture during the formal working day" to attain social and economic gains. In private, however, their lives "may be highly black and monocultural."[65] All ethnic minorities, White and non-White alike, who wish to make social and economic advances are forced to become biethnic to some degree. This is not the case for members of the dominant culture who "can and often do live almost exclusive monocultural and highly ethnocentric lives."[66] Recent research on children and adolescents shows that African American and Mexican American families raise their children to be bicultural far more than do White families.[67]

Stage five is *multiethnicity*. "The individual at this stage is able to function, at least at minimal levels, within several ethnic sociocultural environments and to understand, appreciate, and share the values, symbols, and institutions of several ethnic cultures. Such multiethnic perspectives and feelings . . . help the individual to live a more enriched and fulfilling life and to formulate more creative and novel solutions to personal and public problems."[68]

Stage six is one of *globalism and global competency*. "Individuals within stage six have clarified, reflective, and positive ethnic, national, and global identifications and the knowledge, skills, attitudes, and abilities needed to function in ethnic cultures within their own nation as well as in cultures within other nations. These individuals have the ideal delicate balance of ethnic, national, and global identifications, commitments, literacy, and behaviors. They have internalized the universalistic ethical values and principles of humankind and have the skills, competencies, and commitments needed to act on these values."[69]

Although Banks stresses the "tentative and hypothetical" nature of his typology, even in its rough form it helps illuminate important sociopsychological differences between individual members of an ethnic group. Inside any particular school, we may find the entire array of stages within each ethnic group on campus. An awareness of this ethnic group diversity helps destroy ethnic stereotypes. Individuals do not become open to different ethnic groups until and unless they develop a positive sense of self, including an awareness and acceptance of their own ethnic group. This is an extension of the basic psychological principle that self-acceptance is a necessary condition for accepting others. The typology should not be viewed as a hierarchy; people do not necessarily begin at stage one and progress to stage six. Individuals can move from one stage to another, and depending upon personal experiences could become less open-minded as they go through life. Stages five and six are ideals that help us describe and visualize the goals of multicultural education.

White Racial Identity Development

Several theories of White identity development are available, notably Hardiman's White Identity Development Model (WID), Helms's Model of White Racial Identity Development, and Ponterotto's White Racial Consciousness Development Model.[70] These models share common themes and have been integrated by Sabnani,

Ponterotto, and Borodovsky into "an all inclusive model of White identity development" comprising five stages: Pre-exposure/Pre-contact, Conflict, Pro-minority/Antiracism, Retreat into White Culture, and Redefinition and Integration.[71]

Individuals in stage one, *Pre-encounter/Pre-contact*, lack awareness of themselves as racial beings. They are unaware of societal exploitation of people of color, and oblivious to racial tensions and issues. They are unaware of the role of Whites in an oppressive society, unaware of White privilege, and are unaware of their worldview that includes minority group stereotypes. Some Whites remain in this stage for life.

Whites who enter stage two, *Conflict*, encounter and internalize new information about race relations. For example, knowledge could come from interactions with people of color, readings, the media, or a course on race relations. As a result of their discovery, these individuals feel torn between loyalty to their White peers, family, and friends, and their desire to uphold nonracist values and (frequently) their religious values and beliefs in equality. For the first time they acknowledge their Whiteness; they commonly feel confusion, guilt, anger, or depression. To escape these feelings, individuals in Conflict move on into stage three or four.

Stage three, *Pro-minority/Antiracism*, describes White people who begin to resist racism and identify with minority groups. Sometimes they overidentify with people of color or act in paternalistic ways; these responses are likely to be ridiculed or rejected by people of color as well as other Whites, creating greater confusion, alienation, despair, or withdrawal into White culture (stage four). People who remain in this stage maintain a strong pro-minority position and feel tremendous guilt and anger toward White society.

Individuals who *Retreat into White Culture*, stage four, avoid further racial conflict by withdrawing from situations that are emotionally or physically threatening. "White flight" into White schools and neighborhoods is an example of this, resulting from deep fear and/or anger directed at another racial group. Individuals seek comfort and security in same-race settings, and develop a strong pro-White mentality.

Whites who reach *Redefinition and Integration*, stage five, come to terms with what it means to be White in a racist society. They develop a balanced and healthy sense of racial identity that enables them to "acknowledge their responsibility for maintaining racism while at the same time identifying with a White identity that is nonracist (or antiracist). . . . They see the good and bad in their own group as they do in other groups."[72] Individuals in this stage now devote their energies to social justice and desire the end of all forms of oppression.

Conceptions of stages of ethnic identity, such as those just described need further refinement and may not prove to be the most valid approach for understanding the sense of ethnic identity. Enough is known, however, to realize that students differ in their psychological readiness to interact with people from different ethnic groups. This is true whether the meeting occurs through actual experience or through texts and media. Students and teachers who are ethnically encapsulated will hold more negative prejudices against different ethnic groups than will others. Individuals who are in "ethnic psychological captivity" (Banks's stage one) may be embarrassed by discussions of their group's contributions and characteristics and may reject or deny evidence of individual and institutional racism. Individuals in the highest stages may, if permitted to voice their views, serve as models for others. However, they could be totally rejected by individuals in stage one or two.

 ## The Nature of Stereotypes and Multicultural Teaching

A major goal of multicultural education is the elimination of stereotypes. Although some stereotypes are positive—for example, the overgeneralization that all Jews are highly intelligent—they are still harmful in that they lead to inaccurate perceptions and judgments. Furthermore, many positive stereotypes refer to those who dominate a society and give justification for their preeminent position, as happened with stereotypes about Aryan superiority prior to World War II. When these erroneous beliefs, either favorable or unfavorable, are applied universally and without exception to all members of a group they become stereotypes.

A stereotype is a mental category based on exaggerated and inaccurate generalizations used to describe all members of a group. Some common stereotypes are that athletes are dumb; Jews are stingy; Japanese Americans are highly intelligent; African Americans are violent; fat people are lazy and lack self-discipline; sorority girls are superficial; Whites are racially prejudiced; African Americans are sexually promiscuous; and Hispanics speak Spanish. Often there is just enough fact to make a stereotype seem true. For example, there *are* some dumb blondes, interfering mothers-in-law, cruel stepmothers, and Asian whiz kids, and these kernels of truth work to keep the stereotypes alive.

As psychologists have pointed out, stereotyping is a natural phenomenon in that all humans develop mental categories to help make sense of their environment.[73] According to Triandis,

> We stereotype because it is impossible for the human brain to employ all the information present in man's environment. Furthermore, there is a natural tendency to simplify our problems and to solve them as easily as possible. A "pet formula" such as "Mexicans are lazy" makes it possible for an Anglo employer to eliminate much of his mental effort by simply not considering Mexicans for jobs in his firm. If he were to check on each applicant and to understand the causes of [the applicant's] behavior he would have to work much harder. Furthermore, categorization helps perception. When somebody tells us, "Careful, a drunken driver!" our driving instantly becomes more defensive. The category "drunken" implies many behaviors on the part of the other driver, and we adjust to them quickly and usefully.
>
> But categorization also has a penalty. The broader the categories, the more inaccurate they are likely to be. The more they help us, in that they allow us to simplify our problems, the more likely they are to cause us to perceive the world incorrectly.[74]

In addition to developing stereotypes about others, we can accept social stereotypes about ourselves. Positive stereotypes can give us an exaggerated sense of superiority, while negative stereotypes can cause self-doubt and anxiety. In several recent studies of outstanding African American and White undergraduates at Stanford, for example, psychologist Claude Steele discovered a "stereotype vulnerability" phenomenon that may explain why many bright students of color score lower than their nonminority peers on standardized tests.[75] He administered the most difficult verbal-skills questions from the Graduate Record Exam to all the Black and White students in his studies. Before the test, half the students were told that the purpose of the research was to measure "psychological factors involved in solving verbal problems," while the other group was told that the exam "was a test of your verbal abilities and limitations."[76] Black students in the first group performed as well as their White classmates (who performed equally in both settings), but Black students who were told the test measured their intellectual potential scored significantly lower than all the other students. Why did this occur?

Steele argues that lower test scores among bright African American students result not from a conscious or unconscious acceptance of negative stereotypes about Black intelligence, but rather, "that they have to *contend* with this whisper of inferiority at the moment when their mental abilities are most taxed. In trying not to give credence to the stereotype . . . the students may redouble their efforts only to work too quickly or inefficiently."[77] He also suggests, "much of what is mistaken for racial animosity in America today is really 'stereotype vulnerability.' "[78] When people from different races meet for the first time, they are aware of the stereotypes about their own group; they use up so much psychic energy trying to deflect these stereotypes that they show discomfort and confirm the stereotypes by acting, for example, "racist" or "incompetent."

It is sometimes argued that stereotypes help develop strong in-group feelings and are necessary if cherished ethnic traditions and beliefs are to be preserved. The individual holds positive stereotypes about his or her own group and negative stereotypes about out-groups. From this point of view, multicultural education may seem undesirable. However, based on the theory of cultural pluralism, a basic assumption of multicultural education is that different ethnic groups can retain much of their original culture if they so choose yet be multicultural at the same time. In other words, it is believed that people can learn about multiple ways of perceiving, believing, doing, and evaluating so that they can conform to those aspects of the dominant culture that are necessary for positive societal interaction, without eroding identification with their original ethnicity. It is assumed that ethnic traditions and beliefs can be preserved under conditions of intercultural contact that will reduce myths and stereotypes associated with previously unknown groups. These are big assumptions. Is it possible to destroy ethnic stereotypes and still maintain a sense of ethnic identity in a culturally pluralistic society? In other words, are multiple loyalties possible?

Those who believe in the feasibility of cultural pluralism will find support in the work of Gordon Allport. Allport has written that group loyalty does not necessarily mean one feels hostile toward out-groups. "Hostility toward out-groups helps strengthen our sense of belonging, but it is not required."[79] To illustrate his point, Allport diagrammed some of the in-groups to which one might belong, with the central core being most potent and the outermost circle being the weakest (see Figure 3.3). There is no intrinsic reason, however, why loyalty to humanity ("mankind"—the outermost circle) must be weakest. Allport writes:

> *Race itself has become the dominant loyalty among many people, especially among fanatic advocates of "Aryanism" and among certain members of oppressed races. It seems*

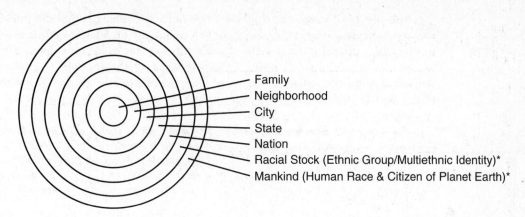

Figure 3.3 ◪ Hypothetical Lessening of In-group Potency as Membership Becomes More Inclusive

From Gordon Allport, *The Nature of Prejudice*, © 1979, Addison-Wesley, Reading, Massachusetts. Reprinted with permission of the publisher. *Modified from the original.

today that the clash between the idea of race and of One World (the two outermost circles) is shaping into an issue that may well be the most decisive in human history. The important question is, Can a loyalty to mankind be fashioned before interracial warfare breaks out?

Theoretically it can, for there is a saving psychological principle that may be invoked if we can learn how to do so in time. The principle states that concentric loyalties need not clash. To be devoted to a large circle does not imply the destruction of one's attachment to a smaller circle. The loyalties that clash are almost invariably those of identical scope. A bigamist who has founded two families of procreation is in fatal trouble with himself and with society. A traitor who serves two nations (one nominally and one actually) is mentally a mess and socially a felon. Few people can acknowledge more than one alma mater, one religion, or one fraternity. On the other hand, a world-federalist can be a devoted family man, an ardent alumnus, and a sincere patriot. The fact that some fanatic nationalists would challenge the compatibility of world-loyalty with patriotism does not change the psychological law. Wendell Willkie and Franklin Roosevelt were no less patriots because they envisioned a United Nations in One World.[80]

If we accept Allport's reasoning, it is clear that loyalty to an ethnic group need not preclude loyalty to the nation and vice versa. Respect and cooperation among different groups can replace prejudice, discrimination, and scapegoating.

The assumption that everyone is prejudiced is neither helpful nor accurate. There are individual differences in the extent to which we reject outsiders. Furthermore, it has been established that the person who rejects one out-group is likely to reject any out-group.[81] Although no single theory adequately explains the development of prejudice, it appears that less prejudiced people feel less aggression toward others, hold a generally favorable view of their parents, and perceive their environment as friendly and nonthreatening. No child is born prejudiced. Prejudices are learned within a context influenced by personal needs and social influence.

Pate suggests that some people reject prejudiced thinking because of intellectual and psychological strengths.[82] He identifies four areas of defense against prejudice: positive view of self; positive view of society (for example, belief in democratic values of equality and justice); positive view of other people; and logical thinking. An individual with low self-esteem is more likely to be prejudiced than one with high self-esteem. A positive view of society means

> a person should have basically democratic views with a belief in equality and a sense of justice. A positive view of other people includes a degree of empathy, a feeling that people are basically worthwhile, and an aversion to manipulating people for selfish reasons. Logical thinking is just that—a quality of reasoning ability which does not jump to conclusions, see only the superficial, reach faulty conclusions, confuse cause and effect, or overgeneralize.[83]

Obviously teachers are limited in what they can do to modify the deeply prejudiced personality. We should remember, however, that not everyone who accepts stereotypes is deeply prejudiced. Furthermore, there is no known reason why we cannot or should not attempt to reduce ethnic group stereotypes and at the same time foster within our students a healthy sense of ethnic pride and respect. Those who feel genuine pride (not superiority) in their own ethnic group are most apt to accept other ethnic groups. Stereotypes impede that acceptance.

Avoiding Ethnic Group Stereotypes: What Can Teachers Do?

It is important to remember that we run the risk of stereotyping when we seek the perspective of a particular nation or ethnic group. People within every national or ethnic group differ from each other in important ways. Not all White Anglo-Saxon Protestants are racially prejudiced. Not all Mexican Americans identify with their native heritage. Not all African Americans are knowledgeable about life in the Black ghetto or can speak for the Black community on race-relations issues. Not everyone with a Spanish surname can speak Spanish. Not every Muslim is an Arab. And not every Arab is a Muslim.

Within any one nation or ethnic group, social conflicts and different viewpoints emerge due to such factors as geographic origins, social class, and gender. Personal qualities such as aptitude, personality, and appearance also make a difference. All these factors interact with the individual's sense of national or ethnic identity; some individuals tend to be assimilated into the dominant culture, others are more ethnically encapsulated, and still others are bicultural or even global in perspective. Geographic origins, social class, and sense of ethnic identity are especially helpful in explaining ethnic diversity.

The following suggestions illustrate how an awareness of diversity within ethnic groups and nations can be developed, along with an understanding of the group's perspective.

- Select a nation or ethnic group and plan ways of portraying the diversity within it. Include male and female viewpoints, different generations and age groups, dissimilar occupations, geographical regions, socioeconomic backgrounds, neighborhoods, and intergroup experiences.

- When social issues are debated, or when students are asked to play roles, include a realistic mix of opinions that portray the different viewpoints within many ethnic groups and nations.
- Help students identify diversity within their own ethnic group and nation, including physical features associated with different races, attitudes, opinions, and socioeconomic factors.
- Provide a variety of role models from each ethnic group present in the school.
- When tracking of students or ability grouping is used, consider a range of placement criteria to ensure ethnic diversity within instructional groups.

Africa: An Illustration of Racism and the Need for Curriculum Reform

The traditional curriculum in most schools in the United States is a classic example of institutional and cultural racism. From elementary school, where uncounted numbers of children have been taught to "sit like an Indian" (which in itself is a racial stereotype), to colleges and universities, where thousands more have learned the misconception that IQ differences are related to race, schools have fostered the belief in White supremacy. The traditional mono-ethnic curriculum has presented one way of perceiving, believing, behaving, and evaluating: the Anglo-Western European way. School texts and educational media have presented negative myths and stereotypes about most of our ethnic minorities, have overlooked important contributions, and have presented a distorted view of past and current history that reinforces the doctrine of White supremacy. The case of Africa and the cultural roots of African Americans provides one example.

Common Misconceptions

The truth about Africa has been so distorted among non-Africans that with the emergence of Africa on the world scene in 1960 (the year most contemporary African nations achieved independence and sent representatives to the United Nations), most Westerners were almost totally ignorant about the earth's second largest continent. For centuries perceptions of the "Dark Continent" had been clouded over with myths and stereotypes, and Africa was greeted then as now with all the myths and stereotypes intact. Some of the simplest myths are most common: lions in the jungles, the isolated Dark Continent, inferior savages, a race of Negroes—heathens developed only by the grace of God and the White man—and a land of turmoil, incapable of self-government. Because these myths and stereotypes are alive today in the school's curriculum (however unintentional the distortions and omissions may be), in the hands of unaware and unskilled teachers the curriculum continues to feed the racist doctrines and practices of White supremacy.

Raised on a diet of Westernized history, Tarzan books and films, and sensationalized news media, many in the United States believe Africa to be a primitive land of hot, steamy jungles inhabited by wild animals and savages. In truth, less than 10 percent of the African continent is jungle. (And of course, lions live in grasslands, not jungles.) Nearly half of the African continent consists of grassy savannah, and approximately one-third is searing desert.[84]

The idea that Africa has been isolated until recently is also false. Ancient Africans had contact with the Greeks, Romans, Chinese, and early Indonesians, and there is evidence that they may have entered the western hemisphere long before the Spaniards. Archaeological evidence reveals active trade with Arabs and Indians via the Indian Ocean and the Sahara, which was at one time a lush fertile nursery of African civilizations. For example, cave paintings and chariot tracks preserved in rock attest to a lively commerce that began before the Sahara dried up and became a desert. Europeans traded with the Moroccans, probably without knowing that many goods (primarily gold, salt, and ivory) originated south of the Sahara. Davidson describes the bustling port of Kilwa from the twelfth to the fifteenth centuries as the chief trading center of East Africa and one of the liveliest in the entire world. "On any given day . . . workers could be seen loading their masters' dhows with African gold, iron, ivory and coconuts, and unloading textiles and jewelry from India and exquisite porcelain from China."[85]

Related to the misconception that Africa was an isolated continent prior to the arrival of the Europeans is the belief that Africans were uncivilized savages. Early writings of Muslim scholars who traveled throughout Africa in the tenth and eleventh centuries provide evidence that African civilization was as advanced, or more so, than that of Europe, even according to the material standards typically used by Westerners. The Arab geographer alBakri, for example, wrote in 1067 (one year after 20,000 Normans conquered England) that "the king of Ghana . . . can raise 200,000 warriors, 40,000 of them being armed with bows and arrows."[86] When Mali's king, Mansa Musa, made his pilgrimage to Mecca in 1324, his "entourage was composed of 60,000 persons, a large portion of which constituted a military escort. No less than 12,000 were servants, 500 of whom marched ahead of their king, each bearing a staff of pure gold. Books, baggage men, and royal secretaries there were in abundance. To finance the pilgrimage, the king carried 80 camels to bear his more than 24,000 pounds of gold."[87] Because King Musa spent so much money in the Middle East, the value of gold in the great commercial center of Cairo was depressed for at least twelve years.[88]

Yet few people have learned about the achievements of the early West African kingdoms of Ghana, Mali, and Songhai, the forest kingdom of Benin, or Kanem-Bornu in the interior. The prosperity and power of the great West African empires, which covered an area almost as large as the United States, arose from the agricultural base of the Niger River Valley, their control of the gold and salt trade between North African Arabs, the existence of the open savannah that foot and horse soldiers could quickly traverse, and their rulers' adoption of Islam, which brought them aid, allies, and smoother trade among Muslims of North Africa and the Middle East.[89]

Although ancient Egypt is a staple of world history and art history courses and a source of fascination for young children and youth, the Black African influences on Egyptian civilization, and therefore Anglo-European civilization, has been hidden. Few people have heard that the ancient kingdom of Kush, which thrived during the Ptolemaic era, was a center of extensive iron smelting, and developed the Meroitic alphabet.

Africa's record of achievement is not limited to the large kingdoms, however. Elaborate social and political systems, complex religions (frequently dismissed as animism), effective health care practices (for example, the herbal-psychological services of the traditional healer), and advanced expressions of music and art all developed in African villages as well as in large empires. Some scholars assert that the greatest genius of the African peoples was their capacity for social organization, a talent that operated at the village level and in the complex kingdoms.[90] In community attitude that "joined man to man in a brotherhood of equals, in moral attitudes that guided social behavior, in beliefs that exalted the spiritual aspects of life above the material," many Africans achieved a kind of social harmony that could exist without the power of a centralized authority.[91] This is not to overlook the fact that prior to European invasions nearly all ethnic groups in Africa practiced some form of slavery. It is important to recognize, however, that although they suffered great liabilities, African slaves were guaranteed extensive rights, had a relatively stable family life, and often experienced a great deal of social mobility. In fact, eventual freedom was often presumed.[92]

Ibn Battuta, a Berber scholar and theologian from Tangiers who crossed the Sahara in 1352 and spent a year in Mali, found some of his hosts' customs unpleasant, but he wrote about the high sense of justice among the people. "Of all peoples, the Negroes are those who most abhor injustice. The Sultan pardons no one who is guilty of it. There is complete and general safety throughout the land. The traveler here has no more reason than the man who stays at home to fear brigands, thieves or ravishers."[93] Furthermore, "the blacks do not confiscate the goods of any North Africans who may die in their country, not even when these consist of large treasures. On the contrary, they deposit these goods with a man of confidence . . . until those who have a right to the goods present themselves and take possession."[94]

In the late fifteenth century, Europeans did not need to rely on the travelogues of Muslim scholars and could see for themselves that Africa was not a primeval wilderness inhabited by savages. Instead, these visitors discovered

> *prosperous, self-contained cities linked to each other by a busy, carefully ordered trade. Their inhabitants—merchants, artisans, laborers, clerks—lived comfortable lives. Their pleasures were the familiar ones cherished by all people—feasting and family gatherings. Africa was in many ways no more savage than Europe—at the time just concluding the Hundred Years' War and only recently occupied with burning Joan of Arc.*[95]

Nevertheless, myths about Africa continued to flourish in Europe and eventually were transported to the colonies in North America. These myths conjured visions of the great White hunter facing primitive tribes with their cannibalism, depraved customs, loincloths, and spears. Early slave-ship records promoted the view that it was only through the grace of God and the White man that these heathen savages would be Christianized and civilized. Sensationalized news stories and films have helped keep the Tarzan image alive, as well as images of the noble savage unspoiled by the evils of industrialized society.

How and why did these myths develop? First, competition among the emerging European nations and houses of commerce led to practices of secrecy lest rivals benefit from knowledge gained through the early explorations of lands unknown to Europe. Second, was the blatant "dishonesty of literary hacks who concocted all sorts of nonsense for a gullible public."[96] Third, was the need to justify slave trade in the minds of Christians and the enlightened. Assurances that slaves were heathen savages who would benefit by becoming Christianized and civilized became a basic rationalization. It should also be noted, however, that Spanish colonists distinguished between Blacks and Indians, thinking the former were subhuman and therefore unworthy of conversion.[97] Related to the desire to expand Christianity is the fact that Europeans launched into an era of imperialism and the quest for new lands and natural resources. To control new colonies, in this case the African colonies, traditional history, culture, and sources of group identity had to be suppressed and were replaced (at least temporarily) by the colonialists' culture, history, and doctrines of White supremacy. Today, many textbooks contain outdated information about African nations. Rapidly changing events on that continent make maps and other content obsolete even in relatively new texts. Furthermore, news media and periodicals, which could be used to supplement outdated materials, are often inadequate sources for understanding current and past events in Africa.

> *The Washington Post, probably the most important news source of American political decision makers, covers Africa's fifty-two nations and 350,000,000 people with one reporter, who within a few days was ordered to cover the independence of Mozambique, the coup against the Emperor of Ethiopia, and the Ali–Foreman fight in Zaire. This is an impossible assignment! (As one Madison, Wisconsin, newspaper editor noted, there is more and better reporting on Africa in one weekly airmail issue edition of the British Manchester Guardian than in all the American national press combined.) Those who know Africa and read the U.S. press's political reporting frequently find that the stories are shallow, and stereotypical, overemphasizing the importance of ethnicity and tribe, fixated on the bizarre and exotic, primarily dependent on white expatriates for information and sometimes covertly allied with white racialist interests.*[98]

In addition to outdated content, most current textbooks that attempt to present Africans to elementary and secondary school students emphasize exotic and irrelevant information about race and overemphasize small groups of people such as the Mbuti, San, and Khoi peoples, commonly referred to as Pygmies, Bushmen, and Hottentots. The combined population of these three groups is estimated to be between 25,000 and 250,000, or approximately 0.007 to 0.07 percent of the total population of Africa (over 350 million).[99]

> *The names chosen to describe these people—"Bushmen," "Pygmies" and "Hottentots"—are not names which are used by the people themselves; rather, they are deprecating and unflattering terms given to them by Europeans who . . . did not learn or use the appropriate names. Pygmy comes from a Greek word meaning short or dwarf. The name Bushman was given to the San people by South African whites who exterminated many of them and drove others from their fertile lands into the desert bush*

areas. . . . Many young Americans come to believe that many or most African people live like these exotic, small atypical groups because so much of the curriculum is devoted to their study.[100]

Given the vast reservoir of African history and cultures available and yet unknown by most people in the United States, the textbook emphasis on Pygmies and Bushmen is telling. These peoples exemplify survival in an inhospitable environment and may be more spiritually developed than many humans who live in higher technological societies, but the texts neither point this out nor establish the array of humanity found on the African continent. Thus, the unsophisticated non-African reader who comes across illustrations and texts that only show Africans in the bush perceives emotionally and physically uncomfortable conditions and "improper behavior" (scanty clothes, scarification, dipping food from a common bowl) and evaluates the people as inferior. American children and youth need to understand the basic human characteristics they share with the various peoples of Africa. This is not achieved by emphasizing exoticism and cultural differences associated with so-called primitive humanity.

Some Effects of Misconceptions about Africa

One result of this deformed view of past and present Africa is that it promotes ignorance and disdain of Africans. These are dangerous outcomes in a world whose peoples are growing closer and more interdependent. Another obvious result of ignorance about Africa is that it feeds the doctrine of White supremacy and the belief that African Americans as a group are inferior because they are genetically related to Africans. Myths and theories from the past that were used to justify slavery continue to serve as a rationalization for inferior schools, substandard homes, low-paying jobs, and segregated restaurants, rest rooms, and transportation. The Council on Interracial Books for Children concludes the following:

> *To justify the treatment of the African slave, and later of the Afro-American citizen, white society encouraged an army of propagandists to "scientifically" prove the inferiority of Black people. While this ideology of racism was applied to all people of color with whom Euro-American society came into contact, its severest application was against Afro-Americans. Because they were the most physically different from whites, because their numbers were the second largest to whites, and because of their geographical and social proximity to whites, Black people have been perceived as the greatest threat.*
>
> *White supremacist ideology has infected every level of national life. Government officials, social scientists, ministers, teachers, journalists and doctors have all played a part, as new and more sophisticated revisions of the myths and rationalizations of white supremacy keep reappearing. Whether it is religious leaders in colonial days pointing to Biblical passages damning Ham; biologists of a hundred years ago "studying" cranial structures; Social Darwinists utilizing theories of evolution and survival of the fittest; geneticists of the 1920s "proving" inborn moral inferiority; Moynihan-like theories of Black "pathology"; recent genetic pronouncements of Shockley and Jensen about Black IQ—all serve as pseudo-scientific apologies for the ongoing oppression directed against Black people.*[101]

Box 3.1
Multicultural Self-Report Inventory

SA = Strongly Agree,   MA = Moderately Agree,   U = Uncertain,
MD = Moderately Disagree,   SD = Strongly Disagree

	SA	MA	U	MD	SD
1. I am interested in exploring cultures different from my own.	1	2	3	4	5
2. I have enough experience with cultures different from my own.	1	2	3	4	5
3. I seem to like some cultures and ethnic groups better than others.	1	2	3	4	5
4. Part of the role of a good teacher is to encourage children to adopt middle class values.	1	2	3	4	5
5. I feel that cultural differences in students do not affect students' behavior in school.	1	2	3	4	5
6. As students progress through school, they should adopt the mainstream culture.	1	2	3	4	5
7. I am comfortable around people whose cultural background is different from mine.	1	2	3	4	5
8. I can identify attitude or behaviors in children that are peculiar to my culture.	1	2	3	4	5
9. I believe I can recognize attitudes or behaviors in children that are a reflection of cultural or ethnic differences.	1	2	3	4	5
10. I feel I can take the point of view of a child from a different culture.	1	2	3	4	5
11. It makes me uncomfortable when I hear people talking in a language that I cannot understand.	1	2	3	4	5

Another effect of these deformed images of Africa is the misconceptions about Black African people that crop up in textbooks and other educational materials. These misconceptions are then transferred to African Americans. According to Beryle Banfield, president of the Council on Interracial Books for Children,

> *Racism in textbooks is usually most evident in five important areas: the historical perspective from which the material is presented; the characterization of Third World peoples; the manner in which their customs and traditions are depicted; the terminology used to describe the peoples and their culture and the type of language ascribed to them; and the nature of the illustrations.*[102]

	SA	MA	U	MD	SD
12. Values and attitudes learned in minority cultures keep children from making progress in school.	1	2	3	4	5
13. Only people who are part of a culture can really understand and empathize with children from that culture.	1	2	3	4	5
14. I have had few cross-cultural experiences.	1	2	3	4	5
15. Multicultural education is an important part of a school curriculum.	1	2	3	4	5
16. I am prejudiced in favor of some ethnic or cultural group or groups.	1	2	3	4	5
17. Some ethnic groups make less desirable citizens than others.	1	2	3	4	5
18. Some ethnic groups are more reluctant to talk about family matters than other cultural groups.	1	2	3	4	5
19. Children from differing ethnic groups are likely to differ in their attitudes toward teacher authority.	1	2	3	4	5
20. Personally, I have never identified any prejudice in myself.	1	2	3	4	5
21. I am prejudiced *against* some ethnic or cultural groups.	1	2	3	4	5
22. In the United States, given equal intelligence and physical ability, every individual has equal access to success.	1	2	3	4	5

Source: From "Multicultural Experiences for Special Educators" by J. C. Slade and C. W. Conoley. *Teaching Exceptional Children*, 22, no. 1 (1989), 62. © 1989 by the Council for Exceptional Children. Reprinted with permission.

Yet another result of our deformed history is the internalized racism exhibited by individuals who internalize, or hold within their psyche, society's negative stereotypes about a group they identify with. They often experience "stereotype threat," or self-doubt and anxiety in situations where they could inadvertently confirm these stereotypes. The theory of stereotype threat helps explain the "extra pressures that can affect the test performance and academics of such groups as African Americans and women in math."[103] In my own work with students of color who hope to become teachers, I find evidence of stereotype threat in many of these students' experience with the praxis exam that is required for admission into our teacher-education programs. Other researchers see evidence of internalized racism in the artwork of young children, and this is a theme in African American literature, such as *The Bluest Eye*, by Toni Morrison.

In a thematic analysis of *The Bluest Eye*, Lisa R. Lazarescu, an English discourse scholar at Eastern Oregon University, writes,

> *Internalized racism occurs both consciously and subconsciously. It can affect any race, group, or person, whether it be due to color, sexual status, or even medical issues. Basically it occurs when a person begins to believe all of the negative stereotypes and images that come from other people, history, media, or any other sources that depict oppressing images, which often lead to self-hatred of the person or group as inferior, such as the white oppression against people of color. Internalized racism occurs in "The Bluest Eye," partly because whiteness is a standard of beauty, but mainly because America, in all avenues during the 1940s was oppressing the black people of its nation.*[104]

 ## Conclusions

Although both cultural and racial differences might be an important source of transitional trauma, misunderstanding, and conflict in the classroom, race is often the more serious factor. White American culture rooted in Anglo-European traditions predominates in most schools, most of which are controlled by White people. We find evidence of this in the growing body of literature that shows alarmingly high rates of dropping out among Latino and American Indian students and the inequitable participation rates of African American students on the college campuses—the result of our society's pervasive legacy of racism. A major goal of multicultural education is to help us understand this legacy and move toward a more just society.

This chapter's discussion of racism has emphasized Africa and African Americans. We must be careful, however, not to regard racism strictly as a Black–White issue. There are parallels to the case of Africa all over the world. The results of ignorance and misunderstanding have been seen in Southeast Asia during the Vietnamese war and its aftermath—and again in Central America, an area many perceive simplistically as the Banana Republics.

Likewise, not only are non-White ethnic groups in United States society affected by racism; many White immigrants, such as the Irish, Italians, and Jews from Eastern Europe also have experienced cruel discrimination. Immigration officials in California sometimes violate the civil rights of Mexican Americans who are assumed to be illegal aliens by stopping them and asking them for identification. Immigrants from Asia—the Vietnamese and Chinese—now face resentment and racial prejudices in many aspects of their lives.

Because space does not permit all-inclusive illustrations, the focus on Africa and African Americans is appropriate. In terms of numbers, African Americans represent the largest ethnic minority. (However, according to the U.S. Census 2000, when Cuban Americans, Mexican Americans, Puerto Ricans, and immigrants from Central and South American are combined, Hispanics are now the largest.) More important, however, is the fact that no other group entered this society primarily through slavery. The experience of slavery and its justification firmly entrenched the doctrine of White supremacy in the minds and institutions that shaped U.S. history and led to the overall suppression of dark-skinned citizens.

Obviously, schools do not exist in a vacuum. They are only one aspect of a broader social context that, despite many changes that help encourage social justice for everyone, is still racist in many ways because it supports White privilege. How do we proceed in the face of this? First, we must accept that schools can and should make a difference. Those who would equate a stand against racism with preaching values can be told that it is un-American, undemocratic, and antihuman to be racist. We can then proceed as follows:

- Recognize racist history and its impact on oppressors and victims.
- Examine our own attitudes, experiences, and behaviors concerning racism.
- Understand the origins of racism and why people hold racial prejudices and stereotypes.
- Understand the differences among individual, institutional, and cultural racism.
- Be able to identify racist images in the language and illustration of books, films, television, news media, and advertising.
- Be able to identify current examples of racism in our immediate community and society as a whole.
- Identify specific ways of combating racism.
- Become antiracist in our own behavior.

In Chapters 4 through 5 the case for multicultural education is further developed through a discussion of the roots of cultural diversity in the United States. They provide a comparative analysis of important ethnic groups in terms of their origins and responses to various forms of oppression.

Selected Sources for Further Study

Adams, M., Blumenfeld, W. J., Castaneda, R., Hackman, H. W., Peters, M. L., & Zuniga, X. (Eds.) (2000). *Readings for Diversity and Social Justice: An Anthology on Racism, Antisemitism, Sexism, Heterosexism, Ableism, and Classism.* New York: Routledge.

Ayres, W., Quinn, T., & Stovall, D. (2009). *Handbook of Social Justice in Education.* New York: Routledge.

Banks, J. A. (2004). "Race, Knowledge Construction, and Education in the United States: Lessons from History," in J. A. Banks & C. M. Banks (Eds.), *Handbook of Research on Multicultural Education,* 2nd ed. (pp. 228–239). San Francisco, CA: Jossey-Bass.

Bennett, C., McWorter, L., & Kuykendall, J. (2006). "Will I Ever Teach? Latino and African American Students' Perspectives on PRAXIS I," *American Educational Research Journal, 43*(3), 531–575.

Bonilla-Silva, E. (2006). *Racism Without Racists: Color-Blind Racism and the Persistence of Racial Inequality in the United States,* 2nd ed. Lanham, NJ: Rowman & Littlefield.

Brown, M. K., et al. (2003). *White Washing Race: The Myth of a Color-Blind Society.* Berkeley: University of California Press.

Delgado, R., & Stefancic, J. (2001). *Critical Race Theory: An Introduction.* New York: New York University Press.

Derman-Sparks, L., & Ramsey, P. G. (2006). *What If All The Kids Are White? Anti-Bias Multicultural Education with Young Children and Families*. New York: Teachers College Press.

Ford, R. T. (2008). *The Race Card: How Bluffing About Bias Makes Race Relations Worse*. New York: Farrar, Straus and Giroux.

Gottschalk, P., & Greenberg, G. (2008). *Islamophobia: Making Muslims the Enemy*. Lanham, MD: Rowman & Littlefield.

Howard, G. (2006). *We Can't Teach What We Don't Know: White Teachers, Multiracial Schools*, 2nd ed. New York: Teachers College Press.

Kennedy, R. (2003). *Nigger: The Strange Career of a Troublesome Word*, 2nd ed. New York: Pantheon and Vintage Books.

King, J. E. (2004). "Culture Centered Knowledge: Black Studies, Curriculum Transformation, and Social Action," in J. A. Banks & C. M. Banks (Eds.), *Handbook of Research on Multicultural Education*, 2nd ed. (pp. 349–378). San Francisco, CA: Jossey-Bass.

Kivel, P. (2002). *Uprooting Racism: How White People Can Work for Racial Justice* (Rev. ed.). Gabriola Island, Canada: New Society.

Madison, J. (2001). *A Lynching in the Heartland: Race and Memory in America*. New York: Palgrave.

Mun Way, L. (Producer and Director). (1994). *The Color of Fear* (Film). Los Angeles.

Ngai, M. N. (2004). *Impossible Subjects: Illegal Aliens and the Making of Modern America*. Princeton, NJ: Princeton University Press.

Pollock, M. (2008). *Because of Race: How Americans Debate Harm and Opportunity in Our Schools*. Princeton, NJ: Princeton University Press.

Race: The Power of an Illusion. (Three videos) California Newsreel. www.newsreel.org.

Root, M. (2004). "Multiracial Families and Children: Implications for Educational Research and Practice," in J. A. Banks & C. M. Banks (Eds.), *Handbook of Research on Multicultural Education*, 2nd ed. (pp. 110–124). San Francisco, CA: Jossey-Bass.

Rothenberg, P. S. (Ed.). (2005). *White Privilege: Essential Readings on the Other Side of Racism*, 2nd ed. New York: Worth.

Singleton, G., & Linton, C. (2006). *Courageous Conversations About Race: A Field Guide for Achieving Equity in Schools*. Thousand Oaks, CA: Corwin Press.

Sleeter, C. E., & Delgado Bernal, D. (2004). "Critical Pedagogy, Critical Race Theory, and Antiracist Education: Implications for Multicultural Education," in J. A. Banks & C. M. Banks (Eds.), *Handbook of Research on Multicultural Education*, 2nd ed. (pp. 240–258). San Francisco, CA: Jossey-Bass.

Steele, C. (2004). "A Threat in the Air: How Stereotypes Shaped Intellectual Identity and Performance," in J. A. Banks & C. M. Banks (Eds.), *Handbook of Research on Multicultural Education*, 2nd ed. (pp. 282–298). San Francisco, CA: Jossey-Bass.

Van Ausdale, D., & Feagin, J. R. (2001). *The First R: How Children Learn Race and Racism*. Lanham, MD: Rowan & Littlefield.

Watkins, W. H. (2001). *The White Architects of Black Education: Ideology and Power in America, 1865–1954*. New York: Teachers College Press.

Wise, T. (2005). *White Like Me: Reflections on Race from a Privileged Son*. New York: Soft Skull Press.

 **myeducationlab**
The Power of Classroom Practice
www.myeducationlab.com

Now go to Topics #2 and 14: **Race** and **Identity Development** in the MyEducationLab (www.myeducationlab.com) for your course, where you can:

■ Find learning outcomes for these topics along with the national standards that connect to these outcomes.

■ Complete Assignments and Activities that can help you more deeply understand the chapter content.

■ Apply and practice your understanding of the core teaching skills identified in the chapter with the Building Teaching Skills and Dispositions learning units.

Part II
Roots of Cultural Diversity in the United States: The Conflicting Themes of Assimilation and Pluralism

Chapter 4

Immigration and the American Dream: European American and Jewish American Perspectives

This section begins our focus on *demographics*, a highly complex aspect of multicultural education. Our population has changed dramatically since the first edition of this book was written (nearly three decades ago), and we need to rethink the old theories of cultural assimilation and pluralism as we attempt to understand contemporary immigration and how the future might unfold. The next four chapters further the case for multicultural education by providing brief histories of major ethnic groups in the United States, including recent newcomers as well as the long-established ones.

Why is this history important? First, we often overlook the different histories of ethnic minority children and youth as a factor in their contemporary school experiences. For example, some people wonder why many Mexican Americans want to maintain fluency in Spanish or have difficulty learning English when many other immigrants master English within a generation. How do we explain the disproportionately high poverty rates among African Americans, American Indians, Puerto Ricans, and Appalachian Whites? Why do language-minority children and low-income students drop out of school at higher rates than students fluent in Standard English and students from middle- and upper-income families? Second, we tend to lump students into broad ethnic categories, as we do with Asian Americans, who are often viewed as the "model minority" and academic whiz kids, and thus overlook the tremendous diversity and learning needs of students within the group. And third, these brief histories illustrate the ethnic pluralism in our contemporary society that is better served by multicultural schools than by monocultural schools. As teachers working toward social justice, we must become informed participants in a society that is increasingly diverse in terms of national origins, languages, religions, and race. In this chapter, I hope to provide a context and framework that will help readers understand the increasingly complex roots and consequences of ethnic diversity in the United States that are explored in Chapters 5 through 7, especially the complexities of contemporary immigration and their implications for our schools and society. We begin with overviews of immigration and the American Dream and continue with perspectives from European American and Jewish American experiences.

Immigration

Ethnic Diversity Present and Past

Today, the American population is more ethnically diverse than ever before in our history.[1] According to scholars of mass migration to the United States, "There has been no comparable massive migration of people entirely different from the native-born population in origin, religion, and even physical characteristics" as what we are experiencing today.[2] This may be a surprise, because we have always been a dramatically diverse people in terms of language, religion, national origin, and race.

The colonial era and early independence years witnessed tremendous cultural diversity among indigenous peoples as well as voluntary and involuntary immigrants. American Indians were comprised of over 500 distinct indigenous peoples at the time of the Conquest.[3] Europeans included Spaniards, French, and British settlers who established civilian outposts, explored the continent, and built settlement communities; there were Dutch, Portuguese, German, and Scandinavian settlers as well. African Americans grew to about 20 percent of the population. Most of the original Africans were brought here as slaves from different ethnic regions in central and western Africa to work on large Southern plantations, but there also existed small free Black populations and smaller slave populations in the North.[4] During the period of "Manifest Destiny," the United States moved west, expanding into territories that were home to indigenous peoples as well as people of European decent. There was the Louisiana Purchase in 1803, the annexation of Texas in 1845, the incorporation of the northern half of Mexico after the Mexican-American War in 1848, and the Gadsden Purchase in 1853. The conquest and settlement of these areas was accomplished by significant numbers of immigrants from Northern Europe. Between 1821–1880, "86 percent of the immigrants were from Northern and Western Europe, mainly Germany, Ireland, and the United Kingdom, with a lesser number from Norway, Sweden, Denmark, the Netherlands, Switzerland, Belgium, and France."[5]

The naturalization of immigrants (citizenship) is a central aspect of this history; our nation was created as a place "where immigrants were welcome and expected to become full-fledged citizens of the new nation."[6] At first, citizenship was limited to "free White" who could "prove two years of continuous residence in the United States."[7] Then, in 1802, Congress established basic requirements for citizenship that remain largely unchanged today: five years of residency, a "declaration of intention" that must be filed two years in advance of naturalization (abolished in 1952), an oath of allegiance, and the recommendation of two citizen witnesses.[8] Race continued to be a factor for decades, and until 1869 citizenship was limited to Whites, particularly Anglo-Saxon Whites.[9] With passage of the Fourteenth Amendment, people of African descent became eligible for naturalization, and they were extended citizenship rights through the 1870 Naturalization Act. For the next hundred years, race remained a "defining aspect of citizenship in the United States" and racial classification became a "fundamental factor in the admission of immigrants to residency and naturalization in the United States."[10]

The evolution of race as a factor in immigration legislation is revealed in three of our most important immigration acts, which were passed between 1924–1965. These acts can be reviewed in Box 4.1 on the next two pages. Four important pieces of immigration legislation in the contemporary era are also summarized in Box 4.1.[11]

The Classic and Contemporary Immigration Eras

The classic period of immigration refers to the five decades between 1880 and 1930 (also known as the "deluge" or "mass migration" period in American history) when approximately 28 million people immigrated to this country.[12] The majority were culturally different from the Anglo European immigrants who arrived in the previous waves of migration from Northern Europe and the British Isles; most were Catholic, Jewish, or Eastern Orthodox Christian immigrants from Southern and Eastern Europe and Russia.[13] It is a classic period in that most of the children were eventually assimilated into American society by the third or fourth generation, much as previous generations had done in earlier waves of immigration. The flood of newcomers was followed by a major decline in immigration due to racial restrictions and national origin quotas that were established in 1924, and the percentage of foreign-born shrunk to about 5 percent of the population by 1970, the lowest in our nation's history.[14] This break in the flow of newcomers contributed to the eventual cultural assimilation of later generations, giving credence to the melting pot perspective.

Today we are experiencing a second immigration boom, known as the contemporary era, which is rooted in changes in the Immigration and Nationality Act Amendments of 1965.[15] As noted in Box 4.1, this legislation abolished nationality quotas, contains no racial or ethnic preferences, and "fundamentally changed the composition and size of immigrant cohorts over the next decades."[16] It gives preference to "immigrants with exceptional professional qualifications and those with close family members who were U.S. citizens the highest priority in the allotment of visas."[17] Today, the "United States issues more permanent and temporary visas to legal immigrants than any country in the world and has millions of foreign nationals living and working illegally in the country. Immigrants to the United States come from every country in the world, although Mexico accounts for the most (30.7%)"[18] followed by India, China, and the Philippines. Table 4.1 on page 114 lists the world regions according to the number of persons (from highest to lowest) who obtained permanent resident status in the United States and identifies the top ten countries of birth for persons who obtained permanent resident status between 1998–2007. It also shows the number who entered under one of the five basic preference categories: family-sponsored, employment-based, immediate relatives of U.S. citizens, diversity, and refugees and asylees. These trends are expected to continue into the foreseeable future.

According to Pyong Gap Min, editor of the recent book *Mass Migration to the United States: Classical and Contemporary Periods*,

The overrepresentation of nonwhite, Third World people among contemporary immigrants is something policymakers neither intended nor expected when they liberalized the immigration law. In 1965, when Congress passed the liberal immigration law, only

Box 4.1
Becoming an American in the United States: A Brief History of Naturalization and Immigration Laws

The evolution of race as a factor in immigration legislation is revealed in three of our most important immigration acts passed between 1924–1965. These are briefly summarized below, followed by a summary of four important pieces of immigration legislation in the contemporary era.[138]

The National Origins Act of 1924 (Fully Effective in 1929)

The National Origins Act was the nation's first comprehensive immigration law; its goal was to protect the White European population base. It assigned nationality quotas of 2 percent of each nation's population in the United States prior to 1890, just prior to the deluge of immigrants from Eastern and Southern Europe and Russia. Therefore, immigration from Southern and Eastern Europe was nearly eliminated. It also restricted immigration from the Eastern Hemisphere by excluding most Asians from citizenship. The total number of immigrants per year was capped at 150,000, but an unlimited number of Canadians and Mexicans were allowed.[139] Priority was given to persons with skills needed in the United States and to family reunification, which was limited to spouses and minor children.[140] The "avowed aim" of this legislation was to maintain the "racial purity" of the American people.[141]

Immigration and Nationality Act of 1952

The Immigration and Nationality Act of 1952 maintained national quotas for immigrants from eastern hemisphere countries, but it banned racial discrimination in the *naturalization* of immigrants (e.g., Japanese and Korean immigrants became eligible for citizenship). The law added the English-language requirement for citizenship, eliminated the declaration of intent requirement, and set up preference criteria for skilled workers and relatives of U.S. citizens.[142] The act was amended to admit refugee groups from Communist or Communist-dominated countries within the general area of the Middle East and established a small quota for the Asia-Pacific triangle.[143]

Immigration and Nationality Act Amendments of 1965

Largely as a result of the civil rights movement in the Unites States during the 1950s and 1960s, this legislation abolished nationality quotas and contained no racial or ethnic preferences. It changed the composition and size of future immigrant cohorts and gave top priority to those with exceptional professional qualifications and those with close family members who were U.S. citizens.[144] The number of immigrants per year was limited to 170,000 from the Eastern Hemisphere, with a maximum of 20,000 per country; Western Hemisphere immigrants were limited to 120,000 per year and could enter on a "first-come, first-served basis," with no limits per nation. However, *immediate* family members were not included in the cap, which set up preferences for family reunification that has created the "chain migration" we see today.[145] Refugees were also not included in the cap. The racially and nationally restrictive immigration policies of previous decades were now officially over.

Immigration Reform and Control Act of 1986

The Immigration Reform and Control Act (IRCA) resulted from debates over how best to handle illegal immigration. It authorized legalization for illegal aliens who had entered the United States before

January 1, 1982, and had lived in the United States continuously since.[146] IRCA also emphasized sanctions against employers who hired illegal workers. It also enhanced enforcement of border controls and restructured the foreign worker permit program to import temporary agricultural workers.[147]

Immigration Act of 1990

The Immigration Act of 1990 established a flexible annual cap of 675,000 per year beginning in 1995.[148] Within this number, 480,000 places are reserved for family-sponsored immigrants (beyond immediate family), 140,000 are reserved for high-need employment areas, and 55,000 are "diversity immigrants" intended to balance out national origins of new immigrant cohorts. However, refugees, asylees, and immediate relatives of U.S. citizens are not included in these limits.

Illegal Immigration Reform and Immigrant Responsibility Act of 1996 (IIRIRA)

This act was generated by concerns for national security after the World Trade Center bombing by terrorists in 1992. IIRIRA beefed up U.S. border control, established protections for legal workers through worksite enforcement and the removal of "deportable aliens," and restricted some public benefits for illegal immigrants. (To date, undocumented workers have the right to certain federal benefits, including free medical emergency care; free public school for minor children; and, in some states, in-state college tuition for young adult children.) Critics of IIRIRA argue that the law treats "law-abiding legal permanent residents the same as dangerous criminals."[149]

Post-World War II Refugee Acts

In the aftermath of the horrific Holocaust in Nazi Germany, President Truman urged that Jewish refugees be given top priority within the nation's immigrant quotas. In 1948, Congress passed the Displaced Persons Act, which was the first refugee policy measure in U.S. history.[150] This act opened the way for 450,000 European refugees to enter the United States through a federally supported relocation program led by civic and religious volunteer groups. Post-World War II refugees from China were also admitted, and 250,000 refugees from Cuba entered the country over the next decade.[151] Eventually, these quotas were officially ignored as the United States responded to later refugee crises in Southeast Asia, the Middle East, and Africa.[152]

It is important to consider the differences between refugees and immigrants in order to understand their resettlement experiences in the United States and how this affects schoolchildren in our classrooms. The fundamental experiential difference between refugees and immigrants is choice. Whether migrant laborers, professionals, or entrepreneurs, immigrants leave their home country by choice and are frequently "pulled" to migrate permanently because of employment or educational opportunities.[153] They have a destination in mind and usually make plans well in advance of departure, although they may need to wait due to quota limitations. In contrast, refugees and asylees are "pushed" from their homeland due to "life-threatening political, economic, religious, and even environmental circumstances. . . . Refugees often do not know their final destination, . . . do not have the luxury of planning their exit before departure (and) experience fears of never seeing their home again."[154] However, their refugee status exempts them from immigration quotas and facilitates their entry into the United States. Refugees, unlike regular immigrants, are eligible for federal and local assistance.[155]

Table 4.1 ☒ Persons Obtaining Legal Permanent Resident Status: Total for Decade Ending 2007 and Admission Category in 2007, by Region and Top Ten Countries of Birth

		Fiscal Year 2007 Admission Category						
Region and Country of Birth	Decade Total	Family-Sponsored Preferences	Employment-Based Preferences	Immediate Relatives of U.S. Citizens	Diversity	Refugees and Asylees	Other	Total for 2007
Region								
Total	9,359,479	194,900	162,176	494,920	42,127	136,125	22,167	1,052,415
North America*	3,362,195	89,582	23,841	174,197	421	33,100	18,214	339,355
Asia	3,155,800	80,081	92,147	160,366	7,498	42,384	1,032	383,508
Europe	1,357,013	5,594	22,198	59,113	12,004	19,894	2,018	120,821
South America	759,917	13,204	16,962	59,747	2,209	14,000	403	106,525
Africa	647,824	5,603	5,810	37,414	19,277	26,178	429	94,711
Oceania	54,638	743	1,073	3,261	678	315	31	6,101
Unknown	22,092	93	145	822	40	254	40	1,394
Country of Birth								
Mexico	1,651,460	45,422	11,900	87,466	10	396	3,446	148,640
India	581,110	15,551	28,703	18,205	57	2,680	157	65,353
China, People's Republic	561,904	15,261	13,886	27,115	22	20,352	19	76,655
Philippines	522,705	13,535	17,182	41,416	4	372	87	72,596
Vietnam	279,282	12,430	D	13,974	D	1,768	317	28,691
Dominican Republic	249,601	13,250	308	14,360	D	D	44	28,024
Cuba	246,647	1,794	14	2,737	229	24,261	69	29,104
El Salvador	246,156	6,145	1,276	6,240	—	493	6,973	21,127
Colombia	207,004	3,177	2,641	17,174	11	10,091	93	33,187
Haiti	193,168	8,028	102	13,569	—	6,261	2,445	30,405

*   Includes Mexico and Canada
D   Data withheld to limit disclosure.
—   Represents zero.

Source: Adapted from *2007 Yearbook of Immigration Statistics*, Table 3 and Table 10, U.S. Department of Homeland Security.

small numbers of Latino, Asian, and Caribbean black immigrants were naturalized citizens. Thus, policymakers never imagined the possibility of the multiplier effects of family-based immigration. However, an increasing number of third world immigrants who came to the United States as beneficiaries of the new immigration law have become naturalized citizens and thus have been able to invite their immediate family members and relatives through "family reunification" preferences. Since family reunification has been the major mechanism for legal immigration to the United States during recent years, new immigrant groups from Third World countries have been able to bring more and more immigrants here from their countries.[19]

Immigration is a core American issue. It "touches our people's most basic beliefs about our freedom to move to new opportunities, about our national identity and sovereignty. It touches our personal experiences and family histories and our philosophies about inclusion, economics, and especially the role of government. It is to most people . . . 'surprisingly emotional.' "[20] It also raises questions about *who is an American* and who should be able to attain American citizenship. Most immigrants come to this country to find work, to create a better life for themselves and their families, and to experience their American Dream.[21]

 ## What Is the American Dream?

The phrase "American Dream" was first coined by James Truslow Adams in his book *The Epic of America*, written in 1931. According to Adams, the American Dream is ". . . that dream of a land in which life should be better and richer and fuller for everyone, with opportunity for each according to ability or achievement. . . . It is not a dream of motor cars and high wages merely, but a dream of social order in which each man and each woman shall be able to attain the fullest stature of which they are innately capable, and be recognized by others for what they are, regardless of the fortuitous circumstances of birth or position."[22]

Thirty-four years later, Dr. Martin Luther King, Jr. delivered a Fourth of July sermon on "The American Dream" at Ebenezer Baptist Church.[23] King found the substance of the American Dream in the Declaration of Independence: "We hold these truths to be self-evident, that all men are created equal, that they are endowed by God, Creator, with certain inalienable Rights, that among these are Life, Liberty, and the pursuit of Happiness." Saying it is a "great dream," he continued, "Never before in the history of the world has a sociopolitical document expressed in such profound, eloquent, and unequivocal language the dignity and the worth of human personality. The American Dream reminds us . . . that every man is an heir of the legacy of dignity and worth." King spoke about the dignity of all work, the need to join the war on poverty in America, and the need to become "one big family of Americans." He argued that God (Creator)

> *somehow called America to do a special job for mankind and the world. Never before in the history of the world have so many racial groups and so many national backgrounds assembled together in one nation. And somehow if we can't solve the problem in America the world can't solve the problem, because America is the world in miniature and the world in America writ large. And God set us out with all the opportunities. He set us between two great oceans; made it possible for us to live with some of the great natural resources of the world. And there he gave us through the minds of our forefathers a great creed: "We hold these truth to be self-evident, that all men are created equal."*

In the book *Seizing Destiny*, Richard Kluger explains how the American Dream has been a beacon of hope and promise for immigrants to the United States over the centuries. He tells "how our founders—the Puritans of New England, the tobacco planters of the South, and President Thomas Jefferson—believed that what truly set

America apart was its virtually unlimited supply of land and the ability to attract the labor to work it."[24] Margaret Orchowski, author of *Immigration and the American Dream*, continues the argument.

> Early colonists, including indentured servants and later homesteaders and land grantees from Europe, all were promised land-ownership as their prize for hard work and long hours of servitude. If they followed the rules, they got freedom and land. The magic of America is that from early on, former servants, workers, farm laborers, craftsmen, and even some slaves could become citizens and leaders if they worked hard enough and played by the rules. All were encouraged to exploit labor and land and to build prosperity just as their former masters had done.
>
> This is the American Dream—equality and opportunity and inclusiveness for those who follow the rules and regulations. This is the basis of why immigrants come and why Americans welcome them.[25]

 ## Classic and Contemporary Immigration Eras: How Are They Alike and How Do They Differ?

Anti-Immigrant Attitudes and Actions

In an examination of anti-immigrant attitudes and actions during these two eras of mass migration, Charles Jaret discusses "the most striking similarities and differences in anti-immigrant phenomena in the 1880–1924 era and the present period."[26] He also examines nativism, the belief that the foreign-born pose a threat to the nation, in both eras. Native-born Americans today, as in the past, are concerned about changes in immigrants' national and racial origins; express public opinion that is hostile to immigration and support restrictions that would reduce the number of immigrants from non-Anglo-European countries; reveal nativist fears that ethnically different immigrants threaten national unity, especially the use of languages other than English; and engage in physical violence against immigrants.[27] However, there are also differences in the anti-immigration attitudes and actions during these two eras.

One important difference is the prominence of illegal immigration today. This phenomena is not new; foreigners have entered and resided in the United States illegally throughout our history. However, in the classic period the public paid little attention to people who entered the country in violation of the law and did not regard it as a major concern.[28] Today, however, many people "fixate on the 'illegal alien' as the main part of the 'crisis' in immigration policy."[29] Another difference is the change in organized labor's position regarding immigration. Typically, unions have felt the need to "protect 'their' jobs or the wage levels they struggled so hard to obtain and that these other immigrant workers (often perceived in a racialized way as 'nonwhite,' hence inferior) were job competitors who drove down wages and working conditions and were used by business owners as strikebreakers."[30] Recently, however, organized labor has modified its stand, and after years of declining membership began to see "illegal immigrants as a potential source of new members. In 2000, the AFL-CIO reversed its longstanding position and came out in favor of an amnesty program that would allow millions of illegal immigrants to become legal permanent residents."[31]

A third difference is local, state, and federal legislation that discriminated against immigrants during the 1880–1924 era. "Aliens" who were ineligible for citizenship, such as immigrants from Asia and immigrants who had not yet requested citizenship, had fewer rights and privileges than native-born Americans.[32] For example, some states passed "licensing laws that explicitly prevented aliens from practicing medicine, surgery, chiropractic, pharmacy, architecture, engineering, surveying, or driving buses."[33] States also passed laws to prevent immigrants who were ineligible for citizenship (e.g., Asians) from land ownership. These laws no longer exist, and today legal immigrants are permitted to work in most private-sector jobs. Moreover, in an important difference from the classic era, many contemporary immigrants are highly educated and have advanced technological skills.

A fourth difference is that the movement to restrict immigration during the classic era was successful in passing restrictive laws that dramatically reduced the numbers of immigrants and changed their national origins.[34] Significant examples include the Chinese Exclusion Act in 1882, the 1917 ban on immigration from most of Asia, and the 1924 Johnson-Reed (National Origins) Act. Today's restrictionists have not succeeded in moving Congress to decrease immigration, and there have been only minor changes in who can be admitted. And fifth, the United States' world position is different today from what it was during the end of the classic era when it wanted to avoid "entanglements" with Europe and became more isolationist after several decades as an important commercial and military power on the world stage. In contrast, "from the mid-1960s to the present the United States has played an active and powerful international role. . . . (And as long as this role continues), it is unlikely to adopt the kind of anti-immigrant restrictions that it instituted in the 1920s."[35]

What Causes Anti-Immigrant Attitudes and Actions?

According to social scientists, "common fears that generate unease, mistrust, and conflict" associated with nativism, or the fear that immigrants threaten national security, is the primary cause of anti-immigrant attitudes and actions.[36] Nativists focus on immigrants as political threats, economic threats, social and cultural threats to the "American way of life," and threats to the natural environment.[37] Those who see immigrants as political threats are afraid that they may work as foreign agents to "weaken, destroy, or conquer the United States."[38] Others believe that the foreign-born lack the qualities needed to become good citizens in a democracy and that they have different values and are unable to fit in. These fears were evident during the 1880–1924 era when anti-German sentiment surged during World War I. Today, contemporary nativists have accused Arab and Mexican immigrants of aiding foreign nations, and after September 11 verbal and physical aggression against Arab and Muslim immigrants increased "as well as widespread government interrogation and detention of them."[39]

Greater Diversity Among Immigrants Today

In an analysis of "the changing face of America," Min Zhou highlights the greater diversity among immigrants today. Compared with immigrants in the classic period, contemporary immigrants differ dramatically in terms of national origins and socioeconomic characteristics.[40] Most newcomers today are from non-European countries. "Since the 1980s, more than 85 percent of the immigrants admitted to the United States come from Asia and the Americas (excluding Canada) and only 10 percent from Europe compared to more than 90 percent at the earlier peak."[41] These changing demographics have had a lasting impact on the growth and composition of the general U.S. population. Immigration has accounted for more than one-third of total U.S. population growth over the past 30 years. In particular, Asian- and Latin-origin populations have grown fast in both absolute and relative sizes. Some groups—Salvadorans, Guatemalans, Dominicans, Haitians, Jamaicans, Asian Indians, Koreans, Vietnamese, Cambodians, and Laotians—have grown at spectacular rates, mainly as a result of immigration.[42] (Refer back to Table 4.1 on page 114. Although not shown in this table's top ten countries of birth, South Korea ranks eleventh, Jamaica ranks twelfth, and Guatemala ranks sixteenth. The ranking number of immigrants from Cambodia and Laos is much lower, but the percentage increase is about 400 percent over the past decade.)

Contemporary immigrants are also more diverse in terms of their socioeconomic backgrounds. In contrast to images of the poor, uneducated, and unskilled "huddled masses" used to depict the turn-of-the-century European immigrants, there are dramatic differences in levels of education, occupations, and wealth among today's immigrants, according to their nation of origin.[43] For example, beginning with the 1990 U.S. Census, foreign-born adults from India reported higher levels of education than the average American population (60 versus 20% had attained college degrees); at 45 percent, over twice as many Indian immigrants as the average population held managerial or professional occupations; and their median household income of $48,000 exceeded the national average of $30,000. In sharp contrast, less than 5 percent from those from El Salvador and Mexico had attained a college degree; fewer than 7 percent from El Salvador, Guatemala, and Mexico held managerial or professional occupations; and the median household income of immigrants from the Soviet Union and the Dominican Republic was under $20,000.[44] Poverty rates also varied, "ranging from a low of 5 percent for Indians and Filipinos to a high of 33 percent for Dominicans and an extreme high of more than 40 percent for Cambodians and 60 percent for Hmong, compared to about 10 percent for average American families."[45] These trends continue today as shown in Table 9.4 on page 269 in Chapter 9.

New Settlements: From Megalopolis to the Heartland

At the turn of the last century, most immigrants were settled along the Northeastern seaboard and the urban areas in the Midwest. Their five favorite states were New York, Pennsylvania, Illinois, Massachusetts, and New Jersey, and their favorite cities were New York, Chicago, Philadelphia, St. Louis, and Boston.[46] This pattern continued into the 1970s and 1980s as newcomers settled in large cosmopolitan cities with ethnically mixed populations where they adjusted and "fit in" fairly easily.[47] In 1990, about 75 percent of the foreign-born population was settled in one of five expansive metropolitan areas, or the *megalopolises* of Boston to Washington, D.C., Chicago to Pittsburgh, San Diego to San Francisco, and Peninsular Florida. This changed in the 1990s with a "distinct shift away from megalopolis towards *nonmegalopolitan areas* distributed throughout the country."[48] Although most of today's immigrants still live in highly concentrated areas, many are settling in states and cities that had few foreign-born immigrants in the past. Today, about 95 percent of the newcomers live in new cities with populations greater than one million, including Dallas, Atlanta, Charlotte, Nashville, Denver, Phoenix, Seattle, and others.[49]

> *The result . . . has been a cultural transformation of the U.S. Heartland, that broad pool of states beyond the peripheral metropolitan swaths. The implantation of new features on the cultural landscape (business, homes, churches, schools, possessions, and the people themselves) is giving many Americans a geography lesson on the "Third World"—at a time when increased world understanding is something the country cannot do without. In some cases these new groups have revitalized declining communities.*
>
> *But this geographic dispersion of immigrants . . . has also created landscapes of conflict and suffering as the immigrants and their hosts adjust to each other. The differences between immigrants and residents tend to stand out starkly on the social landscape of smaller, more demographically homogeneous or bi-cultural places. Some traits, for example religious rituals, marriage practices, economic pursuits, house styles, and language may come into conflict with local norms and laws and generate animosity towards the immigrant group. This animosity may hinder the immigrants' primary goal (arguably the host society's goal for them as well): socioeconomic integration.[50]*

One of the consequences of these new settlement patterns is a change in the dynamic of race relations and ethnic identity among contemporary immigrants and their children. Today, many communities are experiencing difficulties as well as opportunities related to increased ethnic diversity, and the rapid departure of non-Hispanic Whites from metropolitan areas along with the arrival of new immigrants is changing the dynamics of race and ethnicity in significant ways.[51] Ethnicity has become more salient and "all Americans—native-born whites, blacks, Asian and Latin Americans, as well as the newcomers themselves"—face new challenges.[52] We will explore this further in Chapters 5, 6, and 7.

Will the New Second Generation Assimilate?

It is interesting to compare the classic era of immigration with the contemporary era, because, in contrast to previous immigration waves, these two periods in our history are the only times when immigration peaked at the highest levels *and* the majority of immigrants in both periods differed dramatically from the predominant American population in terms of language, religion, national origin, and racial identity. (Although Southern and Eastern European immigrants during the classic era were viewed as "racial inferiors," and for a time were denied citizenship based on "race," they eventually blended into mainstream society.) Thus, we can ask the question:

Will the children and grandchildren of contemporary immigrants eventually assimilate into American society, as did the descendants of immigrants from the classic era? Social scientists who study and compare the two mass migration periods think the new second and third generations are not as likely to follow a "straight-line assimilation path," even if they attain high socioeconomic status quickly.[53]

White immigrant groups in the classic era "lost their cultural traditions quickly in a generation, while it took them three or four generations to catch up with Protestant ethnic groups in socioeconomic status."[54] In contrast, it is likely that contemporary immigrant groups "will be more successful than the turn-of-the-century European immigrant groups in preserving their language and culture over the generations."[55]

Why is ethnic retention more likely today? Why is it easier to pass on religion and cultural traditions, such as language, customs, rituals, and food?[56] One reason is the higher level of residential concentration and segregation among today's immigrants and their families. Immigrant neighborhoods and enclaves provide opportunities to "share a common language" and other aspects of their home culture. This is particularly true among contemporary immigrant groups from Third World countries who live in more segregated neighborhoods compared to White immigrant groups from the classic era, and it is often due to racial discrimination in housing.[57]

A second reason is that today immigrants have stronger connections with their home countries than did immigrant groups in the past due to greater proximity and transnational ties. For example, Latino and Caribbean immigrants typically choose destinations close to their home countries. In addition, advances in international air travel and telecommunication, such as email, and the ethnic mass media enable today's immigrants to keep active connections with family and friends in the homeland despite the barriers of geographical distance.[58] A third reason ethnic retentions are easier today is the multicultural policy in the United States. Prior to the 1960s, immigrants were expected to give up their home language and culture and assimilate into mainstream American society. Today, schools and society are more supportive of cultural pluralism. A fourth reason is the abundant flow of new immigrants today that is expected to continue into the foreseeable future, which serves as a source to "replenish the ethnic community with the culture of their homeland."[59] In contrast, the immigration flow in the classic era was cut off in the early 1930s and contributed to the tremendous loss of ethnic cultural traditions among most immigrant groups of the era.

However, conditions favorable to ethnic retentions do not mean that the children and grandchildren of contemporary immigrants will inherit a "static" ethnic culture. There are many cultural revisions and inventions of new traditions among young people who experience American popular culture and peers, both of which have a stronger influence on youth today than in the past. Furthermore, the second and third generations of contemporary immigrants who are bilingual or multilingual are able to *selectively* assimilate into American society and culture while maintaining a strong sense of ethnic identity. Descendants of immigrants from contemporary Third World countries who experience racial prejudice and discrimination are likely to value ethnic retentions as well as some degree of separatism. And although immigrants from the classic era, such as the Irish and the Italians, also experienced "color-based" prejudice, there is a difference between the two eras regarding racial prejudice and assimilation.

> *Because of their differences in language, religion, and "races," the southern and eastern European immigrants, too, initially encountered prejudice and discrimination by Protestant Americans. But over generations, these "inassimilable races" have melted into white American society. One of the reasons why the third- and fourth-generation white ethnics have lost their cultural traditions almost completely is that as whites they have been accepted as full American citizens. However, the descendants of contemporary Third World immigrants are not likely to be accepted as full American citizens, no matter how many generations they live in this country. When they experience racial prejudice and discrimination, as a defense mechanism they may try to selectively assimilate to American culture while holding on to their positive cultural traditions.*[60]

Many social scientists predict that the descendants of Third World immigrants will encounter color-based prejudice and discrimination in the United States, which often leads to a "reactive ethnicity." Children and youth who experience color-based rejection may try to *selectively* assimilate into American culture and at the same time maintain positive aspects of their cultural traditions or even create new ones that help maintain their separate ethnicity. For example, we find Black Caribbean youth who emphasize their ethnic culture to "avoid being labeled *Black* by White students."[61] Reactive ethnicity may also occur with Asian youth who are seen as "foreigners," even though their families have lived in the United States for generations, have served in the military, and have contributed to society in many ways.

European American Perspectives

Origins and Establishment of the White Anglo-Saxon Protestant (WASP) Core Culture

Although the Spanish and other Europeans settled in North America prior to the English and Welsh, the British were the first Europeans to settle in North America in large numbers. Their migration differed from later European immigration in that it involved the subordination of indigenous peoples and the takeover of their homeland. The King of England supported these early immigrants and viewed the colonies as a source of raw materials and a marketplace for English manufactured goods. We tend to lump all English-speaking immigrants together. However, there were four distinct groups among these early immigrants to North America, and although liberty and economic opportunity (aspects of the American Dream) were highly valued across these groups, important distinctions existed in how each group envisioned them.[62]

First came the Puritans, who were from eastern areas of England and settled in New England; they set up "nucleated settlements, congregational churches, town meetings, and a tradition of ordered liberty" that emphasized the rule of law.[63] Next came a small number of Royalists and numerous indentured servants from southern England who settled in the vicinity of Virginia.[64] They established a way of life characterized by "extreme hierarchies of rank, strong oligarchies, Anglican churches, a highly developed sense of honor, and an idea of hegemonic liberty" where high-status people had the freedom to dominate those of lesser status, such as indentured servants, and involuntary immigrants in slavery.[65] Third were Quakers from the North Midlands of England and Wales who settled in the Delaware Valley and established a " 'pluralistic system of reciprocal liberty' based on spiritual and social equality, austerity, and an intense work ethnic."[66] And fourth, an ethnically diverse group of English, Scots, and "Scotch-Irish" from the borderlands of northern Great Britain and northern Ireland settled in the Appalachian backcountry.[67] Although "extreme socioeconomic inequalities" characterized this group, its members "shared the ideal of natural liberty" that emphasized private interests and advocated minimal government intervention.[68]

Each of these four groups had a distinctive type of culture—distinctive speech pattern, architecture, family ways and child-rearing customs, dress and food ways, religious orientations, and conceptions of liberty and the organization of public life. Over time, their cultural patterns interacted with each other and eventually fused together to create the dominant Anglo-Protestant culture of the colonies and, later, the United States.[69]

Although colonial society was ethnically diverse in terms of race (20 percent of the population was African American), religion, and language, an Anglo-Protestant core culture was established. English became the dominant language and English common law became the basis for the U.S. legal system. Later, public education became a way of socializing non-British immigrants.

With the public school movement that began in earnest in the first decades of the nineteenth century, British dominance of public schools became a fact of life. Urban schools were seen as a means of socializing non-British immigrants into Anglo-Protestant values and the values of the U.S. industrial system. British American industrialists and educators established most public schools, shaped curricula and teaching, and supervised operations. Although some, such as John Dewey, believed education gave greater opportunity to poor immigrants, many educators emphasized the social-control aspects of schools. Americanization pressures on immigrant children were often intense. Whether children were Irish, Jewish, or Italian, Anglicization was designed to ferret out non-Anglo-Protestant ways, to assimilate the children in terms of Anglo-Protestant manners, work habits, and values.[70]

Until recently, influence from American Indian cultures on the Anglo-Protestant core culture has been overlooked. Some scholars argued that the unique form of democracy that emerged in the United States was influenced as much by native people as by the British, the eighteenth-century French, and the Romans and Greeks.

When Americans try to trace their democratic heritage back through the writings of French and English political thinkers of the Enlightenment, they often forget that these people's thoughts were heavily shaped by the democratic traditions and the state of nature of the American Indians.[71]

Native peoples, particularly those who lived in the northeastern part of the continent, provided the models for some aspects of American democracy that differed from what was known in Europe: a federal system of government, the separation of civil from military authorities, the concept of impeachment, admission of new territories as states (partners rather than colonies), political debate that allowed one person to speak at a time, group authority (councils) rather than individual authority, the caucus, an egalitarianism that disallowed slavery (compared with Greek democracy that was based on massive slavery), and a political voice for women.[72] Most of this has been left out of the history books, which is typical of the fate of a colonized people. In his discussion of early Anglo-Saxon cultural dominance, Banks writes:

> *Early in American colonial life, non-English groups began to be evaluated negatively. The New England colonies, which were predominantly English, took steps to bar the settlements of Roman Catholics. The French Huguenots became the focal point of English hostility. Later, the Scots-Irish and the German immigrants were the victims of English antagonism. An English mob prevented a group of Irish immigrants from landing in Boston in 1729. Several years later, another mob destroyed a new Scots-Irish Presbyterian church in Worcester . . . As early as 1727, nativistic feeling toward the Germans in Pennsylvania ran high. (Nativism was a movement designed to restrict immigration to America and to protect the interest of the native-born. It was an extreme form of nationalism and ethnocentrism.) To discourage further foreign settlement in the colony, Pennsylvania passed a statute in 1729 increasing the head tax on foreigners, allegedly to prevent persons likely to become public charges from entering the colony. Other anti-foreign legislation emerged in the eighteenth century. In 1798, Congress, dominated by the Federalists, passed the Alien and Sedition Acts to crush the Republican party by destroying its large base of immigrant support. . . . The Alien and Sedition Acts lengthened the time required to become an American citizen from five to fourteen years and gave the president almost unlimited control over the behavior of immigrants. They virtually nullified the freedoms of speech and the press.[73]*

Over 34.5 million Europeans immigrated into the United States between 1820, when the government began to record immigration, and 1960. Europeans represent 82 percent of the total immigration during this time period.[74] Between 1820 and 1921, when Congress passed the first quota act to restrict immigration, the European immigrants "came in a series of gigantic waves, each more powerful than the last and separated one from another only by short periods of time."[75]

The First & Second Waves: Western and Northern Europeans

The first wave of European immigrants began soon after the end of the Napoleonic Wars and peaked just before the Civil War and at the time was described as "one of the wonders of the age."[76] Over 5 million immigrants arrived, numbering more than "the entire population of the United States at the time of the first census in 1790."[77] The overwhelming majority were from western and northern Europe. Over half were from the British Isles; 2 million were from Ireland, and another three-quarter million were from England and Wales. Germany contributed another million and a half immigrants, including 200,000 German-speaking people from

Alsace and Lorraine who were listed as French citizens. Switzerland, Norway, and Sweden each contributed 40,000 people, and another 20,000 arrived from the Netherlands.[78]

The underlying reasons for this massive movement of people are complex and differ in the various parts of Europe. For example, economic change was a factor in Ireland, while religious factors were important in Norway, Holland, and Prussia as well as among Mormon converts from Great Britain and Scandinavia. In addition to contrasting factors among groups and personal idiosyncrasies among individuals, there are also a number of social and economic factors that underlay the movement as a whole and that gave it most of its impetus:

1. A population explosion in Europe due to better health practices and an increased food supply
2. The growth of the factory system in Europe that displaced artisans and made workers vulnerable to unemployment cycles
3. The shift from a medieval communal system of agriculture to large-scale production that freed serfs and peasants from the land
4. Political and religious discontent
5. A heightened awareness of America as a land of opportunity
6. The removal of legal restrictions on emigration and the development of inexpensive ocean transportation.[79]

As a whole, immigrants into the United States have been characterized as individuals or families who relied on their own strength and resources. They were self-directed, unassisted, and therefore free to determine their own destiny within the constraints most would face in the "New World." The types of people varied greatly over time and country of origin. The Irish immigrant experience illustrates this diversity and corrects a common misconception of the wholly impoverished immigrant. (It would be more accurate to see them as people who feared a future loss of security or status.)[80] Prior to 1830, the majority of Irish immigrants were small farmers burdened by intolerable rents, tithes, and taxes. After 1830 there was a steady flow of laborers and evicted tenant farmers; typically, the younger and most able-bodied family members were sent to the United States "in the confident hope, which only rarely was disappointed," that money would be sent back to Ireland to finance the voyage of remaining family members to the United States.[81]

While the number of departures steadily increased throughout the 1830s and early 1840s, it was not until the Great Famine that the floodgates finally opened and the exodus attained epic proportions. The successive potato blights of 1845–49, leading as they did to untold deaths from starvation and fever and to appalling physical suffering even for those who survived, were a catastrophe which finally broke the Irish peasant's tenacious attachment to the soil and convinced many of the futility of further struggle against hopeless odds. . . . the famine had reversed the peasant's former attitude to emigration; hitherto considered a banishment, it now came to be regarded as a happy release. The prevailing mood of despair gripped not only the laborer and the [tenant farmer] but even those who [were] substantial farmers. Thus all classes were represented in the million and a half people who left Ireland in the decade that followed.[82]

The second wave of European immigrants entered the United States during the decades of industrialization following the Civil War. They continued to come primarily from Northern and Western Europe.

Classic and Contemporary European Immigrants

We have already noted that beginning in the 1880s the number of immigrants from Southern and Eastern Europe increased dramatically. In just a few decades, over 15 million new immigrants entered the United States, primarily from Austria-Hungary, Italy, Russia (including Poland), Greece, Romania, and Turkey.[83] Over 2.5 million were Jews from Russia and Eastern Europe, and nearly 4 million were from southern Italy. Although this "new" immigrant group was diverse in terms of motivations and socioeconomic background, the vast majority of immigrants from Southern and Eastern Europe were culturally very different from the English and Scots who had established the English colonies and from the first waves of immigrants from Northern and Western Europe who had largely assimilated into the Anglo-Eurocentric core culture. Indeed, their arrival triggered legislation to restrict immigration on "racial grounds" (e.g., the 1924 National Origins Act). People from southern and eastern Europe were described by the U.S. Immigration Commission to be "incapable of assimilation and were even biologically inferior to the Nordic stock out of western and northern Europe."[84]

Anti-Immigrant Attitudes and Actions

With the exception of the British immigrants, virtually all the immigrants from Europe experienced harsh prejudice and discrimination after settling in the United States. The Irish and Italians provide examples from the "old" and "new" immigrants, respectively.

Irish Americans suffered verbal abuse, stereotyping, intentional discrimination, and violent attacks from the time of their arrival in North America.[85] Much of the violence has been directed at Irish Catholics, and

> *By 1850 most large cities had seen anti-Catholic demonstrations and riots. Philadelphia became a center for anti-Irish Catholic violence. There, in 1844, two major riots "resulted in the burning of two Catholic churches . . . ; the destruction of dozens of Catholic homes; and sixteen deaths." In the 1850s Protestant nativist groups such as the Know-Nothings played a major role in attacks on Irish Americans.*[86]

Resistance to Irish immigration is also evident in nineteenth-century literature, cartoons, and theater. The Irish were stereotyped as immoral, lazy, violent, and mentally inferior. Influential journals such as *Harpers' Weekly* dehumanized the Irish through apelike images that portrayed the poor Irish as the "missing link" between humans and the gorilla.[87]

The school has been an agent of assimilation for the children of many European immigrant families in the United States.

By the end of the nineteenth century, immigrants from Eastern and Southern Europe, such as the Italians and Slavs, were the new targets of stereotypes and violence. There were myths about disease, illiteracy, and intellectual inferiority. "Popular writers, scholars, and members of congress warned of the peril of allowing inferior stocks from Europe into the United States."[88]

As early as the 1870s, Italians had been stereotyped as criminals, and the Mafia myth has persisted.[89] Films and prime-time television often reinforce the image of Italians as gangsters and hoods. Like all stereotypes, there is a grain of truth to these images, for example, the increased involvement of Italians in organized crime during Prohibition. Yet crime-rate statistics among the Italian-born were lower than for English and Welsh foreign-born in 1910 and were about the same as for all native-born Americans in the 1920s and 1930s. Only a very small percentage of Italians are currently involved in organized crime, which is being taken over by more recent groups from Asia, Latin America, and Russia.[90]

Like the Irish before them, the Italians have also been the victims of violence. For example, they have been lynched at the hands of vigilante mobs for violating racial taboos in the South and they have been executed in "the midst of hysteria over left-wing un-American activities."[91]

Ethnic Pluralism

Distinct geographic patterns of settlement emerged among European immigrants, sometimes in an attempt to preserve ethnic distinctions, and to some degree these persist in the twenty-first century. Typically, immigrants would settle in areas where they could use the skills they brought with them from Europe. The Irish were an exception; although most had been country dwellers, they rejected farming and country life and settled overwhelmingly in the cities. Nearly two-thirds of the Irish settled in New York, Pennsylvania, New Jersey, and New England. Few Germans settled in New England, and over half settled in "the upper Mississippi and Ohio valleys, especially in the states of Ohio, Illinois, Wisconsin, and Missouri,"[92] but there were also large numbers in New York, New Jersey, and Pennsylvania. Norwegians, Swedes, and Danes were heavily concentrated in Minnesota, Illinois, Wisconsin, the Dakotas, and the state of Washington.[93] Nearly two-thirds of the Dutch settled in Michigan, New York, Wisconsin, and Iowa, while the Finnish were concentrated in Michigan, Minnesota, and Massachusetts.[94]

Ethnic pluralism characterized U.S. society throughout this period of massive immigration and the first generations of settlement. Many ethnic communities were named after European towns, and their schools, churches, and newspapers were patterned after European models. The German communities of the Midwest in the latter half of the nineteenth century illustrate this healthy state of ethnic pluralism as it was manifested in bilingual education.

> *The Germans were afforded the most extensive programs of bilingual education in the history of the country. The public school districts in cities within the so-called German Triangle, Cincinnati, St. Louis, Milwaukee, Chicago, Indianapolis, and others, also developed formal offices of German instruction to supervise the programs. . . . In some school districts, as much as 70 percent of the school population took some of their instruction in German as late as 1916. This situation persisted until the beginning of World War I, when anti-German sentiment made German study unpopular.[95]*

With the rise of anti-German sentiment in the twentieth century, German community support for separate schools, churches, and civic organizations declined. In the face of heightened prejudice, threats of violence, and discrimination, many German Americans made the choice to disappear through greater cultural assimilation.

Advocates of the melting-pot theory often use examples of White ethnic groups, such as the Irish, to support their assimilationist position. Indeed, the Irish have moved up the socioeconomic ladder and are strong influences in our nation's political and economic spheres. While assimilationists would argue that Irish ethnic identity among Irish Americans is fading, pluralists would look for signs of cultural retention and a spirit of ethnic identity.

Feagin offers valuable insights into the assimilation of the Irish, along with evidence that there is still an Irish ethnic group to be recognized.[96]

> *While Irish Protestants seemed to have begun blending in relatively early, for Irish Catholics, because of nativistic attacks and discrimination, ethnic identity was less voluntary in the first few decades than it was to become later. In the beginning the Irish Catholic group, concentrated in the cities, had a cultural heritage which was distinctly different from that of the British-dominated host culture; yet there were some modest similarities in language and customs. Over several generations of sometimes conflictual interaction the Irish adapted substantially to the host society. Yet in this interaction process was created a distinctive Irish ethnic group which reflected elements both of its nationality background and of the host culture revised to fit the subordinate situation of the Irish.*

This Irish Catholic group changed over several generations of contact with the public school system and mass media, but it also retained enough distinctiveness from its nationality heritage and its experience as a subordinate group in the nineteenth century to persist as a distinctive ethnic group for many decades, even into the last third of the twentieth century. With future assimilation it may be that this distinctiveness will come to be more in the area of behavior and less in the areas of ethnic identity and sense of one's ethnic heritage. Thus the Irish seem to be moving at cultural, structural, and marital levels in the direction of the core society. But the Irish remain. It is useful to distinguish here between ethnic identity and ethnic impact. Ethnic identity for the Irish, the sense of the past, may be weakening, while the impact of the Irish background on Irish behavior is still obviously strong.

Indeed, an example of the persistence of Irish ethnicity, even of distinctive ethnic communities, and its positive and negative functions, can be seen in the desegregation struggle which took place in Boston in the mid-1970s. There a working-class and lower-middle-class Irish community, South Boston, was involved in a judge's school desegregation plan; the plan was vigorously, even violently, opposed by the Irish. As one reporter noted: "Antibusing demonstrators, wearing tam-oshanter hats in the neighborhood high school colors, have broken up rallies of women's groups and dogged Senator Edward M. Kennedy's appearances. The usually jovial St. Patrick's Day parade was a procession of antibusing floats." This is more than a legal desegregation struggle. Different views of schooling and of urban communities are reflected in the controversy; the South Boston Irish see the schools as a socializing force, reinforcing traditional family and community values, whereas frequently blacks and suburban, Protestant whites now view them as avenues of upward mobility for nonwhite minorities. Irish resistance to the racial desegregation of central city neighborhoods is based in part on protecting one's own ethnic community against all intruders, whoever they may be.[97]

Italian Americans are another example of a White ethnic group that has overcome initial prejudice, discrimination, and violence and has moved upward into the higher economic and political spheres of the host society. Even though the social mobility of Italian Americans over the past few generations makes them an American "success story," they have not been completely assimilated into the dominant culture. Many "have remained enmeshed in kinship-friendship networks predominantly composed of other Italian Americans,"[98] and most prefer Italian American neighborhoods and marry within the Italian American community. Non-Italian marriage partners tend to be from other Catholic groups—Irish, German, or Eastern European. According to Feagin,

Italians came to the United States with significant differences from the dominant British group, but they at least shared some European historical background and a Christian tradition with that group. By virtue of interaction in the public schools and the influence of the mass media, the linguistic and custom gap narrowed substantially, but by no means completely. Nationality characteristics, the immigrant heritage, have had a persistent impact. Italian Americans became in some ways similar to members of the host culture, but in other ways they retained their distinctiveness. Over time, because of their heritage, together with segregation and strong community and kinship networks, a dis-

tinctive American ethnic group was spawned. In the complex adaptation process an Italian American group was formed, distinctive in terms of both certain persisting nationality characteristics and unique experiences in the United States. No longer an Italy-centered group dominated by its heritage, neither has it simply become British Protestant American or simply American. Substantial adaptation without complete assimilation at a number of levels characterizes Italian Americans. The third and fourth generations appear to retain a great deal of Italian Americanness, in their commitment to the family and Italian community. Particularly for working-class Italian Americans there is still a rich family community life in the 1970s.[99]

According to scholars at the National Italian American Foundation, Italian Americans who are fully immersed into the American mainstream continue to maintain a strong sense of ethnic identity. The 2000 Census confirmed a seven percent increase in the number of citizens who affirmed their Italian descent, in contrast to other European groups whose numbers significantly declined since the 1990 Census.[100]

Who Assimilates?

Of all the European immigrants to the United States, the 3 million English immigrants assimilated most swiftly. Job mobility was easy for skilled workers from textile, mining, and manufacturing industries. Eventually displaced by machines or later immigrant groups, many English American workers moved up into managerial and technical positions. As a group they were spared the poverty, language differences, hostility, and discrimination experienced by most other European immigrants.

A study of descendants of seventeenth- and eighteenth-century European immigrants who lived in the New York region found that by the 1980s, most especially those with British ancestry report, "that their ethnic identity had *no importance* to them."[101] Sociologists such as Richard Alba suggest that this may be because they equate

> *their English or British American identity as synonymous with a "truly American" identity. They may have so completely integrated their English or British identity with their definition of what is American that they see no need to identify with their country of origin. In contrast, more recent immigrant groups (for example, Southern European Catholics) were much more likely to identify with a national heritage.*[102]

Today, Europe is no longer the primary source of immigrants to the United States, as Latin America and Asia have replaced Europe as the main source of both legal and illegal immigrants.[103] Who are the immigrants from Europe today? Over the past decade, the top six nations of origin for persons obtaining legal permanent resident status have been the United Kingdom (17,207); Ukraine (17,142); Russia (13,188); Germany (8,436); Romania (7,137); and the former Soviet Union (6,229).[104] Researchers are finding relationships between where these foreign-born migrants from Europe settle in the United States and "their identities, adjustment, and adaptation to American life."[105]

Russian and Ukrainian Refugees in Portland, Oregon

Oregon is a favored destination among refugees to the United States, and it ranks eleventh in total number of new refugees.[106] Like most migrants from the former Soviet Union, Russians and Ukrainians enter the United States as refugees, based on their religious beliefs. Most are members of religious groups that were persecuted in the former Soviet Union, such as Baptists, Pentecostals, and Seventh Day Adventists. (Russian and Ukrainian Jews also enter with refugee status, but they tend to settle in larger cities.)

Susan Hardwick, a geography scholar who studies refugee settlement patterns, conducted a four-year case study of Russian and Ukrainian migrants in Northern California and the Pacific Northwest. Using Census data from 1990 and 2000; documents from refugee and immigrant resettlement files, church records, and business directories; personal interviews of numerous refugees and community leaders; participant observation; and field observations, Hardwick examined immigrants' residential neighborhoods, changes in personal identities, and adjustment to life in the United States, especially in terms of religion and socioeconomic well-being. Fluent in Russian and with over two decades of work with Russians and Ukrainians in the Western United States and Canada, she took time to build up trust among long-term residents and newcomers in order to conduct meaningful interviews. Hardwick had assumed that "the white skin color and Protestant religious belief systems (in addition to the well-developed economic support systems provided to refugees by local social service agencies) would assist groups such as Russians and Ukrainians to blend rapidly into the mainstream of their new place of residence."[107] However, her assumptions proved to be wrong.

First, Hardwick discovered that religious affiliations are the primary means of support for most of the post-Soviet refugees.[108] Prior to migrating, many individuals learned about opportunities in the American West through their church newsletters or Russian-language radio programs that featured migrants with evangelical Slavic backgrounds. Hardwick quotes one young woman who is typical:

> *I heard a sermon one Sunday morning on my old radio in Siberia. The pastor talked about the tulip fields and the freedom that waited for us here. He encouraged us all to come so we could worship in freedom here in Oregon.*[109]

Entire congregations have migrated, settled in the same vicinity, and set up "social, cultural, and economic connections and relationships (that) continue to sustain them, especially in their first years in the United States."[110] Although state and local refugee resettlement agencies provide English language instruction, job training, and up to eight months of financial support, housing, medical care, and psychiatric support for new arrivals from Russia, Ukraine, and elsewhere, religious institutions are more important and support the cultural survival and ethno-religious identity of these Russian and Ukrainian migrants.[111] Two Ukrainian men, who, like most of the people she interviewed, spoke of the importance of church membership in the early years of settlement and revealed this unexpected finding. Victor said,

But you see, having the same God in our lives holds us all together. When we sing our songs in church and listen to the teaching of our same Russian Bible, nothing else can tear us apart. We are Russian Christians. That's just all there is to know, you see?[112]

And according to Sasha,

My church helps me stay connected to my culture and my beliefs for sure. But it is also where I make my connections for jobs. You know, I can't open my own business because it costs too much here—and I need work to be a plumber like I did at home. So sometimes I hear about jobs people need done when we talk at church.[113]

Hardwick's second unexpected finding was that these religious and economic connections among Russians and Ukrainians led to political empowerment by making connections with people of color and their community organizations. For example, they created the Slavic Coalition and then linked up with the Portland community's Coalition of Color. As White, foreign-born migrants, initially they were not included in Portland's Coalition of Color, an organization "that unites coalitions of different minority groups like Latino Network, Asian-Pacific Islanders, African Americans, African Immigrants, Native Americans."[114] The Coalition is charged by the county to provide financial support for projects proposed by various immigrant and refugee groups of color. Eventually the Slavic Coalition members were able to redefine their White ethnic identity, be recognized as a minority group,

Mother, daughter, and granddaughter shopping in Brooklyn's Hasidic neighborhood, NYC.

and join the Coalition of Color. As a result, the Slavic Coalition received a $340,000 grant to provide "cultural programming for the Slavic community."[115]

The Slavic Coalition is now the second major force (after religious affiliations) behind the sense of unity that is emerging among Russians and Ukrainians in Portland. Formed at a retreat in 2004, the primary goals of the Coalition are to help Russians and Ukrainians gain access to social and economic opportunities within the larger community *and* to ensure that coalition members' ethnic and religious identities are preserved during the process of building new lives in Portland. Hardwick concludes that Slavic migrants are seeking a path of "cultural betweeness" within a distinctive ethnic "community of choice." These newcomers can decide what aspects of home they wish to maintain (such as their religious beliefs), what aspects of the new society they wish to accept, and what they will reject. She sees both confusion and possibilities in this path toward "acculturation, assimilation, and adjustment to American life in the years to come."[116]

Jewish American Perspectives

Jewish Americans are unique among European American immigrants in that their sense of peoplehood was not linked to a nationality. The Jews are unified by religion and tradition rather than by national origins. Jews are descendants of the Hebrews, a people who in ancient times lived in what is now Israel and its immediate environs. After the Roman Empire conquered their homeland in A.D. 70, Jews were eventually scattered all over the world (although mainly across Europe and the Mediterranean), where they remained a minority wherever they lived.

Early Origins: Roots of Diversity and Community

Jews from Spain & Portugal

Individual Jews were among the earliest settlers who came to the Atlantic coast colonies in the 1600s. The first group of Jewish immigrants who came to America were Sephardic, coming primarily from Spain and Portugal in the 1700s. Prior to the Spanish Inquisition, Sephardic Jews in Spain enjoyed more freedom and attained greater positions of wealth and power than Jews anywhere else in Europe. Many owned large landed estates and were important political figures, bankers, and industrialists. Jewish wealth, in fact, was used to help finance the explorations of Columbus. Conditions changed suddenly in 1492 when Ferdinand and Isabella decreed that Jews either convert to Christianity or be expelled. Some Jews pretended to convert, remained in Spain, and practiced their faith in secret. Others fled to the eastern Mediterranean, and still others came to the American colonies, which were known for greater religious freedom.

Jews from Central Europe

The stream of German Jews began soon after the arrival of Sephardic Jews. Quickly, the German Jews came to predominate within the Jewish American population, which grew from approximately 3,000 at the time of the American Revolution to over a half million by 1880.[117] Differences existed between Sephardic and German Jews, and those differences are still evident today. According to Thomas Sowell, Sephardic Jews tended to emphasize business over scholarship. Drawing upon their expertise developed in Spain, most recovered from their earlier financial losses and were economically prosperous by the time the war broke out. Furthermore, they tended to look down on other Jews who were not of Sephardic origins, particularly the German Jewish immigrants.[118]

German Jews differed from later Jewish immigrants in that they did not settle in concentrated Jewish communities. Instead they spread out across the nation, working as "small tradesmen and professionals scattered among their non-Jewish clientele."[119] By the time the third wave of Jewish immigrants began in the 1880s (escapees from persecution in Russia), German Jews had become well established.

> *The German Jews were active, not only in their own communities but also in American society at large as businessmen and bankers. . . . Many Jews were destined to play important roles in developing such major American institutions as Macy's Department Store chain, Sears Roebuck, and the New York Times. As of 1880, 40 percent of all German-Jewish families had at least one servant. Only 1 percent of the heads of Jewish families were still peddlers, and fewer than 1 percent worked as laborers or domestic servants.*[120]

The Classic Era: Jews from Eastern Europe

The third (and largest) group of Jewish immigrants came from Eastern Europe, particularly from Russia, where Jews were the victims of Russification and of peasant massacres called *pogroms*. Between 1880 and World War I, approximately 2 million Jews fled to the United States. Sowell writes that their arrival was an acute embarrassment to the German Jews in America.

> *The size of the eastern European Jewish immigration swamped the existing American Jewish community of largely German origin. The eastern European Jews were also heavily concentrated in New York City and, in fact, were even more localized on the lower east side of Manhattan, which contained the largest number of Jews ever assembled in one place on earth in thousands of years. The German Jews already established in America were appalled not only by the numbers but also by the way of life of the eastern European Jews. The eastern Jews were not only poorer—most arrived destitute, with less money than any other immigrant group—but were also far less educated (a 50 percent illiteracy rate), and with rougher manners than the more sophisticated and Americanized German Jews. Eastern European Jews had lived a provincial life, outside the mainstream of the general European culture in which German Jews were immersed. Eastern Europeans even looked different—earlocks, skull caps, beards, old-fashioned Russian-style clothing, scarves about the women's heads, and a general demeanor reminiscent of a painful past that German Jews had long ago left behind. The Orthodox Jewish religious services were full of traditions and practices long abandoned by the modern Reform Judaism of Germans. The very language of the eastern European Jews—Yiddish—was a folk dialect disdained by more educated Jews, who used either the language of the country or classical Hebrew.*[121]

At times the Jewish philanthropic tradition overcame these negative attitudes, however. "German Jewish organizations made strenuous efforts to aid, and especially to Americanize, the eastern Jewish immigrants. Schools, libraries, hospitals, and community centers were established to serve 'downtown' Jews, financed by 'uptown' Jews."[122] However, the lines of distinction between German Jews and Eastern European Jews remained visible.

Most Eastern European Jewish immigrants did manual work, particularly in the garment industries, where they met the demands for cheap labor in the notorious sweatshops. These Jews lived in crowded, filthy slums that averaged more than 700 people per acre and were infected with tuberculosis and other diseases. Because of their religious orthodoxy, Jews from Eastern Europe lived and worked in close proximity with other Jews to satisfy their need for kosher food, a synagogue, and recognition of the Sabbath (many non-Jewish businesses and factories operated on Saturdays). Thus, there were large concentrations of Jews in New York, Chicago, and Philadelphia.

The Jewish American community today reflects both the unity and diversity of its origins in Europe and the Mediterranean. As a group, Jewish Americans have a tradition of humanitarianism, commitment to civil rights issues for all peoples, and political support for most liberal candidates. In contrast to some other groups, most Jewish Americans have not become more conservative as they moved up the socioeconomic ladder. Many Jews were active in the civil rights movement of the 1960s and in protests against the war in Vietnam. Jews are noted for their support of the Anti-Defamation League and numerous other civil rights organizations. However, friction has recently developed between portions of the Jewish and African American communities over issues such as Israel and Zionism, inner-city reforms, and affirmative action programs. Jews also differ among themselves on the issue of Zionism (support of modern Israel) and Arab–Israeli relations.

Orthodox, Conservative, and Reform Judaism

The Jewish religion remains a major source of diversity among Jews, as well as the major source of identity for Jews as a distinct ethnic group. The major religious movements (Orthodox, Conservative, and Reform) differ sharply in their degree of adaptation to the non-Jewish dominant culture, and there are secular Jews who maintain their Jewish identity even though they do not accept any form of religious Judaism. This becomes a more complex issue because, for many Jews, Judaism is the essence of being Jewish.

Although differences exist within each response, retention of the original Jewish faith and tradition is strongest among the Orthodox Jews and weakest among Reform Jews. Conservative Judaism developed in the nineteenth century as an attempt to balance the Reform movement, which many Jews thought had become too secular. The numerical strength of these different responses is difficult to establish, but it seems that Orthodox Judaism is the smallest group in the United States.

Among Orthodox Jews the Sabbath is kept from sundown on Friday until sundown on Saturday. Religious services are in Hebrew with men and women worshiping separately, and daily prayers are said in the morning, late afternoon, and after sunset. Dietary rules are strictly observed; for example, neither pork nor shellfish is eaten, and milk and meat are not consumed at the same meal. Only kosher food, prepared in accordance with Jewish law, may be eaten. For example, meat may be eaten only if it comes from a healthy animal that has been killed quickly and painlessly.

Religious services among Reform and Conservative Jews contain much more English than do traditional Orthodox services. Men and women worship together, and organ music may be part of the service. Conservative Jews generally observe Jewish dietary laws in all public functions of the synagogue, while they may or may not keep a kosher kitchen at home. Reform Jews are least likely to keep kosher, are more likely to attend a synagogue or "temple" only on high holidays (Rosh Hashanah and Yom Kippur), and are more likely to marry non-Jews than are Orthodox or Conservative Jews.

Although Jewish Americans represent an economically prosperous group and although Judaism has become partially Americanized, Jewish Americans have not been accepted into the Anglo-Saxon core. Writing in the late 1970s, Feagin stated that anti-Semitism, or discrimination against Jews, was still a factor in the United States.

> *From the late nineteenth century onward Jewish Americans have been excluded from hotels, restaurants, social clubs, voluntary associations, and housing. Such discrimination has persisted into the 1960s and 1970s. Thus the social ties of Jewish Americans have been firmly cemented together, at least partially, for defensive reasons. The Jewish community and the extended Jewish family—one can underscore this point—have provided the critical defensive context for survival in the face of anti-Semitism. The "Jewish mother" stereotypes have a nucleus of truth in the vigorous protective actions taken by Jewish mothers—and fathers—in defending their children from the onslaughts of non-Jews. Even in recent decades Jewish families have remained cohesive bastions of defense for their members.*
>
> *Consequently, in recent decades the intermarriage rate has not been as high as some analysts have predicted, given the high level of acculturation of Jewish Americans.*[123]

In the 1990s, Feagin and Feagin found persisting anti-Semitism in the United States, as well as a strong sense of ethnic identity among Jewish Americans.[124]

Accommodation in the Face of Anti-Semitism

Despite long centuries of political fragmentation and persecution, Jews have kept alive their religion and cultural traditions. Judaism is one of the world's oldest religions and was the first to teach the existence of one God, giving birth to both Christianity and Islam. Jews were persecuted along with the early Christians prior to the Christianization of the Roman Empire. During the Middle Ages, Renaissance, and Enlightenment, they were attacked as heretics by Christians and have been the victims of scapegoating and discrimination up to the present. Of the estimated 14 to 20 million people killed by the Nazis in World War II concentration camps, at least 6 million were Jews. The Holocaust exterminated three-fifths of the Jewish population in Europe; approximately 1.5 million of the victims were Jewish children. Because Jews maintained their own religion, language, and traditions and lived in segregated communities or ghettos, they became "a marked people—natural targets for whatever passions or fears might sweep over an ignorant and superstitious population."[125] Furthermore, because Jews were typically barred from owning land, they often worked as middlemen, particularly money lenders, tax collectors, and small businessmen, performing the economic functions that "are almost universally unpopular around the world," as seen in the case of the Chinese in Southeast Asia, the East Indians in Uganda, and the Ibos in Nigeria.[126]

Restrictions on Jews were most relaxed in Western Europe, and many Jews began to assimilate to some degree into their host society. In Western Europe, Jews could retain the Jewish religion and still be perceived as French, German, or English. What became Germany was one of the most liberal areas toward Jews, and it was there in the early 1800s that Reform Judaism originated. National policies toward Jews were more restrictive in Russia and Eastern Europe, and most Jews there remained Orthodox.

A Jewish American perspective emerges out of this array of past experiences, beliefs, and opinions. All Jewish Americans are influenced by the challenge of living within a culture that is predominantly Christian. As part of a worldwide Jewish community, Jewish Americans are influenced by a long history of discrimination, which was experienced most recently in the horror of the Holocaust. They are influenced by the existence of Jewish communities in the modern state of Israel and elsewhere, such as the former Soviet Union. These influences help to unify Jewish Americans despite their individual and group differences.

Contrary to popular myths and stereotypes of wealthy Jews in control of U.S. finance, business, and industry, the Jewish community contains sharp socioeconomic differences. It is true that as a group Jewish Americans show the highest family income index of any major ethnic group in this society.[127] However, it is also estimated that out of a population of about 6 million, over half a million Jewish Americans are below the nation's poverty level. While the percentage of Jews on college and university faculties and in other professions is much higher than their 2.6+ percent of the U.S. population, very few occupy top executive positions or positions of political power. The widely held belief that Jews control the nation's business, banking, and finance is a misconception. Most Jewish Americans fall into middle-income categories that include middle-management jobs and small business.[128]

Persistent Anti-Semitism

According to annual reports published by the Anti-Defamation League (ADL), blatant acts of anti-Semitism, such as arson attempts and vandalism of Jewish tombstones or synagogues, are on the increase. Anti-Semitic incidents in the United States have reached their highest level in nine years, according to a 2005 report released by the Anti-Defamation League.[129]

After a slight decline between 2001 and 2003, incidents of harassment "increased by 27 percent, with 1,117 incidents reported in 2004, compared with the 929 reported in 2003." Acts of vandalism against Jewish community institutions, synagogues, and property also continued an upward trend in 2004, with 644 incidents, compared with the 628 reported in 2003. "Continuing a longstanding trend," the states with the highest numbers of reported incidents are New York, New Jersey, California, Florida, Massachusetts, and Connecticut.

The ADL attributes these increases to the distribution of racist and anti-Jewish literature and intensified activity, including Internet messages, by the neo-Nazi National Alliance, various KKK groups, White Revolution, White Aryan Resistance, and David Duke's European-American Unity and Rights Organization (EURO). The report also cites the high number of anti-Semitic acts reported at middle and high schools as a factor in the increase. "These incidents took the form of swastikas painted or written on desks, walls and other school property, as well as anti-Jewish name-calling, slurs, mockery and bullying." Barbara B. Balser, ADL National chair, added a statement of special importance for educators. "Whether these acts reflect a lack of education or exposure to stereotypes in the home, or insensitive misuse of Holocaust imagery in the wider culture, it shows that there is a great need for anti-bias education among young people."

The Audit does not exist in a vacuum. Although crime rates have declined, there are still many groups dedicated to promoting their racist and anti-Semitic worldviews. In addition to their mass mailings of anti-Semitic propaganda and printings of anti-Jewish and racist publications, these extremist groups continue to find in the Internet a growing vehicle for their hate. As a medium that is inexpensive and almost impossible to regulate, the Internet has become an increasingly active component of the anti-Semitic propaganda machine. (Generally, Internet-related anti-Semitism is not part of the findings of the Audit.)

The Contemporary Era

Contemporary Jewish immigrants are similar to Jewish immigrants from the classic era in a number of ways. First, Russian Jews rank among the top ten immigrant groups in both eras and they are the only European group near the top during the contemporary era. Because government statistics rarely report religious affiliations, "Russian" nationality is often used as a proxy for Jewishness because well over half of all immigrants from Russia to the United States have been Jews.[130] A second similarity is refugee status. In both eras, entire families fled, seeking "refuge from prejudice and assault, as well as . . . economic opportunity."[131] Furthermore, in both eras most Jewish immigrants settled in large cities, such as New York, Los Angeles, and Chicago, where they joined established Jewish communities, maintained cooperative economic networks, found access to American schools for their children, and learned English faster than other immigrant groups.[132]

However, there are dramatic contrasts between the Jewish immigrant experience during the classic and contemporary eras. Today, in contrast to the crowded and filthy tenements of the classic era, most Jewish immigrants "settle in established Jewish neighborhoods, which are often middle class. Within them, they find a variety of amenities and services provided by co-nationals, the American Jewish community, and the larger society. As refugees, most Russians and some Iranians are eligible for a variety of benefits."[133]

A second dramatic difference is the reduction in prejudice and discrimination Jewish immigrants encounter today. In fact, "recent Jewish immigrants find themselves among the upper echelon of all migrants largely because of their European origins, high levels of education, legal status, connections to established co-ethnics, and white skin."[134] Third, in contrast to Jewish newcomers of the past, current Jewish immigrants are distinctly different in terms of language, culture, and national heritage (e.g., Russia, Israel, and Iran), and relations with the American Jewish community differ dramatically from earlier eras of immigration. Although recent Jewish immigrants find support in established Jewish communities, they tend to be more conservative politically, focus on national identity over Jewish identity, and prefer Chabad, "an ultraorthodox, Hassidic movement considered exotic by mainstream American Jews," over Reform and Conservative Judaism.[135] According to Steven Gold,

> *Jewish immigrants face a dilemma as they plan for their children's Jewish education. If they do nothing, their children will lose touch with their Jewishness. However, if they enroll the youngsters in American Jewish institutions, they are confronted with another foreign notion of identity: American Judaism. As a consequence, immigrant parents must choose between having their children socialized in either of two unfamiliar cultural traditions—those of non-Jewish Americans and American Jews.*[136]

Who Has Assimilated?

Cultural pluralism can be visualized along a continuum with cultural assimilation at one end and cultural suppression at the other. There are degrees of assimilation and suppression, with cultural pluralism falling somewhere between the extremes. Box 4.2 lists characteristic responses among ethnic minority groups under conditions of assimilation, pluralism, and suppression in contrast with the predominant mainstream cultural responses.

The true test of assimilation is when members of an ethnic group experience the following conditions:

- Change of cultural patterns to those of the predominant society
- Large-scale entrance into cliques, clubs, and institutions of the predominant society on the primary group level
- Large-scale intermarriage
- Development of a sense of peoplehood based exclusively on the predominant society
- Absence of prejudice
- Absence of discrimination
- Absence of value and power conflict[137]

Conclusions

As we think about our nation's contemporary immigrants, and their children and grandchildren, several questions come to mind. Will history repeat itself? Will a pattern of segmented assimilation prevail? How will schools and society be impacted

Box 4.2
The Assimilation–Pluralism–Suppression Continuum

Ethnic Minority Group versus Dominant Culture Responses

Assimilation	Pluralism	Suppression
The Ethnic Minority Group	*The Ethnic Minority Group*	*The Ethnic Minority Group*
■ Gives up its original culture ■ Identifies with and is absorbed into the predominant Anglo-Western European culture ■ Is no longer identifiable as distinct from the predominant Anglo-Western European culture	■ Retains many of its traditions, such as language, religion, artistic expression, and social customs ■ Adopts many aspects of the predominant Anglo-Western European culture such as language; monogamy; military service; local, state, and federal laws; and full rights of citizenship ■ Develops an ethnic perspective and also identifies with the nation as a whole ■ Respects and appreciates different ethnic traditions that it may or may not choose to experience	■ Is segregated from the rest of society, including schools, churches, jobs, housing, restaurants, and clubs ■ Develops a unique culture, retains its original culture, or a combination of both ■ May develop a "dual consciousness" in order to survive
The Macroculture	*The Macroculture*	*The Macroculture*
■ Accepts members of other ethnic groups once they give up their original identity ■ Views other cultures as unacceptable, inferior, or a threat to social harmony and national unity ■ Suppresses the culture and contributions of other groups	■ Respects and appreciates ethnic diversity ■ Encourages ethnic minorities to keep many of their traditions alive ■ May or may not adopt some of society's different ethnic traditions and current way of life	■ Regards the ethnic minority as inferior ■ Controls society's economy, government, schools, churches, and news and other media ■ Accepts the doctrine of White supremacy and sets up policies to preserve it ■ Suppresses the culture and contributions of other groups

by the continuing arrival of newcomers? Will the American Dream take on new meaning? Could it provide a foundation for social justice in our nation's immigration policies? These are questions we will explore in the next three chapters, which focus on American Indians and African Americans who experienced colonialism and involuntary immigration, respectively; Latinos whose experiences include colonialism, refugee status, the migrant stream, and voluntary immigration; and the classic and contemporary immigrant and refugee experiences of Asians, Muslims, and Arab Americans.

Selected Sources for Further Study

Alba, R., & Nee, V. (2003). *Remaking the American Mainstream: Assimilation and Contemporary Immigration.* Cambridge, MA: Harvard University Press.

Banks, J. A. (2008). *Teaching Strategies for Ethnic Studies, 6th ed.* Boston: Allyn & Bacon. (Chapters 8 & 9.)

Feagin, J. R., & Feagin, C. B. (2008). *Racial and Ethnic Relations*, 8th ed. Upper Saddle River, NJ: Prentice Hall.

Gallo, D. R. (Ed.). (2004). *First Crossing: Stories about Teen Immigrants.* Cambridge, MA: Candlewick Press.

Jones, R. C. (Ed.). (2008). *Immigrants Outside Megalopolis: Ethnic Transformation in the Heartland.* Lanham, MD: Lexington Books.

Joselit, J. W. (1995). *The Wonders of America: Reinventing Jewish Culture, 1880–1950.* New York: Hill and Wang.

Joselit, J. W. (2001). *A Perfect Fit: Clothes, Character, and the Promise of America.* New York: Metropolitan Books.

McKee, J. O. (Ed.). (2000). *Ethnicity in Contemporary America.* Lanham, MD: Rowman & Littlefield.

Min, P. G. (Ed.). (2002). *Mass Migration to the United States: Classical and Contemporary Periods.* Walnut Creek, CA: AltaMira Press.

Miyares, I. M., & Airriess, C. A. (Eds.). (2007). *Contemporary Ethnic Geographies in America.* Lanham, MD: Rowman & Littlefield.

Orchowski, M. S. (2008). *Immigration and the American Dream: Battling the Political Hype and Hysteria.* Lanham, MD: Rowman & Littlefield.

Portes, A., & Rumbaut, R. G. (2006). *Immigrant America: A Portrait*, 3rd ed. Berkeley: University of California Press.

Pyong, G. M. (Ed.). (2002). *Mass Migration to the United States: Classical and Contemporary Periods.* Walnut Creek, CA: AltaMira Press.

Ngai, M. M. (2004). *Impossible Subjects: Illegal Aliens and the Making of Modern America.* Princeton, NJ: Princeton University Press.

Suarez-Orozco, C., Suarez-Orozco, M. M., & Todorova, I. (2008). *Learning a New Land: Immigrant Students in American Society.* Cambridge, MA: Harvard University Press.

Now go to Topic #10: **Immigration** in the MyEducationLab (www.myeducationlab.com) for your course, where you can:

- Find learning outcomes for these topics along with the national standards that connect to these outcomes.
- Complete Assignments and Activities that can help you more deeply understand the chapter content.
- Apply and practice your understanding of the core teaching skills identified in the chapter with the Building Teaching Skills and Dispositions learning units.

Chapter 5

Colonialism, Involuntary Immigration, and the American Dream: American Indian and African American Perspectives

American Indians

Who is an American Indian? The answer varies. Some full-blooded native people do not regard a person with one-quarter native heritage as qualifying, while others accept $\frac{1}{128}$. The majority of native peoples accept a person with at least one-fourth tribal heritage as a member. The U.S. Census Bureau lists anyone who claims native identity as a native. One Native American law center has identified fifty-two legal definitions of Native Americans.[1] According to the American Indian Heritage Foundation, the U.S. federal government recognizes 690 tribes and bands of various sizes. Largest, with populations of over 100,000 each, are the Cherokee, Navajo, Chippewa, and Sioux.[2] Approximately 5 percent of U.S. territory, or 94 million acres of land, is currently held by Native Americans and Alaskan Natives. This may be compared to the 2 billion acres of land used by native people in 1492.[3]

Origins: Roots of Diversity

Ten primary culture areas have been identified in North America, beginning with the Arctic, home of the Inuit people, and stretching to Mesoamerica, the southernmost culture area. The ten culture areas are described by Herman Viola in *After Columbus: The Smithsonian Chronicle of the North American Indians* as follows:

- *Arctic*   The last Siberian wanderers to reach America: Ancestors of the Aleuts and Inuits probably arrived starting 5,000 years ago and ranged from Alaska to Greenland.
- *Sub Arctic*   Nomadic hunters of the taiga or northern forests: Carriers, Crees, Dogribs, and Kutchins pursued such big game as caribou and moose and small fur-bearing animals.
- *Northwest Coast*   Premier woodworkers: The sea-faring Haidas, Kwakiutls, and Tlingits crafted totem poles, boats, and elaborate dwellings from the region's giant evergreens.
- *Plateau*   Fishermen, foragers, and hunters: The Nez Perce, Spokane, and Yakima Plateau tribes lived in underground, pit-house villages in Columbia River country.
- *Plains*   The horse and the gun transformed the Arapaho, Cheyenne, Sioux, and other plains tribes from farmers into nomadic buffalo hunters.

- *Northeast* Three great confederacies—Powhatan, Iroquois, and Miami—occupied settlements on the coast and in forested uplands, where they farmed, hunted, and fished.
- *Southeast* Skilled farmers: The Creeks, Chickasaws, Choctaws, Cherokees, Yamasees, and Seminoles built their villages in river valleys.
- *Southwest* Pueblo-dwelling Hopi and Zuni lived on rugged mesas and, along with such desert-dwelling agricultural tribes as the Pima, fought Apache and Navajo hunter-raiders.
- *Great Basin* Making the most of scarce, seasonal resources, bands of Paiutes, Utes, Shoshones, and Bannocks roamed a land of arid basin and snowy range.
- *California* In a bountiful area smaller than today's state, a dense but diverse population of hunter-gatherers lived in tribal bands and spoke hundreds of different languages.[4]

In their culture, language, and physical appearance, native peoples of North America are as dissimilar as are the peoples of Europe.[5] At the time of the European invasion there were hundreds of different Native American societies. Over 200 different languages were spoken, and political, social, and economic systems differed dramatically. And yet there is a shared cultural perspective, a worldview that reflects basic spiritual values and reverence for the earth. When the European settlers and adventurers explored North America, they were oblivious to the history and culture of the native peoples that had developed over the previous 20,000 years. "They did not find monuments of antiquity awaiting them such as existed in the old world (paintings, sculpture, and architecture) . . . the continent seemed silent."[6]

> The continent did not speak to the newcomers because the civilizations of North America did not always speak in loud stone. They spoke in earth and wood, in fiber and textile, in bead and shell. Even when they did choose to speak in stone, they selected small images that could be carved from softer stone, such as the carved animal pipes of the ancient Hopewell people, or the polished red pipe stone of the Plains. Even the stone buildings at Chaco Canyon in New Mexico or Mesa Verde in Colorado spoke in a softer tone, without triumphant arches, expansive domes, soaring pillars, or other modes of imperial adornment and ostentation.[7]

At one time, North America was among the most wooded places on earth. Except for the Great Plains and southwestern desert areas, the American Indians were a forest people, living

> in a virtually eternal "wooden age." . . . The Indians had lived in and around forests for millennia, and had carefully managed and shaped the forests through these years. They consciously followed practices that maximized the growth of trees and plants that they found useful and minimized those that obstructed them.[8]

Through controlled burning, for example, American Indians kept the forests open and allowed large trees to flourish. The trees were harvested for building dugout canoes and making roof beams for homes and community buildings. Controlled fires had additional benefits, such as killing parasitic plants, irritating insects and pests, and poisonous snakes. It also stimulated new growth that attracted large game. In the Plains area, the Indians burned tall prairie grasses to lure buffalo closer to their villages, and after centuries of land management that kept the forests open and attractive to large animals, buffalo had adapted to the forest and moved east to provide "the Indians of the Eastern forest with new sources of food and raw materials."[9] The Indians also developed practices to maintain the wildlife populations of birds, fish, and large animals on which they depended for survival.

American Indians were among the best hunters in the world. In addition to their incredible speed and accuracy, "their genius lay in their intimate knowledge of animal habits and in their sophisticated approach to hunting, which stressed tactics over technology."[10] For example, Native American hunters could reproduce the calls of birds and animals and camouflaged themselves in animal skins, horns, or antlers and used a variety of traps and strategies to ambush their prey. The "universal tool kit" for the entire continent was the bow and arrow, the spear, and (in some areas) the sling shot.[11]

Early Contact with Europeans

Estimates of the Native American population size at the time of the European invasion of North America vary greatly. Early analysts have estimated the indigenous population in North America at between 500,000 and 1,150,000, but more recently the figure has been estimated at nearly 10 million.[12] Current scholars believe that the early estimates did not consider factors such as European diseases, especially smallpox, measles, and syphilis, which wiped out large portions of the Native American population during early years of contact. Furthermore, lower estimates had helped legitimize European takeover of unsettled territories.

The first 250 years of European contact with Native Americans included accommodation as well as conflict. In the eastern portions of the continent, American, British, Dutch, French, and Spanish powers fought each other and Native Americans for control of the land. As long as the natives controlled the balance of power in North America, the European and U.S. governments recognized them (at least on paper) as the "rightful owners of land in the Americas. Land was not to be taken from Indians except in fair exchange. Indians were needed not only as military allies, but also as producers and suppliers."[13] This philosophy was reflected in words from Article 111 in the Northwest Ordinance.

> *The utmost good faith shall always be observed towards the Indians; their land property shall never be taken from them without their consent; and in their property, rights, and liberty, they never shall be invaded or disturbed, unless in just and lawful wars authorized by Congress; but laws founded in justice and humanity shall from time to time be made, for preventing wrongs being done to them and for preserving peace and friendship with them.*[14]

How the Land Was Taken[15]

The Lewis and Clark Expedition: Different Narratives

The American public has been fascinated by recent revivals of the Lewis and Clark Expedition. Events surrounding the expedition's 200th anniversary celebrated the "American narrative" of the "birth of a new nation carved out of 'foreign soil.'"[16] In April 1804, President Thomas Jefferson launched the expedition to enter territories in the Pacific Northwest that were previously uncharted by Euro-American explorers, with the goal of claiming this area for the United States.[17] When Lewis and Clark mapped, described, and named the lands they traversed, they transformed "Native" lands into "American" lands. Rebecca Tsosie, noted Yaqui scholar and professor of Native American Law and Ethics at Arizona State University, writes,

> *Lewis and Clark mapped the mountains, valleys, rivers, and other natural features of the land they traversed. In some cases, they recorded the French names or Native names that had already been given to these natural features. However, in most cases . . . (they) named the places according to their own experience (e.g., whether the water was "muddy" when they visited it), or through incidents that occurred when they visited the places (e.g., the day they ran out of flour), or in commemoration of people that were important to them (e.g., the "Judith River" after Clark's fiancé; "Clark's Fork," after himself). This was a "renaming process" designed to transform indigenous understandings of the land into "American" understanding, and to supplant Native narratives with a new "American" narrative.[18]*

Thus, the narrative celebrated by the American public is very different from Native peoples' narratives about the enduring impact of the Lewis and Clark Expedition. If we think about "how the land was taken," in contrast to "how the West was won," we can uncover American Indian perspectives that many of us are unfamiliar with.

Ethnic geographers describe Native Americans as "a land-based minority" that is deeply cognizant of its relationship to the land.[19] Furthermore, in the United States American Indians differ from other "ethnic" minorities because they are members of sovereign nations. Sovereignty—the inherent right of a people to self-government, self-determination, and self-education—includes "the right to linguistic and cultural expression according to local languages and norms, and the right to (in the words of Henry Giroux) 'write, speak, and act from a position of agency.'"[20] In reality, the sovereignty of Indian tribes and nations does not require complete independence from federal or state governments in pluralistic democracies such as the United States.[21]

Rebecca Tsosie explains how the Earth is simultaneously a source of "physical survival" and "cultural survival" for Native Americans.[22] Particular geographic areas often are central to cultural identity, and "Many Indian Nations speak of the specific 'origin place' of their people as being attached to a river, mountain, plateau, or valley. This origin place becomes a central defining feature of the tribe's religion and cultural worldview," as revealed in creations stories, the cultural boundaries of a tribe associated with mountains and bodies of water, as well as ethical principles associated with certain places.[23] For example, one Apache Elder told Tsosie, "The land is always stalking people. The land makes people live right. The land looks after us. The land looks after people." Non-Indians rarely understand these cultural connections between American Indians and the land and dismiss it as a "romanticized" notion of the past that has little use today.[24]

The Doctrine of Discovery and the Loss of Native Land

The Doctrine of Discovery originated in Europe during the Crusades as a justification for the conquest of "non-Christian" peoples. Later, it was an understanding among European colonizers that "the first nation to 'discover' a foreign land was the only entity to whom the natives could sell their land."[25] Based on Roman Catholic Church edicts, the doctrine was used to justify the European conquest and colonization of "uncivilized" indigenous people throughout the world.[26] A modified version of this doctrine, established by three Supreme Court cases between 1823 and 1832 when John Marshall served as Chief Justice, "gave to the United States all the powers of a conqueror with respect to Native people" and established the principles of federal Indian law in effect today.[27] At the time of the Louisiana Purchase, American Indians were "largely independent and powerful nations who owned land and occupied land located outside the boundaries of any state."[28] However, in the first of these cases Marshall reasoned that the tribes did not own land because of the European Doctrine of Discovery. Therefore, explorations such as the Lewis and Clark Expedition transferred legal title of Indian lands to the United States. In the second case, the Cherokee Nation challenged the State of Georgia's efforts to drive it out of Georgia so it could take over Cherokee land. The Supreme Court decided it did not have jurisdiction to hear the case because the Cherokee Nation is neither a foreign nation, nor a state or citizen of another state. Marshall viewed tribes as "domestic dependent nations" with the right of self-government, or internal sovereignty only. This ruling set up the Trust Doctrine wherein the state can act on behalf of individuals who have few legal rights, as guaranteed by the Constitution.[29] In the third case, the Court ruled that the states have no jurisdiction inside reservation boundaries and that tribes have internal sovereignty and "are free to make their own laws and be governed by them, free from state intrusion, unless Congress deems otherwise."[30] These three cases set the stage for the idea that the federal government could "grant" sovereignty to tribes, ignoring the fact that "sovereignty was an inherent and historic right."[31]

Federal Indian Policy and the Loss of Native Land

Federal Indian policy in the nineteenth and twentieth centuries is frequently described as a pendulum that swings between policies aimed at assimilation of Indians at one extreme and policies that recognized tribes as distinct nations and peoples at the other.[32] Figure 5.1 provides an overview of the major federal government acts. Until the most recent policy phase, known as the "self-determination era," American Indians had little to no voice in the goals and implementation of these policies.

The Indian Removal Act (1830)   Forced migration of Southeastern tribes to settlement lands west of the Mississippi River; requirements for legal removal were not enforced.

The Dawes Act (1887) & Allotment Era   Broke up reservation land and allotted Indian families and non-Indian homesteaders 160 acres of private land for farming; established Indian boarding schools managed by non-Indians to Christianize and assimilate Indian youth.

The Snyder Act (1924)   Granted citizenship to American Indians.

The Reorganization Act (1934)   Recognized tribal sovereignty and authorized tribes to enact constitutions and set up tribal governments; ended land allotments.

Termination Acts (1950–1960)   Abolished over 100 tribes, ended trust relationships, and returned to coercive assimilation.

Self-Determination Era (1960–1990)   Returned to recognition of tribal sovereignty and reinstated some tribes, affirmed tribal self-determination without threat of termination, ended paternalism and moved toward partnership and self-help. Still in place, but faces some challenges today.

Figure 5.1 ▨ Federal Indian Policy: Brief Overview

The Removal Act[33]

The westward expansion of non-Indians created pressures for land held by the Cherokee, Seminoles, Delawares, Choctaws, and Creeks in the Southeastern United States. With westward expansion came the image of savage Indians attacking helpless settlers as they resisted the pressures of farmers and missionaries on the frontiers. Encouraged by President Andrew Jackson, Congress passed the Indiana Removal Act in 1830.[34] This act began the forced migration of American Indians from their homelands. Although the Indian Removal Act stipulated that American Indians could be relocated only on condition of their consent, the end result was that the federal government forcibly removed those living east of the Mississippi to reservations on lands attained through the Louisiana Purchase. On the "Trail of Tears," for example, 4,000 Cherokees died during the forced march out of the South to territory in present-day Oklahoma. "Oklahoma, already the home of the Five Civilized Tribes of the Southeast, was soon to become a vast concentration camp into which Indians from tribes as far apart as the New York Seneca and the West Coast Modace were to be squeezed."[35]

Ethnocentrism and cultural conflict played a large role in the bitter land conflict between the European American and the Native American:

> *It was the permanent settler who transplanted the European market economy and brought the legacy of private property. Sizable investments of labor and capital were made by settlers, for land had to be cleared, homes and whole towns built, and a system of transportation constructed on the frontier. . . . It is estimated that each homestead site required an initial investment of $1,000 to bring it into production. Private ownership of the land gave a settler some sense of security that he would realize a return on his investments, for he had legal title to the land, and the land and the improvements he made on it could not be capriciously taken from him.*[36]

Many European settlers had experienced the oppression of serfdom and found security in the ownership of private property. The Anglo-European worldview concerning land, private property, and exclusive ownership was incompatible with the American Indian worldview, which stressed egalitarianism, nonmaterialism, and opposition to the unnecessary alteration of nature or destruction of any part of the earth. Given these divergent perspectives, the era of treaties before and after the Removal Act would seem to have been doomed by misunderstanding, if not deceit.

The Allotment Act (Dawes Act)

The Dawes Act, passed by Congress in 1887, was the centerpiece of coercive assimilation policies by which most of the large reservation lands were "broken up and parceled out to tribal members and non-Indian homesteaders."[37] The act provided each American Indian family with 160 acres of reservation land, with the titles held in trust by the federal government for twenty-five years. Furthermore, every attempt was made to suppress native traditions, especially religions and education. Indian boarding schools were established that required elementary school-age children to leave their families for the academic year. "Reservation Indians were expected to emulate white settlers . . . by becoming farmers and tilling allotments of privately owned land . . . [and] would eventually assimilate into American society."[38] During this period, tribal lands declined dramatically, falling from "155.6 million acres in 1881 to 104.3 million acres in 1890, to 52.2 million acres in 1934, when the allotment policy was formally abandoned."[39]

The impact of the Dawes Act is yet another illustration of conflicting worldviews. Ben Nighthorse Campbell has described the Dawes Act as "another of Washington's attempts to destroy the sovereignty of tribal governments by substituting in its place private ownership of land to a people who historically and philosophically had no understanding of private ownership. The land was part of the Creator's domain. We may occupy it, but people cannot usurp the Creator by claiming title to it."[40]

The Reorganization Act

During the 1920s, efforts to reform federal Indian policy gathered steam as the failure of coercive assimilation became obvious and reformers argued for the preservation of the tribes. Furthermore, the valiant performance of American Indian soldiers in World War I demonstrated their intelligence and capabilities.[41] As a result, American Indians were declared citizens of the United States in 1924, and the Indian Reorganization Act of 1934 recognized the tribes' authority to establish constitutional governments that would affirm and activate "the inherent sovereignty of the tribes"[42] and recognize American Indian nations as legally autonomous self-governing territories, separate from any state. At the time, the idea that Indians should be in charge of their own affairs was revolutionary—at least to most non-Indians.

The Indian Reorganization Act can be viewed from several angles. In one sense, it indicated a return to the early principle that Native Americans have a right to self-determination: Reservation lands were returned to tribal management, community day schools replaced distant boarding schools, and traditional cultures, including religions, were encouraged. However, the illegally seized lands were not restored, many treaty agreements were ignored, and the reservations were in a sense colonies subject to the political and economic policies of a foreign ruler in Washington, D.C. Most reservations are located on barren land; compared with all other ethnic groups in the United States, the Native American population suffers the poorest health, the shortest lifespan, the highest rate of infant mortality, and the greatest economic impoverishment. Writing about the Reorganization Act several decades ago, Jack Forbes, a noted authority on Native American affairs, expressed views that remain applicable today:

> It must be openly acknowledged that Indians are poor because white people are rich, that the land, timber and minerals which white people use to produce their wealth were virtually all taken by force or deception. It must be recognized that Indian reservations usually exist in marginal land, not originally of value from the perspective of white economic development.[43]

The Termination Acts

During the 1950s, Congress passed a series of acts to end the federal government's involvement in tribal affairs; reservations and tribes were to be abolished and Indians were to be made "subject to the same laws and entitled to the same privileges and responsibilities as are applicable to other citizens of the United States."[44] The acts stated that Indians "should be freed from federal supervision and control" as soon as possible.[45] What could be wrong with these goals of freedom and equality? When federal programs and previously guaranteed protections were withdrawn from over one hundred tribes, thousands of Indians lost their legal status as Indians and 1.4 million acres of trust land were lost to the tribes.[46] And "although the tribal members received distributions of the proceeds from land sales, they failed to prosper. Tribal members became subject to the laws of the states and dependent on the services the states provided. The dislocation of Indian life was profound."[47]

The termination of reservations revived attempts to reduce the land holdings of American Indian tribes, as did "the encouragement of Indian peoples, especially young and middle-aged adults, to relocate from their rural reservations and small towns to metropolitan areas where greater opportunities for employment existed."[48] Although the federal government initiated housing and employment programs designed to support Indians who migrated to urban areas, these efforts were mostly a failure. Urban jobs favored younger persons, and many older Indians returned to the reservations. Those who remained were often exploited by landlords and lived in overcrowded, poverty-stricken neighborhoods where living conditions "were worse than what they had left behind on the reservations."[49] Some scholars believe that termination advocates wanted to do away with the tribes in order to avoid the federal government's legal "obligation through treaties to perform 'trust responsibility' to tribes—not individuals" as a way to save money.[50]

Self-Determination Policy

During the civil rights movement of the 1960s, the termination policy was repudiated. Presidents Kennedy, Johnson, and Nixon all opposed it and actively supported policy changes that affirmed tribal sovereignty. President Johnson proposed a new direction for Indian policy, "a goal that ends the old debate about "termination" of Indian programs and stresses self-determination; a goal that erases old attitudes of paternalism and promotes partnership self-help."[51] As part of Johnson's "Great Society" legislation, tribes became eligible for youth and community action programs and initiatives such as Volunteers of Service to America (VISTA) and Operation Head Start.[52] In contrast to previous eras, the self-determination policy meant that the tribes themselves administered the funding and governance, and this change led to the desire and skills needed to take over other federal programs on the reservations. The policy flourished under President Nixon, who stated, "Self-determination among the Indian people can and must be encouraged without the threat of eventual termination. In my view, in fact, that is the only way that self-determination can effectively be fostered."[53]

What has been accomplished under the policy of self-determination? We see the results in the widespread respect for and preservation of Indian language and culture. Nearly forty tribal colleges and universities have been established; the number of indigenous community-controlled schools has increased;[54] the National Museum of the American Indian sits on the Capitol Mall; and an Indian Arts and Crafts Board assists Indian artists in marketing their work, educates the general public about Indian culture, and establishes criteria for authentic works of art (as opposed to the imitations and phony artifacts sold to an uninformed public). Some sacred lands have been returned to the tribes. Legislation such as the Native American Graves Protection and Repatriation Act of 1990 and the American Indian Religious Freedom Act has been passed. In addition, most of the Bill of Rights has been guaranteed to tribal governments through the Indian Civil Rights Act of 1968. The Indian Child Welfare Act of 1978 put the tribes in charge of native adoptions and foster care. This act ended decades of state, federal, religious, and social service removal of Indian children from their families and placement in non-Indian foster care and adoption systems where very few thrived.[55] Economic development initiatives and natural resource management policies have been established that bring a degree of prosperity to some tribes, through legislation such as the Indian Gaming Regulatory Act and the Mineral Development Act. Tribes with well-managed casinos can provide jobs as well as funding for indigenous schools, tribal colleges, museums, community health services, and craft shops that offer opportunities to sell "market art" (e.g., baskets, weavings, pottery, quill boxes, etc.) that are authentic expressions of traditional artistry.[56]

Will the Indian Self-Determination Policy Survive?

Is the self-determination policy here to stay? Scholars disagree. For example, Kevin Gover of the Pawnee Tribe of Oklahoma, legal scholar and a professor at the Arizona State University College of Law, concludes that after two centuries of Indian policy pendulum swings between "policies that presume the imminent disappearance of the tribes, and policies that foster an ongoing role for tribes in American federalism" it is possible that "the tribes have won a permanent place in the American governmental system and a perpetual and unique relationship with the federal government."[57] In contrast, other scholars argue that self-determination is already being eroded by recent Supreme Court cases; that the general public and much of Congress are misinformed by the media about the realities of "Indian Country"; and that there has been little improvement in the state of American Indian health, educational attainment, or economic well-being in the past two decades.

Tim Johnson, a Mohawk who is executive editor of *Indian Country Today* and cofounder of *Native American Journal* at Cornell University, argues that the survival of a "vibrant American Indian existence is linked to how well the American public and its policy makers are informed about American Indian realities."[58] Furthermore, he argues that the more successful Indians become, especially in terms of increased wealth—the most publicly visible evidence of success—the greater is the threat to their freedom. Johnson describes a compelling case of inaccurate reporting and prejudicial editorializing in the biased press coverage of New York Indian casino issues. He refers to a recent editorial in the *Wall Street Journal* that "made the point that gaming enterprises are bad, bringing 'lowlifes and organized crime, drugs, prostitution, loan sharking, and money laundering. The mob infiltrates and corruptions in local government often follows.'"[59] Johnson shows how the *Wall Street Journal* used misinformation and stereotypes to influence public perceptions that "gaming is going bad and must be addressed." Several months later, *Time* launched a "special investigation" about Indian gaming in a cover story, "Look Who's Cashing In at Indian Casinos."[60] According to Johnson, "A thick layer of anti-tribal attitude permeated the story, which was intended to prove, once and for all, that Indian peoples and their self-governance rights are unfair, corrupt, and inept." By focusing on a few bad examples and ignoring the hundreds of success stories the public received the message that "Indian tribal recognition, economic growth, and advancement are creating more problems than solutions."[61] As a result, Congressional hearings on tribal gaming and federal recognition were held, and the tribal leaders succeeded in making their case concerning the benefits of tribal casinos. Other recent examples of negative press coverage include a national news commentator's statement that Indians stole an election with phony Indian votes and the Governor of California's statement that California's Indians are "ripping us off."[62] In his discussion of "What to Do?" Johnson describes the work of the American Indian Policy and Media Institute (AIPMI), an independent public policy initiative "dedicated to the education and projection of American Indian historical, legal, and contemporary realities within the public's awareness, knowledge, and generally held perceptions."[63] AIPMI's primary goal is to find ways to bridge the gap between people with different "understandings of the historical, cultural, and legal realities that define and empower American Indian peoples and their governments."[64] Members stress the need for tribal governments to tell their story and promote accurate images of today's Indian peoples, otherwise, "The pillars of economic, social, governmental and political success tribes have begun building over the past thirty years will come crashing down."[65] In his concluding comments, Johnson urges tribal leaders, *"Educate America or perish—this is the clarion call to this generation."*[66]

Culture Clash

Many American Indians feel torn between their native culture and that of the surrounding American society. This was illustrated recently at the Wind River Reservation (population 6,000) in Wyoming, where nine young men committed suicide during a two-month period. They ranged in age from 14 to 25. As a result of the tragedy, tribal elders have revived traditional medicine practices not used since a flu epidemic in 1918 and are introducing the school-age population to traditional spiritual practices to help them recover some of their cultural identity.[67]

American Indians have gone through centuries of efforts to Christianize and "civilize" them.[68] Throughout this history of miseducation, American Indians have resisted the pressure to give up their cultural identity. The twenty-four tribal colleges that have developed since the 1970s as a response to the unsuccessful experience of Indian students on mainstream campuses are a symbol of a revitalized ethnic identity among native peoples in the United States.

Today, many Native American leaders openly criticize the Anglo-European core culture and its religion. Christianity is sometimes criticized "as a crude religion stressing blood, crucifixion, and bureaucratized charity rather than practicing sharing and compassion for people."[69] Other criticisms of White Europeans are that they are newcomers to the continent, sharply accelerated war, killed off many animal species, betrayed the Native Americans who had aided them in establishing settlements, destroyed the ecosystem, polluted the environment, and became slaves to technology.[70]

> *They had what the world has lost. They have it now. What the world has lost, the world must have again lest it die. Not many years are left to have or have not, to recapture the lost ingredient. . . . What, in our human world, is this power to live? It is the ancient, lost reverence and passion for human personality, joined with the ancient, lost reverence and passion for the earth and its web of life. This indivisible reverence and passion is what the [Native] American . . . almost universally had; and representative groups of them have it still.*
>
> *If our modern world should be able to recapture this power, the earth's natural resources and web of life would not be irrevocably wasted within the twentieth century, which is the prospect now.*
>
> *True democracy, founded in the neighborhoods and reaching over the world, would become the realized heaven on earth. And living peace—not just an interlude between wars—would be born and would last through ages.*[71]

The ideas expressed in this passage are important because they illustrate how an ethnic minority that comprises only about 2 percent of the population can contribute to the thinking and policies of the dominant culture. The idea of ecology does not belong exclusively to American Indian cultures, nor do all Native Americans subscribe to it. However, American Indians have provided our nation with a strong voice in thinking about environmental issues such as overdevelopment of the land, loss of natural resources, and storage of toxic wastes. More Americans are becoming aware of the connections between the health of the earth, their own personal physical and spiritual well-being, and the wholesomeness of their communities.

African Americans

Today, African Americans comprise about 12.5 percent of the population of the United States. Prior to the massive emigration of peoples from Europe, they made up one-fifth of the population. Throughout nearly four centuries of U.S. history, African Americans have been critically important to the nation's commercial and industrial growth. While all immigrant groups have contributed hard labor to build the nation, African Americans, involuntary immigrants who arrived in chains, are an exception in that they could not reap the benefits of their labor for themselves and their families.

Three Phases of History

African American history and the national experience can be visualized according to three watersheds: First was slavery, beginning with capture and forced migration from Africa, followed by nearly 150 years of bondage; next was emancipation, followed by another 50 years of tenant farming and economic exploitation under the conditions of sharecropping; and third was the great migration north in the first half of the twentieth century that created contemporary Black urban communities and a second emancipation, the civil rights movement of the 1950s and 1960s.[72] The themes of opposition and liberation provide a lens for the following brief overviews of these three periods.

Phase One: Enslavement

It is estimated that over 100 million Black Africans were either killed or transported to the Americas between 1502 when the slave trade began and its actual end in the 1860s.[73] When the legal slave trade ended in 1808, over 400,000 Africans had been forced into slavery in North America and another 10 to 50 million were forcibly transported to South America and the Caribbean.[74] By 1860, the African American population in the United States had grown from 400,000 to more than 4 million, with the majority being born into slavery.[75]

Slaves in the United States were the personal property of their masters. They were in absolute bondage for life and were denied the rights of property and all other civil and legal rights and could hold property only at the will and pleasure of the master.[76] Slaves could neither give nor receive gifts; could make no will, nor, by will, inherit anything. They could not enter contracts for work or for matrimony and "could buy or sell nothing at all, except as (the) master's agent, could keep no cattle, horses, hogs, or sheep and (in some states) could raise no cotton."[77] They were also denied the civic privileges of education and worship. "Every Southern State except Maryland and Kentucky had stringent laws forbidding anyone to teach slaves reading and writing, and in some states the penalties applied to the educating of free Negroes and mulattos as well."[78]

Most historians agree that the earliest Africans who came to the English colonies were indentured servants and, like indentured servants from Europe, gained their freedom after a fixed number of years.[79] (It is also widely agreed that Africans explored and settled in other regions of the Americas prior to the slave trade.) Children of these Black servants were automatically free from birth. The number of free persons of color who acquired this status because they were never slaves was strengthened by African Americans who were freed or escaped slavery prior to the Civil War. Once the concept of chattel slavery evolved in the late 1600s, slaves became property for life and passed the legacy on to their children. Freedom could be attained, however, through voluntary manumission by slave owners, escape, self-purchase, purchase by already free relatives or philanthropic Whites, or through special legislation as a reward for unusual service to the community.[80] Mulatto children of White mothers were also automatically free from birth. Between 10 and 14 percent of the African American population in the United States was free prior to the Civil War.

The status of free African Americans during colonial days and the early 1800s was precarious at best, particularly in the South. Free Blacks could be kidnapped and sold into slavery, especially after the Fugitive Slave law was passed in 1850. Free people of color were denied voting rights, were excluded from the militia and from carrying U.S. mail, and were permitted to bear arms only if they could obtain a permit. Free Blacks could, however, own real estate and some attained great wealth. A Black elite developed in the lower South, for example, where African Americans (formerly subjects of France and Spain) had more legal and customary rights than elsewhere in the South. In the state of Louisiana there developed a large group of prosperous free Black planters, as well as a highly educated free Black elite.[81] Furthermore, in Louisiana free Blacks traveled freely and could testify in court.

Slave life has been revealed in slave autobiographies, numerous history texts, and films such as Alex Haley's *Roots*, *Queen*, and *Amistad*.[82] Scholars have argued about the degree to which slavery was a "paternalistic" system (wherein White masters rationalized slavery in terms of "Christianizing" and caring for the slaves), the degree to which slaves resisted their oppressors, and the degree to which carryovers from African cultures have survived and influenced African American culture today. The most widely accepted view among scholars today is that

> *[in] the face of physical torture and white attempts to eradicate their cultures, the many peoples of Africa among the slaves . . . became a single African American people and forged their own oppositional culture, an African American culture. Drawing on deep African spiritual roots, these new Americans shaped their own religion, their own art and music, their distinctive versions of Afro-English, and their own philosophical and political thinking about racial oppression, liberation and social justice. In the colonies and later in the United States the pressures on black Americans to conform to the white core culture forced them to become bicultural, to know both the dominant Euro-American culture and their own culture as well. Since the days of slavery there has been a centuries-long struggle for the maintenance of this oppositional culture, a culture*

> *part African and part an African American adaptation to the concrete history of white oppression. This culture has provided the foundation of active black resistance to oppression since the seventeenth century.*[83]

The struggle to maintain an African American oppositional culture is described by Roger D. Abrahams, a preeminent scholar of African American culture, in his study of the corn-shucking celebrations throughout the South prior to the Civil War.[84] Originating in the English custom of harvest home, the corn-shucking harvest ceremony became an important autumn event. "It was regarded as a slaves' holiday, one which called for the field workers to enter freely into a work party as a prelude to a feast and a dance."[85] The master would have immense quantities of corn hauled up to the crib, often heaped as high as a house. Slaves would gather from miles around, select two leaders or generals, and choose up two sides. The teams would then compete to see who could shuck the most corn the fastest, amid singing and shouting. An extravagant feast was provided by the master, followed up with dancing that lasted most of the night.

In his study of this particular event, Abrahams sees the corn-shucking ceremony as being

> *characteristic of a dynamic process taking place on the plantation in which the slaves neither divested themselves of their African cultural heritage nor acculturated to the behaviors and performance pattern of their masters. To the contrary, the hands were encouraged to act and perform differently. The practices emerged as forms of active resistance, not in the sense that they attacked the system but rather in the ways in which they maintained alternative perspectives toward time, work, and status.*[86]

The owners and their families and guests observed the slave dances from the big house verandah. Over time these events became an important source of enjoyment for the White ruling elite. As the slave dancers engaged in the performance and self-expression, they transformed the event into one of social and moral mockery. Meanwhile their masters were oblivious to the hidden meanings and ridicule directed at them. Abrahams explains how later the dances developed into the minstrel and vaudeville shows and influenced White culture as well as African American performance style today (e.g., the subversive treatment of authority and interplay with the audience).

Phase Two: Emancipation, Sharecropping, and Tenancy

The decade of Reconstruction following the Civil War was a period of hope for African Americans. The former slaves, nearly 200,000 of whom had fought for the union military (37,000 died), held high expectations for their freedom. They sought independence from White control.[87] A top priority was ownership of land, and the right to determine the use of their own labor, as a basis for control over their family life. Some made Herculean efforts to be reunited with family members, with thousands advertising in the Black press for lost loved ones.[88] They consolidated the network of churches, schools, and mutual aid societies that had been forged during slavery, a "semi-autonomous culture centered on family and church."[89] They withdrew from White-controlled churches and developed independent Black churches, especially Methodist and Baptist.

> *The church played a central role in the Black community; a place of worship, it also housed schools, social events, and political gatherings, and sponsored many of the fraternal and benevolent societies that sprang up during Reconstruction. Inevitably, black ministers came to play a major role in politics. More than 200 held public office during Reconstruction.*[90]

Self-sufficiency and community improvement were also evident in their "thirst for education."

> *Before the war, every Southern state except Tennessee had prohibited the instruction of slaves. Now, adults as well as children thronged the schools established during and after the Civil War. Northern benevolent societies, the Freedman's Bureau, and, after 1868, state governments, provided most of the funding for black education during Reconstruction but the initiative often lay with African-Americans, who pooled their meager resources and voluntarily taxed themselves to purchase land, construct buildings, and hire teachers."*[91]

The Reconstruction Act of 1867 gave Black men in the South the right to vote; three years later the Fifteenth Amendment was ratified, outlawing voter discrimination based on race (gender discrimination was outlawed in 1920). Over 1,500 African Americans were elected to political office in the Reconstruction South, although nowhere was their political representation proportionate with the total population.[92] For the first time in American history there was a biracial government, and it

> *functioned effectively in many parts of the South. Public facilities were rebuilt and expanded, school systems established, and legal codes purged of racism. The conservative oligarchy that had dominated Southern governments from colonial times to 1867 found itself largely excluded from political power, while those who had previously been outsiders—poorer white Southerners, men from the North, and especially former slaves—cast ballots, sat on juries, and enacted and administered laws. (One Northern correspondent reported in 1873) "One hardly realizes the fact that the many Negroes one sees here . . . have been slaves a few short years ago, at least as far as their demeanor goes as individuals newly invested with all the rights and privileges of an American citizen."*[93]

What went wrong? Most historians agree that the failure of Reconstruction lies in the lack of land distribution reform. African Americans gained civil rights and political rights through the Fourteenth and Fifteenth Amendments, but proposals for land distribution legislation were rejected by Congress. Although they were no longer slaves, they became sharecroppers, "working the land of their former master in exchange for part of the crop. Forced to buy goods from the planter's store, they were trapped in a vicious economic cycle, making barely enough to pay off their debts."[94] Thomas Fortune, an editor of the New York *Globe*, testified before a Senate committee in 1883 about "widespread poverty" and government betrayal.[95] A Negro farm laborer in the South was usually

> *paid in "orders," not money, which he could only use at a store controlled by the planter, "a system of fraud." The Negro farmer, to get the wherewithal to plant his crop, had to promise it to the store, and when everything was added up at the end of the year he was in debt, so his crop was constantly owed to someone, and he was tied to the land, with the records kept by the planter and storekeeper so that the Negroes "are swindled and kept forever in debt."[96]*

Sharecropping and tenancy became firmly entrenched during the post–Civil War years, trapping both Blacks and many Whites in a system that lasted until pressures initiated by two world wars and the New Deal initiated its demise.

The long post-emancipation period of sharecropping and tenancy was a time of lynching, race riots, Jim Crow legislation, and the rise of terrorist groups such as the Ku Klux Klan. Lynching became a way for vigilante mobs to keep African Americans (as well as sympathetic Whites) "in their place" after the Civil War and Reconstruction. Recorded lynching shows that nearly 3,500 African Americans were lynched between 1882 and 1951, but actual lynching is believed to be over 6,000.[97] Most of the lynching was carried out in Southern states, but in the North there were race riots, led by Whites against Blacks, at the end of World War I, as well as other forms of White violence and oppression. The 1920s saw a rebirth of the Ku Klux Klan. Its focus was Christian morality versus sin.

> *The enemies of America, the Klan proclaimed, were booze, loose women, Jews, Negroes, Roman Catholics (whose "dago pope was bent on taking over the U.S."), and anybody else who was not a native-born white Protestant Anglo-Saxon. Many churchmen across the nation acclaimed the Klan's program, and in the south especially, Methodist and Baptist clergymen lent the K.K.K. massive support. It was not long before it blossomed into a mighty nationwide organization that claimed to number in its hooded ranks about 4,000,000 members.[98]*

Some of the most blatant evidence against the melting-pot myth is the oppression of African Americans under slavery and later under the Jim Crow laws, which legalized the separation of Blacks and Whites. Separate but equal facilities for Blacks became the law of the land, although separate facilities were rarely (if ever) equal. An extreme dual system pervaded all aspects of life in the American South. Jim Crow laws were passed to keep "coloreds" separate from Whites in schools, public transportation, restaurants, theaters, baseball fields, public bathrooms, swimming pools, doctors' offices, and so on. Many courtrooms had separate Bibles for giving oaths. Intermarriage was illegal in thirty-eight of the forty-eight states until the mid-twentieth century, and Blacks were denied their right to vote through grandfather clauses, poll taxes, and outrageous literacy tests until voting rights legislation was passed between 1964 and 1970.

Phase Three: Northern Migration, a Second Emancipation, and the Civil Rights Movement

Most historians agree that the civil rights movement of the 1950s and 1960s is rooted in political and cultural changes that began with the migration north of African Americans during the first half of the twentieth century.[99] At the end of the Civil War, about 90 percent of the African American population lived in the Southern states, primarily on farms. By the mid-twentieth century, millions of African Americans had migrated north in search of a "promised land," and by 1960 only half of the Black population lived in rural areas, with only a tenth still working on farms.[100] Today most African Americans live in cities, North and South, and the migration pattern has shifted, with more moving into the South than leaving. The 2000 U.S. Census showed that 47 percent of the Black population lived in ten Southern states: Texas, Florida, Georgia, North Carolina, Maryland, Louisiana, Virginia, South Carolina, Alabama, and Mississippi. However, the largest concentration of African American citizens is in two Northern cities, New York and Chicago.

According to the historian Thomas C. Holt,

> These demographic and economic changes laid the basis for the greatest political mobilization of black Americans since Reconstruction. Freed from the constraints of the rural South, blacks began to organize in both formal and informal political arenas. In the North during the 1920s and in southern cities by the 1940s and 1950s, blacks organized once again to protest segregation, Jim Crow, and job discrimination. With the advent of the New Deal, blacks became an important factor in national politics, and federal executive and judicial policies reflected the change. These political changes, together with a greatly augmented black intelligentsia and the revival of racial liberalism in the aftermath of Nazism, were essential precursors to the southern civil rights movement that seemingly exploded full-blown in the 1950s. Before that movement had run its course, the face of southern institutions had been radically transformed: voting and holding office in unprecedented numbers, blacks decisively influenced presidential politics and enticed erstwhile foes, among them Governor George Wallace of Alabama, to recant their earlier racist views.[101]

While it is generally agreed that the urbanization of African Americans in the twentieth century was critical to the destruction of racial segregation in the South, scholars disagree on the personal impact of urbanization on African Americans. Some social scientists emphasize the negative impact on "Black peasants" who were ill prepared for urban life.[102] The author Richard Wright, in *12 Million Black Voices*, shares a perspective that could support the view that African Americans became victims in Northern ghettos. Wright, who ran away from home in the delta country of Mississippi at age fifteen and worked his way up to Chicago, described the feelings of many African Americans who were part of the Great Migration—and their experiences once they arrived.

We see white men and women get on the train, dressed in expensive clothes. We look at them guardedly and wonder will they bother us. Will they ask us to stand up while they sit down? Will they tell us to go to the back of the coach? Even though we have been told that we need not be afraid, we have lived so long in fear of all white faces that we cannot help but sit and wait. We look around the train and we do not see the old familiar signs: FOR COLORED and FOR WHITE.[103]

Wright describes the mixed feelings of freedom and fear the migrants experienced as they disembark in Chicago, Indianapolis, New York, Cleveland, Buffalo, Detroit, Toledo, Philadelphia, Pittsburgh, and Milwaukee. Encountering thousands and thousands of strangers, people in the North at first seem indifferent and distant, especially the "Bosses of the Buildings" who helped African Americans find jobs in the factories and foundries, as well as places to live in crowded and noisy apartments. The migrants soon discover that, far from feeling indifferent, these Bosses

are deeply concerned about us but in a different way. It seems as if we are now living inside of a machine; days and events move with a hard reasoning of their own. We live amid swarms of people, yet there is a vast difference between people, a distance that words cannot bridge. No longer do our lives depend upon the soil, the sun, the rain, or the wind; we live by the grace of jobs and the brutal logic of jobs. In the South, life was different; men spoke to you, yelled at you, or killed you. The world moved by signs you knew. But here in the North cold forces hit you and push you. It is a world of things.[104]

In Chicago, for example, both Black and White migrants experienced a bewildering shortage of housing, which led to competition for available apartments. Wright describes the process of White fright and flight to the suburbs, followed by the conversion of vacated houses into apartments (called "kitchenettes") by the Bosses of the Buildings. As many as five or six persons would live in a one-room kitchenette.[105]

The kitchenette, with its "filth and foul air, with its one toilet for 30 or more tenants," is at the root of the high infant death rate; it is a seed bed for malnutrition and diseases such as scarlet fever, dysentery, typhoid, tuberculosis, and pneumonia; and is an arena for crimes against women and children, while bringing wealth to the Bosses of the Buildings.[106]

While perspectives such as Wright's provide insights into the origins of poverty and injustice in many of the nation's urban centers today, it is unfair to view African American migrants as mere victims. Many African American family histories include people and events connected with the Great Migration, histories laden with courageous individuals and fascinating events, as well as harrowing experiences with discrimination. Like other educators who use personal and family narratives in teaching, I have encountered numerous students with family migration stories worthy of becoming a novel or film, that focus on themes of love, escape, bravery, justice, and mystery, as well as experiences of incredible cruelty and meanness.

These family stories resonate in a study of the African American migration to Chicago, *Land of Hope* (1989).[107]

Black southern migrants were bearers of a deeply ingrained and distinctive culture; from their southern experience a race-conscious world view emerged that informed both their choice to migrate and their responses to the urban environment—responses necessarily different from those of both northern-born blacks and white ethnic immigrants.[108]

Settlement and adjustment in the north was influenced by the migrants' Southern communal and kinship networks, as in the "transfer almost intact of churches, barber shops, and other social institutions from specific southern communities;" and, "from the black perspective, class difference shaped social relations within the black community . . . while outside that community, race was the dominant variable."[109]

Throughout these decades, African Americans resisted postslavery oppression through political organizations, such as the National Association for the Advancement of Colored People (NAACP) and the Urban League, which were both organized in the first decade of the twentieth century. They have resisted with nonviolent civil disobedience, as in the bus boycotts, freedom rides, lunch counter sit-ins, and peaceful protest marches to end segregation during the civil rights movement of the 1960s. Dr. Martin Luther King Jr. epitomized the hope of African Americans in his famous "I Have a Dream" speech before tens of thousands of demonstrators—both Black and White—during the March on Washington in August 1963. African Americans have also resisted oppression with violence, as in the riots in Los Angeles (Watts in 1965 and South Central Los Angeles in 1992), in Detroit (1967), and in Newark (1967). The 1960s were years of growing Black pride and Black community consciousness. The Black Power movement and the Nation of Islam ("Black Muslims") pressed for Black identity and Black self-help enterprises. A group of young African American men formed the Black Panthers, an organization to pro-

African American teens discussing a common perspective, despite gender, socioeconomic, regional, and ethnic identity differences.

vide breakfast programs for school children and protection for the Black community against White police brutality, and a variety of other militant organizations aimed at Black nationalism and Black community support emerged.[110]

Themes of opposition and liberation are also expressed in African American literature, art, music, and film. The Harlem Renaissance was a period of vibrant creativity among African American writers and musicians during the 1920s. Artists such as Romare Bearden and Jacob Lawrence have chronicled African American history, and Black film directors such as Spike Lee portray contemporary African American perspectives.[111]

In a recent essay on Black Americans today, Harvard sociologist Orlando Patterson describes the immense progress achieved by African Americans in most areas of American life as well as the persistent challenges and difficulties that remain, such as the "dysfunctional attitudes among many inner-city youths," increasing segregation, and the achievement gap. He introduces his analysis of an "immense body of data"[112] with the following words:

> *The civil rights movement and subsequent policies aimed at socioeconomic reform have resulted in the largest group of middle-class and elite blacks in the world; yet the bottom fifth of the black population is among the poorest in the nation and, as Hurricane Katrina exposed, often live in abysmal third world conditions. Politically, blacks are a powerful presence and the most loyal members of one of the nation's two leading parties; yet, "race" still remains a central component of American politics. . . . Blacks have a disproportionate impact on the nation's culture—both popular and elite—yet continue to face major problems in the educational system and are badly underrepresented in its scientific and high-end technology. And although legalized segregation has long been abolished and antiexclusionary laws strictly enforced, the great majority of blacks still live in highly segregated communities.[113]*

Despite decades of effort to end racial oppression, and despite dramatic progress in the second half of the twentieth century, we still feel the sting of the nation's legacy of slavery. For example, the "relative fragility of the black middle class's base" is crystal clear when we look at net worth as an indicator of economic well-being. In the first decade of the twenty-first century, the average net worth of non-Hispanic Whites was $88,000, or 14.5 times greater than the $6,000 average net worth of African American householders,[114] due to "the historical legacy of low wages, personal and organizational discrimination, and institutionalized racism."[115] And although African Americans are a vibrant presence in the nation's public life and national identity, most remain "segregated from the intimate, social, communal and cultural life of white Americans," sometimes by choice and sometimes due to informal societal barriers and/or the vestiges of institutional racism.[116]

Conclusions

The histories of American Indians and African Americans differ from most other long-standing ethnic groups in the United States in that they did not enter as immigrants in pursuit of the American Dream. Indians lived throughout the Americas when the Europeans first arrived and were forcibly incorporated into U.S. society through conquest and colonization (as were Mexican Americans and Puerto Ricans as discussed in the next chapter); the vast majority of African ancestors of African Americans were seized in their homelands and forced into slavery that was among the cruelest the world has known because it separated Black families. As noted in this chapter, both the Indians and the Africans were highly diverse in terms of geographic origins, religions, languages, and cultural styles; both were non-Western in orientation and emphasized spiritual and non-material aspects of life over the technological; both experienced centuries of oppression and were denied citizenship despite their crucial, though not widely recognized, contributions to the young nation; both resisted oppression and kept aspects of their cultures alive. American Indians witnessed their lands taken by force, misunderstanding and deception, and those who did not assimilate ended up on ethnically encapsulated reservations; Africans were taken from their lands by force and were denied basic human rights and acceptance despite their close proximity to the White population.

Chapter 9, "Reaching All Learners," reveals the impact of American Indian and African American history on the school-age population, as well as history's impact on today's school children and youth of other major ethnic groups. An understanding of how history contributes to the nation's achievement gap is essential if we are to address and end the inequities in our schools and society that keep this gap alive. History exposes the origins of unequal school and societal conditions that provide unequal opportunities for children of color and the poor to learn and thrive in schools across the nation.

Selected Sources for Further Study

Appiah, K. A., & Gates, H. L., Jr. (Eds.). (2005). *Africana: The Encyclopedia of the African and African American Experience* (2nd ed.). New York: Oxford University Press.

Banks, J. A. (2008). *Teaching Ethnic Studies.* (Chapters 5 & 7.) Boston: Allyn & Bacon.

Baszile, J. (2008). *The Black Girl Next Door: A Memoir.* New York: Touchstone Books.

Bennett, L. (2007). *Before the Mayflower: A History of Black America* (New Millennium Ed.). Chicago: Johnson.

Berry, K. A., Grossman, Z., & Pawiki, L. H. (2007). "Native Americans." In I. M. Miyares & C. A. Airriess (eds.), *Contemporary Ethnic Geographies in America* (pp. 51–70). Lanham, MD: Rowman & Littlefield.

Cajete, G. (2003). *Native Science: Natural Laws of Interdependence.* Santa Fee, NM: Clear Light.

Castagno, A. E., & Brayboy, B. M. J. (2008). "Culturally Responsive Schooling for Indigenous Youth:

A Review of the Literature." *Review of Educational Research, 78,* no. 4:941–993.

Champagne, D. (2007). *Social Change and Cultural Continuity Among Native Nations.* Lanham, MD: AltaMira Press.

Feagin, J. R., & Feagin, C. B. (2008). *Racial and Ethnic Relations,* 8th ed. Upper Saddle River, NJ: Prentice Hall. (Chapter 6, "Native Americans," and Chapter 7, "African Americans".)

Horse Capture, G., Champagne, D., & Jackson, C. C. (Eds.). (2007). *American Indian Nations: Yesterday, Today, and Tomorrow* (Lanham, MD: AltaMira Press).

Levine, L. (1977). *Black Culture and Black Consciousness: Afro-American Folk Thought from Slavery to Freedom.* New York: Oxford University Press.

Lomawaima, K. T., & McCarty, T. L. (2006). *To Remain an Indian: Lessons in Democracy from a Century of Native American Education.* New York: Teachers College Press.

Mann, C. C. (2005). *1491: New Revelations of the Americas before Columbus*. New York: Knopf.

Seale, D., & Slapin, B. (Eds.). (2005). *A Broken Flute: The Native American Experience in Books for Children*. Walnut Creek, CA: AltaMira Press.

Segal, R. (2000). *Islam's Black Slaves: The Other Black Diaspora*. New York: Farrar, Straus & Giroux.

Now go to Topics #1 and 2: **Ethnicity/Cultural Diversity** and **Race** in the MyEducationLab (www.myeducationlab.com) for your course, where you can:

- Find learning outcomes for these topics along with the national standards that connect to these outcomes.

- Complete Assignments and Activities that can help you more deeply understand the chapter content.

- Apply and practice your understanding of the core teaching skills identified in the chapter with the Building Teaching Skills and Dispositions learning units.

Chapter 6

Colonialism, Immigration, and the American Dream: Latino Perspectives

Latinos in the United States: Who Are They?

The term *Latino* embraces a diverse group of peoples that includes recent immigrants from Latin American countries as well as persons whose ancestors lived in what is now the Southwestern United States. According to the U.S. Census Bureau's Department of Racial Statistics, "Hispanic Americans" or Latinos are a "pan-ethnic" category of people that can be from any racial group.[1] Their numbers are estimated to be over 42 million, making them one of the two largest ethnic groups of color in the United States, along with African Americans. Today, roughly 64 percent of Latino Americans trace their ancestry to Mexico; 9 percent are Puerto Ricans living on the mainland; 3.5 percent are Cuban Americans; and the rest have origins in El Salvador, the Dominican Republic, Columbia, Venezuela, and about two dozen other countries of Central and South America.[2] (See Table 2.2 on page 51.)

This chapter begins with a focus on Latinos whose countries of origin are islands in the Caribbean: Puerto Ricans who are citizens by virtue of their birth in an American possession, Cubans who entered primarily as refugees several decades ago, and Dominicans who provide an example of immigration in the contemporary era. The chapter then focuses on Mexican Americans, migrant workers, and four examples of contemporary Latino immigrant experiences in the heartland.

Caribbean Latinos: Puerto Ricans, Cubans, and Dominicans

Puerto Ricans, Cubans, and Dominicans have much in common in their histories and aspects of their culture, such as music, religious practices, food preferences, and political attitudes.[3] The people in all three nations are predominantly Catholic, speak the Spanish language, and come from tropical islands in the Caribbean. They endured a history of Spanish conquest and rule, although Santo Domingo also experienced periods of Haitian and French rule. To some degree they share a common heritage and worldview that stem from the cultural fusion of Spanish and Indigenous peoples' cultural values and the legacy of colonialism. Individuals in all three groups have a shared history of cultural conflicts related to the pressures of Americanization and race relations that are problematic in the United States. However, their experiences in the United States also differ dramatically due to the different times and circumstances of their entry into this country.

Puerto Ricans

As U.S. citizens at birth, Puerto Ricans are free to travel between Puerto Rico and the U.S. mainland as they wish.[4] Today, over 3.7 million Puerto Ricans live on the mainland, primarily in New York City, Chicago, and cities in New Jersey, California, and Florida. Another 3.8 million reside in Puerto Rico itself, including illegal immigrants from the Dominican Republic, many of whom later move on to the United States.[5]

Although only a small percentage of the U.S. population, their significance is great for a number of reasons.[6] According to Boswell and Cruz-Baez,

- They are the only large ethnic group to enter the United States as American citizens, and this gives them the right to move back and forth without immigration restrictions. They are the only Latino group that does not contain a significant element of "illegal aliens."[7]
- They are the first large group of American immigrants who are predominantly of mixed Black and White racial background, with some indigenous Indian mixture, suggesting "that the experience of Puerto Rican tolerance for social differences may be one of their major and enduring contributions to American society."[8]
- The population is highly mobile and returns frequently to the homeland for holidays and family events; most travel is via the 3.5-hour plane flight between San Juan and New York City and costs "an average of about one week's pay."[9] This phenomenon keeps their language and cultural traditions alive.
- The Puerto Rican government maintains offices in U.S. cities with large Puerto Rican settlements to provide a variety of social and economic supports as well as pubic relations programs. Although this involvement helps many Puerto Ricans make the transition to life in a new country, it may also inhibit "the development of powerful grass-root organizations among the Puerto Rican Americans, such as those developed historically among a number of other American immigrant groups."[10]

"Circulatory Migration" and National Identity Issues

The pattern of "circulatory migration" among Puerto Ricans has two important implications for education.[11] First, most Puerto Ricans wish to maintain their language and culture and in fact have a practical need to do so, in contrast to most European immigrants who arrived earlier and have largely assimilated. Second, Puerto Ricans have "redefined immigration from 'a single life-transforming' experience to 'a way of life'" wherein "cultural patterns are renewed, transformed, and recreated."[12] Because maintenance of the Spanish language is so essential, some mainland families send their children back to the island for extended periods to maintain cultural ties and Spanish language proficiency.

In addition to U.S. citizenship and geographic mobility, the Puerto Rican experience is also unique among immigrant groups in the United States in that Puerto Ricans are divided over the issue of national independence, statehood, or maintaining its commonwealth status. As a U.S. commonwealth, Puerto Rico is a U.S. possession subject to most federal laws. Puerto Ricans are subject to military conscription and have fought with the U.S. military in all wars since World War I, but they cannot vote in national elections and are exempt from paying federal taxes. Although Puerto Ricans are U.S. citizens, Puerto Rico is not a state and is represented only by an elected resident commissioner, who is a nonvoting member of Congress. The unsettled status question sometimes divides members of the same family as some actively seek national independence while others advocate statehood.

The Legacy of Colonialism

Colonialism refers to the conquest and rule of an indigenous people by a foreign nation that then uses the conquered people and their natural resources for its own benefit. It is estimated that nearly 40,000 Taino Indians inhabited Puerto Rico when Christopher Columbus arrived in 1493. During the Spanish takeover, indigenous people revolted; many were killed. Others escaped from the island or died from diseases. Black Africans were brought in as slaves, beginning in 1511, to replace the native laborers. Slavery was maintained in Puerto Rico until it was abolished in 1873.[13]

Spain ruled Puerto Rico for nearly 400 years, using the island primarily as a military outpost. The governance was oppressive and inept, controlled primarily by small, upper-class elites who were descendants of the original Spanish colonizers. Although the people suffered from illiteracy, poverty, and poor health, they were filled with the spirit of independence and self-government, particularly after Spain turned Puerto Rico over to the United States at the end of the Spanish-American War in 1898. The Puerto Ricans' hopes for a plebiscite to determine their political destiny were quickly shattered. During the next half a century, Puerto Rico was headed by a series of governors appointed by the U.S. government, and during this time conditions in Puerto Rico changed little from what they had been at the end of Spanish rule.[14] In 1948, Puerto Ricans elected their own governor for the first time, Luis Munoz Marin. Dramatic changes occurred during the sixteen years of his leadership. Marin helped establish Puerto Rico as a commonwealth (a result that satisfied neither the statehood nor independence advocates) and created new economic programs such as Operation Bootstrap, a plan that attracted U.S. investments to build up industry in Puerto Rico. Although the yearly per capita income increased dramatically from 1940 to 1969, Operation Bootstrap critics point out that upper-class Puerto Ricans and U.S. industrialists benefited most from the program.[15]

The legacy of colonialism is still evident in Puerto Rico's high level of unemployment and the impoverished living conditions of the urban poor. It is also evident in the Americanization of Puerto Rican schools that stress the English language over Spanish and historical figures, events, and achievements from the United States rather than Puerto Rican history. As Sonia Nieto points out, bilingual education has been the primary focus to remedy unequal education among Puerto Ricans and other Latinos, more than school desegregation. She writes,

Demands for bilingual education should not be understood outside the American dream, but as part and parcel of it. . . . The main objectives Puerto Ricans envision for education are economic security and what one might call "the good life" . . . (and) there has been no contradiction between getting a good education and retaining ethnic and linguistic identity.[16]

Cubans

Most Cubans arrived in the United States after Fidel Castro overthrew the Cuban dictatorship of Fulgencio Batista in 1959. The majority came to the United States as political refugees. They felt threatened and sought freedom and security, rather than the economic prosperity sought by most immigrant groups. Because they entered the United States during Fidel Castro's revolution in their homeland, Cubans are viewed as refugees fleeing a Communist regime and are entitled to financial assistance under the Refugee Act (see Box 4.1, pages 113–114) that most immigrants are not eligible to receive.

Cubans who entered during the U.S. government airlift between 1965 and 1973 tended to be from upper- and middle-income groups. Caucasians and Chinese Cubans were overrepresented, and there were few Black Cubans among them.[17] Most were admitted to the United States without having to wait for visas or worry about immigration quota restrictions.

The most recent wave of Cuban immigrants arrived in 1980 via the Mariel boatlift. Strongly supported by Cubans who had previously settled in the United States, a flotilla of private boats transported close to 125,000 Cuban refugees to Key

Roughly 60 percent of the Latino population in the United States trace their ancestry to Mexico.

West, Florida, between April and June of 1980. Although the first group of Cuban refugees who entered the United States received a warm welcome from Anglo society, this was not the case for Cuban immigrants who arrived in 1980 via the Mariel boatlift. In contrast to the upper-income professionals and technicians who had arrived in the 1960s, the Mariel Cubans were generally of humble origins, and their reception ranged from warm to hostile. "A Gallup poll conducted nationally in late May 1980 found that 59 percent of respondents felt that Cuban emigration was bad for the United States. In the Miami area, a similar survey conducted by the *Miami Herald* in May 1980 found that 68 percent of the non-Latino White population and 57 percent of the African American population surveyed felt that the new wave of Cuban refugees would have a negative influence on the local community."[18]

Today, there are nearly 1.5 million Cuban Americans in the United States, making them the nation's third largest Spanish-speaking ethnic group. More than half the Cuban population has settled in the greater Miami area, and there are also large communities in New York City and Los Angeles. Most Cuban refugees arrive first in Miami, the Cuban capital in the United States, which is home to over half of all Cubans living in the United States.[19] Individuals with family connections are absorbed into the Miami metropolitan area, while those who are unattached and have no other family members in the United States are forced to "resettle wherever the resettlement agency decides to locate them."[20] For over half a century, the Cuban Refugee Resettlement Program has relocated several hundred thousand Cuban refugees in over fifty cities throughout the United States, with assistance from volunteer organizations such as Catholic Social Services, the International Rescue Committee (IRC), the United Hebrew Immigrant Aid Society, and the Church World Service.[21] The experience of Cubans living in larger cities as well as in smaller isolated communities in the United States is very different from those who remain in Miami where *cubanidad* (a sense of identification with Cuba) remains strong.

Of all the Spanish-speaking ethnic groups in the United States Cuban Americans are the most economically prosperous and the most highly educated. Cuban Americans are more assimilated into U.S. society than either Puerto Ricans or Dominicans. However, they have suffered hardships, particularly those who fled Cuba after Castro took over. Most Cuban Americans express a strong desire to maintain their language and other aspects of their cultural heritage. This has important implications for schools that serve the Cuban American community, such as Dade County, Florida, where Cubans comprise one-third of the school-age population. At the same time, many Cuban Americans are "unashamedly patriotic, grateful to the United States for their freedom."[22]

Dominicans

In contrast with Puerto Ricans and Cubans, Dominicans are more representative of the post-1965 (contemporary) era of immigration to the United States. Beginning in the 1980s, the number of immigrants from the Dominican Republic increased dramatically, up from an average of less than 1,000 per year prior to the new U.S. immigration policies established in 1965.[23] By the early 1980s, "the Dominican Republic was sending more emigrants to the United States than any other country in the Western Hemisphere, except for Mexico."[24] The flow of immigrants from this Caribbean Island did not let up and between 1980–2000, with the Dominican-born population in the United States increasing from 169,147 to 687,677.[25] From 1998–2007, nearly 250,000 additional immigrants from the Dominican Republic were added to the U.S. population. In 2007 alone, over 28,000 Dominicans obtained legal permanent resident status in the United States, nearly all as immediate relatives of U.S. citizens or under family-sponsored preferences. (See Table 4.1 on page 114.)

Dominicans are motivated to immigrate primarily to find work and economic opportunities, because they come from a country with some of the highest rates of poverty in the world. Dominicans benefit from contemporary immigration policies that give preference to family reunification, and many maintain strong connections with their homeland through "financial remittance and social ties to family members still living in the Dominican Republic."[26] More than 80 percent of Dominicans settle in one of three states: New York, New Jersey, or Florida. They are city dwellers, with over 75 percent living in the New York metropolitan area, including northern New Jersey and Long Island.[27] Recently Dominican families have begun to settle in new areas, such as South Florida, Maryland, Georgia, and North Carolina.[28] Compared with Cuban Americans and Puerto Ricans, Dominican Americans have the lowest levels of income, English-speaking abilities, and educational attainment, due their recent arrival in the Unites States, and higher levels of poverty in their country of origin.[29]

Among Dominican Americans, 12.7 percent self-identify as Black, compared to 8.3 percent of Puerto Ricans and 4.9 percent of Cubans.[30] African influences are more evident in the Dominican Republic than in Cuba or Puerto Rico; Santa Domingo was the first seat of the Spanish conquest and rule of the Caribbean Islands, and after African slavery was introduced in 1501 the indigenous population "rapidly disappeared as a result of warfare, enslavement, and disease."[31] However, Latino ethnic identity is more important than racial identity for most Dominicans and Puerto Ricans. Although most Dominicans are of "African or mixed race descent," because they are the majority race in their home country many identify as either "White" or "Other" in response to the U.S. Census' question about racial identity.[32]

Mexican Americans: How Can History Help Us Understand Current Immigration Issues?

Origins of La Raza

The military conquest of the Aztec empire at the hands of Hernan Cortez and his soldiers in 1521 marks the beginning of 300 years of Spanish rule in regions that are now Mexico and the Southwestern United States. With few Spanish women migrating to the Americas, the Spanish conquerors cohabited with indigenous women and

Black women in slavery. However, the Spanish distinguished between Indians and Blacks—the latter being more vilified than the former,[33] even though "many of the Spanish colonizers had some African ancestry *before* they arrived, because of Spain's long centuries of contact with, and invasion by, peoples from Africa."[34] Under the Spanish system, Blacks could be slaves and Indians could only be *peons* (landless laborers who worked for large land owners). Together, these three groups formed a Mestizo population known as *La Raza*, "the race." Also important are the many indigenous groups, ethnically identified Indians, who still live in Mexico and who attempt to preserve their ethnic autonomy from mainstream Mexican culture.[35]

Origins in the Borderlands: Early Settlements and Law of the Indies

Mexican American populations originated in the borderlands that connect the present-day United States and Mexico, stretching nearly 2,000 miles from California to Texas. Between 1521 and 1821, Spanish-speaking people from New Spain (now Mexico) settled in portions of California, Arizona, New Mexico, Colorado, and Texas.[36] During this era of conquest, Spanish settlers sought to "civilize" and Catholicize the indigenous peoples such as the Pueblo and Pima Indians. These settlements followed the dictate of the Law of the Indies, legal codes that explained how new lands should be settled.[37] The initial frontier institutions were the mission, an extension of the Catholic Church, and the presidio, a garrison or military settlement. The third Spanish settlement institution was the pueblo, or town, which was anticipated to become a permanent civil community, in contrast to the religious and military institutions that were seen as temporary, at least in theory. According to the Law of the Indies,

> *Pueblos were to be situated on a grant of . . . approximately forty-two square miles. The center of the pueblo included a plaza, surrounded by government offices and a parish church. A rectangular grid of streets emanating from the plaza accommodated houses. Surrounding these were lands for cultivation, pasture, and woodland. The pueblos became the major nuclei of population, for attracting merchants, artisans, and farmers. Los Angeles, California, and San Antonio, Texas, for example, were founded as pueblos.*[38]

The fourth settlement institution was the land grant, a generous parcel of land deeded to private individuals as an incentive to settle new areas and make them productive as cattle and sheep *ranchos*, as in Texas and California, or farmsteads cultivating wheat and corn, as in New Mexico. Today, many land grants remain as "legal definitions of property in the borderlands."[39]

After Mexico won independence from Spain in 1821, and before the invasion of Anglo-American immigrants in the 1830s, thousands of Mexicans lived on these Mexican land grants and had established prosperous communities throughout Texas, New Mexico, Arizona, and California.[40] Within a few decades of Mexican independence, thousands of European American immigrants moved into the area and soon outnumbered the Mexican population. The Texas revolt and the annexation of Texas by the United States in 1845 triggered war with Mexico, and the United States eventually forced Mexico to cede nearly half of its territory for

$15 million.[41] Given the choice to remain on their lands or move south to Mexico, most Mexicans stayed, guaranteed by the Treaty of Guadalupe Hidalgo full rights of citizenship and protection of property. In the end, however, most Mexican landowners lost their lands to Anglo Americans. The methods of takeover ranged from "lynching, to armed theft, to quasi-legal and legal means such as forcing expensive litigation in American courts to prove land titles."[42] McWilliams explains the situation this way:

> Many of the villagers neglected to bring papers into court and often had lost evidence of title. Most of them lacked funds to defend titles: or, if they retained an Anglo-American lawyer, a large part of the land went in payment of court costs and fees. . . . Litigation over land titles was highly technical and involved; cases dragged on in the courts for years; and . . . control of resources shifted to the Anglo-American.[43]

One of the more popular techniques for expropriating land from Mexicans was taxation. "American politicians would levy property tax rates at levels that only the largest Spanish landholders could afford, thereby forcing small Hispanic entrepreneurs off their land and into wage labor."[44]

Immigration Experience

Among immigrant groups to the United States during the contemporary era, Mexican Americans have the "longest record of significant continuous flow."[45] Immigrants have entered in a variety of ways: "legals" who come with official visas; "illegals" who enter without documents; *braceros*, or "guest workers," who have government contracts to do seasonal farm work; "commuters" who have official visas, live in Mexico, and work in the United states; and "border crossers," those with short-term work permits who often become domestic workers.[46]

First Wave: 1900–1930

It is impossible to know how many people migrated between the United States and Mexico during the decades following the Treaty of Guadalupe Hildago signed in 1848 and the Gadsden Purchase of 1853, because "the border was highly porous and largely unmonitored."[47] However, during the first wave of immigration from Mexico between 1900–1930, it is estimated that millions entered California and the Southwest to meet the demand for unskilled labor in the mining, railroad, and agricultural industries.

At the turn of the twentieth century, Mexican immigrants were "pulled" to the United States by the need for labor. Previous sources of low-wage labor dwindled after the U.S. government excluded new immigrants from China (in 1882) and Japan (in 1908), the decline in European immigration during World War I, and the restrictive immigration acts of the 1920s that cut immigration to a trickle.[48] Because of this need for labor, the border was unpatrolled until 1924; after that, impediments were minor, allowing Mexicans to avoid the literacy tests and fees required for legal immigration. Simultaneously, immigrants were being "pushed from" Mexico due to precarious economic conditions that developed when land was consolidated into large, "privately owned haciendas" at the cost of small farmers, as well as the "bloody strife" and unsafe countryside during the Mexican Revolution (from 1910–1920). Thus, for the first three decades of the twentieth century "labor flowed more or less freely from Mexico into the United States" and provided the "human labor power for the region's agricultural revolution and laid the infrastructure for the modern Southwest's economy: (Mexican workers) laid railroad tracks, cleared ranch lands for farming, and dug irrigation canals."[49] Many found year-round housing on their employers' farms and ranches, while others "settled in small rural hamlets and began to raise families, even as they continued to travel frequently to Mexico."[50] Gradually, as agriculture and farm labor were transformed from small family-owned and operated farms and sharecropping to large farms and agribusinesses, farm workers could no longer find year-round work, and a migratory agricultural workforce was created.

> *Migrant streams of landless laborers, including families, now followed the seasons of cotton, fruit, and vegetable crops on a year-long search for work at wages as low as $1.50 a day. The shift overwhelmed and displaced older patterns of work and settlement. The migratory agricultural workforce drew large numbers of new immigrants from Mexico—an average of 62,000 legal and an estimated 100,000 undocumented entries a year during the 1920s—and swept more established immigrants and Mexican Americans into its embrace as well. Mexican Americans, old immigrants, and new immigrants alike worked the two major migrant streams in Texas and California; at the same time, smaller streams followed the cotton crops in Arizona and New Mexico, and reached northward to the sugar-beet fields of Colorado, Michigan, and Montana.*[51]

With passage of the restrictive immigration laws of the 1920s, the idea of Mexicans as "illegal aliens" was created. In contrast to previous decades of informal border crossings when the lack of a workable border policy encouraged "expansiveness, possibility, and lawlessness," migrants now became "illegal" because they "crossed the border without going through formal entry and inspection and therefore lacked the requisite papers" such as "visas, head-tax receipts, border-crossing cards, inspection certificates, bathing certificates, and the like."[52] The formality and complexity of the new policies generated confusion and fear of "sweeps, detainment, interrogation, and deportation" and stood as "the single greatest indication that Mexicans did not belong"; a vulnerable "alien" workforce was created that "ultimately served the interests of agribusiness."[53]

During the Great Depression, cheap Mexican labor was no longer needed and hundreds of thousands of Mexicans were sent back to Mexico in repatriation efforts carried out by both federal and local government. In some cases, immigrants who had lived in the United States for decades and had become U.S. citizens were deported. "Once back on Mexican soil, the former U.S. residents were not allowed to return. In Los Angeles, repatriation reduced the Mexican population by one-third and transformed the community into one dominated by the second generation."[54] However, when the United States entered World War II, Mexican labor was needed again and immigration policy reversed itself to encourage the inflow of workers from Mexico.

Second Wave: 1942–The Present

The Bracero Program and Encouragement of Undocumented Workers, 1942–1964
The word *bracero* is derived from *brazo*, meaning "arm" in Spanish, and is used to refer to laborers from Mexico who are admitted to the United States to work under contract, usually in agriculture. In 1942, the Emergency Farm Labor (*Bracero*) agreement was reached between Mexico and the United States to once again provide Mexican workers needed for U.S. agriculture. Under the initial wartime agreement, the United States imported several hundred thousand Mexican nationals to work in agriculture as well as railroad construction and maintenance.[55] Over the following two decades, nearly 5 million *braceros* were given contracts to work in the United States at the request of U.S. employers, and they worked in over 25 states. "The Migrant Labor Agreement stipulated that Mexican contract workers could not be used to replace domestic workers or to repress domestic farm wages. *Braceros* were guaranteed transportation, housing, food, and repatriation, and were exempt from American military service."[56] Furthermore, workers were promised wages that matched domestic rates and were guaranteed work for at least 75 percent of the contract period.

Although the program was set up as a way to end illegal immigration, it actually generated more of it. How could this happen? Illegal immigration developed as "an unintended consequence of Mexico's (initial) exclusion of Texas, Arkansas, and Missouri employers from the *bracero* program on grounds of race discrimination."[57] Mexico objected to the Jim Crow laws and racial discrimination in these states, which excluded Mexicans from public accommodations that were "White only," such as hotels, restaurants, movie theaters, swimming pools, and parks. Growers in these states that were "ineligible to use *braceros* increasingly resorted to illegal labor during the 1940s."[58] Moreover, the *bracero* program itself generated illegal immigration because the Mexican government could not accommodate all of the Mexican workers who wanted to work in the program. Those who could not get a government contract often crossed the border anyway to escape poverty in rural Mexico and support their families. Furthermore, some U.S. growers preferred to recruit farm laborers informally, because these workers could be paid lower wages than those under *bracero* contracts.[59] Thus, the recruitment and employment of *braceros* and workers without papers, known as "illegals" or "wetbacks," occurred simultaneously with legal immigration and often under the same employers.

Even though historically the Immigration and Naturalization Service (INS) has allowed "wetbacks" to enter the country whenever there is a need for cheap labor, cruel stereotypes and misinformation accompany the image of "wetbacks"—those who cross the river illegally to find work in the United States. Critics have stereotyped "wetbacks" as dangerous criminals, destitute females engaged in prostitution, and invaders who bring in "misery, disease, crime, and many other evils."[60] Eventually a racial stereotype of the "Mexican" was created and applied to individuals who were local citizens of Mexican descent; in the public mind there was no distinction between "wetbacks" and legal immigrants, even those who were U.S. citizens.

Post-Bracero Immigration

Although a great many Mexican immigrants are low-skilled workers, it is important to underscore the diversity among them. Compared to other foreign-born groups, a relatively large number are in professional occupations and have attained advanced degrees.[61] Throughout the contemporary immigration era, Mexico stands out as the largest single source of persons who obtain legal permanent resident status in the United States. Despite restrictions on immigration from Mexico, such as the 20,000 per country limit (family members are not included in this total), legal immigration has continued to grow. Why? The primary reason, besides the IRCA amnesty program, is their ability as U.S. citizens to bring family members into the nation, coupled with the "push" factors of economic recession and poverty in Mexico.

Settlement patterns established during the previous Mexican immigrant waves continue, and today approximately three-fourths of the Mexican American population lives in the original Southwestern states, the majority in California followed by Texas. Ninety percent live in urban areas, and they are a majority in Los Angeles and San Antonio. However, as noted in Chapter 4, Mexican immigrants are also settling in previously non-Latino cities and in small towns throughout the U.S. interior. Chicago has ranked as one of the top three cities of choice consistently since the 1960s, New York City is a newly preferred choice, and Mexican communities are emerging in areas new to immigration, such as the rural South. In fact, according to ethnic geographer Richard Jones,

> [Mexican] immigrants are the vanguard of new generations outside the Southwest.... Agribusinesses and the growth of new gateway cities have created unprecedented low-wage job opportunities for Mexican migrants in states such as Georgia, North Carolina, Kentucky, Kansas, and Nebraska. We are seeing a cultural transformation of the U.S. heartland as a result.[62]

However, large numbers of Mexican workers in the United States find themselves in a position of "sustained marginality." They "frequently perform 3-D jobs (dirty, dangerous and dead-end)"[63] that do not require pre-existing skill or English-language ability, such as the meatpacking plants in the Midwest and tobacco, textile, forestry, and poultry operations in the Southeast. The profitability and prosperity of agribusinesses depend on low-cost Mexican labor whose low pay and meager benefits place them at the margins of U.S. society, and among those who are undocumented "illegal" status reinforces this marginality.[64] Furthermore, Mexican immigrants and their families often experience social rejection in historically homogenous Midwestern communities as well as in bicultural towns in the Southeast where Blacks and Whites have resided for generations.

Migrant Farmworkers

Although the vast majority of Mexican Americans live in urban areas, about 10 percent are farmworkers, primarily in the migrant stream. Most are based in Texas,

California, and Florida, but they travel throughout the country, following the harvest season in the nation's fields and orchards. Of these, 70 percent are foreign born. Sixty-five percent are born in Mexico, and 5 percent are primarily from other Latin American countries, such as Guatemala and El Salvador, as well as the Caribbean Islands. Of U.S.–born farmworkers, 18 percent are White, 10 percent are Latino, and 2 percent are African American.[65]

Each year millions of farmworkers and their families migrate to the United States from their home countries to follow the agricultural crops. The $28 billion dollar fruit, vegetable, and horticultural industries in the United States are dependent on the labor of 3 to 5 million migrant and seasonal farmworkers. Yet over three-fifths of farmworker households live in poverty, earning less than $10,000 annually. This is an increase from 1990, when only half were living in poverty. Many workers live apart from their families for the agricultural season, but increasingly entire families travel together during a season. Women and children are often left out of the discussion about farmworkers, even though 19 percent of the 3 to 5 million migrant and seasonal farmworkers in the United States are women, and 8 percent are minors.[66]

Child labor is outlawed in every U.S. industry except agriculture. Exemptions under U.S. federal child labor laws allow children under the age of twelve to work as a hired worker in agriculture for an unlimited number of hours before and after school and in excess of forty hours during the school and work week. Migrant farmworker children often work and travel with their families rather than go to school, so many are not able to keep up with their classes, and eventually drop out. The average level of education for a farmworker is fifth grade.[67] Any twelve- or thirteen-year-old can work with his or her parents' consent. A child of any age can labor on farms that are not covered by the minimum-wage law, and many are not. A recent study made for the U.S. Department of Health and Human Services states, "Child labor is an economic necessity for the migrant family due to the low level of income. By the age of four, most children work in the fields at least part of the day. And older children drop out of school well before high school to work full-time in the fields."[68]

Poor health conditions among farmworkers are a major concern,[69] and they are twenty-six times more likely than the national population to contract parasitic diseases because of heavy exposure to pesticides and insecticides.[70] Other preventable diseases such as tuberculosis, influenza, pneumonia, and tooth and gum deterioration occur at a rate 200 to 500 percent higher than among the national population.[71] The rate of infant and maternal mortality is two-and-a-half times higher than the national average, contributing to an average life expectancy of forty-nine years among migrants, compared to the average North American life expectancy of seventy-four years.[72]

Latinos in the Heartland: Are They Integrating into U.S. Society?

Ethnic geographers have begun to study the "cultural landscapes" and socioeconomic adjustment of contemporary immigrants in the United States who are settling in specific communities outside the major gateway cities favored by immigrants in the past. This section presents four case studies of Latino immigrant communities to illustrate major themes and trends as well as the diversity of contemporary Latino experiences. Each study explores the degree to which immigrants are *socially integrated*, or have "established contacts with members of the dominant ethnic group(s) as neighbors, friends, club, or society members"; *economically integrated*, or have matched host society levels of occupational status, income, and education; and *acculturation* (assimilation), the adoption of "host-society cultural traits such as language, religious beliefs, preferences for food, etc."[73]

Mexican Immigrants in San Antonio, Texas

In a case study of Mexican immigrants in San Antonio, Texas, Jones studied the "adjustment of new immigrants from Mexico into an established Hispanic community with its own cultural institutions—Tejano (Texas Mexican American) life ways and language, Hispanic-run businesses, social services serving the Latino population, and strong political representation."[74] Indeed, San Antonio's established Latino neighborhoods are reflective of Mexican cultural landscapes in that the barrios include cultural elements such as "brightly colored houses, fences enclosing house properties, colorful murals in residential and commercial areas, and ethnic shopping streets."[75] Jones anticipated that new immigrants would have an easier time integrating into society in San Antonio, with its substantial Latino population and culture, than would Mexican immigrants in other parts of the country that lacked a Latino community. Instead, social adjustment was as difficult for Mexican immigrants in San Antonio as in most other parts of the United States. Study participants felt prejudice and discrimination from both established Latino residents and Anglos, and preferred to retain their original Mexican culture (which could vary according to their Mexican state of origin), to either Tejano culture or Texan culture. Over time, their socioeconomic status, income, and English-language skills remained largely unchanged and they continued to live at the margins of society.

Cuban Émigrés in Phoenix, Arizona

A case study of Cuban émigrés in Phoenix presents a different story; here "Cuban émigrés are acculturating into the Latino subculture."[76] In Phoenix, the Cuban community that was initially concentrated because of a refugee resettlement policy is largely invisible today.[77] After the first few months of settlement in Phoenix, the refugees began to disperse, and today there are few cultural imprints of the Cuban community in Phoenix. Instead, a "broader, more pan-ethnic Latino identity" has emerged among the immigrants.[78] Many émigrés joined the larger established Latino community, which is about 35 percent of Phoenix's population. Compared with the demographic profile of Cuban refugees in Miami, foreign-born Cubans in Phoenix are more likely to identify as "Nonwhite" (49.3 vs. 7.7% of Cubans in Miami), males are overrepresented (nearly 80% compared to 47% in Miami), their average age is 36.2 years (compared to 48.7 years in Miami), and just over half are married, compared to 70 percent of Cubans in Miami.[79] Cuban refugees who are unattached and have no other family members in the United States come to Phoenix without "a familial or kin social support network in place."[80] Since 1990, over

90 percent of the new Cuban refugees in Phoenix are "younger nonwhite males" who are without family or friends; they often find new sources of friendship, community, and intimate relationships in the larger Latino community.[81] Today, with about 4,000 Cuban Americans living in Phoenix, this case study provides insights into the Cuban American experience in areas beyond Miami.

Mexican Immigrants in Leadville, Colorado

Nancy Hiemstra's case study of Latinos in Leadville, Colorado, illustrates a different immigrant experience of Mexican immigrants working in low-wage jobs in a small town in the U.S. interior. Leadville is located in Lake County, a mountainous area with severe winters, where many immigrants from Mexico have settled since the mid-1980s. The U.S. 2000 Census listed the county's population as 7,812, with over 36 percent Latino.[82] Later estimates that included undocumented workers raised the figure to 50 percent, and for the 2004–2005 school year, 62 percent of the district's student population was Latino. Hiemstra gathered information through her work as a high school Spanish teacher active in the local community; reviews of local newspapers over a five-year period; semi-structured interviews, background surveys, and focus group interviews with immigrants, as well as semi-structured interviews with native-born residents.

Hiemstra writes that prior to their arrival in Leadville most Mexican immigrants "worked as ranchers, farmers, or in *maquiladora* factories" where they experienced severe economic hardships due to declining wages in these industries.[83] Now many of them work six days a week and travel forty-five to ninety minutes to and from Leadville, where they can find affordable housing. They work long hours in neighboring ski resort towns such as Vail and Breckinridge, where there is no affordable housing due to property values that have skyrocketed with the resort industry boom. Thus, these newcomers are cut off from support they might receive from their employers, and they have little opportunity to interact with the local population in Leadville, including native-born residents who are Latino, Anglo, or Asian. Living on the edge of town in isolated trailer parks and low-cost apartments and away from Leadville from dawn until late evening, most are cut off from the townspeople, who often view them with suspicion. There is little or no time for involvement in local schools, English-language classes, or community events; even grocery shopping provides limited chances for interaction with local residents because it takes place when workers with transportation are available, often after 9 P.M.

Mothers with young children and no means of transportation typically remain at home until their husbands return. This isolation has led to confusion, cross-cultural misunderstandings, conflict, and fear.[84] For example, some newcomers are surprised at the U.S. custom of shaking hands, some Anglos are angered by "Latino residents' practice of playing loud music from cars," and one Leadville resident disliked the "tendency of Mexican men to call out flirtations to women on the street" saying he did not like "the way they treat our young ladies and what have you . . . I just don't like them."[85] Schoolteachers, administrators, and social workers are critical of what they see as a lack of parental concern and involvement in the children's lives.

Language emerges as "the great divider" between immigrants and native-born residents. Hiemstra notes,

> *As in most new sites of immigration in the U.S., new Latino immigrants in Lake County usually have very limited English language skills, and the majority of native-born residents do not speak Spanish. All residents may feel frustration or anxiety when they don't understand what is being spoken around them. Sandra, a bilingual non-profit employee, put it this way: "Whenever there's a language barrier, you'll have people that are like, 'what are they saying? They're dishonest,' and they're just talking about the fruit that's on the table, same thing as we are, but it's just the misunderstanding of language."*[86]

The Leadville community typically assumes that the immigrants must learn English, and some native-born residents view their inability to use English as an "unwillingness to 'fit in.'" Some native-born residents perceive Mexican immigrants to be arrogant, conceited, and unwilling to talk with them. Few understand or are willing to accept that many Mexican immigrants act this way because they feel a lack of English-language proficiency and are afraid to speak publicly in English. Limited proficiency in English also prevents some documented immigrants from buying or renting a nice home, even if they have sufficient money, because they are unable to maneuver the paperwork. And among immigrants without legal papers, there are feelings of vulnerability, helplessness, and not belonging. As in the case of Mexican immigrants in San Antonio, Leadville's Mexican immigrants are neither socially nor economically integrated into the larger community.

Mexican Immigrants in Garden City, Kansas

A case study of Mexican immigrants working in Garden City, Kansas, by Donald Stull and Michael Broadway provides a different example of Mexican newcomers in a small town.[87] Compared to the Leadville experience, immigrants in Garden City who come to the area to work in nearby meatpacking plants are far better integrated into the broader community. A century ago, only three Mexicans lived in Garden City; today, Latinos are over 50 percent of the town's population. Meatpackers have always depended on immigrants for their labor, and it was in ready supply when the meatpackers were located in urban areas. However, as meatpacking plants have moved to small towns and rural areas, packers have had to recruit workers to these new locations. Stull and Broadway provide background about immigrants who work in the meatpacking industries that applies throughout the U.S. heartland.

> *High employee turnover, dangerous working conditions, and low wages make meatpacking jobs unattractive to many Americans, so packers have turned to immigrants and refugees for their staffing needs. When a new plant starts up, yearly turnover among line workers often reaches 200 percent or more before it drops to the industry average of 72–98 percent. . . . The industry's insatiable appetite for workers means that local labor pools are soon exhausted and plants must recruit from farther and farther afield. Current employees are frequently paid bonuses of $150–200 for recruiting new workers if they remain on the job past the probationary period of 90–120 days. This practice, in*

turn, fosters chain migration and the emergence of immigrant enclaves in packing towns, often from specific sending communities.[88]

Factory line work in packing houses does not require "preexisting job skills or knowledge of English, and the industry has a long history of hiring immigrants, many believed to be here illegally."[89] At times, the Immigration and Naturalization Service (INS) has cracked down on illegal immigration in Midwestern meatpacking plants in highly publicized raids. Several of these raids have resulted in large reductions of the labor force, causing production to drop by as much as 20 percent. Some people propose that illegal immigrants be able to apply for renewable three-year work permits to "alleviate labor shortages and improve working conditions for illegal immigrants."[90] But critics argue that because each permit applies to only one employer, this approach would put too much power in the hand of employers; other critics argue that jobs provided to these guest workers would hurt the native-born workforce.[91]

As Stull and Broadway point out, "Local communities have no choice over immigration policy or how it is enforced. Nor can they influence the meatpacking industry's working conditions, wages, or recruitment policies. But they can influence public opinion and provide immigrants with a positive context of reception."[92] In their study of Garden City, they tell the story of a city's cultural landscape that is being transformed by Mexican workers, even as the city is facing higher unemployment and poverty after three devastating blows to the town's economy between 2000 and 2003 (a fire that destroyed the ConAgra beef plant and put 2,300 workers out of a job, the aftermath of 9/11, and Tyson's reduction of weekly hours and pay after the confirmation of a case mad cow disease in the United States led to reductions in cattle prices and the blockage of U.S. beef exports to other countries). Despite the economic downturn, immigrants from Mexico, El Salvador, and Guatemala continue to come to Garden City.

Most of the immigrants have school-age children. The local school district reflects these demographic changes and has played a role in meeting the challenge of integrating newcomers who know little English and who also may be illiterate in their native language. For example, "The school district established a Newcomer Center to deal with this challenge. The center provides adult basic education, English-as-a-second-language, and survival English instruction for adults and students in grades 5–12, as well as community information on housing, health care, and education."[93] The elementary schools are racially balanced, reflecting housing patterns that show Latino neighborhoods scattered throughout the community. According to the researchers,

> *the changing demographic of the public schools have been accepted and even applauded by an increasingly progressive school board, administration, and faculty. Intramural sports, especially soccer and basketball, have been instrumental in making immigrant students feel more involved with the schools. The high school has an Asian club and Latin Lingo, a modern dance group that focuses on salsa and other contemporary dances. . . .*[94]

However, when the school held its first Latino dance none of the 250 students who attended were Anglo and "high school students segregate themselves by ethnicity in the cafeteria and most other activities."[95] Despite efforts to integrate Latinos into the school community, "they are significantly underrepresented in high school honors classes and overrepresented among students who drop out and have disciplinary problems."[96] Nevertheless, Stull and Broadway optimistically note that the principal is Latino, "twelve languages are now spoken in Garden City schools," the district is actively recruiting minority and bilingual teachers, and it offers financial incentives for teachers to increase their Spanish-language proficiency. Furthermore, small-scale minority-owned businesses have become "a robust sector of Garden City's economy"; the Mexican American presence "pervades" neighborhoods and commercial activity; interaction between native-born and immigrant Latinos is more common than in the past, and also includes Anglo and Asian Americans; and Latinos are much more visible in the community's "political fabric" than several decades ago.[97] They conclude that the American Dream is being affirmed in Garden City, as immigrants "make a new life in a new land where their children can pursue their own dream." For example, when Garden City's first new-immigrant and first Latina mayor was recently sworn in she said:

> *I am living proof that (the American Dream) is not only possible, but alive and well. . . . I feel like Laura Ingalls of the twenty-first century. Forty-two years ago, I was born in a small village with no electricity, plumbing, or a place to get primary education. . . . I want to thank my parents for having the courage to seek a better life for their children.*[98]

Selected Sources for Further Study

Acuna, R. (2007). *Occupied America: A History of Chicanos*, 6th ed. Boston: Addison-Wesley.

Banks, J. A. (2008). *Teaching Strategies for Ethnic Studies*, 8th ed. Boston: Allyn & Bacon. (Chapters 10, 11, & 12.)

Feagin, J. R., & Feagin, C. B. (2008). *Racial and Ethnic Relations*, 8th ed. Upper Saddle River, NJ: Prentice Hall. (Chapters 8 & 9.)

Ganster, P., & Lorey, D. L. (2008). *The U.S.-Mexican Border into the Twenty-First Century*, 2nd ed. Lanham, MD: Rowman & Littlefield.

Gibson, M. A., Gandara, P., and Koyama, J. P. (Eds.). (2004). *School Connections: U.S. Mexican Youth, Peers, and School Achievement*. New York: Teachers College Press.

Jones, R. C. (Ed.). (2008). *Immigrants Outside Megalopolis: Ethnic Transformation in the Heartland*. Lanham, MD: Lexington Books. (Chapters 3, 5, 6, 7, & 11.)

McKee, J. O. (Ed.). (2000). *Ethnicity in Contemporary America*. Lanham, MD: Rowman & Littlefield. (Chapters 4, 5, & 6.)

Miyares, I. M., & Airriess, C. A. (Eds.). (2007). *Contemporary Ethnic Geographies in America*. Lanham, MD: Rowman & Littlefield. (Chapters 5, 6, 8, 9, & 12.)

Ngai, M. M. (2004). *Impossible Subjects: Illegal Aliens and the Making of Modern America*. Princeton, NJ: Princeton University Press, 2004. (Chapters 3 & 4.)

Nieto, S. (2004). "Puerto Rican Students in U.S. Schools: A Troubled Past and the Search for a Hopeful Future." In *Handbook of Research on Multicultural Education*, 2nd ed. J. A. Banks & C. M. Banks, Eds., 515–541. San Francisco: Jossey-Bass.

Valdes, G. (2001). *Learning and Not Learning English: Latino Students in American Schools*. New York: Teachers College Press.

Now go to Topics #1 and 2: **Ethnicity/Cultural Diversity** and **Race** in the MyEducationLab (www.myeducationlab.com) for your course, where you can:

- Find learning outcomes for these topics along with the national standards that connect to these outcomes.
- Complete Assignments and Activities that can help you more deeply understand the chapter content.
- Apply and practice your understanding of the core teaching skills identified in the chapter with the Building Teaching Skills and Dispositions learning units.

Chapter 7

Contemporary Immigration and the American Dream: Asian, Muslim, and Arab American Perspectives

 ## Who Are the Asian Americans?

Asian Americans, like Latinos in the United States, are a pan-ethnic group of more than a dozen distinct ancestry groups with origins in Asia or the Pacific Islands. (See Table 2.2 on page 51 and Table 9.4 on page 269.) In 2004, Asian Americans numbered 14 million, or 4.7 percent of the U.S. population.[1] This is a dramatic jump from 3.5 million in 1980. As the nation's second fastest growing racial group on a percentage basis, it is estimated that Asian Americans will reach 6.4 percent of the U.S. population by the mid-twenty-first century.[2] The dramatic increase in the number of Asian Americans has been accompanied by equally dramatic shifts in their nations of origin due to passage of the Immigration Act of 1965 and the abolishment of national origins quotas. Prior to 1970, two-thirds of all Asian Americans were of Japanese or Chinese origin; in 1970, Japanese formed the largest group, but the Chinese surpassed them in 1980. Since the end of the war in Vietnam, Laos, and Cambodia in 1975, over a million Southeast Asians and even larger numbers of Koreans, Filipinos, and Asian Indians have immigrated to the United States.[3]

Their reasons for coming to the United States are profoundly different, as are their experiences once they arrived.

The early Chinese, Japanese, and Filipino immigrants were primarily healthy young men with families waiting for them to return with a share of America's wealth. Few got rich. Like gold seekers from our eastern states, many returned poor and embarrassed at their failure. Those who stayed, however, found in the United States an economy eager for muscle power and placing no premium on formal education. Compare that experience to (contemporary) refugees from nations decimated by war. Strong young men have been killed by the thousands, leaving their widows, children, and elderly parents to migrate to safety. . . . In the United States they find few jobs not requiring skill in English and extensive formal education. For many refugee families, only the children can hope to share fully in the American promise.[4]

Our discussion of Asian Americans begins with Chinese, Japanese, and Filipino Americans, as they all had substantial numbers of immigrants prior to 1965 when changes in immigration law opened up the contemporary era. Although, the number of immigrants from Japan has declined in recent years, the number of immigrants from China and the Philippines have increased significantly since 1970 and are second only to Mexico. Our discussion will then turn to Korean, Asian Indian, and Vietnamese Americans, whose countries of origin have (along with China and the Philippines) ranked in the top ten sources of immigrants to the United States during the contemporary era.

Chinese Americans

Chinese Sojourners

The first Asians to enter the United States in sizable numbers were from China, coming not as immigrants, but as sojourners who intended to return to their families in China. When China opened up to outside trade in the mid-1800s, family elders sent their youngest sons to work temporarily under labor contracts in other countries. "Permanent emigration of families was not really an option because Chinese believed in living close to their ancestral grounds."[5] Between 1840 and 1900, 2.5 million Chinese left China for temporary work in other countries such as Cuba, Peru, Hawaii, Sumatra, Malaysia, Australia, New Zealand, and Vietnam. Three hundred thousand came to the United States to work first in the gold mines and mining communities and then later on the railroads.[6]

> The Chinese were first hired to work on the transcontinental railroad because the owners could not attract enough white workers. At the time the lure of gold in the mountains was still greater than the pay of a railroad job. The railroad owners at first did not think the Chinese had the stamina for such difficult work but the Chinese proved themselves excellent workers. Charles Crocker; one of the Big Four, said, "They worked themselves to our favor to such an extent that if we were in a hurry . . . it was better to put the Chinese on at once." In time, workers were recruited directly from China, as the Chinese labor force swelled to nearly 14,000 men.[7]

With the completion of the railroads in the 1870s, anti-Chinese feeling began to intensify as cheap Chinese laborers flooded markets where non-Chinese workers had been employed. After more than a decade of anti-Chinese journalism, violence, and active struggle on the part of the Chinese for civil rights and equality, Congress passed the Chinese Exclusion Act in 1882. This law prohibited Chinese laborers from entering the United States and denied those Chinese already here the right to become naturalized citizens. Implying that they were undesirable solely on the basis of their ethnicity, the Exclusion Act had a devastating impact on the Chinese American community, and their numbers shrank to only 60,000 in 1920.[8] The population was predominantly men since only the very wealthy Chinese had been able to bring their wives and families with them. Mae Ngai summarizes this history in an eloquent paragraph.

The Chinese have the dubious distinction of being the only group to be excluded from immigration into the United States explicitly by name. The Chinese exclusion laws, which barred all Chinese laborers from entry and prohibited Chinese from acquiring naturalized citizenship, generated the nation's first illegal alien citizens. Although the Supreme Court ruled in 1898 that Chinese born in the United States were citizens, the premises of exclusion—the alleged racial unassimilability of Chinese—powerfully influenced Americans' perceptions of Chinese Americans as permanent foreigners. Excluded from the polity and for the most part confined to Chinatown ghettoes and an ethnic economy, Chinese Americans remained marginalized from the mainstream of society well into the twentieth century.[9]

The public's image of the Chinese changed from "despised Oriental 'other'" to friendly ally during World War II, and then to "dangerous Communist threat" during the Cold War.[10]

The Contemporary Era

As noted previously, Chinese immigration to the United States has increased substantially in recent decades. With the arrival of Chinese people from Taiwan, Hong Kong, Southeast Asia, and the Chinese mainland, they are much more diverse than in the past when most came from the rural counties of China's Pearl River Delta. A majority of Chinese newcomers now enter as immediate relatives of U.S. citizens and settle in existing Chinatowns where they find work in "ethnic firms."[11] Most of the others are highly educated professionals who attain advanced degrees from American universities and obtain legal permanent status in the United States under employment-based preferences. Smaller numbers enter as refugees or asylees, such as student protestors after the Tiananmen Square tragedy. There is also a sizable but unknown number of undocumented immigrants, most of whom disappear into Chinatowns in our coastal cities, such as New York, San Francisco, and Los Angeles. As a result, two social patterns have emerged within Chinese American communities today. Some social scientists refer to Chinese immigrants who settle in Chinatowns as the "Downtown Chinese," while the "Uptown Chinese" are those who have moved out of Chinatown, or have never lived there, and are more socially integrated into the mainstream society.[12] Immigrants in the first group typically enter with little income, educational background, or knowledge of English. Many move into large Chinatown communities "where they are culturally protected" but often experience economic exploitation by other Chinese.[13] Today, hundreds of thousands of Chinese still live in Chinatown ghettos.

Because of crowding and poor housing conditions, the incidence of tuberculosis, mental illness, drug abuse, and alcoholism are high; crime is increasing and juvenile street gangs are not uncommon. Chinese in these ghettos still feel the remnants of racial bias from their host cities and believe they are too often left to solve their problems alone. Recent immigrants, often unable to speak English and sometimes here illegally, do not have the same rights and privileges as other Americans and may be abused and exploited by other Chinese who need their inexpensive labor services.[14]

The second settlement pattern refers to recent immigrants with strong educational backgrounds and professional skills, as well as second-, third-, and fourth-generation Chinese immigrants ("Uptown Chinese") who, several decades ago, were highly dispersed and integrated into mainstream society. Today, a somewhat different pattern is emerging. In large metropolitan areas that have large concentrations of new highly educated immigrants as well as traditional Chinatowns, such as Atlanta and Houston, we find

> *the emergence of clustered business areas for Chinese and other Asian-owned commercial establishments such as restaurants, a variety of retail shops, and green groceries. Often nearby are found substantial but not exclusive Chinese and Asian residential communities in middle-income suburban areas; these include not only Chinese but Korean, Vietnamese, and sometimes Filipinos. These new communities are in between the highly segregated Chinatowns and the highly dispersed and better-integrated social patterns of Chinese professionals of the 1970s and 1980s.*[15]

Today, Chinese Americans are highly admired; as a group (along with Korean, Filipino, and Asian Indian Americans) they "are more educated, better employed, and enjoy higher incomes than the average citizen, and they are often lauded as a prime example of success in the 'American Way.'"[16] However, we must also keep in mind the realities of Chinatown that "for many of the first generation and recent immigrants is the American dream unfulfilled."[17]

Japanese Americans

Japanese Laborers

Japanese laborers were the first Asian immigrants to follow the Chinese. When they entered the United States in the late 1800s, the Japanese inherited a climate of anti-Asian feeling directed previously at the Chinese. However, there were important differences as well as similarities in the early Japanese and Chinese experiences.

In 1868, Japan sent 148 contract laborers to work in the sugarcane fields of Hawaii.[18] These laborers were city folk, unskilled in farm work. The experiment ended in an embarrassing failure, and the laborers were sent home. However, the incident led to deeper involvement of the Japanese government in the lives of Japanese workers abroad than was the case for the Chinese and greater protection of Japanese citizens living in other countries. Japanese emigration proceeded slowly and was legalized in 1885. As was true for the Chinese and many other immigrant groups, the Japanese came to the United States to gain wealth.[19]

Despite strong anti-Asian feelings that were directed initially at the Chinese, the number of Japanese immigrants jumped from 25,000 in 1900 to 70,000 by 1910, triggering headlines in California newspapers that protested the "Yellow Invasion of California."[20] Wishing to avoid the embarrassment of another exclusion act, in 1907 President Theodore Roosevelt negotiated the Gentlemen's Agreement between the United States and Japan. The agreement meant that Japan would stop issuing passports to Japanese laborers. However, the wives, children, and parents of laborers already in the United States, as well as professionals, were allowed to immigrate.

Although the agreement drastically reduced the number of Japanese immigrants to the United States, it avoided the bachelor-oriented society the exclusion acts had created for the Chinese. As Japanese men saved enough money to start families, their families in Japan would arrange a marriage between the son and a daughter of good family background. Usually, the son would not return to Japan to be present at the ceremony and was represented by proxy. The bride would then sail to America, where her husband would meet her, using her picture as a means to identify her, creating what was called the "picture bride" phenomenon.[21]

Land Issues

Most Japanese immigrants, known as *Issei*, settled in Hawaii and California. Many worked in agriculture, beginning as tenant farmers and then saving money to buy their own land. Through the use of muscle power rather than machines, the *Issei* converted lands never previously farmed, and by 1920 they worked over 50 percent of the California acreage dedicated to hand-labor crops. These successes triggered actions such as California's alien land law that made it illegal for individuals ineligible for citizenship, that is, the *Issei*, to own land. By 1920, fourteen states passed such legislation. To circumvent these acts, the *Issei* purchased land in the names of their children, for the *Nisei* (the second generation) were U.S. citizens by birth and could own land even as infants.[22]

Imprisonment of Japanese Americans During World War II

By far the most tragic example of prejudice and discrimination directed at Asian Americans occurred after Japan bombed Pearl Harbor. On February 19, 1942, President Franklin D. Roosevelt signed Executive Order 9066, which mandated the relocation of Japanese people living on the West Coast. More than 110,000 of the 126,000 Japanese in the United States were affected, two-thirds of whom were native-horn U.S. citizens.[23] Initially, the evacuees were housed in temporary centers that had been hurriedly converted from fairgrounds, racetracks, and livestock exposition halls. Mine Okubo, an evacuee, describes the conditions:

> *The guide left us at the door of Stall 50. We walked in and dropped our things inside the entrance. The place was in semidarkness; light barely came through the dirty window on either side of the entrance. A swinging half-door divided the 20 by 9 foot stall into two rooms. . . . The rear room had housed the horse and the front room the fodder. Both rooms showed signs of a hurried whitewashing. Spider webs, horsehair, and hay had been whitewashed with the walls. A two-inch layer of dust covered the door, but on removing it we discovered that linoleum . . . had been placed over the rough manure-covered boards. We opened the folded cots lying on the floor of the rear room and sat on them in the semidarkness. We heard someone crying in the next stall.*[24]

Later, the Japanese Americans were moved to one of ten permanent camps that sometimes housed as many as 20,000 people. Germans, Italians, and Japanese in Hawaii were also threatened, and some Japanese were relocated into concentration camps. The camps were bordered with barbed wire, guarded by the military, and offered little privacy. Some object to the label "concentration camp" because it associates the Japanese American relocation experiences with the Holocaust in Germany, where 6 million Jews and another 6 million people from marginalized groups were annihilated. There are, of course, significant differences in the two experiences: Few Japanese were killed, and many who could prove their loyalty were released to fight in the war, participate in work-release programs, or move east. Nevertheless, the experience represents a massive violation of the civil rights of over 100,000 people and brought unjustifiable personal tragedy and financial ruin to many of them. Even though the War Relocation Authority (WRA) was established to supervise the evacuations and the Federal Reserve Bank was ordered to protect their property, most evacuated Japanese Americans suffered great financial losses, ultimately mounting to over $400 million.[25] President Ronald Reagan signed a reparation bill in 1988 that provided $20,000 to be paid to each surviving Japanese American who had been interned, but these people's personal and financial losses can never be fully recovered.

Why did it happen? The forced imprisonment of Japanese Americans has traditionally been explained from a military viewpoint. Japan had attacked the United States, and the West Coast was particularly vulnerable to sabotage because of the military facilities concentrated along the coastline. It was feared that the Japanese (as well as Germans and Italians) were engaged in espionage. Others have emphasized strong racist anti-Japanese prejudice that had long infected California as well as the federal government. (See anti-Japanese legislation at both the federal and state levels.[26]) Still others emphasize the role of farm and business elites eager to eliminate Japanese competition. Most non-Japanese Americans do not understand the impact of the relocation experience on the Japanese American community. The loosening of family ties between *Issei* and *Nisei* is only one example. Also little known is the fact that Japanese Americans did protest and resist their imprisonment, that many Japanese soldiers fought with great valor during the war, and that returning home after 1945 many Japanese Americans could not regain their farms and businesses and faced violence and discrimination in their communities. As a result of this history, many Japanese American adults still feel an anxiety about the security of their daily lives in U.S. society.[27]

From "Yellow Peril" to "Model Minority"

Japanese Americans are often regarded as a classic example of the U.S. success story. Stereotyped earlier as the "Yellow Peril," now they are often stereotyped as the model minority. Japanese Americans have one of the highest literacy rates of any ethnic group in U.S. society, tend to be financially well off, and have been assimilated into the predominant language and religion. The similarity between traditional Japanese values and attitudes and the dominant culture may be a superficial mask hiding some deep cultural differences.

> *Acculturation for the Japanese has in some ways been less difficult, because of a rough similarity in certain Japanese and core culture values. Certain traditional Japanese values such as enryo, the deferential or self-denying behavior in a variety of situations, and*

the ancient Buddhist-Confucian ethic of hard work aimed at individual honor and the success of the group have been useful for the Japanese operating in the United States context. Enryo was useful in coping with oppression and bears some similarity to the Protestant Ethic. As a result, Japanese Americans have sometimes been viewed in recent years as "just like whites." Yet the basic values are, in a number of ways, still fundamentally Japanese. In this sense, then, complete acculturation has not been fully attained. What appears to be Anglo conformity acculturation may not always be so.[28]

The success of Japanese Americans in U.S. society is often used as an example of what other non-Whites, particularly African Americans and Mexican Americans, could also accomplish. However, sociologists point out a number of factors that contributed to the success of Japanese Americans and Jewish Americans that were not available to larger oppressed groups, such as African Americans.[29]

The Contemporary Era

Today there are over 1.2 million Japanese Americans. They have settled primarily in the Western states, especially California and Washington. Among Asian Americans as a whole, Japanese Americans have the highest percentage born in the United States, as a result of their early entry and smaller number of recent immigrants.[30] And among the largest Asian American groups in the United States (Japanese, Chinese, Filipino, Korean, Vietnamese, and Asian Indian), they have the highest number reporting two or more Asian groups and/or some non-Asian ancestry.[31] The *Nisei*, *Sansei*, and *Yonsei* (second-, third-, and fourth-generation Japanese Americans) are more socially and occupationally mobile than the original *Issei* (first-generation), and many of the old Japan towns (ethnic enclaves that provided Japanese American communities with goods and services unavailable in the larger community) have disappeared.[32]

Beginning in the 1980s, Japanese immigration to the United States increased significantly (although it later declined when the Japanese economy was strong and may continue to fluctuate with economic changes).[33] Many of these newcomers are employees of Japanese companies (called *chuzaiin*) operating in the United States who bring their families with them for a two- to five-year period before returning home. The children attend public schools in the United States and also go to private, after-school Japanese schools to help them negotiate their return home in a few years. This phenomenon has created a stereotype of contemporary Japanese immigrants as "fixed-term migrants" who live in separate Japanese-oriented communities that they have created in the United States.[34] However, ethnic geographic researchers point out that there are many other types of Japanese migrants today. For example, many choose to migrate for "personal lifestyle reasons," especially single women who seek alternatives to Japan's strict gender role expectations that limit their opportunities.[35] Both Japanese men and women who are single migrate as a result of widespread media exposure to American culture to seek opportunities as artists, musicians, filmmakers, or fashion designers. Moreover, given the relative ease of obtaining a student visa, many young adults enter the United States as students.

Filipino Americans

The Classic Era

Filipinos were the third major group of migrants from Asia to enter the United States. After Spain ceded the Philippines to the United States and the United States defeated the Philippine independence movement, Filipinos could enter the country with the legal status of "American nationals" and were not included in laws that excluded other Asian immigrants. During the first years of American rule in the Philippines, "the territorial government sponsored several hundred students from elite families" to study law, medicine, higher education, and politics in the United States.[36] The emigration of laborers was discouraged at first, but beginning in the 1920s Filipino immigration to the United States gained momentum, peaking in the 1930s during the Great Depression. Single male laborers (primarily in agriculture) came to "fill the niches left vacant by the exclusion of Japanese, Koreans and South Asians following the Immigration Act of 1924."[37] Similar to the Chinese and Japanese sojourners who preceded them, Filipinos entered the migrant stream to work long hours in the fields of California, Oregon, and Washington as well as the Alaskan salmon fisheries.[38] They, along with Mexicans, became the mainstay of migrant labor in California agriculture. Others found work as household servants or in "hotels and restaurants as bellmen, cooks, janitors, and dishwashers," and by 1930 there were over 56,000 Filipinos living on the West Coast.[39] As sojourners, most expected to return home, but very few did so.

Unlike the early Japanese immigrants, Filipino workers did not send for wives or establish ethnic communities that could provide economic and social support. They also differed from previous Asian immigrants in two significant ways. First, they became active in Filipino labor movements that led to a reputation for "independence" and triggered a backlash from "both white farm owners and laborers from Oklahoma with whom they competed."[40] Second, "interracial dating and marriage between Filipino laborers and white women also provoked the anger of whites, resulting in the extension of the anti-miscegenation law by the California state legislature to include the 'Malay' race in its general prohibition of interracial union applying to the black and 'Mongolian' races."[41]

After more than a decade of near invisibility, Filipinos became the target of violence and major riots throughout California. As a result, in 1934 the U.S. Congress passed legislation granting independence to the Philippines and limiting immigration to fifty persons per year, the lowest of any nation. There was also an offer to repatriate Filipinos, who could then not re-enter the United States unless they were included in the fifty-person quota. Slightly over 2,000 Filipinos accepted the offer of a paid trip back to the Philippines.[42]

The Contemporary Era

The second wave of Filipino immigrants differs dramatically from the first wave of single male sojourners who came primarily as agricultural laborers.[43] As is characteristic of most contemporary immigrants, the majority of Filipino immigrants are well-educated professionals and highly skilled technical workers; only about 10 percent come as laborers. They are fluent in English, financially middle income or higher, and come with families, prepared to settle in the United States. According to Alba and Lee, this second stream of Filipino immigrants is largely invisible, because the immigrants assimilate rapidly into U.S. society, finding jobs in mainstream institutions and living primarily in suburban, mixed neighborhoods.[44] Moreover, as a major source of medical doctors, nurses, and hospital staff, they are helping meet national shortages in the health professions. In contrast to the assimilationist perspective, other scholars point to youth gangs among contemporary Filipino youth from upper- and middle-income families as an indicator of racialized ethnic identity.[45]

Asian Indian Americans

The Classic Era

Although there were fewer migrants from India than from China, Japan, or the Philippines prior to 1965, their early story is an important one. Most were Sikhs from the Punjab region of India, and they, too, first arrived as single male sojourners in response to demands for cheap labor in the United States. They worked in the sawmills, railroads, and the migrant stream of farmworkers. Like the Filipinos, they did not establish ethnic communities, but some eventually leased land from White landowners and established productive farms, "growing crops such as rice and cotton that were familiar to them from their native farms in the Punjab region."[46] Although Indians were classified as Caucasians, they were included in the U.S. government's Asian exclusion acts and were therefore not eligible for naturalized citizenship or continued immigration. Challenging their inclusion in these acts, in 1910 and 1913 the courts ruled in their favor and affirmed that because of their Aryan origins Indians were indeed White and therefore entitled to naturalized citizenship. However, the U.S. Supreme Court later reversed these decisions in 1923 and ruled in accordance with the "common man's understanding" of Whiteness that was limited to "Whites from Europe."[47] This ruling was devastating to Asian Indians living in the United States, some of whom had brought their wives from India and, thinking they were eligible for naturalized citizenship, had raised their children to believe in the American Dream.

The Contemporary Era

Since the passage of the Immigration Act of 1965, Indian Americans have increased their numbers to over 2.5 million today. Three periods, or mini-waves, of migration are evident, beginning with large numbers of skilled (mostly male) professionals in medicine, education, and engineering who entered between 1965 and 1980.[48] Few wives were formally educated; their husbands had little difficulty finding well-paying professional jobs, and together they raised children who are now a new adult generation of Indian Americans. This second generation is well educated, fluent in English, and widely dispersed throughout the United States, but especially in New York City, New Jersey, Los Angeles, Chicago, and Houston.[49] A second group began arriving in the 1970s, and it included more well-educated professional women and a more diverse mix of occupations.[50] The third and larger group of newcomers included many family members sponsored by earlier immigrants. Today we find "The image of the Indian doctor or engineer is slowly being accompanied by that of the computer programmer, motel owner, cab driver, and convenience store clerks . . . (and) many newcomers since the 1980s have entered one of the nation's most dangerous jobs—cab drivers in metro areas."[51] To date, there is little interclass unity between the most recent arrivals and the first group of professionals.[52] However, all are potential victims of racial stereotyping, hate crimes, and attacks on their religion.[53] (Although most Indian Americans are Hindi, the major religious traditions also include Jain, Sikh, Muslim, Hare Krishna, Christian, and Parsi.) Prior to September 11, 2001, South Asians were the victims of more hate crimes than any other Asian American group in the United States and since that tragedy such attacks have intensified.[54] In her 2006 book, *New Roots in America's Sacred Ground*, Professor Khyati Joshi writes about the growing "racialization of religion," whereby physical attributes associated with nationality groups and particular religions are linked, leading to discrimination and violent attacks on schoolchildren and adults. In post–9/11 U.S. society, Hindus, Muslims, Sikhs, South Asian Christians, and Jews are targeted, because many Americans have assumed that people with brown skin are Muslim.[55]

Korean Americans

From the Classic to the Contemporary Era

Small numbers of Koreans entered the United States during the late 1800s and early twentieth-century, first as "students, political exiles, ginseng merchants, and migrant laborers," and later as laborers contracted to work on Hawaiian sugarcane

A multicultural classroom in action.

plantations.[56] Korean women first entered as "picture brides" of earlier immigrants or political refugees until the 1924 Immigration Act cut off immigration from Asian nations.[57] At the end of World War II, after Congress amended the War Brides Act, servicemen who had married Asian women could bring them into the United States where they would be eligible for naturalized citizenship. Many wives were Korean, and Korean orphans adopted by Americans after the war also added to the numbers of Korean immigrants. However, not until the contemporary era of immigration opened up in the late 1960s did Korean immigration become substantial. Indeed, by the end of the 1980s, Koreans were among the top five immigrant groups (after Mexicans and Filipinos).[58] Since the 1990s, however, the rate of immigration has declined with the growth of a burgeoning economy in South Korea. Today, there are over 1.5 million Korean Americans, comprising about 10 percent of the Asian American population.[59]

Selectivity and Homogeneity

Alba and Lee point out the striking selectivity of the Korean immigration, making it a relatively homogenous group.[60] Most Koreans came from just one city, Seoul; most are highly educated professionals from the urban middle class, with over 70 percent having attained college and postgraduate degrees; and because most intend to settle permanently in the United States they arrive with families, having sold their homes and other assets to facilitate the transitions to work in the United States.[61] Why do they emigrate? Dana Reimer argues that the answer is more than economic opportunities or escape from political instability, but rather, "the vast majority of immigrants are both charmed and enchanted by the picture of an America they learned from both the Korean and American media. In Korea, this is described as 'American fever.'"[62] She also credits the powerful military, political, and economic connections established between Korea and the United States during the Korean War and the "American Christian missionaries who first established Western-style schools and hospitals in Korea" at the turn of the nineteenth century.[63] Part of the complex dynamics of Korean immigration, especially after the 1980s when South Korea had become economically prosperous, is the desire of many Korean parents to give their children better educational opportunities, especially a college education.[64]

Today, about half of Korean Americans have settled in California, New York, and New Jersey. The rest are dispersed in urban areas across the country. The cultural homogeneity of Korean society in terms of language and literacy (Korea has only one national language and close to 100% of the population is literate) contributes to a strong sense of ethnic identity among Korean Americans.[65] For example, many Korean immigrants who are unfamiliar with the English language depend on Korean-language media to keep abreast with the news and to gain needed information and, as a result, many first-generation Koreans are slow to adapt to mainstream American society.[66]

The Korean Christian Church

The Korean Christian Church plays an important role in the lives of Korean immigrants and is a center of Korean communal life in the United States. Only about

25 percent of the South Korean population is Christian in a country dominated by Buddhism and Confucianism, but most of those who immigrate to the United States are active Christians.[67] Today, there are about 2,500 Korean Protestant churches in the United States, and they are the center of Korean communal life. According to Alba and Lee, "Korean ministers are heavily involved in community service, from matchmaking to interpreting for newly arrived immigrants and helping them find jobs and housing."[68] Although Korean Americans are widely dispersed in urban areas, they remain connected through church activities. Dana Reimer explains that entire Sundays are "given over to a combination of worship and social activities. Korean small-business success is, in part, promoted by church-sponsored activities."[69] For example, church members organize credit clubs and employment networks. Korean churches also help keep many aspects of traditional Korean culture alive by providing language instruction, sponsoring cultural events for children, and celebrating important Korean holidays.

Entrepreneurship and Socioeconomic Issues

Today, Korean Americans are known for their success as small-scale entrepreneurs, having the "highest self-employment rate of any of the post-1965 immigrant groups."[70] Given that very few Korean immigrants have a business background, one wonders why this is the case. According to Pyong Gap Min, large numbers of Korean immigrants operate a small business of their own because of language barriers and rejection of their Korean credentials, making it difficult to find employment in their areas of training and expertise.[71] Like Japanese and Chinese workers in the past, Koreans have created their own businesses and/or work as "minority middlemen," and many newcomers find initial jobs in Korean-owned businesses that are far below their qualifications. This has led to "a high level of self-segregation that has delayed substantial adaptation to mainstream culture."[72] Furthermore, today's extensive involvement of Korean immigrants in middleman businesses located in Black neighborhoods has resulted in racial conflict and deep mistrust in both communities, as depicted in Spike Lee's film *Do the Right Thing.*

> The climax of Korean-African American conflict came during the Los Angeles riots of 1992. Approximately 2,300 Korean-owned businesses in South Central Los Angeles and Koreatown were damaged or destroyed, primarily by arson and/or looting, totaling more than $350 million in damage. Many of these businesses never recovered. The failure of the police to protect them and of the government to financially help them rebuild has bred long-lasting resentment. . . . [73]

According to Alba and Lee, Korean immigrants are willing to set up businesses that serve the inner city "even in the face of growing hostility toward them from the black community," because it is highly profitable and can enable them to move into more affluent suburban neighborhoods and eventually provide educational opportunities for their children, the second generation.[74] However, among all the Asian American groups, with the exception of Vietnamese Americans, Koreans have the lowest median income and the highest rate of families living below the poverty level

(11.2% in 2005).[75] Furthermore, a recent study of Korean immigrant workers, about 30 percent of them undocumented, reveals that

> *(M)any low-wage service workers—often working in restaurants, groceries, nail salons, construction, and dry cleaning businesses—are seriously exploited by their employers, some of whom are also Asian American. They are often made to work long hours and are not given work benefits to which they are entitled.*[76]

The significant number of undocumented workers living in Korean American communities has led to increased protests against anti-immigrant legislation and support for immigrant-legislation reform.[77]

Vietnamese Americans

The most recent immigrants from Asia are from Southeast Asian countries. In contrast to the early groups of Chinese, Japanese, and Filipino laborers who arrived over a century ago, today's Southeast Asian immigrants are a heterogeneous group that includes large numbers of well-educated families and leaders from South Vietnam, "destitute boat people, who are in large part ethnic Chinese from Vietnam, and largely non-literate mountain tribesmen, like the Hmong and Mieu from Laos and Vietnam."[78] Prior to 1975, there were approximately 10,000 Southeast Asians living in the United States, mostly from Vietnam.

First Wave of Refugees

With the fall of Saigon in 1975, there was a mass exodus of Vietnamese citizens to the United States. It began with the "baby lift," which brought nearly 3,000 children to the United States, most of them orphans, and continued with the evacuation of approximately 145,000 Southeast Asian refugees. Most of these individuals had been associated with the war effort in Vietnam. Approximately 40 percent of them were school-age children.[79]

In contrast to the second wave of refugees that began in 1976 and continues to the present, this first group was relatively homogeneous in terms of nationality, socioeconomic background, education, and familiarity with Western societies. Thuy states,

> *Before their arrival in the United States, a good number of them were not only already well-educated and from well-to-do families by Vietnamese standards, they also had been exposed to Western culture and the English language, due to the French occupation and American involvement in Vietnam. Many were professionals and/or members of the educational and social elite, and, generally speaking, they had occupied relatively high economic statuses in their native country.*[80]

Second Wave of Refugees

The second wave of refugees was much more diverse and, in general, could be characterized as suffering from poorer health, being from lower educational and socioeconomic backgrounds, and having less exposure to Western culture. For the most part, this second group included "the Laotian refugees and the Hmong tribes people of Laos who crossed the Mekong River to Thailand; the Cambodian refugees who escaped famine and the war in Cambodia to enter Thailand; and the Vietnamese and Chinese Vietnamese who set sail from their homeland to seek asylum in refugee camps and who have been known as 'the boat people.'"[81]

It is estimated that over 40 percent of those fleeing perished during the escape. Many of the children and adults who arrived in the United States, as well as in other host countries (such as Australia, Canada, China, and France), experienced traumatic ordeals and harrowing escapes. Those who fled and left family members behind, often because of the desire to spare wives and children the physical dangers, suffer from guilt, depression, and loneliness.

Although the U.S. government passed emergency legislation that provided over $400 million for assistance in the resettling process, the sudden arrival of 150,000 refugees between 1975 and 1976 caught the U.S. public and refugee service providers off guard. This state of unpreparedness added to the culture shock that accompanied resettlement in a new country where the language and way of life, as well as the legal, economic, and transportation systems, were all foreign. Although the U.S. government's original plan was to disperse the refugee population evenly across the fifty states, after a short period of resettlement many of the refugees have moved to ethnic clusters located in Florida, Louisiana, Texas, Washington, D.C., and California. These secondary and tertiary migrations are often inspired by a desire to live among their own people with whom they feel more comfortable, as well as a desire for warmer weather, jobs, and better educational opportunities. In some cases, ugly hostility in the larger community has forced many of the refugees to withdraw into ethnic enclaves for protection and comfort.[82] However, the refugees from Southeast Asia have not faced the severe discrimination and prejudice experienced by their predecessors from China and Japan. In fact, many communities and individual family sponsors have provided warm welcomes.

The Contemporary Immigrant Experience

It is possible that the Japanese American experience will provide a model for the new immigrants from Southeast Asia, the Vietnamese, Cambodians, and Laotians. Butterfield reports that among the children of 6,800 Indochinese who have arrived in the United States since 1978, "one-quarter . . . earned straight As and 44 percent got an A average in math, though two-thirds of them arrived in the United States knowing no English."[83] These successes are attributed to a belief in the efficacy of hard work and the malleability of human nature, part of the Confucian ethic: "The belief that people can always be improved by proper effort and instruction is a basic tenet of Confucianism. This philosophy, propounded by the Chinese sage in the fifth century B.C., in time became a dynamic force not only in China but also in Korea, Japan, and Vietnam, sanctifying the family and glorifying education."[84]

A top priority among Southeast Asians is acquisition of the English language. Learning English can be frustrating for both students and teachers, particularly among second-wave refugees who have had little or no previous exposure to Western languages, because English and the various Southeast Asian languages share little in common linguistically. Nevertheless, as noted previously, many U.S. schoolchildren from Southeast Asian families are successful. However, because they are Asian, many are also victims of the "model minority myth" associated with Japanese Americans. Stereotypes about Asian "whiz kids" and jealousy over the relatively high percentages of Asian Americans in the nation's colleges and universities may blind some non-Asian parents, fellow students, and teachers to the deep cultural conflict many Southeast Asian Americans face in our schools. Thuy describes the kind of clashes that occur in Asian families and within schools.

> *Practices which are quite acceptable in American culture, and the values which are taught and observed in American schools, sometimes collide head-on with those which are taught and observed in Indochinese families. American cultural practices such as dating and reverence of individuality are two possible sources of conflict between Indochinese school children and their parents. This often leads to family disturbances and discord, and, in turn, strains the parent–child relationship and widens the generation gap. In addition, the practice of placement by age rather than academic preparation makes education irrelevant, inappropriate, and inequitable for a significant number of refugee children who are older and/or have received limited or no education in their homelands. Placement problems have led to a high dropout rate among illiterate and semiliterate children, older children, or children with limited past education because, in addition to the tremendous language barrier and unfamiliarity with the American educational system, these children are unable to live up to the academic expectations of the teacher.*[85]

Muslims in the United States (with Salman H. Al Ani)

Islam and the Muslims have a long history in the Americas. Muslims reached Central and South America before Columbus did, sailing from Spain and the African continent.[86] Muslims also accompanied Columbus on his voyages and contributed their expertise during his explorations of the Americas.[87] Moreover, significant numbers of Africans who were transported to the New World during the transatlantic slave trade were believers in Islam and carried their religion with them.[88] Despite efforts to deprive these Africans of their languages, religion, and other aspects of their heritage, Islam took root during colonial and antebellum times.[89]

Today, the majority of these "indigenous Muslims" are African Americans, while only about 70,000 are Caucasian (white). The more recent Muslim immigrants come from diverse parts of the world, including the Middle East and North Africa, Eastern Europe, sub-Saharan Africa, South Asia, and some Southeast Asian countries, such as Malaysia. Muslims constitute about one-fifth of the world's population. Following a substantial increase in their numbers during the past decade, there are between 2.8 and 7 million Muslims in the United States,[90] about one-third of whom are native-born Americans. However, the exact number is not known, because the census that is conducted every ten years does not inquire into religious affiliation.

Community and Diversity: Immigrant and Indigenous Origins

Immigrant Muslims come from a variety of ethnic, linguistic, and cultural backgrounds. They came to the United States in basically three different waves, the first of which started at the end of the nineteenth century and continued to 1925.

First Wave of Immigrants

Most Muslims who came during this period were poor and uneducated and were from Bilad ash-Sham (Greater Syria), the area that after World War I became known as Jordan, Lebanon, Palestine, and Syria. They also came from Turkey, Albania, India, and a few other countries. In the majority of cases they settled in Dearborn, Michigan; Toledo, Ohio; Cedar Rapids, Iowa; Michigan City, Indiana; and other midwestern cities and towns. These groups form the core of the early immigrant Muslims in the United States. Cedar Rapids is unique inasmuch as one of the first mosques in North America, referred to as the Mother Mosque in North America, was built there in 1934.[91]

Second Wave of Immigrants

The second major group began to arrive after World War II, as political and social unrest in the Middle East and North Africa drove many Muslims to immigrate to America. The partition of Palestine and the establishment of the state of Israel in the late 1940s, as well as the creation of Pakistan, also resulted in the migration of Muslims to the United States. Unlike the first wave, the majority this time were educated professionals. A substantial number of students who came to the United States to study eventually settled here.

Third Wave of Immigrants

The third wave, which continues to the present day, came as a result of the liberalization of the immigration regulations in the late 1960s. Many of the Muslims in this group emigrated from Egypt, North Africa, Pakistan, India, and from several other Muslim countries, including Albania and what was then Yugoslavia. The oil-rich Middle Eastern countries have sent a large number of Muslim students to study at U.S. universities and colleges, especially since the 1970s. These students have played active and sometimes leadership roles in Muslim communities and have influenced Muslim Student Association (MSA) branches all over the United States.

The first generation of Muslim immigrants experienced difficulties in adjusting to the U.S. environment. As a result they tend to live in groups formed on the basis of ethnic, cultural, and social origins. Therefore, they do not integrate easily either with indigenous American Muslims or with other Muslims of different ethnic backgrounds. This state of affairs makes it difficult for them to establish a national political base that could give them the sort of influence enjoyed by other ethnic or religious groups.

Religious Beliefs, Practices, and Organizations

Muslims in the United States enjoy the freedom to practice their religion, both as individuals and as groups. They have managed to establish communities in almost every city in this country. Also, they have built or purchased over 600 mosques and Islamic centers, where they worship, celebrate holidays (*Eids*), hold social gatherings, and organize schools that teach Islam and Arabic to adults and children. In addition, American Muslims have established national organizations such as the Islamic Society of North America (ISNA), whose headquarters in Plainfield, Indiana, include a beautiful mosque and adjoining buildings that sit on over 100 acres of land, with a small lake. ISNA holds an annual national convention on Labor Day weekend in various major cities and is attended by Muslims from all over the United States and Canada, as well as from many other countries.[92]

Originally called the Muslim Student's Association (MSA), ISNA was founded in 1963. Local MSAs are still found on virtually every major college and university campus in the United States. The MSA in Bloomington, Indiana, built a beautiful mosque in 1993 where students and other Muslims gather to pray (especially for the Friday, jumah, prayers), to celebrate festivals, weddings, and other social occasions, and to study Islam and Arabic. (Mosques were traditionally used just for worship and the study of Islam and Arabic, but use as multipurpose community social centers has caught on in MSA mosques throughout the United States.) The Muslim community of Bloomington is truly universal. At the jumah prayers on Fridays people of every linguistic, social, and cultural background come together as one group. The one element that brings them together, even with the diversity of their backgrounds, is the universality of the message of Islam.

Muslim Beliefs and Practices

Muslims believe in one God (Allah) and that Muhammad is His Prophet and Messenger. In the seventh century A.D. when Muhammad was forty years old and living in Makkah, the Qur'an (Holy Book) was revealed to him in the Arabic language. It was revealed from God through the Angel Gabriel over the period of twenty-three years leading up to the Prophet's death at the age of sixty-three. The Qur'an is the last revealed word of God and is the prime source of every Muslim's faith. The teachings of the Qur'an and the Hadiths (sayings and deeds of Prophet Muhammad) form the foundation for Islamic law (Shariah) and regulate the daily lives of Muslims. For example, drinking alcohol and eating pork and pork products are prohibited.

Muslims all over the world, including Americans, regardless of their linguistic or ethnic backgrounds, are supposed to recite the Qur'an in Arabic, especially during their prayers. This means that it is important for all Muslims to learn Arabic, at least enough for this purpose. Although the Qur'an has been translated into almost all languages of the world, Muslims still rely on the Arabic text and consider the translations as mere interpretations. Muslims in the United States feel strongly about teaching the Qur'an, the Arabic language, and basic Islamic beliefs to members of their communities, especially to their children. Therefore, wherever there is a large concentration of Muslims, Arabic-Islamic schools have been developed. In smaller areas, the teaching is done in mosques, Islamic centers, or homes.

The Five Pillars of Islam

There are Five Pillars that form the framework of the Muslim faith. These are (1) the Declaration of Faith, or the *Shahadah*, which is a simple formula that all the faithful pronounce. It simply states that "I bear witness that there is no one worthy of worship except God (Allah) and that Muhammad is His Servant and Messenger"; (2) prayer, or *Salat*: Prayers in Islam are obligatory and are performed five times a day—at dawn, noon, mid-afternoon, sunset, and nightfall. (3) Fasting: Every year in the month of *Ramadhan* all Muslims fast from first light until sunset. Those who are sick, elderly, or on a journey and women who are pregnant or nursing are permitted to break the fast and make up an equal number of days later in the year. During the fasting periods no food, drink, or intercourse is allowed; (4) Alms giving, or *Zakat*: In Islam it is believed that all things belong to God and that wealth held by men is held in trust. *Zakat* means purification, and it is a contribution that is collected and distributed to the poor and needy. Zakat usually amounts to two and a half percent of one's capital; and (5) Pilgrimage, or *Hajj*: an annual pilgrimage to the Ka'bah, the holy sanctuary in Makkah, is performed at least once in a lifetime provided one has the means and health to undertake the journey. About 2 million Muslims, from every corner of the globe, go to Makkah each year. The Hajj begins in the twelfth month of the Islamic year, which is based on a lunar rather than a solar calendar. For Muslims in the United States, charter flights and group trips are arranged.

African American Muslims

Muslims in Early America

New scholarship on the trans-Atlantic slave trade indicates that at least 200,000 of the 400,000 to 523,000 Africans brought to British North America came from areas in which Islam was "at least a religion of the minority."[93] Muslim slaves sought each other out, retained their common Islamic heritage, and passed their traditions on to their progeny, according to newly researched "auto biographical and biographical sketches, newspaper articles and advertisements for runaway slaves, slaveholders' records, and the testimony of slaves and their descendants."[94] Compared with other Africans, Muslims were preferred by some slave owners and were given positions of relative privilege and responsibility. In some cases this fueled tensions between Muslim and non-Muslim slaves, as did an attitude of Muslim superiority that may have existed because of factors such as experience with social stratification and slavery in areas of West Africa; devotion to Islamic practices; prominent family backgrounds, including an elite education; and positions as house servants, drivers, and confidants. Although Islam was in competition with other African religions practiced by the slaves, and was eventually overtaken by Christianity, evidence points to a lasting legacy of Islam in African American cultural heritage.[95] The Nation of Islam, founded by men who could have been influenced by African-born practicing Muslims, and today's Black pilgrimage to Islam,[96] may be part of this legacy.

The Nation of Islam

The major movement of African American Muslims today can be traced back to a man named W. D. Fard, who was of Middle East origin. In 1930, Fard founded the first African American movement and named it "The Lost-Found Nation of Islam in the Wilderness of North America," which later became known as the Nation of Islam (NOI), or the Black Muslims. Fard created the NOI mythology and proclaimed himself to be "supreme ruler, Allah or God in Person." He disappeared mysteriously in 1934, but before this he proclaimed his disciple, Elijah (Poole) Muhammad, to be the Messenger of God. The latter assumed leadership of the NOI from the mid-1930s until his death in 1975.[97]

Elijah Muhammad attracted many followers, especially in Detroit and Chicago. The program for his followers was freedom, justice, and equality. He also advocated the establishment of a separate state and the prohibition of alcoholic beverages and of eating of pork and pork products. In addition, he prohibited intermarriage and mixing with the White race. The sources of his teachings were his own interpretations of the Bible, the Qur'an, and the manuals of W. D. Fard. Under his leadership the movement became nationwide. He made Hajj (pilgrimage to Makkah) in 1960, and his book *The Message to the Black Man in America* was published in 1965.[98] This book embodies his basic teachings and philosophy. It is considered the basic source for the movement. The NOI continued to grow under the leadership of Elijah Muhammad, spreading to almost all major U.S. cities and acquiring an international reputation.

At the death of Elijah Muhammad in 1975, the NOI joined the mainstream of Islam and became a true Islamic organization under the leadership of Elijah's son, Warith Deen Muhammad,[99] who changed the name to American Muslim Mission. This reorganization of the NOI is known as "the change." Warith Deen's brother wrote:

> *Elijah Muhammad's doctrine and policies underwent basic modifications and outright reversals with the accession in 1975 of his son, now known as Warith Deen Muhammad. Referring to himself as the "Mujaddid" (Renewer) he discarded the belief in the divinity of Fard, the messengerhood of his father, the evil nature of European-Americans and the superiority of one people over another.*[100]

Imam Warith Deen rejected the doctrine of his father and directed the movement in line with the principles of orthodox Islam. He studied Arabic, the Qur'an, and Islamic jurisprudence. He preached an entirely different message from that of his father. He debunked all forms of racism and abandoned his father's idea of a separate state. Most important, he rejected his father's claim to be the Messenger of Allah and the doctrine that Fard was Allah. Imam Warith Deen preached the orthodox Islamic doctrine that there is only one God and that Muhammad (Peace Be Upon Him) is His Messenger. He changed the name of temples to masjids, or mosques, and ministers to imams. In addition, he taught that the Qur'an is the revealed word of Allah. In February 1990 he headed a delegation to Makkah for the Council of Mosques, and in 1992 he became the first Muslim imam or leader to give an invocation before the U.S. Senate. He is the most highly respected Muslim leader in the United States today. Lately, he has been actively engaged in trying to bring harmony between indigenous American and immigrant Muslims.

In 1985 Imam Warith Deen officially dissolved the American Muslim Mission and integrated its members into the mainstream of the Muslim community in the

United States. This move enhanced his own leadership and position among the Muslims in North America and throughout the Muslim world. The NOI movement did not die completely. In 1988 one of the disciples of Elijah Muhammad, Louis Farrakhan, who disagreed with "the change" that Warith Deen had instituted, revived the NOI. Farrakhan has about 20,000 followers, with headquarters in Chicago, who adhere faithfully to the teachings and philosophy of Elijah Muhammad.

Malcolm X

An interesting phenomenon in the history of Muslims in the United States was the emergence of al-Hajj Malik Shabazz, commonly known as Malcolm X. Both his life and untimely death left a mark on the American scene, for he not only was a distinguished Muslim leader but also proved to be an important African American leader. He was born as Malcolm Little in 1925 in Omaha, Nebraska, the son of a Baptist minister. Prior to joining the NOI movement he was involved in drugs, criminal activities, promiscuity, and wild parties. This led to his being arrested and imprisoned. While he was in prison in the late 1940s, he joined the NOI and began preaching the teachings of Elijah Muhammad to his fellow prisoners. He became one of the close disciples and a strong supporter of Elijah Muhammad.

In December 1963, Malcolm X's relationship with NOI deteriorated due to his well-known statement concerning President John F. Kennedy's assassination: "The chickens are coming home to roost." This statement and his popularity as a leader eventually led to a break between him and the NOI.

Malcolm X made a few trips to Africa and the Middle East, after which he abandoned the teachings of the NOI and its leader. Instead, he then began preaching orthodox Islam and founded the Muslim Mosque, Inc. After performing Hajj, he became known as al-Hajj Malik Shabazz. (The Muslim honorific title al-Hajj is added to any Muslim's name who performs Hajj to Makkah.) While Malcolm was performing Hajj in August 1964, he wrote an article in which he expressed the following thought:

> At Makkah I saw the spirit of unity and true brotherhood displayed by tens of thousands of people from all over the world, from blue-eyed blondes to black-skinned Africans. My religious pilgrimage (Hajj) to Makkah has given me a new insight into the true brotherhood of Islam, which encompasses all the races of mankind.[101]

It is interesting that an FBI file on Malcolm X runs to about 2,000 pages.[102] The bureau opened his file shortly after his release from prison in 1953 and continued collecting information on him even after his death. He was assassinated in New York City in February 1965. A film titled *Malcolm X* that was released in 1993 portrays the various aspects of his life, and in spring 2005 a new exhibit opened in Harlem at the Schomberg Center for Research in Black Culture. The exhibition, Malcolm X: A Search for Truth, includes personal papers, journals, letters, and other evidence that were previously unavailable. It maps out major themes in his life in a "developmental journey" that reflects his driving intellectual quest for truth.[103]

Muslim Concerns

Muslims, while they enjoy freedom of religion and the relaxed atmosphere of a pluralistic environment that tolerates various ideologies and religious practices, feel some prejudices against their way of life. Yvonne Haddad writes on this issue:

> [They] American Muslims are concerned over insensitive and racist statements on radio, television and in the press. They see media coverage of terrorists attacks by Muslims abroad, and particularly what is identified as "fanatic Muslim fundamentalism," as unbalanced and prejudicial, increasingly causing other Americans to equate Islam with terrorism.[104]

As a result of indiscriminate reporting of some criminal acts committed by individuals who happen to be Muslims, it becomes ingrained in the minds of people that all Muslims are fanatics and criminals. This is not the case; the majority of Muslims are peaceful, law-abiding citizens just as in other ethnic groups. It is the style of the media's reporting of events, such as the Gulf War and wars in Afghanistan and Iraq that leaves a negative and prejudicial impression of the Muslim community in the United States.

One myth regarding Muslims is that all Muslims are Arabs. This is not true. In fact, Arabs account for only about one-fifth of the population of Muslims worldwide. The largest Muslim countries are not even in the Arab world. Among these are Indonesia and Pakistan. Furthermore, there is a wide misconception that Iran is an Arab country. Iran is a Muslim country, and the people speak a language called Farsi that belongs to a branch of the Indo-European language family; its lexicon is heavily influenced by Arabic loan words.

Another myth that Muslims feel uneasy about is their religion being referred to as "Muhammadism" instead of Islam. Muslims are not followers of Muhammad in the sense that Christians are followers of Jesus Christ. They follow the teachings of the Qur'an as revealed to Muhammad. The term "Muhammadism" has a negative connotation and is a misconception of the religion of Islam. Muslims not only in the United States but all over the world are insulted when this term is used to refer to their religion.

Although religious pluralism in the United States gives Muslim Americans religious freedom, they often feel restricted in many ways. For instance, it is difficult for them to leave their jobs to attend Friday prayers. Also, Islam forbids interest on loans, and this makes it difficult for strict Muslims to function financially within the Western banking system. Another concern is for Muslim women who adhere to the Islamic dress code. Their religion requires them to cover their heads with a hijab or scarf. This makes it almost impossible for them to obtain jobs, as most businesses in the United States do not accept this mode of dress. Some social customs that are taken for granted in U.S. society, but that are anathema to strict Muslims, such as dating and free mixing between the sexes, also present problems.

Islam is part of the Abrahamic tradition, as are Christianity and Judaism. Muslims feel strongly about their religion being part of this tradition. When religion is discussed and reference is made to the Judeo-Christian tradition, Muslims feel that they are not directly included, on the national scene, as active participants and members of this major religious group. They would like to see active involvement and participation concerning their faith and fate in U.S. religious, cultural, educational and even political dialogues taking place in the United States.

Arab Americans

Arab Americans are people whose ancestors immigrated to the United States from countries in Southwest Asia (the "Middle East") and Northern Africa, where Arabic is one of the primary spoken languages. According to the American-Arab Anti-Discrimination Committee Research Institute (ADCRI), "about 3 million Arab Americans live in the 50 states with about 30% of them living in California, Michigan, and New York and another 35% living in Illinois, Maryland, Massachusetts, New Jersey, Ohio, Texas and Virginia."[105] Box 7.1 provides a global snapshot of Arab and Muslim populations.

First Wave of Immigrants: Christian Majority

Arabs first immigrated to the United States primarily from what is now Syria and Lebanon in the latter part of the nineteenth century, and this trend continued until shortly before World War II. The majority were Christians, merchants, farmers, and even some intellectuals such as Gubran Khalil Gubran, a noted author and artist. Most Arab Americans are now in the second and third generation and have assimilated into the American way of life. Although they have retained some of their cul-

---

Box 7.1
A Global Snapshot

- The 2000 U.S. Census counted 1.2 million Arab Americans, twice the number in 1980.
- The Arab American Institute believes there are around 3.5 million Arab Americans today.
- At least 66 percent of Arab Americans are Christian. Only about 24 percent are Muslim, according to a 2000 survey by pollster John Zogby.
- There are between 2.8 million and 7 million Muslims in the United States. African Americans account for 33 percent to 40 percent of American Muslims.
- Arabs worldwide number about 300 million, just over the U.S. population. The global Muslim population is about 1.2 billion.

Source: L. W. Winik, "Don't Ask Me to Take Off the Uniform," *Parade*, April 17, 2005, p. 7.

tural heritage and have discouraged intermarriage, language and ethnic identity gave way to new realities.[106]

Early Arab immigrants to the United States, in contrast to later immigrants, did not have a direct association or link to specific Arab countries. Most of the Arab countries that exist today were not in existence during this period because, until the beginning of the World War I, the greater part of the Middle East was under the rule of the Ottoman Empire. Therefore, in the majority of cases the early immigrants identified themselves as Syrians since they came from the region of Greater Syria. In fact they established churches and clubs in which the name "Syrian" plays a prominent part.

> *The Syrians' acceptance of America as their permanent home was signaled by establishment of such institutions as Eastern-rite churches, an Arabic-language press, and several educational and charitable associations, mainly in the more populous East Coast urban colonies.*[107]

It is interesting that a number of politicians, film stars, and well-known businessmen trace their ancestry to Syria and Lebanon. Some of these are the late Danny Thomas; Casey Kasem; consumer advocate Ralph Nader; former senator and founder in 1980 of the national organization called the American Arab Anti-Discrimination Committee (ADC), James Abourezk; clothing magnate Farah; Dr. James Zogby, a writer and politician and founder and head of the Arab American Institute; former White House chief of staff and former governor of New Hampshire John Sununu; and Donna Shalala, secretary of health and human services with the Clinton Administration. This is a brief list. Many other professional Americans of Arab descent, such as doctors, engineers, professors, and scientists, contribute greatly to the American way of life.

The period between the first and second world wars did not witness any substantial wave of Arab immigrants. This is partially due to the restrictions of U.S. laws, especially the quota law of 1924 that severely limited the number of Arabs immigrating to the United States.

Second Wave of Immigrants: Muslim Majority

After World War II, many of the present-day Arab countries were established, and the majority of the immigrants at this time, in contrast to those in the earlier period, were Muslims. Political events in the Middle East, such as the establishment of Israel in 1948, contributed to an increase of Arab immigrants to the United States. These new Arab immigrants were generally better off economically than the earlier group. They were educated professionals or students who did not return to their country of origin after studying in the United States. The exact number of Arab Americans in the United States today is not known. However, the available estimates range from 1.2 to 3.5 million, with some estimates as high as 7 million, or approximately 1 percent of the U.S. population.[108] Arab Americans are considered one of the fastest growing groups of immigrants, settling all over the United States, especially in large cities such as Chicago, New York, Detroit, and Los Angeles. Even though they are Arabic-speaking people, there exists no real feeling of Arab solidarity among them.

Former congressman Paul Findley writes about the weak and almost nonexistent political stand of Arab Americans when compared with the Jewish-Israeli lobby that is visible, powerful, and influential, especially in Washington, D.C. He states that, "Arab American lobbies, fledgling forces even today, were nonexistent." He further states, "Even if a congressman had wanted to hear the Arab viewpoint, he would have had difficulty finding an Arab spokesman to explain it."[109] This state of affairs continues, although there is a growing trend for Arab Americans to become more politically organized.

Arab American Origins

Arab Americans are linked ethnically and historically to the Arab people of the Middle East. The Arab people today number approximately 220 million and inhabit the Middle East and African regions that consist of over twenty countries. An Arab can be Muslim, Christian, Jew, or of some other belief. The Arab people are Semites, and their original homeland is the Arabian Peninsula. In the pre-Islamic period, seventh century A.D., the Arabs lived in tribal communities, and some established small kingdoms. There was no clear national consciousness among the various communities in Arabia even though they shared the same language and, to some extent, the same cultural heritage.

The Arabs pride themselves with having an expressive, eloquent, and poetic language. They honor their poets and celebrated the occasions when a poet became recognized as a defender of the tribe. In the pre-Islamic period, annual festivals were held in Makkah where some poets recited their works. Seven of the poets became so famous that some of their poems were written in gold and hung on the walls of the Ka'bah, the religious sanctuary in Makkah. These poems are memorized by many members of the tribes, and this tradition has endured throughout the history of the Arabs even to today.

With the advent of Islam in the seventh century, the Arabs and the Arabic language acquired a new status. The Qur'an was revealed in Arabic and gave the Arabic language a status of glory that it never had before. Arabic became the language of the Islamic civilization and the lingua franca of the entire Islamic empire that extended from the eastern shore of the Mediterranean to the western region of China. Today the Arabic language (including various regional dialects) is still the medium of expression for all Arab countries. The Arabic alphabet is used with many of the Islamic languages, including Farsi (Persian), Urdu, and several other languages of the region. Also, the Arabic language is recognized as one of the six official languages at the United Nations.

Images and Challenges

Both positive images and negative stereotypes surround Arab Americans. Positive images include the strong ties among nuclear and extended families, care and respect for elders, and the generosity and hospitality that are well known by those entertained or hosted by an Arab. But it is the negative images and stereotypes of the Arab world in general, and Arab Americans specifically, that are the most prevalent. As one author states:

> *The Arab-American community, now estimated to be over two million, has suffered and continues to suffer in many ways the curse of negative stereotyping of Arabs. Thus, Arab Americans are made to feel ashamed of their ancestors and their former homeland. As a result, some have avoided reference to their Arab heritage, for instance, often describing themselves in terms of geographic region from which they came or the religious sect to which they belong.*[110]

The negative image of Arab Americans, particularly of Palestinian Arabs, is more widespread and intense because of the Arab-Israeli conflict. Palestinians are often viewed by the media as Arab refugees or terrorists. Many Arab Americans perceive that they are an easy target for insults and slurs. Whenever major events take place in the Middle East, such as the Gulf War, the Arab American community often becomes the focus of investigation and interrogation. After the terrorist attacks on September 11, 2001, discrimination and hate crimes against Arab American citizens increased because the terrorists were of Middle Eastern descent. Despite this unfriendly and sometimes hostile climate, Arab Americans continue to serve in our military. Their knowledge of culture and language in countries like Afghanistan and Iraq are crucial in the United States's attempts to end conflict and help establish peace and justice throughout the area.[111]

The U.S. movie industry has always had a fascination with the Arab character, either real or mythical. A study reviewing a century of Arabs portrayed in U.S. movies states,

> *Over the past century the movies have recorded changes, invariably for the worse, in an Arab image that was tinged with negative elements to begin with. For Americans, the Arab has long been the quintessential Other—fundamentally different from us, both fascinating and repugnant, enacting the taboos of our society. Brought to life on the screen from our collective imagination, the Arab does terrible deeds and receives appropriate punishments.*[112]

Arab Americans are often erroneously perceived as a unified single ethnic group. Their complexity is frequently overlooked. In reality, Arabs in the United States, especially the first generation who in turn influence their offspring, come from different countries with different allegiances and interests. For example, Lebanese Arabs tend to congregate and rally around the specific interests of their origin, as do Egyptians, Palestinians, and Iraqis. However, cultural, linguistic, and possibly religious affiliations play a role in uniting them with a common perspective. In the United States today, the Arab community, especially in large metropolitan areas, has established Arabic newspapers and produced its own television and radio shows. The persistent Arab-Israel conflict contributes to this growing sense of common identity among Arab Americans. The establishment of Israel in 1948 and the war of 1967 resulted in a large number of Palestinian refugees, who were scattered throughout many Arab countries and other parts of the world, including the United States. An estimated 80,000 to 100,000 Palestinians are now living in the United States. Former U.S. president Jimmy Carter wrote concerning this conflict,

> *In simplest terms, the Arab-Israeli conflict is a struggle between two national identities for control of territory, but there are also historic, religious, strategic, political, and psychological issues that color the confrontation and retard its amicable solution. What each wants is no less than recognition, acceptance, independence, sovereignty, and territorial identity. Neither officially recognizes the other's existence, so any testing of intentions must be done through uncertain intermediaries.*[113]

President Carter, who orchestrated a peace treaty between Egypt and Israel in 1979, envisioned a day when the Palestinians and Israelis would settle their conflict peacefully. His dream was partially fulfilled when on September 13, 1993, at the White House in Washington, D.C., official representatives of the Palestinians and the Israelis met to sign a peace agreement. While this treaty signifies the possibility of a new era in Arab-Israeli relations, the long history of conflict continues to influence the Arab American worldview.

Describing the current political scene in the United States, the American-Arab Anti-Discrimination Committee Research Institute (ADCRI) writes, "Arab Americans are evenly divided among Republicans, Democrats, and Independents. Polls show that Arab Americans are more likely to vote than other Americans. In the recent presidential election, the major parties met with leaders of the Arab American community because Arab Americans constitute a powerful voting block in some key states. Arab Americans have held office at all levels. They've served in the U.S Senate, the U.S. House of Representatives, and presidential cabinets. They've been governors and state legislators. More than thirty have been mayors of U.S. cities."[114]

 ## Conclusions

The history of immigration to the United States is marked by openness during periods of economic prosperity and hostility during times of economic decline and political insecurity. Hostility and xenophobia have increased again because the influx of immigration is now at its highest point since the first decade of the twentieth century. Critics of immigration argue that newcomers are taking jobs away from the native-born population and are a drain on the nation's public welfare resources, health services, and the public schools. These assertions are not backed up by most of the recent research conducted by academics and government officials.[115] Most studies show "that immigrants, legal and illegal, are more of a boon than a bane in this country."[116] They indicate that, on average, immigrants actually help create more jobs and are more likely to be self-employed and start their own businesses, and that they pay higher tax rates than do natives. Furthermore, they indicate that immigrants do not make higher use of welfare or unemployment benefits than natives. Nevertheless, the fears and negative images of immigrants persist. Thus, many classroom teachers face difficult challenges as the nation's school-age population becomes ever more diverse and the social climate becomes more xenophobic.

In *Preparing for the Twenty-First Century*, Paul Kennedy identifies global demographic imbalances between richer and poorer nations as the major issue underlying all the other important forces we will face in the twenty-first century.[117] Poorer nations are experiencing population explosions along with shrinking natural resources, while the rich nations (who account for about one-sixth of the world's population and control five-sixths of its wealth) are experiencing problems of stagnant or negative population growth. One result of these changing demographics is massive emigration from "have-not" nations to wealthier nations such as the United States. If we are to benefit from these changing demographics, the massive educational reforms advocated by multiculturalists must be implemented. Multiculturalists argue that if we establish an equitable society based on the ideal of cultural pluralism, we can accommodate the predicted influx of immigrants from poorer nations. Economic, cultural, and spiritual growth will then benefit society as a whole.

Selected Sources for Further Study

Airriess, C. A. (2007). "Conflict Migrants from Mainland Southeast Asia," in *Contemporary Ethnic Geographies in America*, eds. I. M. Miyares & C. A. Airress, 291–312. Lanham, MD: Rowman & Littlefield.

Alba, R., & Nee, V. (2003). *Remaking the American Mainstream: Assimilation and Contemporary Immigration.* Cambridge, MA: Harvard Press, 2003. Chapter 5, "The Background to Contemporary Immigration," and Chapter 6, "Evidence of Contemporary Assimilation."

Banks, J. A. (2008). *Teaching Strategies for Ethnic Studies*, 8th ed. Boston: Allyn and Bacon. Chapter 13.

Brown, C. L., & Pannell, C. W. (2000). "The Chinese in America," *Ethnicity in Contemporary America: A Geographical Appraisal*, 2nd ed., ed. J. O. McKee, 283–289. Lanham, MD: Rowman & Littlefield.

Chacko, E. (2007). "Immigrants from the Muslim World: Lebanese and Iranians," in *Contemporary Ethnic Geographies in America*, eds. I. M. Miyares & C. A. Airress, 313–330. Lanham, MD: Rowman & Littlefield.

Dhingra, P. (2008). "Trying to Be Authentic, But Not Too Authentic: Second-Generation Hindu Americans in Dallas, Texas," *Immigrants Outside Megaloopolis: Ethnic Transformation in the Heartland*, ed. R. C. Jones, 65–68. Lanham, MD: Lexington Books.

Feagin, J. R., Feagin, C. B. (2008). *Racial and Ethnic Relations*, 8th ed. Upper Saddle River, NJ: Prentice Hall. Chapter 10, "Japanese Americans"; Chapter 11, "Chinese, Filipino, Korean, Vietnamese, and Asian-Indian Americans"; and Chapter 12, "Arab and Other Middle Eastern Americans."

Joshi, K. Y. (2006). *New Roots in America's Sacred Ground.* New Brunswick, NJ: Rutgers University Press.

Li, W. (2007). "Chinese Americans: Community Formation in Time and Space," *Contemporary Ethnic Geographies in America*, eds. Ines M. Miyares & C. A. Airress, 213–232. Lanham, MD: Rowman & Littlefield.

Min, P. G. (Ed.). (2002). *The Second Generation: Ethnic Identity Among Asian Americans.* Walnut Creek, CA: Walnut Creek, 2002.

Min, P. G. (2002). "A Comparison of Pre- and Post-1965 Asian Immigrant Businesses," in *Mass Migration to the United States: Classical and Contemporary Periods*, ed. P. G. Min, 285–308. Walnut Creek, CA: AltaMira Press.

Min, P. G. (Ed.). (2006). *Asian Americans: Contemporary Trends and Issues.* Thousand Oaks, CA: Pine Forge Press.

Min, P. G., & Kim, J. H. (Eds.). (2002). *Religions in Asian American: Building Faith Communities.* Walnut Creek, CA: Walnut Creek.

Miyares, I. M., Paine, J. A., and Nishi, M. (2000). "The Japanese in America," in *Ethnicity in Contemporary America: A Geographical Appraisal,* 2nd ed., ed. J. O. McKee, 263–282. Lanham, MD: Rowman & Littlefield.

Ngai, M. M. (2004). *Impossible Subjects: Illegal Aliens and the Making of Modern America.* Princeton, NJ: Princeton University Press.

Reimer, D. (2007). "Korean Culture and Entrepreneurship," in *Contemporary Ethnic Geographies in America,* eds. I. M. Miyares & C. A. Airress, 233–250. Lanham, MD: Rowman & Littlefield.

Skop, E. (2007). "Asian Indians and the Construction of Community and Identity," *Contemporary Ethnic Geographies in America,* eds. I. M. Miyares & C. A. Airress, 271–290. Lanham, MD: Rowman & Littlefield.

Tyner, J. A. (2007). "Filipinos: The Invisible Ethnic Community," in *Contemporary Ethnic Geographies in America,* eds. I. M. Miyares & C. A. Airress, 251–270. Lanham, MD: Rowman & Littlefield.

Now go to Topics #1 and 2: **Ethnicity/Cultural Diversity** and **Race** in the MyEducationLab (www.myeducationlab.com) for your course, where you can:

- Find learning outcomes for these topics along with the national standards that connect to these outcomes.

- Complete Assignments and Activities that can help you more deeply understand the chapter content.

- Apply and practice your understanding of the core teaching skills identified in the chapter with the Building Teaching Skills and Dispositions learning units.

Part III
Individual Differences and Societal Inequities That Affect Teaching and Learning

Chapter 8

Learning Styles and Culturally Competent Teaching

Chapters 4 through 7 have described the dramatic changes in the U.S. population over the past several decades due to changes in immigration policies and the influx of newcomers from Asia, Latin America, and Africa. Immigration engenders ethnicity, and today our school-age population is more diverse than ever before in terms of languages spoken at home, race, religion, and national origins. How does this impact schools? According to one educational administrator in Utica, New York, a community of just under 60,000 that has welcomed over 11,000 refugees since 1979,

> *anytime a district is growing, it presents problems, but certainly some challenges and some opportunities. As your enrollment increases, there's additional funding that comes with enrollment. There's additional growth and space that you need, but . . . it's also a sign of prosperity, that you're growing. . . . It's forced us to change the way we deliver instruction into every classroom, because every single teacher is forced to deal with students that English wasn't their native language . . . And I see that as an advantage, because I think teachers look at kids individually and how they learn, it not only helps kids that are refugees, but it helps (those) that may not learn the same way as everybody else.*[1]

Over the years, Utica has received and resettled refugees from Vietnam, persons from the former Soviet Union (primarily Pentecostal Christians), Bosnians (mainly Muslims), and, most recently, Bantu refugees from Somalia as well as migrants from Liberia, Sudan, and Myanmar.[2] Many people see benefits and opportunities with this influx of newcomers, especially for our schools. Two community leaders put it this way:[3]

> *In terms of cultural and the diversity, what kids from different countries bring to the school is really immeasurable. We . . . if you go into any of our schools, elementary, middle, or high school, and you look at the faces of the kids, you can tell they reflect, you know, the United Nations. They really reflect all different countries all over. And I think that's great for them, and for the kids that were born here. They learn different cultures, they learn from different kids. So that's a real plus, I think, for the kids that go to school here.—Education administrator*

The fact that we have such a wonderfully diverse population here is a very, very good thing for this community, and for the young people in this community to be in school with people from all over the world. . . . That's amazing. . . . And so you're sitting next to someone from somewhere else in the world; what a great geography lesson. What a great sociology lesson; what a great history lesson. So, so I think that our children are having the opportunity to be more accepting, to have a bigger worldview. I see this as extremely positive for our community, on every level that I can possibly think of.—Foundation leader

Teachers need this kind of support from administrators and community leaders as they carry out their work in ethnically diverse classrooms with cultural competence. Culturally competent teachers provide equitable learning environments and are aware of both cultural and individual differences. There is a necessary interaction here. If teachers are unaware of cultural differences when they exist, they may perceive a student as being unacceptably deviant or deficient. However, they must also be aware of the individual diversity that exists within any one ethnic group and guard against stereotypes. And, finally, they must see the similarities among individuals across the range of groups found in their classrooms.

The first half of this chapter begins with an overview of learning-styles theory and research, presents three strategies for identifying learning styles, and continues with discussions of the relationships between culture and learning styles and learning styles and teaching styles. The second half of the chapter focuses on culturally competent teaching, including principles, examples, and the "funds of knowledge" approach to teaching and research.

 ## Learning Styles

Students differ in the ways they approach learning. Some work well in groups; others prefer to work alone. Some need absolute quiet in order to concentrate; others do well with noise and movement. Some need a great deal of structure and support; others are more independent and self-motivated. Some students grasp oral instructions quickly; others need to see the instructions in writing. Some require a warm personal rapport with the teacher, while others do not. Some are intuitive; others prefer inductive or deductive reasoning. Some learn best in a formal environment, while others prefer a more relaxed atmosphere. The list of differences could go on.

Psychologists have been researching the nature of learning styles for a number of decades. Only recently has the utility of this research been made known to educators. Typically, we look for emotional reasons to explain why a child is not learning; we look for an emotional block or conflict, or a learning disability. Many teachers ignore the possibility that children are not learning because they are not given an opportunity to use their own styles of learning in the classroom.

Take, for example, a child who has a slow warm-up period of twenty to thirty minutes. He or she does not easily get into something new, but once involves he may show a good deal of perseverance. He may also be a physical learner who needs to become involved in the learning process. This takes time.

Once immersed, he may go deeper than his classmates. The quick learning activity typical in most elementary classrooms can make it impossible for the slow-to-warm-up learner to get past the point of warming up. Thus, she is rarely able to complete work expected by the teacher. The frequent change of activity may also be frustrating and discouraging because once into an activity she has difficulty shifting to a new one. If she makes it past the eighth grade, the slow-to-warm-up learner will also find it difficult to learn within the rigid time schedules of most secondary schools. Unless helped, the slow-to-warm-up student gets caught in a vicious cycle of anxiety, inability to concentrate, and failure.

The idea that we must gear our teaching to students' learning style needs is revolutionary and, perhaps, unsettling. It triggers the fear that we sometimes create the conditions of failure for some students. Fortunately, the movement has progressed far enough to provide some of the tools we need to discover the important differences that affect learning and to design appropriate instructional strategies and materials.

As noted in Chapter 2, the notion that certain learning styles are related to certain ethnic groups is both dangerous and promising. It is dangerous because it can foster stereotypes. It is promising to the degree that it illuminates cultural variables that influence the way children learn and helps teachers discover ways of strengthening academic achievement among learners of diverse cultural backgrounds. Recall that intellectual modes, that is, both the styles of learning and the types of knowledge most valued, are one of the five aspects of ethnicity Longstreet uses to mediate cultural differences in the classroom.

What Is Learning Style?

The National Task Force on Learning Style and Brain Behavior adopted the following definition of *learning style* with the understanding that it would be revised if necessary:

> *Learning style is that consistent pattern of behavior and performance by which an individual approaches educational experiences. It is the composite of characteristic cognitive, affective, and physiological behaviors that serve as relatively stable indicators of how a learner perceives, interacts with, and responds to the learning environment. It is formed in the deep structure of neural organization and personality [that] molds and is molded by human development and the cultural experiences of home, school, and society.*[4]

The fact that this definition is offered as tentative should alert us to the fact that learning style is an emerging concept. Despite decades of research, there are more questions than answers about learning styles. Nevertheless, knowledge about learning styles has become one of the most promising avenues to improving education. We must be careful, however, not to view learning styles as the panacea that will eliminate failure in the schools. To address learning styles is often a necessary, but never sufficient, condition for effective teaching.

Why Be Concerned about Learning Styles?

The rationale behind learning styles is similar to the broader rationale for multicultural education. Knowledge about learning styles provides insights that move us beyond the rhetoric associated with "individual differences," "human potential," and "creating the independent learner."[5] First of all, when a student is having difficulty learning, it is now possible to pinpoint which of the many individual differences affect his or her learning. Understanding individual differences has been especially challenging for junior high and high school teachers. Gerald Kusler, a specialist on learning-style theory, wrote:

> Most secondary teachers want to know the students they teach. But, two factors tend to block even the most committed. First, teachers don't really know what they need to know about learners. . . . Second, the typical secondary teacher spends about 90 hours in class with between 125 and 150 youngsters. "Getting to know you" can become "putting the name with the face (or the seat)."[6]

Recent developments in learning-style research have produced a variety of efficient measurements to gather information about students and assess their strongest or preferred approach to educational experiences. Thus, if a student has a strong modality preference, a teacher can provide visual, auditory, or kinesthetic experiences that will enhance the student's learning. Teachers can provide more structure for those who need it, or assist reflective thinkers in developing skills needed for standardized tests. The possibilities are endless.

Second, by focusing on how students learn, we assume that they can learn. This is basic to the humanists' view that all of us have the capacity to grow and develop to our fullest potential. Third, when students discover *how* they themselves learn they become involved in a teaching-learning partnership. In schools where learning styles are assessed and shared with learners, students become involved in structuring how they will approach what is being taught. This is an important step in creating the independent learner.[7]

The concept of learning style can also provide some of the teeth needed to move us beyond the rhetoric of educational equity for those ethnic groups that have not yet been well served by our nation's schools. This notion warrants some discussion.

One can assume that teachers, unless they learn to do otherwise, expect their students to learn the same way that they themselves do. Teachers who dislike group work rarely use it with their students. Teachers who require the written word remember to write the assignment on the board, but they may not think of taping the text for their auditory learners. Teachers who are incremental learners tend to spell out short-term objectives, while the intuitive teachers may seem less organized. A teacher's learning style does not have to become a teaching style straitjacket; teachers can learn to be flexible and teach in a variety of ways. Being flexible is important because research shows that students do better in classes taught by teachers with the same learning style as their own. Students also tend to like these teachers better.[8]

The concept of learning styles offers a value-neutral approach for understanding some of the individual differences among ethnically diverse students, and within any one group. Many learning styles are bipolar, representing a continuum from one extreme of a trait to another. Usually, no value judgment is made about where one falls on the continuum. "It is acceptable for example, to be a kinesthetic or an audio or visual learner, to reason abstractly or concretely."[9] The assumption is that everyone can learn if teachers respond appropriately to individual learning needs.

Learning style is believed to be a combination of both heredity and environment. While it is to some degree rooted in the individual's neurological structure, learning styles do change with age and experience. Young children, for example, seem to be more kinesthetic and tend to develop a visual or auditory preference as they mature. In highly technical societies, such as the United States, cognitive styles tend to move in the direction of analytical thought.

Numerous instruments now exist for diagnosing students' learning styles. In her selected bibliography of learning-style assessment instruments, for example, Cornett lists thirty.[10] Keefe and others have organized the available measurement tools into four categories: cognitive-style instruments, affective-style instruments, physiological-style instruments, and comprehensive or multidimensional instruments.[11] Cognitive style instruments are those that measure intellectual attributes, such as the learner's typical mode of perceiving, thinking, problem solving, and remembering.[12] Affective style instruments are those that measure emotional attributes related to preferences or needs that improve concentration and ability to pay attention, motivation, and need for structure. Physiological style instruments are those that measure physical or biologically based responses, and how they are influenced by nutrition intake needs, and perception of aural or visual stimuli. Comprehensive or multidimensional instruments are those that assess dimensions from more than one of these three categories of learning style.[13] Because comprehensive instruments that can measure all three aspects of learning style (cognitive, affective, and physiological dimensions) do not yet exist, it is wise to select instruments from two or more categories to better understand a student's learning-style profile.

Three Strategies for Discovering Learning Styles

Field Independence-Dependence: Group Embedded Figures Test (GEFT)

Imagine yourself in a psychology laboratory, seated on a chair in a tilted room. The experimenter asks you to adjust the chair and your body to the true upright position. Can you do it?

Now imagine that you are seated in a darkened room with a luminous rod in a luminous picture frame, which is set aslant. You are instructed to set the rod to the true vertical position. Are you able to do so?

These two experiments were part of the dramatic research begun by Herman Witkin and his associates in 1954. The research illustrates the field independence-dependence dimensions of learning style. Those participants labeled field dependent consistently aligned themselves to the tilt of the room, leaning perhaps as much as thirty degrees but perceiving themselves to be sitting upright. They also tended to be influenced by the slant of the picture frame and were unable to place the rod in its true upright position. Other participants, those labeled field independent, ignored their immediate surroundings. In the tilted-room test they used internal cues to adjust their bodies to an upright position. In the luminous-rod test, they tended to ignore the frame and set the rod in its true upright position.[14]

Diagnosis of field independence-dependence is now greatly simplified through use of a simple embedded-figures test. Figure 8.1 illustrates the task as it appears in the Hidden Figures Test.[15] If we visualize people along a continuum from extreme field dependence to extreme field independence, we find that people at the field-dependent end are unable to locate simple figures embedded in the complex pattern. Field-independent people, however, can quickly separate the simple figure from the background.

For years, knowledge generated about learning styles by Witkin and others has been unavailable to teachers and counselors. Only recently have classroom implications been discussed. When trying to identify students who are relatively field independent-dependent, think in terms of clusters of personality and intellectual characteristics. These clusters include the characteristics listed in Table 8.1.[16]

Field independence-dependence does not appear to be correlated with intelligence, with the exception of analytical intelligence, which requires the separation of component parts from the whole. It is not related to other aspects of intelligence, such as verbal comprehension. However, most schools and tests tend to be geared to the highly analytical learner who can think abstractly (field-independent learn-

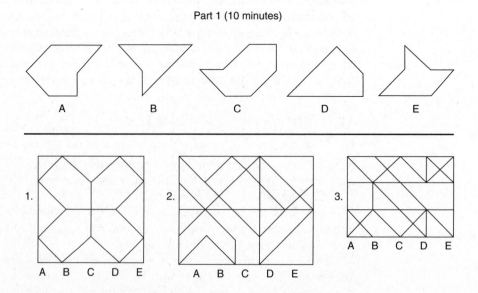

Figure 8.1 ⊠ Hidden Figures Test

Adapted from Hidden Figures Test (Cf-1), Kit of Factor-Referenced Cognitive Tests. (Ans. 1, A; 2, B; 3, E.) Copyright © 1962 by Educational Testing Service. Reprinted by permission.

Table 8.1 Field-Independent versus Field-Dependent Learners

Field-Independent Learner	Field-Dependent Learner
1. Perception of discrete parts	1. Global perception
2. Good at abstract analytical thought	2. Poor at analytical problem solving
3. Individualistic and insensitive to others, poorly developed social skills	3. Highly sensitive and attuned to social environment, highly developed social skills
4. Favors "inquiry" and independent study, provides own structure to learning	4. Favors a "spectator approach" to learning, adopts organization of information to be learned as given
5. Intrinsically motivated, unresponsive to social reinforcement	5. Extrinsically motivated, responsive to social reinforcement

ers). Some psychologists suggest that people can be helped to develop cognitive strategies, that people can be taught to make conscious choices about which cognitive process to use in certain situations. Thus, field independents might learn to be more sensitive to other people, and field dependents might increase their analytical skill.

Research by Ramirez and Castañeda suggests that learning style is related to worldview, that certain learning styles tend to be predominant in certain cultures.[17] They indicate that Mexican Americans tend to be relatively field dependent or global in orientation. Furthermore, their research suggests that bilingual individuals tend to be bicognitive; that is, fluent speakers of Spanish and English tend to have greater cognitive flexibility than monolinguists, being able to move back and forth between global and analytical orientations as needed.

The field independence-dependence approach to learning styles is the most widely researched, with over two thousand studies completed to date.[18] There are some problems, however. The Embedded Figures Test (EFT) makes field dependents, now more frequently known as "field-sensitive learners," feel like failures. The more field sensitive the individual, the less likely he or she will be successful in locating a simple figure within a complex whole. Given a school's emphasis on testing, it becomes difficult to convince the student who scores between zero and eight out of thirty-two possible points that the test reveals little about learning potential. Another problem is that the terms *field sensitive* and *field independent* tend to label students and can lead to stereotyping. Therefore, the EFT should be administered with care and with a full discussion of the insights it offers into how the individual approaches learning.

Castañeda and Gray have developed observation guidelines based on field independence-dependence research that can help teachers discover where a student falls on the continuum without testing. They also describe the teacher characteristics and curriculum approach that are most compatible with each learning style. These are summarized in Boxes 8.1, 8.2, and 8.3, on pages 228–231.[19]

Students' Need for Structure

Students in any classroom may differ greatly in their ability to rely on themselves, to take on new assignments, to make choices, and to organize themselves and their materials. Some need frequent reassurance from the teacher and continually ask if what they are doing is right and what they should do next.

Students also differ in their need for an explanation of the instructions before beginning a test or assignment. Teachers often give instructions to a group of thirty to forty students, expecting all of them to understand the first or second time. A teacher may become irritated at students who never seem to listen or pay attention. In many cases, perhaps, the student is not paying attention, but students can differ in their need for directions from the teacher. Students at all age levels differ from one another in their ability to carry out independent projects and activities. Some can handle long-term assignments while others can work independently only for short periods of time.

Need for structure is sometimes regarded as a manifestation of learning style. David Hunt, of the Ontario Institute for Studies in Education, conceptualizes learning style on the basis of the amount of external structure needed by the student. He identifies the characteristics of students who require much, some, and little structure and teaching approaches that are most desirable for students who require a certain degree of structure.

The paragraph completion method has been used since the 1960s by Hunt and his associates to assess a student's conceptual level.[20] This method, which requires special training to administer, asks the learner to complete six to eight open-ended statements by writing two or three sentences about his or her feelings for each one (*What I think about rules . . . , When I am . . . , What I think about parents . . . , When someone does not agree with me . . . , When I am not sure . . . , When I am told what to do . . .* and so on).[21] Learner responses are then coded and scored according to the structure of the response, not the content. The result is a general indication of the amount of structure the student needs at the time. He also emphasizes that there are many high-ability students who require structure and warns that many teachers confuse learning style with ability. This confusion is particularly likely with younger (i.e., grade six) students because "teachers tend to equate high level verbal ability with a learning style that requires little structure."[22] While many high achievers do require structure, it is less likely that students who are at lower achievement levels will need less structure. Hunt writes that, therefore, "learning style and ability show a low, but significant relation, yet they are distinct from one another" and furthermore, "the relation decreases as students grow older."[23]

Hunt's approach to learning style is practical for teachers, most of whom know that certain students are more independent than others, and that others need more guidance and support. Hunt makes it possible for teachers to sharpen these observations by providing specific behaviors to look for. Box 8.4 on pages 231–233 summarizes some of these behaviors and can be used as a guideline for identifying a student's need for structure.

Hunt also offers some valuable suggestions about teaching strategies that best meet a student's need for structure. These are summarized in Box 8.5 on pages 233–234.

Self-motivated students who require little structure can pursue independent projects with relative ease.

Many of these suggestions may seem like common sense. The point is, however, that most teachers do not act on them; instead, they insist on the same amount of structure for all students. Hunt provides guidelines for flexibility as educators match their teaching with the amount of structure a student requires.

Perceptual Modalities

The Edmonds Learning Style Identification Exercise (ELSIE) is an effective technique for discovering perceptual modes. Classroom teachers can administer, score, and roughly evaluate the ELSIE in less than a half-hour of class time. The ELSIE can be used in grades seven to adult, and possibly as early as fourth grade.

The ELSIE provides a profile of modality strengths, based on the individual's response to a selected list of fifty common English words that are read once at ten-second intervals. Students are asked, as they hear each word, to indicate on their answer sheet which of the following responses is their "own immediate and instantaneous reaction to the word itself."[24]

1. Visualization: a mental picture of some object or activity
2. Written word: a mental picture of the word spelled out
3. Listening: the sound of the word with no mental picture
4. Activity: a "physical or emotional feeling about the word, such as a tightening of a muscle or a feeling such as warmth, sorrow, etc."[25]

Students can tally the number of responses in each response category and then plot their own profiles to discover their own perceptual strengths and weaknesses. The learner's scores in all four categories are charted on a stanine scale displayed as bands above and below the mean. A sample profile is shown in Figure 8.2. These profiles are interpreted such that "the further the individual varies from the mean in any one of the four categories, the stronger or weaker will be that mode of learning for that individual, that is, the more (or less) easily the individual is able to learn by using that approach. Scores at the extremes (either in the ± 3 or ± 4 band) may be considered indicative of a strongly dominant influence—positively or negatively—of that mode."[26]

Students who score high on visualization learn best when they can actually see objects and activities. Visual media such as films, pictures, demonstrations, and models would enhance their learning.

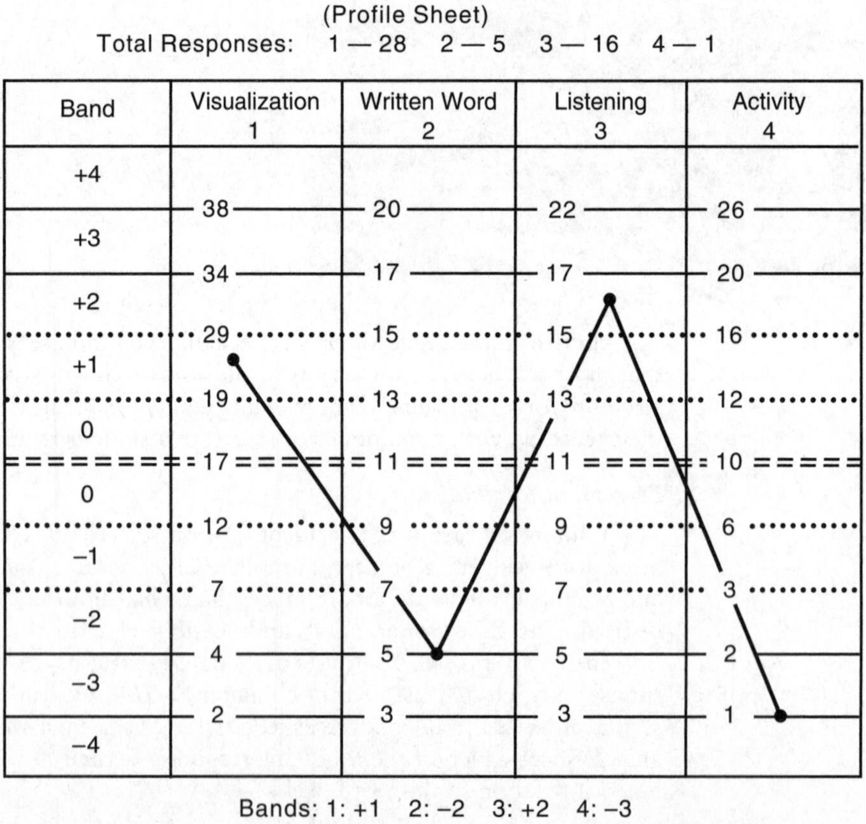

(Profile Sheet)

Total Responses: 1 — 28   2 — 5   3 — 16   4 — 1

Band	Visualization 1	Written Word 2	Listening 3	Activity 4
+4				
	38	20	22	26
+3				
	34	17	17	20
+2				
	29	15	15	16
+1				
	19	13	13	12
0				
0	17	11	11	10
	12	9	9	6
−1				
	7	7	7	3
−2				
	4	5	5	2
−3				
	2	3	3	1
−4				

Bands: 1: +1   2: −2   3: +2   4: −3

Figure 8.2 ◼ Edmonds School District, Learning-Style Identification Exercise

From Harry Reinert, "One Picture Is Worth a Thousand Words? Not Necessarily!" *The Modern Language Journal*, 60 (April 1976): 164. Reprinted by permission of the author.

Learners who score high on the written word portion learn best by reading about what is to be learned. "Persons scoring very high in this category have a great dependency on the written word. . . . Persons scoring very low in this category may read quite well, but they tend to translate written words into another category (visual images or sounds) rather than being able to get meaning from the words immediately."[27]

Learners with a modality strength in listening are auditory learners. The higher the score for listening, the better the individual can learn from hearing the spoken language without recourse to some other mode. Listening labs and tapes are usually very effective with auditory learners.

Learners who score high on activity require some manner of physical activity in order to facilitate learning. Many activity or kinesthetic learners are compulsive underliners or notetakers "in class or at lectures (and even films), but they will seldom need to refer to their notes at a later time, for the activity of writing seems to impress the information on their memory."[28]

Reinert reports finding far greater diversity between individual learning profiles than he had originally anticipated and suspects that "many slow learners are 'slow' only because they have never had a chance to learn in the way they could have learned."[29] The ELSIE provides teachers with specific information about students' learning strengths and weaknesses, making it possible for teachers to give individual students the kind of help they need. For some students, drills, outlining, or copying definitions is helpful; for others it is a waste of time. Some students benefit from listening to a tape of the text as they read; some even require it if they are to comprehend. For others, auditory stimuli are a hindrance.

The ELSIE can also be valuable for understanding the overall learning style makeup of a particular class. Reinert suggests that each class has a unique profile. Once teachers know what it is, they can plan instruction that should be most effective for the class as a whole. For example, Reinert gives evidence that casts doubt on the overall effectiveness of films with some groups. One picture is not always worth a thousand words.

Young children can develop understanding of abstract concepts, such as cooperation, through concrete experiences that use all of the learning modalities.

In summary, *learning-style theory* emphasizes the different processes people use to absorb information, solve problems, and create objects. It also emphasizes the thoughts and feelings associated with these processes[30] and thus helps us understand the distinct *styles* of our students.

Relationships between Culture and Learning Style

How does culture influence the way individuals learn to know and understand the world? How does it influence the way they think, perceive, remember, and solve problems? In her research into relationships between culture and individual learning styles, Worthley has identified five cultural factors that appear to have an effect on learning styles.[31] One is the socialization process, particularly where a society's child-rearing practices fall along a continuum from authoritative to laissez-faire. The more control a society exercises over its children, the more field dependent they become. A second factor is sociocultural tightness. The more the established social structures exert pressure to conform, as in high-context cultures, the more field dependent are its people. Third is the factor of ecological adaptation. In some societies survival depends upon keen observations of the environment, for example, accurate reading of the snow conditions of the arctic region or wave patterns of the sea or facial expressions of an oppressor. These environments produce people with highly developed perceptual skills, as with the Alaskan Natives, the Trukee of the South Pacific, and African Americans in a community of hostile Whites. A fourth factor is the biological effect, particularly nutrition and physical development. Some research has shown, for example, that children who lack protein tend to be more field dependent. (This relationship is not necessarily causative, however.) Finally, language exerts an important influence on learning style, especially the degree to which a society is literate. Contemporary literate societies emphasize written language, while traditional preliterate societies emphasize direct experience observation and modeling.[32]

In discussing her findings, Worthley writes that

> while diversity among individuals within any culture is the norm, research has shown that these individuals tend to exhibit a common pattern of perception when the members of that culture are compared to the members of another culture. A "cultural personality" is more than a myth or stereotype. In addition, individuals from relatively pluralistic cultures such as that of the United States (actually a polyglot of many subcultures) tend to exhibit greater diversity in learning style than individuals from relatively singular cultures such as that of the African Kpelle tribe.[33]

Another illustration of the connections between learning style and culture is the work of Wade Boykin and his associates at Howard University.[34] Boykin has developed a conceptual framework for the study of African American child socialization that reflects the bicultural nature of the African American community and captures the "uniformity, diversity, complexity and richness of Black family life."[35] This framework is based upon the premise that African American culture encompasses three different realms of experience: mainstream, minority, and Black cultural or Afro-cultural.

African Americans whose life experiences are "mainstream" share the beliefs, values, and behavioral styles that are common to a majority of people living in the United States, especially middle- and upper-income Anglo Europeans. In contrast, African Americans who live a "minority" experience are bicultural and have adopted coping strategies and defense mechanisms that have been developed by many minority groups to face life in an oppressive environment. African Americans whose lived experiences are more ethnically encapsulated are likely to be socialized within Boykin's Black cultural or Afro-cultural orientations. The Afro-cultural experience is essentially the link between contemporary African descendants throughout the Diaspora and traditional West African worldviews.[36]

Based on a distillation of scholarly writing on linkages between West African cultural ethos and the core character of African American culture, Boykin identified nine "interrelated but distinct dimensions" that are manifested, mostly in terms of stylistic behaviors, in the lives of African Americans:

1. Spirituality, a vitalistic rather than mechanistic approach to life
2. Harmony, the belief that humans and nature are harmoniously conjoined
3. Movement expressiveness, an emphasis on the interweaving of movement, rhythm, percussiveness, music, and dance
4. Verve, the especial receptiveness to relatively high levels of sensate stimulation
5. Affect, an emphasis on emotions and feelings
6. Communalism, a commitment to social connectedness where social bonds transcend individual privileges
7. Expressive individualism, the cultivation of a distinctive personality and a proclivity for spontaneity in behavior
8. Orality, a preference for oral/aural modalities of communication
9. Social time perspective, an orientation in which time is treated as passing through a social space rather than a material one.[37]

Boykin and his colleagues have conducted a series of basic research studies guided by Boykin's conceptual framework of African American culture. One set of studies focused on verve, a second focused on movement expressiveness, and a third set focused on communalism. Overall, the results of this research supported the conclusion that aspects of African American culture can be incorporated into classroom pedagogy to facilitate learning among African American children. These studies lend support to the view that cultural discontinuity between home and school settings contributes to the academic difficulties many children of color experience in mainstream schools.

The late Asa Hilliard, a noted scholar of African American culture and history at Georgia State University, argued that learning styles are a component of cultural behavioral styles—the habits, values, predisposition, and preferences that develop during the child's cultural socialization process.[38] Children of equivalent intellectual potential who grow up in different cultural milieus learn "to manifest their mental power in somewhat different ways."[39] Hilliard's research, which contrasted African and African American culture with European and European American culture, identified "a unique African American core culture that could be empirically described."[40] Realizing that there are many individual differences within each group, he focused on "central tendencies" and reported that "a given individual in many ways may be very much like most of the members of his or her historical groups of reference."[41] Hilliard wrote that "most individual African Americans are very much a part of core African American culture," even though some may operate on the behavioral margins of their historical group of reference . . . [and] others may operate in ways that are quite outside the norms of [the African American community]."[42] He concluded, "most African Americans, and even a few European Americans, shared in this core culture to a greater or lesser degree."[43]

When teachers misunderstand their students' cultural behavioral styles, they may underestimate their intellectual potential and unknowingly misplace, mislabel, and mistreat them. They may underestimate their students' cognitive abilities, academic achievement, and language skills. Hilliard found that when teachers have low expectations for student learning, they will simplify, concretize, fragment, and slow the pace of instruction, or fail to offer abstract, conceptually oriented instruction to the child. "Thus, we see that it is not the learning style of the child that prevents the child from learning; it is the perception by the teacher of the child's style as a sign of incapacity that causes the teacher to reduce the quality of instruction offered."[44]

There has been a great deal of study focused on the learning styles of African American children and youth.[45] A number of scholars report that the schools take a "White Studies" approach in both subject matter and teaching strategies.[46] Black children and youth who are not bicultural, having grown up outside the dominant culture, tend to process information differently from the predominant way it is processed in schools. Their learning styles are often described as relational, as opposed to the analytical style rewarded in schools.[47] Hilliard observes learning-style tendencies among African Americans that are very compatible with high-context culture (discussed in Chapter 2) and with the core of African American cultural style. He argued that African American people who identify with the African American core culture tend to

1. Respond to things in terms of the whole picture instead of its parts
2. Prefer inferential reasoning to deductive or inductive reasoning
3. Approximate space, numbers, and time rather than stick to accuracy
4. Focus on people and their activities more than on things
5. Have a keen sense of justice and are quick to analyze and perceive injustice
6. Lean toward altruism, a concern for one's fellow man
7. Prefer novelty, freedom, and personal distinctiveness
8. Be very proficient in nonverbal communications and not "word" dependent[48]

Although all researchers might not agree with Hilliard, a growing body of research tends to confirm his conclusions.[49] Learning styles have been identified as an important variable in the school success (or failure) of ethnic minorities in the United States. The fact that our schools tend to be monoethnic, despite the array of diverse learning styles associated with different ethnic groups, may help explain the high dropout rates among African Americans, Latinos, and Native Americans. Further consideration of learning-style characteristics of several ethnic minorities will illustrate how they are often incongruent with learning styles accepted in our schools.

With over 500 American Indian and Alaskan tribal groups, there are differences as well as similarities in the learning styles of children from these groups. The degree to which children are raised in traditional culture communities also makes a difference; many families live in urban areas and may reflect the "mainstream" or "minority" experiences Boykin describes for African Americans and assimilate into the mainstream or become bicultural. However, there is some suggestive research with Indian children raised in traditional communities. Recent studies on the learning styles of some Native American and Alaskan Native youth have established the importance of visualization in learning. Children learn to learn through careful observation of, for example, the behavior and expressions of adults, changing weather conditions, the terrain, and wildlife. Overall, the research on Native American students presents a common pattern in the way they "come to know or understand the world. They approach tasks visually, seem to prefer to learn by careful observation which precedes performance, and seem to learn in their natural settings experientially."[50] This is in contrast to African Americans, who tend to be relational and field dependent. Where Native Americans fit on the continuum of relational/analytical or field dependent/field independent is not clear. What is clear, however, is that the learning style of many American Indian students is different from that of mainstream students.[51] Phillips describes how this difference can cause problems in school:

> [Native] American students customarily acquire the various skills of their culture (i.e., hunting, tanning, beadwork) in a sequence of three steps. First, the child over a period of time watches and listens to a competent adult who is performing the skill. Secondly, the child takes over small portions of the task and completes them in cooperation with and under the supervision of the adult, in this way gradually learning all of the component skills involved. Finally, the child goes off and privately tests himself or herself to see whether the skill has been fully learned: a failure is not seen by others and causes no embarrassment, but a success is brought back and exhibited to the teachers and others. The use of speech in this three-step process is minimal. When these same children go to school they find themselves in a situation where the high value placed on verbal performance is only the first of their cross-cultural hurdles. . . . Acquisition and demonstration of knowledge are no longer separate steps but are expected to occur simultaneously. Furthermore, this single-step process takes place via public recitations, the assumption apparently being that one learns best by making verbal mistakes in front of one's peers and teachers. Finally, the children have little opportunity to observe skilled performers carrying out these tasks, for the other children who perform are as ignorant and unskilled as they. Under these circumstances, it is small wonder that these [Native] American students demonstrate a propensity for silence.[52]

In contrast to the mainstream adage, "If at first you don't succeed, try, try, again," the Native American view is likely to be, "If at first you don't think, and think again, don't bother trying."[53]

Compared with the research on learning styles of other U.S. ethnic groups, there is a paucity of research on Asian American learners.[54] The education research that does exist on Asian Americans, particularly on Japanese American students, has indicated that many are hardworking, high achieving, relatively nonverbal, and seek careers in math and science.[55] As a result,

> many teachers stereotype Asian and Pacific American students as quiet, hardworking, and docile, which tends to reinforce conformity and stifle creativity. Asian and Pacific American students, therefore, frequently do not develop the ability to assert and express themselves verbally and are channeled in disproportionate numbers into the technical/scientific fields. As a consequence, many Asian and Pacific American students undergo traumatic family/school discontinuities, suffer from low self-esteem, are overly conforming, and have their academic and social development narrowly circumscribed.[56]

Perhaps the successful "model minority" myth associated with Asian Americans explains why there has been little study of their educational problems and learning styles. Particularly needed is insight into the learning styles of the most recent immigrants from Southeast Asia, many of whom face major difficulties in our schools. A recent study of the learning styles of Hmong refugees, hill people from northern Laos who have settled in the Midwest, offers valuable insights into learning-style characteristics that may be applicable to recent Southeast Asian refugees in general.[57] The Hmong students studied tend to be primarily field dependent and to use global rather than analytical problem-solving techniques. They are also reported to be passive and receptive, rather than active; unaccustomed to dealing with abstractions; and dependent upon mimesis (memorization), close identification with the teacher, peer influence, group support, and cooperation.

Learning Styles and Teaching Styles

As teachers we tend to teach the way we learn best, unless we make a conscious effort to do otherwise. We can, therefore, discover a great deal about our teaching style by analyzing our learning style. Indeed, this is important, for just as students may be negatively affected by learning-style mismatches, teachers are often negatively affected by teaching-style mismatches.

Gregorc writes, "Teachers whose teaching styles closely approximate their *major learning preferences* report comfort, ease, and authenticity."[58] Teachers who consistently mismatch their learning and teaching styles "report feelings of awkwardness, lack of efficiency and authenticity, and pain—mental and physical."[59] Many teachers are not aware of their teaching-style and learning-style preference and view pain and fatigue as natural results of hard work and study—"not as possible indicators of *dis-ease.*" Many teachers attempt to conform to a distinct image of what a teacher should be, even if the image is unnatural for them. Others are influenced by traditional or required practice. "There are teachers, for example, who tell us that 'poetry *must* be taught this way,' and that 'we can't individualize and still meet mandated behavioral objectives,' or that 'students are not permitted to move around my room.'"[60]

Stress and teacher burnout can result from extended periods of mismatch. Thus, educators' understanding of their own learning and teaching styles benefits them as much as their students. Fortunately, it is not difficult to attain this self-awareness.

Teachers find the ELSIE (see page 219) and the GEFT (see page 215) useful approaches for assessing their own perceptual modality preferences and their tendency toward field insensitivity-sensitivity or field independence-dependence. Most often these teachers agree that they expect their students to learn the same way they do. They also report that this self-awareness gives them insight into some of the "disease" they experience when trying to be more flexible in their teaching. The insight itself often leads to feeling greater ease as they add new teaching styles to the old.

The idea of teaching style must not be confused with a teacher's method of instruction, such as the lecture, small group work, or oral reports. Teaching style refers to the teacher's pervasive personal behaviors and media used during interaction with learners. It is the teacher's characteristic approach, whatever the method used.[61]

In one recent review of learning-style research, Dunn and Dunn examined a large number of "well-designed and carefully conducted research"[62] studies. They reported that when students are taught through their individual learning styles, their academic achievement increases significantly, their attitudes toward school improve significantly, and school discipline problems are significantly reduced.[63] Furthermore, "students have significantly more positive attitudes toward a subject when their learning styles are similar to their teachers' teaching styles."[64] Other research has documented that students perform better in classes taught by teachers with learning styles similar to the student.[65] This makes sense if one assumes that most teachers teach in ways that match their own learning styles. Only recently have demands been made that teachers become more flexible and use a variety of teaching styles in order to respond to the diversity of learning styles among their students.

Conclusions on Learning Styles

In her anthology *Culture, Style and the Educative Process*, Shade reviews a wide range of literature and research on the cultural styles of African Americans, Asian Americans, American Indians, Latinos, and European Americans. Her contributors wrote at different times and in different geophysical environments, yet their "suggestions for promoting the academic success of culturally different children are remarkably similar."[66] Four major suggestions emerged to help teachers use culture and cognitive style in their teaching:

1. Inclusion of "multisensory presentations to open all pathways to the brain"[67]
2. Acceptance and understanding of different behavioral styles that otherwise could lead to unwarranted discipline problems
3. Restructuring of the classroom social environment to make it more inclusive and less exclusive
4. Inclusion of a variety of communication and thinking styles to strengthen information processing by *all* students[68]

Without alternative paths to success, we will continue to thwart the learning of some, and often many. If classroom expectations are limited by our own cultural orientations, we impede success for learners guided by another cultural orientation. If we teach only according to the ways we ourselves learn best, we are also likely to

Box 8.1
Field Sensitivity   *Alfredo Castañeda and Tracy Gray*

Field-Sensitive Behaviors
Relationship to Peers
1. Likes to work with others to achieve a common goal
2. Likes to assist others
3. Is sensitive to feelings and opinions of others

Personal Relationship to Teacher
1. Openly expresses positive feelings for teacher
2. Asks questions about teacher's tastes and personal experiences; seeks to become like teacher

Instructional Relationship to Teacher
1. Openly expresses positive feelings for teacher
2. Seeks rewards that strengthen relationship with teacher
3. Is highly motivated when working individually with teacher

Characteristics of Curriculum That Facilitate Learning
1. Performance objectives and global aspects of curriculum are carefully explained
2. Concepts are presented in humanized or story format
3. Concepts are related to personal interests and experiences of children

Field-Sensitive Teaching Style
Personal Behaviors
1. Displays physical and verbal expressions of approval and warmth
2. Uses personalized rewards that strengthen the relationship with students

Instructional Behaviors
1. Expresses confidence in child's ability to succeed, is sensitive to children who are having difficulty and need help
2. Gives guidance to students; makes purpose and main principles of lesson obvious; presentation of lesson is clear, with steps toward "solution" clearly delineated
3. Encourages learning through modeling; asks children to imitate
4. Encourages cooperation and development of group feelings, encourages class to think and work as a unit
5. Holds informal class discussions; provides opportunities for students to see how concepts being learned are related to students' personal experiences

Curriculum-Related Behaviors

1. Emphasizes global aspects of concepts; before beginning lesson ensures that students understand the performance objectives; identifies generalizations and helps children apply them to particular instances
2. Personalizes curriculum; teacher relates curriculum materials to the interests and experiences of students, as well to her or his own interests
3. Humanizes curriculum; attributes human characteristics to concepts and principles
4. Uses teaching materials to elicit expression of feelings from students; helps students apply concepts for labeling their personal experiences

Source: Alfredo Castañeda and Tracy Gray, "Bicognitive Processes in Multiracial Education," *Educational Leadership, 32* (December 1974). Reprinted with permission of the Association for Supervision and Curriculum Development. Copyright © 1974 by the Association for Supervision and Curriculum Development. All rights reserved.

Box 8.2
Field Independence   *Alfredo Castañeda and Tracy Gray*

Field-Independent Behaviors

Relationship to Peers

1. Prefers to work independently
2. Likes to compare and gain individual recognition
3. Task oriented; is inattentive to social environment when working

Personal Relationship to Teacher

1. Rarely seeks physical contact with teacher
2. Formal; interactions with teacher are restricted to tasks at hand

Instructional Relationship to Teacher

1. Likes to try new tasks without teacher's help
2. Impatient to begin tasks; likes to finish first
3. Seeks nonsocial rewards

Characteristics of Curriculum That Facilitate Learning

1. Details of concepts are emphasized; parts have meaning of their own
2. Deals with math and science concepts
3. Based on discovery approach

continued

Field-Independent Teaching Style

Personal Behaviors

1. Is formal in relationship with students; acts the part of an authority figure
2. Centers attention on instructional objectives; gives social atmosphere secondary importance

Instructional Behaviors

1. Encourages independent achievement; emphasizes the importance of individual effort
2. Encourages competition between individual students
3. Adopts a consultant role; teacher encourages students to seek help only when they experience difficulty
4. Encourages learning through trial and error
5. Encourages task orientation; focuses student attention on assigned tasks

Curriculum-Related Behaviors

1. Focuses on details of curriculum materials
2. Focuses on facts and principles; teaches students how to solve problems using shortcuts and novel approaches
3. Emphasizes math and science abstractions; teacher tends to use graphs, charts, and formulas in teaching, even when presenting social studies curriculum
4. Emphasizes inductive learning and the discovery approach; starts with isolated parts and slowly puts them together to construct rules or generalizations

Source: Alfredo Castañeda and Tracy Gray, "Bicognitive Processes in Multicultural Education," *Educational Leadership, 32* (December 1974). Reprinted with permission of the Association for Supervision and Curriculum Development. Copyright © 1974 by the Association for Supervision and Curriculum Development. All rights reserved.

Box 8.3
Curricula for Field Sensitivity and Field Independence   *Alfredo Castañeda and Tracy Gray*

Field-Sensitive Curriculum

Content

1. Social abstractions: Field-sensitive curriculum is humanized through use of narration, humor, drama, and fantasy. Characterized by social words and human characteristics. Focuses on lives of persons who occupy central roles in the topic of study, such as history or scientific discovery.
2. Personalized: The ethnic background of students, as well as their homes and neighborhoods, is reflected. The teacher is given the opportunity to express personal experiences and interests.

Structure

1. Global: Emphasis is on description of wholes and generalities; the overall view or general topic is presented first. The purpose or use of the concept or skill is clearly stated using practical examples.
2. Rules explicit: Rules and principles are salient. (Children who prefer to learn in the field-sensitive mode are more comfortable given the rules than when asked to discover the underlying principles for themselves.)
3. Requires cooperation with others: The curriculum is structured in such a way that children work cooperatively with peers or with the teacher in a variety of activities.

Field-Independent Curriculum

Content

1. Math and science abstractions: Field-independent curriculum uses many graphs and formulae.
2. Impersonal: Field-independent curriculum focuses on events, places, and facts in social studies rather than personal histories.

Structure

1. Focus on details: The details of a concept are explored, followed by the global concept.
2. Discovery: Rules and principles are discovered from the study of details; the general is discovered from the understanding of the particulars.
3. Requires independent activity: The curriculum requires children to work individually, minimizing interaction with others.

Source: Alfredo Castañeda and Tracy Gray, "Bicognitive Processes in Multicultural Education," *Educational Leadership, 32* (December 1974). Reprinted with permission of the Association for Supervision and Curriculum Development. Copyright © 1974 by the Association for Supervision and Curriculum Development. All rights reserved.

Box 8.4
Learning Styles and Students' Needs   *David Hunt*

Characteristics of Students Who Require Much Structure

1. They have a short attention span, cannot sit still for the period—in constant movement.
2. They have no inner control as individuals, do not know how to function in group situations (many physical and verbal fights).
3. They (usually boys) are physical with each other and try the rules often.
4. They ask for direction often. (They do not rely on themselves or want to think.)

continued

5. They are literal and unable to make inferences or interpretations.
6. They lack self-confidence, generally have a poor self-image.
7. They have difficulty organizing themselves and their materials.
8. They do not reveal anything of themselves or express personal opinions—everything is very objective. They are afraid to get emotionally involved with a story or film.
9. They have a wide range of abilities.
10. They see things in black and white with no gray in between.
11. They want to know the basic information or process and are not interested in the sidelights.
12. They are incapable of handling general questions or thinking through a problem; they guess and let it go at that.
13. They do not assume responsibility for their own actions.
14. They work only because the teacher tells them to work and look to peers for approval.
15. They are laconic; they give brief answers with little elaboration.

Characteristics of Students Who Require Some Structure

1. They are oriented to the role of the good student (one who gets the right answers, has neat work, and good work habits).
2. They seek teacher approval and strive to please the teacher; they go along with what the teacher says.
3. They want to work alone at their own desks.
4. They are reluctant to try anything new; they do not like to appear wrong or dumb.
5. They do not express personal opinions.
6. They do not ask questions.
7. They are confused by choices.
8. They are incapable of adjusting to a different teacher; they are upset by visitors or alterations of the schedule.
9. They look for reassurance and frequently ask, "Is this right?" "What should I do now?" "What should I write?"
10. They are not particularly imaginative.
11. They participate well in the class as a whole but do not work well in small groups.
12. They are grade conscious.

Characteristics of Students Who Require Little Structure

1. They like to discuss and argue; everybody wants to talk at once with few listening; therefore the noise level is high and progress somewhat slower.
2. They will question and volunteer additional information.
3. They want to solve things themselves; they don't want the teacher's help until they have exhausted all resources.
4. They are averse to detail and dislike going step by step, are able to see the entire picture and tend to ignore the steps required to get there, are creative and like to formulate and act on their own ideas, and often get so involved that they do not hear the teacher.

5. They are capable of abstract thinking; they do not require concrete objects.
6. They are less afraid of making mistakes than other students, are more imaginative, go off on sidetracks, and are able to see alternatives.
7. They can stay at one thing for a longer time and can work by themselves with little or no supervision.
8. They have a greater depth of emotions and are more open about themselves than other students.
9. They display greater ability in making interpretations and drawing inferences than other students do.
10. They are somewhat self-centered and not very concerned with others.

Source: Adapted from David E. Hunt, "Learning Style and Students Needs: An Introduction to Conceptual Level," in *Student Learning Styles: Diagnosing and Prescribing Programs* (Reston, VA: National Association of Secondary School Principals, 1979). By permission of the author.

Box 8.5
Structure Requirements
David Hunt

Teaching Approaches for Students Who Require Much Structure
1. Have definite and consistent rules—let them know what is expected of them.
2. Give specific guidelines and instructions (step by step); even make a chart of the steps.
3. Make goals and deadlines short and definite—give them the topic, how many lines/pages, how it is to be done and the exact date it is due.
4. Provide a variety of activities during the period, incorporating some physical movement whenever possible.
5. Make positive comments about their attempts; give immediate feedback on each step; give much assurance and attention; praise often.
6. Use visuals and objects they can see, feel, and touch.
7. Get them to work immediately and change pace often.
8. Display their work—it is a form of reinforcement to which they respond.
9. Capitalize on their interest to assist them in learning the various skills (for example, stories or projects dealing with cars with grade nine boys).
10. Begin with factual material before discussion.
11. Move gradually from seat work to discussion; provide more group work as they are able to handle it.
12. Leave them at the end of each period with the satisfaction of having learned new material and having success in what they have been studying—almost a complete lesson each period with minor carry-over to the next period with the mention of something interesting to come.

continued

13. Give short quizzes and objective tests initially.
14. Provide opportunities for choice and decision making as they appear ready for them.

Teaching Approaches for Students Who Require Some Structure

1. Arrange students initially in rows and gradually get them working in pairs, then in small groups.
2. Have definite and consistent rules—let them know what is expected of them.
3. Use creative skits to encourage spontaneity, self-awareness, and cooperation.
4. Tell them what to do each day. Some teachers find that initialing the students' work daily provides the contact they desire and the impetus to continue—they can see how much they have accomplished.
5. Provide nonthreatening situations where they have to risk an opinion.
6. Provide a lot of praise and success-oriented situations.
7. Give them group problems to encourage sharing.
8. Provide opportunities for choice and decision making as students appear ready for them. Push them gently into situations where they have to make decisions and take responsibility.

Teaching Approaches for Students Who Require Little Structure

1. Allow them to select their own seats.
2. Give them many topics from which to choose.
3. Set weekly or longer assignments and allow students to make up their own timetables.
4. Encourage them to use each other as resources.
5. Allow more mobility and give them more opportunities to take part in planning and decision making.
6. Give them freedom to pursue projects on their own.
7. Have them work in groups with the teacher serving as a resource person.
8. Train them to listen to instructions (and to listen in general) as they tend to go off on their own.
9. Remind and encourage them to take an interest in others.

Source: Adapted from David E. Hunt, "Learning Style and Students Needs: An Introduction to Conceptual Level," in *Student Learning Styles: Diagnosing and Prescribing Programs* (Reston, VA: National Association of Secondary School Principals, 1979). By permission of the author.

thwart success for learners who may share our cultural background but whose learning style deviates from our own.

Everyone knows of gifted teachers, whose awareness and human sensitivity enable them to bridge cultural and individual gaps. They manage to provide each student with what he or she needs to be successful. But to what extent this flexibility and openness depend on basic personality traits may never be known. In any case, every teacher who wants to can take steps that will open the channels of success to all learners, regardless of their cultural or individual ways. To do this, we should adopt the following guidelines:

- Know our own teaching and learning styles.
- Determine how far we can stray from these strengths and preferences and still be comfortable.
- Begin with a few students, those who are having difficulty in our classes.
- Know the learning-style patterns that seem to characterize various ethnic groups.
- Build classroom flexibility slowly, adding one new strategy at a time.
- Use all modes (visual, auditory, tactile, and kinesthetic) when teaching concepts and skills.

The Promise of Culturally Competent Teaching

What is *culturally competent teaching*? It refers to teachers who have the dispositions, attitudes, knowledge, skills, and resources needed to ensure high levels of learning and the personal development of culturally different learners—students whose lived experiences, culturally developed knowledge, and sometimes language differ from their teachers and/or their classroom peers. Becoming a culturally competent teacher is probably a career-long endeavor, but the journey is hastened with open-mindedness and an inquiry orientation when one first encounters "strangers" in the classroom. Karen Manheim Teel identifies eight characteristics of teachers who have attained a high level of racial and cultural competence. Similar to teachers who practice culturally responsive teaching, these are teachers who

1. Are very comfortable with the students
2. Engage students all of the time
3. Have a positive personal connection with each student
4. Have very high expectations for each student and follow through with them
5. Accept total responsibility for any student's lack of success
6. Have a strong, positive relationship with all of the parents
7. Constantly reflect on their practice and include others in the assessment of their practice
8. Develop and use culturally relevant lessons on a regular basis[69]

Culturally relevant teaching has focused primarily on "reversing the underachievement of students of color."[70] It is defined as "using the cultural knowledge, prior experiences, frames of reference, and performance styles of ethnically diverse students to make learning encounters more relevant to and effective for them. It teaches *to and through* the strengths of these students. It is culturally *validating and affirming*."[71] Thus, culturally relevant teaching is appropriate for *all* students, including those who are ill served by the school because of their ethnicity, first language, or low-income background. It originated in research aimed at understanding and mediating mismatches between students' home culture and the culture of the school through teaching that has been labeled "culturally appropriate," "culturally congruent," "culturally compatible," or "culturally responsive."

The work of Gloria Ladson-Billings, a former teacher in Philadelphia Public Schools who is now a professor at the University of Wisconsin, is among the most important on this topic and uses the term "culturally relevant teaching."[72] Let's consider her award-winning research based on three years of qualitative inquiry in a California school district that serves primarily African American families.

The first step in the Ladson-Billings research was the identification of successful teachers of African American children. She asked both the parents and principals in four schools to nominate "excellent teachers." What the parents and principals looked for differed dramatically. The parents' criteria included: (1) enthusiasm their children showed in learning while in the teacher's classroom; (2) consistent levels of respect they (the parent) felt from the teacher; and (3) their perception that the teachers "understood the need for the students to operate in the dual worlds of their home community and the White community."[73] Principals, however, used the following criteria: (1) low number of discipline referrals; (2) high attendance rates; and (3) high standardized test scores. Nine teachers were on both the parents' and the principals' lists. Eight agreed to participate in the study.

Funded for two years, the Ladson-Billings study included in-depth ethnographic interviews with each teacher, unannounced classroom visitations, extensive video-taping of classroom instruction, and collaborative reflection and inquiry with all the teachers in the study. She extended her study for a third year to focus on literacy teaching.

At first this researcher despaired of discovering any patterns or themes that could help her identify some principles that would explain why these teachers were so outstanding. Her teachers differed dramatically in terms of structure, style, strategies, and personality. Eventually, however, it became clear that these teachers (who were either African American or White) were very similar in how they viewed themselves as teachers and how they viewed their students, parents, and others in the community; in how they structured social relations inside and outside their classrooms; and in how they viewed knowledge. First of all, they were proud of teaching as a profession and had chosen to teach in this low-income, primarily African American community. Each of these teachers felt a strong sense of purpose and believed it was his or her responsibility to ensure the success of each student. Second (whether African American or White), they were aware of the societal conditions of discrimination and injustice for African Americans and understood how this influenced the school's academic expectations for students of color. Third, they avoided "assimilationist" approaches to teaching and wanted to prepare their students to become change agents, not just to fit into mainstream society. And fourth, they capitalized on their students' home and community culture by creating a flexible, fluid, and collaborative learning climate where everyone (including the teacher) learned from everyone else.

Principles of Culturally Relevant Teaching

Three promising principles of culturally relevant teaching have developed from the Ladson-Billings research. Some educators describe it as "just good teaching," which leads us to wonder why it is so rare among students of color, as well as among rural and low-income White students.

1. Students must experience academic success, including literacy; numeracy; and the technological, social, and political skills they need to be active participants in a democracy. This is not false self-esteem building. Rather, self-esteem accompanies genuine academic success.
2. Students must develop and/or maintain cultural competence, and the student's home culture becomes a vehicle for learning. For example, one of the teachers in the study whose teenaged son was an avid rap fan encouraged her second graders to write and sing rap as a tool for writing poetry and for becoming bilingual and bidialectical. (The students' raps had to be something they would sing at home!)
3. Students must develop a "critical consciousness" through which they may challenge social injustice. Some of the teachers studied engaged their students in rewriting out-of-date textbooks; others got involved in community information drives and community problem solving.

Similarly, Geneva Gay identifies and describes six characteristics of culturally responsive teaching.[74]

1. First, it is *validating*, in that
   - It acknowledges the legitimacy of the cultural heritages of different ethnic groups, both as legacies that affect students' dispositions, attitudes, and approaches to learning and as worthy content to be taught in the formal curriculum.
   - It builds bridges of meaningfulness between home and school experiences as well as between academic abstractions and lived sociocultural realities.
   - It uses a wide variety of instructional strategies that are connected to different learning styles.
   - It teaches students to know and praise their own and each other's cultural heritages.
   - It incorporates multicultural information, resources, and materials in all the subjects and skills routinely taught in schools.
2. Second, it is *comprehensive*, in that it focuses on the whole child and uses community cultural connections to

   develop intellectual, social emotional, and political learning. . . . Along with improving academic achievement, these approaches to teaching are committed to helping students of color maintain identity and connections with their ethnic groups and communities; develop a sense of community, camaraderie, and shared responsibility; and acquire an ethic of success. . . . Students are held accountable for each others' learning as well as their own.

3. Third, it is *multidimensional* in that it "encompasses curriculum content, learning content, classroom climate, student-teacher relationships, instructional techniques, and performance assessments."

4. Fourth, it is *empowering*, in that "it enables students to be better human beings and more successful learners. Empowerment translates into academic competence, personal confidence, courage, and the will to act."

5. Fifth, it is *transformative*, in that it

defies conventions of traditional educational practices with respect to ethnic students of color.... It is very explicit about respecting the cultures and experiences of African American, Native American, Latino, and Asian American students, and it uses these as worthwhile resources for teaching and learning. It recognizes the existing strengths and accomplishments of these students and then enhances them further in the instructional process.... (A)cademic success and cultural consciousness are developed simultaneously.... Students ... must learn to become change agents committed to promoting greater equality, justice, and power balances among ethnic groups.... (T)he transformative agenda ... is double focused. One direction deals with confronting and transcending the cultural hegemony nested in much of the curriculum content and classroom instruction of traditional education. The other develops social consciousness, intellectual critique, and political and personal efficacy in students so that they can combat prejudices, racism, and other forms of oppression and exploitation.

6. Sixth, it is *emancipatory*, or liberating, in that it

releases the intellect of students of color from the constraining manacles of mainstream canons of knowledge and ways of knowing.... it helps students realize that no single version of "truth" is total and permanent.... Students are taught how to apply new knowledge generated by various ethnic scholars to their analyses of social histories, issues, problems, and experiences. These learning engagements encourage and enable students to find their own voices, to contextualize issues in multiple cultural perspectives, to engage in more ways of knowing and thinking, and to become more active participants in shaping their own learning.

Examples of Culturally Relevant Teaching

In *The Dreamkeepers: Successful Teachers of African American Children*, Ladson-Billings presents vivid portraits of the eight teachers in her study. One of them, Ann Lewis, is a forty-four-year-old Italian American woman who has taught sixth grade in a low-income, predominantly African American community for fourteen years.[75] Most of the African American young men in Ann's classroom have a history of "misbehavior" and are considered to be "at risk" of school failure. Ann encouraged them to lead discussions and other class activities, to initiate inquiry, and to challenge the status quo. In her class it was "cool" or "hip" to be academically excellent. She emphasized a learning community based on cooperation and collaboration, rather than competition, and encouraged her students to rely on and support each other. Ann included the students' real-life experiences as legitimate parts of the "official curriculum," and often learned from her students. Although she selected literature for her students, such as Candy Dawson Boyd's *Charlie Pippin* (a story about a young African American girl who launches an antinuclear war protest), she allowed her students to ask their own questions and search for their own answers. She relied on her students' own lives to build and extend the curriculum. For example, the discussion of *Charlie Pippin* led a student to comment that he lived in a "war zone," which led to discussion and writing about living in a community plagued by violence. On another occasion Ann used her students' fears about attending an integrated camp as an opportunity to read, write, and talk about threatening social conditions. When some of her students did encounter a racial incident at the camp, they were better prepared to deal with it without violence.

Another powerful example of culturally relevant teaching is Martha Demienti-eff, a Native Alaskan teacher of Athabaskan Indian students, who is described in Lisa Delpit's book, *Other People's Children: Cultural Conflicts in the Classroom.* Martha's students live in a small, isolated village of about 200 people. Martha builds upon her students' knowledge of their own language and culture to help them understand the language of power in our society; her goal is intercultural competence, not assimilation through eradication of the village culture. For example, she analyzes their writing for examples of "Village English" and writes them on the blackboard under the heading "Our Heritage Language." Opposite each example she writes an "equivalent statement" under the heading "Formal English." Delpit describes what happens next in Martha's classroom:

She and the students spend a long time on the "Heritage English" section, savoring the words, discussing the nuances. She tells the students, "That's the way we say things. Doesn't it feel good? Isn't this the absolute best way of getting that idea across?" Then she turns to the other side of the board. She tells the students that there are people, not like those in the village, who judge others by the way they talk or write.[76] Martha tells them:

> *We listen to the way people talk, not to judge them, but to tell what part of the river they come from. These other people are not like that. They think everybody needs to talk like them. Unlike us, they have a hard time hearing what people say if they don't talk exactly like them. Their way of talking and writing is called "Formal English."*
>
> *We have to feel a little sorry for them because they have only one way to talk. We're going to learn two ways to say things. . . . One will be our Heritage way. The other will be Formal English. Then, when we go to get jobs, we'll be able to talk like those people who only know and can only listen to one way. Maybe after we get the jobs we can help them to learn how it feels to have another language, like ours, that feels so good. We'll talk like them when we have to, but we'll always know our way is best.*[77]

Martha does many follow-up activities to help students understand informal or Heritage English and Formal English. She also helps them see differences between "wordy" academic language and the metaphoric style of Athabaskan. The students are helped to see how "book language always uses more words" while in Heritage language "the shorter way is always better."[78] Martha encourages her students to write enough to "sound like a book" and then to reduce the message to a "saying" brief enough to fit on a T-shirt!

A third example of culturally relevant teaching is seen with Kathy, a Head Start teacher who works in a rural school in Northern Michigan that serves low-income White students.[79] In contrast to most Head Start teachers, who follow curriculum guidelines provided by their Head Start coordinator, Kathy builds her teaching around her children's interests and questions. Like Ann and Martha, Kathy chooses to teach in a low-income community and believes it is necessary to connect her teaching with the lives of her children. Kathy, too, is an advocate for her children and their families. She rejects the idea that her role as an "at-risk" teacher is to instruct the children and families in how to fit into middle-class society. She said:

> I believe that it is my responsibility to learn as much as I can about the child's family and their culture and then implement that into my classroom, so that the child can see that his/her culture is a part of our classroom and that I respect them and their family and their culture. It can be hard; I don't want to pre-sent any new stereotypes to these kids, so I ask the parents a lot of questions. Sometimes I get the answers and sometimes I don't, but at least they can see I am trying.[80]

Kathy watches her children to discover what interests them. For example, one warm winter day a fly was in the classroom, and her students were fascinated. "They talked about and followed that fly all day!"[81] That evening Kathy gathered books and other materials about flies and insects, and she and the children spent two weeks on bugs.

Kathy does not find much collegial support for her approach to teaching and is likely to lose her current job with Head Start. She might find encouragement in the collaborative research among a team of teacher-researchers who, like herself, want to know and understand their students' funds of knowledge.

Funds of Knowledge Research and Teaching

A team of educators and anthropologists working with schools and communities in southern Arizona is developing another promising line of research, *funds of knowledge*, that is compatible with culturally relevant teaching. They view *culture* as the historically accumulated knowledge and lived experiences of students; each family household has funds of knowledge that establish a knowledge base for schoolchildren to draw upon. They write,

> Our purpose in this work is to provide a broad anthropological context for possible educational reforms of the public schools that serve U.S.–Mexican populations in the southwestern United States. Our position is that public schools often ignore the strategic and cultural resources, which we have called funds of knowledge, that households contain. We argue that these funds not only provide the basis for understanding the cultural systems from which U.S.–Mexican children emerge, but they are also important and useful assets in the classroom.[82]

Through their study of household and classroom practices within working-class, Mexican-origin communities in Tucson, they are developing "innovations in teaching that draw upon the knowledge and skills found in local households."[83] Although this research has focused on Mexican-origin and Yaqui families living in the borderlands, it has exciting implications for multicultural teaching throughout the country.

Their work includes three components: (1) the *ethnographic study* of "the origin, use, and distribution of funds of knowledge among households in a predominantly Mexican, working-class community of Tucson, Arizona"; (2) *after-school "lab"* or *study groups* where teachers and researchers collaborated and planned strategic instruction based on their research findings; and (3) *classroom research* that examined the impact of instruction based on the household study of funds of knowledge developed in the study groups.[84]

In the original study, ten teachers each conducted research in three households of children in their classroom. In partnership with an anthropologist skilled in ethnographic inquiry, the teachers entered these households as learners, or ethnographers who wanted to know and understand their students and their students' households' "funds of knowledge."[85] A basic assumption of this research is that students will learn more in classrooms where teachers know and understand these funds of knowledge. To discover these assets, the teachers interviewed family members and served as participant observers, keenly listening and watching, and learned about the lived practices of their students' households.

As they approached the households these "teacher researchers" noted gardens, recreational areas, tools, equipment, physical and spatial layouts of the homes, books, toys, and any other material clues that might lead to the discovery of household strategies and resources. They engaged in a series of open-ended interviews with parents that focused on family histories and social networks, labor histories of households, and language and child-rearing ideologies. In this way, teacher-researchers came to appreciate the repertoire from which households draw in order to subsist and validated household knowledge as worthy of pedagogical notice.[86]

The household funds of knowledge the team initially gathered are based on a sample of about 100 families who have knowledge and skill in areas such as ranching and farming, including horse and riding skills, animal management, soil and irrigation systems; mining and timbering, including minerals and blasting; business, such as market values, appraising, renting and selling, loans, labor laws, building codes, accounting, and sales; household management, like budgeting, child care, cooking, and appliance repairs; home construction, design, and maintenance; repair of airplanes, automobiles, and heavy equipment; contemporary and folk medicine; and religion, such as catechism, baptism, Bible stories, moral knowledge, and ethics.[87]

While they were engaged in this research, the teachers worked together in after-school study groups to develop innovative teaching practices that made strategic connections between homes and classrooms. As a result, their approach avoids ill-founded attempts at teaching a "culture-sensitive curriculum" that is based on "folkloric displays, such as storytelling, arts, crafts, and dance performance."[88] Instead, the students' funds of knowledge are drawn upon to enhance student learning in all the content areas, such as mathematics, language arts, science, social studies, and physical education. For example, one teacher-researcher built upon her students' households' knowledge of the medicinal value of plants and herbs, and created a unit on the curative properties of plants. Another teacher developed an inquiry-based unit on candy that explored nutritional content, production, marketing, and a cross-national preference survey report, when she learned that one of her students regularly participated in transborder activities and often returned from northern Mexico with candy to sell.[89]

The research described above is inspiring; hopefully it will be replicated in schools and communities across the country. In the examples of culturally relevant teaching and teaching based on funds of knowledge, we see evidence of the *empowering nature of respect* as envisioned by Sara Lawrence-Lightfoot in her book, *Respect: An Exploration* (1999).

Conclusions on Culturally Competent Teaching

Culturally competent teaching requires teachers to create learning communities that are socioculturally and linguistically meaningful for *all* the learners in the classroom. We have seen successful examples of culturally responsive teachers working with diverse students from the same community. But what about classrooms where students come from several or many different communities? What about communities in the heartland where children of recent immigrant families are newcomers in schools, many of them English–language learners? These questions will be addressed in Chapters 10 and 11, but teachers cannot do it alone. Culturally competent teachers require community and broad societal support to meet these challenges and to turn them into opportunities for all learners to become multiculturally competent.

A number of scholars who are working with projects to help educators become more culturally competent are inspired by the work of Terry Cross, the executive di-

A discussion of "Funds of Knowledge" research and the importance of culturally relevant teaching.

rector of the National Indian Child Welfare Association in Portland, Oregon.[90] In 1989 and 1993, Cross and his associates published the monograph *Toward a Culturally Competent System of Care*. Although it was written for mental health providers, it is also used in industrial and educational settings because it provides "a model for individual and organizational change."[91] Their vision of a culturally competent system is one that

- Respects the unique, culturally defined needs of various student populations.
- Acknowledges culture as a predominant force in shaping behaviors, values, and institutions and that culture has an impact on education.
- Views natural systems (family, community, church, healers) as primary mechanisms of support for minority populations.
- Recognizes that the concepts of family, community, and the like are different for various cultures and even for subgroups within cultures.
- Understands that minority students are usually best served by persons who are part of or in tune with their cultures.
- Educates students in the context of their minority status, which creates unique educational issues for them, including issues related to self-esteem, identity formation, isolation, and assumptions about the role of schooling.
- Recognizes that the thought patterns of non-Western peoples, though different, are equally valid and influence how students view problems and solutions.
- Respects cultural preferences that value process rather than product and harmony or balance within one's life rather than achievement.
- Recognizes that taking the best of both worlds enhances the capacity of all.
- Recognizes that minority people have to be at least bicultural, which in turn creates educational and health issues such as identity conflicts resulting from assimilation.
- Understands when values of minority groups are in conflict with dominant society values.[92]

Taken together, these statements provide a framework to help educational institutions create environments that support culturally competent teaching and to progressively evaluate their assumptions, goals, purpose, policies, and practices over time.

Selected Sources for Further Study

Conchas, G. Q. (2006). *The Color of Success: Race and High-Achieving Urban Youth*. New York: Teachers College Press.

Cushner, K., & Brennan, S. (Eds.). (2007). *Intercultural Student Teaching: A Bridge to Global Competence*. Lanham, MD: Rowman & Littlefield.

Diller, J. V., & Moule, J. (2005). *Cultural Competence: A Primer for Educators*. Belmont, CA: Thompson Wadsworth.

Gay, G. (in press). *Culturally Responsive Teaching: Theory, Research, & Practice*, 2nd ed. New York: Teachers College Press.

Gonzalez, N., Moll, L. C., & Amanti, C. (Eds.). (2005). *Funds of Knowledge: Theorizing Practices in Households, Communities, and Classrooms.* Mahwah, NJ: Lawrence Erlbaum Associates.

McIntyre, E., Rosebery, A., & Gonzalez, N. (Eds.). (2001). *Classroom Diversity: Connecting Curriculum to Students' Lives.* Portsmouth, NH: Heinemann.

Nieto, S. (2004). "Puerto Rican Students in U.S. Schools: A Troubled Past and the Search for a Hopeful Future." In *Handbook of Research on Multicultural Education*, 2nd ed., eds. J. A. Banks and C. M. Banks, 515–541. San Francisco: Jossey-Bass.

Pang, V. O., Kiang, P. N., & Pak, Y. K. (2004). "Asian Pacific American Students: Challenging a Biased Educational System." In *Handbook of Research on Multicultural Education*, 2nd ed., eds. J. A.

Banks and C. M. Banks, 542–563. San Francisco: Jossey-Bass.

Robins, K. N., Lindsey, R. B., Lindsey, D. B., Terrell, R. D. (2006). *Culturally Proficient Instruction: A Guide for People Who Teach*, 2nd ed. Thousand Oaks, CA: Corwin Press.

Sercu, L. (2004). "Assessing Intercultural Competence: A Framework for Systematic Test Development in Foreign Language Education and Beyond." *Intercultural Education, Vol. 15*, No. 1, pp. 73–89.

Sheets, R. H. (2005). *Diversity Pedagogy: Examining the Role of Culture in the Teaching-Learning Process.* Boston: Pearson Allyn & Bacon.

Teel, K. M., & Obidah, J. E. (Eds.). (2008). *Building Racial and Cultural Competence in the Classroom: Strategies from Urban Educators.* New York: Teachers College Press.

Now go to Topics #1 and 12: **Ethnicity/Cultural Diversity** and **Strategies** in the MyEducationLab (www.myeducationlab.com) for your course, where you can:

- Find learning outcomes for these topics along with the national standards that connect to these outcomes.

- Complete Assignments and Activities that can help you more deeply understand the chapter content.

- Apply and practice your understanding of the core teaching skills identified in the chapter with the Building Teaching Skills and Dispositions learning units.

Chapter 9

Reaching All Learners: Perspectives on Gender, Class, and Special Needs

Addressing the Achievement Gap

One of the greatest challenges we face as a nation is the inequity in educational attainment based on race, class, and gender. The achievement gap between children from lower- and upper-income families, especially in the case of children of color, threatens the well-being of our society as a whole. The gap is rooted in historical inequities that stem from our legacy of racism and classism that result in denied opportunities to learn. Although much of the challenge lies in societal contexts beyond the school, teachers can help, and many of them *are* making a difference.[1]

As we saw in Chapter 8, an appropriate response to students' learning and cultural styles is often a necessary condition for success in the classroom. However, these styles are only part of a cluster of characteristics that, along with societal contexts and inequities, need to be considered. For example, a student may be so interested in a particular subject that he or she will learn it regardless of the teacher's approach. However, students who lack confidence, who are bullied at school, who are English-language learners, who are haunted by memories of a war zone, or who face hunger or other severe problems outside the classroom may be unable to learn even under the best classroom conditions. This chapter explores the nation's educational achievement gap in terms of societal conditions related to gender, poverty level, and special needs and how these categories interact and are differentiated by race and sexuality as well as personal experiences and desires. We begin with a look at measures of student learning revealed in the "nation's report card" and then consider the nation's high school dropout crisis.

What Does the Nation's Report Card (NAEP) Tell Us?

The National Assessment of Educational Progress (NAEP) is a nationally representative and ongoing assessment of what students know and can do in the following subject areas: mathematics, reading, science, writing, the arts, civics, economics, geography, and U.S. history.[2] Assessments in world history and foreign language are anticipated in the near future.

Because NAEP assessments are administered uniformly using the same sets of test booklets across the nation, NAEP results give us a picture of student performance for all states and selected school districts in urban areas. The assessment stays essentially the same from year to year, enabling us to examine student academic progress over time, since the 1960s. From the very beginning, the NAEP has revealed an achievement gap, with White students scoring higher than African American and Latino students in all subject areas. Although the average score for all student groups has steadily improved in all subjects over the years, the achievement gap has not disappeared and is especially pronounced in the South and large cities. The figures and tables presented in this chapter give a snapshot of this gap; additional information and updates are available in an online format through the Nation's Report Card (http://nces.ed.gov/nationsreportcard/).

Figure 9.1 provides an overview of scores in seven content areas broken down by ethnic group. The students' best scores are in geography, mathematics, reading, and U.S. history; the lowest scores are in civics, science, and writing. The figure also shows that White students score higher than African American and Latino students in all the subject areas. Latinos score higher than African Americans in all subjects, due to their improved scores on the most recent tests.

What happens when we consider gender as well as ethnic group? Table 9.1 shows us the scores for males and females within the three ethnic groups. Within each ethnic group, girls score notably higher than boys in reading and writing, somewhat higher in civics, but lower than boys in mathematics and science. Latino and White females also score lower in U.S. history than males in their group, while African American females and males score equally on that test.

When we take a look at class, or family income as measured by eligibility for school lunch programs, we see the most dramatic differences. Table 9.2 shows that low-income students in all three ethnic groups score significantly lower than higher-income students in all the content areas. What is especially noteworthy, however, is

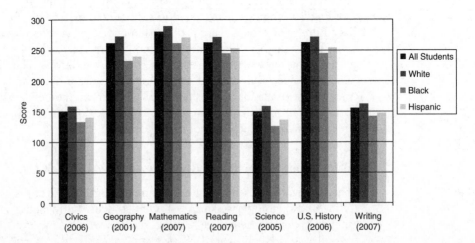

Figure 9.1 Average Scores on NAEP Eighth-Grade Examinations by Race

Source: (http://nces.ed.gov/nationsreportcard/)

Table 9.1 ⬛ Average Scores on NAEP Eighth-Grade Examinations by Race and Gender

Test (Year)	All	White		Black		Hispanic	
		Male	*Female*	*Male*	*Female*	*Male*	*Female*
Civics (2006)	150	158	159	129	136	138	142
Geography (2001)	262	275	270	236	233	242	237
Mathematics (2007)	281	291	288	263	262	273	270
Reading (2007)	263	266	276	240	251	249	257
Science (2005)	149	161	156	128	125	138	134
U.S. History (2006)	263	274	269	245	245	257	252
Writing (2007)	156	152	173	134	151	139	155

Source: (http://nces.ed.gov/nationsreportcard/)

Table 9.2 ⬛ Average Scores on NAEP Eighth-Grade Examinations by Race and Family Income

Test (Year)	All	White		Black		Hispanic	
		E	*N*	*E*	*N*	*E*	*N*
Civics (2006)	150	140	160	125	146	131	149
Geography (2001)	262	259	176	228	243	232	248
Mathematics (2007)	281	273	295	257	271	264	279
Reading (2007)	263	256	275	240	254	246	262
Science (2005)	149	143	164	120	137	126	146
U.S. History (2006)	263	255	276	239	257	245	264
Writing (2007)	156	146	168	137	149	139	156

Family Income: Eligible/Not Eligible for Free/Reduced Lunch Program

Source: (http://nces.ed.gov/nationsreportcard/)

that upper-income African Americans score *lower* than low-income Whites in geography, mathematics, reading, and science, and just slightly higher in writing and U.S. history. Civics is the one content area where higher-income Black students score notably higher than low-income White students, in a reversal from the previous civics test in 1998, where they scored lower. This income disparity is no longer true for Latinos, except in geography, where upper-income Latinos score lower than low-income White students. In previous tests administered prior to 2003, upper-income Latinos did score lower than lower-income Whites in all content areas except writing. Thus, we see academic gains on the NAEP for higher-income Latino students, as measured by ineligibility for school lunch programs, although there is still a wide achievement gap compared to higher-income White students.

Both race and family income make a big difference in students' academic attainment as measured on the NAEP. But, contrary to what is commonly believed among many educational scholars, race remains a greater factor than class.

High School Dropping Out and the Graduation Rate Crisis

In an introduction to their report on the nation's invisible dropout crisis, *Losing Our Future: How Minority Youth Are Being Left Behind by the Graduation Rate Crisis*, the editors write:

> *Every year, across the country, a dangerously high percentage of students—disproportionately poor and minority—disappear from the educational pipeline before graduating from high school. Nationally, only about 68 percent of all students who enter ninth grade will graduate "on time" with regular diplomas in twelfth grade. While the graduation rate for white students is 75 percent, only approximately half of Black, Hispanic, and Native American students earn regular diplomas alongside their classmates. Graduation rates are even lower for minority males. Yet, because of misleading and inaccurate reporting of dropout and graduation rates, the public remains largely unaware of this educational and civil rights crisis.*[3]

Table 1.1 on page 14 provides an overview of these national graduation rate findings, and Table 9.3 shows the four states with the lowest high school graduation rates for Black, Latino, and White students. Given that high school graduation is an indicator of academic attainment, like the NAEP reports, this study documents a persistent nationwide achievement gap based on race/ethnicity, gender, and class (family income), as well as geographic region of the country.

In its entirety, the report includes graduation rates for each state and the nation's largest school districts, showing those with the highest and lowest graduation rate disparities, along with interviews of state education officials and narratives of

Table 9.3 ◼ Four Lowest State High School Graduation Rates by Race/Ethnicity

Race/Ethnicity	*Four Lowest States*			
Black	New York (35.1%)	Ohio (39.6%)	Nevada (40.5%)	Florida (41.0%)
Latino	New York (31.9%)	Massachusetts (36.1%)	Michigan (36.3%)	Iowa (40.5%)
White	Florida (57.9%)	Nevada (62.0%)	Georgia (62.4%)	Mississippi (63.3%)

Source: Orfield, G., Losen, D., & Swanson, C. (2004). *Losing Our Future: How Minority Youth Are Being Left Behind by the Graduation Rate Crisis*. Cambridge, MA: The Civil Rights Project at Harvard University/UCLA.

students who have either dropped out or felt "pushed out" of school. It provides evidence to support the following conclusions:

1. *The racial disparities in graduation rates that exist at the federal, state, district, and school levels are pervasive and deep.*
2. *Graduation rates for Black and Hispanic males are averaging under 50 percent nationally.*
3. *At the national and state level, the racial gap in graduation rates between White and most minority groups is pronounced.*[4]

This is a crisis for all of us. Educators at every level, but especially teachers, have a unique and potentially powerful role to play in helping the nation address this achievement gap. My hope is that this book, and other publications and programs in multicultural education, can help teachers make this difference, despite the societal and global challenges beyond our schools and classrooms.

What about Immigrant Children and Youth?

We do not have a clear understanding of the academic achievement of immigrant and refugee children and youth, even though they comprise over 20 percent of our school population. National reports of academic achievement, such as the No Child Left Behind (NCLB) Act, separate data according to ethnicity, socioeconomic status, gender, special needs, and home language. However, not all immigrant children are classified as English-language learners and they are lumped in with one of the following broad categories: African/African American, American Indian, Asian/Asian American, Hispanic, and White.[5] Despite this limitation, researchers find academic achievement disparities between immigrant and refugee children and youth as well as an achievement gap when compared with nonimmigrant peers.

According to the NAEP, English-language learners (ELL) "tend to lag behind their English proficient peers in reading and mathematics."[6] At the elementary level (grade four), the achievement gap between English-language learners (those who could be assessed) and non–English-language learners is very slowly narrowing, but the gaps are wide in both reading and mathematics. At the twelfth-grade level, ELLs score below English-proficient *eighth-graders* in reading.[7] However, *the gap is greater between high- and low-performing ELLs than between English-language learners and non–ELLs.*[8] Their varying degrees of educational success are linked to nation of origin, family circumstances, knowledge of their new country's language and culture, where they settle in the United States, and the degree to which their welcome as newcomers is warm and supportive. For example, students from higher socioeconomic status (SES) ethnic groups, such as Koreans and Russians, tend to score higher on English-language development tests, whereas students from lower (SES) ethnic groups, such as Hmong and Khmer, tend to score lower on these tests. Unfortunately, too many newcomers, especially young adolescents of color, encounter racism and other forms of prejudice and discrimination and give up on their original hopes and dreams about coming to America.[9]

An Inside View of the Achievement Gap

Immigrant Youth and Teachers Caught in School Structures and Societal Contexts

Immigrant youth today enroll in a variety of schools, ranging from "well-functioning" schools with "a culture of high expectations and a focus on achievement, to dysfunctional (schools), with an ever present fear of violence, distrust, low expectations, and institutional anomie."[10] Too often, immigrant youth from low-income families who are most in need of academic support end up in low-quality schools.[11] We know that a classroom climate of respect, where students are engaged in important intellectual pursuits, feel safe, and are affirmed by teacher and peers alike, is important for *all* students. However, these positive school and classroom climates are especially important for immigrant youth, because the school is the major avenue for learning about their new culture and developing their full potential. Too often, well-meaning dedicated teachers who respect and care about their students are limited by school and classroom social structures beyond their control, and students fall into the achievement gap.

For example, a recent study of Latino immigrant youth by Susan Katz[12] examined "how teachers' attitudes and practices that the Latino students perceived as racist were linked to structural conditions within the school that went beyond the responsibility of the individual teachers."[13] Katz conducted a year-long ethnographic study at Coolidge Middle School, rated as one of the city's best in terms of standardized test scores, and located in a quiet middle-class Asian and European American neighborhood in Southern California. As a result of a federal court order to desegregate in 1984, 270 of the school's 1,400 students were bused in from the barrio of Las Palmas (historically one of the city's most vibrant neighborhoods but known for intense poverty and the highest level of gang activity) or from Oakdale,

Positive classroom climates are characterized by genuine respect and caring.

an African American community. However, through tracking or ability grouping, segregation was maintained. One-third of the student population was enrolled in the gifted and talented program,[14] where 43 percent were Asian and 49 percent were European American, with only 1 percent Latino, 2 percent African American, and 5 percent other. In contrast, among the Latino students 31 percent were in ESL classes (located in dingy "cottages" outside the school building) and another 6.5 percent were in special education (located in the school basement); 21 percent of the African American students were in special education. Latino and African American students rarely participated in after-school activities (due largely to the busing schedule) and none were in school government; on the other hand, 75 percent of the students on the dean's list of discipline problems were African American or Latino.

Katz focused on the school experiences of eight Latino students at the school, and observed and interviewed them throughout the school year. She also interviewed five of their teachers. Students selected for the study included four females and four males, six of whom were first-generation immigrants (two were second-generation) from Central America and Mexico. Spanish was spoken at home and all had experienced bilingual education in elementary school, where most were perceived to be bright and promising. At the time of the study all were enrolled in the grade-seven intermediate-level ESL class (where Spanish was actively discouraged), had developed "well-defined friendship groups within the class," had older siblings or close friends involved in gangs and were viewed to be "at risk" because of poor grades (D average or below), standardized test scores below 26 percent, and/or poor attendance.[15]

Despite their good or excellent elementary school records, all eight students became increasingly alienated from school during grades six through eight. Both the Latino students and their teachers felt tensions in their relationships. Students perceived that their teachers discriminated against them as a group and preferred the Asian students; they felt the teachers regarded them as criminals, prostitutes, and unable to learn. As a result of feeling uncared for and disrespected at school many of them developed a reshaped Latino identity through "their own styles of language, literacy, and representation"[16] and formed social groups to create a space of their own at school. Teachers, however, stated that they assessed Latino students as individuals and put their energy into those that were worth investing in and had a chance to score well on the tests, which were used to evaluate the teachers as well as the students. They also saw the peer-group pressure among Latino students (manifested in dress and hair styles, graffiti-style writing, and nicknames) as a negative force and tried to single out the higher-achieving students for encouragement and support.

Katz concluded that social structures at the school shaped teacher attitudes and practices, which led to the students' perceptions of racism against them as Latinos. "The structural factors of tracking, resegregation, English-only curriculum, and reliance upon standardized test scores along with high teacher turnover in all but the GATE programs together contributed to an environment that greatly limited the Latino students' opportunities for success. They also discouraged the establishment of productive teacher–student relationships."[17] Although all eight students completed the seventh grade, three dropped out in eighth grade and only two made it to their senior year.

Can scenarios such as this be avoided when classroom environments are inclusive and respectful? The teaching concepts and strategies presented in Chapters 8 and 10 and in this chapters section on cooperative learning provide ways to create positive classroom climates that are based on decades of classroom research. In each one, teaching strategies or social structures within the school and/or classroom are designed to facilitate positive interpersonal interactions and equitable student achievement.

In this chapter, we will further explore student-achievement differences related to gender, ethnicity, and family income. But first we begin with the true story of Kevin Armstrong, an elementary-school student whose family has just moved from Denver to a college town in the Midwest.

Ms. Dixon's conclusion after less than two days of observation that Kevin was not capable of third-grade work warrants questioning. She was aware of his geographical move, and the adjustment to a new home, new school, and new friends

The Example of Kevin Armstrong

It is 2:15 P.M. on the second day of a new school year. The phone rings and Ms. Armstrong answers it.

"Hello, Ms. Armstrong?" a voice inquires. "This is Ms. Dixon over at Wildwood Elementary School. Kevin's teacher. I—"

Ms. Armstrong, a striking Black woman in her early thirties, interrupts, "What's wrong?"

"Nothing is wrong," answers Ms. Dixon. "I'm just calling to let you know that we've decided to put Kevin back in second grade. He just isn't ready for third-grade work."

Ms. Armstrong is stunned. Kevin had done superior work in Denver, in a desegregated school that was considered good. Over half the students were White. "What do you mean he isn't ready for third grade?" she asks coldly. "Teacher last year didn't say nothin' about him having problems."

"Ms. Armstrong, what I'm suggesting is for Kevin's own good. He's way behind the other children in my class. He'll feel like a failure if he stays."

"How you think he'll feel if you put him back?" she snaps. "He been lookin' to third grade all summer long."

"I hoped you would understand that we want to do what's best for Kevin," responds Ms. Dixon. "Would you like to come to the school and talk this over with the principal?"

"We comin'." Ms. Armstrong hangs up and turns to face her husband.

Wildwood is considered by many to be the best elementary school in town. Standardized achievement test scores are among the highest in the state, and the school boasts many innovative academic programs. Except for a few who, like Kevin, live in a string of apartment buildings bordering the school district, most of the children come from wealthy homes. The community is largely professional. A handful of Black and Latino children attend the school, most of whom have been adopted by Anglo parents.

Mr. Peters, the principal, explains to Mr. and Mrs. Armstrong why he and Ms. Dixon believe Kevin would be better off in second grade. Ms. Dixon, also present, remains silent.

"Kevin is too immature for third grade. Ms. Dixon picked this up immediately. Physically he is small for his age, and his attention span is very short. During music class he is unable to sit still. In class he can't wait for his turn to speak, and in general it's clear that he hasn't learned to control himself the way our other third graders do. Ms. Dixon has already given the children some pretests to see how much they remember. And, of course, Kevin's reading, writing, and math skills are way below grade level."

"Can't you give him a chance? This is just the second day. Can't we get him some tutoring or something? I read somewhere about some special programs for kids in the district who have problems," Ms. Armstrong asks.

"Some schools in the city do, but not us. We don't have enough students who need them to justify the expense. If we keep Kevin in third grade, he'll be isolated from his classmates, working by himself. That doesn't seem fair to Kevin."

"But still that's better than puttin' him back," counters Ms. Armstrong. "We'll be goin' back to Denver in a year and a half."

Stating that it is against their best judgment, Ms. Dixon and Mr. Peters agree to keep Kevin in the third grade on a trial basis.

---

can be difficult for any child. The additional adjustments an African American child must make to a setting such as Wildwood can be traumatic. Many children like Kevin are raised in a cultural environment significantly different from that which predominates at school. For these children, the school's expectation of appropriate behavior requires so much energy that little remains for the business of learning.

Let's reconsider the case of Kevin Armstrong and then meet one of his schoolmates, Rachael Jones, both of whom are perceived by their teachers strictly as failing individuals. However, these teachers like all their children and believe in treating each one the same. Ironically, by treating Kevin and Rachael the same as their classmates, teachers are probably stacking the deck against them. In order to provide equal opportunity for all students, it is sometimes necessary to offer unequal treatment, according to relevant (though not frivolous) differences.

Kevin Reconsidered

Anyone who knows Kevin around the apartment complex is struck by his clever wit, his mischievous nature, and the way he gets other kids of all ages to do just what he wants. Kevin somehow manages to outsmart the other children and many of their parents as well. The apartment children often get into a lot of trouble, though usually it's not too serious, and Kevin is always there. Somehow, though, he always escapes blame. Physically, he is tough: although he is very small for his age, he can get the better of kids almost twice his size.

On rainy days Kevin usually plays in a friend's apartment. He often builds complicated structures with Legos. He seems to know all the television programs, channels, and times by heart, but can read the *TV Guide* if necessary.

Kevin organized a week-long toy sale and earned a commission as manager. He kept all the financial records and supervised the cash flow for an entire week. To the casual observer, Kevin is a bright and lively eight-year-old.

It is a different story inside Ms. Dixon's classroom, where Kevin lags far behind everyone else in class, though he sits in his desk a lot better than he did at the beginning of the year. He works by himself in a cubby much of the time, but still hams it up any chance he gets. The other kids love that and see Kevin as a kind of class clown.

Ms. Dixon is concerned about Kevin. His progress this year is very slow, slower than any child she has known in her three years of teaching (all at Wildwood). Kevin does not concentrate on one activity long enough to finish anything, and he is easily distracted by his classmates. Often he does not listen to her directions and, thus, cannot do the assignments or does them incorrectly. Although she is often amazed at his creative and unusual ideas, Ms. Dixon is distressed by his sloppy and careless writing habits and his lack of effort in math.

Ms. Dixon is unable to entertain the thought that Kevin might require a different approach, because deep inside she fears this may be a racist notion. Therefore, she dismisses his blackness as irrelevant. Ms. Dixon has had a Black student before, the adopted daughter of a prominent physician in town. The girl performed beautifully in class, was a top student, and confirmed Ms. Dixon's view that there are smart Blacks and dumb Blacks. For her, Kevin falls into the second category.

Kevin's schoolmate Rachael is White. The conditions of her life are largely unknown to her teacher who, thus, has no reason to believe there is any possible explanation for her failure other than her lack of ability to learn. Her Whiteness masks the possibility that she might need unequal treatment in order to attain success in school.

The Example of Rachael Jones

Rachael lives in Kevin's apartment complex and is a second-grader at Wildwood. This is her first year there, too. Rachael's mother, a hardworking and good-hearted woman in her thirties, cleans apartments in the complex. Her work has become so steady that she is off Aid to Dependent Children (ADC) for the first time in six years. Although Rachael's stepfather has a college degree, he has been unable to find work in his field and works as a city bus driver. Rachael's natural father is continually in and out of prison and pays no support for any of his five children. Her eldest brother has also been in prison. While money is a continual problem for the family, Rachael's mother's remarriage has brought a degree of stability and security.

Like Kevin, Rachael is at the bottom of her class. She is often sick and is frequently absent from school. Rachael complains to her mother that her schoolwork is too hard. Homework assignments are usually put off until 9:30 or 10:00 P.M., and Rachael's mother is unable to help her. On occasion she will ask one of the women she works for to help Rachael. Unlike Kevin, Rachael fears adventure, even the three-quarter-mile walk to school, and has few friends. Her long blonde hair hangs limply and her clothes seldom fit properly, a fact that sometimes elicits cruel remarks from schoolmates.

Miss Bryant, Rachael's second-grade teacher, sees Rachael as a shy, quiet little girl who is doing the best she can. She has placed Rachael in her slowest reading and math group, where Rachael's progress is so slow that it is doubtful she will be able to go on to third grade next year.

Reflections about Reaching All Learners

It is unlikely that Kevin and Rachael will perform well on the NAEP when they take it in another year or so. Some people argue that for students like Kevin and Rachael, the problem is a lack of basic intelligence—their ability to learn from experience, or to acquire and retain knowledge. They argue that intelligence is predetermined at birth and that it is only natural for the brightest students to score highest on these tests, that boys are naturally smarter in mathematics and science, and so on. Others believe that intelligence develops primarily through environmental experiences and argue that students cannot be expected to perform well on these tests unless they have been taught or have had an opportunity to develop the knowledge and skills included on the NAEP and other standardized tests.

Our position in this text is that a child's highest potential is determined at conception, that high potential is evenly distributed across our society's ethnic and socioeconomic groups, and that the degree to which this potential is fulfilled depends largely on what the child experiences during the formative years. The mother's emotional and physical health during pregnancy, as well as the nutrition provided the infant and young child, can influence how this potential is developed. But we can assume that, barring cases of extreme nutritional and emotional deprivation, the vast majority of students have the capacity to succeed in school.

Students who experience conflict between their home and school culture, as in the example of Fred Young (page 48), and students from low-income families, such as Rachael Jones, are often perceived as being culturally disadvantaged, deficient, and lacking in academic ability. But they may have the same potential for high achievement and just differ in the learning opportunities they have had. A suburban child, for example, may not know as much about animals and nature as a child who has grown up on a farm. An inner-city child may know little about fishing. A rural child may never have flown in an airplane or visited a large city. Although these children's horizons may be broadened through vicarious experiences on television, much remains to be learned about the impact of that medium on their cognitive development. Tests that ask students to use knowledge they have not been taught, or to perform tasks they are not ready for—because of slower rates of maturation or absence of necessary experiences—may trigger the student's feelings of frustration, self-doubt, and failure.

Moreover, what students already know or do not know about what we plan to teach is of obvious importance to their success in the classroom, and eventually on tests like the NAEP. We need to ask ourselves if they have the basic knowledge needed to understand new material. Can they read musical notes? Can they comprehend the textbook? Have they mastered their multiplication facts? Do they already know most of what we plan to teach this year? Perhaps a student is obsessed with reading about space or dinosaurs, has had years of experience helping in a parent's store, is already an expert mechanic, is an authority on Beethoven, or has a hobby collecting fossils. Perhaps a student has grown up in a world of crime and injustice or has developed more insight into the problems of alcohol and drug abuse than could be provided in any college text. When students show a special interest in or aptitude for what is being taught, they will probably learn at a rapid rate. Students who show little interest in or readiness for a subject will require more time to learn it.

Teachers must be careful not to assume, however, that a slow rate of learning means low potential. There may be other explanations: the student may lack basic knowledge needed for the task at hand; not be ready to handle abstractions; lack self-confidence; be reflective rather than impulsive learners and therefore appear "slow"; or experience transitional trauma due to cultural conflict between home and school. The challenge is to keep our expectations high for *all* students and to know when it is necessary and fair to expect more, and when it is not.

When considering the academic readiness of students whose socioeconomic and cultural background differs from the Anglo-European middle-class culture that predominates in school, it is important to remember the following factors:

- The past experiences and opportunities of ethnically different and low-income students are often not the ones teachers recognize and value.
- Measures of achievement and aptitude, as well as instructional content and strategies, have traditionally been most appropriate for White, middle-income groups.
- Teachers often lack understanding of cultural difference and have lower expectations for the success of ethnically different, low-income students.
- The student may not be fluent in standard English or may speak a dialect the teacher regards as slang.
- The student may learn better in a style not accommodated by the teacher.
- The student may not be accepted by a majority of classmates, a factor found to lower achievement levels among children in the minority.

Teachers cannot control the student's world outside the classroom. We cannot solve problems such as poverty and hunger, family conflicts, child abuse, or a child's inability to make friends. And neither a hungry child nor a rejected child is likely to place a high priority on learning. Teachers, nevertheless, are in a prime position for helping students meet needs at all levels and must do what we can to work toward the goal of helping all students fulfill their potential. Some of the strategies known to maximize motivation, development, and achievement among students are suggested in Box 9.1. These suggestions are arranged in four categories: instructional qualities, content, personal qualities, and classroom climate.

How Does Gender Make a Difference?

Gender-related differences and assumptions affect and influence learning in many ways. One that comes immediately to mind is the old belief that boys are more adept at math and science, while girls excel in English and the humanities. During the 1970s and 1980s, research was motivated by concerns about the underachievement and marginalization of girls in education.[18] For example, the Project on Equal Education Rights of the Legal Defense and Education Fund of the National Organization of Women found that schools discouraged girls from taking math, science, computer, and vocational classes.[19] Other examples of gender-related differences are

Box 9.1
Teaching Strategies

Instructional Qualities

- Provide each student with an opportunity to make an important contribution to class activities.
- Provide each student with an opportunity to experience success.
- Provide students with effective feedback or helpful information about their progress; be prompt; be clear about the criteria for success.
- Shift patterns of instruction; use a variety of strategies and sensory channels.
- Alter the physical learning environment when necessary to make it compatible with the purpose of the lesson. (For example, desks in a circle facilitate equal communication, rows may be more effective for a film, and opposing blocks of chairs can enhance a classroom debate.)

Suggestions about Content

- Begin with clear objectives that are challenging but attainable.
- Make clear why the objectives are important and worth attaining.
- Cultivate curiosity and creativity.
- Invite students to participate in planning and evaluating their curriculum.
- Build on students' existing interests while trying to create new ones.
- Organize at least part of the curriculum around real-life problems.

Suggestions about Personal Qualities

- Search for ways to express care for each student.
- Never belittle or ridicule a student.
- Project enthusiasm.
- Avoid distracting behaviors and overuse of terms such as "uh" and "you know."
- Use movement—don't stay behind the desk.
- Be genuine.

Suggestions about Climate

- Get to know the students. Learn their names right away.
- Find ways to help students know each other.
- Insist that students show respect for each other; create a classroom climate of trust and acceptance.

that girls mature physically and emotionally at an earlier age than boys, that boys are more susceptible to infant disease and mortality, and that they are much more likely than girls to be suspended, expelled, or placed in special education. Still other research in moral development and epistemology pointed to even more important, although less understood, differences in the ways that girls and boys learn and understand the world.

Since the 1990s, girls have begun to catch up and even outperform boys on some indicators of academic achievement, which has led to a "moral panic" about boys and new attention to gender issues related to masculinity.[20] Both boys and girls have improved in reading and mathematics over the past decade, but girls have nearly matched boys' scores in mathematics, whereas the achievement gap between boys and girls on reading tests remains large. Although *all* students have gained in mathematics and reading, the gap between White students and African American and Latino students persists as well.

Conceptions of Masculinity and Femininity

The terms *sex* and *gender* are often used interchangeably to refer to an individual's status as either male or female. *Sex* refers to the biological differences between males and females, whereas *gender* refers to the cultural expectations regarding men's and women's behavior. Like race, gender is a social construction: the roles and responsibilities for males and females are culturally determined but may change over time.

Boys' constructions of gender is a new area of interest among educators, especially how predominant views of masculinity negatively affect girls as well as males who might be viewed as effeminate. Indeed, contemporary research has moved away from its concerns about gender socialization patterns and the reproduction of gender inequality in schools[21] and shifted instead to the ways boys and girls construct gender identities in relation to each other as well as societal structures.

According to traditional sex-role socialization theory, boys and girls learn "appropriate" sex roles and ways of being through observation and/or "experiencing rewards and sanctions which reinforce such behaviors."[22] Females are expected to be "caring, nurturing and self-less," while males are expected to be aggressive, independent, and competitive. School and classroom gender-equity programs based on this theory try to broaden children's views of what is appropriate behavior for males and females, introducing "gender fair" options. For example, fairy tales were revised to show heroines who act "aggressively" and heroes who engage in traditional female endeavors that boys found distasteful, such as ballet. Most children rejected this approach. Such interventions overlooked the fact that "boys and girls invest heavily in demonstrating that they belong to their 'own' gender and the last thing that the majority wants to do is to appear not to fit in with their same-sex group."[23] Nevertheless, curriculum strategies based on stereotypical sex roles continue and are likely to remain unless expanded images of gender identities are included in teaching theory and practice.

Pro-Feminist and Men's-Rights Perspectives on Masculinity

The pro-feminists, both men and women, see schools as "masculinizing agencies" that privilege a stereotypic view of maleness over femaleness. They are concerned about the imbalance of power between males and females, as well as between males and males. Furthermore, they focus on the different ways of being male that arise from "different culture groups through the influence of social class, age, ethnicity and sexuality as well as the connections between them."[24] Pro-feminists argue that school programs working toward gender equity must address power structures in school and society as well as foster conversations about a range of masculine identities. Boys and men can be caring and sensitive without losing their masculinity, and girls and women can be rational and assertive without losing their feminine identity. For example, Connell argues that there are multiple ways of being masculine that can be categorized according to "social, cultural and institutional patterns of power" that evolve over time and place.[25] *Hegemonic masculinity* describes the mode of masculinity that is dominant and defines "what it means to be a 'real' man or boy," generally the attributes of "physical strength, adventurousness, emotional neutrality, certainty, control, assertiveness, self-reliance, individuality, competitiveness, instrumental skills, public knowledge, discipline, reason, objectivity and rationality."[26] *Complicitus masculinity* refers to "that cluster of masculinities whereby men reap the benefits of hegemonic masculinity without actively seeking or supporting it."[27] *Subordinate masculinity* refers to the various ways of 'being male' in school settings "which stand in direct contrast to hegemonic masculinity," such as "gay masculinity."[28] *Marginal masculinity* includes those male identities that emerge out of interactions with subordinated ethnic groups or social classes.

Although many boys and men do not identify with hegemonic masculinity, they all benefit from the "*patriarchal dividend* which is the advantage men gain from the overall subordination of women without actually being at the forefront of the struggles involved with hegemonic masculinity."[29]

In contrast, the men's-rights perspective views boys as a homogenous group based on a view that masculinity is "strong, active, hard, and rational" as opposed to femininity, which is "weak, passive, soft, and emotional."[30] Through this lens, boys' school experiences are believed to be basically the same, irrespective of race, class, religion, sexuality, age, or culture. Some men's-rights advocates see boys as victims and blame the "feminization" of schools as the cause of academic declines among boys. They argue for stronger models of masculinity, stricter school and classroom discipline, more competition, and other policy changes, such as allowing boys to start school a year later than girls, who mature earlier. Some suggest dividing classrooms or schools by gender, while others advocate grouping boys who have difficulty with language and literacy with girls who are superior in these areas.

Gender Differences in the Classroom

The "Ethic of Care" and the "Ethic of Justice"

Some of the most important and useful research in the area of gender differences has been done by Carol Gilligan in her work *In a Different Voice*.[31] Gilligan undertook her study in an attempt to include a female perspective in the male-dominated field of psychology and moral development. She found that when measured against a male standard, women were often ranked at "lower" stages of moral development than men. But when Gilligan listened to women, the voice she heard was not inferior or superior, it was simply different. The two different voices or ethics that she heard she named the "ethic of care" and the "ethic of justice." Although these two ethics are not gender specific, the ethic of care is more commonly a female ethic and the ethic of justice a male ethic.

The ethic of care, according to Gilligan, has to do with connection, responsibility, and nurturing relationships, rather than with securing rights. The world of those rooted in this ethic is grounded in personal experience, and moral judgments are made based on concrete circumstances and the need to take care of others. The ethic of justice, on the other hand, relies on a more abstract notion of individual rights and the application of universal principles in making moral decisions. These differences in moral perspectives are related to identity development: for those operating within an ethic of care, *self* is understood in connection and relatedness to others, whereas those whose ethic is one of justice understand themselves more in terms of autonomy and separation.

These differences have important implications in the classroom. Because the Western intellectual heritage upon which our educational system is based relies heavily on abstract, objective reasoning and an atomistic understanding of the world, those who operate under the ethic of care—usually girls—are at a disadvantage. Although Gilligan has asserted that this voice is merely different, in the classroom it is often heard as inferior—or worse, it is not heard at all.

Metaphors of "Silence" and "Finding a Voice"

In their work *Women's Ways of Knowing*, Belenky and her associates found the metaphors of "silence" and "finding a voice" to be very important in the development of women's selves, minds, and ways of learning.[32] In extensive interviews of 135 women from varying ethnic, socioeconomic, and educational backgrounds, they found that a great many women had gone or were still going through a period of feeling "deaf and dumb." One woman, looking back on her educational experiences, said, "I could never understand what they were talking about. My schooling was very limited. I didn't learn anything, I would just sit there and let people ramble on about something I didn't understand and would say Yup, yup. I would be too embarrassed to ask, 'What do you mean?' "[33] Although this woman's experience was extreme, a surprisingly large number of women surveyed reported having felt similarly about their abilities to communicate and understand through language. Although not literally deaf and dumb, these women felt incapable of hearing and learning from the words of others and unable to speak and have a voice themselves.

This metaphor of silence can actually be substantiated by examples of literal female voicelessness. Contrary to the myth that women and girls talk in excess, studies have found that men interrupt women far more than they interrupt other men, and more than women interrupt men or other women.[34] Furthermore, in naturally occurring conversation between women and men who describe themselves as sexually liberated, it was found that although women initiated 62 percent of conversations, only 36 percent of their topics succeeded in fostering conversation, while men had a 96 percent success rate.[35]

It appears that in the classroom, boys have dominant voices as well. Sadker found that teachers praise—and criticize—boys far more than girls. She also found that boys call out for the teacher's attention eight times more than girls do, and that teachers accept boys' unsolicited remarks as contributions. When girls do the same, they are told to raise their hands.[36]

This voicelessness—both metaphorical and literal—that girls experience in the classroom is only reinforced by the absence of females in the curriculum. Literature courses still focus largely on a White male canon; history and social studies continue to lean toward the male-dominated world of politics rather than the more female-oriented social realm; and the fact that math and science are still heavily dominated by males is seldom questioned or criticized in the classroom. Voicelessness not only restricts the student's ability to contribute to the learning experience, it also restricts all of us from a vital portion of the curriculum.

Issues of Gender and Sexuality in Schools

In her introduction to "Gender, Sexuality, and Social Justice in Education,"[37] Mara Sapon-Shevin writes,

> *We live in a highly gendered and gender-troubled world. Thirty-five years after the publication of the "X: A Fabulous Child's Story" by Lois Gould (www.trans-man.org/ baby_x.html) in which parents refused to tell people the gender of their child—and were assailed by distress and confusion—we continue to live in a state of categories. Ambiguity—because a child is intersexed, or transgendered, or simply doesn't "act like a girl" or "look like a boy"—shakes many people to their core.[38]*

She uses the analogy of canaries who were released deep in coal mines to test the air for carbon monoxide and to warn miners if the levels of poisonous gas reached dangerous levels; sometimes the canaries had so much trouble breathing that they died, alerting the miners to escape while they could.

Metaphors of "silence" and "finding a voice" are important in the development of young girls' sense of self, their minds, and their ways of learning.

In many ways, LGBT youth are our canaries in the coal mine; the experiences of gender-and-sexuality nonconforming youth tell us much about the school culture and climate in general—the air quality, if you will—for all kids. We should look at what happens to nonconforming students and know we have a serious problem.[39]

Most of us are familiar with examples of brutality and violence directed at lesbian, gay, bisexual, and transgender (LGBT) youth. Indeed violence, bias, and harassment directed at LGBT students are commonplace in our schools.[40] The following example of abuse is extreme, but all too common.

Jesse Montgomery was subjected to frequent and continual teasing from the time he was in kindergarten. To his classmates, he was never quite enough of a "boy," so throughout his school years other students referred to him as a girl, calling him "Jessica," as well as fag, homo, freak, princess, fairy, lesbian, femme boy, bitch, queer, pansy, and queen. The harassment became physical in sixth grade, when he was punched, knocked down, and even super glued to his seat. He was also subjected to insults of a more sexual nature. . . . Over the years, officials and school staff did little to address the ongoing harassment that Jesse experienced.[41]

The predominant view of sex-role socialization sets up masculinity and femininity as mutually exclusive categories. It is assumed that males will be attracted to females and vice versa; there is an unspoken "compulsory heterosexuality" that is learned at an early age. Consider the following classroom incident recently reported by a kindergarten teacher, an extreme and unusual example of student harassment involving very young children.

Two girls had been in the "house and home" center, pulling clothes out of the dress-up box, arranging pretend food on the table. They draped scarves and lace over their heads and around their shoulders. One said to the other, "I know. Let's get married. We'll be lesbians." The two girls stood together with their arms linked as if they were walking down an aisle. Another girl who had been playing nearby jumped up, yanked a scarf from one of the bride's heads and screamed, "You are in trouble—you're going to burn up or get really sick because people like you are bad, so stop it!" By this time a few other children had joined in saying things like, "Yeah, that's nasty," or "I'm gonna tell!" One boy ran into the fray . . . he kicked one of the dressed-up girls and slugged the other. All of this occurred in the few moments it took the teacher to disentangle herself from the yarn and other art materials she was using with a group across the room. She had heard the interaction and called out several times to stop it. She reached the scene in time to prevent the boy's next blow and began the process of deescalating the conflict and comforting the two girls. The little girl who had first opposed the imaginary marriage stood back from the scene and said to the teacher, "My mama won't let me come here anymore. I'll tell her, too. People who do like them are the baddest. They make other people sick and they kill other people. My daddy said we have to kill them first."[42]

Here we see an example of what could be age-appropriate imaginary play that triggered anger and fear in some of the other children. (It occurred in a city where human rights for LGBT people had been a public concern for nearly a decade; the authors write that for these little girls, "'lesbian' is not a sexual term but instead a

What images of masculinity and feminity do children bring to the classroom?

name for women who are in adult pairing with women."[43]) Although this situation is unusual, it shows that homophobia is learned at an early age and raises questions about how teachers and counselors can best mediate these fears and related aggression. Physical and psychological harassment of young men and women who do not fit accepted "norms for gendered appearance and behavior" is well documented and takes place at all levels of education.[44] Research in secondary schools shows the "pervasive presence of homophobia" among teenage boys, and that young men are often haunted by the fear of being called gay.[45] It notes

> *the ways in which homophobic abuse could be carefully codified and ritualized within male peer groups and could incorporate a seemingly endless range of features such as clothes, posture, mannerisms, hobbies, tone of voice, patterns of friendship and attitude toward schoolwork.*[46]

According to the 2003 National School Climate survey, 80 percent of LGBT students report being physically, sexually, or verbally harassed at school.[47] Schools that have sexual-harassment policies frequently overlook homophobia, and it is well known that many gay and lesbian students leave school due to bullying and are at high risk for suicide, and that "gay bashing" is conducted primarily by young people.[48]

Achieving Gender Equity in Schools and Classrooms

Much work is needed to bring about effective gender-equity programs. It is not easy. Often, boys and men are identified as the problem and the focus of change efforts.

Instead, the *school* must see its role as central to the problem and solutions. Programs must avoid making boys feel guilty, avoid alternative images of masculinity that boys find unappealing, and recognize that some girls and women as well as gay men take on the cloak of hegemonic masculinity. Some of the most effective approaches in gender-equity education are structured discussions and activities such as brainstorming, journaling, and roleplay, but these literacy-based approaches tend to appeal more to girls than to boys.

Perhaps the greatest challenge is selection of the best theoretical framework to guide appropriate gender-equity programs. One established scholar in this field argues that children work hard to establish their gender identity and, rather than being presented with alternatives to the dominant gender characteristics, they need to learn how to question and discuss these conventional gender images. She lists four key questions to guide schools as they develop their own programs:

1. *What images of masculinity and femininity are children bringing with them to school, and what types are they acting out in the classroom and playground?*
2. *What are the dominant images of masculinity and femininity that the school itself reflects to the children?*
3. *What kinds of role models does the school want and expect of its teachers?*
4. *What kinds of initiatives/strategies/projects should teachers be undertaking with children to question gender categories?*[49]

What about gender equity for LGBT youth? Every school corporation's plans for gender equity programs should include LGBT individuals, both students and teachers, regardless of any one person's sex, gender, or sexual orientation.[50] Over the years I have found that support for LGBT individuals is the *acid test* for many of my students who are otherwise advocates for social justice and human rights. Some educators are reluctant to affirm the needs of LGBT children and youth because they feel this violates their religious beliefs, and some parents and students may argue that they have the right to express their negative views of homosexuality. While it is true that all members of the school community have the right to express their views, especially religious beliefs, "they cannot do it in a way that makes LGBT students feel unsafe, or feel as if their education is being imperiled."[51]

Over the last two decades a large body of gender-equity research has generated implications for creating positive school cultures for all students, including LGBT children and youth.[52] For example, an inclusive curriculum could incorporate LGBT material in English classes through a study of LGBT themes in famous literary works and opportunities to research and write about LGBT issues; biology classes could include a focus on the biological basis for sexual orientation (i.e., genetic, hormonal, physical attributes); and government classes could include legal and legislative responses to "the endemic problem of discrimination, violence, and harassment" directed at students who are *perceived* to be LGBT.[53] (Any school "misfit" is at risk.) Everyone in the school community would benefit from learning new content that clears up misconceptions about many LGBT issues, as well as better understand what it means to live in a socially just school community. In the inspired words of Mara Sapon-Shevin,

> *The good news is that this is not a zero-sum game. Making life better for LGBTQ youth will not make things "worse" for students who identify as heterosexual or for those with other identities related to race, ethnicity, religion, or language. Indeed, if we don't make it right for everyone, then we've made it wrong for everyone, even those who don't know it![54]*

How Does Class Make a Difference?

A recent inquiry into class in America, "Shadowy Lines That Still Divide," finds that social class is a powerful force in American life today. It states,

> *Over the past three decades, (class) has come to play a greater, not lesser, role in important ways. At a time when education matters more than ever, success in school remains linked tightly to class. At a time when the country is increasingly integrated racially, the rich are isolating themselves more and more. At a time of extraordinary advances in medicine, class differences in health and lifespan are wide and appear to be widening.[55]*

Determination of a person's social class is compared to a card game where "everyone is dealt four cards, one from each suit: education, income, occupation, and wealth."[56] Although an American meritocracy (where success is based on the hard work and talents of the individual) is believed to have replaced the old system of inherited wealth as the key to achievement, "merit, it turns out, is at least partly class-based. Parents with money, education and connections cultivate in their children the habits that the meritocracy rewards."[57] As one economist states, "Being born in the elite in the U.S. gives you a constellation of privileges that very few people in the world have ever experienced, and being born poor in the U.S. gives you disadvantages unlike anything in Western Europe and Japan and Canada."[58]

Poverty in America: What Are the Facts?

The "glaring truths about poverty in America" were revealed to the world in the aftermath of Hurricane Katrina.[59] The families left behind were physically trapped in areas of Louisiana, Mississippi, and Alabama because they were also trapped by poverty. Those who lacked cash, assets, credit cards, bank accounts, or access to an automobile or phone had no way out. Much of the nation was oblivious to the hunger, hardship, and extraordinarily high rates of child poverty that existed in the area prior to Katrina. Hopefully, we are now wide awake and aware of the latest economic reports from the U.S. Census Bureau that poverty is increasing across the nation, with nearly 40 million Americans now living below the poverty line and many more existing in precarious economic circumstances. As a result, we find many schoolchildren in every state who experience hunger and other conditions of poverty that make it difficult for them to thrive, from a "low" of about 6 percent of children in New Hampshire to a "high" of 33 percent in Mississippi. Research tells us that "poverty is the greatest threat to children's well-being," but also that is not unalterable.

Low-Income Families[60]

In 2008, the federal poverty level (FPL) was pretaxable income at or below $21,200 for a family of four, $17,600 for a family of three, and $14,000 for a family of two. Research shows that an average family (depending on locality) needs at least twice the FPL to provide for basic necessities such as food, housing, and health care. As shown in Figure 9.2, of the 73 million children living in the United States in 2008, 28 million (nearly 40% of all children) are living in low-income families; 18 percent of all American children live at or below the poverty level, and another 21 percent live in families that are at the FPL or up to twice the FPL limit, which is considered precariously low income. When we look deeper into these statistics, we see in Figure 9.3 that among all of the nation's children younger than age eighteen who live in low-income families the largest number (38%) are White, compared to 33 percent who are Latino, 25 percent who are African American, 3 percent who are Asian, and 1 percent who are American Indian.

"Families who live in this gray area between official poverty and minimum economic security have many of the material hardships and financial pressures that officially poor families face. As their income grows, they rapidly lose eligibility for public benefits, making it harder for them to reach economic self-sufficiency."[61] Low-income families cannot provide the economic security that comes from a stable and predictable income; savings or other economic assets, such as home owner-

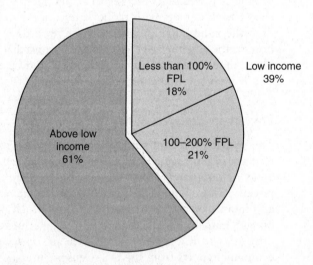

Figure 9.2 ▧ Children by Family Income, 2007

Note on Federal poverty level (FPL): There are over 73 million children in the United States. 39%—28.8 million—live in low-income families. 18%—13.2 million—live in poor families.

Source: Reprinted with permission of National Center for Children in Poverty (www.NCCP.org), by Morris Ardoin, Director of Communications NCCP. Basic Facts About Low-Income Children: Birth to Age 18.

ship, rental properties, land, or investment income; and cultural and social capital, such as education, specialized training, and support systems that help families make lasting financial gains.

Overrepresentation of Racial and Ethnic Minority Children[62]

Although the largest percentage of children in poverty is White, children from racial and ethnic minorities are tremendously overrepresented. As shown in Figure 9.4, 61 percent of Latino children (9.4 million), 60 percent of African American children (6.5 million), 30 percent of Asian children (0.9 million), and 26 percent of White children (10.9 million) are members of low-income families. And 58 percent of children of immigrant parents (7.4 million) live in low-income families, compared to 35 percent of children of native-born parents (20.2 million). The actual numbers are likely higher, because Figures 9.3 and 9.4 do not reflect the most recent economic downturn and rising unemployment.

Although the percentages of low-income families vary by race and ethnicity, there are also sharp differences *within* these racial/ethnic groups. Levels of poverty as well as income and educational attainment differences within these large pan-ethnic categories are striking. Table 9.4 shows the socioeconomic diversity among Asian Americans compared to Whites, Blacks, Hispanics/Latinos, and Native Americans.[63] (I have selected Asians as the comparison group because they are frequently perceived to be a monolithic "model minority" with high levels of socioeconomic

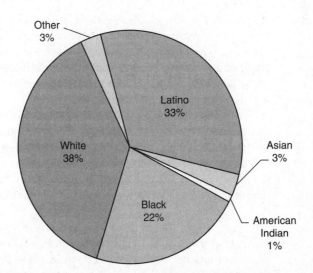

Figure 9.3 ▨ Percent of Total U.S. Children Living in Low-Income Families, by Race/Ethnic Group, 2007

Source: Reprinted with permission of National Center for Children in Poverty (www.NCCP.org), by Morris Ardoin Director of Communications NCCP. Basic Facts About Low-Income Children: Birth to Age 18.

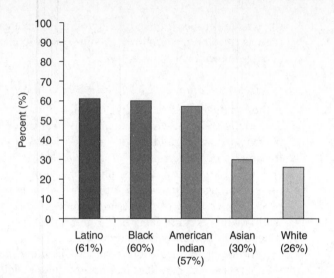

Figure 9.4 Percent of U.S. Children Living in Low-Income Families by Race/Ethnic Group, 2007

Source: Reprinted with permission of National Center for Children in Poverty (www.NCCP.org), by Morris Ardoin Director of Communications NCCP. Basic Facts About Low-Income Children: Birth to Age 18.

attainment.) Although these socioeconomic characteristics go beyond poverty measures, all are related to the quality of life for children as well as their educational attainment. The poverty figures in Table 9.4 do not include low-income people who are at or twice the "official" poverty level (FPL), only those below. Thus is it helpful to consider a wider range of socioeconomic factors to get a sense of our preschool and school-age children's well-being.

First, in contrast to monolithic views of Asian Americans and the "model minority" stereotype, we find sharp differences among the seven largest Asian American groups on the eight socioeconomic variables listed in Table 9.4. Cambodian, Hmong, or Laotian Americans have the highest percentage of people who are not proficient in English and have not graduated from high school and the lowest percentage with college or advanced degrees. In contrast, Japanese Americans have the lowest percentage of non–high-school graduates, whereas Asian Indians have the highest percentage of college graduates and holders of advanced degrees (over twice as many as Whites for both), the highest median family income (over $20,000 more than the median family income for Whites), the highest percentage (74.9%) of married two-parent families, and the highest percentage (51.6) in high-skill occupations, such as executive, professional, technical, or upper management positions. This last figure is dramatically higher than the 21.4 percent of Whites, 12.3 percent of Blacks, 11.9 percent of Native Americans, and 9.6 percent of Latinos in high-skill occupations. Chinese Americans have the second highest percentage in high-skill occupations

Table 9.4 ☒ Socioeconomic Characteristics of the Largest Asian and other Racial/Ethnic Groups

Asian Groups

	Not Proficient in English	Less than High School	College Degree	Advanced Degree	Median Family Income	Poverty	Public Assistance	Married with Spouse Present	Homeowner	High Skill Occupation
Asian Indians	8.4%	12.6%	64.4%	12.5%	$69,470	8.2%	0.9%	74.9%	56.8%	51.6%
Cambodian Hmong or Laotian	44.3%	52.7%	9.2%	0.4%	$43,850	22.5%	9.9%	66.6%	53%	9.8%
Chinese	31.3%	23.6%	46.3%	8.5%	$58,300	13.1%	1.8%	67.1%	65.7%	41.9%
Filipinos	7.0%	13.1%	42.8%	4.3%	$65,400	6.9%	1.6%	62.7%	67.6%	29.7%
Japanese	10.0%	9.5%	40.8%	4.6%	$61,630	8.6%	0.9%	60.7%	70.8%	32.0%
Korean	32.9%	13.8%	43.6%	5.6%	$48,500	15.5%	1.6%	69.0%	51.9%	21.0%
Pacific Islander	7.1%	21.7%	13.6%	1.6%	$50,000	16.7%	4.4%	61.4%	48.1%	13.8%
Vietnamese	40.4%	37.8%	13.8%	2.5%	$51,500	13.8%	4.8%	61.2%	60.0%	22.6%

Non-Asian Groups

	Not Proficient in English	Less than High School	College Degree	Advanced Degree	Median Family Income	Poverty	Public Assistance	Married with Spouse Present	Homeowner	High Skill Occupation
Whites	0.7%	15.3%	25.3%	3.3%	$48,500	9.4%	1.3%	64.5%	78.2%	21.4%
Blacks	0.8%	29.1%	13.6%	1.2%	$33,300	24.9%	4.5%	38.0%	54.4%	12.3%
Hispanic/ Latinos	30.3%	48.5%	9.9%	1.6%	$36,000	21.4%	3.5%	56.3%	53.4%	9.6%
Native Americans	2.6%	27.4%	10.8%	0.9%	$32,240	25.1%	6.1%	50.2%	64.2%	11.9%

Source: C. N. Le, Director of Asian & Asian American Studies Certificate Program at the University of Massachusetts, Amherst and author of Asian-Nation <www/asian-nation.org/>.

(41.9%), whereas Cambodian, Hmong, or Laotian Americans have the lowest percentage among Asians (9.8%) and it is close to Hispanics/Latinos, who have the lowest percentage of all (9.6%).

In addition to being fluent in English, the language of power in our schools and society, Whites show a distinct advantage in one characteristic: home ownership, at close to 80 percent. Although net worth is not included in Table 9.4, the relative economic security of middle-class Whites is an enormous advantage when we take a look at net worth, the most comprehensive indicator of economic status. For example, in 2002 the median net worth of non-Hispanic Whites was $88,000, almost fifteen times higher than that of Black householders, which was estimated at $6,000.[64] Today the gap is widening.

Home ownership is an asset that contributes significantly to one's net worth and provides financial security as well as equity in times of emergency or to finance the education of children or grandchildren. Blacks have significantly lower levels of home ownership, and yet they have been part of the nation's fabric as long as Whites. As we noted in Chapter 5, lower percentages of home ownership is part of our persistent legacy of slavery that for centuries prevented African Americans from benefiting from their own labor and accumulating earned wealth, that continued in the era of sharecropping and Jim Crow, and that lives on in racist loan sharking and practices that limit access to equitable home loans and housing in desirable neighborhoods.

Filipinos have the lowest poverty rates (6.9%), and Native Americans have the highest (25.1%), just a bit higher than Blacks (24.9%). Public assistance in some form of cash welfare benefit(s) is highest among Cambodian, Hmong, or Laotian Americans (9.9%), to some extent due to their refugee status, nearly as high among Native Americans (6.1%), and lowest among Asian Indian and Japanese Americans, with only .09 percent receiving public assistance in both groups. The high rates of poverty and public assistance among American Indians reflect "the dire situation of many Native Americans who still live on reservations that offer little employment and opportunities for socioeconomic mobility."[65] The roots of these socioeconomic problems, as well as tribal efforts to address them with the casino and gaming businesses, were discussed in Chapter 5.

Family Characteristics of Low-Income Children

Over half (55%) of all children living in low-income families have at least one parent who works full time (15.7 million), 26 percent have at least one parent who works part time or full time part of the year (7.6 million), and 19 percent do not have an employed parent (5.5 million). Half of these children live in families with two parents and half live in families headed by a single parent. Over 75 percent of the children live in families where parents have a high school education or more.

Children and adolescents from low-income families and the *underclass*, a term describing the poorest of the poor who are trapped in a vicious cycle of poverty, are the least likely to graduate from high school. Accurate dropout rates by race and income are not readily available, but in the mid-1980s the dropout rate for non-poor Whites was 8.6 percent, compared to 27.1 percent for poor Whites, and 9.3 percent for non-poor Blacks, compared to 24.6 percent for poor Blacks.[66] Children raised in poverty are likely to suffer from hunger and chronic malnutrition that can stunt their growth and development and sap their energy for schoolwork. "The Physicians Task Force on Hunger in America estimated that in 1985, about 20 million Americans, including 12 million children, were hungry at some point every month. They also concluded that malnutrition affected almost half a million children in 1985."[67] With the increasing numbers of children living in low-income families over the past decade, many of our nation's children still suffer from malnutrition, and millions experience hunger at some point every month. Moreover, the number of homeless children and youth (K–12)—youth who lack a fixed, regular, and adequate nighttime residence and might be sharing the housing of others; living in cars, motels, campgrounds, homeless shelters, or bus stations; or awaiting foster care placement[68]—increased from around 843,000 in 1997 to more that 930,000 in the year 2000.[69]

Impact on Young Children's Development and Health Risks

A recent report published by the National Center for Children in Poverty (NCCP), *Low Income and the Development of America's Kindergartners*, shows that "by the time they begin formal schooling, children in low-income families already lag significantly behind their more affluent peers academically, socially, and physically."[70] This longitudinal study of a nationally representative sample of 21,255 children in the kindergarten class of 1998–99 discovered significant difference in cognitive development (based on standardized test scores in reading, mathematics, and general knowledge); social-emotional development (based on parent and teacher ratings); and physical development (based on observation). After looking at the well-being of *all* kindergartners (children across all income levels and ethnic groups), it concluded,

> *The more income a family has, the better their children do academically, socially, and physically. This research shows a dramatic linear pattern between family income and children's positive development. . . . [For all racial ethnic groups, including Whites,] living in low-income families exacts a measurable toll on children's overall healthy development.*[71]

Despite these stark group differences in school readiness based on social class, it is important to remember that there is diversity within these categories. Not all children from wealthy homes scored high on these measures, and many children in low-income families scored at high levels. These students are sometimes called resilient because they are able to overcome the challenges they face.

What Do We Know about Schools in Low-Income Communities?

Several school-level factors are linked with poor academic achievement for students, regardless of the student's individual background. A school's sociodemographics make a difference, such as school-level poverty, region, and ethnic/racial composition of the students and teachers.[72] As we learned from the Nation's Report card on pages 245–247, students in high-poverty schools scored significantly lower on the NAEP test in all content areas. Moreover, students in high-poverty schools are more likely to be retained, fewer graduate, and their access to financial and human resources is limited by low property-tax bases that restrict school budgets.

Furthermore, class size is typically larger in poor schools. This is unfortunate, because some research shows that students in smaller classes (13–17 students in grades K–3) have higher levels of academic achievement than students in regular classes (22–26 students).[73] Poor schools in urban areas are large schools where health and safety risks are greater; more teachers are on temporary or emergency licenses; school climate is often monitored with surveillance techniques, even though some research shows this approach is less effective than an emphasis on rules and consequences; and school policies related to tracking and ability grouping, hotly contested practices, are often based on teacher discretion rather than student merit.[74] This means there are many more teachers teaching out of license; so, for example, science and mathematics teachers may not have academic majors or minors in these subjects, and few if any advanced-placement courses are offered.

Another issue in high-poverty schools is special education. Nationwide, there are about 6 million six- to seventeen-year-old students who receive services under the Individuals with Disabilities Education Act (IDEA), or about 11 percent of the school-age population.[75] However, in some high-poverty urban schools, one-fourth to one-third of the students are placed in special education. Of these, the majority are categorized as having a specific learning disability. African American and male students are overrepresented in many special-education programs, in some cases even when they are in high-income families with well-educated parents.

Retention, a policy designed to counteract "social promotion" of students who have not met grade-level academic achievement expectations, and suspensions and expulsions are also salient factors. Moreover, African American and male students are disproportionately represented in rates of retention, suspension, and expulsion, all of which are related to dropping out of school.[76]

Finally, many low-income urban schools are characterized by a "pedagogy of poverty," in which teachers stress drill and practice and students are cast in the role of passive listeners and observers. Expectations are low and students are not encouraged to engage in higher-level thinking. Warren Benson, a dedicated teacher in a high-poverty school, serves as an example of what is happening in too many classrooms.

It is evident that Warren Benson's class typifies one of the most difficult teaching situations imaginable. The problems Benson faces—problems of poorly prepared students, high absenteeism, and unruly classes—are faced by teachers in most high-poverty schools across the nation.

The Example of Warren Benson's Classroom

It is 2:00 P.M., beginning of the sixth-period class, and Warren Benson, a young teacher, looks around the room. Only eight students out of a possible thirty are present.

"Where is everybody?" he demands. "They don't like your class," a girl volunteers. Three girls saunter in. Cora, who is playing a cassette recorder, bumps over to her desk in tune with the music. She lowers the volume. "Don't mark us down late," she shouts. "We was right here."

Benson, a first-year teacher who spent four years in the Navy between high school and college, had requested this school. Here he found students from poor homes, students who couldn't read, students who hated school and teachers, students with drug problems, students waiting to drop out. Almost one-third of the students came from homes where one or both parents speak only Spanish.

For years Benson's dream was to teach on a Native American reservation. He believed this school would be good preparation. Now, after two months in the classroom he has real doubts. Doubts about these kids. Doubts about himself.

Benson tells everyone to take out today's vocabulary words. "Aw, come on man, give us a break," a student called Spark moans. Cora turns up the volume and croons, "Hey-ey-ey, bay-bee . . . ah wants ya to know-o-o-o . . ." Then, lowering the volume, she asks, "Mr. Benson, you got a pencil?" Another straggler walks in. "You late, boy," one student says. "So what, boy," the straggler answers. Benson asks for a definition of the first word, *tariff*.

No response. "Ricardo?" "What?" Ricardo asks, tuning in briefly. A few students busily leaf through the text, trying to locate the glossary.

Spark tells some nearby students his ancestors are Aztec Indians. "You an Indian?" Ricardo asks. "You got a tomahawk and all?" Benson defines *tariff* for Ricardo, who listens for a second, then throws a paper airplane over Benson's head and hits a girl in the neck. Benson continues. "Number two is Treaty of Guadalupe. Who can tell us what the Treaty of Guadalupe is?"

"Mr. Benson," Cora interrupts, "I got to go to the bathroom." Benson tells her no. "Goddammit, motherf_____, I got to go to the bathroom," she yells. "I'll give you a pass today," says Benson, "but this is the last time."

Benson tries to get back into the lesson. "Who can tell us what the Treaty of Guadalupe is?" "Ain't no word Treaty of Ha-wa-da-loop in here," shouts Spark. A blonde student sits silently in a corner chair; everyone else is talking.

Cora returns to the classroom. She grabs Benson's hand and pats it. "You ain't mad, is you?" Benson ignores her. Then he shouts to make himself heard above the din of conversation. "Get quiet!" Benson slams his fist on the lectern. Then he glares at the students until he has their attention. "Okay. It's obvious that you haven't learned these words. Everybody take out a paper. I'm going to give you a vocabulary test."

Class and Peer Interactions in School Success

The social structure of the classroom and the social status of the individual student with respect to classmates can affect student learning. Researchers have discovered a positive relationship between a student's popularity among classmates and social interactions; others have found that social acceptability is also related to achievement.[77] Sociologists have also identified a suspicion among poor Whites, often from rural areas, of schools and teachers who represent "middle class" values and behaviors. A peer-group dynamic can emerge among poor Whites in urban schools that is similar to what researchers discovered among Black adolescents who experience peer pressure not to work in school (i.e., act White).

School desegregation research has shown that students who represent a numerical minority tend to achieve better in classroom climates of acceptance.[78] Indeed,

for students from working-class and immigrant families, peers often play an even more significant role in shaping school performance patterns than do peers for youth from more advantaged circumstances. This is because their parents in many cases do not possess the educational background or have easy access to the institutional knowledge needed to help their children succeed in high school or prepare for college.[79]

Social Capital and Latino Youth

Scholars interested in the school achievement of Latino youth are looking at ways peers and peer relationships influence their school performance.[80] When a large number of diverse Latino students attend a school, peers can help ease new students' transition into the school environment. Veteran peers, especially bilingual peers, can provide "social capital" to new students, such as information about social values, networks, organizational structures, expectations, and disciplinary practices found in mainstream schools. When newcomers have this kind of access, they learn about adolescents' connections and peer networks that offer "institutional resources and funds of knowledge that enable low-status students to decode the system and participate in power sharing."[81]

Latino youth in families whose parents are recent immigrants, or even first or second generation, tend to stick with peers in their own ethnic group. Thus, a pool of available, academically informed peers is important for school success.[82] We need to look at how schools collaborate in structuring these peer relationships and how they can create caring communities Latino students will identify with.

However, when the percentage of veteran Latino students is small or the majority is placed in separate classes or lower tracks, bilingual peers cannot supply the types of social capital related to academic success or help English language learners negotiate an unfamiliar school context. And when schools do not provide pathways to academic success that could lead to college, such as challenging curricula and advanced-placement classes, as well as opportunities for campus leadership and cocurricular activities, students' . . . access to a group of peers with whom they may interact and form friendships is restricted,[83] and many develop a limited view of themselves as students. For example, a researcher in California finds that "some groups of working-class, Mexican-descent youth—most frequently males—are influenced by their peers to perform for one another in their classes, all the while not learning what their teachers are attempting to teach."[84] Here we see peer group solidarity in action, "the backing up of a peer when he or she disrupts class, interrupts learning, or challenges authority—that gives the appearance of resistance but may be reflective of . . . 'willful not-learning.' " This not-learning is evident in classrooms where teachers do not understand their students' backgrounds and motivations, where the curriculum is boring and unchallenging, and where students feel devalued or misunderstood.[85] Other researchers who focus on peer relations among street-socialized youth and members of gangs argue that school structures and practices actually contribute to the alienation these Latino youth feel. They argue that because these youth have weak academic skills and little to no support apart from their gang family, misbehavior may result from not knowing how to be a student, not necessarily a rejection of mainstream culture and schooling.[86]

Fears of Acting White

In a famous study of African American high school students, Fordham and Ogbu argued that peer pressure not to act White, that is, not to strive for academic achievement, is one major reason Black students do poorly in school.[87] Based on their research in Washington, D.C., Fordham and Ogbu wrote that many Black adolescents identify attitudes and behaviors such as the following as acting White and therefore unacceptable:

- Speaking standard English
- Listening to White music and White radio stations
- Going to the opera or ballet
- Spending a lot of time in the library studying
- Working hard to get good grades in school
- Getting good grades in school (those who get good grades are labeled "brainiacs")
- Going to the Smithsonian
- Going to a Rolling Stones concert at the Capital Center
- Doing volunteer work
- Going camping, hiking, or mountain climbing
- Having cocktails or a cocktail party
- Going to a symphony orchestra concert
- Having a party with no music
- Listening to classical music
- Being on time
- Reading and writing poetry
- Putting on airs

They argued that this view of acting White is shared by many Black adolescents in other areas of the nation, as well as by other minorities, such as those "American Indians and Mexican Americans [who] perceive the public schools as an agent of assimilation into the white American or Anglo frame of reference . . . [and as] detrimental to the integrity of their cultures, languages, and identities."[88]

Their research with academically successful and unsuccessful Black high school students revealed that because they fear being labeled a brainiac, "many academically able black students do not put forth the necessary effort and perseverance in their schoolwork, and consequently, do poorly in school. Even black students who do not fail generally perform well below their potential for the same reasons."[89]

The problem developed partly out of our racist past, where many White Americans refused to acknowledge the intellectual potential of Black Americans, and partly because many Black Americans subsequently learned to doubt their own intellectual ability, began to define academic success as White people's prerogative, and began to discourage their peers, perhaps unconsciously, from emulating White people in striving academically, that is, from acting White.[90]

Ogbu and Fordham found that the more successful Black students have developed strategies for coping with their peers and the "burden of acting white." Through participation in athletics, clowning and "acting crazy," or trading academic assistance for protection, males are able to obtain good grades without being rejected by their peers. Females tend to maintain a low school profile through strategies such as cutting classes selectively so as not to accumulate enough absences in any one class to fail it, "putting brakes" on their academic performance, and refusing to participate in the school's academic clubs and academic competitions.

Peer pressure related to perceptions that academic achievement means acting White is only one important reason for some Black students' lack of achievement in school. Some scholars argue that a better explanation for why students of color are not academically motivated is that they feel a lack of respect and a lack of caring from teachers and administrators,[91] or they feel alienated because they live in communities where high rates of poverty and racial segregation are combined.[92] Other important factors are the social and economic barriers many Black Americans face as adults (for example, a job ceiling) and the fact that traditionally, many Black Americans have been provided with substandard schooling. Until changes in the opportunity structures occur, many Black adolescents, as well as adolescents in other subordinate minorities, are likely to view academic school success as "a kind of risk which necessitates strategies enabling them to cope with the burden of acting white."[93]

In the face of these barriers, what can teachers do? If school personnel and parents understand these problems, they can help students learn to separate the pursuit of academics from the idea of acting White and can reinforce students' sense of ethnic identity in ways that are compatible with intellectual achievement. The possibilities are noted in the case of E. Sargent, a journalist with the *Washington Post*, who attended public schools in Washington, D.C. Sargent describes how his knowledge of African American history, acquired outside the schools, strengthened his sense of Black identity and his ability to deal with the burden of acting White.

> *While I had always been a good student, I became a better one as a result of my sense of black history. I began to notice that my public school teachers very rarely mentioned black contributions to the sciences, math, and other areas of study. . . . They never talked about ways blacks could collectively use their education to solve the great economic and social problems facing the race.*
>
> *My mind was undergoing a metamorphosis that made the world change its texture. Everything became relevant because I knew blacks had made an impact on all facets of life. I felt a part of things that most blacks thought only white people had a claim to. . . . Knowing that there is a serious speculation that Beethoven was black—a mullato [sic]—made me enjoy classical music. "Man, why do you listen to that junk? That's white music," my friends would say. "Wrong. Beethoven was a brother." I was now bicultural, a distinction most Americans could not claim. I could switch from boogie to rock, from funk to jazz and from rhythm-and-blues to Beethoven and back. . . . I moved from thinking of myself as disadvantaged to realizing that I was actually "superadvantaged."[94]*

Special Education: The Simultaneity of Race, Culture, Class, and Gender

The Promise of Special Education and Inclusive Classrooms

Before 1975, when Congress passed the Education for All Handicapped Children Act (renamed the Individuals with Disabilities Act, or IDEA), close to half of the 4 million children with disabilities were not receiving a public education.[95] Those who did attend public schools were often sent to separate facilities or were "relegated to a ghetto-like existence in isolated, often run-down classrooms located in the least desirable places within the school building."[96] With passage of the IDEA, all children with disabilities have the right to a "free and appropriate public education."

The law also requires that these children be educated in regular education (inclusion) classrooms unless the nature of the disability is so severe that the child could not receive an appropriate education in this setting, even with supplementary aids and services.[97] Research supports the benefits of this policy. Thus, the process of evaluation and diagnosis to establish the nature of the disability and to develop an Individualized Education Program (IEP) for each child is critical. Today, over six million are reaping the benefits of improved special education,[98] but these benefits are not distributed equitably.

> *Minority children with disabilities all too often experience inadequate services, low-quality curriculum and instruction, and unnecessary isolation from their nondisabled peers. Moreover, inappropriate practices in both general and special education classrooms have resulted in overrepresentation, misclassification, and hardship for minority students, particularly black children.*[99]

Racial Disparities in Special Education

The numbers of children and youth in the so-called soft categories (learning disability, emotional and behavioral disorders) have increased dramatically since 1975, with 40 percent of all children in special education being categorized with a learning disability (such as Attention Deficit Disorder [ADD] and Attention Deficit Hyperactivity Disorder [ADHD]). The overrepresentation of African American students in the soft categories, especially males, is a major concern, because definitions of exceptionalities in these categories are difficult to pin down. For example, emotional and behavior disorders include difficulties with academic learning, peer relations, and self-control that are not explained by "intellectual, sensory, or health factors."[100] However, no widely accepted definition of this exceptionality exists because disordered behavior is a socially constructed concept and there is disagreement about what it means to be mentally healthy. Language disorders, the second most common category, has become an issue for English-language learners who have been misplaced in special education. The so-called hard categories are easier to define and include sensory impairments, such as deafness or blindness, physical disabilities, health impairments, and moderate to severe mental retardation.

According to the National Center for Education Statistics, about 60 percent of the public-school population is White, 17 percent African American, 17 percent Latino, 4 percent Asian/Pacific Islander, and 1 percent American Indian/Alaskan Native.[101] However, the percentages of students in the largest special-education categories (mental retardation, emotional disturbance, and specific learning disability) do not match their ethnic group's percentage of the total public-school population. For example, 53.97 percent of the students classified as mentally retarded were White, 33.04 percent were African American, 10.04 percent were Latino, 1.90 were Asian/Pacific Islander, and 1.04 were American Indian/Alaskan Native.[102] These disparities also exist among students classified as emotionally disturbed, with

Approximately 13 percent of the nation's school children are exceptional learners; most of them are in mainstream classrooms.

African Americans again overrepresented. Mental retardation and emotional disturbance are the two categories that most often result in separate special-education placements; this leads to widespread concern that African American students are being resegregated in many of our nation's schools.

A recent report from the Civil Rights Project at Harvard University identifies five areas of concern that contribute to racial inequities in special education. It lists overidentification of students of color needing special education; educational placement wherein African American and Latino children are less likely than White children to be mainstreamed into inclusive classrooms; poor-quality evaluations, supports, and services that can lead to inappropriate placements and flawed IEPs; racial discrimination; and "multiple contributing factors." The editors write,

> The evidence suggests that black over-representation is substantial in state after state. The studies reveal wide differences in disability identification between blacks and Hispanics and between black boys and black girls that cannot be explained in terms of social background or measured ability.
>
> Both the statistical and qualitative analyses in this (report) suggest that these racial, ethnic, and gender differences are due to many complex and interacting factors, including unconscious racial bias on the part of school authorities, large resource inequalities that run along lines of race and class, unjustifiable reliance on IQ and other evaluation tools, educators' inappropriate responses to the pressures of high-stakes testing, and power differentials between minority parents and school officials.[103]

One research team included in this report questioned why this overidentification existed and explored whether ethnic groups are differentially susceptible to disability. For example, since African American, Latino, and American Indian children are also overrepresented in poverty and thus may experience malnutrition, exposure to lead poisoning, and other negative environmental conditions, they might be more susceptible to disabilities such as mental retardation and emotional disturbances. They also explored the possibility that overrepresentation "is the result of special education referral, assessment, and eligibility processes and instruments that are culturally and linguistically loaded and that measure and interpret the ability, achievement, and behavior of students differently across ethnic groups."[104] They studied the effects of gender, ethnicity, and school demographics on students who were identified with mental retardation (MR), serious emotional disturbance (SED), or learning disability (LD), using White females as the comparison group to see if there were gender or ethnic differences in who was identified as MR, SED, or LD. Initial findings showed that "white males were 3.8 times as likely as White females to be identified as a student with SED, while Black males were 5.5 times as likely."[105] American Indian and Latino males were 2.9 and 2.1 times as likely, respectively.

Later, these researchers combined school demographics (level of poverty, percentage of students of color, and per pupil spending) with race and gender. School poverty level showed some unexpected findings. For example, the number of African American students identified as MR dramatically declined as poverty increased. In schools with the *lowest poverty rates*—usually schools with more White students—the percentages of African American and Native American students identified as MR are highest. For African American and Latino students identified as SED and LD, the percentages do increase as poverty increases. These findings suggest that overrepresentation in the SED and LD categories may be related to differential susceptibility attributable to the conditions of poverty. However, overidentification of African American students in low-poverty schools as MR smacks of systemic bias. The study also discovered that African American and Latino students were more overrepresented in the MR and SED categories when White students were a large majority (60% or more) of the school population.

Socioeconomic Disparities and Cultural Clash in the Special Education System

One explanation for the overrepresentation of African American, Native American Indian, and Latino children in special education is the cultural clash between home and school, particularly for low-income families. Teachers, the majority of whom are White and middle- to upper-middle income, tend to regard individual differences based on ethnic or cultural differences as deficits or disadvantages. The fact that disproportionately large numbers of ethnic minorities are below the U.S. poverty level reinforces this idea, even though nearly half of the nation's low-income children are White.

In an insightful article, "Framework for Reducing the Cultural Clash between African American Parents and the Special Education System," Boyd and Correa point out that many African American parents have become alienated and disillusioned by the special-education system.[106] They show how African American parents' perceptions of special-education professionals and the professionals' perceptions of the parents both contribute to cultural clash that leads to the negative outcomes described previously. Low-income African American parents are "more likely to hold cultural values and beliefs different from middle-class professionals with whom they interact."[107] For example, conceptions of "disability" based on a wider view of what is normal, the importance of religion as a source of strength and affirmation of inclusiveness, and the role of extended family as a social-support group are likely to affect how parents view and interact with the special-education system. Many parents initially see special education as an opportunity for their children to catch up with their peers, but they become disillusioned with the system when their children are placed in separate classrooms and see this as a form of segregation. Moreover, low-income African American parents are unlikely to possess the social and cultural capital to make their voices heard. These feelings have led many parents to withdraw, and with the silencing of the parents' voices, African American children and communities are left without their most important advocates and potential mediators. This alienation and withdrawal can only exacerbate the problems of systemic racial bias.

The structure of the special-education system itself contributes to a dichotomous relationship with the families in at least three ways. First, it relies on a one-sided parent-education model that tells parents how to treat their children; second, it does not seek input from parents in planning a program for their child and relegates them to a passive recipient role needed mainly to sign consent documents; and third, it uses professional jargon that gets in the way of effective interpersonal communication.[108] Some scholars argue that the field of special education is unaware of its middle- and upper-class mainstream cultural assumptions, and that new professionals inducted into the field have little if any preparation to become multiculturally competent.

Ethnicity, however, is not always the issue. The majority of children who are in special education are White, and many middle- and upper-income children are having difficulty in school. Max Britten provides an example.

The Example of Max Britten

There had always been something different about Max that his teachers couldn't quite understand. As early as kindergarten his teachers sensed something. He tuned out a lot during class, and his work was inconsistent, ranging from very high to very low. The teacher suspected he was capable of doing better, although a learning disability was also a strong possibility. At the school's request Max was completely tested by the head of the Children's Neurology Clinic. The physician reported that Max was a bright, exceptionally independent child who could learn anything he wanted to learn. But that would be the key: his interest. Max also suffered from a severe case of sibling rivalry regarding his younger brother that might require future attention.

After kindergarten, Max's parents (both college professors) divorced, and he moved with his mother and brother to the Midwest, where he attended the same school as Rachael and Kevin (see pages 254 and 252). Max became quite shy and had a difficult time making friends. At school he was often teased and scapegoated in subtle ways unobservable by his teachers. At home he was continually taunted by his peers, with the exception of one friend who suffered similar rejection.

Max's schoolwork deteriorated. His teacher felt he was immature, easily distracted, and did not listen well. He was in the lowest reading and math groups. In contrast, Max's younger brother was a top student at Wildwood. He was liked by teachers and classmates and was involved in sports and music. As one teacher said to Max's mother, "Your sons are like night and day, salt and pepper." In the third grade, for some unknown reason, the school did not receive the results of Max's Iowa Tests. There was no record of his past test scores, and the fourth-grade teacher wondered if Max was mildly retarded or perhaps suffered from some sort of learning disability.

Despite his parents' divorce, Max's home environment was highly supportive, and during summer vacations with his maternal grandparents, Max was a different person. He was an avid stamp collector and through stamps had come to know more about geography than most adults did. He read *Time* and *National Geographic* regularly and frequently consulted his *World Book* encyclopedias, a gift from his grandparents. Yet it became clear that Max was becoming increasingly miserable at school. One day he cut school and hid at home. When his mother returned from work he told her he just couldn't go back. The school decided to test Max to see if he was eligible for special education.

The confidential psychological evaluation of Max in the fourth grade stated that "Max is a handsome, blond-haired, blue-eyed boy. He is somewhat quiet but friendly. Max reportedly gets along well with his classmates although the teacher notes that he tends to keep to himself. . . . Max frequently does not attend to critical instructions regarding assignments that often results in missed work and/or poor performance on assignments. When singled out for individual attention Max's work tends to improve; his work also improves when he is specifically requested to redo an unsatisfactory assignment."

On the day Max was given a variety of IQ tests, his teacher excitedly told him to tell his mother that he had done a fantastic job on the tests. He had done so well in fact, that none of the socioemotional tests were administered.

The written report stated that "The results of the current psychological evaluation show Max to be a child of superior intellectual ability. . . . Interviews with Max's teacher suggest that Max can perform academically when he is given large amounts of individual attention or when required to redo unsatisfactory assignments. However, there is only a limited amount of individual attention that can be afforded to any individual child in a typical classroom.

"There is some suggestion that Max finds the individual attention he receives very soothing and rewarding and therefore sees little incentive in performing well consistently. This is not unusual in view of Max's family situation. . . . It is recommended that Max be reassured about his academic ability but also, it should be explained that he must satisfy certain criteria in order to complete the fourth grade successfully. Max is not eligible for special services at the present time."

Later, during the case conference, Ms. Johnson stated that Max became a different person as a result of doing well on the tests and his schoolwork began to improve. Max's mother reported that he was beginning to make new friends in the neighborhood and that he seemed happier at home.

Suppose Max, for emotional reasons, was unable to perform well on the test. What would have happened? The example of Max illustrates that factors related to school success are very complex and not necessarily linked to cultural conflicts or racial differences. Both Max and his teacher were from White, economically advantaged backgrounds.

It is possible that problems faced by children like Kevin and Rachael and the students in Warren Benson's classroom (see pages 272–273) grow out of conflict between their worldview and the school's culture, or of negative prejudices on the part of teachers and classmates. It is also possible that, like Max, their failure is due to a mismatch between teaching and learning styles, or to some special personal qualities that need to be understood. Teachers must be sensitive to all the possibilities, which is not an easy task.

Although teachers often have no idea about what their students' home conditions are like, they make assumptions. Kevin does poorly in pretests the first day of school in a new city; thus, he is not ready for third grade in an academically oriented elementary school. Max comes from a privileged family and has many advantages; thus, the fact that he is not doing well in school must be due to poor aptitude or a learning disability. Moreover, Max lives in a single-parent household; therefore, he feels rejected and needs extra attention in school, but a teacher with thirty-three other students can't provide it. Rachael lives in the poor section of town, has not been exposed to good books or music, and does not value school; thus, little can be expected from her.

Too often, we assume that children and youth from low-income backgrounds or single-parent homes receive insufficient love and support from their families. We tend to assume the opposite for the child from the typical all-American family in suburbia. Although there is some truth to these stereotypes, parents and students are rightfully offended when schools assume that children from low-income backgrounds are deprived of love and emotional support. Divorced parents are also rightly offended at the single-parent stereotypes. Research on the long-term effects of divorce on children shows that after a period of transition and under supportive conditions some children recover sufficiently to resume progress in school, and that children raised in single-parent homes often develop greater independence, responsibility, and initiative.

Reaching *All* Learners in Inclusive Schools and Classrooms

There exist many promising ideas to foster academic success and resilience among students. For example, programs that are making a difference for students identified as having emotional and behavioral disabilities (these are students who are the most likely to get failing grades, to drop out, and to be incarcerated) are also appropriate ways to provide support for *all* learners.

Successful schools create learning environments that "are supportive of children's total social, cognitive, physical, ethical, and emotional development, and that are responsive to their needs as individuals;"[109] work to achieve a caring school community that connects with families; focus on effective teaching strategies, social-skills instruction, and cultural competence; value *all* students as members of the school community, regardless of their strengths and weaknesses; provide children who have special needs with an opportunity to learn with same-age peers; and help general-education students develop empathy and respect for others with diverse abilities and limitations. When inclusion is implemented effectively, everyone benefits. Cooperative learning is one promising teaching strategy that can be appropriate for *all* learners whether or not they are in inclusive classrooms.

Cooperative Learning

Student team learning has emerged recently as one of the most promising strategies for working with diverse groups of students. Developed originally for racially desegregated schools, the approach has been extended to virtually all types of schools. Most recently, student team learning techniques have been used to help integrate mainstreamed learners into the "least restrictive environments" with "normal-progress" classmates, and with language-minority at-risk students.[110]

Various learning techniques have been developed as alternatives to the competitive incentive structure and individualistic task structure of traditional classrooms. The success of the student team learning approach developed by Robert Slavin, David DeVries, and Keith Edwards at Johns Hopkins University, however, has been most fully documented.[111]

Research results show that student team learning improves both academic achievement and students' interpersonal relationships. All students (including high, average, and low achievers) appear to benefit. One of the most consistent findings is that African American students, and possibly Latinos, "gain outstandingly in cooperative learning."[112] Further research is needed before these race-by-treatment interactions can be fully explained. There is some evidence to support the possibility that children raised in African American or Latino communities tend to be more motivated by cooperation than competition, while the reverse is often true for those raised in the White middle-class milieu.[113] In contrast to the orientations of many African American and Latino students, the traditional classrooms in U.S. society stress competition and individual achievement. This emphasis can be stressful when students are faced with the conflict of "attempting to excel academically and risk alienating their peers, or to do the minimum needed to get by."[114] Given the fact that disproportionate numbers of African American and Latino students are low achievers, Slavin suggests that student team learning may help close the school success gap between minority and nonminority students. This is not to imply that the needs of White students are overlooked in the process. Although the achievement gains among nonminority White students tend to be less dramatic, says Slavin, their school achievement is not hindered by cooperative learning, and they reap many benefits in intergroup relations.

> *For improving race relations, our results have been phenomenal. In seven field studies in desegregated schools, most of them inner-city Baltimore junior high schools, we found out team learning classes had much better racial attitudes and behaviors than traditional classes. In many cases, when we asked students to name their friends, they named as many or almost as many friends of other races as they would have if race were not a criterion. This was quite different from our pretests in these classes and in our control classes; in fact, in most of our control classes there were fewer cross-racial friendships on the posttest than there were on the pretest.*
>
> *In addition to positive effects on race relations the team classes learned as much or more than the traditional classes. In five of the seven studies in desegregated schools, the team classes learned significantly more language arts and mathematics than did the traditionally taught students. In many of the studies, students in the team classes engaged in less off-task behavior than did control students. This indicates that team learning techniques may also improve discipline in desegregated schools. Team learning techniques don't have to cost anything, and they are easy to learn and use. Instead of the usual one-day workshop in which speakers try to reduce teachers' prejudice, we can spend the same time to teach teachers to use an instructional system that is far more likely to improve students' racial attitudes and behaviors as well as their achievement.*[115]

The three student team learning methods used most widely are Student Teams-Achievement Divisions (STAD), Teams-Games-Tournaments (TGT), and Jigsaw II. The following descriptions are taken from the teacher's manual available from the Johns Hopkins Team Learning Project.

> *In the Jigsaw method, students are assigned to six-member teams. Academic material is broken down into as many parts as there are students on each team. For example, a biography might be broken into early life, first accomplishments, major setbacks, and so on. Members of the different teams who have the same section form "experts groups" and study together. Each then returns to his or her team and teaches the section to the team. Often, the students take a quiz on the entire set of material. The only way students can do well on this quiz is to pay close attention to their teammates' sections, so students are motivated to support and show interest in each other's work.*
>
> *Teams-Games-Tournaments (TGT) is the best researched of the classroom techniques that use teams. In TGT, students are assigned to four- or five-member learning teams. Each week, the teacher introduces new material in a lecture or discussion. The teams then study work sheets on the material together, and at the end of the week, team members compete in "tournaments" with members of other teams to add points to their team scores. In the tournaments, students compete on skill-exercise games with others who are comparable in past academic performance. This equal competition makes it possible for every student to have a good chance of contributing a maximum number of points to his or her team. A weekly newsletter, prepared by the teacher, recognizes successful teams and students who have contributed outstandingly to their team scores. The excitement and motivation generated by TGT is enormous. Teachers using this method have reported that students who were never particularly interested in school were coming in after class to get materials to take home to study, asking for special help, and be-*

coming active in class discussions. In one project in a Baltimore junior high school that contains a large number of students bused from the inner city, almost every student in two classes stayed after school (and missed their buses) to attend a tie-breaker playoff in the TGT tournament competition [see Figure 9.5].

Student Teams-Achievement Divisions (STAD) is a simple team technique in which students work in four- or five-member teams, and then take individual quizzes to make points for their team. Each student's score is compared to that of other students of similar past performance, so that in STAD, as in TGT, students of all ability levels have a good chance of earning maximum points for their teams. Thus, STAD is like TGT, except that it substitutes individual quizzes for the TGT game tournament.[116]

A fourth technique, Team-Assisted Individualization (TAI), has been developed and evaluated more recently. Developed originally for math, TAI is a unique form of cooperative learning in that it uses individualized rather than class-paced instruction. TAI is designed especially for classrooms where students are too heterogeneous to progress at similar rates. In TAI, students are assigned to four- to five-member heterogeneous teams as in other forms of team learning. After diagnostic testing, each team member works through the appropriate set of programmed mathematics units at his or her own pace.[117]

Why is student team learning so successful? For one thing, the strategy avoids problems caused by diffusion of responsibility often associated with small-group

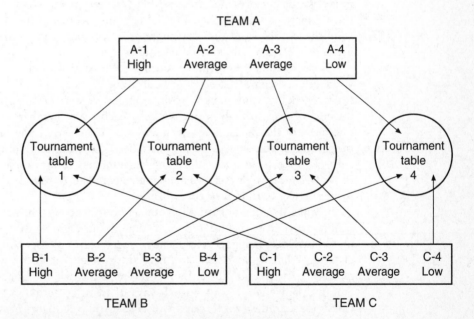

Figure 9.5 ▨ Assignment of Tournament Tables

Source: From Robert E. Slavin, *Teacher Manual for Student Team Learning* (Baltimore, MD: Center for Social Organization of Schools, Johns Hopkins University, 1978), p. 10. Reprinted by permission of the author.

work. Many people have worked in groups where some individuals were rewarded even if they contributed little or nothing to the group and where those who contributed most, or who worked to their fullest potential, received no recognition. Team learning avoids these problems because *group rewards are based on each individual member's learning*. The strategy is structured so that "the achievement of all group members does in fact contribute to group success. . . . [Furthermore,] the contributions of each group member can be easily seen, so that praise or blame among group members can be correctly applied.[118]

An important aspect of student team learning is equal-opportunity scoring. Team scores are derived from the improvement on test scores of individual members in STAD and Jigsaw II and from game competition with equals in TGT. This enables all students, no matter what their entry-level skills, to contribute to the team if they do their best. This scoring system is believed to increase student achievement and is necessary for several reasons. First, it avoids the problem of low student motivation under traditional grading systems, in which some students are virtually guaranteed high marks while others do poorly no matter how hard they try. When grades correspond to ability rather than effort, high-ability students can often take things easy, while lower-ability students become discouraged over too difficult tasks. When improvement is the criterion for success, both success and failure are within the reach of all students. This is believed to enhance motivation and personal responsibility.

A second advantage of equal-opportunity scoring is that it lessens the chances that the less able group members will be devalued by their group mates. A system that rewards performance increases makes every team member a potential contributor. Experience shows that more able team members often become motivated to tutor the less able students who might otherwise be ignored or resented because they are perceived as a liability to the group.

Because equal-opportunity scoring is embedded in the student team learning strategies, its separate effect is difficult to determine. The results to date do suggest, however, that it may have a positive effect on student achievement.[119] The effectiveness of task specialization, whereby each team member becomes an expert on one piece of the puzzle (e.g., Jigsaw) is not conclusive either. Positive results have been obtained in courses like social studies, science, and literature when content can be broken into subtopics. When the learning task requires mastery of a specific set of skills, concepts, or facts, as in a language, then group study (i.e., STAD and TGT) is more effective than task specialization.

Cooperative team learning is not without problems, however. One of the most serious arises from the differences in students' academic status (e.g., entry-level skills and knowledge, language proficiency), social status as ascribed by the outside society (e.g., ethnicity and sex), and peer status (e.g., friendship network).[120] The extensive research and curriculum development work by Cohen and associates at Stanford University has identified ways of treating status problems in cooperative classrooms, grades two through five. Successful treatments include:

- Training students to use cooperative behaviors, such as listening to peers, giving everyone a chance to talk, and asking for assistance

Cooperative team learning can strengthen intergroup friendships as well as academic achievement when it is implemented well.

- Assigning of rotating roles, such as facilitator, to each group member
- Using rich, stimulating learning materials that are intrinsically motivating and not entirely dependent on reading materials
- Including tasks that are open ended so that "precocious students can carry them further, while less mature students can complete them on a simpler level."[121]
- Introducing each set of activities as requiring multiple abilities.
- Assigning competence to low-status students through specific and public praise of behaviors such as reasoning or imagining, or of skills that require spatial ability or activities that require precision.[122]

Cohen's text, *Designing Groupwork: Strategies for Heterogeneous Classrooms*,[123] is an invaluable source for teachers. In it she clearly explains the theoretical framework for small-group instruction in terms of students' gains in academic learning (e.g., conceptual learning and improved oral language proficiency) and social development, as well as the benefits for classroom management. The theory is translated into practice by means of classroom examples at the elementary, middle, and high school level, and can include multilingual classrooms. The book's appendix contains team-building activities and suggestions for helping students learn the various team roles.

Conclusions

Successful teachers in inclusive classrooms have discarded the ethnocentric view that low-income and ethnic-minority students are "culturally disadvantaged" and "at risk." They reject the idea that anyone who has not had the "normal" advantages of a middle-income home life is culturally deprived. They realize that a "deficit" view is harmful because it focuses on where our students *aren't* and blinds us to where they *are*.

A good example of this deficit way of thinking is a young elementary-school teacher in Chicago who was appalled to learn that some of her inner-city children did not know that beds go in a bedroom. What she did not realize is that many of her children's homes had beds in the kitchen, as a matter of course, particularly in the cold of winter. Furthermore, she confused and degraded (however unintentionally) her children with such comments as "Johnny! We don't speak that way!" She is unaware that Johnny is speaking the way all the important people in his life speak. Another student of mine who had attended a prestigious magnet school for the arts in New York City was appalled that several of the rural Indiana schools she visited did not have a school symphony. Although there were talented musicians in the student body, she detested their music, dismissed their farming and hunting abilities, and had difficulty relating to them.

To overcome this mentality, it is important to ask ourselves, "Are we talking about groups of individuals whose backgrounds, attitudes, and general capabilities have failed to equip them adequately for a life of opportunities or are we talking about minority cultures of a country where the attitudes of the majority have inhibited the participation of the minorities in these opportunities?"[124] Do these children fail because their intellectual development is deficient from what is expected at school? Or do they fail because they can't fit in?

When we look through deficit lenses we perceive that the child from a low-income home is failing in school because he or she is unready. The low-income home is viewed as an environment that retards children's overall development and leads to their disadvantage in school. Deficit lenses focus our vision on developmental lags in students' cognitive development and shut out visions of "turn-around teachers" who can accommodate and affirm cultural and individual diversity in the classroom while maintaining high levels of academic achievement for all students. For many, taking off these old glasses is a difficult first step.

When teachers do put on new glasses, they see that overall, the United States is a polycultural society with monocultural schools. They accuse the school, rather than the child, of unreadiness. They see the damage done to a child's self-esteem when school success requires a denial of family and community. They are disturbed when some teachers say, "If only we didn't have to send the children home at night," or "What can we expect of kids with parents like that?" They know that, given a choice of fitting in at home or school, most children choose the former, and these teachers work to lessen the conflict between home and school. They know that children are powerless to change the school, and it is their responsibility to find out where the child is and build from there. They are well aware that the achievement levels of students like Kevin and Rachael are deficient, but they keep their expectations and standards of achievement high. They continually work to reverse the existing patterns of failure in schools and to equalize the chances of all students to achieve success. They know that "the poor and racial or ethnic minorities can and actually have been able to learn at the same level as others when the proper environmental support was provided."[125]

It would be impossible to know and fully understand the family backgrounds of all students. Teachers can realize, however, that sometimes a student is unable to learn in school because of problems at home or because of a conflict between home and school. Teachers can avoid diminished expectations based on erroneous assumptions that a student is simply slow or unmotivated. We can provide encouragement and support in school and better the chances that eventually a child will be resilient and catch up. We can avoid stereotypes and misconceptions by asking ourselves the following questions:

Does the family provide love and emotional support?

Does the family provide adequate food and shelter?

Does the student have unusual family responsibilities?

Are there mutual feelings of respect and ease between family members and school personnel?

Is there any cultural conflict between home and school expectations?

Selected Sources for Further Study

Anderson, J. D. (2007). "The Historical Context for Understanding the Test Score Gap." *National Journal of Urban Education and Practice, 1,* no. 1:1–21.

"Annotated Bibliography for the Mini-Series on Lesbian, Gay, Bisexual, Transgender, and Questioning Youth: Their Interests and Concerns as Learners in Schools." *School Psychology Review, 29,* no. 2 (2000): 231–234.

Aronson, E., & Patnoe, S. (1997). *The Jigsaw Classroom.* New York: Longman.

Ashcraft, C. (2008). "So Much More Than 'Sex Ed': Teen Sexuality as Vehicle for Improving Academic Success and Democratic Education for Diverse Youth." *American Educational Research Journal, 45,* no. 3:631–667.

Au, W. (2008). *Unequal By Design: High Stakes Testing and the Standardization of Inequality.* New York: Routledge.

Ayers, W. (1997). *A Kind and Just Parent: The Juvenile Justice System in Chicago.* (For peer relations, race, and low-income families.)

Calderon, A. E., & Minaya-Rowe, X. (2003). *Designing and Implementing Two-Way Bilingual Programs: A Step-by-Step Guide for Administrators, Teachers, and Parents.* Thousand Oaks, CA: Corwin Press.

Carrol, R. (Ed.) (1997). *Sugar in the Raw: Voices of Young Black Girls in America.* Ntozake Shange. (For gender and peer relations.)

Chapman, C., & King, R. (2005). *Differentiated Assessment Strategies: One Tool Doesn't Fit All.* Thousand Oaks, CA: Corwin Press.

Cohen, E. G., & Lotan, R. A. (1997). *Working for Equity in Heterogeneous Classrooms: Sociological Theory in Practice.* New York: Teachers College Press.

Conchas, G. Q. (2006). *The Color of Success: Race and High-Achieving Urban Youth.* New York: Teachers College Press.

Council for Exceptional Children website, www.cec.sped.org.

Crawford, James. (2004). "No Child Left Behind: Misguided Approach to School Accountability for English Language Learners. Forum on Ideas to Improve the NCLB Accountability Provisions for Students with Disabilities and English Language Learners. Center on Education Policy, September 14, 2004, 10 pages. Available from jwcrawford@compuserve.com.

Eckes, E., & McCarthy, M. M. (2008). "GLBT Teachers: The Evolving Legal Protections." *American Educational Research Journal, 45,* no. 3:530–554.

Gibson, M. A., Gandara, P., & Koyama, J. P. (Eds.) (2004). *School Connections: U.S. Mexican Youth, Peers, and School Achievement.* New York: Teachers College Press. (For gender, class, ethnicity, and peers.)

GLSEN, Inc. (2004). *No Dissing: No Name-Calling*

Week. New York: GLSEN & Simon & Schuster Children's Publishing. (Kit includes video, *Creating Safe environments*, curriculum guide, copy of *The Misfits*.)

Gregory, G. H., & Chapman, C. (2002). *Differentiated Instructional Strategies: One Size Doesn't Fit All*. Thousand Oaks, CA: Corwin Press.

Gunderson, L. (2004). *The Language and Literacy, and Social Consequences of an English-Only Program for Immigrant Students*. 53rd NRC Yearbook. Milwaukee: National Reading Association.

Habitat World, The Publication of Habitat for Humanity International, www.habitat.org. (For global, national, state and local perspectives on addressing world hunger and poverty.)

Henning-Stout, M., James, S., & Macintosh, S. (2000). "Reducing Harassment of Lesbian, Gay, Bisexual, Transgender, and Questioning Youth in Schools." *School Psychology Review, 29*, no. 2: 180–191.

Irvine, J. J., & Armento, B. J. (2001). *Culturally Responsive Teaching: Lesson Planning for Elementary and Middle Grades*. New York: McGraw-Hill.

"It's Elementary: Gay and Lesbian Issues in the Classroom." (1996). (Video, 78 minutes). San Francisco: Women's Educational Media.

Kivel, P. (1999). *Boys Will Be Men: Raising Our Sons for Courage, Caring and Community*. Gabriola Island, British Columbia: New Society Publishers.

Klein, S., Richardson, B., Grayson, D. A., Fox, L. H., Kramare, C., Pollard, D. S., & Dwyer, C. A. (Eds.) (2007). *Handbook for Achieving Gender Equity through Education*, 2nd ed. Mahwah, NJ: Lawrence Erlbaum.

Kohn, A. (2001). *The Case against Standardized Testing: Raising the Scores, Ruining the Schools*. Portsmouth, NH: Heinemann.

Lacy, K. R. (2007). *Blue-chip Black: Race, Class, and Status in the New Black Middle Class*. Berkeley: University of California Press.

Ladson-Billings, G. (2006). "From Achievement Gap to the Educational Debt: Understanding Achievement in U.S. Schools." *Educational Researcher, 35*, no. 7:3–12.

Lareau, A. (2003). *Unequal childhoods: Class, Race, and Family Life*. Berkeley: University of California Press.

Lee, S. J. (1996). *Unraveling the "Model Minority" Stereotype: Listening to Asian American Youth*.

New York: Teachers College Press. (For ethnicity, peers, class, and gender.)

Lesbian, Gay, Bisexual, and Transgender People in Education. (1996, Summer). *Harvard Educational Review, 66*, no. 2 (Special Issue).

Levin, H. M. (2009). "The Economic Payoff to Investing in Educational Justice." *Educational Researcher, 38*, no. 1:5–20.

Losen, D. J., & Orfield, G. (2002). *Racial Inequality in Special Education*. Cambridge, MA: Harvard Education Press.

McNeil, L. M. (2000). *Contradictions of School Reform: Educational Costs of Standardized Testing*. New York: Routledge.

Meier, D. (2002). *In Schools We Trust: Creating Communities of Learning in an Era of Testing and Standardization*. Boston: Beacon Press.

Morris, J. E., & Monroe, C. R. (2009). "Why Study the U.S. South? The Nexus of Race and Place in Investigation of Black Student Achievement." *Educational Researcher, 38*, no. 1:21–36.

National Center for Children in Poverty, Mailman School of Public Health, Columbia University, www.nccp.org.

Oakes, J. (1985). *Keeping Track: How Schools Structure Inequality*. New Haven: Yale University Press.

Popham, W. J. (2004). *America's Failing Schools: How Parents and Teachers Can Cope with No Child Left Behind*. New York: Routledge-Falmer.

Reyes, P., Scribner, J. D., & Paredes Scribner, A. (eds.) (1999). *Lessons from High-Performing Hispanic Schools*. New York: Teachers College Press.

Skiba, R. J., Knesting, K., & Bush, L. D. (2002). "Culturally Competent Assessment: More Than Nonbiased Tests." *Journal of Child and Family Studies, 11*, no. 1: 61–78.

Steele, C. M., & Aronson, J. (1998). "Stereotype Threat and the Test Performance of Academically Successful African Americans." In C. Jencks & M. Phillips (eds.), *The Black-White Test Score Gap* (pp. 401–427). Washington, DC: Brookings Institution Press.

Sternberg, R. J. (2007). "Who Are the Bright Children? The Cultural Context of Being and Acting Intelligent." *Educational Researcher, 36*, no. 3:148–155.

Stringfield, S., & Land, D. (eds.) (2002). *Educating At-Risk Students: One Hundred-First Yearbook of the National Society for the Study of Education*, part II. Chicago: The University of Chicago Press.

Stritikus, T., & Nguyen, D. (2007). "Strategic Transformation: Cultural and Gender Negotiation in First-Generation Vietnamese Youth." *American Educational Research Journal, 44*, no. 4: 853–895.

Tschannen-Moran, M. (2004). *Trust Matters: Leadership for Successful Schools*. San Francisco: Jossey-Bass.

Watson, M. (2003). *Learning to Trust: Transforming Difficult Elementary Classrooms through Developmental Discipline*. San Francisco: Jossey-Bass.

Now go to Topics #3, 6, 7 and 12: **Exceptionality, Class, Gender** and **Strategies** in the MyEducationLab (www.myeducationlab.com) for your course, where you can:

- Find learning outcomes for these topics along with the national standards that connect to these outcomes.

- Complete Assignments and Activities that can help you more deeply understand the chapter content.

- Apply and practice your understanding of the core teaching skills identified in the chapter with the Building Teaching Skills and Dispositions learning units.

Chapter 10

Teaching in Linguistically Diverse Classrooms

James S. Damico

In the documentary film *Do You Speak American?*, journalist Robert MacNeil travels the United States to explore the status and practices of American English across the country. What he finds is a language that is dynamic and rich with regional distinctiveness, that there is not one American English but many American Englishes. What he finds is a language inseparable from culture and history, political forces, economic changes, and demographic shifts. Through conversations with Maine lobstermen, Texas ranchers, patrons in a Cajun restaurant, among many others, MacNeil reveals the importance of understanding the social and cultural worlds of speakers and appreciating the inextricable link between language and identity. MacNeil provides us with much evidence to challenge any deficit view of language differences or of speakers of distinct dialects—any view that dialect differences equate with deficiencies. Rather, *Do You Speak American?* brings to light that the variation in language use across the country is something to be celebrated, an enduring reminder that we live in a multicultural, polyglot society.

An understanding of the dynamism and pluralism of language use in the United States as depicted in this documentary also sets the stage for this chapter about teaching linguistically diverse students. This chapter centers upon the experiences of English-language learners in U.S. schools and ways to best meet their needs. The significant increase of English-language learners in U.S. schools makes this a historic time for multicultural education.

English-Language Learners in U.S. Schools

According to the U.S. Census Bureau, the estimated number of foreign-born people in the United States in 2002 was 32.5 million, an increase of 64 percent since 1990. As noted in Chapter 4, this more recent wave of immigration differs from previous waves. Before 1950, close to 90 percent of immigrants came from Europe or Canada; today more than half of all immigrants come from Latin America and more than 25 percent come from Asia.[1] Correspondingly, the demographics of American K–12 classrooms are changing significantly.

Schools in the United States now serve millions of children who come from homes in which English is not the primary language spoken. English-language learners made up 10.5 percent of the K–12 student population in 2003[2] and are the fastest growing segment of students in the United States. The highest percentage growth has occurred in grades 7–12, where there was a 70 percent increase of English-language learners between 1992 and 2002.[3] Some researchers estimate that the percentage of U.S. schoolchildren whose dominant language will not be English will reach 40 percent by the year 2050.[4] Although Spanish is the heritage language of the majority of English-language learners (approximately 80%), school districts across the country have identified over 350 different first languages for their second-language learners.[5] California, Florida, Texas, New York, and Illinois have the highest numbers of English-language learners, yet populations of English-language learners are also surging in the South and the Midwest.[6]

As with any segment of the population, English-language learners are not a homogeneous group. They differ in many ways in terms of cultural background, levels of oral proficiency in English, literacy abilities in both English and the heritage language, background knowledge in academic content areas, mastery of age and grade-level skills, the amount of English spoken in the home, how much they identify with the heritage culture and with U.S. culture,[7] how many social and economic hardships they have endured, and the challenges they continue to face. Many English-language learners are children of immigrants who have come to the United States seeking economic advancement, educational opportunity, or safe haven from war or political turmoil. Other English-language learners have deep roots in American soil, such as American Indians of many tribal heritages whose ancestral ties go back many generations.[8] We also know that English-language learners, especially immigrant students, on average struggle academically more than native English speakers. In 2005, 4 percent of English-language learners in eighth grade reached the proficiency level on the reading component of the National Assessment of Educational Progress (NAEP), while 31 percent of all students achieved proficiency.[9] Non-native English speakers were also 21 percent less likely to have graduated from high school than their native-English-speaker peers.[10] We also know that a disproportionate number of English-language learners are misidentified as learning disabled when in fact their school-related difficulties are because of cultural and linguistic differences.[11] Many English-language learners are also tracked into courses with less challenging content, are often separated from mainstream students, and attend schools where there are many students like themselves.[12]

With each passing year it becomes more clear that a robust, equity-focused multicultural education must embrace the multilingual knowledge and needs of students in U.S. classrooms. The rest of this chapter addresses ways to do this. After a historical review of bilingual education in the United States and a description of programs designed for English-language learners, sets of guiding principles and classroom practices for linguistically diverse classrooms are described. This includes windows into classrooms where high academic standards and achievement are realized with English-language learners through culturally and linguistically relevant instructional approaches. Because the ways we as teachers view and understand programs, principles, and practices in education are shaped by the theories or perspectives we hold, this section of the chapter is framed by culturally responsive teaching[13] with English-language learners in mind.

Bilingual Education

National strategies for language policy tend to fall into three categories: (1) emphasis on a national language at the expense of indigenous languages, such as in Australia, Canada, and the former Soviet Union; (2) elevation of a local language that symbolizes sociocultural, religious, or political unity to the status of national language, as in Quebec (French) and India (Hindi); or (3) retention of the language of a previously occupying nation, or colonial languages, as the official language when there are numerous traditional language groups competing for power, as in Nigeria. The history of language policy in the United States is best described by the first strategy, an emphasis on national language at the expense of indigenous languages.

The nineteenth- and early twentieth-century waves of immigration from Europe, China, and Japan prior to World War I led initially to the establishment of private and public schools that used heritage or native languages as the primary medium of instruction.[14] These multilingual education programs and a national tolerance for cultural diversity were soon submerged by Americanization programs in the schools. By 1923, thirty-two states had adopted English-only instruction as a number of schools attempted to prohibit any kind of foreign language instruction. World War II, however, led to the realization that the trend toward educational monolingualism had left the United States at a global disadvantage. And in 1958, after the Soviets launched Sputnik, the United States more fully realized the disadvantage of a policy of linguistic isolation. The National Defense Education Act of 1958 had as its primary goal the facilitation of foreign-language instruction in the United States. One ramification of this act came in the form of assertive efforts on behalf of linguistic minorities during the 1960s, including the efforts of a group of Spanish-speaking immigrants from Cuba at the Coral Way School in Miami.

The concept of bilingual education steadily gained momentum in the United States after the formation of Miami's Coral Way School in 1963. Established by the wave of Cuban immigrants who entered Florida in the early 1960s—most of whom were highly educated, skilled professionals who held social and educational values compatible with Miami's mainstream—the school provided Spanish–language-dominant and English–language-dominant children proficiency in two languages and an appreciation of knowledge of two cultures. The success of this Dade County, Florida, school greatly influenced language education policy over the next twenty years.

This more hospitable view of bilingual education, however, began to change in the mid-1980s as "critics won increasing support for the contention that this experiment, however well intentioned, has failed to meet expectations."[15] This has led to efforts to politically establish English as the official language of the United States. Although this type of bill has failed in Congress on numerous occasions, individual states have been successful with this policy initiative. In 1984, the state senates in Indiana, Kentucky, and Tennessee passed a bill that established English as the official language. By 1988, there were sixteen "official English" states in the United States, and today there are twenty-eight.[16]

A chronology of bilingual education in the United States is provided in Box 10.1.

Box 10.1
Chronology of Bilingual Education in the United States

1963   Dade County, Florida, initiated a bilingual program for Spanish-speaking Cuban children and English-dominant children who want to become bilingual.

1965   The Elementary and Secondary Education Act (ESEA) granted funds to schools to upgrade education, including the areas of languages and linguistics.

1966   The first Navajo/English school was created in Rough Rock, Arizona.

1967   The Elementary and Secondary Education Act provided funds for schools that wished to implement bilingual education designed for language minority students. Seventy-two bilingual programs started in 1969.

1968   The Bilingual Education Act was passed by Congress. The act was reauthorized in 1974, 1978, 1984, 1988, and 1990.

1971   Massachusetts became the first state to pass a law mandating bilingual education for limited-English-proficient students.

1973   The Bilingual Education Reform Act updated the 1968 law and mandated the study of history and culture in bilingual programs.

1974   The United States Supreme Court decision *Lau v. Nichols* decreed that limited-English-proficient students have a legal right to special assistance as part of equal educational opportunity.

1974   The National Council of Teachers of English (NCTE) affirmed the right of a student to use his or her own language.

1979   Ann Arbor, Michigan, court decision on dialects stated that use of Black English vernacular is not an indication of intellectual inferiority or learning disability.

1979   The President's Commission on Foreign Language and International Studies reported, "The inability of most Americans to speak or understand any language except English and to comprehend other cultures handicaps the U.S. seriously in the international arena."

1983   The National Commission on Excellence in Education called for renewed efforts in teaching foreign languages.

1988   The Bilingual Education Act was reauthorized and amended by the three-year enrollment rule, implying that three years of bilingual education was sufficient for most students with limited English proficiency.

1998   Proposition 227 was approved in California, where 40 percent of the nation's English language learners attend school. This initiative tragically eliminates most instruction in bilingual children's first language, with very few exceptions.

2002   The English Acquisition Act, part of the NCLB legislation, replaced the Bilingual Education Act and had broad bipartisan support.

Source: C.I. Bennett. (2007). *Comprehensive Multicultural Education: Theory and Practice* (6th ed.) p. 297.

After more than three decades of bilingual education since the Bilingual Education Act was passed in 1968 by a unanimous vote in Congress, bilingual education came under serious attack in the 1990s.[17] In 1998, the State of California passed, by a margin of 61 to 39 percent, Proposition 227, an initiative that eliminated most bilingual programs in the state. Although scholars and advocates of bilingual education do not claim that it is a panacea, they argue that too often it is not implemented properly. For example, in California only 30 percent of the children with limited proficiency in English were receiving any type of bilingual education, and among those who did only 18 percent were taught by certified bilingual teachers; the remaining 12 percent were taught by monolingual English-speaking teachers with a bilingual aide.

Despite consistent research findings that bilingual education is highly effective when done well, public support for bilingual education has continued to decline.[18] In 2002, after thirty-four years, the Bilingual Education Act expired.[19] In its place, the No Child Left Behind Act (NCLB) provided funds to support the education of English-language learners, but the emphasis moved from the previous goal of maintaining native-language skills, wherever possible, as the child develops proficiency in English, to a focus on English only. These political decisions run counter to much research as well as some common sense ideas about second-language learning. In their book *Learning in Two Worlds: An Integrated Spanish/English Biliteracy Approach*, Perez and Torres-Guzman write:

> For children who come to our schools speaking Spanish, developing literacy in the language for which they have oral forms is essential. Children who use their first language to solve problems and discuss abstract ideas also learn to use a second language in similar ways. A substantial amount of research . . . has shown that the most effective route to English language literacy for language minority students is through their first language.[20]

Programs to Meet the Needs of English-Language Learners

Federal law requires that schools provide English-language learners with opportunities for English-language development and access to the core curriculum, while state laws govern more of the specifics of program requirements.[21] Local school districts are then given a great deal of latitude to choose the particular types of programs to support English-language learners in their schools. Thus, the design of these programs varies according to the underlying philosophy of a local community or state. These philosophies fall along a continuum of cultural assimilation (i.e., ESL and English immersion) at one end and cultural pluralism (i.e., two-way or maintenance) on the other (see Figure 10.1). Most scholars believe that the most effective programs are two-way bilingual/bicultural education, or when that is not possible, a language-maintenance program rather than the quick-exit transitional programs now favored by Congress.

Cultural Assimilation
(English Only)

Cultural Pluralism
(English Plus)

English as a Second Language (ESL)
Goal: Proficiency in English;
transition into English as
soon as possible; academic content
taught in English with varying degree
of support in native language

Participants: English language
learners; 1–3 years is common

Maintenance Bilingual Education
Goal: Proficiency in
English and in native
language; academic content
taught in native language until
sufficient proficiency in English is achieved;
affirmation of home culture and mainstream culture

Participants: English language
learners; 3 years plus (varies)

Two-Way Bilingual Education
Goal: Full proficiency in two languages
(English and native language), appreciation and understanding of the two
related cultures; high academic attainment; school climate of equity and
respect.

Participants: Native English speakers
and English language learners
(e.g., Spanish, Navajo, Korean,
etc. at home); K–12.

Figure 10.1 ⊠ Overview of Approaches to Bilingual Education: A Continuum
Showing Degree of Native Language Instruction While Learning English

Source: C.I. Bennett. (2007). *Comprehensive Multicultural Education: Theory and Practice* (6th ed.) p. 299.

Transitional Programs

Transitional programs focus on the goal of mainstreaming students with limited
English-language skills into English-only classes as soon as they have the English
proficiency to succeed, and cultural assimilation is often stressed. A goal of transitional programs is to provide instruction in the children's native language to assist
them in learning school subjects as they study English in programs designed for

second-language learners.[22] The goal is to prepare students for English-only classrooms, typically within two to three years.[23] Unfortunately, transference is often expected prior to the consolidation of language, skills in the native language and this premature transference can harm children's cognitive development by disallowing use of the home language.

English as a Second Language (ESL) programs use only English as a medium of English-language instruction. The goal is to assimilate learners into the English language as quickly as possible. ESL programs may be found as a language arts component of a bilingual education program or used alone to simultaneously teach English to a variety of students with different first-language backgrounds. ESL programs seem most effective when more than one home language is represented in a classroom. They provide English-only instruction but may include a multicultural emphasis. Although research indicates that an English-only classroom is not as cognitively effective as a sound bilingual program,[24] ESL programs can be effective and appropriate for students who are motivated to learn the new language in a mainstream English-only classroom. Often ESL programs are "pullout" programs where English language learners receive most of their instruction in mainstream classrooms with monolingual or English–language-dominant peers but are pulled out of the classroom to receive additional instruction from an ESL teacher, such as reinforcement of academic content taught in the mainstream classrooms.

Maintenance or Developmental Programs

Maintenance or developmental programs are designed to help children develop cognitive skills in both their native language and English. Maintenance of the native language supports and facilitates transition into English while strengthening a sense of ethnic identity. An ideal maintenance program provides dual-language instruction for students from kindergarten through twelfth grade, although few programs exist at the secondary level. The student develops cognitively in both languages and also receives instruction in the history and culture of his or her ethnic group. A goal is for students to retain and expand their heritage language while also becoming proficient in standard English.

Two-way bilingual education is another way to approach maintenance or developmental bilingual programs. In two-way immersion programs, both language-minority (English-language learners) and language-majority (English speakers) students are placed together in a bilingual classroom. They learn each other's languages and work academically in both languages while developing and maintaining their home languages. Different versions of this two-way program model have been carefully documented and evaluated and proven successful in school districts throughout the United States.[25] Enrichment immersion programs have been widely successful among language-majority children who wish to acquire a second language, as in the French language-immersion program in Quebec and the Chinese language-immersion program in Indiana.

Whatever approach is used, we know that a variety of factors affect the motivation of students to learn the English language, as well as their motivation to retain

Table 10.1 ☒ Factors Encouraging Language Retention and Loss

Language Retention	*Language Loss*
Political, Social, and Demographic Factors	
Large number of speakers living in concentration (ghettos, reservations, ethnic neighborhoods, rural speech islands)	Small number of speakers, dispersed among speakers of other languages
Recent arrival and/or continuing immigration	Long, stable residence in the United States
Geographical proximity to the homeland; ease of travel to the homeland	Homeland remote and inaccessible
High rate of return to the homeland; intention to return to the homeland, homeland language community still intact	Low rate or impossibility of return to homeland (refugees, Indians displaced from their tribal territories)
Occupational continuity	Occupational shift, especially from rural to urban
Vocational concentration, i.e., employment where co-workers share language background; employment within the language community (stores serving the community, traditional crafts, homemaking, etc.)	Vocations in which some interactions with English or other languages is required; speakers dispersed by employers (e.g., African slaves)
Low social and economic mobility in mainstream applications	High social and economic mobility in mainstream occupations
Low level of education, leading to low social and economic mobility; *but* educated and articulate community leaders, familiar with the English-speaking society and loyal to their own language community	Advanced level of education, leading to socio-economic mobility; education that alienates potential community leaders.
Nativism, racism, and ethnic discrimination, because they serve to isolate a community and encourage identity with the ethnic group rather than the nation at large.	Nativism, racism, and ethnic discrimination, as they force individuals to deny their ethnic identity in order to make their way in society
Cultural Factors	
Mother-tongue institutions, including schools, churches, clubs, theaters, presses, broadcasts	Lack of mother-tongue institutions, from lack of interest or lack of resources
Religious and/or cultural ceremonies requiring command of the mother tongue	Ceremonial life institutionalized in another tongue or not requiring active use of mother tongue
Ethnic identity strongly tied to language; nationalistic aspirations as a language group; mother tongue, the homeland national language	Ethnic identity defined by factors other than language, as for those from multilingual countries or language groups spanning several nations; low level of nationalism
Emotional attachment to mother tongue as a defining characteristic of ethnicity, of self	Ethnic identity, sense of self derived from factors such as religion, custom, race rather than shared speech
Emphasis on family ties and position in kinship or community network	Low emphasis on family or community ties, high emphasis on individual achievement

Table 10.1 ▨ (Continued)

Cultural Factors

Emphasis on education, if in mother-tongue or community-controlled schools, or used to enhance awareness of ethnic heritage; low emphasis on education otherwise	Emphasis on education and acceptance of public education in English
Culture unlike Anglo society	Culture and religion congruent with Anglo society

---

Linguistic Factors

Standard, written variety is mother tongue	Minor, nonstandard, and/or unwritten variety as mother tongue
Use of Latin alphabet in mother tongue, making reproduction inexpensive and second-language literacy relatively easy	Use of non-Latin writing system in mother tongue, especially if it is unusual, expensive to reproduce, or difficult for bilinguals to learn
Mother tongue with international status	
Literacy in mother tongue, used for exchange within the community and with homeland	Mother tongue of little international importance
	No literacy in mother tongue; illiteracy
Some tolerance for loan words, if they lead to flexibility of the language in its new setting	No tolerance for loan words; if no alternate ways of capturing new experiences evolve, too much tolerance of loans, leading to mixing and eventual language loss

---

Source: Reprinted with permission of The Free Press, a Division of Macmillian, Inc., from *A Host of Tongues* by Nancy Faires Conklin and Margaret A. Lourie. Copyright © 1983 The Free Press.

and continue learning their native language. Table 10.1 summarizes major factors that affect language retention and language loss. It is essential for teachers to recognize that some ethnic groups, given their life situations, tend to be more motivated than others to learn English. Among Spanish-speaking communities of the Southwest, for example, fluency in Spanish is essential to maintaining family, community, and economic bonds on both sides of the border. Newly arrived students from East Asia, Eastern Europe, or South Asia, however, who are eager to build a new life in the United States, may be more eager to master English. When family members encourage the acquisition of English or are themselves bilingual, the child's acquisition of the new language is enhanced.

Readiness and ability to learn English are also shaped by a student's "affective filter," what Stephen Krashen describes as the variables, such as motivation, self-confidence, self-image and level of anxiety, that play a role in second-language learning.[26] Learners who are highly motivated and confident with low levels of anxiety and self-doubt are more likely to acquire a second language than learners with low motivation, poor self-esteem, and greater levels of anxiety. For this latter group of students, the self-doubt and anxiety function as a filter between the teacher (or other English speakers) and the English-language learner, making it more challenging to understand and communicate in the second language, English.

What We Know about Literacy and Language Learning

Fortunately, we know a lot about the ways children become literate.[27] We know that by the age of three children begin to master the phonological, semantic, and syntactic components that all languages have.[28] These sound, meaning, and grammar systems develop in generative stages referred to as holophrastic (one-word utterances), telegraphic ("me go home"), and pivot/open grammar ("allgone egg"). The vocabulary, intonation patterns, and nonverbal gestures that accompany language production are learned from models (parents, siblings, and neighbors) and are culture bound. Research has also shown that language learning involves an integration of reading, writing, speaking, listening, and thinking and that this learning is best achieved when children use language for meaningful, authentic purposes[29] in classrooms where risk-taking and making mistakes are encouraged.[30]

We also know that becoming proficient in a language includes social and academic language. Social language, also called *basic interpersonal communication skills* (BICS), refers to the type of language skills necessary to communicate in more informal social settings, such as school hallways, playgrounds, and cafeterias. In these *context-embedded* settings, language learners can rely on additional nonverbal cues such as body language, gestures, and facial expressions to facilitate communication.[31] Academic language, commonly called *cognitive academic language proficiency* (CALP), is much different. CALP focuses on communication within content areas (science, math, social studies, literature) where specialized vocabulary and key concepts are essential for understanding. These settings tend to be *context-reduced* because related nonverbal communication features are much less prominent than in informal settings. Peregoy and Boyle describe several components of academic language use that "students must control with increasing sophistication as they progress from elementary through middle school and high school."[32] Academic language is needed to proficiently read and write texts, especially essays, where the skills of comparison and contrast, description, persuasion, summarizing, and synthesizing are prominent. Academic learning also involves sophisticated uses of oral language, comprehending as well as communicating oral explanations of complex concepts in subject matter disciplines.[33]

It is also essential to note that academic language skills develop significantly more slowly than social language skills. While social language skills often develop within two years, cognitive academic language proficiency often takes an average of five to seven years.[34] Cummins criticizes quick-exit transitional bilingual education programs that don't allow children time to develop beyond basic interpersonal communication skills. Cummins believes that children must attain cognitive academic language proficiency in their first language in all the school subjects before they are ready to learn these subjects in English. He advocates five to seven years of native language instruction in reading, writing, mathematics, and social studies, along with communication-based ESL and sheltered English classes. Sheltered instruction, also called Specially Designed Academic Instruction in English (SDAIE), is an academic content-based approach in English with modifications for English language learners to ensure comprehension.[35] The term *sheltered* "indicates that such instruction provides refuge from the linguistic demands of mainstream instruction" as teachers use a range of strategies (clarification of concepts in home language, use of supplementary materials, building on students' backgrounds) to support English-language learners.[36]

What We Know about African American Language (AAL)

Multicultural educators inquire into the experiences of different groups of people to broaden and deepen their understandings about the world and the places they and their students occupy. One generative area of inquiry for educators is linguistic diversity: learning about the development and key features of different languages, especially the home languages of their students. Consider, for example, African American Language (AAL) and speakers of AAL—speakers who are part of a particular group of English-language learners. Unlike newly arrived immigrants with no background in English, most AAL speakers have lived in the United States all of their lives and possess a great deal of conversational English yet many are learners of mainstream Academic English.

There is a great deal of scholarship in the fields of history, linguistics, sociology, among others, about the development of AAL in the United States. For instance, some of the seminal work in linguistics, beginning in the 1960s and 1970s, demonstrated clearly that AAL was systematic and rule-governed with distinct, identifiable features, such as the grammatical form of copula absence (no use of the verb form *to be*, as in "He tired").[37] Other identifiable features of AAL or some discourse strategies that African American speakers use include call and response, signifyin', tonal semantics, narrative sequencing, historically Black words, and directness of speech.[38] Developing understandings about distinctive linguistic and performative features of AAL can also address negative attitudes and views of AAL, which can be persistent.[39] When teachers have at least some working knowledge of these features, they can also enact more culturally responsive curriculum with African American students. Carol Lee, for example, has demonstrated how African American readers can draw upon their knowledge of signifyin'—a form of figurative language use or verbal play that typically involves witty insults (is also called "playing the dozens")—to enrich their interpretations and deepen their understandings of literature.[40]

An emphasis on AAL here highlights the relationship between a teacher learning and developing knowledge about a language and culture and then designing learning opportunities for students that build on this knowledge. All students' home languages in a classroom are worthy of similar focus, inquiry, and curricular attention.

Classroom Considerations for English-Language Learners

Obviously, the best teachers for students who are English-language learners are bilingual teachers who are fluent in the students' home language as well as English. However, bilingual teachers for some languages are difficult to find, and most teachers, new and experienced, in K–12 classrooms in the United States are monolingual

English speakers. Given these realities, along with an increasing population of English-language learners in K–12 classrooms, *what can teachers do to best meet the needs of English language learners?* The next section of the chapter offers a response to this important question, a response framed by culturally responsive teaching, grounded in sound instructional and learning principles, and demonstrated through examples of specific classroom practices.

Culturally Responsive Teaching: Implications for English-Language Learners

As discussed in Chapter 8, culturally responsive teaching, at its core, validates and affirms the "cultural knowledge, prior experiences, frames of reference and performance styles of ethnically diverse students."[41] When teachers use culturally relevant approaches, students have opportunities to draw on their cultural and linguistic knowledge and resources to foster more meaningful learning experiences.[42] In her 1994 book *The Dreamkeepers*, Gloria Ladson-Billings outlined a set of principles for culturally responsive teaching. These principles include possessing positive views of families and communities, communicating and holding high expectations for academic achievement, employing active teaching methods, and reshaping the curriculum to facilitate culturally relevant learning experiences. According to Geneva Gay, this enables teaching and learning to be comprehensive, transformative, and emancipatory.[43]

While much scholarship in second-language acquisition theory has taken place in linguistics and cognitive psychology, more recent work has focused on how issues of identity, context, politics, and power shape language acquisition.[44] This emphasis on the social and cultural factors of language learning aligns with the guiding principles of culturally responsive teaching and provides an integrative framework to consider principles and practices for working with English-language learners.

Principles and Practices for Working with English-Language Learners

The population of English-language learners in U.S. schools is increasing dramatically, leaving many school districts with little time to more fully prepare teachers to manage this population shift. Fortunately, leading professional organizations and advocacy groups have been taking a lead to help schools and teachers best meet the needs of the growing number of linguistically diverse students in their classrooms. In 2001, the International Reading Association (IRA) issued a position statement on English-language learners and second-language literacy instruction. This statement begins with the research-based stance that literacy and language learning are best when instruction builds on children's knowledge and strengths in their home or heritage language—and all children come to school with strengths in their home language. Beginning with a child's home language is especially advantageous for children affected by poverty.[45] The cultivation of language skills in a child's heritage language can then be applied to learning English. The IRA recognizes that initial instruction often takes place in English-due to limited school resources and also acknowledges that parents of English-language learners might prefer that the school provide initial instruction in English. What is most important from the IRA's perspective is the right of students and family members, when feasible, to choose the language of initial literacy instruction, whether it is English or their heritage language. Overall, the IRA is clear about the benefits of second-language literacy instruction, with one of the primary benefits being tolerance—"tolerance of majorities for minorities; tolerance of speakers of all languages for speakers of others; and especially tolerance on the part of monolingual speakers of the world's politically dominant languages for multilingualism."[46]

An emphasis on tolerance—and moving beyond tolerance to critical understanding—is especially significant when anti-immigration sentiment and xenophobia are running high. During these times it is also more likely that myths about language learning and English-language learners take hold, and it is imperative for teachers to be able to distinguish between rhetoric and reality and to identify and debunk myths when it comes to English-language learning. Toward this end, the National Council of Teachers of English (NCTE) published a policy brief debunking six common myths about English-language learners (see Table 10.2). Understanding the realities and truths about English-language learners enables teachers to stand on more solid ground when it comes to designing learning opportunities for students.

NCTE also offers research-based recommendations to ensure quality instruction for English-language learners. These recommendations can serve as guiding principles for all teachers with English-language learners in their classrooms. A summary of six key principles appears in Box 10.2. Teachers can enact these principles in a range of ways, as the following classroom examples illustrate.

Language and Literacy Learning Through Reading, Writing, and Drama

One approach to help make children's lives—their language and their cultural, familial, and community experiences—an integral part of the curriculum is through reading and writing opportunities with autobiography and memoir. Cecilia Espinosa describes how dual-language teachers (Spanish and English) guided elementary school bilingual students in a study of memoir reading and writing.[47] In this unit of study the teachers led a group of fifth-graders in readings and discussions of memoirs written for children and young adults. These texts, written in English and/or Spanish, included *My Very Own Room/Mi Propio Cuartito* by Amada Irma Pèrez, *Women Hollering Creek and Other Stories* by Sandra Cisneros, *America Is Her Name* by Luis Rodriguez, and *La Mariposa* by Francisco Jimenez. After close readings and discussions of these high-quality published memoirs, the teachers guided their students to draw from these models to compose their own memoir stories. With a goal to help "the children to see that everyone's life is filled with memories worth writing about," the teachers first modeled the story-writing process by sharing memoir moments from their own childhoods.[48] The teachers then guided the students through several phases of the writing process (drafting, revising, and editing) as the children composed their own memoir pieces.

Table 10.2 ⊠ Debunking Common Myths about English-Language Learners (ELLS)

Myths	Reality
1. Many ELLs have disabilities, which is why they are often overrepresented in special education.	1. A disproportionate number of ELLs are represented in special education. However, often assessments do not distinguish between disabilities and language differences which leads to misdiagnosing ELLs.
2. Children learn a second language quickly and easily.	2. Many factors affect language learning, including different experiences acclimating to a new culture and level of language proficiency in first language.
3. When an ELL student is able to speak English fluently, he or she has mastered it.	3. Everyday oral language includes different structure and vocabulary than written and oral academic language.
4. All ELL students learn English the same way. Students need to learn forms and structures of academic language and understand the relationship between forms and meaning in written language so they can express complex meanings.	4. Prior schooling, level of academic content knowledge and lexical similarity to English (e.g., prevalence of cognates), among other factors, lead to different learning experiences for ELLs.
5. Providing accommodations for ELL students only benefits those students.	5. Research shows that instructional strategies with ELLs can also benefit native English speakers.
6. Teaching ELLs means only focusing on vocabulary.	6. Students need to learn forms and structures of academic language and understand the relationship between forms and meaning in written language so they can express complex meanings.

Source: National Council of Teachers of English, English Language Learners: A Policy Research Brief. 2008. www.ncte.org/ell. Retrieved August 18, 2009.

While this type of instructional approach—immersion in high-quality literature, modeling of storytelling and writing, and guidance through the writing process—benefits all students, Espinosa points out that the English-language learners in this classroom benefited particularly from several instructional strategies. First, the teachers created opportunities for the children to tell their stories out loud in Spanish or English, which helped "create an environment filled with storytellers, caring and active listeners, and an abundance of stories to share."[49] Second, the teachers also selected for reading and discussion examples of culturally relevant texts—memoirs that dealt with bicultural, bilingual, and immigrant issues and experiences as well as memoirs that confronted more universal issues and themes related to childhood. Third, the teachers addressed specifically the needs of the bilingual students

Box 10.2
Guiding Principles for Teaching Linguistically Diverse Students

- Develop awareness and deepen understanding of students' cultural, familial, and community backgrounds.
- View native languages and home-family knowledge as vital classroom and curricular resources.
- Have high expectations for academic achievement for English-language learners.
- Provide English-language learners with challenging, rigorous curricular content.
- Maintain a teaching focus on academic literacy (content-specific vocabulary) with English-language learners across K–12 classrooms.
- Integrate technology meaningfully into classroom instruction.

Source: Adapted from English Language Learners: A Policy Research Brief produced by the National Council of Teachers of English (Urbana, IL: NCTE, 2008).

by guiding the children to use their bodies to dramatize key moments of each other's own stories. Having other students "act out" one's memoir provided each writer with essential feedback about, for example, the need to include more concrete details and vivid imagery to pull readers into a story. In all, these strategies reflect a stance of high academic and intellectual expectations for all students, especially English-language learners.

We can also see the guiding principles from Box 10.2 in action in Gerald Campano's elementary classroom in California. In a classroom where more than a dozen different languages were spoken in his students' homes, Campano demonstrates how high academic achievement is possible when spaces are created in the curriculum for students to access cultural and familial stories and experiences, especially immigrant and migrant experiences, to compose autobiographical migrant narratives. These stories of struggle, survival, perseverance, and hope are deeply personal and evocative, yet "the emotions they convey have social import, reflecting readings of the world that are embedded in collective history and group experience."[50] It is also essential to note that these narratives were deeply embedded in Campano's ethnographic and practitioner inquiry stance as a teacher. The narratives were not solely an "activity" that students were required to complete. Rather, Campano was working from what he describes as an "inquiry stance into the larger socio and political contexts of the students' lives and learning" that "was informed by the theories that acknowledge the epistemic status of their experiences and identities."[51]

As Campano emphasizes, this approach to curriculum—where the reading and writing of migrant narratives are core language-learning practices—can also provide opportunities for students to situate their own stories in relation to broader goals or ideals of democratic and multicultural education. This can be seen in a narrative of one of Campano's fifth-grade students, Ma Lee, who links her own family experiences with "a more universal need for everyone to live in freedom."[52]

Multicultural schools that serve ELLs help prepare students for life in an interconnected world.

In our Hmong culture we have to wake up very early to go to our garden. Even a little girl like me has to go. You also have to sew your own clothes. You can put red, blue, yellow or you can put any color you like. You can go to the store to buy it, but it costs a pack of money for just one dress, so we prefer to sew our Hmong clothes. We sewed clothes for ourselves, but we didn't even have shoes to wear.

I want everyone to know about my life and know how to respect my culture to make our Hmong people full of freedom. I know someday if no one wants to go out there and talk what they believe, I will because I don't want people to make fun of me and my culture. I know everyone wants to live in freedom. If someday my dreams come true, the world I live in will always be radiant and never be dim with prejudice. This is what I believe in my heart.[53]

Campano also describes how an academically rigorous curriculum for language learning can be enacted through drama, or *teatro*, where students investigate subjects, such as the shared histories of Mexican and Filipino workers, and then compose and perform their own skits and plays based on their investigations. In another example of the ways drama can be used to promote language and literacy learning, Medina demonstrates how a fifth-grade boy used drama to deepen his interpretations of children's literature, especially Latina feminist literature.[54] What is most important across these examples is a culturally relevant stance that sees curriculum connected to or emerging from the knowledge and needs of students.

Parents as Partners in Language Learning

The principle of valuing home and family languages and knowledge as vital classroom resources can lead to powerful learning experiences for all students when teachers invite parents and other family members to be partners in creating curric-ular activities. Joel Dworin describes just such a project.[55] Building from a "funds-of-knowledge" orientation[56] in which students are encouraged to access and use knowledge from their homes and communities to support academic learning in school, Dworin outlines how a bilingual Spanish and English teacher guided her stu-dents in a "family stories project." The children in this fourth-grade classroom were Latino and in the process of transitioning to all English-instruction-classes. The "family stories project" occurred in several phases. After first reading and discussing children's literature examples of bilingual family stories, the children collected sto-ries from their own family members about their lives. These stories were predomi-nately in Spanish. The children then wrote, revised, illustrated, and translated these stories in Spanish and English. The project culminated with the students publishing two books of these stories, one in Spanish and one in English. Looking across the entire project, several features seem most central to its success. The children were able to use their funds of knowledge and meaningfully involve family members in a project to accomplish academic goals. Peer sharing and collaboration was essential throughout the project, with the children providing feedback on each other's stories and jointly coming up with the best translations. The project also brings to light the significance of children translating their own stories because it "demonstrates that bilingual children have sophisticated levels of language knowledge and abilities that teachers can easily make part of literacy learning by valuing biliteracy."[57] As the "family stories project" aptly demonstrates, children's intellectual and academic de-velopment can be enhanced when the sophisticated use of both Spanish and English are cultivated in the classroom.

Culturally Relevant Texts in the Classroom and Academic English Mastery

The previous classroom examples highlight the ways culturally relevant texts can play a vital role in the academic, intellectual, and social growth of English-language learners. Culturally relevant texts affirm and validate identities of students and can motivate them toward deeper engagement with reading and writing and with aca-demic content.[58] Culturally relevant texts can also directly facilitate language learn-ing. There are a number of books written in two languages, especially Spanish and English, which help students with comprehension. Some texts also represent the dis-tinctive features of a particular language or variant of English, though it remains im-portant to evaluate these, as with all books, for bias, stereotypes, and other misrepresentations.

Walter Dean Myers, for example, an accomplished author of literature for chil-dren and young adults, imbues his stories and characters with the distinctiveness of AAL and culture and situates his stories in the context of political, economic, his-torical, and social struggles of African Americans. Carmen Kynard describes how Myers accomplishes this in the book *The Blues of Flats Brown*.[59] Kynard explains how the blues motif in the book represents the Great Migration and the collective struggle of African Americans against the persistent sting of racism and oppression. The characters in *The Blues of Flats Brown* also employ African American discourse modes in their speech, including tonal semantics and call and response. Tonal semantics refers to ways that intonation of a word or phrase can change its meaning,[60] and Myers consistently accentuates this discourse mode by keeping "the ideas of a talking guitar and blue-playing dog in sharp focus and rhythm."[61] Call and response is a practice in which the statements (calls) from a speaker are affirmed by expressions (responses) from a listener.[62] Myers has the narrator of the story directly address readers throughout the text, invoking responses from readers. What is perhaps most important about *The Blues of Flats Brown* and Kynard's analysis of this book is that AAL "is not used merely for dialogue but as the very structure and theme of folklore, identity, cultural politics, and history."[63]

Using literature like *The Blues of Flats Brown* can help educators honor language variation and differences in their classrooms while also guiding students to acquire mainstream academic English. One such educator is Linda Christensen, a veteran language arts teacher and social justice educator. She selects literature of authors who often write in languages that correspond to the home languages of many of Christensen's students such as Lucille Clifton, August Wilson, Lois Yamanaka, and Jimmy Santiago Baca. She then leads class discussions with her students about how and when to "code-switch" from their home languages to mainstream English in their own writing. The students identify poetry and dialogue in narratives as appropriate places for home language and decide that college essays, state exams, and job applications are genres that necessitate the use of mainstream English.[64]

While many English-language learners develop everyday conversational English or basic interpersonal communication skills, they experience much greater difficulty with academic English, or cognitive academic language proficiency. This group of English-language learners includes newcomers to the United States with no background in English as well as students fluent in conversational English but not proficient in academic English. One program in Los Angeles, California, called the Academic English Mastery Program, addresses the needs of English-language learners, especially those in the latter category, including African American, Mexican American, Native American, and Hawaiian American non-native speakers of mainstream academic English.[65] Teachers in this program help students identify features of their home language and then translate or code-switch to mainstream English. For example, students learn to identify the zero copula rule in AAL (the absence of *is* or *are* in a sentence) and then code-switch to mainstream English ("She funny" to "She is funny"). This approach does three important things. It builds from the extensive scholarship that documents AAL as a systematic, rule-governed language;[66] it values the linguistic knowledge and experiences of the students; and it moves them to mastery of mainstream English. What is most important about the work of educators like Linda Christensen and programs such as the Academic English Mastery Program is that honoring and building from students' home language use is not in conflict with becoming proficient in academic English.

Academic English Mastery Through Thematic Integrated Units

Another way to promote academic English mastery is for teachers and school leaders to create and organize curriculum around themes or integrated units of study. The goal is for students to learn academic language and academic content together.[67]

Freeman and Freeman suggest this can perhaps be best achieved when curriculum is framed with big ideas or questions,[68] such as "What are the political, economic, and sociological effects of global warming?"[69] This type of complex question can foster rigorous, scholarly inquiry in mathematics, science, social studies, and language arts. This approach to curriculum can also connect to students' lives and build from their interests and experiences, which can foster deeper engagement with the content and more successful learning.[70] The meaningful integration of technology—for example, using computers to conduct Internet searches to investigate topics and using digital authoring software (e.g., iMovie and Photovoice) to communicate results of investigations—can also further support English-language learners.

A Curricular Emphasis on Issues of Language and Power

From a critical multicultural perspective, all language issues involve power dynamics, and teachers can choose to make issues of language and power a curricular focus in their classrooms. Linda Christensen does this with high school students, guiding them to think critically about the relationship between language and power. Whether it is helping students gain more accurate historical knowledge about the evolution of African American vernacular English or using popular culture texts for careful analysis of language use, Christensen makes language and power the focus of study—part of scholarly inquiry in her engaged curriculum. She does this in a range of ways with her students, including showing films and leading discussions of the films, engaging students in different role-play activities, and guiding them to write narratives building from their own experiences. All these pedagogical decisions are designed for students to gain a better understanding of the ways language works in society. Christensen describes her rationale for this approach in this way:

> *During thirty years as language arts classroom teacher, I realized that if I wanted my students to open up in their writing, to take risks and engage in intellectually demanding work, I needed to challenge assumptions about the superiority of Standard English and the inferiority of the home language of many of my students . . . I finally realized that I needed to create a curriculum on language and power that examined the roots of language supremacy and analyzed how schools perpetuate the myths of the inferiority of some languages. I also discovered that students needed stories of hope: stories of people's resistance to the loss of their mother tongues and stories about the growing movement to save indigenous languages from extinction.[71]*

As Christensen demonstrates, explicit attention to language and power issues can help both teachers and students identify and work through their own beliefs and assumptions about the intersections among language, race, class, and power.

Global Englishes and Language Preservation

A number of scholars, practitioners, and language advocates are in favor of a national policy initiative that would recognize and honor the rich and diverse languages that students speak.[72] H. Samy Alim and John Baugh describe how this list of English-language learners would include "Vietnamese English learners in the San Francisco Bay area, Jamaican Creole speakers in the Bronx, Chicano English speakers in East Los Angeles, isolated white Appalachian English speakers in the mountains of the Northeast, Gullah speakers on the Carolina Sea Islands, Lumbee English speakers in southeastern North Carolina, Arabic–dominant Palestinian English learners in New Jersey, and the millions of undocumented students of various immigrant backgrounds in America's schools."[73] Considering this list of English-language learners also helps bring to light two language-related movements taking place that will likely shape our understandings of linguistic diversity well into the twenty-first century: (1) the rise and spread of English or Englishes as the lingua franca in a globalized world and (2) language preservation and revitalization efforts with many indigenous languages.

As the forces of globalization—the movement of goods, capital, ideas, information, etc.—continue to intensify and escalate across the world and English further solidifies as the lingua franca of globalization, the result is the emergence and development of an increasing array of Englishes practiced around the globe (e.g., Singaporean English as different than Taiwanese English). These Englishes are always evolving and are inflected with national, regional, and local cultures and languages. At the same time, there are efforts to preserve and revitalize indigenous languages, which are dying at an alarming rate (roughly one language every two weeks). These efforts are taking place around the world in, for example, New Zealand with Maori languages and in the Andes in South America with Quechua languages.[74] Language restoration and revitalization efforts are also taking place in the United States. Stephen Greymorning, for example, describes how an Arapaho community on the Wind River Reservation in Wyoming created a language-immersion program to restore and preserve Arapaho language and culture.[75] The potential long-term success of a program like this must also be placed in historical context, as Greymorning points out:

> In spite of perceived advancements in human rights, Indigenous peoples remain colonized within their homelands. In the face of a long history of political oppression, the struggle to maintain the integrity and uniqueness of being Indigenous continues. It is for this reason that the hope for the future remains strongly rooted in Indigenous peoples' proven resilience to survive.[76]

Conclusions

This chapter addresses the need for culturally responsive teaching and curriculum for English-language learners. Fortunately, the topic of teaching linguistically diverse students is moving more to the center of professional development concerns and initiatives across the United States. Leading professional organizations have issued policy briefs and position statements about English-language learners,[77] and a host of resources—in print and online—are available that describe curricular approaches and instructional strategies to better meet the needs of linguistically diverse learners.

For teachers today, learning about diversity and becoming a multicultural educator requires learning about linguistically diverse children and youth. This entails learning about the vast cultural and linguistic resources and knowledge students bring to school and cultivating an inquiry stance with English-language learners guided by goals of culturally responsive teaching.

Selected Sources for Further Study

Adger, C. T., Snow, C., & Christian, D. (2002). *What Teachers Need to Know About Language.* McHenry, IL: Delta Systems.

Alim, H. S. & Baugh, J. (2007). *Talkin Black Talk.* New York: Teachers College Press.

Ashburn, E. (2007). A Race to Rescue Native Tongues. *Chronicle of Higher Education,* 54(5): B15.

Barbieri, M. (2002). *"Change My Life Forever": Giving Voice to English-language Learners.* Portsmouth, NH: Heinemann.

Campano, G. (2007). *Immigrant Students and Literacy: Reading, Writing and Remembering.* New York: Teachers College Press.

Christensen, L. (2000). *Reading, Writing & Rising Up: Teaching About Social Justice and the Power of the Written Word.* Milwaukee, WI: Rethinking Schools.

Dong, Y. R. (2004). *Teaching Language and Content to Linguistically and Culturally Diverse Students: Principles, Ideas, and Materials.* Greenwich, CT: Information Age Publishing.

Freeman, R. (2004). *Building on Community Bilingualism.* Philadelphia: Caslon.

Freeman, Y., & Freeman, D. (2009). *Academic Language for English-language Learners and Struggling Readers.* Portsmouth, NH: Heinemann.

Greymorning, S. (2004). *A Will to Survive: Indigenous Essays on the Politics of Culture, Language, and Identity.* Boston: McGraw-Hill.

Lee, C. (2007). *Culture, Literacy, and Learning: Taking Bloom in the Midst of the Whirlwind.* New York: Teachers College Press.

Peregoy, S., & Boyle, O. (2008). *Reading, Writing, and Learning in ESL: A Resource Book for Teaching K–12 English Learners,* 5th ed. Boston: Pearson.

Reyes, M. L., & Halcon, J. (2001). *The Best for Our Children: Critical Perspectives on Literacy for Latino Students.* New York: Teachers College Press.

Smitherman, G. (1977). *Talkin and Tesifyin: The Language of Black America.* Detroit, MI: Wayne State University Press.

Suàrez-Orozco, M. M., Suàrez-Orozco, C., & Baolian Qin, D. (eds.). (2005). *The New Immigration: An Interdisciplinary Reader.* New York: Routledge.

Valdès, G. (2001). *Learning and Not Learning English: Latino Students in American Schools.* New York: Teachers College Press.

Van Sluys, K. (2005). *What if and why?: Literacy Invitations in Multilingual Classrooms.* Portsmouth, NH: Heinemann.

Part IV
Strengthening Multicultural Perspectives in Curriculum and Instruction

Chapter 11

Multicultural Curriculum Development: A Decision-Making Model and Lesson Plans

In the late 1960s, Bill Cosby narrated the film *Black History: Lost, Stolen, or Strayed?* The film documents numerous stereotypes, omissions, and biased interpretations of history that characterized the school curriculum at that time. Cosby discusses the negative impact on young African American children and youth, and how Whites were socialized to accept negative stereotypes and misconceptions about African Americans. Although the film is over three decades old, I still show it. Many of my students today find it to be disturbing and similar to the school curriculum they are taught today. Most of them have learned very little about *any* of the diverse ethnic groups that have contributed to our national development over the centuries. In fact, the curriculum they describe seems quite similar to what I was taught in high school decades ago.

This chapter is about curriculum reform, one of the four basic dimensions of multicultural education. Curriculum reform is aimed at rethinking and transforming the traditional curriculum that is primarily Anglo-European in scope, including bias in textbooks, trade books, and other instructional media. It requires active inquiry to discover and include knowledge and perspectives that have previously been ignored or suppressed. It recognizes that textbook knowledge is contested and constructed, and that a Eurocentric curriculum in a multicultural society such as the United States is a tool for cultural dominance.

Multicultural Teaching

What does it mean to teach in a multicultural manner? It means creating classroom environments where students are respected, cared for, and encouraged to develop their fullest potential. It means creating curricula that include diverse and multiple perspectives. It means helping students develop some degree of intercultural competence. And it means fostering fair-minded critical thinking, compassion, and social action to improve societal conditions. This chapter provides a curriculum development model and sample lessons to illustrate the possibilities. Let's revisit Sam Johnson, the middle school science teacher introduced in pages 8–9.

The transformation of Sam's classroom (compared with what we saw earlier) illustrates that it is possible to incorporate multicultural perspectives into the ongoing curriculum. These changes reflect a rationale based on Sam's conceptions of his

Sam Johnson's Classroom Revisited

It is the second week in October. Sam Johnson's classroom is filled with the students' preparations for World Food Day as part of their life science unit on the causes and effects of hunger. The students have brought in collections of pictures and articles on food and hunger across the world and in the United States. There are student-created posters and diagrams showing the biological impact of starvation and malnutrition. Student-made graphs show that approximately one out of every eight people on earth suffers from hunger, and that 40,000 children die of hunger every day, or 15 million a year. Additional posters show that crop failures, floods, and other natural disasters do contribute to hunger, but the most important cause of hunger is poverty. Several world maps have been created to show global facts and trends such as the following:

Most of the world's hungry live in Third World nations, located primarily in the Southern Hemisphere, Central America, South America, Africa, the Middle East, and Southeast Asia, but hunger does exist in the so-called First World—North America, Western Europe, Australia, and Japan—and in Second World nations—the former Soviet Union and Eastern Europe.

- The Third World has 74 percent of the world's population, but only 26 percent of the world's wealth.
- The First World has 17 percent of the world's population, and 56 percent of the world's wealth, and in the Second World, the ratio is 9 percent to 18 percent, respectively.
- The Third World nations contribute a significant portion of the world's natural resources, or raw materials, from which First and Second World nations generate wealth.

A bulletin board labeled "Working to End World Hunger" lists the addresses of local, national, and worldwide organizations that are working to end world hunger. Sam's students have organized a recycling drive, a community garden project, and a Thanksgiving food drive, and have prepared an educational program for parents and students entitled "Ending World Hunger: Think Globally and Act Locally." Most have written letters to a congressional representative or senator to express their concerns that millions die every year of starvation despite the fact that we produce sufficient food to provide over 3,000 calories per day for every human on earth.

When Sam's principal questioned him about how much life science his students were learning, Sam was able to report that student motivation and achievement were higher than in previous years. Even on the textbook publisher exams, most of Sam's students were well above mastery on core concepts related to the nature and continuity of life, human biology, and ecological relationships.

students, his community, his subject matter, and the goals and values of multicultural education. The curriculum model that guides Sam's revisions will be explained in this chapter.

This model integrates aspects of multicultural and global education by combining Hanvey's *Attainable Global Perspective* and the work of global educators such as Becker and Reardon with my original model of a multicultural curriculum.[1] It is based on the belief that neither multicultural education alone (with an emphasis on ethnic groups within a society), nor global education alone (with an emphasis on worldwide trends and issues) is sufficient for the twenty-first century.

 ## Rethinking the Curriculum

The idea of using students' own culture and history as a context for learning and helping them relate socially and psychologically to other cultural perspectives is at the heart of multicultural curriculum development. It also involves rethinking history itself and the history of the specific disciplines (physics, mathematics, American literature, music, art, etc.) through a lens of race, ethnicity, culture, class, and gender. Major events, persons, themes, and societal, cultural, or political developments are studied from multiple perspectives and experiences to create an inclusive curriculum.

An illustration of how historical inquiry can help correct curriculum bias is the study of Chinese, Japanese, Korean, Indian, Filipino, Vietnamese, Cambodian, and Laotian American stories and perspectives by Ronald Takaki.[2] In *Strangers from a Different Shore: A History of Asian Americans*, Takaki corrects the misconception that the United States is a nation of immigrants from Europe who were the only pioneers in a westward expansion movement. In this narrative study of Asian immigrants Takaki shows that

> the term "shore" has multiple meanings. These men and women came from Asia across the Pacific rather than from Europe across the Atlantic. They brought Asian cultures rather than the traditions and ideas originating in the Greco-Roman world. Moreover, they had qualities they could not change or hide—the shape of their eyes, the color of their hair, the complexion of their skin. They were subjected not only to cultural prejudice, or ethnocentrism, but also racism. . . . Unlike the Irish and other groups from Europe, Asian immigrants could not become "mere individuals, indistinguishable in the cosmopolitan mass of population.[3]

Asians migrated east, through Oahu, Hawaii, or Angel Island in San Francisco Bay, not through Ellis Island, and contributed to such national undertakings as the transcontinental railroads and development of agriculture in Hawaii and California. Takaki documents the diversities and similarities in their experiences and perspectives, as well as the history of racism—such as the anti-Asian immigration laws and the internment of Japanese American citizens during World War II—and the resurgence of racism directed at the "model minority" today. Despite the privileging of Anglo-European peoples and cultures, Takaki argues that America also has a countertradition and vision, springing from the reality of racial and cultural diversity.

Likewise, in a content analysis of California textbooks, Joyce King[4] challenged the "immigrant perspective" that "distorts the historical continuity of African Americans, Native Americans, and the indigenous peoples now known as Chicanos, Hispanics, or Latinos, who did not come to America in search of material gain or freedom but were conquered by European American settlers."[5] She argued that the "reified immigrant experience" affirms visions of *individual opportunity for upward mobility and economic advancement, more so than collective struggle for justice. For the descendents of indigenous peoples forced off and forced to give up their lands, one political consequence of accepting this ideology is the forfeiture of any basis of collective claims for redress and justice. On the other hand, to identify with one's collective interests is not "excessive veneration of one's ancestors," but a logical antidote to domination and alienation. . . .*

Black students' ancestral origins are doubly tainted within the cultural model framework that naturalized the immigrant experience. Not only did their ancestors "come" to this land as slaves, but the masses of black folk still live in poverty. The reality of the African presence, then, as now, contradicts the myth of America as a land of freedom, justice, and equality of opportunity . . . [and] inherently implies that Black people's failure is a failure to assimilate and acculturate. The immigrant bias in the textbooks obscures the contradictions occasioned by racial injustice and misequates the Middle Passage with Ellis Island, thus distorting the African experience and making it an anomaly rather than a paradox of the American reality.[6]

This chapter presents ways to create a multicultural curriculum by including multiple perspectives, as advocated by scholars such as Takaki and King, within the curriculum development model introduced in Chapter 1. The model's six goals are explained and illustrated with sample lesson plans to show how multicultural education can be integrated into the ongoing curriculum and academic standards without sacrificing the basic skills, concepts, and understandings our students need to learn in the various subject areas. The process can begin with thinking about reasons curriculum revision is needed and coming up with a strong rationale.

Developing a Course Rationale

According to curriculum designers Posner and Rudnitsky, an adequate course rationale must address three value areas: conceptions of the learner, the society, and the subject matter.[7] As shown in Figure 11.1, these valuative considerations influ-

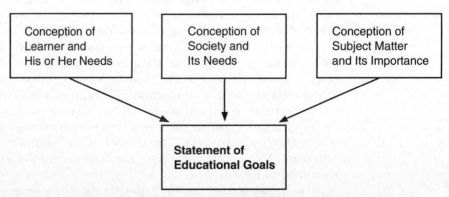

Figure 11.1 Components of a Course Rationale

ence or determine the educational goals of a particular course. This model provides extremely useful guidelines for teachers who are designing curriculum. The model clarifies the values that are related to three essential components, assuring a comprehensive approach rather than one that is only society centered, or child centered, or subject-matter centered.[8] When it comes to designing a multicultural curriculum, however, more is needed. The core value concepts must also be articulated because multicultural education has ideological overtones that are lacking in less controversial aspects of the curriculum. These values serve as a perceptual filter through which the conceptions of learner, society, subject matter, and goals are determined (Figure 11.2).

It is unlikely that the process will be linear as implied in the diagram, however. I envision a circular process of curriculum design and development, where teachers enter and revisit the processes at any point, or at multiple points simultaneously. Sam Johnson illustrates this process as we see how multicultural perspectives can be built into the curriculum once the core values and goals have been established. Sam used the model in Chapter 1 to clarify his conception of learner needs, society needs,

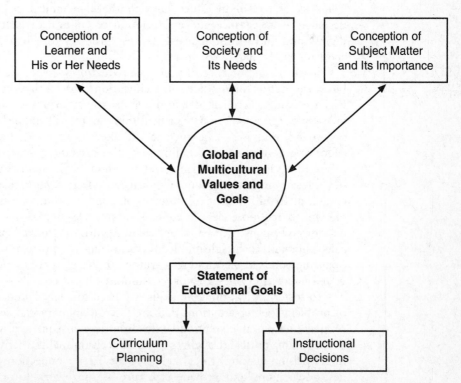

Figure 11.2 ◾ Instructional Decisions

and the nature of his subject area. He viewed his students as being overly ethno-centric, racially prejudiced, uninformed, and lacking compassion for their fellow humans. The same characteristics were reflected in the school's broader community, which found itself in a global economy, however unwillingly. Sam valued the tradi-tional science curriculum but wanted to focus it on state-of-the-planet issues. His course goals and objectives, therefore, included knowledge, attitudes, and skills re-quiring multicultural perspectives that fit the proposed curriculum model.

Effective multicultural lessons contain the same ingredients as any effective les-son (Figure 11.3). Plans for instruction are based on decisions about the nature of the learner, the nature of the subject matter, societal needs, and what is known about effective pedagogy. In addition, however, multicultural and global lessons are based on a special rationale that clarifies the instructor's values and goals. The decision-making worksheet in Box 11.1 is designed to help teachers clarify these values and goals and to select one or more goals as a basis for their own classroom instruction.

 ## The Importance of Fair-Minded Critical Thinking

Fair-minded critical thinking is necessary in multicultural teaching. If teachers and their students are not continually engaged in critical thought, multicultural educa-tion is likely to result in indoctrination rather than ethical insights based on core val-ues such as acceptance and appreciation of cultural diversity, respect for human dignity and universal human rights, responsibility to a world community, and re-spect for the earth.

Given the importance of prejudice reduction, perspective taking, and responsi-ble social action in multicultural education, critical-thinking skills are essential. Richard Paul, a major leader in the international critical-thinking movement, pro-vides an eclectic definition of critical thinking that distinguishes between uncritical and critical thinking.[9] The uncritical thinker is one whose thoughts are shaped by egocentric desires, social conditioning, and prejudices. Uncritical thinkers are un-aware of assumptions, relevant evidence, and inconsistent reasoning. They tend to be "unclear, imprecise, vague, illogical, unreflective, superficial, inconsistent, inac-curate, or trivial."[10] Critical thinkers, in contrast, think about their thinking in an attempt to be "more clear, precise, accurate, relevant, consistent, and fair."[11] They attempt to be constructively skeptical and work to remove bias, prejudice, and one-sided thought. To be fair-minded, critical thinkers must show empathy for diverse opposing points of view and seek truth without reference to one's self-interest or the vested interests of one's friends, community, or nation.

To foster critical-thinking skills, we need to engage students in complex issues or problem-solving situations that are interdisciplinary and contain multiple points of view and possible solutions with differing consequences. One excellent way of strengthening critical thought is to build decision-making activities into the curricu-lum. Decision-making "trees" help students to see connections among thoughts, val-ues, and actions and provide structure as they work through the stages in the decision-making process.[12]

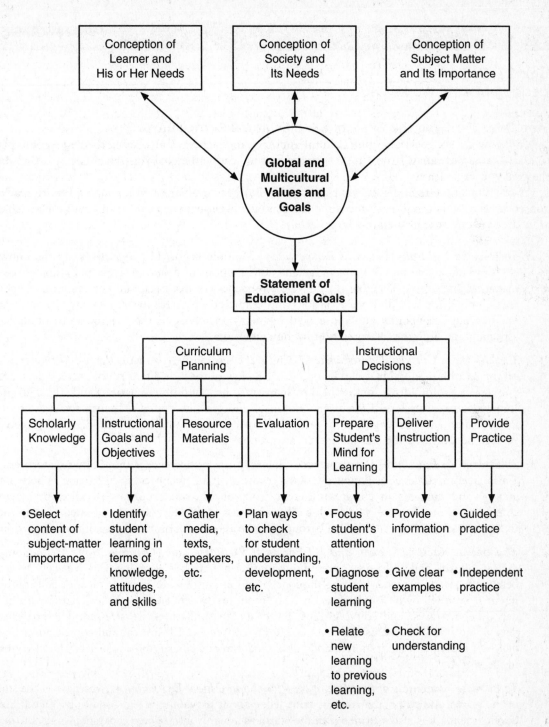

Figure 11.3 ▨ Extended Guidelines for Instructional Decision

Box 11.1
Decision-Making Worksheet

Step One: Clarifying the Goals of a Multicultural Curriculum

Listed below are six goals of a multicultural approach to teaching. Considering the courses you plan to teach, rank these goals from 1 to 6, with the first indicating the goal you value most and the sixth the goal you value least.

Work alone first; then discuss your decision with other members of your team and try to reach a consensus as to which goal seems most important. You will choose one member of your group to share your decision and reasons with the larger group.

1. ***To Develop Multiple Historical Perspectives*** Multiple historical perspectives are the knowledge and understanding of the heritage and contributions of diverse nations and ethnic groups, including one's own. The goal is to develop awareness of historical and contemporary experiences among the world's diverse nations and ethnic groups. This awareness includes both minority-group viewpoints and those held by many members of the macroculture or nation, especially the differing interpretations of human events.

2. ***To Strengthen Cultural Consciousness*** Cultural consciousness is the recognition or awareness on the part of an individual that he or she has a view of the world that is not universally shared and differs profoundly from that held by many members of different nations and ethnic groups. It includes an awareness of the diversity of ideas and practices found in human societies around the world and some recognition of how one's own thoughts and behaviors might be perceived by members of differing nations and ethnic groups.

3. ***To Strengthen Intercultural Competence*** Intercultural competence is the ability to interpret intentional communications (language, signs, gestures), some unconscious cues (such as body language), and customs in cultures different from one's own. Emphasis is on empathy and communication. The goal is to develop self-awareness of the culturally conditioned assumptions that people of different cultural backgrounds make about each other's behaviors and cognitions.

4. ***To Combat Racism, Sexism, and All Forms of Prejudice and Discrimination*** Reduction of racism, sexism, and all forms of prejudice and discrimination is lessening negative attitudes and behaviors based on gender bias and misconceptions about the inferiority of races or cultures different from one's own. Emphasis is on clearing up myths and stereotypes associated with gender, different races, and ethnic groups. Basic human similarities are stressed. The goal is to develop antiracist, antisexist behavior based on awareness of historical and contemporary evidence of individual, institutional, and cultural racism and sexism in U.S. society and elsewhere in the world.

5. ***To Increase Awareness of the State of the Planet and Global Dynamics*** Awareness of the state of the planet and global dynamics is knowledge about prevailing world conditions, trends, and developments. It is also knowledge of the world as a highly interrelated ecosystem subject to surprise effects and dramatic ramifications of simple events.

Box 11.1 *(continued)*

6. *To Build Social Action Skills*   Social action skills include the knowledge, attitudes, and behavior needed to help resolve major problems that threaten the future of the planet and well-being of humanity. One emphasis is on thinking globally and acting locally; the goal is to develop a sense of personal and political efficacy and global responsibility resulting in a participatory orientation among adult members of society. Another emphasis is enabling minorities and nonminorities to become change agents through democratic processes.

The statement we believe identifies the most important multicultural education goal is:

_____

_____

_____

Our reasons for this are the following:

1. _____

2. _____

3. _____

The goal we value least is _____

_____

_____

Our reasons are the following:

1. _____

2. _____

3. _____

continued

Box 11.1 *(continued)*

Step Two: Identifying Objectives for Student Learning

My teaching area is _____. I can build multicultural curriculum goals into this area with objectives for student learning such as the following:

1. _____

2. _____

3. _____

Step Three: Writing the Lesson Plan

By yourself or in a small group, write a lesson plan that will help you begin to realize your objectives.

The Curriculum Model: Goals, Assumptions, and Content

Goal One: Understanding Multiple Historical Perspectives

Most of us tend to be ahistorical when it comes to understanding contemporary issues, whether they are local, national, or global in scope. We also tend to view these issues from the viewpoint of the predominant society. It is difficult to be otherwise, given the nature of the traditional curriculum, which emphasizes the political development of Euro-American civilization. For example, informed and ethical decisions about affirmative action programs in education and employment require an understanding of the nation's history, as well as the perspectives of minorities and nonminorities, that few people possess. An important goal of a multicultural curriculum, therefore, is the development of multiple historical perspectives that will correct this Anglo-Western European bias. Past and current world events must be understood from multiple national perspectives, and both minority and nonminority points of view must be considered in interpreting local and national events.

Among the assumptions underlying this goal are the following:

- People must possess a degree of self- and group-esteem, as well as personal security, before they can be empathetic in their interrelations with others.
- Awareness of the achievements of one's culture group will enhance one's self- and group-esteem.
- Knowledge that corrects misconceptions about certain people (for example, that nonindustrialized people are less civilized than industrialized people) helps destroy the myth of Euro-American superiority.
- People can achieve a psychological balance between cultural pride and identity on the one hand and appreciation of cultures different from their own on the other. (For example, increased group pride does not necessarily increase ethnocentrism.)

Chun-Hoon in "Teaching the Asian-American Experience" expresses the importance of minority perspectives:

The greatest danger to an open society is an education that homogenizes its people into limited and fixed conformity; the greatest danger to a small minority like Asian-Americans is that they will be imprisoned in the images created for them by mass society and that their own personal reality will not be able to transcend the imposed psychological colonization of society-as-a-whole.[13]

Chun-Hoon asserts that schools bear a large responsibility for ensuring that minorities are accurately represented. He believes this can happen only when both the majority and the minority perspective are used in teaching the experience of minority groups:

Unless, for example, we can understand the relocation of Japanese-Americans during World War II, both from the perspective of those who were interned as well as from the perspective of those who interned them, we achieve only a partial understanding of the event itself. For in this instance, the fullness of the historical event is not measured by the inconsequential effects experienced by the overwhelming American majority, but by the extreme effects experienced by the Japanese minority. History is not made or experienced impartially, and attempts to report it or teach it neutrally all too often merely neutralize the real significance of events themselves. Accordingly, the major imperative of teaching the Asian-American experience, or any minority's history, is the ability to represent these dual perspectives fairly and completely.[14]

But how are multiple historical perspectives developed? Such perspectives are based on knowledge and understanding of the worldviews, heritage, and contributions of diverse nations and ethnic groups, including one's own. Subject matter from the fields of history, literature, and the arts can be used to provide understanding about people's contemporary culture, worldview, and differing interpretations of human events. This knowledge builds an awareness of historical and contemporary developments among the world's diverse nations and ethnic groups, awareness of traditional and contemporary attitudes held by the members of the dominant culture with respect to these groups, and knowledge about minority perspectives.

Content that builds within each student a sense of ethnic pride and identity is central, as is content about the achievements of people from other nations and cultures. Therefore, teachers could use subject matter that has traditionally been confined to ethnic studies courses such as Black history, Mexican American literature, Native American cultures, and White ethnics, as well as world culture courses. Teachers could use this content in ways that would encourage students to get at the underlying values and patterns of socialization of a particular culture rather than focusing only on the more superficial cultural trappings (such as foods and holidays), heroes, and historical events.

Every classroom offers opportunities for developing historical perspectives. Students can interview family members about their own ethnic roots and experiences. Bulletin boards can display people of the week or points of view on a variety of topics, or who's who in math, music, science, and so on. A multicultural calendar provides an excellent way to introduce students to people from many ethnic groups and nations, and can become a springboard for more in-depth study. Tiedt and Tiedt offer several suggestions of ways the calendar can be used: "Celebrating the birthdays of specific men and women can bring these people to life as students learn about their contributions. Focusing on events significant in the history of various ethnic groups in the United States is an effective way of informing all students about this country's multiethnic heritage. Information about these groups will provide the minority group student special opportunities to identify with his or her history."[15] The multicultural calendar is a helpful teaching aid that can be used for immediate reference and display. The calendar could be modified for junior and senior high school students to highlight people who have contributed to specific fields, such as sports and athletics, science and industry, mathematics, literature, politics, and the arts. Students can help create the calendar by doing research, planning the displays, and doing the artwork.

If multiple historical perspectives are to be understood, textbook distortions, stereotypes, and serious omissions surrounding ethnic minorities and Third World nations must be corrected. Acceptable revisions of the curriculum must be guided by an understanding of ethnic minority and Third World viewpoints, as well as the traditional majority point of view. Consider two phenomena that have traditionally been examined only from the Anglo-European viewpoints: slavery and manifest destiny.

Slavery

Slavery and emancipation are classic examples of how textbooks have excluded the African American point of view. Slavery is often introduced as an economic necessity. Later slavery is treated as a problem for Whites.

The African American perspective on slavery would include African cultural origins and histories of the array of African civilizations (just as England and Europe are discussed prior to colonization by Whites). It would also include evidence of Black people's strength under conditions of extreme oppression (in many cases the strongest and most intelligent Africans were sold into slavery and survived the middle passage), and of the expressions of African American culture that emerged in United States society.

A vivid example of how one's thinking can be dulled by limited frames of reference is the erroneous assumption often made concerning the social status structure among American slaves: House slaves, drivers, artisans, and mulattoes are accorded higher status than field slaves. According to Berry and Blassingame, however, the social structure from the slaves' viewpoint was far more complex.

Occupations translated into high social standing only if they combined two of the following features: mobility (frequently allowing the slave to leave the plantation); freedom from constant supervision by whites; opportunity to earn money; and provision of service to other blacks. . . . At the bottom of the ladder were those slaves who had the most personal contact or identified most closely with masters (house servants, concubines, drivers, mulattoes). Since conjurors and physicians helped to maintain the slave's mental and physical health, they received more deference than any other black.[16]

Native-born Africans were revered as links to the ancestral home, as were the educated. "Old men and women with great stores of riddles, proverbs, and folktales (creators and preservers of culture) played a crucial role in teaching morality and training youths to solve problems and to develop their memories. Literate slaves had even more status than the sources of racial lore because they could read the Bible, tell the bondsmen what was transpiring in the newspapers, and write letters and passes."[17]

Rebel slaves who resisted floggings, violated racial taboos, or escaped from their masters were held in the highest esteem by the slaves and were preserved as heroes in slave folktales and songs. "Physical strength, skill in outwitting whites, possession of attractive clothes, and ability to read signs and interpret dreams also contributed to a slave's social standing."[18]

Hamilton has described the lack of Black perspectives in the curriculum as part of the reason many Black parents give up on traditionally desegregated schools and prefer Black community control of schools serving Black children and youth. He quotes Killens and Bennett to illustrate how African Americans may view history differently from what is in the textbooks.[19] According to Killens,

> *We [black Americans] even have a different historical perspective. Most white Americans, even today, look upon the Reconstruction period as a horrible time of "carpetbagging," and "black politicians," and "black corruption," the absolutely lowest ebb in the Great American Story.*
>
> *We black folk, however, look upon Reconstruction as the most democratic in the history of this nation; a time when the dream the founders dreamed was almost within reach and right there for the taking; a time of democratic fervor the like of which was never seen before and never since.*
>
> *For us, Reconstruction was the time when two black men were Senators in the Congress of the United States from the State of Mississippi; when black men served in the legislatures of all the states in Dixie; and when those "corrupt" legislatures gave to the South its first public-school education. . . .*[20]
>
> *Even our white hero symbols are different from yours. You give us moody Abe Lincoln, but many of us prefer John Brown, whom most of you hold in contempt as a fanatic; meaning of course, that the firm dedication of any white man to the freedom of the black man is prima-facie evidence of perversion or insanity.*[21]

And Bennett challenges the traditional role and image of Abraham Lincoln, who he believes "was not the Great Emancipator. As we shall see, there is abundant evidence to indicate that the Emancipation Proclamation was not what people think it is and that Lincoln issued it with extreme misgivings and reservations."[22]

Manifest Destiny and the Native American and Latino Perspectives

One of the most blatant examples of Anglo-European bias in the curriculum is the fact that United States history is traditionally taught as an east-to-west phenomenon. The northward flow of peoples and cultures from central Mexico is largely overlooked. Our legacy from the Spanish colonizers who imposed Catholicism, the Spanish language, and an economic system of mining and agriculture on the native populations, and who helped create Mestizo and Creole populations, is largely ignored. If, however, history were taught according to a larger frame of reference, alternative perspectives to manifest destiny could be presented, particularly Chicano and Native American perspectives. Our legacy from the native peoples, which is just beginning to be discovered, would be recognized. People would realize that American Indian contributions penetrate all aspects of society, including our form of government, a federation modeled after the Iroquois League.[23]

What is the native perspective that should become part of the revised curriculum? Forbes provides excellent guidelines in the following illustrations of what teachers must do to teach the history of Indian people from their own viewpoint.

- The unsubstantiated theories of white anthropologists should be treated as such. For example, Native Americans are not mongoloid because . . . there is not a shred of evidence linking Indians exclusively with any single race.
- The Bering Straits migration theory should be treated with great skepticism since there is absolutely no evidence (except logic) to support it. Indian people generally believe that they evolved or were created in the Americas. This viewpoint should be respected although it is acceptable to discuss the possibility of migration as an alternative explanation. The point is that there is no empirical evidence to support any particular migration theory.
- American Indians should be treated as the original Americans, and the first 20,000 years of American history must be discussed prior to any discussion of European, African, or Asian migrations to the Americas. Likewise, in the discussion of the pre-European period, data derived from archaeology should be supplemented by American Indian traditional literature (as found in *The Book of the Hopi, The Sacred Pipe, The Constitution of the Six Nations*, and other available paperback books).
- The ongoing evolution of Indian groups must be dealt with, from 1492 to the present. That is, one must deal with the internal history of native tribes and not merely with European relations. For example, the development of the Iroquois confederation, the Cherokee Constitution of 1824, the Handsome Lake religion, the Comanche–Kiowa–Apache–Cheyenne–Arapaho alliance system, the westward movements of the Otchipwe, Cree, Dakotas and others, the teachings of the Shawnee Prophet, the Kickapoo Prophet, and so on, must be discussed as significant developments in the heartland of the United States at a time when Europeans were only marginal (i.e., along the Atlantic Coast).
- The teacher must deal truthfully with European expansion; native wars of liberation and independence must be dealt with as such and not as acts of aggression carried out against so-called peaceful Whites.

- The teacher will want to try to use accurate names for the American Indian groups in his or her region (such as Otchipwe in place of Chippewa). The correct names can usually be found in Hodge's *Handbook of Indians North of Mexico*.
- Native heroes and resistance leaders of the post-1890 period (such as Carlos Montezuma and Yukioma) must be dealt with—American Indian resistance did not cease with the "last Indian war."
- American history, from a native perspective, is not merely a material success story (bigger and bigger, more and more, better and better), nor does it consist solely in the reverse (that Whites have actually brought about the near-destruction of this land). History is not progressive, but cyclical. That is, the evils of the White man and some Indians and others are a repetition of previous eras wherein other people went astray and contributed to the destruction of a cycle. We are now in the fourth or fifth world from the native perspective.
- This world may be self-destroyed because of man's evil.... More inventions . . . may not lead to any great utopia in the future but simply to the end of this epoch. Furthermore, what really matters is the spiritual struggle of all creatures, the struggle for perfect character development, not a great invention.
- White people, for example, may exult over the development of a new type of rocket ship and regard a flight to the moon as an event worth recording in a history book. But from a wholly different perspective the decision of an ordinary man to give up a needed job whose demands run counter to his ethics is more significant because it is a spiritual act directly relevant to man's highest level of aspiration. From the traditional American Indian perspective, at least, the history of America should focus on man's spiritual development and not on his material progress.[24]

Establishing Multiple Historical Perspectives—The Challenge

An accurate representation of multiple historical perspectives is not always possible. Even when one wants a full, unbiased depiction of ethnic minority viewpoints and experiences, for example, lack of available information is a major problem. Political history in the schools has emphasized White males in power positions, and past omissions and inaccuracies make it difficult to establish the experiences and contributions of all groups.[25] Racist and sexist practices of the past make rediscovery of history difficult. Because copyrights and patents were not available to women and non-Whites until relatively recently, many early contributions remain unrecognized. Literature, art, even monuments are all tainted with bias. One example is African American soldiers in World War I. Of the 200,000 African Americans sent to France, nearly 30,000 fought on the front lines and received high accolades from the French. Yet no Black American soldiers were permitted to march in the glorious victory parade up the Champs Elysees. "The ultimate injustice was the U.S. War Department's insistence that African American soldiers not be depicted in the heroic frieze displayed in France's *Pantheon de la Guerre*."[26]

Chinese Americans experienced a similar fate after contributing most of the labor needed to complete the western portion of the transcontinental railroad. Nearly 10,000 Chinese workers had been involved, and much of their labor was high risk, using explosives and working at dangerous heights. Yet not a single Chinese face appears in a famous photograph that captured the first meeting of locomotives from east and west.[27]

Although oral history and folklore are not free of distortions and are often inaccessible to outsiders, oral literature and oral history along with music and the visual arts remain some of the best means of discovering ethnic minority perspectives. The facts that most enslaved people were barred from learning to read or write and that many immigrant groups, such as the Chinese, Japanese, Mexicans, and Eastern European Jews, entered initially as illiterate laborers mean that few pieces of literature or documents written by these people for themselves are available. Oral history, including songs, folktales, jokes, proverbs, aphorisms, verbal games, and (among African Americans) toasts offer the richest sources for understanding ethnic perspectives. Levine's exceptionally fine study of Black folklore, for example, has led him to paint a picture of slavery that differs dramatically from the view traditionally accepted by popular culture as well as by many scholars.

> *I have only begun to touch upon the reservoir of tales and reminiscences which stress slave courage, self-respect, sacrifice, and boldness. The accuracy of this picture is less important for our purposes than its existence. These stories were told and accepted as true—a fact of crucial importance for any understanding of post-slavery Afro-American consciousness. Once again a vibrant and central body of Black thought has been ignored while learned discussions of the lack of positive reference group figures among Negroes, the absence of any pride in the Afro-American past, the complete ignorance Negroes have concerning their own history, have gone on and on. The concept of Negro history was not invented by modern educators. Black men and women dwelt upon their past and filled their lore with stories of slaves who, regardless of their condition, retained a sense of dignity and group pride. Family legends of slave ancestors were cherished and handed down from generation to generation. Postbellum Negroes told each other of fathers and mothers, relatives and friends who committed sacrifices worth remembering, who performed deeds worth celebrating, and who endured hardships that have not been forgotten.[28]*

Table 11.1 provides an overview of the lesson plans included in this chapter. These lessons are examples of how the six multicultural curriculum goals and core values presented in this book can come to life in the classroom. The table gives the page number where each lesson begins and suggests content areas, grade levels, and possible modifications for each lesson.

It should be clear that minority perspectives are not built only from heroes and success stories, or from an emphasis on foods, fads, and festivals. Cortez cautions against this in "Teaching the Chicano Experience" with words that can be applied to every ethnic group.

Table 11.1 🖾 Overview of Lesson Plan Examples in This Chapter

<table>
<tr><td colspan="5" align="center">**Goal: Multiple Historical Perspectives**</td></tr>
<tr><td>**Lesson Title**</td><td>**Page in Text**</td><td>**Content Area**</td><td>**Grade Level(s)**</td><td>**Modifications**</td></tr>
<tr><td>1. *Three Views of History*</td><td>Page 336</td><td>Social studies</td><td>7 and above</td><td>Use any historical or current event</td></tr>
<tr><td>2. *Maps as a Metaphor: The Power of Perspectives*</td><td>Page 337</td><td>Science and social studies</td><td>5 and above</td><td></td></tr>
<tr><td>3. *Introducing the Blues!*</td><td>Page 339</td><td>Music</td><td>7 and above</td><td>Enrichment in language arts or social studies</td></tr>
<tr><td>4. *World War II in Historical Fiction and Multicultural Education*</td><td>Page 341</td><td>Language arts and social studies</td><td>Elementary</td><td>Expand to high school with adolescent literature</td></tr>
<tr><td colspan="5" align="center">**Goal: Cultural Consciousness**</td></tr>
<tr><td>**Lesson Title**</td><td>**Page in Text**</td><td>**Content Area**</td><td>**Grade Level(s)**</td><td>**Modifications**</td></tr>
<tr><td>5. *The Many Faces (and Shoes) of Cinderella*</td><td>Page 350</td><td>English, language arts, and social studies</td><td>5 and above</td><td>Use in early grades with teacher-read stories</td></tr>
<tr><td>6. *Five Great Values of the Lakota Sioux*</td><td>Page 357</td><td>Social studies</td><td>7 and above</td><td>Any content area to get at assumptions</td></tr>
<tr><td>7. *Modeling toward Understanding*</td><td>Page 360</td><td>Poetry</td><td>7 and above</td><td>Any content area; use content-specific prompts</td></tr>
<tr><td>8. *Building Bridges to Islam: Lanterns and Quilts*</td><td>Page 363</td><td>Mathematics and Art</td><td>Elementary</td><td>Tie in with social studies and language arts</td></tr>
<tr><td colspan="5" align="center">**Goal: Intercultural Competence**</td></tr>
<tr><td>**Lesson Title**</td><td>**Page in Text**</td><td>**Content Area**</td><td>**Grade Level(s)**</td><td>**Modifications**</td></tr>
<tr><td>9. *Faces, Families, and Friends*</td><td>Page 375</td><td>ESL, Bilingual Language Arts</td><td>Early elementary</td><td>Ice breaker for any level</td></tr>
<tr><td>10. *Nobody Speaks My Language*</td><td>Page 377</td><td>ESL, Bilingual Language Arts, Spanish</td><td>All levels</td><td>Choose age appropriate materials</td></tr>
<tr><td>11. *Spirituals for the School Choir*</td><td>Page 382</td><td>Choir</td><td>High School</td><td>Use as primary sources in social studies & English</td></tr>
<tr><td>12. *Misunderstandings in Cross-Cultural Interactions*</td><td>Page 385</td><td>Spanish</td><td>High School</td><td>Create vignettes for any language/culture</td></tr>
</table>

continued

Table 11.1 ☒ (Continued)

Goal: Combating Racism, Sexism, Prejudice, and Discrimination

Lesson Title	Page in Text	Content Area	Grade Level(s)	Modifications
13. "All Men Are Created Equal"	Page 394	U.S. history	High school	Adapt for social studies grade 7 and up
14. Can You Recognize Racism?	Page 398	Multicultural teacher ed & adolescent workshops	7 and up	Revise "test" with people and events from any content area
15. Hidden Messages in Children's Literature	Page 401	Multiple	All ages	Select literature from any content area
16. Reading, Constructing, and Interpreting Graphs	Page 404	Mathematics	High school 7 and up	Select data to fit any content area
17. Women in the World	Page 409	Social studies, career ed		Use global data in mathematics

Goal: State of the Planet Awareness

Lesson Title	Page in Text	Content Area	Grade Level(s)	Modifications
18. Thinking Peace/Doing Peace	Page 413	Social studies	All levels	Can be a theme in any content area
19. Poverty and World Resources	Page 420	Multiple	All levels	Adapt to age level and content
20. Global Connections in the World of Science	Page 422	Physics	High school	Use cross age tutoring with younger learners or other areas of science
21. Acid Rain	Page 425	Social studies, biology, physics	7 and up	Apply to global environmental concerns

Goal: Social Action for Social Justice

Lesson Title	Page in Text	Content Area	Grade Level(s)	Modifications
22. Promoting Youth Social Activism Using Hip-Hop and Technology	Page 429	Technology and social studies	7 and up	
23. The Little Rock Nine	Page 432	Social studies and english	7 and up	Use other literature with examples of youth activism
24. To Take a Stand or to Not Take a Stand	Page 437	All areas U.S. government	All ages	Create new examples to fit classroom content and concerns
25. No Man Is an Island: The Importance of Perspective in Decision Making	Page 438		High school	Adapt for social studies in grades 7 and up
26. Global Economics and the U.S. Consumer: Nike Goes Global	Page 442	Economics	High school	Adapt for social studies grades 7 and up

Certainly heroes and success stories comprise part of the Chicano experience. Chicanos can develop greater pride and non-Chicanos can develop greater respect by learning of Chicano lawyers, doctors, educators, athletes, musicians, artists, writers, businessmen, etc., as well as Mexican and Chicano heroes (heroes either to their own culture or to the nation at large). However, the teaching of the Chicano experience often becomes little more than the display of Emiliano ZaPata, Pancho Villa, Benito Juarez, and Miguel Hidalgo posters or an extended exercise in "me too-ism"—the list of Mexican Americans who have "made it" according to Anglo standards.

In falling into these educational cliches, the very essence of the Chicano experience is overlooked. For this essence is neither heroes nor "me too" success stories, but rather the masses of Mexican-American people. . . . [The] teacher should focus on these Chicanos, their way of life, their activities, their culture, their joys and sufferings, their conflicts, and their adaptation to an often hostile societal environment. Such an examination of the lives of Mexican Americans—not Chicano heroes or "successes"—can provide new dimensions for the understanding of and sensitivity to this important part of our nation's heritage.[29]

Obviously, people differ in their awareness of alternative ethnic and national perspectives. Most of us are more aware of some minority perspectives than others, particularly if we have lived a minority experience. Each of us, however, needs to become more informed about ethnic and national perspectives beyond our own—especially when we have grown up in a racist society, with an incomplete, biased curriculum.

The challenge to become knowledgeable about new ethnic and national perspectives may seem overwhelming at first, but it is a challenge that teachers are obliged to meet. The following suggestions are offered as possible ways of proceeding; with effective guidance, students can participate in all these steps.

- Start small. Begin by selecting one or two nations and/or ethnic groups, preferably those that hold special meaning for your students, the community, and yourself.
- Become informed about their perspectives regarding current events and the subject areas you teach. Consult global and/or ethnic primary source materials, such as literature, films, art, news media, and music. A list of key questions can help guide the research, or you may prefer to avoid preconceptions and let the issues emerge.
- Become acquainted with community resources (both people and organizations) in your area that can provide knowledge about your selected nations or ethnic group(s). Complete a list of local residents who would be willing to visit your school or be interviewed by students.
- Examine your texts and supplementary materials for bias.
- Develop a resource file of primary source materials and teaching strategies that will help you present the selected group's perspectives to your students. Everything from news articles containing statistics that can be converted into math problems, to songs, speeches, and cartoons can be collected.
- Select one or more areas of your course in which the group's contributions and viewpoints have been overlooked. Create and teach a lesson that provides more accurate knowledge by including the group's perspectives.

Lesson Plans That Develop Multiple Historical Perspectives

Lesson 11.1
Three Views of History   *David Page*

Introduction

On December 7, 1941, Japanese armed forces attacked Pearl Harbor. That night, 600 Japanese immigrants were picked up by the FBI and held in detention centers. Two months later, President Roosevelt signed Executive Order 9066 authorizing exclusion of all people with Japanese ancestry from the West Coast, and their relocation into internment camps. One hundred twenty thousand people were forced from their homes and put into these camps. Sixty percent of these people were U.S. citizens. Personal possessions of those evacuated were either confiscated by the government or sold at a fraction of their real worth. Over 30,000 Japanese and Japanese American families were forced to live in these camps from 1942 until 1945. The ostensible reason for their imprisonment was national security. A closer look reveals that many other forces were at work.

Objectives

1. Students will understand some of the many factors that enable institutionalized racism to exist and the different points of view on why it happened.

2. Students will identify with victims of racism as fellow human beings.

3. Students will see that not all laws are necessarily just, and that in some cases we must work to change laws for the better.

Materials

Copies of Executive Order 9066, which gives the U.S. Military the right to exclude any person from any area during wartime.

Video recording: *The Politics of War: Japanese Americans* 1941–1945, Chelsea House Educational Communications, 1970 (ten minutes). Narrator portrays situation of U.S. citizens of Japanese ancestry in the wake of Pearl Harbor, explaining war relocation and authority activities, such as Nisei detention camps, property losses, and abridgment of civil rights.

Sound recording: *They Chose America: Conversations with Japanese Immigrants*. Princeton, NJ: Visual Education 5302–05-p, 1975 (twenty-nine minutes, use side one only). A Japanese American talks about his experiences in the United States, before, during, and after the war.

The three items listed above give three very different views of the same event. All are true, but each is incomplete when viewed alone.

Executive Order 9066 gives the official view for the internment. It bases its reason for enactment on national security and the right of the federal government to enact such a law during wartime.

Lesson 11.1 *(continued)*

The video records the events that preceded the enactment of Order 9066; it starts with a description of the social and political position of Japanese and Japanese Americans living on the West Coast before and during the war. This video recording provides an impersonal view of the Japanese internment. It speaks of the Japanese only as a group, not as individual people. The only people who speak are Caucasian historians and a narrator.

The sound recording features an older Japanese American man who was sent to an internment camp as a young adult during the war. He gives his view of what it was like to lose his home and possessions, and the uncertainty he felt about his future.

Each point of view will be presented to a student separately, after which the student will be asked to rate seven statements about the internment of Japanese aliens and Japanese Americans. The statements are as follows:

Strongly agree 1 2 3 4 5 Strongly disagree

1. Japanese and Japanese Americans were interned mainly for national security.
2. Japanese and Japanese Americans were interned mainly for their own safety because Caucasians might think they were the enemy.
3. Japanese and Japanese Americans were interned because of racism.
4. Japanese and Japanese Americans were interned because of scapegoating.
5. Japanese and Japanese Americans were interned because of the economic competition experienced with Caucasians.
6. Americans of Japanese descent were more dangerous than citizens of Italian or German descent.
7. The internment of Japanese Americans during World War II was justified.

Evaluation

After all questions have been answered, students should compare the three ratings to each other. In most cases students will have changed answers for at least a couple of the questions. Ask the students to write a short paper that details how and why their answers changed.

Reprinted with permission of the author.

Lesson 11.2
Maps as a Metaphor: The Power of Perspectives

Introduction

In this lesson, geographical maps are used as a metaphor for understanding cultural perspectives or worldview. Maps both shape and are shaped by our views of the world.

continued

Lesson 11.2 *(continued)*

The objectivity of contemporary world maps is so taken for granted that most of us are unaware of their inherent biases. All maps reflect the assumptions and conventions of the society and the individuals who create them. Such biases seem blatantly obvious when one looks at ancient maps but usually become transparent when one examines maps from modern times. Only by being aware of the subjective omissions and distortions inherent in maps can a user make intelligent sense of the information they contain.[30]

Most of us take for granted our own view of the world and are unaware of the basic assumptions that guide our thoughts and perceptions. In the same way, the objectivity of contemporary world maps is so taken for granted that most of us are unaware of their inherent biases. By studying a variety of modern maps of the world we can see how scientific inquiry, as well as our understanding of human events, literature, and arts, is shaped by our limited perspectives. The search for truth is enhanced when we become aware of our biases and erroneous assumptions.

Goals

- Students will understand that all maps contain distortions and that different maps send different messages.
- Students will understand how maps affect our interpretations of the world.
- Students will realize that by gaining insight into basic assumptions, values, and beliefs we can think more critically about human events, creations, and scientific inquiry.

Materials

Maps and globes (e.g., Mercator Projection, Peters Projection, McArthur Projection, the Earth Ball, the Endangered Species Ball, National Geographic Map of Africa, and graphic maps).

Newsprint, markers, masking tape, and background reading.

Activities

1. Students work in groups of two to four. Each group is given a different type of world map. The students are instructed to locate Africa (or another part of the world) on their map and list on newsprint all the information they can find about Africa. They are to pretend that they know nothing about Africa other than what they can find on their map.

2. All groups report to the class, explaining their map and the information they have garnered. The maps and lists are displayed together to show the different types of information each group discovered.

3. In a follow-up discussion, students identify the strengths and weaknesses of each map, define what a "perspective" is, and develop implications for what they will be studying (e.g., the scientific method; differing points of view in history, or current events; the perspective of an author or character; and perspectives in art or architecture).

Sources
Phil Porter and Phil Voxland. "Distortions in Maps: The Peters Projection and Other Developments." *Focus*, Summer 1986, 22–30.
Denis Wood. "The Power of Maps." *Scientific American*, May 1993, 88–93.

Lesson 11.3
Introducing the Blues!
Allison Hoadley

Introduction
The purpose of the following lesson plan for a music listening class is to expand the student's understanding and enjoyment of the art of music through the development of perceptive listening abilities. This lesson is designed for high school juniors and seniors.

Goals
- To develop historical perspectives and Black and White culture consciousness through the study of a form of music originated by African Americans as an expression of their own emotions and experiences, and through investigating the influence of this musical form on the music of both White and Black Americans.
- To increase intercultural competence through understanding how Blacks and Whites use music as a form of communication to express their attitudes and beliefs.
- To help eradicate racial prejudice through learning a little of the history of Black people in the United States; recognizing the widespread influence of a Black style of music; working with students of another race to achieve a common goal.

Behavioral Objectives
1. Students will demonstrate knowledge of how the blues style originated in the United States by getting at least 75 percent of the answers correct on a short quiz to be given the following class period.
2. Students will accurately describe the general harmonic structure of a standard twelve-bar blues progression on the above quiz.
3. Students will correctly harmonically analyze a twelve-bar progression in a blues song through listening.
4. Students will describe the characteristics of a blues melody and explain how these characteristics affect the moods of the style.
5. Students will create, with the help of a few fellow students, their own blues with original words and melody, to be performed the next class period.

Materials
Recordings:

"That's All Right," Louis Myers, from *Sweet Home Chicago*

"Graveyard Dream Blues," Bessie Smith, from *Any Woman's Blues*

"Billie's Blues," Billie Holiday, from *Billie Holiday's Greatest Hits*

"It Ain't Necessarily So," George Gershwin, *Porgy and Bess* (Odyssey Records)

"The South's Gonna Do It Again," Charlie Daniels Band, from *Fire on the Mountain* (Epic Records)

A piano

continued

Lesson 11.3 *(continued)*

Motivation

A recording of Black blues music—"That's All Right" (Louis Myers)

Activities

1. Introduce students to the blues and rouse their interest in the topic by playing a recording of Louis Myers singing "That's All Right." Discuss with them in general terms the type of music they just heard, and briefly define the blues as a form of African American folk music that later gave birth to jazz.

2. Play the recording again; instruct the class to listen for a pattern in the harmony. Once they can perceive the repeating harmonic pattern, play part of the recording once more and tell students to listen for the number of measures of the harmonic pattern. Introduce the term twelve-bar blues.

3. Play the chord progression slowly on the piano. Students will listen and write out the chords being played in each bar:

1	2	3	4	5	6	7	8	9	10	11	12
I^7	I^7	I^7	I^7	IV^7	IV^7	I^7	I^7	V^7	IV^7	I^7 V^7	

   Discuss the chord progression in a standard twelve-bar blues.

4. Play a recording of "Graveyard Dream Blues" (Bessie Smith). Instruct the students to hold up one, four, or five fingers according to the I, IV, and V chords they hear. Play part of the recording again; instruct students to listen to the melody and determine what mood they think is being conveyed, and how the melody contributes to that mood. Discuss briefly melodic differences between this song and the second movement of Haydn's Symphony no. 94 (*Surprise*). Show them the first few bars of the blues melody written out on a blackboard; have students give the pitch inventory. Show and explain the blues scale (with flatted third and seventh); explain how the use of blues notes contributes to the overall mood.

5. Explain the historical development of the blues, importance of emotion in presentation, development of performance practices.

6. Expose the class to additional recordings:

   "Billie's Blues" (Billie Holiday)

   "It Ain't Necessarily So" (*Porgy and Bess*, George Gershwin)

   "The South's Gonna Do It Again" (Charlie Daniels Band)

   Discuss similarities and differences between these and previous examples.

7. Have students team up with one or two other students to create their own blues on a standard progression with words that reflect their own personal feelings and experiences. This will be performed later in the week.

Lesson 11.3 *(continued)*

Evaluation

1. Students' knowledge concerning the origin, historic developments, and structure of the blues will be assessed through a short quiz to be given the next class period.

2. Students' understanding of the terms and concepts presented will be evaluated through their participation or lack of participation in the discussion.

3. Students' harmonic listening ability may be perceived through checking their written analysis of the chords of a blues progression played on the piano and through watching them raise the correct number of fingers when listening to a recording.

4. Students' ultimate understanding of the nature of blues can be observed through experiencing their own original performance in this style.

Reprinted with permission of the author.

Lesson 11.4
World War II in Historical Fiction and Multicultural Education
John Kornfeld

Introduction

Students in the United States studying World War II in school usually learn about the war from the Allied perspective, in terms of black and white: Hitler bombed England, which was bad, and we bombed Japan, which was good; the Allies won and the Axis lost, which was good. Obviously, no historical period is that simple. Students need to learn that different societies viewed World War II in a variety of ways, and that regardless of who won or lost, there were ramifications of the war that textbooks cannot adequately communicate to students. Historical fiction offers one way to introduce and reinforce these ideas. Stories of earlier times are intriguing to people of all ages, and they can provide a kaleidoscopic picture of the world in all its diversity and commonalities. It is up to the teacher to help students interpret these stories and, in doing so, provide a coherent, global picture for the students.

World War II has spawned a rich profusion of historical fiction with which to create a powerful multicultural unit of study. A tantalizing variety of books presents perspectives from all over the world—of soldiers throughout Europe and the Pacific, of Jews caught in the Holocaust, of orphaned and abandoned children in Eastern Europe, of Dutch, Danish, and French resisting the Nazis, of Japanese Americans interned in relocation camps, of ordinary people helplessly watching bombs fall on their homes in England, Poland, Italy, Germany, Japan, and what was then the Soviet Union. (See annotated list of representative titles.)

This unit explains how to use historical fiction in an interdisciplinary multicultural unit on World War II. Obviously, the methods described could be used in any number of multicultural units at almost any grade level.

continued

Lesson 11.4 *(continued)*

Goals

- Students will learn that World War II—and any historical event—should be examined and understood from a variety of perspectives.
- Students will develop myriad reading, language arts, art, and social studies skills in an interdisciplinary unit.

Preparing for the Unit

Gather as many books about World War II as possible from your school library, the public library, garage sales, and the like. Be sure to include books for every reading level, from easy picture books to adult level. There are literally hundreds of World War II historical fiction books available, told from every conceivable perspective. In addition to works of fiction, bring in lots of nonfiction books for reference. Finally, choose a few titles of varying difficulty that present different points of view, and order them in sets of six to eight books for reading groups.

Now comes the best part: read as many of the books as you can before starting the unit!

Getting Started

To begin the unit, divide students into groups and assign each group a book to read. You might begin, for example, with *The Devil's Arithmetic, The Machine Gunners, The Road to Memphis, Journey to Topaz,* and *Maus.* Give them reading assignments as you would for any other book. You may want to assign a minimum number of pages per night, but allow students to read more if they wish. Daily meetings with reading groups will enable you to monitor students' progress, clarify ideas in the books, and answer any questions they might have about events in the book.

As soon as the students start reading the books, they will begin asking questions. Why were the Nazis rounding up Jews in *The Devil's Arithmetic?* Where were the bombers coming from in *The Machine Gunners?* What were they hoping to accomplish? Why did the Japanese bomb Pearl Harbor (*Journey to Topaz*)? Thus, the stories the students read will stimulate their curiosity, motivating them to find out more historical information than the books provide. By helping students find the answers to their questions, you will help them make connections between the stories they are reading and the historical events surrounding the stories. Here are a few suggestions:

- Assign readings in the textbook.
- Direct students to encyclopedias, atlases, and other reference books.
- Create vocabulary lists based on words common to many of the stories (Nazi, Gestapo, Allies, Axis, resistance, refugee, concentration camp, etc.).
- Teach geography skills to help students understand the stories' settings.
- Assign research exercises to assess the historical accuracy of events in the books.

Discussions

Class discussions are an integral part of this unit. Students will want to share with one another the stories they have been reading. Each book offers only a narrow perspective of a global conflict; listening to one another will help everyone understand that many events were happening at the same

Lesson 11.4 *(continued)*

time in different places, that the war was a different experience for different people. While Japanese Americans in *Journey to Topaz* were being interned in the western United States, Artie's father in *Maus* was hiding from the Nazis in Poland, and the Soviets were deporting Esther and her family to Siberia in *The Endless Steppe*. Resulting conversations about racism, prejudice, and discrimination are inevitable.

Discussion should also reveal differences and commonalities among different peoples. Most of the books give us a sense of the unique character of a particular culture, from the food they eat, to their family life, to their beliefs and hopes. But in comparing different people's experiences in the war, students will also discover that people on both sides, in many different places, suffered similar tragedies in this War. At the same time that the Allies were enduring bombing attacks (*The Machine Gunners*, *Along the Tracks*, etc.), the people in the Axis countries (*The Little Fishes*, *Faithful Elephants*, *Hiroshima No Pika*, etc.) were suffering bombing raids as well.

What and How Much Should Students Read?

Some of the best works of children's historical fiction happen to be "easy" books (for example, *Hiroshima No Pika*, *Faithful Elephants*, and *Rose Blanche*). Read some of them to the class and encourage everyone to read them; in this way, everyone benefits from these excellent books, and the stigma of reading "baby books" will be removed as well for those who are unable to read anything more difficult. As your students will soon learn, there is nothing childish about the subject matter in these books.

While a few students will read at the minimum pace you assign, most will simply devour their books and ask for more; encourage students to read as many different books as possible, and ask them to share the different perspectives that the stories depict. Soon the original groups will have disappeared, but you may want to continue to meet with groups of students who are reading or have read particular books.

Open-Ended Activities That Grow Out of the Books

Good historical fiction is about poverty, disagreement, oppression, cowardice, and hatred, as well as kindness, camaraderie, compassion, joy, and love. Reading an array of World War II fiction will not just teach students "facts"; it will also induce rage, laughter, sadness, guilt, and hope. The stories will cause the students to care deeply about people all over the world whose lives were changed by the war; they will elicit questions, arguments, confusion, and discussion. Plan a variety of activities which allow students to consider the many issues the books raise and to express their thoughts and values about the events of the war. Here are some activities you could assign to your students:

Write a fictional diary, letter, or story that relates events in the book from a particular point of view.

Write or record (video or audio) a fictionalized interview or news story related to the book.

Create a newspaper, including editorials, on "current events" from the book.

Paint pictures based on the story.

Compose poetry expressing your reactions to events in the story.

Perform skits or spontaneous roleplays based on events in the book.

continued

Lesson 11.4 *(continued)*

Using Excerpts

What about the students who are slow readers and those who are able to read only the easiest books? How will they benefit from all the books you brought into the classroom? And what if you have only one copy of a book that you feel everyone should read?

You can use excerpts from the books to familiarize the whole class with issues and perspectives that you feel everyone should examine. For example, you might want all students to learn about the fate of vagabond children around the world orphaned and made homeless by nightly bombings. You could read aloud short sections from *Along the Tracks* or *The Little Fishes* and generate discussion or an assignment related to this topic. Or you could arrange the class in heterogeneous groups—low readers with higher readers—and have them read the passage together before doing the related assignment. In this way, every student can become conversant with many different perspectives, even if they do not actually finish many books.

Completing the Unit

This unit could go on for months. With the number of books available, the complexity of the events and issues involved, and sheer number and variety of people affected by World War II, a class could conceivably spend an entire semester studying it. You will never be able to "finish" the war, but when you are ready to move on to another topic, individual or group projects are a wonderful way to complete the unit. Possible projects include:

Write a historical novella or a children's picture book about the war from a particular perspective.

Complete a project that illuminates the war experiences of a particular group of people (African Americans, German citizens, Italian children, American women, etc.).

Write and film a video play about the war.

Conduct a research project on any aspect of the war.

Create dioramas, murals, or other art projects.

Design maps, charts, time lines, etc.

When the projects are completed, plan some kind of culminating event in which students can share what they have created and learn from each other. With a variety of projects about people from all over the world, this event will not only be a retrospective on the war, but it also should be a celebration of global diversity as well.

Selected World War II Historical Fiction

* = picture book

+ = easy reading

^ = intermediate reading

= more difficult reading

* Ahlberg, Janet and Allan. *Peek-A-Boo!* Puffin Books, 1981. A day in the life of a British toddler during World War II.

Bergman, Tama. *Along the Tracks*, translated from the Hebrew by Michael Swirsky. Boston: Houghton Mifflin, 1991. The true story of a young Jewish boy who flees Nazi-occupied Poland with his family, then is separated from his family and becomes one of the thousands of abandoned children wandering through Russia.

Lesson 11.4 *(continued)*

+ Bishop, Claire Huchet. *Pancakes-Paris*. New York: Viking Press, 1947. In postwar Paris, a poor French family is befriended by American soldiers, who help make Mardi Gras a festive occasion, complete with American pancakes.
+ Bishop, Claire Huchet. *Twenty and Ten*. New York: Viking Press, 1952. In occupied France, twenty Gentile children bravely hide and protect ten Jewish children from the Nazis.
+ Coerr, Eleano. *Sadako and the Thousand Paper Cranes*. New York: Dell Publishing, 1977. Ten years after the Allies dropped the atom bomb on her home in Hiroshima, Sadako is diagnosed with leukemia, caused by the bomb's radiation.
^ Dahl, Roald. *Going Solo*. London: Penguin Books, 1986. Dahl relates his experiences as a fighter pilot in Africa, Greece, and the Middle East. This true story is as amazing and almost as surreal as Dahl's fiction.
^ Degens, T. *Transport 7-41-R*. New York: The Viking Press, 1974. A thirteen-year-old girl traveling alone describes her journey from the Russian sector of defeated Germany to Cologne on a train carrying returning refugees in 1946.
# Forman, James. *Ceremony of Innocence*. New York: Hawthorne Books, 1970. This is the story of Hans and Sophie Scholl, German citizens who produced the "White Rose" leaflets denouncing Nazism, until they were caught and executed by the Gestapo.
^ Garrigue, Sheila. *The Eternal Spring of Mr. Ito*. New York: Bradbury Press, 1985. A young girl sent from London to stay with relatives in Canada during the blitz learns about racism and hysteria toward Japanese citizens.
# Greene, Bette. *Summer of My German Soldier*. New York: The Dial Press, 1973. In Arkansas a Jewish teenage girl befriends and protects a German soldier who has escaped from a nearby prisoner-of-war camp.
# Haugaard, Erik Christian. *The Little Fishes*. Boston: Houghton Mifflin, 1967. This story traces the odyssey of three homeless orphan children from Naples to Cassino in war-ravaged Italy.
# Hautzig, Esther. *The Endless Steppe*. New York: Thomas Y. Crowell Co., 1968. A Jewish family, exiled from Poland to Siberia, endures bitter hardships in its struggle for survival.
* Innocenti, Roberto. *Rose Blanche*. Mankato, Minnesota: Creative Education Inc., 1985. Rose Blanche lives in a small German town. At first, the war seems to cause little change in her life. Then she discovers the concentration camp outside of town.
^ Kerr, Judith. *When Hitler Stole Pink Rabbit*. New York: Coward, McCann & Geoghegan, Inc., 1972. Nine-year-old Anna must leave the protected world she knows and loves because of the articles her father, a well-known Jewish journalist, writes about the Nazis. As a refugee, she grows in many ways as her family moves from Berlin to Switzerland, Paris, then London.
+ Leitner, Isabella. *The Big Lie*. New York: Scholastic, 1992. Isabella and her family are taken to Auschwitz, but not all of them survive the ordeal.
^ Levitin, Sonia. *Journey to America*. New York: Atheneum, 1970. In 1938 Lisa and her family leave Berlin to escape the Nazis. After many hardships and separations, they are reunited in America.
+ Levoy, Myron. *Alan and Naomi*. New York: Harper and Row, 1977. In New York City, Alan befriends and tries to help Naomi, who is haunted by her recent experiences in France at the hands of the Nazis.
^ Lowry, Lois. *Number the Stars*. New York: Dell Publishing, 1989. In German-occupied Denmark, a ten-year-old girl and her family use courage and cunning to help their Jewish friends escape the Nazis.
* Maruki, Toshi. *Hiroshima No Pika*. New York: Lothrop, 1980. Young Mii is eating breakfast at home in Hiroshima when the atom bomb hits. This story chronicles her ordeal.
^ Maser, Harry. *The Last Mission*. New York: Delacorte Press, 1979. Young Jack falsifies his age so that he can fight the Germans. He learns the horrors and the futility of war.
# Murray, Michele. *The Crystal Nights*. New York: Seabury Press, 1973. Elly and her family must adjust to the arrival of Jewish relatives fleeing Nazi Germany.
^ Reiss, Johanna. *The Upstairs Room*. New York: HarperCollins, 1972. Annie must hide for the entire war in an upstairs room, protected by a courageous Dutch family.
^ Shemin, Margaretha. *The Empty Moat*. New York: Coward, McCann & Geoghegan, 1969. In German-occupied Holland, Elizabeth must decide whether or not to overcome her fears and help the Dutch underground hide Jewish refugees from the Nazis.
+ Shemin, Margaretha. *The Little Riders*. New York: Coward-McCann, Inc., 1963. In a small Dutch town, Johanna saves the "Little Riders," metal figures that have come to represent resistance to the Germans who occupy the town.
+ Spiegelman, Art. *Maus I: A Survivor's Tale*. New York: Scholastic, Inc., 1986. Written in comic book form, with Polish mice and Nazi cats, an old Jewish mouse tells his son the story of his life during the war, of Nazi persecution and his family's attempts to avoid capture.

continued

Lesson 11.4 *(continued)*

^ Taylor, Mildred. *The Road to Memphis*. New York: Dial Books, 1990. This is the fifth book about the Logans, a close-knit African American family faced with White hatred and bigotry in the South. The year is 1941 and Stacy Logan is old enough to join the army. Although far away, the war is never far from anyone's mind.

^ Taylor, Theodore. *The Cay*. New York: Doubleday, 1969. In 1942, young Phillip's ship is torpedoed by a German U-Boat. He and an old Black man drift to a deserted island, where they develop an unexpected friendship.

* Tsuchiya, Yukio. *Faithful Elephants: A True Story of Animals, People, and War*, translated by Tomoko Tsuchiya Dykes. New York: Trumpet Club, 1988. In Tokyo, zookeepers must kill the wild animals because the army fears that bombs may hit the zoo and permit the animals to escape.

Tunis, John. *His Enemy, His Friend*. New York: William Morrow and Co., 1967. A German soldier stationed in occupied France befriends the French villagers until he is ordered to kill six of them.

^ Uchida, Yoshiko. *Journey to Topaz: A Story of the Japanese American Evacuation*. New York: Charles Scribner's Sons, 1971. After the Japanese attack on Pearl Harbor, Japanese American families, although loyal to the United States, must move to internment camps far from home.

Westall, Robert. *The Machine Gunners*. New York: William Morrow and Co., 1976. In a northern English town that suffers from nightly bombing raids, Chas and his friends make a game of collecting souvenirs from enemy war planes that have been shot down. But when they find a machine gun, build their own bunker, and capture an enemy flier, the game becomes very real.

^ Yolen, Jane. *The Devil's Arithmetic*. New York: Viking Kestrel, 1988. Hannah wishes her Jewish parents would forget the Holocaust: after all, those things happened years ago. But one Passover, she opens the door and finds herself in a Polish village during the war. As she is relocated to the concentration camp, she begins to understand why no one should ever forget what happened.

Historical Fiction Activities

Here are some of the activities you may wish to assign your students—or have them choose for themselves.

Write a diary from a character's point of view.

Write a letter from one character to another describing important events in the book.

Write a poem about one of the characters or events in the story.

Based on the story and on what you have learned about this period in history, write a sequel to the book.

Write about a character with whom you identify strongly. How are you and the character alike? How are you different?

Produce a news feature on a character in the story.

Pretend you are a reporter (newspaper, radio, or TV) summarizing the events in the book.

Write a news editorial discussing events or actions in the story.

Draw a political cartoon commenting on an event in the story from your point of view, or from a character's perspective.

Perform a "Newscast from the Past" depicting events from this story, along with events that were going on elsewhere at the same time.

Pretend that you are a book reviewer and write a critique of the book.

Re-create the clothes of one of the characters and come to class dressed as that character.

Lesson 11.4 *(continued)*

Prepare a meal that the people in the story might have eaten.

Describe a typical day in the life of a character in the story. Compare it (using words or pictures) to a typical day of a character in another time or country.

Compare (using words or pictures) events, settings, customs, etc. portrayed in this book to those in other books.

Choose a character and explain how that person makes a living in the story.

Choose five examples of the latest technology in the story, draw a picture of each, tell how each was made, and explain its use.

List all the places mentioned in the book that could be put on a map, and make a map using this list.

Make a map of the world and show the location(s) of this story, as well as the settings of related stories and historical events.

Make a time line of the book's main events, or of historical events happening while the story takes place.

Choose some real (as opposed to fictional) characters and events in the story and do some research to find out more about them.

List all the historical "facts" that you learned in this book.

Write or record an interview with one of the historical characters in the book.

Make a list of important vocabulary words you learned from reading this book.

Make a picture time line of the book's main events.

Draw or paint pictures, make dioramas, create a poster or mural, or make a collage of some or all of the events in the book.

Take a series of photographs that represents your response to events in the book.

Make a book cover, complete with picture on the front and blurb on the back.

Draw a picture of or build a character's house.

Make a mobile about the book.

Make a diorama or draw a picture that shows details of the story's setting.

Write music that evokes the mood of part or all of the book.

Perform a pantomime of certain events in the story.

Perform some music or a dance that the characters may have enjoyed at the time they lived.

Make puppets of characters in the story and perform a puppet show about them.

Stage a debate between characters in the story who represent opposing viewpoints.

Choose the most important or moving section of the book and give an oral reading of this excerpt.

Make a video dramatizing some or all of the story.

continued

Lesson 11.4 (*continued*)

Analyze or debate the ethics or morality of a character's actions.

Examine the author's perspective in this story. What do you think is the author's opinion of events in the story? Does the author seem to have any biases that affect the way that the story is told?

Goal Two: Developing Cultural Consciousness

Closely linked to the development of multiple historical perspectives is the second goal, the development of cultural consciousness. This goal makes the following assumptions:

- An individual must have an understanding of his or her own worldview.
- Humans have the capacity to reduce their ethnocentrism.

Cultural consciousness is defined in terms of two dimensions of Hanvey's "attainable global perspective": perspective consciousness and cross-cultural awareness. Perspective consciousness is

> [t]he recognition or awareness on the part of the individual that he or she has a view of the world that is not universally shared, that this view of the world has been and continues to be shaped by influences that often escape conscious detection, and that others have views of the world that are profoundly different from one's own.[31]

Most Japanese, for example, do not see themselves as racist. Yet, their deep assumptions about the inferiority of certain races has resulted in statements by Japanese officials about the "inferiority" of American Blacks and Hispanics, as well as discrimination against Japanese citizens of Korean or Chinese parentage. As another example, Westerners have assumed until very recently that human dominance over nature is both attainable and desirable. Teachers can foster the development of perspective consciousness by helping students examine their assumptions, evaluations, and conceptions of time, space, causality, and so forth.

The second aspect of cultural consciousness, Hanvey's cross-cultural awareness, refers to

> an awareness of the diversity of ideas and practices to be found in human societies around the world, of how such ideas and practices compare, and including some limited recognition of how the ideas and ways of one's own society might be viewed from other vantage points.[32]

Cross-cultural awareness, a difficult but attainable goal, is seen by Hanvey as an antidote for the human "practice of naming one's own group 'the people' and by implication relegating all others to not-quite-human status." This human trait of chauvinism

> *has been documented in nonliterate groups all over the world . . . [and] shows itself in modern populations as well. It is there in the hostile faces of the white parents demonstrating against school busing . . . [it lurks] in the background as Russians and Chinese meet at the negotiating table to work out what is ostensibly a boundary dispute. And it flares into the open during tribal disputes in Kenya.*[33]

Hanvey identifies four levels of cross-cultural awareness, which are shown in Table 11.2.[34] According to Hanvey's scheme, believability is achieved only at levels 3 and 4. He argues that believability is a necessary condition "if one group of humans is to accept other members of the biological species as human."[35] The attainment of these higher levels of cross-cultural awareness is an integral part of the third multicultural curriculum goal, development of intercultural competence.

As the world becomes a smaller place, cultural consciousness is an essential ingredient in mediating cultural conflicts along the "fault lines" that separate the

Table 11.2 ▧ Levels of Cross-Cultural Awareness

Information	*Mode*	*Interpretation*
1. Awareness of superficial or very visible cultural traits: stereotypes	Tourism, textbooks, *National Geographic*	Unbelievable (i.e., exotic, bizarre)
2. Awareness of significant and subtle cultural traits that contrast markedly with one's own	Culture conflict situations	Unbelievable (i.e., frustrating, irrational)
3. Awareness of significant and subtle cultural traits that contrast markedly with one's own	Intellectual analysis	Believable, cognitively
4. Awareness of how another culture feels from the standpoint of the insider	Cultural immersion: living the culture	Believable because of subjective familiarity

Source: R. Hanvey, *An Attainable Global Perspective* (New York: Center for War/Peace Studies), 4.

world's seven or eight main civilizations.[36] For example, Huntington argues that, with the end of the cold war in Europe, "the Velvet Curtain of culture has replaced the Iron Curtain of ideology as the most significant dividing line in Europe."[37] This cultural division "between Western Christianity on the one hand, and Orthodox Christianity and Islam on the other, has re-emerged,"[38] for example, in the former Yugoslavia, in the Persian Gulf, and in Italy, France, and Germany, where violence against Arab and Turkish immigrants increased in the 1990s. Huntington cautions that the Western worldview, which is based on "ideas of individualism, liberalism, constitutionalism, human rights, equality, liberty, the rule of law, democracy, free markets, the separation of church and state, often have little resonance in Islamic, Confucian, Japanese, Hindu, Buddhist or Orthodox cultures."[39] It can also be argued that the desire for basic inalienable rights, human dignity, and liberty is universal. But to achieve these conditions on a global scale, foreign policy makers must be conscious of culture.

 Lesson Plans That Develop Cultural Consciousness

Lesson 11.5
The Many Faces (and Shoes) of Cinderella   *Patricia A. O'Connor*

Rationale
In today's multicultural world, students need to realize that while people from different cultures may look different and may see and experience events in a different way, deep down people all across the world are the same. By utilizing the well-known fairy tale, Cinderella, and its many cultural variations, students will be able to see that each culture experiences and conceptualizes the Cinderella motif in a unique way—the Cinderellas of the world look different, dress differently, have different skills, and live in a different "world." And yet the theme is the same all across the world. In addition, students will utilize the timeless and cross-cultural Cinderella motif to create a modern version of the tale. By doing so, they will be able to relate a very old tale to their world and experience firsthand the influences that a culture has on a piece of literature. This will be good preparation for analysis of future literature—how a culture and a historical period influence literature (both oral and written) and how a piece of literature relates to our world today.

Learning Objectives
1. Students will be able to compare and contrast cross-cultural versions of Cinderella by reading a selected version of the tale, by summarizing and reporting excerpts (both orally and visually) to the class, and by completing the variant analysis guide (see guide below).

Lesson 11.5 *(continued)*

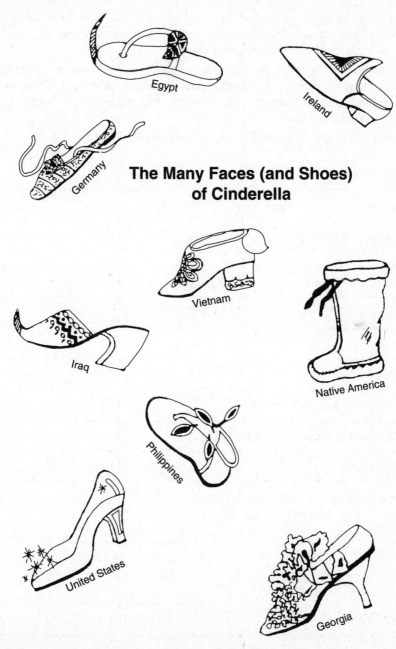

The Many Faces (and Shoes)
of Cinderella

continued

Lesson 11.5 *(continued)*

2. Students will be able to recognize cultural influences on the Cinderella motif by preparing a written report summarizing the differences between the U.S. version and the version they read and analyzing how the culture influenced each tale.

3. Students will learn firsthand how a culture influences the expression of the tale by creating a modern version of the Cinderella tale that reflects current culture. In doing so, they will utilize past knowledge of setting, character development, and descriptive writing.

The Many Faces of Cinderella: Variant Analysis Guide
TITLE:

COUNTRY OF ORIGIN:

Opening
Hero/heroine's (H/H's) innocence/ guilt (with respect to siblings)
H/H's passivity/activity
Sibling rivalry
Father's role
Midnight prohibition
Prince/princess' role in finding H/H
H/H's treatment of stepsiblings/stepparent
Level of violence
Helpful spirit/being
Role of animals
Flight from the event (Why?)
Presence of dead mother/father
Type of shoe, clothing, or ring
Ending

Lesson 11.5 *(continued)*

Day 1
Teaching Strategies

Opening exercise: Students are asked to recall the fairy tale, Cinderella, and to write a brief description of Cinderella's physical features and the shoe she drops. Discussion of descriptions will follow. Students are shown a poster of the various shoes different cultures envision Cinderella wearing and a few overheads of illustrations from different versions. A brief introduction to the unit will follow, in which students will be given the theme ("The Many Faces of Cinderella"), an outline of the unit, and a brief description of intended projects: analysis of different versions, discussion of different interpretations, creation of a modern version of *Cinderella* (or *Cinder "fella"* as the case may be). We also discuss the importance of being aware of the multicultural variations of the motif and of multicultural influences in general.

    Group exercise: Working in small groups of varying abilities (see explanation of group work roles below), students read a selected version of the tale (each group will have a different version—see descriptions below), discuss the differences, prepare an illustration of four scenes from the tale (to be posted on the wall), and give a five-minute oral presentation to the class. A discussion of similarities and differences follows, and students are given a variant analysis guide to be completed on the version they read. We go through the guide in class, discuss the terms, and complete it for the U.S. version.

    Assignment: Complete the variant analysis guide.

Day 2
Teaching Strategies

Review the variant analysis guide that follows and discuss any problems. A copy of a completed variant analysis guide for each version is posted with the illustration prepared on Day 1. A brief lecture on the history of the Cinderella motif, the particular history surrounding the U.S. version, and the various interpretations follows. As a class, students discuss the cultural influences in the U.S. version and some ideas of how the other stories were influenced culturally. A one- to two-page written report summarizing the differences between the U.S. version and the version read by the particular groups is assigned, with completed reports due on Day 3.

    Writing project: Students are asked to create—with their subgroup partner—a modern version of the Cinderella tale. A handout of directions and rules is discussed at this time. Prior to breaking into pairs, students briefly review setting, character development, and descriptive writing. The subgroups/pairs begin working on a modern version, with an initial focus on setting and characters.

    Assignment: Work individually (at home) on modern versions. This individual work is turned in the next day to assure that everyone works on the project.

Days 3–4
Teaching Strategies

Students break into subgroups, review individual work, and compile the information into a complete story by revising and editing on the computer. Then students return to main groups and decide which version to prepare for the dramatic reading. The subgroup whose version is not selected critiques the selected version and makes suggestions for changes and improvement. (It may be that a compilation

continued

Lesson 11.5 *(continued)*

of the two versions can be attempted.) Visuals for the presentation are encouraged. If a decision acceptable to all members cannot be reached, the instructor decides by tossing a coin.

Day 5

Projects are turned in, and presentations ensue.

Additional Activities

Additional activities—from collecting marriage divination rituals to examining feminist and historical perspectives—can be found in the *Oryx Multicultural Folktale Series: Cinderella and Writing and Reading across the Curriculum*. Most of the activities can be adapted to the age of the students.

Group Work

Students will be working in preassigned groups of four or five that were selected based on varying abilities and intelligences of the students. Within that group, they have also been assigned to a subgroup partner, with the same selection qualities used for the main group.

Their main group roles are as follows:

The Eye: This person makes sure that everyone in the group has a chance to talk and explain his or her ideas and that the group stays on task.

The Ear: This person listens and participates in the group discussion, takes notes during the group's brainstorming sessions, and provides team members access to these notes.

The Mouth: This is the spokesperson for the group and facilitates the oral reports and presentations for the group.

The Legs: This person listens for group problems and/or questions and acts as a liaison with the teacher.

The Heart: This person is attentive to the feelings of the individual members and helps the group reach compromises when conflict arises.

Our Cinderella: Writing Project Instructions

Objective: Following the Cinderella motif, write a modern version of the tale that reflects the culture, language, and events of today. By "culture," I do not specifically mean U.S. culture; I mean culture as it relates to YOU, in your school, home, and ethnicity.

Note: You do not need to include every element of the motif. Your version should be based on the following theme:

> *A young man or woman persecuted by his/her family who receives magical help from unusual sources so that his/her true worth can be known by a potential mate of higher rank.*

And it should incorporate at least eight features of the motif (see variant analysis guide).

1. With subgroup partner, decide what culture you wish to represent, your basic setting, characters, and plot. Pay attention to the following questions when working on this section:

   Where is this story taking place? What city/neighborhood? What ethnic group?

Lesson 11.5 *(continued)*

Who are the main characters?
What do they look like?
How do they sound?

2. Each partner should then work individually on development of the story. Then partners will get back together, combine versions, revise story, and add new information. Pay attention to your answers to the above questions when writing.

3. Reconvene with your main group. Exchange and critique versions. Decide which story you will present as a group. Each subgroup will have the opportunity to make suggestions and changes at this point. It may be possible to do a compilation of the two versions.

4. Prepare for presentation of your story. You have a total of ten minutes to present your story to the class. You can act it out or give a dramatic reading. Illustrations of the text are highly encouraged.

5. LET IT ALL HANG LOOSE!! Be creative, use slang, and provide illustrations, but most of all, let your imagination guide the story.

Rules
Completed versions must incorporate three metaphors and three similes.

Only three forms of the verb "to be" can be used in the entire story. (Be descriptive, don't just tell us!)

Evaluation
Oral and Visual Report

Students are graded on understanding of the story and selection of main scenes for illustration.

Written Report

Students are graded on understanding of differences between the versions and the influence of culture on the versions. In addition, reports will be checked for punctuation, grammar, and sentence structure. Revised reports may be requested.

Modern Version

Students will be graded on application of motif to modern times and incorporation of the main theme and elements. While use of slang and colloquialisms will be allowed and encouraged, correct spelling, appropriate punctuation, and grammar of nondialogue writing will be stressed.

Bibliography
Behrens, Laurence, and Rosen, Leonard J. *Writing and Reading across the Curriculum.* Boston: Little, Brown, 1985.
Cooper, J. C. *Fairy Tales: Allegories of the Inner Life.* Wellingborrough, Northamptonshire, England: Aquarian Press, 1983.
Luthi, Max. *Once upon a Time: On the Nature of Fairy Tales.* New York: F. Ungar Publishing, 1970.
Meyer, Rudolf. *The Wisdom of Fairy Tales.* Edinburgh, Scotland: Floris Books, 1981.
Philip, Neil. *The Cinderella Story.* New York: Penguin Books, 1989.
Sierra, Judy. *The Oryx Multicultural Folktale Series: Cinderella.* Phoenix, AZ: Oryx Press, 1992.

continued

Lesson 11.5 *(continued)*

The Invisible One (Native American/Micmac)

Oochigeaskw, a member of the Micmac people of eastern Canada who is mistreated by her sisters, goes forth wearing a dress made of tree bark. Her future husband is no mere human prince; he is an invisible supernatural being. Oochigeaskw passes a different kind of test than the other heroines of Cinderella tales; she passes a test by seeing what other young women do not.

Nomi and the Magic Fish (Africa)

Nomi, a girl who is mistreated by her stepmother, is helped by a magical talking fish. Her naughty tattle-tale dog is different from pets in other Cinderella tales who are faithful and helpful even after death. This particular version was recorded by a young woman of the Zulu people of South Africa.

How the Cowherd Found a Bride (India)

This male Cinderella story features many of the elements of the Cinderella motif—mistreatment by family, a food-giving cow, magic tree, falling in love through finding a gold object, helpful animals, and marriage of the hero to a person of royal status.

Ashpet (U.S./Appalachian)

Ashpet is a servant in the house of a cruel woman and her two daughters. As in many of the Cinderella tales, Ashpet's troubles are not over after her wedding. The two daughters come to see her after her marriage and end up pushing her into a river where she is captured by the Hairy Man.

The Story of Tam and Cam (Vietnam)

This story of Cam and her evil stepsister Tam mirrors the other Cinderella tales, but Cam shows higher resilience and adaptability than many of the Cinderellas. While Tam and her mother might win a contest for the cruelest stepmother/sister, they certainly get two of the worst punishments.

Cap o' Rushes (England)

This story of Cap o' Rushes is told in the regional dialect of the storyteller. It is a different strain of the Cinderella motif, where the heroine is driven out of the house by her father and is later reconciled with him at her wedding feast. This version is thought to be the source of Shakespeare's *King Lear*.

Reprinted with permission of the author.

Lesson 11.6
Five Great Values of the Lakota Sioux   *Gayle Reiten*

Objectives

- Students will develop some familiarity with the traditional cultural values of the northern Great Plains Sioux that still govern and influence their society today.
- Students will understand how these values shape the worldview of the Sioux and influence their response, both individually and as a group, to the dominant culture in the United States.

Introduction

The primary cultural symbol among the Sioux is the circle. It represents Wakan Tanka, the Great Spirit, and is found everywhere within the Lakota worldview. The horizon and the four directions form a circle. The traditional dwelling house, the tipi, is a circle. All nature is circular. This circularity means that the Lakota view the world as a whole, not in parts and pieces to be separately ana-

Lesson 11.6 *(continued)*

lyzed. In this lesson plan the Siouan values will be examined separately, but it is important to remind the class of their interrelatedness.

The First Great Value: Generosity and Sharing

Among the Sioux people the idea of the value of generosity and sharing is very strong. This idea springs from their belief that the earth is the mother from whom they all came. Therefore the land and the food to be found upon it belongs to all; the food that resulted from the hunt or from gathering is to be shared with all others in the band who needed it.

Generosity and sharing as an ideal led to the custom of the GiveAway, in which any or all of one's possessions are given away in a ceremony to honor someone. The honoree could be a recent college graduate, a young man home from the army, or a dead relative. In this process one honors the Great Spirit, the person to whom one gives, and, lastly, oneself. However, paradoxical as this may seem, if one gives or shares with the idea of getting honor in return, one destroys the essence of sharing.

For this reason, when someone does something for you unasked, out of kindness, it is very rude to thank the person, for it is as if you were paying for the generosity—a terrible insult among the Sioux. However, if you ask someone to do something for you and the person complies, a thank-you is acceptable.

Another aspect of sharing is that doing and giving of oneself for the benefit of the group is a requirement in Siouxan culture. If one has a talent or talents and denies these to one's people, it is wrong. As a result, the Sioux share both praise and shame. For instance, they share in pride for Ben Reifel, one-time congressman from South Dakota, and they share the shame of Siouan drunks lying in the gutter.

Historically: Since the land belonged to all, the Sioux had no concept of property ownership and often believed when they signed treaties that they were ceding use of the land rather than ownership.

Currently: When a Siouan family moves to an urban area from the reservation in order to better their economic well-being, they often "fail" by non-Indian standards. Many family and friends will come to visit, spend time, create an extended family. However, this may lead to crowded housing conditions and financial strain as all are given only enough money to function within the urban environment.

Questions: For the Lakota, what are the strengths connected with holding the value of generosity and sharing in the modern world? What are the weaknesses?

Activity: Some members of the class might wish to research the lives of famous Sioux such as Crazy Horse, Red Cloud, Sitting Bull, Spotted Tail, Billy Mills, Ben Reifel, Ella Deloria, and Vine Deloria (both senior and junior).

The Second Great Value: Respect for Old Ones

The Lakota Sioux have always had great respect for their old ones. The Lakota believed one could not speak from ignorance, and wisdom came only with age. One would be considered a young man or woman until the age of forty-five or fifty; then perhaps one might be considered a "wicasa"—a man— and to become "really a man" one needed to be more than sixty.

This respect for the old ones has led to respect for anyone in authority—a priest, a teacher, a policeman, a judge. One way respect is shown is through aversion of the eyes. Another consequence of

continued

Lesson 11.6 *(continued)*

respect for elders is the custom whereby children of hospitalized parents spend much of their time, if not all their time, in the hospital with their parents. This is a matter both of respect and of generosity and sharing—the Lakota seldom leave a sick member of the family alone.

Historically: Early missionaries and teachers were confused by the Sioux. "They seem so shifty and dishonest!" "William Noheart never looks me in the eye." These comments reflected non-Indians' lack of understanding of behavior meant to reflect respect. It is still a problem.

Currently: A few years ago, the federal government gave the tribal government of the Standing Rock Sioux money to build a nursing home for the elderly on the reservation. But the home stood empty for years and was finally converted to government offices.

Questions: Why did the Standing Rock Sioux not make use of the government-built nursing home? In what ways does our dominant culture treat older ones with respect? In what ways does it not? Do others of us have the same respect for the elderly as do the Sioux? Do we express it differently? In what ways do we show respect to authority, and what kinds of body language do we use?

Activity: Demonstrate the difference between a non-Indian greeting a stranger and the way a Sioux would greet a stranger.

The Third Great Value: Getting Along with Nature

For the Sioux, getting along with nature meant more than not misusing the natural world. The Lakota people traditionally believed that Wakan Tanka, the Great Spirit, was in all things, in a rock or tree as much as in a person. And this being, this existence of the Great Spirit within each thing, was called that entity's "Innermost"—a concept that might be compared to the non-Indian idea of a soul or spirit. Furthermore, the Sioux saw the earth, through the Great Spirit's power, as mother to all—and all therefore are related to each other.

This leads to the Siouan ideas about respect for the Innermost. Since everyone's Innermost should be respected, out of politeness the Sioux will tell others what they want to hear, and never with the feeling that this is untruthful. They will also avoid telling someone what that person doesn't want to hear. The Sioux believe that when the Innermost is not respected, hurt is always the result. From this develops their great desire to get along with one another and to respect each person's Innermost.

Historically: The buffalo was the heart of the Siouan culture in the eighteenth and nineteenth centuries. Every part of the buffalo was used in some way. Nonetheless, because the Sioux people believed they were related to the buffalo, it could not be wantonly slaughtered. The Sioux would pray for understanding and forgiveness on the part of the buffalo before they began the hunt, and the entire process had a sense of sacred ritual about it.

Currently: Because of the belief among the Sioux that they must "get along together," one will often observe group togetherness, especially among children. But the group togetherness ideal, while a strength, can also be a weakness. For example, there is strong peer pressure among the reservation Sioux not to appear "better" or "different." And the ideal is often shattered by problems with drug and alcohol abuse, the biggest Native American health problem.

Questions: Can you think of some other ways the value of getting along with nature is a strength? A weakness? How does the non-Indian react to these ideas?

Activities: Research the buffalo's history and find out why these animals are now so few in number. Art classes might want to research paintings that portray the Sioux and the buffalo.

Lesson 11.6 *(continued)*

On the subject of current Sioux life, learn more about Native American problems with substance abuse, or about the adjustments that urban American Indians must make in cities such as Minneapolis, Oakland, Boston, Chicago, and Cleveland.

The Fourth Great Value: Individual Freedom

Individual freedom is strongly related to all the other values, for it involves the essence of choice. No one can ever force anyone else's decision. But this is not freedom to run amok. Individual freedom for the Sioux meant freedom to choose to do the right thing. And the most important thing, the most right thing, was whatever would enable survival of the group. The value of sharing was also involved in choosing to help one's relatives and friends.

Since no Sioux had any right to impose his or her will upon another, the Lakota form of government was the most basic of democracies, with all the men and older women meeting together and making decisions. If any of those within the group did not agree with the decisions made, they were free to go. Many times this is exactly what happened, and new bands of the Sioux were created out of disagreement over some fundamental decision.

The respect for individual rights and abilities also led to the Siouan style of leadership. The idea of a "chief," one overall leader, really came from the non-Indian. Leadership depended upon the situation. One man might be best at leading raids on other tribes for horses. Another might be called upon to lead and organize the buffalo hunt. The style of making war was also not forced. If a man wanted to get up a raiding party, only those who chose to go went with him.

There were never any jails among the Sioux. They had two primary methods of social control: ridicule and banishment. Ridicule could run the gamut from gentle teasing of an adolescent who had behaved in a socially unacceptable manner to intense ridicule for an adult who had committed a more serious offense. Stealing among the Sioux was practically unknown, and still is to this day, because of the great respect for the individual. Serious crimes, such as murder, were punished by banishment. Survival on the northern Great Plains without the group was difficult at best—therefore banishment could be equivalent to a death sentence.

Historically: Sitting Bull is among the most famous of Sioux leaders, but few non-Indians know that he was not a great warrior leader. Rather, Sitting Bull was a "wicasa wakan," a holy man. Others were the military leaders during the Battle of the Little Big Horn.

Currently: The style of government on Sioux Indian reservations today often leads to a virulent form of reservation politics. Tribal government has democratic forms based on the past; and because of the strong belief in individual freedom, political disagreements can be strong. However, groups who disagree with one another are no longer free to move.

Questions: In what ways are dominant culture beliefs about individual rights the same as the beliefs the Sioux held? In what ways are they different? Does the dominant culture value social freedom more than individual freedom, or vice versa? Give examples.

Activity: Read Marie Sandoz's novel *Crazy Horse* and try to determine how Lakota values functioned in making Crazy Horse one of the greatest Sioux leaders.

The Fifth Great Value: Bravery

For the Sioux, eagle feathers were the mark of bravery, and they had to be earned. Bravery was a matter of individual freedom; one had to choose to do the right thing. One could never boast about

continued

Lesson 11.6 *(continued)*

one's own exploits in battle; one allowed someone else, a friend or relative, to do so. Training for bravery began young. Little babies were not allowed to cry, for their cry could give away the location of the people in a tight situation.

A famous war cry the Sioux gave at the Battle of the Little Big Horn was: "Today is a good day to die!" This can be understood only within the context of the Lakota value of bravery. The Sioux believed that if the worst thing one had to fear was death—and if death itself was not really something to be afraid of—then if one died in the process of protecting one's family and people, today was indeed a good day to die. But the Sioux were not fanatic about death, as in some other cultures, and were as afraid of battle as any humans might be. Life itself was the most precious thing the old-time Sioux had, and to give it was the greatest sharing a Sioux warrior could offer.

Historically: The image of the war bonnet with many eagle feathers sweeping down to the ground is basically incorrect. Seldom did any warrior earn enough eagle feathers to create such a bonnet, though headdresses with a number of eagle feathers were possible. Young women could also earn eagle feathers or wear them by inheritance.

Currently: The Sioux people are intensely patriotic, and in the twentieth century have contributed soldiers for U.S. wars out of all proportion to their population. To fight in the U.S. armed forces for them is still the way to protect the people.

Questions: Is our definition of bravery in the dominant culture the same as or different from that of the Sioux? Are some or all of the Siouan values found within the U.S. dominant culture? To what degree are these values visible within the dominant culture's literary and film images of the American Indians?

Activity: Obtain Arthur Kopit's play *Indians* and have the class read, discuss, and/or present it using Sioux values as a basis for the discussion.

Additional Resources

Brown, Dee. *Bury My Heart at Wounded Knee*. New York: Holt, Rinehart and Winston, 1970.

Bryde, John F. *Modern Indian Psychology*. Vermillion: University of South Dakota Press, 1971.

Malan, Vernon D., and Clinton J. Jesser. *The Dakota Indian Religion: A Study of Conflict in Values*. Bulletin 473. Brookings: South Dakota State College, 1959.

Reprinted with permission of the author.

Lesson 11.7
Modeling toward Understanding   *Elizabeth Ellis*

Introduction

This lesson was developed for freshmen or sophomores in general ability groups. Prior to this lesson, students ask parents and grandparents about the countries of their ancestry. Through this vehicle, with

Lesson 11.7 *(continued)*

library research if necessary as a supplement, students are to bring to class at least eight facts about one country of their ancestors. Six of these facts should pertain to the physical characteristics of the country and two should be emotional, feelings these families carry about those roots. This plan is designed to develop culture consciousness.

Objectives
The twofold goal is to let students begin to look into their own cultural backgrounds and to take the first step of writing poetry through imitation. On a larger scale, they will become aware of their classmates' cultural backgrounds.

Strategy
Using the following outline, students will plug in the information indicated to complete the poem. Their role will be to assume the guise of someone who really knows and loves the country in question. Sentences do not have to be complete, and traditional grammar concerns are secondary to creativity. They will be given a copy of my attempt as a guide to show the task does not need to be difficult, and to provide motivation through that reassurance. At the end, copies of Langston Hughes's poem will be distributed for comparison and discussion. Also, each student will later receive copies of the entire class collection of poems.

Outline

I've known _____ (place) _____.

I've known _____ (physical fact) _____ and _____ (physical fact) _____.

_____ (emotion—translate feelings about place) _____.

I _____ (verb) _____ in _____ (place) _____ when.

_____ (time) _____.

I _____ (verb) _____ and _____ (verb) _____.

I looked _____ (physical fact) _____ and _____ (verb) _____.

I heard _____ (physical fact) _____ when _____ (time) _____.

I've known _____ (place) _____.

continued

Lesson 11.7 *(continued)*

(physical fact)

_____.

(emotion—summarize feelings about place)

_____.

Materials

Copies of outline and of teacher's trial run

Copies of Langston Hughes's "The Negro Speaks of Rivers"

Teacher's Try
I've known Ireland.
I've known the interminable staunch greenness and the endless drifting rain.
The pall of its rain echoes the cloud of upheaval Lying over it.
I cry in Ireland when the bombs rip through.
I learned of the desperation and how it destroys the proud history.
I looked at Dublin and saw a girl sobbing as she walked by the Liffey.
I heard the anger and boredom of its young when all seems fruitless and false.
I've known Ireland.
Poor, sad, endlessly proud in its ballys and knocks.
Does the horror ever end?

The Negro Speaks of Rivers[40]
I've known rivers.
I've known rivers ancient as the world and older than the flow of human blood in human veins.
My soul has grown deep like the rivers.
I bathed in the Euphrates when dawns were young.
I built my hut near the Congo and it lulled me to sleep.
I looked upon the Nile and raised the pyramids.
I heard the strong of the Mississippi when Abe Lincoln went down to New Orleans, and I've seen
*   its muddy bosom turn all golden in the sunset.*
I've known rivers:
Ancient, dusky rivers.
My soul has grown deep like the rivers.
—Langston Hughes

Evaluation

Students will be asked in a writing assignment for their journals or a similar nongraded (nonthreatening) situation to point out any new facts that they learned about themselves through this assignment and what they learned about their classmates. This would tell me if the poem was worth writing.

Lesson 11.8
Building Bridges to Islam: Lanterns and Quilts   *Nivan Saada and George McDermott*

Introduction

As a result of recent world events, Islam has been brought to the forefront. Many myths and untruths and much misinformation exist in the general media concerning the Islamic faith and its followers. So much about the religion is unknown here in the United States, yet Islam is the second largest religion in the world and one of the fastest growing religions in the United States. Indiana alone is home to over twenty-three mosques. In fact, the headquarters of the Islamic Society of North America is located in Plainfield, Indiana.

Addressing the topic of religion in school is very confusing to most teachers. Many teachers don't know if they are allowed by law to even bring up the subject in class, or, if it is brought up, how to go about discussing religion in a proper manner. In response, we developed a series of lessons for elementary school teachers that illustrate how mathematics activities can be imbedded within Islamic culture. Two are included here, along with a selected bibliography. These lessons represent small steps in building bridges to Islam, and they fit well with the development of *cultural consciousness* in Bennett's multicultural curriculum development model. We invite readers to contact us through our website for more teaching ideas, including photos and video clips of students and teachers in action (www.irvingtonmathcenter.com).

Ramadan Lanterns

Launching a mathematics activity through culturally specific children's literature

Content:	Geometry—reasoning about shapes
Grades:	Second and third
Objectives:	■ Gain knowledge of the religion of Islam
	■ Recognize and name pattern block shapes
	■ Construct new shapes from pattern blocks
	■ Create shapes that are symmetric
	■ Determine the relationship between the red, yellow, green, and blue pattern blocks
	■ Problem solve and explore various solutions
Materials:	A copy of *Magid Fasts for Ramadan*
	Pattern blocks
	Pattern block triangular paper
	Create lantern outline sheets
	Colored pencils
Launch:	Read the book *Magid Fasts for Ramadan*. This can be accomplished in a single reading or over several days.
	Mathews, M. (1996). *Magid Fasts for Ramadan*. New York: Clarion Books.

continued

Lesson 11.8 *(continued)*

This is a fictional story about a boy named Magid and his family. The story is situated in Egypt and tells of Magid's determination and struggle to fast for the first time. The author describes some of the traditions and customs observed during Ramadan. For example, children carry special Ramadan lanterns (or *Fanoose Ramadan* in Arabic) and sing to their family, friends, and neighbors. This book is suitable for students in the second through fifth grades.

After reading the book, ask if the students have any questions. Ask if any students observe the fasting of Ramadan and encourage them to share their family traditions. Facilitate a class conversation to highlight cultural connections. For example, although the story of Magid is situated in Egypt, Magid has an uncle who lives in the United States, where he observes Ramadan.

The author of the story of Magid also includes some background information that can be utilized during the class conversation. Depending on the grade level of the students, some local, national, and international demographic information can be presented regarding the Moslem population.

Development

Return to the story of the book and ask if any of the students remember what Magid and some of his friends did with their lanterns in Ramadan. Ask the students if they would like to construct their own lanterns today.

After organizing the students in groups of four, explain that each student will be using pattern blocks to construct their own lantern and color the lantern outline sheet appropriately. Once the students have accomplished this, pose the question, If one green triangle cost 10 cents to buy, how much would your lantern cost?

While circulating to assess the students' progress, ask questions to encourage students' use of geometric vocabulary and their exploration of the relationship between the shapes.

- *What shape are you looking for? I wonder, what shape would fit in the area you still have empty? Do you think you could use one block instead of these two triangles? . . . two trapezoids?*
- *What if I removed the hexagon? Can you fill its area with other shapes? I wonder, how many green triangles would fit in the space of the blue rhombus?*
- *Is your lantern design symmetrical? How can you tell? Can you make it so it is symmetrical? How? How could you use your colored lantern sheet to see if your lantern is symmetrical or not?*

Summary

After twenty-five minutes, bring the class together to discuss and share their findings. Ask the students to sort their lanterns according to the descriptions: *My lantern is symmetrical* and *My lantern is* not *symmetrical*. Ask the students to examine the sorting and raise their hands if they have questions about any of the lanterns. Discuss discrepancies, making sure to highlight reflective symmetry.

Have the students share their strategies for finding the price of their lantern. Ask why some lanterns cost the same although they are colored differently (looking for reasoning such as, the same area is covered therefore should cost the same).

Lesson 11.8 *(continued)*

Assessment

Note students' geometric reasoning and various strategies for counting money. For example: counting by tens, using the price of one triangle to find the prices of other shapes, and using conventional money notation. Also, note students' methods of recording and organizing their thinking.

Adaptations

Some students may require two outline sheets: one to construct their design and the other to color.

Extensions

Ask students to predict the price of the lantern if the green triangle is worth only 5 cents? Why do you think so? How did you try to predict? How can you check your prediction?

Quilting Designs
Launching a mathematics activity through culturally specific arts and crafts

Content:	Geometry—Applying transformations and symmetry
Grades:	Fourth through sixth
Objectives:	■ Gain knowledge of the religion of Islam
	■ Predict the results of flipping and turning two-dimensional shapes
	■ Describe line and rotational symmetry in two-dimensional designs
	■ Create and describe mental images of patterns and designs
	■ Problem solve and explore various solutions
Materials:	Video *Egyptian Quilt Makers* (see www.irvingtonmathcenter)
	Photos of some of the quilts
	Mirrors
	Paper
	One-inch-square paper
	Colored pencils
Launch:	Begin the lesson by asking the students if they know what a quilt is. Students then share their quilt stories. Explain that today the class will be viewing a short video that describes how quilts are made in Egypt. After showing the video, ask where the quilters got their designs ideas from (walls and doors of the many mosques in Cairo). Also ask the students about the methods the quilters used to create their patterns and designs (looking for utilization of symmetry and folding to reduce amount drawn by hand).

continued

Lesson 11.8 *(continued)*

Development

Distribute the sets of quilt photos to the six groups of students, and ask them to sort the designs according to the type of symmetry they exhibit. Each group will then describe one of the photos highlighting vertical and/or horizontal lines of reflection, rotational symmetry, angles of rotation, and the number of possible folds that would create their specific design.

While circulating to assess the students' progress, ask questions to encourage students' use of geometric vocabulary and their exploration of the symmetry of the designs.

- *How do you know this design has four lines of symmetry? Can you show us using the mirror? Can you show us a different way?*
- *How many times would I have to rotate this section of the design to get the whole quilt? How do you know that? What if the angle of rotation was 60 degrees? . . . 30 degrees?*

Next, have each student create their own symmetric quilt design. Students should record the types of symmetry they used when creating their designs. The designs will then be displayed as if in a gallery.

Summary

After 25 minutes, bring the class together to discuss and share their designs. Students should visit the gallery and choose a quilt other than their own to describe to the rest of the class. The creator of the described design then has the last word in describing their quilt, adding to the description and agreeing or disagreeing with it. Discussion should be based on sound geometrical reasoning.

Assessment

Note students' various strategies for finding symmetry, their use of geometric reasoning, geometric vocabulary, and their openness to others' reasoning and ideas.

Adaptations

Some students may require the photos to be copied on regular paper to allow for folding along the lines of symmetry. Some may not be able to mentally visualize the end result, and thus may require scissors to cut a part of the design and rotate it to achieve the final design.

Mathematics Extensions

Ask students to produce a quilt with specific attributes. For example: a quilt that has two diagonal lines of symmetry, or 60-degree rotation.

Cultural Extensions

The following community-building activity increases students' knowledge of their own and their peers' cultures and provides an open and respectful forum for students to share, inquire, and discuss their findings. The students will explore cultural designs by incorporating cultural symbols from their own experiences and backgrounds into quilts.

Development

Each student is to design and create a quilt panel (8.5 × 8.5) representing themselves. These panels will constitute the cultural class quilt. Each person will describe their panel and note the similarities and differences across the various cultures.

Lesson 11.8 *(continued)*

Participants are encouraged to use a combination of words, pictures, fabric, symbols, and icons that best represent their culture. This activity can allow students the opportunity to research their ancestry using library and Internet resources as well as by interviewing their family members. The panels can be created at home and assembled into the quilt in class. The following categories are examples of possible included information:

- Languages spoken by participant and/or family members
- Specific family customs and traditions
- Holidays you and your family observe
- Religious traditions observed by you and/or your family
- Clothes worn traditionally by you and/or your family
- Special foods prepared for specific occasions

Note students' various strategies for finding symmetry, their use of geometric reasoning and geometric vocabulary, and their openness to others' reasoning and ideas.

Selected Bibliography

Ben Jelloun, T. (2002). *Islam Explained.* New York: The New Press.
   The author is a French Muslim of Moroccan descent. He wrote the book in the aftermath of the 9–11 tragedy. Through his writing, he aims to (a) present Islam as a part of the universal human heritage and (b) educate young Muslims and non-Muslims about the teachings of Islam. Thus, the author chose to write this book as a conversation between himself and his 10-year-old son. The book is written from the perspective of the insider, is an easy read, and provides a great deal of history concisely and clearly. The chapter layout and the question-and-answer format facilitate teachers' (third through ninth grade) use of parts of the book without the loss of continuity.

Demi. (2003). *Muhammad.* New York: Margaret K. McElderry Books.
   This is a beautifully written and illustrated book about the life of the Prophet Muhammad. The book also provides a concise history of the rise of Islam. This book is well researched, as evident by its bibliography. This book is suitable for students in grades three through seven and their teachers.

Douglas, S. L. (2004). *Ramadan.* Minneapolis, MN: Carolrhoda Books.
   This author describes the demography of Muslims around the world and provides introductory information regarding Islam and its holy book, the Quran. The main focus is the fasting month of Ramadan. She addresses the rules for fasting and some of the cultural traditions. This book is suitable for students in grades two through six and their teachers.

El-Moslimany, A. P. (1994). *Zaki's Ramadan Fast.* Seattle, WA: Amica Publishing House.
   This is a fictional story about a boy named Zaki and his sister, who are the children of a cross-cultural marriage between their African American mother and Indian father. The story tells us of Zaki's first day of fasting, his determination and struggle through that day, and his accomplishment. This book is suitable for students in grades two through five and their teachers.

Ghazi, S. H. (1996). *Ramadan.* New York: Holiday House.
   This book is written from the insider's perspective. Although the author was born in the United States, he is of Saudi Arabian descent and lived there for six years. The story revolves around a little boy named Hakeem. The reader is introduced to Islam in general and fasting in particular by observing Hakeem throughout one day in Ramadan. This book is beautifully illustrated and suitable for students in grades two through six and their teachers.

Hoyt-Goldsmith, D. (2001). *Celebrating Ramadan.* New York: Holiday House.
   This is a nonfictional story about a boy named Ibraheem, his sister, and brother, who are the children of a cross-cultural marriage between their Egyptian American mother and Bosnian father. This is an up-to-date snapshot into the lives of American Muslims. The book follows Ibraheem and his family through the fasting month of Ramadan and the ensuing feast of Id al-Fitr. It also has an explanation of the Muslim prayers. The author enriched the book by including many photographs and a useful glossary of terms. This book is suitable for students in grades two through five and their teachers.

continued

Lesson 11.8 *(continued)*

MacMillan, D. M. (1994). *Ramadan and Id al-Fitr*. Hillside, NJ: Enslow Publishers.

    This book can be utilized in grades two through five. It provides a good initial introduction to the religion of Islam, and describes how American Muslims practice in the United States. The book explains the pillars of Islam and focuses on the fasting of Ramadan and the ensuing feast of Id al-Fitr. The author includes photographs of American Muslims and some mosques, and a useful glossary of terms.

Smith, D. (2002). *If the World Were a Village*. Tonawanda, NY: Kids Can Press.

    The author invites the readers to imagine the world as if it were a village. He goes on to describe the constituents of such a village. This description encompasses the constituents' ages, nationalities, languages, and religions. In addition, the author addresses literacy rates, food and economic resources, and environmental issues. This book is a valuable resource when focusing on diversity and multicultural issues. It shrinks the world to a size that is easier for students in grades two through nine to comprehend. A possible classroom activity is to think of the United States as a village and research the demographics of its population.

Stanley, D. (2002). *Saladin: Noble Prince of Islam*. New York: HarperCollins.

    This is a historical tale of Salah al-Din, a generous and chivalrous Muslim leader who was a courageous fighter but longed for peace. This book is beautifully illustrated and well researched, as evident by its bibliography. Teachers can utilize this book in grades three through eight, especially when identifying role models across multicultural lines.

Wilkinson, P. (2002). *Islam*. New York: DK Publishing.

    This is a picture book that encompasses a wide variety of historical information about Islam and Muslims. The author takes the reader on a geographical tour, visiting the various regions of the world where Muslims live. He accomplishes this through beautiful and aptly described photographs. This book is a good general-information resource on Islam for fourth through eighth graders and their teachers.

Reprinted with permission of the author.

Goal Three: Developing Intercultural Competence

Intercultural competence is the ability to interpret intentional communications (language, signs, gestures), some unconscious cues (such as body language), and customs in cultural styles different from one's own. The emphasis is on empathy and communication. This goal recognizes that communication among persons of different cultural backgrounds can be hindered by culturally conditioned assumptions made about each other's behavior and cognitions. It is also based on the fact that, as Kraemer states, "the effects of cultural conditioning are sometimes so pervasive that people whose experience has been limited to the norms of their own culture simply cannot understand a communication based on a different set of norms. . . . [and] cannot understand why a 'self-evident' communication from them cannot be comprehended by others."[41]

    Some of the assumptions underlying this goal are as follows:

- Language is at the heart of culture and cognition.
- People's effectiveness in multicultural communication can be improved by developing their cultural self-awareness (their abilities to recognize cultural influences on their own cognitions).

■ There are modes of human communication that can transcend cultural barriers.

■ Although cultures are continually changing, some aspects of the diverse cultures within a larger society, such as an African American core culture in the United States, or Navajo culture in the Southwest, can be identified, defined, and taught.

■ Persons can achieve a psychological balance between cultural pride and identity on the one hand, and appreciation of cultures very different from their own on the other (that is, increased intercultural contact will not necessarily lead to cultural assimilation).

Although this goal clearly overlaps the goals of developing historical perspectives and cultural consciousness, to teach for intercultural competence means going beyond the study of worldviews, heritage, and contributions associated with a particular people. It means building an understanding of how one is influenced by the values, priorities, language, and norms of one's culture. This knowledge then can grow into the realization that every person's perception of reality is shaped by experience. Once people understand how their own language, experience, and current modes of cognition relate to their own culture, contrasts may be made with the cultural experience and modes of cognition of culturally different others. Ultimately, they are able to move to a level of transpection, what Hanvey refers to as "the capacity to imagine oneself in a role within the context of a foreign culture."[42]

Gudykunst and Kim define intercultural competence in terms of the *intercultural person*. As noted in Chapter 1,

> [t]he intercultural person represents one who has achieved an advanced level in the process of becoming intercultural and whose cognitive, affective, and behavioral characteristics are not limited but are open to growth beyond the psychological parameters of any one culture. . . . The intercultural person possesses an intellectual and emotional commitment to the fundamental unity of all humans and, at the same time, accepts and appreciates the differences that lie between people of different cultures.[43]

According to Gudykunst and Kim, intercultural people are individuals who

■ Have encountered experiences that challenge their own cultural assumptions (e.g., culture shock, dynamic disequilibrium) and that provide insight into how their view of the world has been shaped by their culture

■ Can serve as facilitators and catalysts for contacts between cultures

■ Come to terms with the roots of their own ethnocentrism and achieve an objectivity in viewing other cultures

■ Develop a "third world" perspective "which enables them to interpret and evaluate intercultural encounters more accurately and thus to act as a communication link between two cultures"[44]

■ Show cultural empathy and can "imaginatively participate in the other's world view"[45]

It is one thing to develop knowledge and awareness of human similarities and another to develop empathy. Knowledge is a necessary but insufficient ingredient. According to Dufty et al., the goal is informed empathy, or "knowledge plus sensitivity in trying to imagine oneself in another's shoes or bare feet. Empathy varies from trying to understand how other people think and view the world to how other people emote, feel or sense."[46] As an illustration, consider the following three responses made by students who were asked to imagine themselves as someone from another culture, based on pictures of an unfamiliar culture. Responses A and B exemplify informed empathy, while response C seems totally lacking in empathy, however informed it may be. Negative empathy or nonempathy, as illustrated in response C, shows "a lack of skill in identifying with others, a lack of cultural imagination, or an inability to think in terms other than those of your own culture."[47]

> *Student A's response:* The holy man came to ward off the spirits which were giving my daughter headaches.
> *Student B's response:* When I die I hope my body will be cremated and my ashes thrown into the sacred Godavari River.
> *Student C's response:* I live in a typical agricultural village in a crude mud hut. I am a New Guinea highlander. Our tribe's religion is animism. My diet is essentially vegetative. The natural vegetation is chopped away with primitive stone axes, the lower story plants are burnt, producing nutrient for the soil. After fifty years, the ecology of my area returns to its original state.

The goal of intercultural competence is a major objective of curriculum writers connected with UNESCO'S efforts toward international understanding through education.[48] Although these educators have limited the scope of intercultural competence to the international scene, many of the accompanying theories and practices are appropriate for education within a domestic multicultural society.

The work of Triandis and his associates has led to a form of cross-cultural training called the culture assimilator, a programmed learning approach designed to increase understanding between members of two cultures.

> As the reader of the assimilator goes through the items, he learns to what features in the episodes he should attend, and which aspects he should ignore [discrimination learning]. The episodes are selected so that they expose the trainee to situations that emphasize the distinctive features of social situations [that] he must learn to discriminate. The items are also selected to give the trainee contrasting experiences with situations differing sharply on such features. The training, then, emphasizes the distinctive features of events [that] make the situation in the other culture most different from the situations that the trainee has already learned in his own culture. As he receives more and more training with related items, he can abstract features which such items have in common. We call such invariances "cultural principles." After the trainee goes through a half a dozen items featuring the same principle, he is presented with a summary sheet in which the principle is stated as a conclusion. Thus, if he has not abstracted the principle by that point, it is given to him.

> *As an example . . . consider some recent work on black/white subcultural differences. Black subjects have a tendency to assume that all white persons are prejudiced against blacks. This has major implications for social perception in interracial encounters. Almost any behavior of the white can be misinterpreted, if the context in which it is seen reflects prejudice.*[49]

Culture assimilators have been developed for a number of nations, such as Israel and Iran, and for Black and White cultures within the United States. To date, these assimilators have been developed primarily for industrial work settings. Similar approaches to multicultural education, however, can be developed for school settings.

Although the culture assimilator can alert teachers to potential sources of misunderstanding in verbal and nonverbal communication, it typically does not provide instruction in the host language or host dialect. Language, chorus, drama, and speech teachers have multiple opportunities for building intercultural competence by teaching accurate pronunciation, intonation, syntax, and word meanings associated with different languages and dialects. In classrooms where multiple dialects of English are spoken, for example, teachers can draw from each one to teach the parts of speech and rules of grammar. Similarly, they can build up student vocabulary and analytical thinking skills. Speech teachers can develop understandings of culturally different styles of posturing and other nonverbal cues. Business teachers could include instruction on culturally different expectations concerning punctuality, eye contact, and handshaking or bows during job interviews. Physical educators and directors of athletic events can alert students to culturally different rules, notions of fair play, and body moves associated with certain sports.

Language is one of the great barriers to intercultural competence in U.S. society and to empathy and respect among culturally different people. Writing from a Chicano perspective, Feliciano Rivera states the following:

> *Historically, state and local institutions have insisted that to become "good Americans" all minority and immigrant groups have to abandon their native languages and cultures, give up their group identity, and become absorbed as individuals into the dominant group. If any group has resisted . . . it has been regarded as uncivilized, un-American, and potentially subversive. Furthermore, it is difficult for many people to accept the idea that a native-born Mexican American who happens to speak Spanish and who retains many of the values of his native culture might well be a loyal American. As a result, social and educational institutions in the Southwest and California have directed their activities toward the elimination of both the Spanish language and Mexican culture.*[50]

Ironically, millions of dollars are spent to encourage schoolchildren to learn a foreign language.

A multicultural curriculum offers guidelines for moving beyond these contradictions. When teachers accept the goal of developing competencies in multiple systems of standards for perceiving, evaluating, believing, and doing, it becomes

A repertoire of multiethnic songs from around the world can strengthen cultural consciousness and intercultural competence.

obvious that knowledge about multiple dialects and languages is part of becoming educated. A society and a world comprised of linguistically different peoples require the ability to interpret an array of verbal and nonverbal communication modes to at least minimal degrees, and accurate interpretation requires some degree of empathy. Of course, it is unrealistic to expect that most people could ever become proficient in more than a few languages. Most U.S. Americans thrive with only one language, provided that language is English, so there is often little motivation to become bilingual or multilingual. The opportunity exists, however. Consider Table 11.3, which gives some indication of the language diversity within the United States.

At the very least, it is possible and imperative that we become proficient with one or more of the most prevalent dialects or languages that coexist with our native tongue, be it English, Spanish, Chinese, or Appalachian dialect. The process of adding even one new dialect or language to our repertoire strengthens awareness of cultural conflicts and misconceptions that emerge from verbal and nonverbal cues associated with different languages. It becomes easier to understand how others misperceive and are misperceived.

Literature and the arts provide other rich sources for developing informed student empathy. Short stories, poems, song lyrics, drama, and pieces of visual art often hold messages about universal human experiences and emotions such as love, grief, anger, protest, and death. Affirmations of the human spirit, which thrives under even the most oppressive conditions, are found in spirituals created by African

Table 11.3 ▧ Language Diversity in the United States: Percentage of School-Age Population Speaking Language Other Than English at Home

Location	Language
15% and Over	
California	German, Italian, Spanish, Polish, Yiddish, French, Russian, Hungarian, Swedish, Greek, Norwegian, Dutch, Japanese, Chinese, Serbo-Croatian, Portuguese, Danish, Arabic, Tagalog, Armenian, Turkish, Persian, Malay (Indonesian), Scandinavian, Basque, Mandarin, Gypsy (Romani)
Arizona	Spanish, Uto-Aztecan
New Mexico	Spanish
Texas	Spanish
Alaska	South Alaskan, Inuit, North Mexican
Florida	Spanish
New York	German, Italian, Spanish, Polish, Yiddish, French, Russian, Hungarian, Swedish, Greek, Norwegian, Slovak, Dutch, Ukranian, Lithuanian, Czech, Chinese, Portugese, Danish, Finnish, Arabic, Rumanian, Balto-Slavic, Celtic, Hebrew, Armenian, Near Eastern Arabic dialects, Turkish, Uralic, Albanian, Persian, Scandinavian, Amerindian, Dalmatian, Breton, Mandarin, Egyptian, Georgian, Gypsy (Romani), Athabascan
Hawaii	Japanese, Tagalog, Polynesian
10.0–14.9%	
Nevada	Spanish
Colorado	Spanish
Illinois	German, Italian, Spanish, Polish, Yiddish, Russian, Swedish, Greek, Norwegian, Slovak, Dutch, Ukranian, Lithuanian, Czech, Serbo-Croatian, Danish, Balto-Slavic
New Jersey	German, Italian, Polish, Yiddish, Russian, Hungarian, Slovak, Dutch, Ukrainian
Connecticut	Italian, Polish, French

Sources: Theodore Andersson and Mildred Boyer, *Bilingual Schooling in the United States* (Washington, DC: U.S. Office of Education, 1970), p. 2627; and U.S. Bureau of the Census, *General Social and Economic Characteristics* (Washington, DC, 1980), Figure 7, p. 10g.

American people during slavery in the American South and in poems and drawings created by young Japanese American children and Jewish children who were imprisoned in concentration camps during World War II. A story such as *Annie and the Old One* can help young non-Indian children relate to humans who live in a culture that differs from their own.[51] Annie is a young Navajo girl who tries to halt time to delay the death of her beloved grandmother. Each night Annie unravels the rug her grandmother is weaving in order to delay her grandmother's death, which will come when the rug is completed. Although Annie is unable to prevent the inevitable, her grandmother teaches her how to face life and accept death. The experience or fear of losing a loved one is something most children can empathize with.

Literature and artistic achievements by one's own people provide sources of identity and pride within the individual, and sources of respect from others. They can help expand students' readiness for empathy. Self-knowledge, self-acceptance, and security are necessary before people can understand and accept others with whom they may disagree. Furthermore, literature and the arts provide numerous opportunities for asking students to imagine themselves as someone else. What is a certain character feeling? What is the artist or composer expressing?

The selection and interpretation of appropriate materials from literature can be problematic, however. In an excellent publication by the National Council of Teachers of English, *Black Literature for High School Students*, authors Dodds, Stanford, and Amin state that most teachers agree that Black literature can help foster interracial understanding. However, teachers differ in their interpretations of literature and in their views about what literature is appropriate.

> *Whites tend to react favorably to books in which white people behave generously and kindly, and often do not notice when behavior is somewhat patronizing and fails to bring about meaningful change for black people. To Kill a Mockingbird . . . is probably the best example of a book which many white teachers feel promotes positive interracial attitudes by showing Atticus' courage. Most black teachers, however, point out that Atticus, in fact, compromised and survived in a destructive social system, and that for the blacks in the novel, Atticus' "heroism" was a paternalistic insult. In a just system, Tom Robinson would never have needed defending—and Atticus would not have been a hero.*[52]

A curriculum that includes the performing arts can strengthen students' cultural consciousness and intercultural competence.

These caveats are not limited to Black literature. They apply to all literature, where racist or sexist themes are evident.

However, in books that avoid White paternalism and provide the realities of barrio, reservation, or ghetto life—such as *The Autobiography of Malcolm X* and Dick Gregory's *Nigger*—four-letter words and dialect are often objected to. Some teachers, minority and nonminority alike, fear these works will reinforce negative stereotypes about the ethnic groups portrayed. They also find that White students are sometimes so disturbed by Black, Chicano, or Native American hatred of Whites that they cannot get beyond feelings of anger, grief, or guilt. Such reactions are understandable and need to be expressed, provided the environment is caring and supportive. However, there is often a danger that students will remain in a state of either nonempathy or overempathizing.

These risks can be minimized with careful instruction. For example, among ethnically encapsulated students whose only contact with culturally different people has been through myths and cruel stereotypes, it may be helpful to begin with ethnically different people of similar backgrounds, values, and social class. Regional and class prejudices will then not have to be dealt with along with their ethnic bias. Dodds, Stanford, and Amin state that, "White middle-class students, even if they are from prejudiced backgrounds, should be able to empathize with the characters in *It's Good to Be Black, Mary McLeod Bethune,* and *My Life with Dr. Martin King, Jr.* Working-class, urban, white students may find that they can identify with Althea Gibson, Connie Hawkins, or Gordon Parks."[53]

Lesson Plans That Develop Intercultural Competence

Lesson 11.9
Faces, Families, and Friends

This lesson is designed for the multilingual primary-level classroom in which children differ in their English-language proficiency and academic progress. Some children are monolingual and speak only English, Spanish, or various Vietnamese dialects. Others are proficiently bilingual in both English and their mother tongue. Some have a limited proficiency in English but can read and write in their first language. Others have had no access to formal education and thus have not acquired basic academic skills.

Part of each day the children work in heterogeneous groups (cooperative teams) to strengthen oral language proficiency and develop creative problem-solving skills. A proficiently bilingual child is placed in each team, along with monolingual children (speakers of English and Spanish or Vietnamese

continued

Lesson 11.9 *(continued)*

dialects). Children have been taught cooperative teamwork and can effectively use the roles of group facilitator, translator, reporter, setup officer, and harmonizer. The children work for an hour each day in discussion groups to strengthen conceptual learning and oral language proficiency. They also work an hour each day in math and science learning centers to strengthen their creative problem-solving skills. The following lesson illustrates how the discussion groups work. Children become more interculturally competent as they learn about each other's verbal and nonverbal modes of communication.

Goals

- Students will develop increased language proficiency in two or three languages, one of which is English.
- Students will develop increased conceptual learning in two or three languages, one of which is English.
- Students will develop increased intercultural competence.

Objectives

1. The children will create a mask portrait of a member of their family (real or imagined) and describe the person to their group (using the bilingual interpreter as needed).
2. Teams write and act out a brief skit based on the characters created by the members.

Activities

1. The teacher gives each team facilitator a card that explains the task. Everyone in the group makes a mask. The mask is the face of a real or imaginary person in your family. Explain your mask (person) to your team. Help write a skit about all the people (masks) in your group.
2. The teams discuss the task card and the translator (who is bilingual) makes sure that everyone understands the task.
3. The setup officer gets the supplies needed to create the masks. (Supplies are clearly organized and identified with pictographs.)
4. Once the masks are finished (about 30 minutes), the facilitators and checkers work together to give everyone a chance to explain his or her mask. As the skit is being developed, they make sure that everyone has input and listens to the ideas of others. Reporters write words in two languages, aided by a bilingual pictionary (30 minutes today, 30 to 60 minutes tomorrow).
5. The skits are acted out, videotaped, and discussed on the third day (30 to 60 minutes).

Materials

Task cards (trilingual and pictographs).

Team roles posted in room. These should be trilingual and include pictographs.

Paper plates, multicolored construction paper, scissors, glue sticks, and water-based markers for the masks.

Video camera and tape.

Lesson 11.9 *(continued)*

Recommended Resource for Teachers

Elizabeth G. Cohen, *Designing Groupwork: Strategies for the Heterogeneous Classroom.* Teachers College Press, New York, 1986. The theory and practice of groupwork are clearly explained, including the development of leadership roles that give everyone an essential part to play. Chapter 10 describes the "finding out" approach used in math and science. Teams discuss activity cards before they begin, as in the lesson above. Once everyone understands the task, they can move to the "interesting manipulative materials" that don't require English language proficiency. This approach has significantly enhanced higher-order thinking and problem-solving skills of young children and helps them to work at or well above grade level in math and science, whether or not they are highly proficient in English.

Lesson 11.10

Nobody Speaks My Language   *Pamela L. Tiedt and Iris M. Tiedt*

Introduction

Give students a taste of what foreigners experience by setting up the classroom as a foreign country. For a brief period, everyone (including the teacher) will pretend that they cannot understand what anyone else says (or writes). Hide all written material so that students will not see anything in a familiar language. Students will have to communicate by pointing, gesturing, and acting out.

At the end of the specified time, discuss how everyone felt. How would this experience be similar to or different from that of a foreigner coming to this country for the first time? Was there anything they wanted to communicate but could not? How could they help someone in a similar situation?

A Local Language Survey

Do students know what languages are spoken in their area? Begin with the local place names. What languages have influenced local names? Ask families. What languages are spoken in the students' families? Do students know people who speak different languages?

Make a map or chart of the area on which to record the information students find. Have them research local history to see what the earliest languages were. Were there any Native American groups living nearby? What language did they speak and what happened to them? Ask who the first settlers were and what languages they brought with them. Trace the language history down to the present time. Students should be able to discover what the major local language groups are and how long their speakers have been in the area.

Once the major languages are identified, this can become an important resource for further study. Plan lessons around examples from these languages. Bring people in who speak various languages so that students can hear what the languages sound like.

continued

Lesson 11.10 *(continued)*

Focusing on Spanish

Spanish is the most commonly spoken language in the United States other than English. Spanish-speaking Americans have their roots in Mexico, Spain, Puerto Rico, Cuba, and other countries. Most Spanish speakers are located throughout California and the Southwest. However, students may be surprised to learn that there are large groups of Spanish speakers in Colorado, Massachusetts, and Florida, for example. In addition, almost all major cities such as Chicago and New York have large Spanish-speaking communities. All children should be aware of the Spanish language and the variety of Spanish-speaking cultures represented in the United States.

The following activities are designed to acquaint all students with the Spanish language. They can be used with bilingual programs or classrooms in which only English is spoken. You can use these activities easily whether or not you know Spanish. Encourage Spanish-speaking students to contribute vocabulary and pronunciation information and reward them for their knowledge. If you have no Spanish-speaking students, bring in Spanish-language teaching tapes or records for the class to become accustomed to Spanish sounds. The activities given here are not intended to teach students Spanish. They are useful to make non-Spanish speakers aware of Spanish as an interesting and important language and to assure Spanish-speaking students that their ability to speak two languages is valued. Although the activities refer specifically to Spanish, they can be adapted for use with any language.

Comparing Alphabets

Show students how the Spanish alphabet is similar to the English alphabet. Show them how it differs. Write or print the letters on the board, circling the letters that are added, thus:

a	b	c	(ch)	d	(e)	f
g	h	i	j	k	l	(ll)
m	n	(ñ)	o	p	q	r
(rr)	s	y	u	v	w	x
y	z					

Explain that the letters *k* and *w* are used in the Spanish language only when words have been borrowed from other languages ("kilómetro" and "Washington").

Letter Names

What are the names of the letters of the alphabet? English-speaking children will be interested in learning how Spanish-speaking children say the alphabet. Have a child who speaks Spanish say these letters slowly for the group. This is more effective than reading or saying them yourself, for it makes the students aware that knowledge of Spanish can be important in school.

Lesson 11.10 *(continued)*

Spanish Letter Names

a	äj	j	hōtä	r	ārā
b	bā	k	kä	rr	ārrā
c	sā	l	ālā	s	āsā
ch	chā	ll	āyā	t	tā
d	dā	m	āmā	u	ü
e	ā	n	ānā	v	bā
f	āffā	ñ	ānyā	w	dūblä bā
g	hā	o	ō	x	ākēs
h	ächā	p	pā	y	ē grē āgä (Greek i)
i	ē	q	kü	z	sātä

Comparing Phonemes and Graphemes

After examining the alphabet letters that are used in writing Spanish, show students the phonemes used in speaking Spanish, some of which are similar to English but none of which are exactly the same. Also show them corresponding graphemes for these phonemes. Here they will notice many differences between Spanish and English.

Consonants	Spanish	English
b	también	ri<u>b</u>
	abrir	like v, but with lips almost touching
c	casa	<u>c</u>ase (before a, o, u)
	nación	<u>c</u>ent (before e, i)
ch	chico	<u>ch</u>urch
d	donde	<u>d</u>own
	madre	<u>th</u>e
f	familia	<u>f</u>amily
g	gente	like exaggerated h (before e, i)
	gordo	<u>g</u>ame
h	hacer	silent
j	jugar	like exaggerated h
k	kilómetro	<u>k</u>itchen
l	làstima	<u>l</u>ittle
ll	llena	<u>y</u>ellow, mi<u>ll</u>ion } regional variation

continued

Lesson 11.10 *(continued)*

Consonants	Spanish	English
m	mañana	morning
n	nada	nothing
ñ	niño	canyon
p	piña	supper
q	queso	key
r	pero	rich
	rico	trilled r
rr	perro	trilled r
s	sala	sad
t	trabajar	time
v	enviar	like b in también
	la vaca	like b in abrir
w	Wáshington	wash
x	examen	exam
	extranjero	sound
	México	hit
y	yo	yes
z	zapato	save

Vowels		
a	padre	father
e	es	they
i	nida	police
o	poco	poem
u	luna	spoon
	querer	silent after q
ai, ay	traiga	nice
au	auto	mouse
ei, ey	aceituna	tray

Lesson 11.10 *(continued)*

Vowels (continued)

eu	deuda	<u>ay</u> plus <u>oo</u>
ia, ya	hacia	<u>y</u>onder
ie, ye	nieve	<u>ye</u>s
io, yo	dios	<u>y</u>olk
iu	ciudad	<u>y</u>ule
oi, oy	soy	b<u>oy</u>
ua	guante	<u>wa</u>nder
ue	vuelve	<u>wei</u>ght
y	y	<u>e</u>ven
ui, uy	muy	<u>we</u>
uo	cuota	<u>woe</u>

Spanish Pronunciation

Whether or not you have ever studied Spanish, it is important to be able to pronounce the Spanish that you introduce in your classroom as easily as possible. Use the chart of Spanish phonemes to become familiar with Spanish sounds. Ask Spanish-speaking students to share their knowledge of Spanish and contribute words or demonstrate pronunciations. There is no reason for you as the teacher to be afraid of making mistakes. You can help by making an effort to try Spanish words without having to speak Spanish fluently. Taking at least an introductory Spanish class is, of course, recommended for any teacher's professional development.

Varieties of Spanish

The information on Spanish presented in this book is very general. There are many varieties of Spanish spoken in the United States, depending on where the speakers live, how long they have lived in this country, and where they came from originally. Spanish in the Southwest is different from Spanish in the Midwest (Chicago), the Northeast, and Florida. Even in New York City, there are important cultural and linguistic differences between persons from Puerto Rico, Cuba, Dominican Republic, Colombia, Ecuador, Peru, Mexico, Venezuela, Bolivia, and other South American communities.

The differences in the Spanish of Latin America are primarily vocabulary and pronunciation. Some vocabulary differences are due to influence from local Indian languages, others to independent development of Spanish.

The following are examples of different words used in Latin America for *boy*.

Mexico—chamaco	Panama—chico
Cuba—chico	Colombia—pelado
Guatemala—patojo	Argentina—pibe
El Salvador—cipote	Chile—cabro

continued

Lesson 11.10 *(continued)*

Pronunciation also varies regionally. The following are some of the differences found: syllable final *s* becomes *h* or disappears—*estos* is [éhtoh] or [éto]; *ll* becomes the same, as *y*—*valla* and *vaya* are alike; and syllable final *r* sounds like *l*—*puerta* is [pwelta], *comer* is [komel].

Introduce vocabulary specific to local Spanish-speaking groups by having a variety of children's books available. Many books, written about members of particular groups, take pride in presenting common Spanish words that are special to that group.

Excerpted from P. L. Tiedt and I. M. Tiedt, *Multicultural Teaching: A Handbook of Activities, Information, and Resources* (Boston: Allyn & Bacon, 1979), 84–88. Reprinted by permission.

Lesson 11.11
Spirituals for the School Choir   *Arlessa Barnes*

Introduction
This lesson is for a high school choir and is primarily an introduction to the teaching of one or two Negro spirituals to add to the choral repertoire. The plan, of course, would extend beyond one lesson.

Goals
Developing culture consciousness and intercultural competence.

Objectives
- Students will understand and become aware of the unique characteristics evident in spirituals sung by African Americans during slavery.
- Students will become aware of the contributions made to the spiritual movement by several Black composers and artists.
- Students will develop skill in correct pronunciation of Black dialect used in the spirituals.

Suggested Motivating Activities
1. Have students attempt to harmonize by ear when choir is learning the spirituals.
2. Allow students to move. Movement, such as foot tapping, swaying, facial expressions, and clapping, is an important part of the African American music culture and shows a true Black aesthetic.

Lesson 11.11 *(continued)*

3. As a follow-up to class, visit a Black church choir rehearsal or service. For those students who are unfamiliar with Black gospel music, observing the emotional energy will help them relate to the Black aesthetic.

4. Attend a Black religious choral concert if one is scheduled nearby.

Procedure

1. Listen to and discuss the characteristics of one or two spirituals that have been passed down from the African tradition.

   Suggested listening: any of the below or [any] selected from the Materials (discography)

   Note to teacher: Spirituals have certain distinctive features, syncopated rhythms, call and response technique (or leader and chorus), rich harmonies, etc. Spirituals are emotional expressions of Black individuals about their particular experiences (an example of an emotional spiritual is "Sometimes I Feel Like a Motherless Child"). Spirituals also tell of biblical incidents, for example "Joshua Fought the Battle of Jericho." The call and response song form, which is directly of African origin, is present throughout the African American repertoire. A song that employs the leader and chorus arrangement is "Swing Low, Sweet Chariot." Some of the spirituals undoubtedly had hidden or double meanings and served as signals for escape purposes. "Steal Away to Jesus" is a classic example.

2. Select one or two spirituals to teach to your choir. Stress the importance of the spiritual as a part of our American heritage.

   Suggested songs: see Materials (song collections)

   Note to teacher: Stress that your singers use proper Black dialect when singing spirituals. Black dialect may present some difficulties to White people who have never lived in the South, but most of the spirituals lose charm when they are sung in straight English. *Examples*:

   (dialect) "I ain't gonna study war no mo"

   (English) "I am not going to study war anymore"

   (dialect) "Gaud's go'nuh trouble duh watah"

   (English) "God's going to trouble the water"

3. Discuss the Fisk Jubilee Singers, who acquainted the masses with spirituals during their American and European tours from 1871 to 1878, and continue today.

4. Discuss Marian Anderson, who perfected these songs with her skilled technique and culture.

5. Discuss J. Rosamond Johnson and Harry T. Burleigh (spiritual composers).

continued

Lesson 11.11 *(continued)*

Materials

1. Discography:

   Fisk Jubilee Singers (Folkways FA 2372)

   Tuskegee Institute Choir (Westminster 9633)

   He's Got the World, Marian Anderson (Victor LSC 2592)

2. Song collections:

   Chambers, H. A., ed. *The Treasury of Negro Spirituals*. New York: Emerson Books, 1963. The book is divided into two sections: "Traditional Spirituals" and "Modern Compositions." The Spirituals are tastefully arranged.

   Johnson, James Weldon, and J. Rosamond Johnson. *The Book of American Negro Spirituals*. New York: Viking Press, 1954. Very useful and most recommended.

   Landecks, Beatrice. *Echoes of Africa in Folk Songs of the Americas*, 2nd rev. ed. New York: David McKay, 1969. Part Four, titled "Songs Roots of Jazz in the U.S.," has street cries, Spirituals, and shouts, work and minstrel songs, and blues. Good selections, with notes and suggestions for performance.

   Lloyd, Ruth Norma, comp. and arr. *The American Heritage Songbook*. New York: American Heritage, 1969. Part Seven of this book, "Songs of the American Negro," contains thirteen Spirituals and folk songs with information about each one.

3. Suggested reading (for the teacher who may not be familiar with African American music):

   Heilbut, Tony. *The Gospel Sound*. New York: Simon and Schuster, 1971. A solid contribution to the literature, good discography.

   Marsh, J. B. T. *The Story of the Jubilee Singers: With Their Songs*. New York: Negro University Press, 1969.

   Reeder, Barbara. "Getting Involved in Shaping the Sounds of Black Music." *Music Educators Journal, 59* (October 1972): 80. This article delineates pertinent rhythmic aspects in Black music with activities to help students feel and respond.

   Work, John Wesley. *American Negro Songs and Spirituals*. New York: Bonanza, 1940.

Evaluation

1. Listening exam(s): Test can be matching, multiple choice, and/or short essay. Construct tests whereby students would be required to pinpoint and describe various characteristics of the Negro spiritual.

2. Ask students to prepare reports on one of the artists/composers studied.

3. If you have an opportunity to observe a live performance of a Black religious choir, instruct students to do a report, critiquing the performance and discussing various characteristics.

Reprinted with permission of the author.

Lesson 11.12
Misunderstandings in Cross-Cultural Interactions   *Delora Medina and Hilda Vazquez*

Introduction
This lesson is for high school Spanish classes.

We live in a diverse community that has undergone a rapid increase in our Hispanic population. It is important for the entire community to recognize that different cultures have different ways of looking at our world and interacting interpersonally. One of the most effective ways to reach the community is through our students. A better understanding of the way in which ethnic groups communicate consciously (such as language and gestures) and unconsciously (such as body language) can be taught in the classroom. In addition, it is important for the students to recognize how their *own* thoughts and behaviors might be misinterpreted by people from *other* cultures. Being unaware of these differences could undoubtedly result in conflicts. As foreign language teachers it is our responsibility to teach not just Spanish, but also the Hispanic culture. *Language is at the heart of culture.* The main goals of our lessons are to strengthen cultural consciousness and intercultural competence.

Objectives
- Students will become aware that communication with others can be affected by their self-perception and their perception of others.
- Students will develop empathy toward interpreting the behavior of other cultural ethnic groups with a more positive attitude.
- Students will engage in group discussions about the feeling and emotions that occur when one is misunderstood.
- Students will sharpen their verbal and writing skills through discussions and compositions of a movie and skits.

Materials
- Video camera
- Videocassette of skits
- Television
- VCR
- Video *Fools Rush In* (Columbia Pictures, 1996), 109 minutes. Romantic comedy of the relationship between a Mexican American woman and an Anglo-Saxon man and the conflicts that arise because of their cultural differences
- Handouts of instructions for writing activities and assignment

Daily Lesson Plan and Activities
I.   Introduction Lesson

    A. Show skits of interpersonal interactions (See Appendix A)

    B. Discussion of skits in class (See Appendix B)

continued

Lesson 11.12 *(continued)*

    II. Development Lesson

        A. Show video, *Fools Rush In*

        B. Group discussion of movie

        C. Fill out worksheet while watching movie (See Appendix C)

        D. Composition assignment (See Appendix D)

    III. Conclusion/Evaluation

        A. Students act out own skits in front of class (See Appendix E)

Skits of Interpersonal Interactions

- The skits portray interactions between two friends, one of Hispanic and the other of Anglo-Saxon background. Our high school students are beginning to form more complex social bonds and are dating. These are situations they may encounter and, possibly, misinterpret when interacting with a Hispanic person.
- Four sample skits (See Appendix A):
  1. Guy and girl walking on sidewalk
  2. Holding hands
  3. Casual touching while talking
  4. Kissing on the cheek
- Discussion Questions (See Appendix B)

Video: *Fools Rush In*

- The video provides an accurate portrayal of an interracial relationship between Isabel Fuentes, a Mexican American woman, and Alex Whitman, an Anglo-Saxon man. Problems arise between the couple and the respective families due to negative misconceptions about each other's cultures.
- Students are required to:
  1. Write a few Spanish sentences on key scenes during the movie (See Appendix C)
  2. Write a composition over the movie for homework (See Appendix D)
- Also, the class will have an open discussion in Spanish after watching the movie (sample questions below)
  1. To what extent were these interactions simply misunderstandings rather than displays of ethnocentrism?
  2. What do you feel you have gained from this video?

Evaluation
Oral and Visual

- In groups of four, students will write their own skit to represent a misunderstanding between two different cultures. They do not need to portray a dating/friendship situation between the Hispanic

Lesson 11.12 *(continued)*

and Anglo-Saxon cultures. Students may research other cultures, but they have to make sure they are not basing the skits on stereotypes. Each skit should be 3 to 5 minutes in length and in Spanish. All groups will perform the skit in class and will be videotaped.

- Handout with instructions on Appendix E.

Written

- Movie compositions will be peer-evaluated before they are turned in.
- Grades will be based on correct grammar, punctuation, and sentence structure.

Appendix A
Teacher Fact Sheet

Homemade Skits on Dating and Friendship

- When a guy and a girl are walking down a sidewalk, it is customary for the guy to walk on the "street side" and for the girl to walk on the "inside" of the sidewalk. It is a sign of security and protection toward the girl.

    Sample take: When a guy and a girl get to a sidewalk, the girl tries to move to the inside of the walk. He resists her attempt to cross in front of him and looks confused.

- Holding hands is very common among friends in Hispanic cultures. Friends can hold hands without it being a "serious" move or sexual in nature.

    Sample take: While walking down a sidewalk the girl reaches out to hold the guy's hand. He instantly pulls his hand out of the way. She tries to hold his hand once more and he pulls it away again.

- Hispanic cultures are known for having very limited (or no) personal space. Ordinarily, Hispanic people will reach over and touch the person they are talking to without realizing it. A problem arises when a Hispanic person talks to someone from a different culture where personal space is well defined and respected. A small, unconscious touch can be misinterpreted as flirting, invasion of space, or disrespect.

    Sample take: The skit may involve a situation such as having a guy come over to watch TV at a girl's house.

Guy: Hi, how are you?

Girl: Fine, come on in. How are you?

Guy: What were you doing?

Girl: I was just sitting here flipping through the channels. (They sit on the couch)

Guy: There's a football game on channel 2, if you want to watch that . . .

Girl: Oh really, who's playing?

Guy: The (team 1) vs. the (team 2).

continued

Lesson 11.12 *(continued)*

Girl: Oh, I'm a big fan of the (team 1)! (reaching over and touching his leg)

Guy: (overreacts either by saying he has a girlfriend or taking the girl's touch as a sexual come-on)

- Hispanic friends and families kiss on the cheek when greeting each other hello and saying goodbye. It is not unusual for a Hispanic person to extend this expression to people from other cultures, unknowingly (possibly) invading their personal space.

    Sample take: The girl sees her guy friend sitting at a table in the library and goes up to him to say hello. She leans in to kiss him on the cheek but he leans back trying to avoid getting "too close."

Appendix B
Discussion Questions over Skits

- How does being aware of differences in personal interactions with people from other cultures help you become more aware of your own culture?
- Do you think that being unfamiliar with the Hispanic culture presented in the skits might lead you to make assumptions about their behavior (that may not necessarily be true)?
- How would you react to an unfamiliar action directed to you? Would you confront the person?
- What do you think you can do to resolve a situation of misunderstanding?

Appendix C

Nombre _____

Fecha _____

Película: *Fools Rush In*

Instucciones: Escribe de tres a cinco oraciones sobre cada una de las siguientes escenas de la película.

1. Cena de familia en case de Isabel

_____

_____

_____

_____

2. Alex regresa a su casa y está decorada la familia de Isabel

_____

_____

_____

Lesson 11.12 *(continued)*

3. La visita inesperada de los padres de Alex

    _____

    _____

    _____

    _____

4. Celbración del 5 de Mayo con los padres de Alex e Isabel

    _____

    _____

    _____

    _____

Appendix D

Nombre _____

Fecha _____

Composición sobre la película *Fools Rush In*

Instrucciones: Escribe tres o más párrafos sobre la película que vimos en clase. !Sé creativo! Cuenta la historia tal y como sucedió o describe lo que pasó después que nació el bebé de Alex e Isabel.

_____

_____

_____

_____

_____

Appendix E

Nombre _____

Fecha _____

Actividad Especial

continued

Lesson 11.12 *(continued)*

La última actividad de esta lección es una actividad en grupo. Tú y tres de tus compañeros de clase (grupos de cuatro personas) escribirán su propio "dramita" de un malentendido entre dos culturas. Las culturas no tienen que ser las mismas que utilizamos en clase (Hispana y Anglo-Sajona). El dramita, de no más de 3 a 5 minutos de largo, va a ser actuado en español y grabado en clase. Piensa bien en lo que tú quieres hacer y trata de no representar estéreotipos negativos e innecesarios de las culturas que uses.

_____

_____

_____

_____

_____

Reprinted with permission from the authors.

Goal Four: Combating Racism, Sexism, Prejudice, and Discrimination

Combating racism, sexism, prejudice, and discrimination means lessening negative attitudes and behavior that are based on gender bias and misconceptions about the inferiority of races and cultures different from one's own. Emphasis is on clearing up myths and stereotypes associated with gender, different races, and ethnic groups. Basic human similarities are stressed. The following lists several crucial assumptions that underlie this goal:

- It is worthwhile for educators to focus on the reduction of racial/ethnic prejudice and discrimination even though powerful sectors of the society and the world do not presently value this goal.
- It is appropriate for schools to teach certain humanistic and democratic values, such as the negative effects of racism and sexism.
- A reduction of racial/ethnic prejudice and discrimination is possible through appropriate educational experiences.

The goal is to develop antiracist, antisexist behavior based on awareness of historical and contemporary evidence of individual, institutional, and cultural racism and sexism in the United States and elsewhere in the world. It is directed at developing greater awareness of the existence and impact of racism, sexism, and ethnic prejudice and discrimination in U.S. society as well as within other nations and across national boundaries. Distinctions between cultural, individual, and institutional racism and sexism are important. Prejudice and discrimination are studied within the contexts of American and world history, science, literature, and the arts. Teaching efforts to reduce prejudice and discrimination are directed at clarifying students' values and at building moral reasoning skills. This, it is hoped, leads to understandings, attitudes, and behaviors that are consistent with basic democratic ideals, such as liberty, justice, and equal opportunity. Global issues related to Western colonialism and violations of human rights are also a focus.

Science and health teachers can debunk myths surrounding the concept of race and teach facts about the biological attributes shared by all humans. Scientists estimate that over 90 percent of one's genetic makeup is shared with all members of the human species, leaving only 6 to 7 percent related to gender and racial attributes and the remainder to individual variance. Misconceptions about the origins of the races and erroneous beliefs about the superiority of some races must be cleared up. Social studies educators can focus on the power dimension of racism. The fact that racial justice still eludes us must be made clear, and the possibility that our quest for racial justice has been misdirected (and needs to be redirected) must be considered.[54]

Teachers in all content areas can help students develop skills in detecting bias in texts and media. In math and general business classes, students can learn about racist loan shark practices that keep people in poverty while also learning percentages and interest rates. Typing teachers can include news articles that discuss racism in their typing skill assignments. Teachers in the humanities can use selected pieces of literature, art, and music to discuss themes related to racism and prejudice.

Positive interracial attitudes can also be fostered without modifying the curriculum extensively if the school population is racially and culturally diverse. Wherever students have a chance to work together to achieve a common goal, chances are excellent for improving mutual respect and appreciation. Sports and team efforts of every kind, musical or dramatic performances, and cooperative class projects are examples of activities many teachers use to develop positive interracial contact experiences.

A necessary first step in creating a revised curriculum is to face the facts of a racist past and present. It is essential to recognize the impact of racism on the oppressor as well as on the oppressed.

As painful as it may be, children and young adults must face facts about the racist past. Under the guidance of knowledgeable and caring teachers, minorities and nonminorities can gain insight into a social context that helps explain current patterns of poverty, protest, and apathy as well as interracial isolation, stereotypes, misconceptions, and conflict. These insights can help convert anger, rage, denial, guilt, and paternalism into the commitment and knowledge needed to combat racism and social injustice wherever it occurs.

Since racial equality and justice still elude us, an emphasis on combating racism is imperative. This necessity, however, must not blind us to other manifestations of

Positive intergroup contact experiences can be built into the curriculum.

prejudice and discrimination, such as those directed at lower socioeconomic groups, the gay community, and certain religious groups (e.g., the Baha'is, Universalists). The fight against racism can be extended into a broader fight for universal human rights and respect for human dignity.

Emphasizing unity through human similarities is one of the most positive and important ways to reduce racism and other types of prejudice and discrimination. Awareness of the common features of human life and the ways humans are interconnected is vital to intergroup cooperation and harmony. Lee Anderson, a social scientist and one of the founders of global education, vividly illustrates the possibilities of what might be achieved in his imaginary world-centered school, Terra.[55] The philosophy behind Terra school generates five overarching purposes:

- To develop students' understanding of themselves as individuals
- To develop students' understanding of themselves as members of the human species
- To develop students' understanding of themselves as inhabitants and dependents of planet Earth
- To develop students' understanding of themselves as participants in global society
- To develop within students the competencies requisite to living intelligently and responsibly as individuals, human beings, earthlings, and members of global society[56]

The following list of questions captures how these purposes can be turned into classroom activity.

What Do You Know about Being Human?

1. How are human beings like all other living things?
2. How are human beings more like some living things than others? Are you more like animals than plants? How? Are you more like a jellyfish or a bird? How? Are you more like a bear or a lizard? How? Are you more like a monkey or a cow? How?
3. How are human beings unlike all other living things.[57]

In Anderson's school, the emphasis is on understanding human culture, and the curriculum is based on a program called The Human Way of Living. The curriculum at this twenty-first century high school is organized around five major programs:

- Studies of individual development and behavior
- Studies of the human species
- Studies of humankind's planetary and cosmic environments
- Development of human competencies
- Social service, political action, and work-study[58]

How can we develop this world-centered perspective in the absence of adequate resources and curriculum materials? Considerations such as the following can be used as evaluative criteria with even the weakest materials.

- Look for evidence of ethnocentrism, the view that one's culture is the standard by which other cultures should be judged.
- Look for evidence that foreign countries are seen too simplistically, with no discussion of the various microcultures within each society. Make the same evaluation with respect to ethnic groups: Are all members of a particular group assumed to share similar ideas, habits, and values, or is the diversity within each group recognized?
- Consider whether the text presents conflicts between groups, nations, or cultures in an overly simplified manner: White settlers versus Indians, the North versus the South during the American Civil War, labor versus management, the Communists versus the Free World.
- Watch for subtle suggestions that the so-called advanced civilizations are superior to, or must offer guidance to, less modern societies.
- Look for evidence of confusion arising from ignorance of specific cultures: for example, traditional Chinese women pictured in the dress of traditional Japanese women.
- Look for the erroneous use of Western assumptions to evaluate non-Western settings. For example, if an author states that "Many Islamic males are non-monogamous," does the word "nonmonogamous" itself carry overtones that may mislead the reader?

- Consider whether the learner is encouraged to imagine the world as others might see it, to understand the perceptions and interpretations of other cultures.
- Look for a recognition that, despite cultural differences, people in all societies share the basic similarities of being human.[59]

Lesson Plans That Combat Racism, Sexism, Prejudice, and Discrimination

Lesson 11.13

"All Men Are Created Equal"   *Don Adams*

Essential Question
Has America lived up to its own ideals?

Goals and Rationale
Perhaps more than any nation in history, the United States is founded on a set of definable ideals. Indeed, even before the nation itself existed, the so-called new world seemed to offer almost limitless possibilities to those who came from Europe. The Puritans, for example, hoped to establish a "city upon a hill" which would serve as a model for others to follow. Others saw it as a "blank slate" on which they could write a new destiny of their own making. To be sure, not all of those who came here did so for idealistic purposes—the pursuit of wealth, the sometimes forcible conversion of natives to Christianity, and other less high-minded purposes were at work as well. Yet from the early days of its "discovery" by Europeans, the new world has been seen as a place in which men could create societies from scratch, and in so doing leave behind the problems of the old world.

None of America's ideals is more profound than the statement "all men are created equal." Formally expressed in our Declaration of Independence, it has served as the organizing principle of much of our history. It has been the rallying cry for the oppressed, the lure for immigrants from all over the world, and the basis for many of our laws. At the same time, its very simplicity and profundity has made America's shortcomings stand out in painful relief. Many of the same men who wrote it into our founding documents owned slaves; women have been able to vote for less than half of our history; Native Americans have been systematically robbed of their land. This disparity between American ideals and American practices is among the most important aspects of American history, and no understanding of America is complete without examining it.

This lesson (and Lesson 9.23) will give students the opportunity to examine this disparity. After an opening lesson that introduces the theme and analytical framework for the unit, the students could examine five specific episodes in American history: the creation of Mount Rushmore, the internment

Lesson 11.13 *(continued)*

of Japanese Americans in World War II, the integration of Central High School in Little Rock, the passing of the 1964 Civil Rights Act, and the Supreme Court's ruling in *Grutter v. Bollinger*. Episodes such as these should be examined within their historical and cultural context, and students could compare American practice with the ideal of "all men are created equal." The students would not only gain important knowledge about these episodes, they would be able to trace the evolution of American practice over time. Ultimately, they should be able to critically assess the impact of the phrase "all men are created equal" on American history, up to and including the present.

National Council for the Social Studies Themes

USH 1.1—Explain major ideas about government and key rights, rooted in the colonial and founding periods, which are embedded in key documents.

NCSS Theme VI—Power, Authority, and Governance

    i. evaluate the extent to which governments achieve their stated ideals at home and abroad

NCSS Theme I—Culture

    a. interpret patterns of behavior reflecting values and attitudes that contribute or pose obstacles to cross-cultural understanding

Objectives

By the end of the lesson, students will be able to:

- Identify passages from key American documents which speak to the idea of equality.
- Distinguish race as a biological consideration from race as a social construct
- Distinguish between "male/female" and "masculine/feminine"
- Begin to compare American ideals with American conduct

Materials

Term sheet
Handout for response groups
PowerPoint slides/transparencies

- Title
- Quote: Declaration of Independence
- Quote: Notes on the State of Virginia
- Image: William Massey
- Image: Sean Combs
- Image: Lebron James
- Lecture slide: What is race?
- Lecture slide: What is gender?

continued

Lesson 11.13 *(continued)*

- Image: Rosie the Riveter
- Quotation: Virginia Declaration of Rights
- Quotation: Fourteenth Amendment
- Quotation: Martin Luther King Jr.

PowerPoint projector/transparency overhead projector

Procedures

1. Anticipatory set: (5 minutes)

   - Free-write in interactive notebooks: What makes America different from other nations?

2. Lecture with slides: (20 minutes)

   - Using slides, review dichotomy between Jeffersonian practices
   - Pose question: How can one man hold such contradictory views?
   - Transition to discussion of race and gender construction
   - Discuss difference between "intergroup variation" and "intragroup variation" even if one group performs better than another by certain measures, does that automatically mean the difference is innate? Even if it is, what do group averages tell us about any given individual?
   - Ask class to analyze the Rosie the Riveter image. How does the image compare to the old nursery rhyme about "sugar and spice and everything nice?" How do coveralls and muscles compare to standard notions of femininity? At the same time, why are her eyebrows plucked and her nails polished? Why is she pretty?
   - Discuss power, significance of the idea that "all men are created equal." Discuss passages from the Constitution. Discuss the impact of Martin Luther King Jr. Trace over time.

3. Response groups (10 minutes)

   - Place students into four groups, hand out instruction sheets
   - Have students answer questions and be prepared to discuss with class

4. Debrief (10 minutes)

   - Ask groups for answers to questions, invite others to agree/disagree

Evaluation

1. Formative questions and work with pairs will establish degree of engagement and comprehension.

2. Group responses will determine distinction between biological versus cultural identities.

3. Summative project at end of unit will serve as final gauge of learning.

Appendix

For copies of Declaration of Independence and other documents, see Avalon Project (www.yale.edu/lawweb/avalon/avalon.htm).

Lesson 11.13 *(continued)*

Term Sheet
Fourteenth Amendment
Virginia Declaration of Rights
Martin Luther King Jr.

Answer these questions following the lecture, reading, or your own research:

1. What is race?

2. What is the difference between "masculine/feminine" and "male/female?"

3. What does the Rosie the Riveter poster tell us about gender roles during WWII?

4. Compare Thomas Jefferson's words in the Declaration of Independence to his words in *Notes on the State of Virginia*.

5. How can we understand the contradiction between America's founders' ideals and their practices?

Response Group Instructions
Answer the questions for your group *not* from your own perspective but from society's. Be prepared to share your answers with the class.

Group 1

What does it mean to be a man? List some of the traits associated with men.
Do boys cry?

continued

Lesson 11.13 *(continued)*

What kind of jobs are appropriate for men? What kind of jobs are inappropriate?
If two working people have a young child, and the child gets sick, who stays home from work, the
   husband or the wife?
Which is more important for a man: looks or intelligence?
Where do these ideas come from? List some of the sources.

Group 2

What does it mean to be a woman? List some of the traits associated with women.
Are women tough?
What kinds of jobs are appropriate for women? What kinds of jobs are inappropriate?
Should women work outside the home, or stay at home as full-time mothers?
Which is more important for a woman: looks or intelligence?
Where do these ideas come from? List some of the sources.

Group 3

What does it mean to be White? List some of the traits associated with White people
If a Black person is walking down the street and a group of young White men is walking toward him,
   should he be afraid? Will he cross the street or simply walk by them?
Can White men jump? Can they dance?
Is it more desirable for a White person to be good at sports or academics?
Where do these ideas come from? List some of the sources.

Group 4

What does it mean to be Black? List some of the traits associated with Black people.
If a White person is walking down the street and a group of young Black men is walking toward him,
   should he be afraid? Will he cross the street or simply walk by them?
Is it more desirable for a Black person to be good at sports or academics?
How does the media portray Black people?
Why are there black magazines, TV stations, and other media?

Reprinted with permission of the author.

Lesson 11.14

Can You Recognize Racism?

Instructions

First work alone. Put a check before each statement you think is an example of racism. Then work
with your small group and try to agree on the examples of racism. (Your group will receive a packet

Lesson 11.14 *(continued)*

of statement cards to make the task easier.) Choose one member of your group to share your decisions with everyone.

A. Which of the following quotations or descriptive statements are examples of racism? Indicate these with a check (✓).

1. _____ "A Black family moved into our neighborhood this week."

2. _____ The principal interviewed two equally outstanding candidates, one Black and the other Latino. She selected the Black teacher because her school had several Latino teachers but no Black teachers.

3. _____ In 1882 immigration laws excluded the Chinese, and the Japanese were excluded in 1908.

4. _____ During the 1960s civil rights movement, Mrs. Viola Liuzzo, a White civil rights worker from Michigan, was shot by White southern segregationists.

5. _____ Between 1892 and 1921 nearly 2,400 African Americans were lynched by vigilante mobs who were never brought to justice.

6. _____ "The best basketball players on our team this year are Black."

7. _____ The band director discouraged Black students from playing the flute or piccolo because he believed it was too difficult for them to excel on these instruments.

8. _____ When Mrs. Wallace, an African American woman from Detroit, visited a predominantly White university in northern Michigan to see her son play basketball, she was seriously injured in a car accident. She refused a blood transfusion because she was afraid of being contaminated by White blood.

9. _____ When Stacey Russell, an African American undergraduate, went through rush, the girls of an all-White sorority decided not to pledge her because several members threatened to move out if they did.

10. _____ The geography textbook described the peoples of Nigeria as primitive and underdeveloped.

11. _____ The children who attended an elementary school in southwest Texas spoke only Spanish at home. When they came to school all the books and intelligence tests were in English. Nearly all of the children were placed in remedial classes or in classes for the mentally retarded.

12. _____ Mr. Jones said, "It is true that Indians who still live on reservations live in extreme poverty. But this is because they refuse to give up their traditions and a culture which is obsolete in the modern world."

13. _____ The U.S. Constitution allowed each slave to be counted as three-fifths of a person.

14. _____ The reporter wrote that "Toni Morrison is a brilliant writer who accurately portrays much of the Black experience in America."

15. _____ When John brought home a new friend, his father was shocked and angry. Peter, the new friend, was of Japanese origin and John's father had been seriously wounded by the Japanese in World War II. John's father refused to allow Peter to visit again.

continued

Lesson 11.14 *(continued)*

16. _____ In 1896 the Supreme Court ruled that separate facilities for the races were legal as long as they were *equal*. This resulted in separate schools, churches, restaurants, restrooms, swimming pools, theaters, doctors' offices, neighborhoods, Bibles used in court, and so forth.

17. _____ When Mary Adams wanted to find a place in the school cafeteria, the only vacant chair was at a table seating five Black girls. Mary, who is White, was afraid to join them.

18. _____ In California today, approximately 10 percent of the population is Black, while 41 percent of those in prison are Black. Blacks generally have more financial difficulty than Whites in hiring a lawyer and plea bargaining.

B. Select one member to write your group's decisions below on the decision sheet and another person to share the results with the rest of us. Be prepared to explain your reasons if necessary.

1. The following statements are examples of either individual or institutional racism: (Write numbers and a word or two for description, and arrange them according to those that refer to racist individuals or to racist policies and institutions.)

Individual Racism	Institutional Racism

2. Our group's definition of racism is:

_____

_____

_____

3. The main difference between individual and institutional racism is:

_____

_____

_____

Lesson 11.14 *(continued)*

4. Examples of individual and institutional racism that we know about in our community are:

Individual racism:

_____

_____

_____

Institutional racism:

_____

_____

_____

Lesson 11.15
Hidden Messages in Children's Literature

Introduction
This lesson can be used at any grade level; the written decision-making sheet can be omitted for young children, and the wording made more appropriate for advanced high school youth. Eventually, the lesson could lead to an examination of ethnic bias in literature. Experience has shown that it is often most effective to begin with sex bias, since everyone can identify with being either male or female. The lesson could fit into a variety of subjects. Possible units of study include images in literature or advertising, family relationships and sex role expectations, Title Nine and athletics, careers, and political behavior.

Objectives
- Students will analyze how children's literature and other socialization agents work to shape the attitudes and behaviors of male and female children.
- Students will begin to develop strategies for detecting biased images in media.

continued

Lesson 11.15 *(continued)*

Student Activity

Each class member is given one or more children's stories.

For Sexism	For Racism
Hansel and Gretel	*Mary Poppins*
Snow White	*Robinson Crusoe*
Little Red Riding Hood	*The Ugly Duckling*
Policeman Small	*The Slave Dancer*
Cinderella	*Pippi Longstocking*
Rumpelstiltskin	*The Five Chinese Brothers*
Sleeping Beauty	*Charlie and the Chocolate Factory*
The Three Little Pigs	*Doctor Doolittle*
The Giving Tree	*Sounder*
I'm Glad I'm a Boy	*Magdalena*
I'm Glad I'm a Girl	
Pippi Longstocking	
Tomas Takes Charge	

1. I have examined the following books:

   _____

   _____

   _____

   I would like to include these other books:

   _____

   _____

   _____

2. Females tend to be described in these ways:

   _____

   _____

   _____

Lesson 11.15 *(continued)*

Males tend to be described in these ways:

_____

_____

_____

3. One or more of these books try to make children think and behave in these ways (list as many examples as possible):

_____

_____

_____

4. The five most common characteristics associated with women and girls are:

_____

_____

_____

In what ways does our society support these images of females?

_____

_____

_____

In what ways does our society reject these images of females?

_____

_____

_____

5. The five most common characteristics associated with men and boys are:

_____

_____

_____

continued

Lesson 11.15 *(continued)*

In what ways does our society support these images of males?

_____

_____

_____

In what ways does our society reject these images of males?

_____

_____

_____

6. Based on this evidence, what differences do you predict between the behavior of males and females in our society?

_____

_____

_____

Lesson 11.16
Reading, Constructing, and Interpreting Graphs   Jean Seger

Introduction
This lesson is designed for high school students. It takes approximately two class periods. Students
should have had preliminary instruction on percents, elementary statistics, and the construction of bar,
line, and circle graphs. The lesson will instruct students on constructing, reading, and interpreting
graphs and tables while having them formulate ideas on discrimination based on racial prejudices.

Lesson 11.16 *(continued)*

Performance Objectives

- The student will be able to correctly read Tables 1, 2, and 3. Upon looking at the tables the student will be able to answer orally or in writing questions concerning the information in the tables.
- Given access to Table 1, the student will be able to construct a line graph comparing the median incomes of males and females among Blacks, Asians and Pacific Islanders, Hispanics, and non-Hispanic whites. The student will construct a second line graph to show the percentage of persons in each ethnic group that lives below the poverty line.

Table 1 ▨ Median Income, Number and Percent Below Poverty Level of Noninstitutionalized Persons 18 Years Old and Over, by Sex, Race and Hispanic Origin in 1998

| | 1998 | | | | | |
| | Number with Income (1000) | | Median Income | | Number below Poverty (1000) | Percent below Poverty |
Persons	Male	Female	Male	Female		
Black	9,776	12,272	19,321	13,137	9,091	26.1
Asian and Pacific Islander	3,500	3,591	25,124	15,228	1,360	12.5
Hispanic	9,617	8,405	17,257	10,862	8,070	25.6
Non-Hispanic White	71,707	74,106	29,862	15,217	23,454	10.5

Source: Adapted from U.S. Census Bureau, *Statistical Abstract of the United States: 2000*, No. 751. Median Income of Persons with Income in Constant (1998) Dollars by Sex, Race, and Hispanic Origin: 1980 to 1998, and No. 754. Persons Below Poverty Level and Below 125 Percent of Poverty Level: 1970 to 1998.

- Given access to Tables 2 and 3, the student will be able to choose three professions and the corresponding data and construct circle graphs for each one.
- The student will be able to express his or her opinion, either orally or in writing, on the causes and effects of the income similarities and differences among males and females across the ethnic groups. (As an alternative, students could generate questions that could help explain the similarities and differences. These questions could lead to small group research projects to find answers to the students' questions. Interactions between income by schooling across race and sex could also be investigated using new Census 2010 data not available for this edition.)
- The student will be able to express his or her opinion either orally or in writing on the economic, social, and psychological ramifications for individuals in the upper and lower income levels, compared with those in poverty. Students should also be able to express an opinion about why some ethnic groups have higher poverty rates than others.

continued

Lesson 11.16 *(continued)*

Table 2 ✖ Occupation of Employed Persons 16 Years Old and Older by Race and Sex, 1999 (percentage of total)

	1999			
			Percent of Total	
Occupation	Total Employed (1000)	Female	Black	Hispanic
Total	133,488	46.5	11.3	10.3
Managerial and professional specialty	40,467	49.5	8.0	5.0
Technical, sales, and administrative support	38,921	63.8	11.2	8.4
Service occupations	17,915	60.4	18.3	15.2
Precision production, craft, and repair	14,593	9.0	8.0	12.8
Operators, fabricators, and laborers	18,167	24.1	15.7	16.6
Farming, forestry, and fishing	3,426	19.7	5.0	23.1

Source: Adapted from U.S. Census Bureau, *Statistical Abstract of the United States: 2000*, No. 669. Employed Civilians by Occupation, Sex, Race, and Hispanic Origin: 1983 to 1999.

Table 3 ✖ Profession of Employed Persons 16 Years Old and Older by Race and Sex, 1999 (percentage of total)

	1999			
			Percent of Total	
Occupation	Total Employed (1000)	Female	Black	Hispanic
Professional Specialty	20,883	53.5	8.4	4.5
Architects	194	15.7	2.3	4.4
Engineers	2,081	10.6	4.6	3.5
Mathematical and computer engineers	1,847	31.1	7.5	3.6
Natural scientists	578	30.1	3.7	3.6
Physicians	720	24.5	5.7	4.8
Dentists	173	16.5	1.9	3.1
Registered nurses	2,128	92.9	9.6	3.1
Teachers, college and university	978	42.4	6.5	4.2
Teachers, except college and university	5,277	74.9	9.9	5.4
Social workers	813	71.4	24.2	7.4
Clergy	352	14.2	10.3	5.2

Lesson 11.16 *(continued)*

Table 3 ☒ *(continued)*

| | | 1999 | | |
| | | | Percent of Total | |
Occupation	Total Employed (1000)	Female	Black	Hispanic
Lawyers and judges	964	28.9	5.2	3.9
Writers, artists, entertainers, and athletes	2,454	49.9	6.6	5.3
Authors	148	55.2	7.3	2.3
Musicians and composers	172	35.6	9.2	7.1
Actors and directors	129	38.8	10.7	5.1
Announcers	50	21.4	8.9	9.2
Athletes	110	28.0	19.0	3.4

Source: U.S. Census Bureau, *Statistical Abstract of the United States: 2000*, No. 669. Employed Civilians by Occupation, Sex, Race, and Hispanic Origin: 1983 to 1999.

Strategy

In all lessons students will work in groups of two.

Day 1

Materials

1. Poster displaying the information in Table 1
2. Individual copies of the table
3. Rulers

Activities

1. Each group will receive a copy of Table 1, and a larger model of the table will appear on the front blackboard.
2. The teacher will direct students in the method for reading the table to find the median income of individuals within each race and sex group; the teacher will also explain the meaning of the numbers and percents in each column.
3. The teacher will ask students to orally (*a*) state the median income earned by individuals; (*b*) compare the incomes of males and females in each ethnic group; and (*c*) compare the poverty rate across the ethnic groups.

continued

Lesson 11.16 *(continued)*

4. Working in pairs, each group will construct a line graph based on the table.

5. Using the line graphs that students have constructed, the teacher will ask students to state their views on the following questions: Is there a correlation between income and sex or race? Are the large differences in median income between racial groups fair? What about the income difference between males and females? Do we have enough information here to answer these questions? What else do we need to know? How can we find some answers?

Day 2
Materials

1. Poster displaying the information in Tables 2 and 3
2. Individual copies of the table
3. Rulers, protractors, and compasses

Activities

1. Each group will receive a copy of Tables 2 and 3, and a larger model of these tables will appear on the front blackboard.

2. The teacher will direct students in the method of reading the chart to find the number and percent of population each racial group comprises in a profession.

3. The teacher will ask students to orally (*a*) state the percent of females, Whites, Blacks, and Hispanic Americans in each of the professions listed; (*b*) compare the percents between racial and gender groups; and (*c*) compare the percent of a race in each profession to the percent that race comprises of the U.S. population; repeat the comparison for gender.

4. Working in pairs, each group will construct circle graphs for three of the professions listed.

5. Using the circle graphs that groups have constructed, ask students to orally state their views on the following: Are Blacks and Hispanic Americans adequately represented in professions, based on their population in the United States? Are females? What are the negative ramifications for groups who are not adequately represented in professions? Students should consider economic, social, and psychological ramifications. Will the percent of women and minority races in professions increase or decrease in the future?

Source: This lesson is an updated and modified version of a lesson by Jean Seger that appeared in previous editions. The updates were supplied by C. Bennett.

Lesson 11.17
Women in the World *Georgia Duncan-Ladd*

Goal
To combat racism, prejudice, and discrimination perpetrated globally, nationally, and locally[60]

Core Values
Respect for human diversity and universal human rights.

Educational Goals
Students will understand the global experiences of women and their contributions to their communities.

Objectives
Students will be able to identify, list, and compare the similarities and differences, the continuities and contrasts among women around the world.

Lesson Opener
Present the students with two exercises using the handouts: "Traits That Are Female or Male" and "Traits That Jobs Require." Compare the results upon completion of the lesson. (See lists below.)

Traits That Are Female or Male
Which traits do you believe are naturally female or male?

1. Emotional
2. Creative thinking
3. Dependent
4. Cruel
5. Forceful
6. Passive
7. Yielding
8. Aggressive
9. Gossipy
10. Natural leader
11. Desires to be protected
12. Selfish
13. Good in math
14. Intuitive
15. Caring
16. Creative
17. Intelligent
18. Dominant
19. Warm personality
20. Holds up in a crisis

Traits That Jobs Require
Using the twenty traits as a checklist, pick the two traits you consider most important for each of the occupations listed here. The jobs are suitable for women and men.

1. U.S. senator
2. Nurse
3. Secretary
4. Electrician
5. Salesperson
6. Soldier
7. Banker
8. Cook
9. Librarian
10. Florist

continued

Lesson 11.17 *(continued)*

11. Lawyer
12. Painter
13. Bartender
14. Mathematician
15. Nursery-school teacher

16. Engineer
17. Construction worker
18. Housekeeper
19. Interior designer
20. Social worker

Instructional Activities

Most women in the world, like most men, lead humble lives. What is striking, though, is how different women's ordinary lives are from men's ordinary lives. We cannot understand our world without understanding the everyday experiences of women. We cannot assume that all women are the same or in the same situation, but we can assume that women everywhere are worse off than men. They have less power, less autonomy, more work, less money, and more responsibility. Nowhere in the world are women [societally] equal to men.

For women, there are no developed countries. While many countries provide formally for sexual equality in law, very few governments have legislation to protect specific job and marriage rights. Nowhere do women have full equal rights with men. Women are biologically stronger, they live longer than men, and naturally outnumber them. In countries where they do not, it is only because of the effects of war, forced migration in search of work, or severe and systematic discrimination. (See the first section, "Women in the World," from *The Penguin Atlas of Women in the World*, Third Edition, 2003.)

Women everywhere share primary responsibility for having and rearing children, for forming and maintaining families, and for contraception. Globally they share the fight for women's rights, for other civil rights, and for peace. They are victims of rape, health traumas from illegal abortions, and pornography. The fate of women is a critical detriment to human society.

1. Discuss one historian's view of the development of the traditional American life. (Adapted from "Backgrounds of the American Family" by Willystine Goodsell, from *Marriage and the Family* by Howard Becker and Reuben Hill, eds.)

2. Have students answer and discuss the following questions:
   a. What was the position of women in England and America in the 1700s?
   b. How does Goodsell think the American family has changed?
   c. What are the key factors that influenced the American family to change?

3. Have the students submit a brief analysis of their view of the following question: What do you think was gained by the changes in the American family just described? What may have been lost? What other conditions in the United States might have led to role changes?

4. Using the *Penguin Atlas of Women in the World* (see above), present and discuss the following topics and data:

Marriage:	Young brides, domestic disorders, social surgery, single states
Motherhood:	Mothers, population policies, contraception and abortion, birth and death, birth care, families
Work:	Time budgets, agriculture, labor force, out to work, migrant workers, job ghettos, earnings, job protection

Lesson 11.17 *(continued)*

Resources:	Access to means, education, refugees
Welfare:	Illness and health, poverty
Authority:	The vote, government, crime, military service, body and mind, the media
Body politics:	Beauty contest, sex for sale, rape
Change:	Channels of change, protest

Materials

Handouts "Traits That Are Female or Male" and "Traits That Jobs Require," *Male and Female in Today's World, Curriculum Development*, Harcourt Brace Jovanovich Inc., 757 Third Avenue, New York, NY, 10017, 14–15, 20–21.

Copies of "What's the Difference" trivia by Jane Barr Stump, in *How Men and Women Compare*, William Morrow, 1985.

Blackboard

Overhead projector

Practice Activities

Guided practice: The reading of graphs and tables to understand the data presented along with questions and discussions of the status of women in the world. (See above source *The Penguin Atlas of Women in the World*, 2003.)

Independent practice: Students will be divided into groups and asked to bring in evidence of male and female roles in other cultures. These will be presented to the class by the groups as a paper.

Evaluation

Based on student verbal and written demonstration of the objectives of the lesson.

Reprinted with permission from the author.

Goal Five: Raising Awareness of the State of the Planet and Global Dynamics

An awareness of the state of the planet and global dynamics consists of the second and fourth dimensions of Hanvey's "attainable global perspective." Hanvey defines his second dimension as an "awareness of prevailing world conditions and developments, including emergent conditions and trends, e.g., population growth, migrations, economic conditions, resources and physical environment, political developments, science and technology, law, health, inter-nation and intra-nation conflicts, etc."[61]

- The world can best be understood as a singular, complex global system.[62]
- An individual's private and collective decisions and behaviors influence for better or worse the future of the world system.[63]
- Multiple loyalties are possible, that is, humans can be committed to a series of concentric groups such as family, religion, nation, and all of humankind.[64]
- Knowledge and understanding of problems facing the global ecosystem will enable and motivate students to participate effectively and responsibly in the world community.

Hanvey stresses examination of the media and political thought when attempting to gain further awareness of global conditions and dynamics. What is important is not whether the information from these sources will shed any light on the subject, but rather the recognition of the students that these sources lack and distort information and, in some cases, even withhold it. Typically, the media focus on extraordinary events, for example, an outbreak in influenza or a rapid decline on the stock exchange rather than on the long-standing poverty of hundreds of millions or endemic malaria. There are significant limits to and distortions in what we can learn from the news media. Political ideology is another source of distortion since it limits access to information about certain nations; for example, the former Soviet Union, Cuba, South Africa, and China during the Cultural Revolution. Political ideology also distorts what we know about the testing of nuclear weapons, and the disposal of nuclear wastes.

Hanvey points out that the technical nature of much of the data about the world is another important deterrent to developing an awareness of the state of the planet. He illustrates his case with an example of the depletion of ozone in the stratosphere. Is this a problem that can be widely understood by the world's populace? Or is it destined to remain "within the private realms of specialists?" Hanvey makes a strong case for the former, provided that educators become involved. "If from the earliest grades on students examined and puzzled over cases where seemingly innocent behaviors—the diet rich in animal protein, the lavish use of fertilizer on the suburban lawn and golf course—are shown to have effects that were both unintended and global in scope, then there could be a receptivity for the kind of information involved in the ozone case."[65] The notion of global "unintended effects" brings us to dimension four, knowledge of global dynamics, which Hanvey defines as "some modest comprehension of key traits and mechanisms of the world system, with emphasis on theories and concepts that may increase intelligent consciousness of global change."[66]

Knowing both that causes and effects are complex and interactive and that "simple events ramify—unbelievably" is essential to an understanding of the world as a system.[67] There are often surprise effects. Hanvey illustrates this with descriptions of unanticipated results, from adding new species to a pond, farm wagons to the Papago community, and the introduction of bottle feeding technology to Third World nations, which led to such surprise effects as infant mortality, poor growth and brain development, and economic loss. How can this goal be developed in the curriculum? Hanvey provides teachers with four targets to help students comprehend technological innovation and change:

1. Sensitize students to the global consequences of technological decisions; for example, stratospheric ozone depletion.
2. Help students imagine the unimaginable, for example, abolishing certain technologies such as nuclear energy because of the problem of nuclear wastes.
3. Examine our beliefs about the naturalness and goodness of technological change and the naturalness and goodness of economic growth.
4. Help students understand the dynamics of feedback and the characteristics of exponential growth.

A world system paradigm similar to Hanvey's is central to the work of most, if not all, global educators in the United States. (It is also an essential part of this book's vision of multicultural education!) Lee Anderson, for example, who is a founding leader in global education, identifies four characteristics of the world system paradigm that are essential to the curriculum:

1. *Humankind as a biologically, historically, and culturally interlinked species of life*
2. *Planet Earth as a global ecosystem*
3. *The global social order as the basis for human social and ecological organization*
4. *Each member of the human species as responsible participatory citizens in the global social order* [68]

 ## Lesson Plans That Develop State of the Planet Awareness

Lesson 11.18
Thinking Peace/Doing Peace
Anna S. Ochoa-Becker

Introduction: A Rationale
The core values of the Bennett model combined with Hanvey's concept of "state of the planet awareness" were used to develop these learning experiences for junior and senior high school students. In this lesson, the focus is *peace*. The activities are designed to promote reflection on the meaning of peace and to promote peaceful practices for the benefit of the future of life on this planet. To bring about a better and more peaceful world, we need to have an awareness of the planet's past and present, as well as a strong recognition of its potential for a more peaceful future. If we cannot visualize a more just and peaceful future, we are not likely to have one.

Central to the existence of peace is the presence of social justice. The theme in the following set of classroom activities is that we cannot have one without the other. When human beings feel oppressed and abused, they are more likely to be angry, degraded, disillusioned, and hostile. They are also more likely to act on those feelings. Hostile actions about injustice were evident in the past: in such events as the storming of the Bastille in France (1789), in our own War of Independence (1776),

continued

Lesson 11.18 *(continued)*

in the riots of the 1960s, frequently among teenage gangs, and in dysfunctional, violence-prone families. The Bennett and Hanvey models advance such core values as responsibility to the world community, appreciation for cultural diversity, reverence of the future, and respect for human dignity and human rights. Taken together, these values serve as a recipe for peace.

"Peace" is a simple five-letter word. Nonetheless, its presence, however important, has been illusive throughout history. Just as importantly, peace is often missing in our personal lives. Someone once wisely said, "Peace begins in the minds of men [and women]" which suggests that peace depends on our ability to come to grips with the issues of social justice as well as in our hopes and dreams for a better future not only for ourselves, but for generations not yet born.

The peoples of this planet have known times when there was no war. However, we cannot conclude that during such times, peace has replaced war. Too often, the end of overt hostilities only means that such activities as bombing, exchange of gunfire, and the taking of war prisoners have terminated. Perhaps, even a peace treaty has been signed. While it is desirable to bring such activities to a close, we all know that it is very easy for hostilities to resume when underlying injustices continue to exist. So, it is in the Middle East, in East Timor, in Kosovo, and among urban gangs who desperately seek power because, from their perspectives, no other avenues appear to be open. We can also look further into our own backyards at civil rights abuse and at the rise in domestic violence that repeatedly targets women and children. These abuses will continue until the underlying injustices are firmly addressed.

Goals

In the learning experiences below two goals have significance:

- to have student-citizens reflect on the meaning of peace personally as well as peace as applied to the public arena
- to have students actively participate in creating a more peaceful and respectful environment.

The second goal represents the phrase coined by Rene DeBois, "thinking locally, acting globally." To reflect about the meaning of peace and social justice followed by deliberate actions that foster a better future is the foundation of peaceful and democratic citizenship.

Classroom Activities: Middle and Secondary Levels

Many of these activities can be adapted for the elementary level.

Activity #1: Discussing Peace: A Beginning

A Startup Activity: Select four or five photographs that depict war and violence (from magazines, newspapers). For older students, teachers can present a print of *Guernica*, Picasso's famous painting that was his response to the Spanish Civil War. (This painting serves as a universal representation of the horror of any and all wars and visually challenges us to explain why human beings permit such violence. It is a dramatic starting point to capture student interest.) After a few moments to examine the pictures carefully, the class can be asked to respond to questions such as: (The teacher can adapt and adjust these questions as appropriate for particular classes.).

- What may have prompted the violent actions in the photograph?
- What do you think are the reasons for such violence?

Lesson 11.18 *(continued)*

- Can war ever be justified? This is an open question. We sometimes hear people say that the last good war was World War II. What is meant by that?
- Can these problems be settled in other ways? How?
- How can we reduce the chances of war?
- What are the ways we can help to prevent war? What can we do to encourage peace? Are these the answers to ways for encouraging peace?

Activity #2: Peace—Making a Conceptual Map

Involve the class in making a conceptual map by asking students to think of ideas that come to mind when they hear the word "peace." Their ideas can be placed on an overhead transparency, on the blackboard, or on a newsprint pad as students present them. When 10–12 ideas have been presented, the class could be asked to participate by responding to, disagreeing with or elaborating on the ideas of their classmates. A concluding question for discussion is, How would you define peace?

Activity #3: Sharing the Meaning of Peace

As a follow-up, the teacher can divide the class into groups of three with each of the groups selecting one of the perspectives on peace listed below. The small size of the group increases the possibility of participation of students who would not speak up in a larger group. Designate one person as the reporter. In a bag or box, have each of the statements below on a separate piece of paper. Have each reporter pick one for his or her group. Each group will then have a different point to discuss.

- Peace is a time of quiet and serenity. Are all times of quiet peaceful? (Think of a parent whose child is going through a serious surgery waiting for the doctor's report in a hospital lobby late at night when it is very quiet. Is this a peaceful scene?)
- Peace is something other than the absence of war. Rather, it is a time when justice and fairness are more prominent in our lives and in the lives of those around us. If we really want peace we must work very hard to act in just and fair ways in how we treat people in our daily lives. What are some things each of us could do to make our lives more peaceful?
- Rodney King, a victim of police brutality, pleaded for peace when he said, "Can't we all get just along?" He realized that getting along with others was basic to peace. Peace has to happen not only on a worldwide basis, but at home in our daily lives and with people who appear to be different from ourselves. It sounds so easy to say: Why can't we just get along? Why is it so hard?
- Peace is based on love—love of family, love of friends, and in the broadest sense, a love for people all across this planet. We must also respect ourselves or we will not have the generosity to extend love and respect to others. This is basically saying, We must be at peace with ourselves. How can we help ourselves be at peace?
- Peace does not have to be quiet. Some people may find peace in the middle of a heated conversation, as they listen to a rock band or an opera (depending on their musical taste), in a celebration such as a wedding, hearing the intense cry of a newborn baby, or among giggling or screaming children running through a sprinkler on a summer afternoon. Do you agree? Can you give an example of peace in your life?

continued

Lesson 11.18 *(continued)*

■ The search for peace does not mean that we never disagree or never get angry. However, it does mean that despite differences in ideas or disappointments with others, we can still love and appreciate them. In other words, we may not like what they do, but we still love them as family, friends, and human beings who share this planet. Do you think this is possible?

■ Violence breeds violence. Do you agree? If you believe this is true, what suggestions would you make about how we might deal with violence?

Activity #4: The Opposite of Peace

Here's a question to think about! Do you think that hatred and violence are the opposite of peace? Why? Sometimes such questions can sustain a class discussion that is meaningful to the class. Follow student comments with responses that ask them to more fully explain their views (Tell me more!!) or that build on their idea (Why do you think so?) or that repeat the idea for reactions from the class.

Activity #5: Defining Peace

Place students in small groups of three. Each person in the group is asked to provide a definition of peace. Prior to group discussion, the teacher selects one person in each group to serve as a reporter and to take down the key ideas mentioned by each group member. After 15 minutes of discussion time, have each group of three join another group of three to discuss the similarities and differences in their comments. The larger group will provide them with a broader base of ideas for their own. Finally, ask each student to write a definition of peace as they see it after hearing the views of others. If possible, type, sign, and submit to the school or local paper in order to give class members some recognition for their views of peace.

Activity #6: The Peacemakers

The following quotations come from people who have earned a reputation as peacemaker: Ask students what the quote means to them. Do you agree? Why?

"... [To have peace] we must subordinate *power* in all its manifestations to our shared human values." Mahnaz Afkhami, a leading proponent of women's rights in the Islamic World (Iran).

"Music more than anything has the power to bring people together—people of different ages, races, religions." Carlos Santana, guitarist, founder of the Santana Blues Band, awarded nine Grammy awards in 1999 (Mexico). Having students hear a recording of his band would be especially compelling for young people.

(These quotes are taken from Michael Collopy and Jason Gardner, *Architects of Peace* [1999] Novato, California. New World Library. Others can be found in this attractively photographed volume, in which each "architect" presents a short essay on peace. This is a wonderful classroom resource.)

Activity #7: "A Time For Peace"

Ask the class to think about a time when they feel they have experienced peace, and to explain why they found it peaceful. It is important that teachers start this activity by sharing, in some detail, an experience of their own.

Lesson 11.18 *(continued)*

Suggestions

- I (the teacher) feel very peaceful when I go outside in the very early morning, see the sunlight dancing through the trees and the dew upon the grass and hear the sounds of early morning creatures—like frogs and birds. I think this means I like quiet times, but it also says that I find peace in nature.
- When I disagree with a friend and we talk about the disagreement and work it out—either by agreeing to disagree or in some other way, I feel very satisfied because we are still friends. For me that is a very peaceful feeling.

The first suggestion is a mild, nonthreatening peaceful experience. The second models a way of dealing with differences that is more challenging and therefore serves as a more powerful example. The important condition here is that the teacher is both authentic and honest. If the teacher can be at least this open, it is much more likely that students will follow suit. This teaching suggestion reflects an age-old piece of wisdom about teaching: "Do not ask students to do what you are not willing to do yourself."

Activity #8: A Place For Peace

Is there a particular place where you feel more peaceful than in others? Outdoors? Indoors? By yourself? With others? What is special about that place? What makes it peaceful?

Activity #9: A Person of Peace

This is an out-of-class assignment to interview someone who students think is a person of peace. This person may be a family member, a friend, a neighbor. They can select anyone who says and does things that create a peaceful setting. They should recognize that no one is peaceful in everything they do. However, some people demonstrate peaceful ideas at very important times.

If students are not able to arrange an interview, they can choose from a list of people who have been identified as peacemakers and write a short paper (two to three pages) on how they have contributed to peace. Again, be sure to emphasize that even peacemakers may not always be peaceful but some people have the courage to act at very important times and in ways that diminish the chance of violence. Selections from the following list can be helpful.

Eleanor Roosevelt	Jimmy Carter
Martin Luther King Jr.	Helen Caldicott
Nelson Mandela	the Dala Lama
Mother Teresa	Cesar Chavez
Marian Edelman	

Activity #10: Doing Peace

At any age, students can be asked how they could contribute to peace in the course of their lives. Though it is difficult to have an effect on a worldwide basis, the Internet or even the mail provide ways to send messages to other young people abroad. However, students can also concentrate on what

continued

Lesson 11.18 *(continued)*

they can do in their classroom, their school, their neighborhood, and among their friends and families. It is important to have students make their own decisions about what they want to do. Pursuing other people's ideas is not as productive. It is also important that the teacher provide a personal example. At a later time, the teacher and the class can share their experiences at making peace. Each student can make a list entitled "What I Did for Peace" or "What Worked for Peace/What Didn't." We all can make life more peaceful in small but meaningful ways. A brief list of suggestions follows:

By being helpful, even when not asked

By befriending someone who is often left out

By collecting clothes for the homeless

By writing a play about peace for a school assembly

By writing letters to your Congressional representative and/or Senators that urge them to support peace and devote themselves to the preservation of peace. Usually, staff members will respond routinely to such letters, but they are represented in the phone calls received by the elected representative

By taking a flower to a person who is ill, elderly, or housebound

By writing letters to the school or local paper that describe small acts of peace that anyone can do

By asking your priest, minister, rabbi, or religious leader to make a statement about peace to the members of his faith

Any activity that makes life better for people who face difficult situations is contributing to peace. Any act that replaces a hostile act with a nonhostile act is also contributing to peace. Hostile acts are often followed with additional hostile acts. These are points for all of us who care about peace to keep in mind on a regular basis and as we relate to others.

To expand on the "Doing Peace" aspect of the peace curriculum, teacher and students would find the following publication extremely helpful: *Ten Ways to Fight Hate* (26 pp.). It is published by the Southern Poverty Law Center, 400 Washington Avenue, Montgomery, Alabama 36104. Phone: 334-264-0286. If each student had a copy, it could serve as a point of departure to get involved more substantially in efforts to promote tolerance, respect, and peace.

Classroom Activities for Younger Children
Activity #1: Pictures of Peace

- Ask children to bring in a picture from a magazine that makes them feel peaceful.
- Ask children to draw a picture of a place where they feel at peace.

Activity #2, #3, #4, #5: Books about Peace

Certain trade books provide an excellent way to start a conversation about peace. A few such titles are:

Lesson 11.18 *(continued)*

#2 *Hiroshima No Pika*, by Toshi Maruki (New York: Lothrop, Lee and Shepard Books, 1980). Translated, this title means: "After the Flash." This book tells the story of the bombing of Hiroshima in vivid illustrations and ends with a child's hope that if no one ever drops another bomb, this can never happen again. The author wrote it with the view that knowing about this tragic event might prevent it from happening again.

#3 *Children Just Like Me*, by Barnabas and Anabel Kindersley (New York: UNICEF 1995). This book depicts through thoughtful, authentic photographs the similarities of children in all parts of the world. Even poor readers can get the message from the photographs. This is a beautiful book.

#4 *The Butter Battle Book*, by Dr. Seuss (New York: Random House, 1995). Through a series of delightful cartoons, this book traces the course of battles between the Yooks and the Zooks and their escalation until each side threatens the other with annihilation. One side insists that bread be eaten with the butter side up while the other insists that it should be eaten with the butter side down. It is easy to draw parallels about how violence begets violence using experiences from the playground or other experiences the children or the teacher have had.

#5 *Annie and the Old One*, by Miska Miles. (Boston: Little Brown and Company, 1971). A Navajo child, Annie, hears her grandmother say that when she completes the rug she is weaving, she will return to the earth (die). Annie does everything she can to prevent her grandmother from finishing the rug. Finally, the child finds peace when her grandmother explains the Navajo view of the connection between life and death. A Caldecott Winner. Illustrated by Peter Parnell.

Many trade books are available. With the help of the school or children's librarians it would not be difficult to identify additional peace-oriented stores.

Resources

The activities above represent a beginning effort to introduce peace education. History textbooks emphasize wars. It seems appropriate to suggest that *peace* should be given equal time. Teachers need to integrate peace-oriented activities into their ongoing curriculum. References that are useful for teachers who are determined to so involve their students are:

Betty A. Reardon. *Educating for Global Responsibilities: Teacher Designed Curricula for Peace Education, K–12*. New York: Teachers College Press, 1988. Note that these activities have been created by classroom teachers.

Educators for Social Responsibility, 475 Riverside Drive #554, New York, NY 10115. This Center produces widely-used curriculum materials that support social justice and peace. Phone: 1-800-370-2575.

The Southern Poverty Law Center, 400 Washington Avenue, Montgomery, Alabama 36104. Internet: www.splcenter.org. This Center monitors hate activities and produces educational materials for classrooms that have been extremely popular with teachers.

Reprinted with permission of the author.

Lesson 11.19
Poverty and World Resources

Susan Hersh and Bob Peterson

Introduction

Media stories of street children in Brazil, war-ravaged lives of children in Bosnia, and starving kids in Sudan occasionally give students in North America a glimpse of the ways many children live in other parts of the world. Such news reports are possible starting places for increasing students' understanding of global inequity and the need for justice. At times we will take a particularly poignant photo and make a transparency of it to use it as a trigger for discussion in our fifth grade classes.

Invariably, the question kids ask is, "Why?" "Why don't the people in Sudan have enough food or water?" "Why are there so many street children in Latin America?" And most news reports or student newsweeklies offer shallow answers that rarely go beyond famine, drought, and war.

Schools need to help them understand the basic divisions between rich and poor in the world, and the reasons behind such inequity. Key terms include: resources, GNP, wealth, distribution, income, power, and colonialism.

Hunger may be a good place to start addressing the issue of world poverty, but it's important that even the youngest children have the issue placed in broader contexts. One way to help upper elementary and secondary students understand the unequal distribution of people and wealth is an activity that combines math, geography, writing, and social studies.

Depending on the sophistication of the students, this activity can be more or less teacher directed, with either the teacher providing most of the information or having the students take the data and arrange themselves accordingly.

Materials

- 11 × 17 inch maps for each student or pair of students to write on
- 50 chips (25 of one color, and 25 of another) for each map
- 25 slips of paper with "I was born in [name of continent, based on chart]"
- 25 chocolate chip cookies
- Playground map, or signs with names of continents and yarn to distinguish boundaries
- Transparency of resource chart
- Writing paper

Procedure

- Give each student or pair of students a world map. Have them identify the continents and other places that you may have been studying.
- Ask students how many people they think are in the world. After students have guessed, show them an almanac with the current estimate. Ask: If we represent all the people in the world with 25 chips, how many people is each chip worth? (Each chip represents approximately 200 million people.)
- Give 25 chips to each student/group and have them distribute the chips by continent according to where they think people live. Discuss student estimates and then tell them the accurate figures. Have them rearrange their chips to reflect the facts. Ask students to draw conclusions based on their differing stacks of chips.

Lesson 11.19 *(continued)*

■ Explain to the students that you are now going to give them another 25 chips of a different color and that they represent all the wealth produced in the world (the worth of all the goods and services produced every year—from health care to automobiles). Tell them to put the chips on the continents to indicate their estimate of who gets this wealth. (Each chip represents 1/25 of the world's total amount of goods and services produced.)

■ Discuss student estimates and record them on the chalkboard. Have students reflect on the size of the two different stacks of chips, population and resources. Collect the chips.

■ Tell the students you are going to demonstrate how population and wealth are distributed by continent. Have each student pick a slip of paper from a container. (The "I was born . . ." slips) They may not trade what continent they are from. (As you distribute the slips listen for any stereotypical reactions to the continents—these will indicate possibilities for future lessons.)

■ Have students go to an area in the room that you have designated to represent that continent. (Playground maps work great for this!) After the students are in their areas, remind them that they each represent about 200 million people and that you are going to distribute the world's riches.

■ Use a popular treat—Rice Krispies Treats or chocolate chip cookies—and distribute them according to the percentages given in the chart. Announce the number of treats you are giving to each continent as you do so. Allow students to divide their share within the group. Don't encourage intergroup sharing, but don't forbid it.

■ Ask each continental group to write down what they think of the wealth distribution.

Table 1 ▨ World Population and Wealth by Continent

Continent	Population			Wealth		
	(in billions) *1992*	*% of* *World*	*# in Class* *of 26*	*Per Capita* *GNP in U.S. $*	*% of* *World*	*# of Treats* *Out of 25*
Africa	.682	12.5%	3	630	3	1
Asia*	3.334	61.0%	17	1,680	22	5
Australia	.027	0.5%	—	3,380	0.4	0
Europe	.695	13.0%	3	12,990	39	10
N. America	.283	5.0%	1	21,580	30	7
S. America	.458	8.0%	2	2,170	6	2
World Total	5.479	100.0%	26	—	100	25

Sources: Population figures are from the United Nations Population Fund, *The State of World Population 1993*, quoted in the *Universal Almanac, 1994*. GNP figures are from the World Bank, quoted in the *Universal Almanac, 1994*. GNP is defined as the total national output of goods and services. Percentage of world wealth is an estimate based on total GNP. (Not shown in the graph.)

*Note: The figures for Europe and Asia are estimates because the available data segregates data from the USSR. For purposes of this lesson the authors folded the figures from the former USSR into Europe and Asia based on a 2 to 1 ratio.

continued

Lesson 11.19 *(continued)*

- Bring the students back together and discuss their feelings. Have a report-back from the continents and individuals. Show students the information from the chart via a transparency or handout. Connect their emotions and feelings of fairness to the information on the chart.
- Some questions worth posing if the students don't ask them themselves:

  "How did the distribution of wealth get to be so unequal?"
  "Who do you think decides how wealth is distributed?"
  "Should wealth be distributed equally?"
  "Do you think that within a particular continent the wealth is distributed fairly?"
  "How does the unequal distribution of wealth affect the power that groups of people hold?"
  "Within our community is wealth distributed fairly?"
  "What can be done about the unequal way wealth is distributed?"
  "Who can we talk with to find out more information about these matters?"

- After the discussion, have students write an essay about their feelings, what they learned, and what they might want to do about world poverty.
- Students can do follow-up research on related topics, such as the role colonialism played in the wealth disparity; how current policies of U.S. corporations and the U.S. government are affecting people in the poorer nations; the role government taxes and budgets play in distributing resources, and what different organizations and politicians are doing about world poverty.

Susan Hersh developed this lesson while teaching fifth graders at La Escuela Fratney in Milwaukee, Wisconsin.

Bob Peterson teaches fifth grade at La Escuela Fratney. He is an editor of *Rethinking Schools*.

Lesson 11.20
Global Connections in the World of Science

Physics and the other areas of science are essential in helping us meet the fifth goal of a multicultural curriculum: *To increase awareness of the state of the planet and global dynamics.* Since World War II, scientists around the world have collaborated on numerous projects that affect the entire human family. They have bridged national, cultural, and language barriers to work together in such areas as biotechnology and health, energy and environment, national security, and the International Space Station. These global connections among international scientists can become a basis for establishing worldwide conditions of peace, equity, health and prosperity, all of which are required for social justice and lasting security at home. This lesson engages high school physics students in an exploration of international collaboration at the International Space Station (ISS) and the Brookhaven National Lab.

Lesson 11.20 *(continued)*

According to the ISS web page, "The International Space Station is the largest and most complex international scientific project in history. And when it is complete just after the turn of the century, the station will represent a move of unprecedented scale off the home planet. Led by the United States, the International Space Station draws upon the scientific and technological resources of 16 nations: Canada, Japan, Russia, 11 nations of the European Space Agency, and Brazil."

Brookhaven National Laboratory was established in 1947 on Long Island and is a multiprogram research center operated by Brookhaven Science Associates for the U.S. Department of Energy. An international group of approximately 3,000 scientists, engineers, and support staff work at the lab, as well as over 4,000 guest researchers each year. Nations involved in these collaborations include Brazil, China, Croatia, Czech Republic, Denmark, France, Germany, Hungary, India, Israel, Japan, Netherlands, Pakistan, Poland, Romania, Russia, South Korea, Sweden, Taiwan, and the United States. Major facilities described at the website include the Relativistic Heavy Ion Collider (RHIC), "the world's newest and biggest particle accelerator for nuclear physics;" the National Synchrotron Light Source (USLSU), that attracts "more users annually than any other research machine in the world;" the Alternating Gradient Synchrotron, "home to Nobel Prize-winning research and many pivotal discoveries in high-energy and nuclear physics;" the Accelerator Test Facility, "the nation's proving ground for new concepts in generating, accelerating and monitoring particle beams;" and the Tandem Van de Graaff Facility, "ion sources for hardware testing and supplier of ions for RHIC." The home page also lists an impressive array of current research projects: "Pollution-eating bacteria; Structural studies of the Lyme disease protein for new vaccines; Studies of the brain, including the roots of drug addiction, psychiatric disorders, and brain metabolism; Asbestos-digesting foam; Quiet jackhammers; Promising cocaine addiction treatments; Large-scale studies of the effect of increased carbon dioxide on ecosystems; Cleaner, more efficient oil burners; Testing of the space worthiness of satellite and spacecraft parts with heavy ions produced in Brookhaven accelerators; Investigation of the basic building blocks of matter using the Relativistic Heavy Ion Collider; (and) Testing the Standard Model of physics, a theory which attempts to explain the fundamental forces of nature such as gravity, with the g-2 experiment."

The lesson can be implemented in one- or two-week segments, as an ongoing semester project, or as independent study enrichment. It is linked with curriculum Standard 2 for high school physics.

High School Physics Standard 2: Historical Perspectives of Physics

Students gain understanding of how the scientific enterprise operates through examples of historical events. Through the study of these events, students understand that new ideas are limited by the context in which they are conceived, are often rejected by the scientific establishment, sometimes spring from unexpected findings, and grow or transform slowly through the contributions of many different investigators.

Objectives

- Students will conduct Internet inquiry on international projects at Brookhaven National Laboratory or the International Space Station.

continued

Lesson 11.20 *(continued)*

- Students will present their findings at a mock international symposium.
- Students will explain how scientists can contribute to wider understanding of global dynamics and the state of the planet awareness.

Materials and Resources

- Computer lab with Internet access
- "The Brahms Collaboration." *BRAHMS*. December 2002. Accessed May 18, 2005. www4.rcf.bnl.gov/brahms/WWW/collaboration.html
- "Building the Space Station." *National Aeronautics and Space Administration*. 2005. Accessed May 25, 2005. www.nasa.gov/mission_pages/station/structure/index.html
- "Europe's Contribution to the Space Station." *Centre National d'Etudes Spatiales*. Accessed May 23, 2005. www.cnes.fr/html/_455_461_1422_1426_.php
- "International Space Station." *European Space Agency*. 2005. Accessed May 20, 2005. www.esa.int/esaHS/iss.html
- "International Space Station." *Norwegian Space Center*. 2003. Accessed May 24, 2005. www.spacecentre.no/artikkel.cfm?aid=42&bid=69&oid=53
- "International Space Station Facts and Figures." *Canadian Space Agency*. January 17, 2005. Accessed May 23, 2005. www.space.gc.ca/asc/eng/iss/facts.asp
- "Phenix Institutions, as of March 2005." *PHENIX*. March 2005. Accessed May 17, 2005. www.phenix.bnl.gov/PHENIX_Inst.html
- "The Phobos Collaboration." *PHOBOS Home Detector Internal Search*. 2004. Accessed May 18, 2005. www.phobos.bnl.gov/Collaboration/index.htm
- "Star Member Institutions." *The Star Experiment*. January 7, 2005. Accessed May 17, 2005. www.star.bnl.gov/central/collaboration/institutions.php
- "Total and Differential Cross Sections, and Polarization Effects in pp Elastic Scattering at RHIC." The pp2pp Experiment. Accessed April 25, 2005, and May 18, 2005 www.rhic.bnl.gov/pp2pp/documents/Collaborators.pdf

Procedures

1. Anticipatory set (5 minutes):

   Show photo of International Space Station. Ask, "What is this a picture of?" Use spiral questions to see what students know and would like to know about the Station.

2. Brief lecture with slides about Brookhaven and the International Space Station (15 minutes):

   Slides and a concise summary of important content are available at the website for each.

3. Explain inquiry project. Students in your class are invited to participate in an international symposium for high school physics students from around the world. The purpose of the symposium is to encourage talented young physics students to think about college majors in physics, as well as think about ways to collaborate worldwide for the good of planet earth and all its inhabitants. The event takes place in Australia over spring break. All expenses will be paid and there will be opportunities to work with top international scholars as well as high school students from

Lesson 11.20 *(continued)*

over fifty nations. To prepare for the event students will work in teams of four to five classmates to conduct inquiry on an international physics project of their choice. (A variety of projects should be selected overall.) Each team will present its findings and the team's evaluation of its international physics project, in a professional-quality PowerPoint with animation and sound effects. Students will evaluate their selected project in terms of its significance and potential for worldwide human good.

Assessment

Each team's PowerPoint and essay or speech can be assessed using a teacher-created rubric. Possible assessment categories include brief history of the selected project, including how scientific knowledge has changed over time, countries and scientists involved, major accomplishments, challenges, future goals, an evaluation of who is benefiting from the research, and the project's potential to contribute to the common good, worldwide.

I would like to thank Robert Gottlieb and Rebekah Miller, physics students at Bloomington High School South, for providing background research used in this lesson.

Lesson 11.21

Acid Rain
Maureen Reynolds

Global Education Rationale

Acid rain is a form of environmental pollution caused by industrial activities. Because the acids that fall in acid rain can travel for hundreds of miles in the atmosphere, they cross national boundaries, causing pollution in countries that do not produce the acid pollution. Some of the damage done by acid rain is probably irreversible. Students need to be sensitive to the global consequences of technological and industrial activities on the environment and to consider the possibility that preserving the environment may mean that people, including Americans, may have to dramatically alter their lifestyles. The core values stressed in this lesson plan are responsibility to the world community and reverence for the earth.

Goals

- Students will become familiar with the causes and effects of acid rain.
- Students will consider which course of action should be taken with respect to acid rain.

Objective

All the students will participate in a values clarification lesson concerning acid rain and the environment.

continued

Lesson 11.21 *(continued)*

Materials

Blackboard

Videocassette recorder

Television

Video: *Acid Rain: More Bad News*, NOVA, John D. & Catherine T. MacArthur Foundation Library Video Classics Project. New York: Ambrose Video Publishing, Inc., 1985 (57 minutes). The video shows damage done by acid rain to forests, lakes, and buildings in the United States, West Germany, and Sweden. It discusses how acid rain is formed and how it travels in the atmosphere. Scientists, public officials, and private citizens are interviewed.

Activities

1. Ask the students what acid rain is and what it does when it comes into contact with flesh, paints, animals, rocks, or soil. Based on their answers, have them guess what acid rain is.

2. Show the video *Acid Rain: More Bad News*.

3. After the video is viewed, ask the students what things can be done to reduce acid rain or its effects. Have assigned students write each alternative with its resulting consequences on the blackboard (each alternative will have its own student).

4. Have students orally propose what they think are the economic, environmental, lifestyle, and health consequences for each listed alternative.

5. By hand, have all students vote for an alternative. Note who voted for what alternatives. Ask students why they voted for a particular alternative. If the class is unanimous, ask why they did not vote for the other alternatives.

6. Ask students how they feel about acid rain and their choice. Does acid rain scare them? Would they rather not think about it? Are they willing to give up material things and conveniences to reduce acid rain? Why do they feel that way? What is more important, a healthy environment or a productive economy? Why do they feel that way? Do they really think that their choice would help the acid rain problem? Do they feel that knowing about acid rain is important? Why?

7. Ask the students what they can do now about acid rain. If the students cannot think of anything, suggest that they write public officials and government agencies to find out their stand on acid rain and other environmental issues and to urge them to take action on such issues. Also, they may attend rallies and be more conscious of themselves as polluters.

Evaluation

- Through observation during the class, the teacher will determine whether most of the students are giving or are able to give reasons for their position.
- On their unit test, the students will be able to accurately discuss the effects of acid rain on lakes, forests, and buildings.

Reprinted with permission of the author.

Goal Six: Developing Social Action Skills

Major problems threaten the future of the planet and the well-being of humanity. The aim of this goal is to give students the knowledge, attitudes, and skills that are necessary for active citizen participation. The emphasis is on thinking globally and acting locally and engendering a sense of personal and political efficacy and a participatory attitude, both of which are essential to the development of global responsibility among the citizens of the earth.

Underlying this goal are the following assumptions:

- The subjugation and unjust treatment of any cultural group dehumanizes everyone.
- Most people will, at some time in their lives, find themselves in the position of being a political minority.
- All groups in society should have equal opportunity to bring about social and political change.
- We value political access and participation for all citizens.
- The more learners can actively participate in decision-making activities and work on self-selected problems beyond the classroom, the more likely they are to increase their feelings of personal and political effectiveness.
- Citizens have a right to know about global crises that threaten human survival, and about actions that can be taken to lessen these problems.

This goal moves us beyond study, reflection, and analysis into a state of action. In view of the fact that certain ethnic groups and Third World nations are cut off from their fair share of the world's resources, suffer from poverty and starvation, serve as the world's dumping ground for toxic wastes, and are unable to gain, maintain, and effectively use political power, to ignore this goal would make the other goals meaningless.

The development of social action skills encompasses Hanvey's fifth dimension. He defines this dimension as "some awareness of the problems of choice confronting individuals, nations, and the human species as consciousness and knowledge of the global system expand."[69]

Decision-making skills are an integral part of these social action skills. This assumes that students can learn to identify alternative choices for themselves as well as for public policymakers and that they can reflect upon the possible consequences of their choices.

There are special impediments to social action in the global arena that deserve attention. There is a lack of a global government and other appropriate institutions to carry out action plans at a global level. Joyce and Nicholson explain the situation this way:

> *Although there are a number of agreed-on domains of international action in such fields as health, postal service, air traffic, weather observation, and international communications, most issues must be negotiated specifically in the absence of general policy. There is no universal language of learning comparable to Latin in the Middle Ages. The problem of creating international institutions, moreover, involves much more difficulty than merely extending existing national institutions to international dimensions. The deficiencies of the*

international monetary and legal systems point up this fact only too well. Added to this inherent difficulty are the differences in perceived self-interest among nations.[70]

Lack of mutual trust, cross-cultural misunderstandings, and differing worldviews compound the problem. A dramatic, if narrowly focused, incident concerning a novel written for young adolescents, *Monsoon: A Novel to End World Hunger*, illustrates the point.[71] The novel has received wide acclaim from American teachers and is thoroughly enjoyed by young American readers. But several visiting scholars from East Asian and Central African nations had a different reaction to the book. They found it offensive, patronizing, unrealistic, and misleading about the causes of world hunger. This criticism should not stop us from looking at this problem. Rather, it should be a point of departure for discussing how people from different parts of the globe view the same problem. It could also lead to an examination of the necessary conditions for global collaboration for solving world hunger.

In her exemplary collection of teacher-designed curricula for peace education, Betty Reardon offers a variety of concepts and skills related to global responsibility.[72] Her book, *Educating for Global Responsibility*, contains thirty-five curricula plans for kindergarten through high school. The curricula cumulatively develop concepts, skills, and understandings related to peace education. Children begin with creative imagining in the early elementary grades and learn to express their fears about such things as nuclear war and share ways of coping with these fears. Teachers must be careful not to introduce materials that produce these fears in children. Children in grades four to six are introduced to problem-solving skills and learn that "people can and frequently do change society and resolve very grave, and overwhelming social problems."[73] Reardon stresses empowerment through the development of creative capacities and imagination via brainstorming, imaging, and model building. She urges that critical and analytical thinking skills be introduced during preadolescence, and high school students move on to ethical reflection and informed action. She writes:

> *Perhaps the most important attitude to be engendered [at this age level and above] is objectivity in the analysis of problems, an intention to examine all available evidence and views. It is also important to impart an understanding that to be objective is not to be neutral. One can hold values that have a direct bearing on an issue and still pursue objective knowledge of the facts. Ethical reflection is as important as consideration of the evidence.*[74]

The case of apartheid in South Africa illustrates this point well. In examining the historical perspectives of Black South Africans, Coloreds, and White South Africans (both British and Dutch Afrikaans), students will better understand current events in South Africa. Knowledge about Afrikaaner nationalism, which includes the belief in a God-given right to settle the land (similar to manifest destiny in the United States) and the racist socialization of young, White, South African children, will give students insight into the national government's actions. This understanding, however, is not the same as acceptance or approval of a system that violates the human rights of the Black population.

Although many educators feel schools should encourage students to be more effective agents of social change, the present curriculum is inadequate to meet this end.[75] Political socialization research, however, offers numerous insights into what kind of curricula and instructional strategies may be effective.[76] These insights range from simply encouraging class discussion of social issues, to political change case studies, small-group problem solving, and community action research. Writing in the early 1970s, an era of political activism, Bradbury Seasholes outlined the ingredients for teaching students to be active agents of change:

> *Perhaps the greatest contribution educators can make to school-age . . . [youth] who will be tomorrow's adult citizens is to reorient their thinking about the development and use of political strategy. This means spelling out with approval the various techniques of bargaining, forced demands, concession, and occasional retreat that are used by politically successful subgroups in our society. It means being candid on two scores when dealing with heterogeneous groups of students in the classroom—candid about the probable maximum of political potential that a given subgroup could have (just how successful groups can expect to be, given their total resources of numbers, money, effort, education, and so forth) and candid about the kind of political techniques that are in fact being used currently or may be used in the reasonably near future.*
>
> *Political activity in this day and age, after all, involves not only voting, contributing money, and writing letters to congressmen. It sometimes involves street demonstrations and civil disobedience. These need talking out in the classroom too, not in normative terms but in terms of strategies which sometimes succeed or fail because they tread so close to the border of normatively acceptable political behavior.*[77]

Today there may be a renewed interest in social activism, as seen in precollegiate service learning programs and revived interest in moral issues in education. Our students need opportunities to make choices and evaluate their decisions. They need to practice self-expression, decision-making skills, and problem resolution. This work practice can begin in kindergarten with opportunities to make simple choices, express opinions, set goals, and discuss classroom rules. Participatory learning can be expanded at the high school level to include simulations, service learning, and community or political action projects.

 ## Lesson Plans That Develop Social Action Skills

Lesson 11.22
Promoting Youth Social Activism Using Hip-Hop and Technology   *Paulette Patterson Dilworth*

Introduction and Rationale
This lesson is designed to incorporate core principles from Bennett's model relating to multicultural competence and teaching toward social justice. The goal of this lesson is to introduce middle

continued

Lesson 11.22 *(continued)*

school and high school students to a social studies project that integrates hip-hop content and technology to engage students with inquiry and social action knowledge and skills. Students will be introduced to themes and topics centered on a controversial political issue: free expression and the First Amendment. Using primary sources, digital cameras, and iMovie, iPhoto, and collaborative small-group activities, students will create a documentary to increase peer and community awareness about free speech, freedom of expression, and First Amendment rights.

Hip-hop culture began in the inner cities of the United States during the 1970s, as a way for marginalized urban youth experiencing harsh socioeconomic conditions to express their views. Using a variety of hip-hop elements, including emceeing, disc jockeys, break dancing, and graffiti, urban youth have created and re-created their own cultural identity. The musical antecedents to hip-hop include the African drum beat, spirituals, blues, jazz, and rhythm and blues. Today, a shared sense of hip-hop cultural identity has spread throughout the world, uniting youth to a global society by engaging them in this art form of free expression. To some degree, hip-hop has become the most important form of free cultural expression for young people from diverse ethnic and racial backgrounds. The term has since come to be synonymous with rap music, fashion, oral expression, and political activism. Although some people view hip-hop as a tool for social change, critics see it as a corrupting influence that alienates youth from schools and communities. Hip-hop critics believe that access to some hip-hop music and videos should be restricted or even censored. For example, sexually explicit messages, the N-word, and disparaging language referring to women are prominent in lyrics and videos of some rap music.

As a worldwide forum, hip-hop offers a multicultural space for youth to assess and critique family, community, economic, social, and political issues. Free expression is embedded in hip-hop culture. Yet, a recent survey of youth in the United States found weak support for fundamental First Amendment rights. The authors of the report found deep student unawareness and apathy about the meaning and significance of the First Amendment, which is the foundation of U.S. civil liberties. Approximately 75 percent of youth reported that they never consider the First Amendment or its connection to their everyday lived experiences. The study, which included the opinions of more than 100,000 teenagers, also found that:

- 36 percent of students believe newspapers should not publish certain stories without government approval
- 32 percent say the press has "too much" freedom
- 83 percent say people should be allowed to express unpopular views

Providing opportunities for middle school and high school students to explore the significance of First Amendment rights to hip-hop can provide youth with the knowledge and skills needed to engage in social justice and social action–oriented activities.

In this lesson students will participate in collective group work to further their own understanding.

Lesson Objectives

- Students will explore First Amendment rights and free speech
- Students will examine the historical antecedents of free expression and hip-hop culture

Lesson 11.22 *(continued)*

- Students will analyze how features of hip-hop culture shape the free-expression attitudes and behaviors of youth in their community and schools
- Students will explore and critique free-expression elements of hip-hop culture
- Students will create an iMovie featuring content from their research on the First Amendment, free expression, and hip-hop culture

Materials and Resources

- Computer lab with Internet access
- Digital video camera
- DVD Player/Television
- iPhoto
- iTunes
- iMovie
- www.firstamendmentcenter.org
- www.urbanthinktank.org
- www.brownpride.com/latinrap/default.asp
- www.csulb.edu/~jvancamp/intro.html#Site

Additional Readings

Baraka, Imamu Amiri. (1963). *Blues people: Negro Music in White America.* New York: William Morrow.

Bynoe, Yvonne. (2004). *Stand and Deliver: Political Activism, Leadership, and Hip-Hop Culture.* Brooklyn, NY: Soft Skull Press.

George, Nelson. (1988). *The Death of Rhythm and Blues.* New York: Penguin Books.

George, Nelson. (1998). *Hip-Hop America.* New York: Viking Penguin.

Kitwana, Barkari. (2002). *The Hip-Hop Generation.* New York: Perseus Press.

Kitwana, Bakari. (2005). *Why White Kids Love Hip-Hop.* New York: Basic Civitas Books.

Peck, Robert. (2000). *The First Amendment and Cyberspace.* Chicago: American Library Association.

Post, Robert C., ed. (1998). *Censorship and Silencing: Practices of Cultural Regulation (Issues and Debates).* Los Angeles: J. Paul Getty Museum Publications.

Rose, Tricia. (1994). *Black Noize: Rap Music and Black Culture in Contemporary America.* Hanover, NH: University Press of New England.

Activities

To begin this lesson, have students take out a sheet of paper and make two columns. At the top of each column, have students write the following questions:

1. What do you know about free expression, free speech, and the First Amendment?

2. What would you like to know about free expression, free speech, and the First Amendment?

   - Allow students approximately 15 minutes to respond to each question. Use a transparency to record and summarize students' responses to both questions. Involve the class in a discussion about their responses and clarify issues and concerns as necessary.

continued

Lesson 11.22 (continued)

- Next, explain the purpose of the lesson and outline instructional activities and plans for the inquiry and production of the documentary. Students will be assigned to work in small groups. Care should be taken to emphasize the collective responsibility of group work and have students identify a group leader and assign roles for each group member.
- Group Assignments and Roles:

  Group 1 History of the First Amendment (Research and develop a history of the First Amendment)
  Group 2 Musical antecedents (Research and develop a time line of musical antecedents to hip-hop)
  Group 3 History of hip-hop (Research and develop a history of hip-hop)
  Group 4 Ethnic images in hip-hop (Research the ways in which multicultural and ethnic images are represented)
  Group 5 Portraits of student and community views (Survey students in school and community and compile results)

- Each group will identify essential concepts and questions that will guide inquiry activities.
- Groups develop list of websites, primary sources (music lyrics, videos, textbook sections, documents, photographs, etc).
- After completing the research, each group will develop a storyboard of their work to be incorporated in the documentary project. Each storyboard will include a title, content narration, and transitions for each section.
- After completing the project, the class reviews the finished documentary and discusses what they learned about the significance of First Amendment rights and free speech to hip-hop culture.
- The iMovie can be copied on CDs or burned as a DVD. The CDs or copies of the DVD can be presented to the school media center, other social studies classes, and community after-school programs.

Assessment

- Each group's storyboard can be assessed using a teacher-created rubric. DVD versions of the iMovie projects can be included in the students' portfolios.
- Each student will write a reflection essay on the efficacy of group work and collective responsibility, focusing on what they learned about this topic.

Reprinted with permission of the author.

Lesson 11.23
The Little Rock Nine   *Don Adams*

National Council for the Social Studies Themes and Indiana State Learning Standards
USH 6.2–Identify and explain the importance of key events, people, and groups connected to domestic problems and policies during the administrations of Truman and Eisenhower.

Lesson 11.23 *(continued)*

USH 6.5–Analyze the cause, conditions, and consequences of the struggle for civil rights by African Americans

NCSS Theme VI–Power, Authority, and Governance

a. examine persistent issues involving the rights, roles, and status of the individual in relation to the general welfare

b. explain the purpose of government and analyze how its powers are acquired, used, and justified

NCSS Theme X–Civic Ideals and Practices

h. evaluate the degree to which public policies and citizen behavior reflect or foster the stated ideals of a republican form of government

Objectives

By the end of the lesson, the students will be able to:

- Define key terms (people, events, ideas, etc.) relating to the integration of public education in the South
- Describe the course of events surrounding the integration of Little Rock's Central High in 1957, including the personal experiences of the nine African American students who first attended
- Compare the ruling in *Brown v. Board of Education* to stated American ideals and constitutional tenets
- Evaluate the concept of "inherently unequal" in social arrangements

Materials/Equipment

Book: *Warriors Don't Cry* by Melba Patillo Beals (1995). New York: Washington Square Press, pp. 1–52, 134–175, 299–312

Transparencies/PowerPoint slides for Day 1:

- Picture: Elizabeth Eckford
- Jim Crow: de jure segregation
- Jim Crow: *Plessy v. Ferguson*
- Jim Crow: segregated theater entrance photo
- Jim Crow: segregated water fountains photo
- Jim Crow: segregated restroom photo
- Jim Crow: de facto segregation
- Jim Crow: cross-burning photo
- Jim Crow: lynching definition
- Jim Crow: lynching photo
- Integration: *Brown v. Board of Education*
- Integration: Southern Manifesto
- Central High, Little Rock, Arkansas, photo
- September 3, 1957, photo of crowd
- September 3, 1957, photo of Elizabeth Eckford
- September 3, 1957, photo of Alex Wilson

continued

Lesson 11.23 *(continued)*

Central High Today

One of Arkansas' most prestigious high schools
- Named one of top 19 open admission high schools in nation by universities
- One of 2 in Arkansas named a "Model School" by National Governors Association
- More National Merit Scholar semi-finalists than any school in Arkansas, including 50% of all black semi-finalists

Source: www.centralhigh57.org/today.htm

Central High Today

Fatima McKindra—Central High student body President 1997–98

Still segregated, but in reverse:
- Little Rock is 1/3 white, but Central High is 2/3 black

Integration in the 1990s

Source: Brown University,
www.s4.brown.edu/schoolsegregation/

Integration in the 1990s

Why continued, even increasing, segregation?
- Increasingly segregated housing
- Elimination of forced busing and other policies designed to created integrated schools

Today's Assignment

Drawing primarily upon *Warriors Don't Cry*, but also on class notes and discussion, write one page about each of the following:
- First, write from the perspective of one of the white protesters outside Central High on September 3, 1957. Why are you there? What do you think and feel about integration? What are you willing to do to achieve your goals?
- Second, write from the perspective of one of the Little Rock Nine. Why are you there? What do you think and feel about integration? What are you willing to do to achieve your goals?

Make sure to include at least three terms from your study guide.

Lesson 11.23 *(continued)*

Transparencies/PowerPoint slides, Day 3:

- Central High today: photo w/ President Clinton
- Central High today: background information
- Central High today: photo of Fatima McKindra
- Integration in the 1990s: graphic
- Integration in the 1990s: information
- Today's assignment: writing for understanding

Equipment: PowerPoint or transparency projector

Procedures
Note: This lesson must begin on a Thursday or a Friday so that students have the weekend to read.

Day 1

Anticipatory set: display picture of Elizabeth Eckford. Ask class to write in response to the question, Why are these people yelling at this girl? When done, ask students for their guesses (5 minutes).

Lecture: Hand out study guide, Go through slides 2–16, provide background on segregation, *Brown v. Board of Education* (30 minutes).

Group discussion: display photo of Elizabeth Eckford. Ask class to write again. Why are these people yelling at this girl? What do you think the rest of her day was like? What about the rest of her year: did things improve? (5 minutes).

Display picture of Alex Wilson and read aloud excerpts from *Warriors Don't Cry*.

Homework assignment: begin reading assigned passages (pp. 1–52, 134–176, 299–312), identify terms on review sheet, and highlight at least two passages of interest.

Day 2

Debrief: group discussion on previous night's reading. What did students learn about the course of events for the Little Rock Nine? What has surprised them? What passages or events stood out? (5–10 minutes).

Read alone from book, highlight one passage of interest (35–40 minutes).

Debrief: ask students to read the passages they selected. Discuss.

Day 3

Lecture: go through slides 1–5, provide update on Central High and integration (5 minutes).

- Group discussion: review terms from review sheet (5 minutes).
- Writing for understanding: display slide 6, have class write for 15 minutes on each question (30 minutes).

continued

Lesson 11.23 *(continued)*

- Work in pairs: have all students pair up and exchange papers. Edit one another's papers, make suggestions, ask questions, etc. (10 minutes).
- Homework: revise work, hand in final draft.

Evaluation

- Written assignment on Day 3 to serve as assessment of learning
- Formative questions throughout to provide broad picture of engagement and progress
- Review of term sheet on Day 3 to confirm knowledge
- Summative assessment at end of unit to include one or more elements from lesson

Web Resources

www.ardemgaz.com/prev/central/ (Archive of Little Rock newspaper accounts)

www.centralhigh57.org/ (Memorial website for 40th anniversary)

www.cr.nps.gov/nr/travel/civilrights/index.htm (U.S. Park Service website for "Historic Places of the Civil Rights Movement")

The Little Rock Nine: A Review

The Little Rock Nine

Orval Faubus

Thurgood Marshall

Brown v. Board of Education

Plessy v. Ferguson

Southern Manifesto

Jim Crow

Integration

Answer these questions after the lecture, reading, or conducting your own research:

1. What reasoning did the NAACP use in its argument before the Supreme Court in *Brown v. Board of Education*?

2. What arguments did southern Whites use against forced integration?

Lesson 11.23 *(continued)*

3. In your own opinion, has integration been good for America? How does it compare to American laws and ideals?

Lesson 11.24
To Take a Stand or to Not Take a Stand

Students can develop decision-making skills if they are given an opportunity to act out a problematic situation in roleplay before they actually encounter it. Young children can use dolls, puppets, or masks made of decorated paper plates during the roleplay. Older students can be given role cards that define their new personality or they can be asked to empathize with a person in an open-ended situation. Examples of roleplaying that help build decision-making skills related to multicultural education goals are listed below. Students can be asked whether they would take a stand or not, depending on who they are (themselves, another actual person, or a contrived character). Wording would be modified according to students' grade level.

1. Your best friend uses a racial slur to insult a classmate.
2. You feel that your teacher is racist because Black/White/Latino students get away with murder in the classroom and you get punished for much less.
3. Your parent tells a cruel ethnic joke that cuts down (insert name) at a family gathering.
4. You find out that the sorority/fraternity you want to join will not pledge anyone from a different race. You are/are not a member of the same race.
5. You are White and have a new job in a sporting-goods store. Your boss asks you to make a note of any Black person who cashes a check in the store.
6. One of your best friends in school is Black/Latino/White. You want to invite this friend to your birthday party but your parent(s) says no.
7. You catch a classmate cheating on an exam. The cheater is of a different race from you and you are afraid of being called prejudiced. Yet you know the cheater shared the exam with a small group of close friends, which raised the class curve, causing you and others to do poorly.

continued

Lesson 11.24 *(continued)*

8. A teacher's purse was stolen by a tall Black person wearing an Afro. You are innocent, but because you fit the description you are called in for questioning and accused of the crime.

9. You have just learned that you will be transported by bus to a new school next year in a distant part of town. You hear that the parents in that neighborhood are angry and upset that you and classmates from your neighborhood are being brought in.

10. Before you came to the United States you loved school and were a good student. Now you understand little of what the teacher and classmates say, and you have been placed in a classroom for the mentally retarded.

Lesson 11.25
No Man Is an Island: The Importance of Perspective in Decision Making   *Karen Kulp*

Topic
An introduction to *jury selection* from a multicultural perspective for a unit on the *American Legal System*, Senior High School, Government class, one to two days.

Rationale
The making of decisions and facing the consequences of decisions made by others will occur in many contexts and at all levels throughout a student's life: global, national, local, and family. It is therefore crucial that the student understand that decisions are rarely made in a vacuum. Just as one's own life history influences one's judgment and perspective when faced with decision, so too does personal history influence the judgment and perspective of every person involved in a decision-making process.

The concept of a jury is a particularly interesting way to illustrate the above point. Because all U.S. citizens of voting age, who are of sound mind and who have not committed a felony, may be called to serve on a jury, the verdict reached by a jury will necessarily reflect the multitude of experiences and attitudes of those who serve.

In the course of this lesson, the student will find it necessary to exercise critical thinking skills by taking into account the variety of factors that may influence an individual's attitude, as well as demonstrate the ability to negotiate with a partner whose interest in the outcome of the case is diametrically opposed to his or her own. These factors make this lesson particularly suitable for use by a teacher interested in multicultural and global education.

Objective
Students will demonstrate critical thinking/inquiry skills by choosing prospective jurors for a court case involving drunk driving. In making their choices, students will be asked to consider the pos-

Lesson 11.25 *(continued)*

sible impact and interplay of various factors on the jurors' reaction to the case. Among these factors are race, sex, age, religious belief, and life history.

Procedure

1. Prepare the students' minds for learning by posing the following questions:
   - How many of you know someone who has ever driven a car while under the influence of alcohol?
   - How many of you know anyone who has suffered injury or death as a result of a driver who was under the influence of alcohol? How do, or would, you feel if this happened?

   Allow time for discussion.

2. Introduce the lesson by explaining that you want the class to simulate the selection of a jury in a drunk driving case.

3. Hand out the Student Information Sheet and the list of prospective jurors.

4. Present the following information to the students:
   - Read your Student Information Sheet carefully. While reading it consider the impact (if any) that a prospective juror's race, sex, religious beliefs, and life history might have on his or her attitudes toward the defendant.
   - Each student will select his or her prospective jurors from the perspective of an attorney for either the prosecution or defense. (Teacher should assign roles and opposition partners at this time.)
   - Students should write down the three potential jurors they wish to eliminate, giving their reasons. They then join their partner who is playing an attorney for the opposing side. The two attorneys must negotiate in order to seat a jury of twelve. When they have come to an agreement, each attorney will explain in writing the decisions and compromises that were made (on a separate sheet of paper).
   - Students will staple and hand in all three sheets. They should be sure their individual sheet had their name on it as well as whether they are a prosecution or defense attorney. The joint sheet should also have both names on it.

Materials

Student Information Sheet

List of prospective jurors

Pencils and paper

Evaluation

Evaluation will be on the basis of students' active participation in the exercise and on the basis of their written responses to the exercises. Particular attention should be paid to the reasoning the student used in his or her choices for elimination.

continued

Lesson 11.25 *(continued)*

Student Information Sheet

You will be assigned to play the role of either an attorney for the prosecution or attorney for the defense. Your job in this exercise will be to select a jury that will be impartial, if not sympathetic, to the side of the case you represent.

Attached to this information sheet is a list of fifteen potential jurors. You will need to eliminate three, but remember that you will need to negotiate with another attorney in order to complete the exercise.

Instructions

1. Read the case below and the attached sheet with descriptions of the prospective jurors. Keep in mind any factors such as race, age, sex, religious persuasion, and attitude toward alcohol that you believe may influence a prospective juror's attitude.

2. On a sheet of paper write your name and the side of the case you represent.

3. List those jurors you are inclined to challenge and your reasons. Then list those jurors that you definitely want on the jury and, again, your reasons.

4. When you have completed your list, join your assigned partner and negotiate to set a jury of twelve.

5. On a separate sheet of paper, name the three jurors that you and the other attorney eliminated as a team. Explain the decisions and compromises that you each made in order to come to an agreement. Staple all three sheets together and hand them in.

People versus Robin Carusa

The defendant, Robin Carusa, is Caucasian, 43 years old, and a resident of Bloomington, Indiana. He is Catholic. Upon graduation from Bloomington High School North, Carusa joined the Marines and served for three years in Vietnam. He is single, has one noncustodial child, and is an attorney.

On the night of October 3, 20____, Carusa and his fiancee, Cindy Freitag, went to a popular nightclub called The Island to hear the local band Voyage. According to the deposition taken from John Donne who is a bouncer at The Island, Carusa and Freitag arrived sometime after 9:00, but before 9:30 P.M. Again, according to Donne, Carusa and Freitag left the nightclub at around 1:00 A.M.

At approximately 2:30 A.M., Carusa's Mercedes crossed the center line on College Avenue and struck an oncoming Volkswagen head-on, killing both occupants instantly. The deceased have been identified as Lilly Mitchell and her 2-year-old son, Damon. Mitchell was Black, 35 years old, and the mother of three children. According to her husband Robert Mitchell, Lilly Mitchell was taking Damon to the emergency room of Bloomington Hospital for a severe case of the croup. Neither Carusa nor Freitag was seriously injured.

Carusa was given a Breathalyzer test at the scene, and his blood alcohol level registered 0.12 percent (1 percent is considered legally intoxicated under Indiana State law). According to Carusa, he drank three beers while at The Island and for the next hour while he and Freitag sat talking in his car, he claims, he did not drink at all. Freitag substantiates his statement. However, five empty beer cans and one unopened can were found on the floor of Carusa's car. Carusa claims that he had a cold that

Lesson 11.25 *(continued)*

could have skewed the test. He also claims that due to a recent rainfall the road was wet, and his car hydroplaned, causing him to lose control.

Carusa is being charged with one count of operating a motor vehicle while intoxicated resulting in death, and two counts of reckless homicide. Both counts are considered Class C felonies under Indiana State law.

Prospective Jurors

- *Harlan Curry*, Caucasian, age 66, retired auto mechanic. Married, three children, seven grandchildren. World War II veteran, no active church affiliation, recovered alcoholic.
- *Susan Andros*, Caucasian, age 40, office manager. Married (spouse is a local attorney), two children at home. Member of local Episcopal church, social drinker.
- *John Davis*, Black, age 33, assistant professor in the Indiana University School of Business. Single, no children. Member of Unitarian-Universalist Church. Davis does not drink, because his father, a retired police officer from Detroit, is an alcoholic.
- *Mark Sampson*, Caucasian, age 29, high school dropout, employed at Kinser Lumber four years. Divorced, two noncustodial children. One previous arrest DWI (no conviction). No church affiliation.
- *Jane Long*, Caucasian, age 20, Indiana University student (School of Education). Graduated from Bloomington High School North, active in Youth for Christ, does not drink.
- *Alice Murray*, Black, age 71, retired to Bloomington after teaching school in Georgia for 35 years. Widowed, one child (died of scarlet fever at age two). Member local Baptist Church, does not drink.
- *James Fanelli*, Caucasian, age 45, sales manager Tom O'Daniel Ford. Married, four children at home. College graduate, Vietnam veteran, active member of St. Charles Catholic Church, social drinker.
- *Julie Chase*, Caucasian, age 36, doctor, Bloomington Hospital, Emergency Room. Divorced, one child at home. Member of and medical consultant to Alcoholics Anonymous. No church affiliation.
- *Shelly Arno*, Caucasian, age 28, unemployed. Widowed (husband killed in a car accident), two children at home. Engaged to Assistant Minister at the Bloomington Pentecostal Church. Does not drink.
- *Jack Allen*, Black, age 33, graduate student at Indiana University. Married (wife Caucasian), one child at home. Worked as an insurance investigator before returning to school. No church affiliation, social drinker.
- *Joe Chin*, Vietnamese American, age 52, teacher, elementary school. Married, one child (deceased). Member of St. Charles Catholic Church, does not drink.
- *Sally Frank*, Caucasian, age 69, owner of local bookstore. Widowed (deceased husband was career military), two children, one grandchild. No church affiliation, social drinker.
- *Edward Said*, Lebanese American, age 40, Professor of Arabic at Indiana University. Single, no children. Muslim, does not drink.
- *John Marks*, Caucasian, age 23, musician in a local rock band. Single, no children. No church affiliation, social drinker.
- *Maya Davis*, Black, age 32, novelist. Married, one child at home. No church affiliation, social drinker.

Reprinted with permission of the author.

Lesson 11.26
Global Economics and the U.S. Consumer: Nike Goes Global   *Kathy Ellis*

Objectives

1. The student will be able to give specific details concerning one company's (Nike's) move of production out of the country.

2. The student will examine his or her feelings and attitudes as to the buying power and decisions to be made by an informed consumer.

3. The student will exercise consumer power by writing a letter to Nike headquarters requesting further information, voicing support, or criticizing Nike's decision to move production elsewhere. (If a student does not wish to communicate with Nike, the student may write a one- to two-page essay on "A Company's Right to Move Production.")

Method/Activities

1. Gain student attention by showing a Nike commercial. (Kathy created her own 15-minute video using Nike's television commercials.) Ask the students these three questions and have someone write the answers on the board:
   a. What do you think the commercial was trying to establish?
   b. What do you know about the Nike company?
   c. What does it mean to be an informed consumer? (Does it mean that you base decisions on the information learned?) (This should take approximately 20 minutes.)

2. Pass out the article from *Harper's* magazine: "The New Free-Trade Heel."

3. Ask the students to read the article and answer the reading guide questions. The article is short, so it could be easily read out loud in class.

4. Then have the students, working in groups, answer the following two questions on overhead transparencies:
   a. List two or three concerns or questions that a U.S. consumer/citizen might have regarding the Nike company.
   b. What are some options for citizens/consumers who question a company's business practices? (This should complete the first period.)

5. Pass out paper to the students. Their assignment is to write a letter to Nike headquarters supporting Nike's decision to move production out of the country, criticizing the decision, or asking questions about the decision. Each letter should contain at least two questions to the Nike company. The letter will be graded on logical reasoning and application of knowledge of global economics. It will not be graded on grammar, but since these letters will actually be mailed, the students might edit each other's letters.

Lesson 11.26 *(continued)*

Materials

Video of a Nike commercial

Article: "The New Free-Trade Heel," *Harper's*, August 1992, 46–47.

Reading guide with questions

Assessment

The object of this lesson is for students to see that they actually are a part of global economics and that the decisions that people of their age group make might possibly have an effect. Another part of the lesson is that being an informed consumer does not necessarily make decisions easier. There are no right or wrong "answers" in the students' letter-writing assignment just as there are sometimes no right or wrong decisions regarding consumer decisions. The real assessment of the lesson will be whether or not the students showed any critical thinking about the Nike company's move of operations.

Reading Guide for "The New Free-Trade Heel"/Name

1. Answer these questions as you read "The New Free-Trade Heel," *Harper's*, August 1992.
   a. What product does Nike produce?
   b. In what state is Nike based?
   c. How many Nike footwear factories are currently operating in the United States?
   d. Between 1982 and 1989, how many footwear jobs did the United States lose?
   e. How many pairs of shoes does Nike produce annually?
   f. List the five countries in which Nike contracts to have shoes made.
   g. What was Nike's net profit in 1991?
   h. How much is Sadisah paid *per day*?
   i. How much is Sadisah paid *per hour*?
   j. What are Sadisah's living conditions?
   k. What is the labor cost for a pair of Nike's that sells in the United States for $80.00?

2. Think about this question: How would a U.S. shoeworker be affected by Nike's decision to move its factories out of the country?

3. Working in groups, answer these two questions, using overhead transparencies.
   a. List some concerns or questions that a U.S. citizen/consumer might have regarding the Nike company.
   b. What are some options for citizens/consumers who question a company's business practices?

Assignment

Write a letter to the Nike company expressing your support of its decision to move production out of the country, criticizing its decision to move production out of the country, or asking questions for more information. Every letter should be at least a page long and should include a couple of questions relating to global economics.

continued

Lesson 11.26 *(continued)*

We are hopeful that Nike will respond. A response might be more likely if you include a little information about yourself.

(If you are opposed to writing a letter to Nike, the alternative assignment is to write a one- or two-page essay on the subject of a company's right to move production out of the country.)

Grading

There are no right or wrong opinions, but the letters and essays will be graded on the basis of logical reasoning and depth of explanation. Extra credit will be given to a person who receives a response from Nike.

Reprinted with permission of the author.

Conclusions

The curriculum model described in this chapter provides a rationale for multicultural education (i.e., the core values and goals) that gives teachers the support they may need when they face pressures and questions from colleagues, the community, and students. The chapter's instructional units and lessons breathe life into the model and illustrate how teachers have used it to create both interdisciplinary and single-discipline plans for teaching.

If teachers are to include multicultural perspectives in their curriculum, they will need to develop new plans for instruction. A curriculum model such as the one proposed here can guide us as we gather sources of information (media, texts, speakers, etc.); select subject matter content, resources, and materials; identify instructional goals and objectives; and decide on teaching strategies and learning activities. Teachers who seek a more comprehensive transformation of their curriculum—one that goes beyond the series of new lessons or units exemplified in this chapter—can use the model's core values and goals to restructure the curriculum so that students can examine "concepts, issues, events, and themes from the perspectives of diverse ethnic and cultural groups."[78]

We can see that a multicultural curriculum is inclusive of diverse cultural perspectives and histories, and also fosters fair-minded critical thinking, compassion, and social action. Furthermore, it is based on the belief and assumption that teachers can make a difference in students' lives and that students can eventually make a difference in society. Thus, a multicultural curriculum is highly interactive with the three other dimensions of multicultural education identified in Chapter 1: the movement toward educational equity, the process of becoming interculturally competent, and the commitment to combat racism, sexism, and all forms of prejudice and discrimination.

Selected Sources for Further Study

Andrzejewski, J., Baltodano, M., & Symcox, L. (2009). *Social Justice, Peace, and Environmental Education: Transformative Standards*. New York: Routlege.

Bigelow, B. (2006). *The Line Between Us: Teaching about the Border and Mexican Immigration*. Milwaukee, WI: Rethinking Schools.

Bigelow, B., & Peterson, B. (2002). *Rethinking Globalization: Teaching for Justice in an Unjust World*. Milwaukee, WI: Rethinking Schools.

Cahan, S. and Kocur, Z. (eds.) (1996). *Contemporary Art and Multicultural Education*. New York: Routledge & The New Museum of Modern Art.

Cai, M. (2002). *Multicultural Literature for Children and Young Adults: Reflections on Critical Issues*. Westport, CT: Greenwood Press.

Carney, J. A. (2001). *Black Rice: The African Origins of Rice Cultivation in the Americas*. Cambridge, MA: Harvard University Press.

Chastoff, D., & Cohen, H. S. (2008). *It's Still Elementary: Talking About Gay Issues in School*. San Francisco, CA: Groundspark. (DVD and 140-page softcover curriculum guide.)

Christensen, L. (2000). *Reading, Writing, and Rising Up: Teaching about Social Justice and the Power of the Written Word*. Milwaukee, WI: Rethinking Schools.

Christensen, L. (2008). *Teaching for Joy and Justice: Reimagining the Social Justice Classroom*. Milwaukee, WI: Rethinking Schools.

Cornelius, C. (1999). *Iroquois Corn in a Culture-Based Curriculum*. Albany: SUNY Press.

Diamond, J. (1997). *Guns, Germs, and Steel: The Fates of Human Societies*. New York: Norton.

Glendon, M. A. (2001). *A World Made New: Eleanor Roosevelt and the Universal Declaration of Human Rights*. New York: Random House.

Gutstein, E., & Peterson, B. (2005). *Rethinking Mathematics: Teaching Social Justice by the Numbers*. Milwaukee, WI: Rethinking Schools.

Kramarae, C., Part IV Editor. (2007). Gender Equity Strategies in the Content Areas, pages 231–463 in Klein, S. S., General Editor, *Handbook for Achieving Gender Equity through Education*, Second Edition. Mahwah, NJ: Lawrence Erlbaum Associates.

Menkart, D., Murray, A. D., & View, J. L. (2004). *Putting the Movement Back Into Civil Rights Teaching*. Teaching for Change and the Poverty & Race Research Action Council (PRRAC): www.civilrightsteaching.org.

Multicultural Perspectives (the magazine of the National Association for Multicultural Education, NAME).

Multicultural Review (a highly rated librarian's journal on ethnic studies literature).

Rethinking Columbus. Special Issue of *Rethinking Schools*, 1001 E. Keefe Ave., Milwaukee, WI, 53212 tel.: 414-964-9646.

Rethinking Our Classrooms: Teaching for Equity and Justice. Special Issue of *Rethinking Schools*, 1001 E. Keefe Ave., Milwaukee, WI, 53212 tel.: 414-964-9646.

Wood, D., Kaiser, W. L., & Abramms, B. (2006). *Seeing through Maps: Many Ways to See the World*. Amherst, MA: ODP Press.

Zavlasky, C. (1993). *Multicultural Mathematics*. Portland, OR: J. Weston Walch.

(Additional resources are noted in many of the lessons in this chapter.)

Websites

- **The National Association for Multicultural Education (NAME):** www.nameorg.org
- **National Clearinghouse for English Language Acquisition and Language Instruction Educational Programs:** www.nclea.gwu.edu

- **Rethinking Schools:** www.rethinkingschools.org
- **Teaching for Change:** www.teachingforchange.org.
- **Teaching Tolerance:** www.teachingtolerance.org.

Now go to Topic #11: **Curriculum** in the MyEducationLab (www.myeducationlab.com) for your course, where you can:

- Find learning outcomes for these topics along with the national standards that connect to these outcomes.

- Complete Assignments and Activities that can help you more deeply understand the chapter content.

- Apply and practice your understanding of the core teaching skills identified in the chapter with the Building Teaching Skills and Dispositions learning units.

Endnotes

Chapter 1

1. A portion of this section is adapted from an article published previously: C. E. Bennett, "Genres of Research in Multicultural Education," *Review of Research in Educational Research*, 72, no. 2 (2001): 171–217.

2. H. M. Kallen, *Culture and Democracy in the United States* (New York: Boni and Liveright, 1924). See also M. R. Konvitz, "Horace Meyer Kallen (1882–1974): Philosopher of the Hebraic American Idea," in *American Jewish Yearbook, 1974–1975*, ed. M. Fine and M Himmelfarb (Philadelphia: Jewish Publication Society of America, 1974), 65–67.

3. D. L. Sills (ed.), "Assimilation," in *International Encyclopedia of the Social Sciences*, Vol. 1 (New York: Macmillan/Free Press, 1968), 438–444.

4. Gonzalez, N., "Processual Approaches to Multicultural Education," *Applied Journal of Behavioral Sciences*, 31, no. 2, (1995): 234–244.

5. R. Hanvey, *An Attainable Global Perspective* (New York: Center for War/Peace Studies, 1975), 4.

6. M. Gibson, "Approaches to Multicultural Education in the United States: Some Concepts and Assumptions," *Anthropology and Education Quarterly*, 7, no. 4 (1976): 7–18. Reprinted in *Anthropology and Education Quarterly*, 15, no. 1 (1984): 99–120.

7. W. B. Gudykunst and Y. Y. Kim, *Communicating with Strangers: An Approach to Intercultural Communications* (New York: Addison-Wesley, 1984), 230.

8. Ibid., 231.

9. Ibid.

10. Gibson, "Approaches to Multicultural Education."

11. See acknowledgments in Chapter 11.

12. P. V. Beck, A. L. Walters, and N. Francisco, *The Sacred: Ways of Knowledge, Sources of Life* (Tsaile, AZ: Navajo Community College Press, 1977), 12.

13. This quote is taken from the Planetary Citizens Registry (P.O. Box 2777, San Anselmo, CA 94960) and was quoted in D. Dufty, S. Sawkins, N. Pickard, J. Power, and A. Bowe, *Seeing It Their Way: Ideas, Activities and Resources for Intercultural Studies* (London: Reed Education, 1976), 29. Reprinted by permission.

14. See, for example, J. Kozol, *Savage Inequalities* (New York: Crown, 1991).

15. G. E. Foster, "Cultivating the Thinking of Low Achievers: A Matter of Equity," *Journal of Negro Education*, 58, no. 4 (1989): 461–467.

16. Y. Padron, "Teaching and Learning Risks Associated with Limited Cognitive Mastery in Science and Mathematics for Limited English Proficient Students," in *Proceedings of the Third National Symposium on Limited English Proficient Students' Issues. Focus on Middle and High Schools*, Vol. 2 (Washington, DC: U.S. Department of Education, OBEMLA [Office of Bilingual Education and Minority Language Affairs], 1994).

17. National Center for Education Statistics.

18. See, for example, Asia Society, *Asia in American Textbooks: An Evaluation* (New York: Asia Society, 1976); J. Friedlander, *The Middle East: The Image and the Reality* (Los Angeles: University of California Press, 1980); S. J. Hall, *Africa in U.S. Schools, K–12: A Survey* (New York: African Institute, 1978); and *In Search of Mutual Understanding, Japan/United States Textbook Study Project, Joint Report* (Washington, DC: National Council of the Social Studies, 1981).

19. National Center for Education Statistics, Participation in Education: Elementary/Secondary,http://nces.ed.gov/programs/coe/2009/section1/indicator07.retrieved 8/20/09.

20. See Chapter 9, pages 265–270.

21. M. Walzer, E. T. Kantowicz, J. Higham, and M. Harrington, *The Politics of Ethnicity* (Cambridge, MA: Belknap Press of Harvard University Press, 1982).

22. Ibid.

23. R. Muller, "The Need for Global Education" (from a speech presented by World Federalists of Canada, 1988, available from Sally Curry, 25 Dundana Avenue, Dundas Ontario, Canada L9H 4ES). See also "Can Man Save This Fragile Earth?" *National Geographic*, 174, no. 6 (1988).

24. A. Rose, *The Condensed Version of Gunnar Myrdal's an American Dilemma* (New York: Harper Torchbooks, 1964), 1–2.

25. C. North, "Delving into the Substantive Meaning(s) of Social Justice," *Review of Educational Research*, 76, no. 4 (2006): 507–535.

26. H. A. Sagar and J. W. Schofield, "Integrating the Desegregated School: Problems and Possibilities," in *Advances in Motivation and Achievement: The Effects of School Desegregation on Motivation and Achievement*, Vol. 1, ed. D. E. Bartz and M. L. Maehr (Greenwich, CT: JAI Press, 1984), 203–242. Following quotation is reprinted by permission of the publisher. Copyright © 1984 by JAI Press.

27. Ibid., 208.

28. Ibid., 212.

29. Ibid., 220–221.

30. Ibid., 231–232.

31. W. E. B. DuBois, "Does the Negro Need Separate Schools?" *Journal of Negro Education*, 4, no. 103S: 326, as quoted in Derrick Bell, *And We Are Not Saved: The Elusive Quest for Racial Justice* (New York: Basic Books, 1987), 120–121. For a discussion of some exemplary schools serving African American children and youth today, see *EBONY*, special issue on Save the Children, 43, no. 10 (August 1988).

32. T. Pettigrew, "The Case for the Racial Integration of the Schools," in *Report on the Future of School Desegregation in the United States*, ed. O. Duff (Pittsburgh: University of Pittsburgh, Consultative Resource Center on School Desegregation and Conflict, 1973).

33. R. Rosenthal and L. Jacobson, *Pygmalion in the Classroom: Teacher Expectation and Pupils' Intellectual Development* (New York: Holt, Rinehart and Winston, 1968).

34. T. L. Good, "Two Decades of Research on Teacher Expectations: Findings and Future Directions," *Journal of Teacher Education*, July–August (1987): 33. See also H. Cooper and T. Good, *Pygmalion Grows Up: Studies in the Expectation Process* (New York: Longman, 1983); and J. Dusek (ed.), *Teacher Expectancies* (Hillsdale, NJ: Erlbaum, 1985). For a discussion of the disproportionately high numbers of ethnic minorities among the nation's school dropouts due to "a dysfunctional education system that produces dropouts," see B. N. Kunisawa, "A Nation in Crisis: The Dropout Dilemma," *NEA Today*, 6, no. 6 (1988): 61–65.

35. C. Cornbleth, O. L. Davis, Jr., and C. Bennett Button, "Expectations for Pupil Achievement and Teacher–Pupil Interaction," *Social Education*, 38, January (1974): 54–58.

36. Described in G. Gay, "Differential Dyadic Interactions of Black and White Teachers with Black and White Pupils in Recently Desegregated Social Studies Classrooms: A Function of Teacher and Pupil Ethnicity," Office of Education, Project no. 2F113, 1974.

37. C. Bennett and J. J. Harris III, "Suspensions and Expulsions of Male and Black Students: A Study of the Causes of Disproportionality," *Urban Education*, 16, no. 4 (1982): 399–423.

38. C. Bennett, "A Study of Classroom Climate in Desegregated Schools," *Urban Review*, 13, no. 3 (1981): 161–179.

39. Gay, "Differential Dyadic Interactions"; also see R. Rist, "Student Social Class and Teacher Expectations: The Self-fulfilling Prophecy in Ghetto Education," *Harvard Education Review*, 40, no. 3 (1970): 411–451; U.S. Civil Rights Commission, Teachers and Students, *Report V: Mexican-American Education Study. Differences in Teacher Interaction with Mexican-American and Anglo Students* (Washington, DC: Government Printing Office, 1973).

40. G. Allport, *The Nature of Prejudice* (Reading, MA: Addison Wesley, 1954), 281.

41. Ibid.

42. G. A. Forehand and M. Ragosta, *A Handbook for Integrated Schooling* (Princeton, NJ: Educational Testing Service, 1976), 79.

43. E. Cohen, "Status Equalization in the Desegregated School" (paper presented at the annual meeting of the American Educational Research Association, San Francisco, April 1979); and E. Cohen, "Student Influence in the Classroom" (paper presented at the annual meeting of the American Educational Research Association, Toronto, 1978).

44. Forehand and Ragosta, *A handbook for Integrated Schooling*. In 1994, on the fortieth anniversary of the Supreme Court's school desegregation ruling, we find that nearly 70 percent of the nation's African American students attend segregated schools. See the *New York Times*, May 18, 1994, for a series of articles on the nation's struggle to desegregate schools.

45. K. M. Teel and J. E. Obidah (eds.), *Building Racial and Cultural Competence in the Classroom: Strategies from Urban Education* (New York: Teachers College Press, 2008), 2.

46. Ibid., 3.

47. Ibid.

48. R. Hanvey, *An Attainable Global Perspective.*

49. Ibid., 6.

50. R. Paul, *Critical Thinking: What Every Person Needs to Survive in a Rapidly Changing World*, Rev. 3rd ed. (Santa Rosa, CA: Foundation for Critical Thinking, 1993), 123.

51. C. Sleeter, "An Analysis of the Critiques of Multicultural Education," in *The Handbook of Research on Multicultural Education*, eds. J. A. Banks and C. A. Banks, 81–94 (New York: Macmillan, 1995).

52. Ibid.

53. I am grateful to Bradley Levinson, a colleague at Indiana University, for bringing this phrase to my attention.

Chapter 2

1. E. B. Tylor, *Primitive Culture* (1871; reprint, New York: Harper Torchbooks, 1958).

2. C. Geertz, *Interpretation of Culture* (New York: Basic Books, 1973), 89.

3. J. P. Spradley and D. W. McCurdy, *Anthropology: The Cultural Perspective* (New York: John Wiley & Sons, 1975), 5.

4. W. H. Goodenough, "Cultural Anthropology and Linguistics," Georgetown University Monograph Series on Language and Linguistics, no. 9, 1957, 167.

5. R. A. LeVine, "Properties of Culture: An Ethnographic View," in *Culture Theory: Essays on Mind, Self and Emotion*, eds. R. A. Sweder and R. A. LeVine, 67–87 (Cambridge, England: Cambridge University Press, 1986).

6. H. C. Triandis, "Cultural Training, Cognitive Complexity and Interpersonal Attitudes," in *Cross-Cultural Perspectives on Learning*, eds. R. W. Brislin, Stephen Bachner, and Walter J. Lonner (New York: John Wiley & Sons, 1975).

7. M. Gibson, "Approaches to Multicultural Education in the United States," *Anthropology and Education Quarterly*, 15, no. 1 (Spring 1984): 94–119.

8. J. P. Spradley and D. W. McCurdy, *Conformity and Conflict* (Glenview, IL: Scott, Foresman, 1990), 480.

9. A. J. Kraemer, "A Cultural Self-Awareness Approach to Improving Intercultural Communication Skills," ERIC ED 079 213 (April 1973).

10. T. B. Saral, "Consciousness Theory and Intercultural Communication" (paper presented at the International Communication Association, Portland, Oregon, April 14–17, 1976).

11. C. Kluckhohn, *Mirror for Man* (Greenwich, CT: Fawcett, 1965), 19.

12. R. D. Abrahams, "Cultural Conflict in the Classroom" (videotape from symposium sponsored by the Alachna County Teacher Center, Gainesville, Florida, January 30, 1975).

13. J. Lynne McBrien, "Educational Needs and Barriers for Refugee Students in the United States: A Review of the Literature," *Review of Educational Research*, 75, no. 3 (2005): 329–364.

14. Ibid., 353.

15. Ibid. Several colleagues and I have encountered this misunderstanding about plagiarism with a number of our graduate students from East Asian countries.

16. G. Valdes, *Con Respeto: Bridging the Distance Between Culturally Diverse Families and Schools* (New York: Teachers College Press, 1996).

17. McBrien, "Educational Needs and Barriers for Refugee Students in the United States," 346.

18. Ibid., 352.

19. Chapters 8–10 focus on promising practices and exemplary school programs. Also see G. Q. Conchas (2006). *The Color of Success: Race and High-Achieving Urban Youth*, New York: Teachers College Press and exemplary programs listed in McBrien noted above.

20. E. T. Hall, *The Silent Language* (New York: Doubleday, 1959). See also by Hall, *The Hidden Dimension* (New York: Doubleday, 1966); *Beyond Culture* (New York: Doubleday, 1976); *The Dance of Life*

(New York: Doubleday, 1983); and "Proxemics: The Study of Man's Spatial Relations," in *Intercultural Communication: A Reader*, eds. L. A. Samouar and R. E. Porter, 172–180 (Belmont, CA: Wadsworth, 1972).

21. C. Bennett, "Teaching Intercultural Competence and Informed Citizenship." (Table 2.1 was developed for the paper presented at the Annual Conference of the National Council of the Social Studies in New York, November 1986.)

22. See C. C. Mukhopadhyhy, R. Henze, and Y. T. Moses, *How Real Is Race? A Sourcebook on Race, Culture, and Biology* (Lanham, MD: Rowman & Littlefield Education, 2007) for an outstanding discussion of this topic, including ideas for classroom teaching as well as the underlying theory and research.

23. Ibid., 21.

24. Ibid., 35.

25. J. Kelso, "The Concept of Race," *Improving College and University Teaching*, 15, no. 95 (Spring 1967): 7.

26. A. Montagu, *Man's Most Dangerous Myth: The Fallacy of Race*, 5th ed. (New York: Oxford University Press, 1974), 7.

27. Ibid.

28. Kelso, "The Concept of Race."

29. H. J. Ehrlich, *The Social Psychology of Prejudice* (New York: Oxford University Press, 1974), 7.

30. M. M. Gordon, *Assimilation in American Life* (New York: Oxford University Press, 1966).

31. Noted in O. Patterson, "Black Americans," in *Understanding America: The Anatomy of an Exceptional Nation*, eds. P. H. Schuck and J. Q. Wilson (New York: Public Affairs, 2008), 376.

32. Ibid., 377.

33. Ibid., 380.

34. Ibid., 376–382.

35. J. Phinney, "When We Talk About Ethnic Groups, What Do We Mean?" *American Psychologist*, 51, no. 9 (1960): 923.

36. This paragraph is taken from my chapter, "Research of Racial Issues in American Higher Education" in *Handbook of Research on Multicultural Education*, 2nd ed., eds. J. A. Banks and C. M. Banks (San Francisco: Jossey-Bass, 2004), 862.

37. M. Navarro, "Who Are We? New Dialogue on Mixed Race," *New York Times*, March 31, 2008, A1.

38. M. P. P. Root, "Multiracial Families and Children: Implication for Educational Research and Practice," in *Handbook of Research on Multicultural Education*, 2nd ed., eds. J. A. Banks and C. M. Banks (San Francisco: Jossey-Bass, 2004), 110–124.

39. T. Arboleda, *In the Shadow of Race: Growing Up as a Multiethnic, Multicultural, and "Multiracial" American* (Mahwah, NJ: Lawrence Erlbaum, 1998).

40. Ibid., 1.

41. Navarro, "Multiracial Families and Children."

42. L. Wirth, "The Problem of Minority Groups," in *The Science of Man in the World Crisis*, ed. R. Linton (New York: Columbia University Press, 1945).

43. As discussed in J. R. Feagin and C. B. Feagin, *Racial and Ethnic Relations* (Englewood Cliffs, NJ: Prentice Hall, 1993), 10.

44. D. L. Sills (ed.), "Assimilation," in *International Encyclopedia of the Social Sciences*, Vol. 1 (New York: Macmillan/Free Press, 1968), 438.

45. E. P. Cubberly, *Changing Conceptions of Education* (Boston: Houghton Mifflin, 1909), 16.

46. D. L. Sills (ed.), "Pluralism," in *International Encyclopedia of the Social Sciences*, Vol. 12, 438–444.

47. H. M. Kallen, *Culture and Democracy in the United States* (New York: Boni and Liveright, 1924); see also M. R. Konvitz, "Horace Meyer Kallen (1882–1974): Philosopher of the Hebraic American Idea," in *American Jewish Yearbook*, 1974–1975, eds. M. Fine and M. Himmelfarb (Philadelphia: Jewish Publication Society of America, 1974), 65–67.

48. G. Gay, "Multiethnic Education Historical Development and Future Prospects," *Phi Delta Kappan*, 64, no. 8 (April 1983): 560–561.

49. A. Portes and R. G. Rumbaut, *Immigrant America: A Portrait*, 3rd ed. (Berkeley: University of California Press, 2006).

50. B. Purkayastha, *Negotiating Ethnicity: Second-Generation South Asian Americans Traverse a Transitional World* (New Brunswick, NJ: Rutgers University Press), 2005.

51. Portes and Rubaut, *Immigrant America.*

52. Ibid.

53. W. Longstreet, *Aspects of Ethnicity: Understanding Differences in Pluralistic Classrooms* (New York: Teachers College Press, 1978). These excerpts have been reprinted with the permission of the author.

54. Ibid., 19.

55. Ibid.

56. Ibid., 22.

57. M. Benitez, "A Blueprint for the Education of the Mexican American," ERIC ED 076 294 (March 1973): 7. Also see B. Perez and M. E. Torres-Guzman, *Learning in Two Worlds* (New York: Longman, 1992).

58. R. D. Abrahams and G. Gay, "Talking Black in the Classroom," in *Language and Culture Diversity in American Education*, eds. R. D. Abrahams and R. C. Troike (Englewood Cliffs, NJ: Prentice Hall, 1972), 201–202.

59. Longstreet, *Aspects of Ethnicity*, 50.

60. Ibid., 51–52.

61. S. B. Heath, *Ways with Words: Language, Life, and Work in Communities and Classrooms* (Cambridge, England: Cambridge University Press, 1983); L. Delpit, *Other People's Children: Cultural Conflict in the Classroom* (New York: The New Press, 1995).

62. J. Daniels, I. Hines, G. Ross, and G. Walker, "Teaching Afro-American Communication," ERIC ED 082 247 (November 1972). See also G. Gay and W. Barber, *Expressively Black* (New York: Praeger, 1988).

63. See, for example, B. Shade, ed., *Culture, Style, and the Educative Process* (Springfield, IL: Charles C Thomas, 1989).

64. M. Bennett, "Culture and Changing Realities" (Society of Intercultural Education Training and Research [SIETAR], preconference workshop, Third Annual SIETAR Conference, Chicago, February 25, 1977).

65. T. Kochman, *Black and White Styles in Conflict* (Chicago: University of Chicago, 1981), 4–5.

66. W. LaBarre, "Paralinguistics, Kinesics, and Cultural Anthropology," in *Intercultural Communication: A Reader*, eds. L. A. Samouar and R. E. Porter, 172–180 (Belmont, CA: Wadsworth, 1972).

67. Ibid., 173.

68. Hall, *Beyond Culture*, 58.

69. Ibid.

70. Ibid.

71. M. Rokeach, *Attitudes, Values and Beliefs* (San Francisco: Jossey-Bass, 1969).

72. Spradley and McCurdy, *Anthropology*, 495.

73. G. Gay and R. D. Abrahams, "Black Culture in the Classroom," in *Language and Culture Diversity in American Education*, eds. R. D. Abrahams and R. C. Troike (Englewood Cliffs, NJ: Prentice Hall, 1976), 80.

74. B. Levinson, personal communication, July 1997.

75. G. Valdes, *Con Respeto: Bridging the Distance between Culturally Diverse Families and Schools: An Ethnographic Portrait* (New York: Teachers College Press, 1996).

76. K. A. Appiah and H. L. Gates, *The Dictionary of Global Culture* (New York: Knopf, 1997), 262.

77. M. I. Herskovitz, *The Myth of the Negro Past* (Boston: Beacon Press, 1969). See also C. Keil, *Urban Blues* (Chicago: University of Chicago Press, 1966); and L. Jones, *Blues People: The Negro Experience in White America and the Music That Developed from It* (New York: William Morrow, 1963). Information was also gathered at "African Perspectives," a panel at the annual meeting of the National Council for the Social Studies, NCSS, Orlando, Florida, November 19, 1988.

78. B. J. Shade, "Afro-American Cognitive Style: A Variable in School Success?" *Review of Educational Research*, 52, no. 2 (Summer 1982): 219–238. See also J. H. Benson, *Black Children: Their Roots, Culture, and Learning Styles*, rev. ed. (Baltimore: Johns Hopkins Press, 1986).

79. A. Hilliard, "Alternatives to IQ Testing: An Approach to the Identification of Gifted Minority Children" (Final Report to the California State Department of Education, 1976).

Chapter 3

1. S. Erlanger, "After U.S. Breakthrough, Europe Looks in Mirror," *New York Times*, November 12, 2008.

2. J. R. Feagin and H. Vera, *White Racism* (New York: Routledge, 1995), 193.

3. S. A. Holmes, "A Rose-Colored View of Race," *New York Times*, Sunday June 15, 1997, p. 4.

4. A. Goodheart, "Change of Heart." *AARP: The Magazine*, May/June 2004, 46.

5. Ibid., 47.

6. Ibid., 93.

7. A. Nagourney and M. Thee, "Poll Finds Obama Isn't Closing Divide on Race," *New York Times*, July 16, 2008, pp. 1–4.

8. Ibid., 2.

9. C. N. Lee, "Continuing Violence Against Asian Students," *Asian-Nation: The Landscape of Asian American.* Available at: www.asian-nation.org/headlines/2005/11continuing-violence-against-asian-students. Accessed March 16, 2009.

10. Ibid.

11. Ibid.

12. S. Mydans, "Los Angeles Policemen Acquitted in Taped Beating," *New York Times*, April 30, 1992, pp. A1, B8.

13. P. Applebome, "Opponents' Moves Refueling Debate on School Busing," *New York Times*, September 26, 1995, p. 1.

14. *Intelligence Report*, October 1994, Southern Poverty Law Center, 9–12.

15. M. Janofsky, "Anti-Defamation League Tells of Rise in Web Hate Sites," *New York Times*, October 22, 1997, p. A17.

16. A. Elliott, "Muslims Report 50 Percent Increase in Bias Crimes," *New York Times*, May 12, 2005, p. A24.

17. S. Fries, "Burial Exposes Racial Rift in Texas," *New York Times*, July 5, 2008, pp. 1–3.

18. J. Steinhauer, "Immigration and Gang Violence Propel Crusade," *New York Times*, May 15, 2008, pp. 1–3.

19. Feagin and Vera, *White Racism*, 146.

20. B. Crossette, *New York Times*, March 4, 2001, p. 8.

21. G. Allport, *The Nature of Prejudice* (Reading, MA: Addison Wesley, 1954), xiii–xiv.

22. J. Forbes, *Education of the Culturally Different: A Multi-Cultural Approach* (San Francisco: Far West Laboratory for Educational Research and Development, 1969), 50.

23. R. Dennis, "Socialization and Racism: The White Experience," in *Impacts of Racism on White Americans*, eds. B. P. Bowser and R. G. Hunt, 71–85 (Beverly Hills, CA: Sage, 1981).

24. Ibid.

25. Ibid., 82.

26. Ibid.

27. M. Rokeach, *Beliefs, Attitudes, and Values* (San Francisco, CA: Jossey-Bass, Inc., 1968).

28. J. G. Ponteratto and P. B. Pedersen, *Preventing Prejudice: A Guide for Counselors and Educators* (Newbury Park, CA: Sage, 1993).

29. G. Allport, *ABC's of Scapegoating* (New York: Anti-Defamation League of B'nai B'rith, 1979). The quotations on the following pages are from Gordon Allport, *The Nature of Prejudice*, © 1979, Addison-Wesley, Reading, Massachusetts. Reprinted with permission of the publisher.

30. J. L. Gwaltney, *Drylongso: A Self-portrait of Black America* (New York: Random House, 1980), 73–74. The following quotations are reprinted by permission of Random House, Inc., and John Brockman Associates. Copyright © 1980 by John Langston Gwaltney.

31. J. M. Jones, "The Concept of Racism and Its Changing Reality," in *Impacts of Racism on White Americans*, eds. B. D. Bowser and R. G. Hunt (Beverly Hills, CA: Sage, 1981), 118.

32. See C. R. Ridley, "Racism in Counseling as an Adverse Behavioral Process," in *Counseling across Cultures*, 3rd ed. (Honolulu: University of Hawaii Press, 1989), 55–77.

33. Jones, "The Concept of Racism," 131.

34. J. R. Feagin and C. B. Feagin, *Racial and Ethnic Relations* (Englewood Cliffs, NJ: Prentice Hall, 1993), 224.

35. S. Carmichael and C. V. Hamilton, *Black Power: The Politics of Liberation in America* (New York: Random House, 1967).

36. L. L. Knowles and K. Prewitt, *Institutional Racism in America* (Englewood Cliffs, NJ: Prentice Hall, 1969).

37. J. R. Feagin and C. B. Feagin, *Discrimination American Style: Institutional Racism and Sexism* (Englewood Cliffs, NJ: Prentice Hall, 1978), 30.

38. M. A. Jones, *American Immigration* (Chicago: University of Chicago Press, 1960), 79.

39. G. Gay, *Racism in America: Imperatives for Teaching Ethnic Studies* (Washington, DC: National Council for the Social Studies), 27–49.

40. Jones, "The Concept of Racism," 148.

41. Ibid., 18.

42. Graves, J. L. Jr., *The Emperor's New Clothes: Biological Theories of Race at the Millennium* (New York: Rutgers University Press, 2002).

43. A. Montagu, *Man's Most Dangerous Myth: The Fallacy of Race*, 5th ed. (New York: Oxford University Press, 1974), 7.

44. H. J. Ehrlich, *The Social Psychology of Prejudice* (New York: John Wiley & Sons, 1973).

45. M. Adams, "Conceptual Frameworks Introduction," in *Readings for Diversity and Social Justice*, eds. M. Adams, et al., 5–14 (New York: Routledge, 2000).

46. P. S. Rothenberg (ed.), *White Privilege: Essential Readings on the Other Side of Racism* (New York: Worth, 2005), 1.

47. G. Howard, *We Can't Teach What We Don't Know: White Teachers, Multiracial Schools*, 2nd ed. (New York: Teachers College Press), 65.

48. B. Tatum, "The Complexity of Identity: 'Who Am I?' " in *Why Are All the Black Kids Sitting Together in the Cafeteria?* (New York: Basic Books, 1997).

49. See, for example: Brown, C. S. (2002). *Refusing Racism: White Allies and the Struggle for Civil Rights*. New York: Teachers College Press; Derman-Sparks, L. & Ramsey, P. G. "A Short History of White Resistance to Racism in the United States," Chapter 6 in Louise Derman-Sparks & Patricia G. Ramsey (2006), *What If All the Kids Are White?: Anti-Bias Multicultural Education with Young Children and Families*. New York: Teachers College Press; Tatum, B. D. (1994). "Teaching White Students about Racism: The search for White Allies and the Restoration of Hope." *Teachers College Record*, 95, no. 4, 462–476.

50. P. Kivel, "How White People Can Serve as Allies to People of Color to End Racism," in *White Privilege: Essential Readings on the Other Side of Racism*, ed. P. S. Rothenberg, 139–147 (New York: Worth, 2005).

51. Ponteratto and Pedersen, *Preventing Prejudice*, 39.

52. J. Phinney. "When We Talk about Ethnic Groups, What Do We Mean?" *American Psychologist*, 51, no. 9, 923.

53. Ibid.

54. W. E. Cross, Jr., "The Negro to Black Conversion Experience: Toward a Psychology of Black Liberation," *Black World*, 20 (July 1979). Synopsis used by permission of the author.

55. Ibid.

56. W. E. Cross, Jr., "A Two-Factor Theory of Black Identity: Implications for the Study of Identity Development in Minority Children," in *Children's Ethnic Socialization: Pluralism and Development*, eds. J. S. Phinney and M. J. Rotheram (Newbury Park, CA: Sage, 1987), 121.

57. Ibid.

58. Ibid., 123.

59. Ibid.

60. Ibid., 126.

61. J. A. Banks, *Teaching Strategies for Ethnic Studies*, 3rd ed. (Boston: Allyn & Bacon, 1984). Synopsis and quotations from this work are used by permission of Allyn & Bacon, Inc. and J. A. Banks. Copyright © 1984 by Allyn & Bacon, Inc.

62. Ibid., 55–56.

63. Ibid., 56.

64. Ibid.

65. J. A. Banks, *Multiethnic Education: Theory and Practice* (Boston: Allyn & Bacon, 1981), 132.

66. Ibid.

67. D. A. Rosenthal, "Ethnic Identity Development in Adolescence," in *Children's Ethnic Socialization: Pluralism and Development*, eds. J. S. Phinney and M. J. Rotheram (Newbury Park, CA: Sage, 1987), 156–179.

68. Banks, *Teaching Strategies*, 56.

69. Ibid.

70. Ponteratto and Pedersen, *Preventing Prejudice*, 63–83.

71. Ibid.

72. Ibid., 78.

73. H. C. Triandis, *Attitude and Attitude Change* (New York: John Wiley & Sons, 1971), 102–103. Quotation reprinted by permission of the publisher. Copyright © 1971 by John Wiley & Sons, Inc.

74. Ibid.

75. E. Watters, "Claude Steele Has Scores to Settle," *The New York Times Magazine*, September 17, 1995, pp. 45–47.

76. Ibid., 45.

77. Ibid., 46.

78. Ibid., 47.

79. G. Allport, *The Nature of Prejudice* (Reading, MA: Addison-Wesley, 1979), 42. The quotations on the following pages are from Gordon Allport. *The Nature of Prejudice*, © 1979, Addison-Wesley, Reading, MA. Reprinted with permission of the publisher.

80. Ibid., 44.

81. Ibid.

82. G. S. Pate, "The Ingredients of Prejudice" (paper presented at the College and University Faculty Assembly of the National Council for the Social Studies, Boston, November 24, 1982).

83. Ibid.

84. B. Davidson, *African Kingdoms* (New York: Time-Life Books, 1966).

85. Ibid., 29.

86. E. A. Toppin, "The Forgotten People," *Christian Science Monitor*, March 6, 1969 (special insert).

87. J. H. Franklin, *From Slavery to Freedom* (New York: Alfred A. Knopf, 1967), 15.

88. Davidson, *African Kingdoms*, 83–84.

89. Toppin, "Forgotten People."

90. Davidson, *African Kingdoms*, 22.

91. Ibid.

92. M. F. Berry and J. W. Blassingame, *Long Memory: The Black Experience in America* (New York: Oxford University Press, 1982), 1–6.

93. Davidson, *African Kingdoms*, 82.

94. Ibid.

95. Ibid., 21.

96. Ibid.

97. I am again indebted to Bradley Levinson for this observation.

98. D. Wiley, "The African Connection," *Wisconsin Alumnus*, 77, no. 2 (January 1976): 7–11.

99. A. Zikiros and M. Wiley, Africa in Social Studies Textbooks (East Lansing: African Studies Center, Michigan State University, 1978), 15.

100. Ibid.

101. *Stereotypes, Distortions and Omissions in U.S. History Textbooks* (New York: Council on Interracial Books for Children, 1977), 16.

102. B. Banfield, "How Racism Takes Root," *UNESCO Courier*, March 1979, 31.

103. C. M. Steele and J. Aronson "Stereotype Threat Does Not Live by Steele and Aronson (1995) Alone," *American Psychologist*, 59, no. 1 (2004): 1.

104. See www.cocc.edu/lisal/thebluesteye/themes.htm.

Chapter 4

1. I. M. Miyares and C. A. Airriess, "Creating Contemporary Ethnic Geographies—A Review of Immigration Law," in *Contemporary Ethnic Geographies in America*, ed. I. M. Miyares and C. A. Airriess, 27–50 (Lanham, MD: Rowman & Littlefield, 2007), 27.

2. P. Gap Min, "Introduction," in *Mass Migration to the United States: Classical and Contemporary Periods*, ed. P. Gap Min, 1–19 (Walnut Creek, CA: Alta Mira Press, 2002), 7.

3. K. Berry, Z. Grossman, and H.-M. Pawiki, "Native Americans," in *Contemporary Ethnic Geographies in America*, ed. I. M. Miyares and C. A. Airriess (Lanham, MD: Rowman & Littlefield, 2007), 51.

4. Miyares and Airriess, "Creating Contemporary Ethnic Geographies," 29.

5. J. McKee, "Humanity on the Move," in *Ethnicity in Contemporary America*, ed. J. McKee 19–46 (Lanham, MD: Rowman & Littlefield, 2000), 24.

6. D. Schneider, "Naturalization and U.S. Citizenship in Two Periods of Mass Migration (1890–1930 and 1965–2000)" in *Mass Migration to the United States: Classical and Contemporary Periods*, ed. P. Gap Min, 161–197 (Walnut Creek, CA: Alta Mira Press, 2002), 163.

7. Ibid.

8. Ibid.

9. S. Shanahan and S. Olzak, "Immigration and Conflict in the United States," in *Mass Migration to the United States: Classical and Contemporary Periods*, ed. P. Gap Min, 99–133 (Walnut Creek, CA: Alta Mira Press, 2002), 102.

10. Schneider, "Naturalization and U.S. Citizenship in Two Periods of Mass Migration," 164.

11. For an excellent overview and more detailed discussion of major immigration legislation from 1795–1996 see J. McKee, "Humanity on the Move," in *Ethnicity in Contemporary America*, ed. J. McKee 19–46 (Lanham, MD: Rowman & Littlefield, 2000). For more discussion of contemporary immigration legislation see M. Sands Orchowski, *Immigration and the American Dream: Battling the Political Hype and Hysteria* (Lanham, MD: Rowman & Littlefield, 2008).

12. Gap Min, "Introduction," 1.

13. McKee, "Humanity on the Move," 20.

14. I. M. Miyares and C. A. Airriess, "Exploring Contemporary Ethnic Geographies," in *Contemporary Ethnic Geographies in America*, eds. I. M. Miyares and C. A. Airriess, 1–26 (Lanham, MD: Rowman & Littlefield, 2007), 3.

15. McKee, "Humanity on the Move," 23.

16. Schneider, "Naturalization and U.S. Citizenship in Two Periods of Mass Migration," 177.

17. Ibid., 177–178.

18. Ibid., 74.

19. Gap Min, "Introduction," 3.

20. M. Sands Orchowski, *Immigration and the American Dream: Battling the Political Hype and Hysteria* (Lanham, MD: Rowman & Littlefield, 2008), 5.

21. Ibid., 74.

22. William Moyers Journal. http://www.pbs.org/moyers/journal/blog/2007/08/a_new_american_dream_1html. Retrieved 12/18/08.

23. Martin Luther King, Jr.

24. Richard Kluger, *Seizing Destiny: How America Grew from Sea to Shining Sea* (New York: Alfred A. Knopf, 2007, as quoted in Orchowski, *Immigration and the American Dream*, 75.

25. Orchowski, *Immigration and the American Dream*, 75.

26. C. Jaret, "Troubled by Newcomers: Anti-Immigrant Attitudes and Actions During Two Eras of Mass Migration," in *Mass Migration to the United States: Classical and Contemporary Periods*, ed. P. Gap Min, 21–63 (Walnut Creek, CA: Alta Mira Press, 2002), 23.

27. Ibid., 21–29.

28. Ibid., 30.

29. Ibid.

30. Ibid., 31.

31. Ibid., 32.

32. Ibid., 33.

33. Ibid.

34. Ibid., 34.

35. Ibid.

36. Ibid., 36.

37. Ibid.

38. Ibid., 37.

39. Ibid., 39.

40. Min Zhou, "The Changing Face of America: Immigration, Race, Ethnicity, and Social Mobility." Chapter 2 (pages 65–98) in Pyong Gap Min, ed. *Mass Migration to the United States: Classical and Contemporary Periods*, Walnut Creek, CA: AltaMira Press, p. 68.

41. Ibid.

42. Ibid.

43. Ibid., 69.

44. Ibid.

45. Ibid., 70.

46. Ibid., 69.

47. R. C. Jones, "Immigrants Transform and Are Transformed by the U.S. Heartland," in *Immigrants Outside the Megalopolis* (pp. 3–22), ed. R. C. Jones (Lanham, MD: Lexington Books), 3.

48. Ibid., 4.

49. Ibid.

50. Ibid.

51. Min Zhou, The Changing Face, 79.

52. Ibid.

53. Gap Min, "Introduction" 10.

54. P. Gap Min, "Contemporary Immigrants' Advantages for International Cultural Transmission," in *Mass Migration to the United States: Classical and Contemporary Periods*, ed. P. Gap Min (Walnut Creek, CA: Alta Mira Press, 2002), 153.

55. Ibid.

56. Ibid., 156.

57. Ibid., 139.

58. Ibid., 142–144.

59. Ibid., 148.

60. Ibid., 150.

61. Ibid.

62. J. R. Feagin and C. Booher Feagin, *Racial and Ethnic Relations*, 8th ed. (Upper Saddle River, NJ: Prentice Hall), 66.

63. D. Fischer, quoted in Feagin and Booher Feagin, *Racial and Ethnic Relations*, 66.

64. Feagin and Booher Feagin, *Racial and Ethnic Relations*, 66.

65. Ibid.

66. Ibid.

67. Ibid.

68. Ibid.

69. Ibid.

70. J. R. Feagin and C. Booher Feagin, *Racial and Ethnic Relations*, 4th ed. (Upper Saddle River, NJ: Prentice Hall), 73.

71. J. Weatherford, *Indian Givers* (New York: Fawcett Columbine, 1988), 129.

72. Ibid., 117–149.

73. J. A. Banks, *Teaching Strategies for Ethnic Studies* (Boston: Allyn & Bacon, 1991), 247, 249.

74. J. Hraba, *American Ethnicity* (Itasca, IL: F. E. Peacock, 1979), 9.

75. M. A. Jones, *American Immigration* (Chicago: University of Chicago Press, 1960), 93.

76. Ibid., 92.

77. Ibid., 94.

78. Ibid.

79. Ibid., 94–101.

80. Ibid., 107.

81. Ibid., 109.

82. Ibid.

83. Jones, *American Immigration*, 180.

84. Hraba, *American Ethnicity*, 8.

85. Feagin and Feagin, *Racial and Ethnic Relations*, 92.

86. Ibid., 93.

87. Ibid., 91.

88. Ibid., 119.

89. Feagin and Feagin, *Racial and Ethnic Relations*, 120–121.

90. Ibid., 121.

91. Ibid., 123.

92. Jones, *American Immigration*, 118.

93. Ibid., 209.

94. Ibid., 118, 209.

95. R. Ruiz in C. Sleeter, *Empowerment through Multicultural Education* (Albany: SUNY Press, 1991), 225.

96. Feagin, *Racial and Ethnic Relations* (Englewood Cliffs, NJ: Prentice Hall, 1978). The following ethnic capsules and other quotes are from this work and are reprinted by permission of the publisher.

97. Ibid., 108–109.

98. Ibid., 140.

99. Ibid., 141–142.

100. John Marino, *Milestones of the Italian American Experience* (Washington, DC: The National Italian American Foundation, 2005). www.niaf.org.

101. Feagin and Feagin, *Racial and Ethnic Relations*, 79.

102. Ibid.

103. Miyares and Airriess, "Exploring Contemporary Ethnic Geographies," 2.

104. Table 3. "Persons Obtaining Legal Permanent Resident Status by Region and Country of Birth: Fiscal Years 1997 to 2006. U.S. Department of Homeland Security; Office of Immigration Statistics.

105. S. Hardwick, "Slavic Dreams: Post-Soviet Refugee Identity and Adaptation in Portland, Oregon," in *Immigrants Outside Megalopolis: Ethnic Transformation in the Heartland*, ed. R. C. Jones, 25–42 (Lanham, MD: Lexington Books), 25.

106. Ibid., 27.

107. Ibid.

108. Ibid., 35.

109. Ibid., 34.

110. Ibid., 35.

111. Ibid.

112. Ibid., 36.

113. Ibid.

114. Ibid., 37.

115. Ibid., 38.

116. Ibid., 40.

117. T. Sowell, *Ethnic America: A History* (New York: Basic Books, 1980), 77. The quotations from this source are reprinted by permission of the publisher. Copyright © 1981 by Basic Books.

118. Ibid., 76.

119. Ibid., 77.

120. Ibid., 78.

121. Ibid., 80.

122. Ibid., 81.

123. Feagin, *Racial and Ethnic Relations* (Englewood Cliffs, NJ: Prentice Hall, 1978), 179–180.

124. Feagin and Feagin, *Racial and Ethnic Relations*, 146–149.

125. T. Sowell, *Ethnic America*, 71–72.

126. Ibid., 73.

127. Ibid., income index, appendix.

128. Feagin and Feagin, *Racial and Ethnic Relations*, 170.

129. www.adl.org/PresRele/ASUS_12/4671_12.htm.

130. S. J. Gold, "From *The Jazz Singer* to *What a Country!* A Comparison of Jewish Migration to the United States 1880–1930 and 1965–1998," in *Mass Migration to the United States: Classical and Contemporary Periods*, ed. P. Gap Min (Walnut Creek, CA: Alta Mira Press, 2002), 253.

131. Ibid., 255.

132. Ibid.

133. Ibid., 261.

134. Ibid., 264.

135. Ibid., 275.

136. Ibid., 274.

137. D. L. Sills (ed.), "Assimilation," in *International Encyclopedia of the Social Sciences*, Vol. 1 (New York: Macmillan/Free Press, 1968), 438.

138. For an excellent overview and more detailed discussion of major immigration legislation from 1795–1996, see J. O. McKee's "Humanity on the Move," in *Ethnicity in Contemporary America*, ed. J. O. McKee, 19–46 (Lanham, MD: Rowman & Littlefield Publishers, 2000). For more discussion of contemporary immigration legislation, see M. S. Orchowski's *Immigration and the American Dream: Battling the Political Hype and Hysteria* (Lanham, MD: Rowman & Littlefield Publishers, 2008).

139. McKee, "Humanity on the Move," 22.

140. Orchowski, *Immigration and the American Dream*, 33.

141. See M. M. Ngai's "The Johnson-Reed Act of 1924 and the Reconstruction of Race in Immigration Law," Chapter 1 in *Impossible Subjects: Illegal Aliens and the Making of Modern America* (Princeton, NJ: Princeton University Press).

142. Schneider, "Naturalization and U.S. Citizenship in Two Periods of Mass Migration (1890–1930 and 1965–2000)," 177.

143. McKee, "Humanity on the Move," 34–35.

144. Schneider, "Naturalization and U.S. Citizenship in Two Periods of Mass Migration (1890–1930 and 1965–2000)," 177.

145. Orchowski, *Immigration and the American Dream*, 36.

146. McKee, "Humanity on the Move," 26.

147. Orchowski, *Immigration and the American Dream*, 38.

148. McKee, "Humanity on the Move," 23.

149. Orchowski, *Immigration and the American Dream*, 39.

150. Ibid., 39.

151. Ibid.

152. Ibid.

153. C. Airriess and D. Clawson, "Mainland Southeast Refugees," in *Ethnicity in Contemporary America*, ed. J. O. McKee, 311–346 (Lanham, MD: Rowman & Littlefield Publishers, 2000), 316–317.

154. Ibid.

155. Ibid.

Chapter 5

1. A. Hirschfelder, *Happily May I Walk: American Indians and Alaska Natives Today* (New York: Charles Scribner, 1982).

2. J. A. Banks, *Teaching Strategies for Ethnic Studies*, 5th ed. (Boston: Allyn & Bacon, 1991), 151.

3. Hirschfelder, *Happily May I Walk*, 4.

4. H. J. Viola, *After Columbus: The Smithsonian Chronicle of the North American Indians* (New York: Orion Books, 1990), 18.

5. Viola, *After Columbus*, 27.

6. J. Weatherford, *Native Roots: How the Indians Enriched America* (New York: Crown Publishers, 1991), 27.

7. Ibid., 16–17.

8. Ibid., 41.

9. Ibid., 42.

10. Ibid., 67.

11. Ibid.

12. J. Hraba, *American Ethnicity* (Itasca, IL: F. E. Peacock, 1979), 212; and J. Feagin and C. B. Feagin, *Racial and Ethnic Relations*, 4th ed. (Englewood Cliffs, NJ: Prentice Hall, 1993), 120.

13. Ibid., 212–213.

14. D. McNickle, "Indian and European: Indian–White Relations from Discovery to 1887," in *The Emergent Native Americans*, ed. D. E. Walker, Jr., 75–86 (Boston: Little, Brown, 1972).

15. R. Tsosie, "How the Land Was Taken: The Legacy of the Lewis and Clark Expedition for Native Nations," in *American Indian Nations: Yesterday, Today, and Tomorrow*, eds. G. Horse Capture, D. Champagne, and C. C. Jackson, 227–239 (Lanham, MD: AltaMira Press, 2007), 240.

16. G. R. Campbell and Neyooxet Greymorning, "What's in a Label? Native American Identity and the Rise of a Tradition of Racism," in *American Indian Nations: Yesterday, Today, and Tomorrow*, eds. G. Horse Capture, D. Champagne, and C. C. Jackson, 22–28 (Lanham, MD: AltaMira Press, 2007), 22.

17. Ibid.

18. Tsosie, "How the Land Was Taken," 244.

19. J. M. Goodman and D. Heffington, "Native Americans," in *Ethnicity in Contemporary America*, ed. J. O. McKee, 49–79 (Lanham, MD: Rowman & Littlefield, 2000), 56.

20. K. T. Lomawaima and T. L. McCarty, *"To Remain an Indian": Lessons in Democracy from a Century of Native American Education* (New York: Teachers College Press), 9.

21. Ibid.

22. Tsosie, "How the Land Was Taken," 244.

23. Ibid., 244–245.

24. Ibid., 246.

25. W. Echo Hawk, "An Overview and Patterns in Federal Indian Law," in *American Indian Nations: Yesterday, Today, and Tomorrow*, eds. G. Horse Capture, D. Champagne, and C. C. Jackson, 210–223 (Lanham, MD: AltaMira Press, 2007), 217.

26. Ibid., 242.

27. Ibid.

28. Ibid., 216.

29. Ibid., 218.

30. Ibid., 219.

31. Ibid.

32. K. A. Berry, Z. Grossman, and L. H. Pawiki, "Native Americans," in *Contemporary Ethnic Geographies in America*, eds. I. M. Miyares and C. A. Airriess, 51–70 (Lanham, MD: Rowman & Littlefield, 2007), 54.

33. Campbell and Greymorning, "What's in a Label?" 2–5.

34. J. R. Feagin and C. Booher Feagin, *Racial and Ethnic Relations*, 8th ed. (Upper Saddle River, NJ: Prentice Hall, 2008), 139.

35. V. J. Vogel, *This Country Was Ours* (New York: Harper & Row, 1972), 70.

36. Hraba, *American Ethnicity*, 214.

37. K. Gover, "Federal Indian Policy in the Twenty-first Century," in *American Indian Nations: Yesterday, Today, and Tomorrow*, eds. G. Horse Capture, D. Champagne, and C. C. Jackson, 187–209 (Lanham, MD: AltaMira Press, 2007), 187.

38. Hraba, *American Ethnicity*, 225.

39. Gover, "Federal Indian Policy," 127.

40. Campbell and Greymorning, "What's in a Label?" 3.

41. Gover, "Federal Indian Policy," 190.

42. Ibid.

43. J. D. Forbes, "Teaching Native American Values and Cultures," in *Teaching Ethnic Studies: Concepts and Strategies*, ed. J. A. Banks (Washington, D.C.: National Council for the Social Studies, 1973), 217.

44. Gover, "Federal Indian Policy," 193.

45. Ibid.

46. Ibid.

47. Ibid.

48. Goodman and Heffington, "Native Americans," 55.

49. Ibid.

50. Campbell and Greymorning, "What's in a Label?" 3.

51. Gover, "Federal Indian Policy," 195.

52. Ibid., 194.

53. Ibid.

54. Lomawaima and McCarty, *"To Remain an Indian,"* 117–134.

55. Gover, "Federal Indian Policy," 195.

56. D. Penny, "Native Art," in *American Indian Nations: Yesterday, Today, and Tomorrow*, eds. G. Horse Capture, D. Champagne, and C. C. Jackson, 51–56 (Lanham, MD: AltaMira Press, 2007), 56.

57. Gover, "Federal Indian Policy," 208.

58. T. Johnson, "Press Coverage of American Indian Issues," in *American Indian Nations: Yesterday, Today, and Tomorrow*, eds. G. Horse Capture, D. Champagne, and C. C. Jackson, 157–164 (Lanham, MD: AltaMira Press, 2007), 157.

59. Ibid., 160.

60. Ibid.

61. Ibid.

62. Ibid., 161.

63. Ibid., 162.

64. Ibid.

65. Ibid., 163.

66. Ibid., 164.

67. "Wind River's Last Generation," *Time*, October 21, 1985, p. 40. For a compelling discussion of land issues and the reservation, see W. La Duke and W. Churchill, "Native America: The Political Economy of Radioactive Colonialism," *Journal of Ethnic Studies, 13*, no. 3 (Fall 1985): 107–132.

68. W. G. Tierney, "Native Voices in Academe: Strategies for Empowerment," *Change, 23*, no. 2 (1992): 36–39.

69. Feagin and Feagin, *Racial and Ethnic Relations*, 219.

70. Ibid.

71. J. Collier, *Indians of the Americas* (New York: New American Library, 1947), 4.

72. T. C. Holt, "African-American History," in *The New American History*, E. Foner, ed. (Philadelphia, PA: Temple University Press, 1990), 212.

73. M. F. Berry and J. W. Blassingame, *Long Memory: The Black Experience in America* (New York: Oxford University Press, 1982), 7. Quotations reprinted with permission from Oxford University Press. Copyright © 1982.

74. Ibid., 7.

75. E. D. Genovese, *Roll Jordan Roll: The World the Slaves Made* (New York: Random House, 1976), 5.

76. S. M. Elkins, *Slavery* (New York: Grosset and Dunlap, 1963), 59.

77. Ibid.

78. Ibid., 60.

79. H. Zinn, *A People's History of the United States* (New York: Harper Perennial, 1992).

80. T. Sowell, ed., *Essays and Data on American Ethnic Groups* (Washington, DC: Urban Institute, 1978), 7–64.

81. Berry and Blassingame, *Long Memory*, 37.

82. A. Haley, *Roots: The Saga of an American Family* (New York: Doubleday, 1977).

83. Feagin and Feagin, *Racial and Ethnic Relations*, 217.

84. R. D. Abrahams, *Singing the Master: The Emergence of African American Culture in the Plantation South* (New York: Pantheon Books, 1992).

85. Ibid., 3.

86. Ibid., xxii.

87. E. Foner and O. Mahoney, *America's Reconstruction: People and Politics after the Civil War* (New York: Harper Perennial, 1995).

88. Ibid.

89. Ibid.

90. Ibid., 38.

91. Ibid., 41.

92. Ibid., 44.

93. Ibid., 112.

94. R. Takaki, *A Different Mirror: A History of Multicultural America* (Boston: Little, Brown, 1993), 134.

95. Zinn, *A People's History of the United States*, 204.

96. Ibid.

97. J. H. Franklin and I. S. Starr (eds.), *The Negro in 20th Century America: A Reader on the Struggle for Civil Rights* (New York: Random House, 1967).

98. Ibid., 189.

99. T. C. Holt, "African-American History," in *The New American History*, ed. E. Foner (Philadelphia, PA: Temple University Press, 1990), 212.

100. Ibid.

101. Ibid., 225.

102. Ibid.

103. R. Wright, "We Are Leaving!" from *12 Million Black Voices*, 1939, quoted in *The Negro in American History*, Vol. 2: *Which Way to Equality?* by Stanley Seaberg. The Scholastic Great Issue Series (New York: Scholastic Book Services, 1969, pp. 48–53), 48.

104. Ibid., 50.

105. Ibid., 51.

106. Ibid., 52.

107. Holt, "African American History," 228.

108. Ibid.

109. Ibid.

110. Feagin and Feagin, *Racial and Ethnic Relations*, 225.

111. N. I. Huggins, *Harlem Renaissance* (London: Oxford University Press, 1971); D. L. Lewis, *When Harlem Was in Vogue* (New York: Alfred A. Knopf, 1981).

112. M. Schwartzman, *Romare Bearden: His Life and Art* (New York: Harry N. Abrams, Inc., 1990); E. H. Wheat, Jacob Lawrence: The Frederick Douglas and Harriet Tubman Series of 1938–40 (Hampton, VA: Hampton Museum Press, 1991); P. K. Maultsby, "Africanisms in African-American Music," in Africanisms in American Culture, Joseph E. Holloway, ed. (Bloomington, IN: Indiana University Press, 1991), 185–210.

113. P. H. Schuck and J. Q. Wilson (Eds.), *Understanding America: The Anatomy of an Exceptional Nation* (New York: Public Affairs, 2008), 375.

114. O. Patterson, "Black Americans," in *Understanding America: The Anatomy of an Exceptional Nation*, ed. P. H. Schuck and J. Q. Wilson (New York: Public Affairs, 2008), 375–376.

115. Ibid., 392.

116. M. Oliver and T. Shapiro, *Black Wealth, White Wealth* (New York: Routledge, 1997), 5, quoted in Ibid.

117. Patterson, "Black Americans," 409–410.

Chapter 6

1. O. Patterson, "Black Americans," in *Understanding America: The Anatomy of an Exceptional Nation*, eds. P. H. Schuck and J. Q. Wilson, 375–410 (New York: Public Affairs, 2008), 376.

2. "Hispanics: a Melding of Cultures," *Time* (Special issue on "Immigrants: the changing face of America"), July 8, 1985, 36; and 2004 Census Bureau press release.

3. T. Boswell and A. D. Cruz-Baez, "Puerto Ricans Living in the United States," in *Ethnicity in Contemporary America: A Geographical Appraisal*, 2nd ed., ed. J. O. McKee, 181–226 (Lanham, MD: Rowman & Littlefield, 2000), 181.

4. S. Nieto. "Puerto Rican Students in U.S. Schools: A Troubled Past and the Search for a Hopeful Future," in *Handbook of Research on Multicultural Education*, 2nd ed., ed. J. A. Banks and C. M. Banks, 515–541 (San Francisco: Jossey-Bass, 2004), 518.

5. Thomas D. Boswell and Terry-Ann Jones, "Caribbean Hispanics: Puerto Ricans, Cubans, and Dominicans," pages 123–150 in Innes M. Miyares and Christopher A. Airriess, eds., *Contemporary Ethnic Geographies in America*. Lanham, MD: Rowman & Littlefield Publishers, Inc., 2007).

6. Boswell and Cruz Baez, "Puerto Ricans Living in the United States," 181.

7. Ibid.

8. Ibid.

9. Ibid.

10. Ibid., 182.

11. Nieto, "Puerto Rican Students in U.S. Schools," 518.

12. Ibid., 519.

13. J. P. Fitzpatrick, "Puerto Ricans," in *Harvard Encyclopedia of American Ethnic Groups*, 4th ed., eds. S. Thernstrum, A. Arlov, and O. Handlin (Cambridge, MA: Harvard University Press, 1980), 859; and Banks, *Teaching Strategies for Ethnic Studies*, 358.

14. Ibid.

15. Ibid.

16. Nieto, "Puerto Rican Students in U.S. Schools," 530–531.

17. C. Diaz, "Puerto Ricans in the United States: Concepts, Strategies, and Materials," in *Teaching Strategies for Ethnic Studies*, 7th ed., ed. J. A. Banks, 376–403 (Boston: Allyn & Bacon, 2003).

18. Ibid., 386.

19. E. Skop, "Emigres Outside Miami: The Cuban Experience in Metropolitan Phoenix," in *Contemporary Ethnic Geographies in America*, ed. I. M. Miyares and C. A. Airriess, 43–63 (Lanham, MD: Rowman & Littlefield Publishers, Inc., 2007), 43.

20. Ibid., 59.

21. Ibid., 43.

22. J. S. Olson, *The Ethnic Dimension in American History,* Vol. 2 (New York: St. Martin's Press, 1979), 379.

23. Boswell and Jones, "Caribbean Hispanics," 131.

24. Ibid., 131.

25. Ibid.

26. Ibid., 123.

27. Ibid.

28. Ibid., 147.

29. Ibid., 140.

30. Ibid.

31. W. L. Langer (ed.). *An Encyclopedia of World History* (Boston: Houghton Mifflin, 1948), 486.

32. Boswell and Jones, "Caribbean Hispanics," 139.

33. Bradley Levinson, personal memo.

34. J. R. Feagin & C. Booher Feagin, *Racial and Ethnic Relations,* 8th ed., p. 207 (Upper Saddle River, NJ: Prentice Hall, 2008).

35. Bradley Levinson, personal memo.

36. D. Arreola, "Mexican Americans," in *Ethnicity in Contemporary America*, ed. J. O. McKee, 111–138 (Lanham, MD: Rowman & Littlefield, 2000), 111.

37. Ibid., 113.

38. Ibid., 114.

39. Ibid., 115.

40. Feagin and Feagin, *Racial and Ethnic Relations*, 207.

41. Ibid.

42. Feagin and Feagin, *Racial and Ethnic Relations*, 288–289.

43. C. McWilliams, *North from Mexico*: 77. The Spanish-Speaking People of the United States (New York: Greenwood Press, 1968).

44. J. Habra, *American Ethnicity* (Itasca, IL: F. F. Peacock, 1979) 241.

45. R. Alba and V. Nee, *Remaking the American Mainstream: Assimilation and Contemporary Immigration* (Cambridge, MA: Harvard University Press, 2003), 184.

46. Feagin and Feagin, *Racial and Ethnic Relations*, 208.

47. Ibid.

48. Alba and Nee, *Remaking the American Mainstream*, 185.

49. M. M. Ngai, *Impossible Subjects: Illegal Aliens and the Making of Modern America* (Princeton, NJ: Princeton University Press, 2004), 129.

50. Ibid., 130.

51. Ibid., 130–131.

52. Ibid., 131.

53. Ibid.

54. Alba and Nee, *Remaking the American Mainstream*, 185–186.

55. Ngai, *Impossible Subjects*, 138–139.

56. Ibid., 139–140.

57. Ibid., 147.

58. Ibid., 147–148.

59. Ibid., 148.

60. Ngai, *Impossible Subjects*, 149.

61. Alba and Nee, *Remaking the American Mainstream*, 188.

62. R. C. Jones, "Cultural Retrenchment and Economic Marginality: Mexican Immigrants in San Antonio," in *Immigrants Outside Megalopolis: Ethnic Transformation in the Heartland*, ed. R. C. Jones, 135–160 (Lanham, MD: Lexington Books, 2008), 136.

63. Ibid., 137.

64. Ibid.

65. Farmworkers USA: Background information, www.globalexchange.org (February 2, 2002).

66. Ibid.

67. Ibid.

68. HCR, Migrant and Seasonal Agricultural Areas, 2021 L Street, N.W., Washington, DC, June 28, 1985, p. 45.

69. Farmworkers USA.

70. R. Acuna, *Occupied America: A History of Chicanos*, 3rd ed. (New York: Harper & Row, 1988), 438.

71. Ashabranner, *Dark Harvest*, 44.

72. Ibid.

73. Jones, "Cultural Retrenchment," 140.

74. R. C. Jones, "Immigrants Transform and Are Transformed by the U.S. Heartland," in *Immigrants Outside Megalopolis: Ethnic Transformation in the Heartland*, ed. R. C. Jones, 3–32 (Lanham, MD: Lexington Books, 2008), 15.

75. Arreola, "Mexican Americans," 128.

76. Skop, "Emigres Outside Miami," 56.

77. Ibid., 47.

78. Ibid., 51.

79. Ibid., 59.

80. Ibid.

81. Ibid.

82. N. Hiemstra, "Spatial Disjunctures and Division in the New West: Latino Immigration to Leadville, Colorado," in *Immigrants Outside Megalopolis: Ethnic Transformation in the Heartland*, ed. R. C. Jones, 89–113 (Lanham, MD: Lexington Books, 2008), 90.

83. Ibid., 102.

84. Ibid., 105.

85. Ibid., 103.

86. Ibid., 103.

87. D. Stull and M. Broadway, "Meatpacking and Mexicans on the High Plains: From Minority to Majority in Garden City, Kansas," in *Immigrants Outside Megalopolis: Ethnic Transformation in the Heartland*, ed. R. C. Jones, 115–133 (Lanham, MD: Lexington Books, 2008).

88. Ibid., 118.

89. Ibid., 119.

90. Ibid.

91. Ibid.

92. Ibid. 119.

93. Ibid., 124.

94. Ibid., 125.

95. Ibid.

96. Ibid., 126.

97. Ibid., 127–128.

98. Ibid., 130.

Chapter 7

1. U.S. Census 2000.
2. "Asians: To America with Skills," *Time* (special issue, "Immigrants: The Changing Face of America"), 44–46, and 2004 U.S. Census press release.
3. Ibid.
4. T. Knoll, *Becoming Americans: Asian Sojourners, Immigrants, and Refugees in the Western United States* (Portland, OR: Coast-to-Coast Books, 1982), 5–6.
5. Ibid., 14.
6. Ibid.
7. "Chinese Americans: Realities and Myths," in *Teacher's Guide* (San Francisco: Association of Chinese Teachers, n.d.), 11.
8. Knoll, *Becoming Americans*, Foreword.
9. M. M. Ngai, *Impossible Subjects: Illegal Aliens and the Making of Modern America* (Princeton, NJ: Princeton University Press, 2004), 202.
10. Ibid., 203.
11. R. Alba and V. Nee, *Remaking the American Mainstream: Assimilation and Contemporary Immigration* (Cambridge, MA: Harvard Press, 2003), 202.
12. C. L. Brown and C. W. Pannell, "The Chinese in America," in *Ethnicity in Contemporary America: A Geographical Appraisal*, 2nd ed., J. O. McKee, ed., 283–209 (Lanham, MD: Rowman & Littlefield, 2000), 283.
13. Ibid.
14. Ibid., 306.
15. Ibid., 305.
16. Ibid., 306.
17. Ibid.
18. T. Knoll, *Becoming Americans*, 52.
19. Ibid., 52–54.
20. Ibid., 54.
21. Ibid., 58.
22. Ibid., 62.
23. Feagin, J. and Feagin C. Booher, *Racial and Ethnic Relations*, 4th ed. (Englewood Cliffs, NJ: Prentice Hall, 1993), 338.
24. B. Hosokawa, *Nisei: The Quiet Americans* (New York: William Morrow, 1969), 329–330.
25. J. R. Feagin and C. B. Feagin, *Racial and Ethnic Relations*, 8th ed. (Upper Saddle River, NJ: Prentice Hall, 2008), 286–287.
26. M. B. Carrott, "Prejudice Goes to Court: The Japanese and the Supreme Court of the 1920s," *California History* (Summer 1983): 122–139.
27. Feagin and Feagin, *Racial and Ethnic Relations*, 8th ed., 286–288.
28. Feagin and Feagin, *Racial and Ethnic Relations*, 4th ed., 356.
29. Ibid., 359–360.
30. Feagin and Feagin, *Racial and Ethnic Relations*, 8th ed., 280–281.
31. Ibid.
32. I. M. Miyares, J. A. Paine, and M. Nishi, "The Japanese in America," in *Ethnicity in Contemporary America: A Geographical Appraisal*, 2nd ed. J. O. McKee, ed., 263–282 (Lanham, MD: Rowman & Littlefield, 2000), 272.
33. Alba and Nee, *Remaking the American Mainstream*.
34. Miyares, Paine, and Nishi, "The Japanese in America," 274.
35. Ibid.
36. Ngai, *Impossible Subjects*, 101.
37. Alba and Nee, *Remaking the American Mainstream*, 205.
38. Ibid., 206.
39. Ngai, *Impossible Subjects*, 103.
40. Alba and Nee, *Remaking the American Mainstream*, 206.
41. Ibid.

42. Ngai, *Impossible Subjects*, 119–126.

43. Alba and Nee, *Remaking the American Mainstream*, 207.

44. Ibid.

45. B. D. Alsaybar, "Filipino American Youth Gangs, 'Party Culture,' and Ethnic Identity in Los Angeles," in *The Second Generation: Ethnic Identity Among Asian Americans*, P. G. Min, ed., 129–152 (Walnut Creek, CA: Walnut Creek, 2002).

46. Alba and Nee, *Remaking the American Mainstream*, 208.

47. Ibid., 208–209.

48. P. Dhingra, "Trying to Be Authentic, But Not *Too* Authentic: Second-Generation Hindu Americans in Dallas, Texas," in *Immigrants Outside Megalopoolis: Ethnic Transformation in the Heartland*, R. C. Jones, ed., 66–68 (Lanham, MD: Lexington Books, 2008); Alba and Nee, *Remaking the American Mainstream*, 207; Feagin and Feagin, *Racial and Ethnic Relations*, 8th ed., 307.

49. Pawan, "Trying to Be Authentic," 66.

50. Feagin and Feagin, *Racial and Ethnic Relations*, 8th ed., 307.

51. Pawan, "Trying to Be Authentic," 67.

52. Ibid.

53. Ibid., 68.

54. Ibid.

55. K. Y. Joshi, *New Roots in America's Sacred Ground* (New Brunswick, NJ: Rutgers University Press).

56. D. Reimer, "Korean Culture and Entrepreneurship," in *Contemporary Ethnic Geographies in America*, I. M. Miyares and C. A. Airress, eds., 233–250 (Lanham, MD: Rowman and Littlefield, 2007).

57. Ibid.

58. Alba and Nee, *Remaking the American Mainstream*, 203.

59. Feagin and Feagin, *Racial and Ethnic Relations*, 8th ed., 307.

60. Alba and Nee, *Remaking the American Mainstream*, 203.

61. Ibid., 204.

62. Reimer, "Korean Culture and Entrepreneurship," 236.

63. Ibid., 237.

64. Ibid.

65. Ibid., 241.

66. Ibid.

67. Ibid.

68. Alba and Nee, *Remaking the American Mainstream*, 204.

69. Reimer, "Korean Culture and Entrepreneurship," 242.

70. Alba and Lee, *Remaking the American Mainstream*, 204.

71. P. G. Min, "A Comparison of Pre- and Post-1965 Asian Immigrant Businesses," in *Mass Migration to the United States: Classical and Contemporary Periods*, P. G. Min, ed., 285–308 (Walnut Creek, CA: AltaMira Press, 2002), 302.

72. Reimer, "Korean Culture and Entrepreneurship," 243.

73. Ibid., 244.

74. Alba and Nee, *Remaking the American Mainstream*, 205.

75. Feagin and Feagin, *Racial and Ethnic Relations*, 8th ed., 330.

76. Ibid.

77. M. S. Orchanski, *Immigration and the American Dream: Battling the Political Hype and Hysteria* (Lanham, MD: Rowman & Littlefield, 2008).

78. Knoll, *Becoming Americans*, Foreward.

79. V. G. Thuy, "The Indochinese in America: Who Are They and How Are They Doing," in *The Education of Asian and Pacific Americans: Historical Perspective and Prescriptions for the Future*, D. T. Nakanishi and M. Hirano-Nakanishi, eds. (Phoenix, AZ: Oryx Press, 1983).

80. Ibid., 107.

81. Ibid., 103.

82. Ibid.

83. F. Butterfield, "Why Asians Are Going to the Head of the Class," *New York Times*, Education, August 3, 1986, pp. 18–19.

84. Ibid., 21.

85. Thuy, "The Indochinese in America," 103.

86. S. Mufti, "Islamic Community in North America: Prospects and Problems," www.masnet.org, posted: November 23, 2004.

87. Ibid., 1.

88. M. A. Gomez, "Muslims in Early America," *The Journal of Southern History,* 60, no. 4 (November 1994): 671–710.

89. Ibid.

90. For further discussion on this issue see C. L. Stone's "Estimate of Muslims Living in America," in *The Muslims of America,* Yvonne Yazbeck Haddad, ed. (New York: Oxford University Press, 1991), 25–36.

91. Y. Aossey, Jr., *Fifty Years of Islam in Iowa 1925–1975* (Cedar Rapids, IA: Unity Publishing Co., n.d.), 2.

92. For further information on Muslim organizations, see Gutbi Mahdi Ahmed's article "Muslim Organizations in the United States," in Y. Haddad, ed., *The Muslims of America,* 11–24.

93. Ibid., 682.

94. Ibid., 673.

95. Ibid., 709.

96. R. Dannin, *Black Pilgrimage to Islam* (New York: Oxford University Press, 2002).

97. For further information regarding the NOI movement and Elijah Muhammad, see the chapter entitled "Muslims in the United States: An Overview of Organizations, Doctrines and Problems" by Elijah's son, Akbar Muhammad, in *Islamic Impact,* Y. Haddad et al., eds. (Syracuse, NY: Syracuse University Press, 1984), 195–217.

98. This 355-page book was published by Muhammad's Temple No. 2, 7351 Stony Island Avenue, Chicago, IL, 1965.

99. The name Warith Deen is an Arabic name that means "the inheritor of the religion."

100. "Muslims in the United States: An Overview of Organizations, Doctrines and Problems," in *Islamic Impact,* Y. Haddad et al., eds. (Syracuse, NY: Syracuse University Press, 1984), 208.

101. This quote appeared in an article Malcolm X wrote for an Egyptian newspaper, August 1964.

102. A summary of the FBI file on Malcolm X was published in C. Carson, *Malcolm X: The FBI File* (New York: Carroll & Graf Publishers, 1991).

103. E. Rothstein, "The Personal Evolution of a Civil Rights Giant," *New York Times,* May 19, 2005, p. B1. This exhibition includes samples from a much more extensive collection of Malcolm X's personal papers that is on 75-year loan to the New York Public Library's Schomberg Center.

104. Y. Y. Haddad, "A Century of Islam in America," Occasional Paper (Washington, DC: American Institute for Islamic Affairs, 1986).

105. American-Arab Anti-Discrimination Committee Research Institute, *Washington Times in Education* supplement, February 10, 2004, p. 3.

106. J. Zogby, *Arab America Today* (Washington, DC: Arab American Institute, 1990), v.

107. A. Naff, *Becoming American: The Early Arab Immigrant Experience* (Carbondale, IL: Southern Illinois University Press, 1985), 12–13.

108. B. Abu-Laban, *Social and Political Attitudes of Arab-Americans,* ADC Issue Paper No. 24 (Washington, DC: ADC Research Institute, 1990), vi.

109. P. Findley, *They Dare to Speak Out* (Westport, CT: Amana Books, Lawrence Hill & Company, 1985), 1–2.

110. M. W. Suleiman, *The Arabs in the Mind of America* (Brattleboro, VT: Amana Books, 1988), 150–151.

111. Winik, "Don't Ask Me to Take Off the Uniform," 4–7.

112. L. Michalek, "The Arab in American Cinema: A Century of Otherness," *The Arab Image in American Film and Television* (Washington, DC: ADC Research Institute, n.d.), 2.

113. J. Carter, *The Blood of Abraham* (Boston: Houghton Mifflin, 1985), 112.

114. American-Arab Anti-Discrimination Committee Research Institute, *Washington Times in Education* supplement, p. 3.

115. "Immigrants: A Cost or a Benefit?" *New York Times,* September 3, 1993, A11; D. Stoll, "In Focus: The Immigration Debate." *U.S. Foreign Policy in Focus,* a project of the Institute for Policy Studies and the Interhemispheric Resource Center, 2, no. 31 (2001).

116. Larry Rohter, "Revisiting Immigration and the Open-Door Policy," *New York Times*, September 19, 1991, p. 4.

117. P. Kennedy, *Preparing for the Twenty-First Century* (New York: Random House, 1993).

Chapter 8

1. E. P. Kraly, "'An Anchor of Hope': Adjustment of Refugees in Utica, New York," in *Immigrants Outside Megalopolis: Ethnic Transformation in the Heartland*, ed. R. C. Jones, 263–288 (Landham, MD: Lexington Books, 2008), 281.

2. Ibid., 267–268.

3. Ibid., 282.

4. J. W. Keefe and M. Languis (untitled article), *Learning Stages Network Newsletter 4*, no. 2 (Summer 1983): 1.

5. G. E. Kusler, "Getting to Know You," in *Student Learning Styles and Brain Behavior* (Reston, VA: National Association of Secondary School Principals, 1983), 13.

6. Ibid., 11–12.

7. Ibid.

8. H. A. Witkin, C. Moore, and F. J. McDonald, "Cognitive Style and the Teaching/Learning Processes" (American Educational Research Association Cassette Series 3F, 1974).

9. J. W. Keefe, "Assessing Student Learning Styles: An Overview," in *Student Learning Styles and Brain Behavior* (Reston, VA: National Association of Secondary School Principals, 1983), 44.

10. C. E. Cornett, "What You Should Know about Teaching and Learning Styles," *Fastback 191* (Bloomington, IN: Phi Delta Kappa Educational Foundation, 1983), 32–37.

11. Keefe, "Assessing Student Learning Styles."

12. S. Messick (Ed.), *Individuality in Learning* (San Francisco: Jossey-Bass, 1976).

13. Keefe, "Assessing Student Learning Styles."

14. Witkin, Moore, and McDonald, "Cognitive Style."

15. Hidden Figures Test (Cf-l), from the *Kit of Factor-Referenced Cognitive Tests* (Princeton, NJ: Educational Testing Service, 1962).

16. Witkin, Moore, and McDonald, "Cognitive Style."

17. M. Ramirez and A. Castañeda, *Cultural Democracy: Bicognitive Development, and Education* (New York: Academic Press, 1974).

18. P. Cross, *Accent on Learning* (San Francisco: Jossey-Bass, 1976), 116.

19. A. Castañeda and T. Gray, "Bicognitive Processes in Multicultural Education," *Educational Leadership, 32* (December 1974): 203–207, Tables 1–3.

20. D. E. Hunt, "Learning Style and Student Needs: An Introduction to Conceptual Level," in *Student Learning Styles: Diagnosing and Prescribing Programs* (Reston, VA: National Association of Secondary School Principals, 1979).

21. D. E. Hunt, quoted in Cornett, *What You Should Know About Teaching and Learning Styles*, 36.

22. Ibid., 31.

23. Ibid.

24. H. Reinert, "One Picture Is Worth a Thousand Words? Not Necessarily!" *Modern Language Journal, 60* (April 1976): 163. Reinert's article is summarized and quoted here by permission of the author. The *Modern Language Journal* is published by the National Federation of Modern Language Teachers Associations (Madison, WI: University of Wisconsin Press).

25. Ibid., 162.

26. Ibid., 165.

27. Ibid., 169.

28. Ibid., 166.

29. Ibid., 161.

30. R. Dunn and K. Dunn, *Teaching Secondary Students through Their Individual Learning Styles: Practical Approaches for Grades 7–12* (Boston: Allyn & Bacon, 1993), 2.

31. K. M. Evenson Worthley, "Learning Style Factor of Field Dependence/Independence and Problem Solving Strategies of Hmong Refugee Students" (master's thesis, University of Wisconsin-Stout, July 1987).

32. Ibid., 45.

33. Ibid., 34.

34. A. W. Boykin, "Psychological/Behavioral Verve in Academic Task Performance: Pretheoretical Considerations," *Journal of Negro Education, 47,* no. 8 (1978): 343–354; A. W. Boykin, "Task Variability and the Performance of Black and White School Children: Vervistic Explorations," *Journal of Black Studies, 12,* no. 4 (1982): 469–484; A. W. Boykin, "Afrocultural Expression and Its Implications for Schooling," in *Teaching Diverse Populations: Formulating a Knowledge Base,* eds. E. R. Hollins, J. E. King, and W. C. Hayman, 243–256 (Albany: SUNY Press, 1994); B. A. Allen, and W. A. Boykin, "African-American Children and the Educational Process: Alleviating Cultural Discontinuity through Prescriptive Pedagogy," *School Psychology Review, 21,* no. 4 (1982): 586–598; W. A. Boykin and B. A. Allen, "Rhythmic Movement Facilitated Learning in Working-Class Afro-American Children," *Journal of Genetic Psychology, 149,* no. 3 (1988): 335–347.

35. W. A. Boykin and F. D. Toms "Black Child Socialization: A Conceptual Framework," in *Black Children: Social, Educational, and Parental Environments,* eds. H. P. McAdoo and J. L. McAdoo (Beverly Hills, CA: Sage, 1985), 38.

36. Allen and Boykin, "African-American Children and the Educational Process," 588.

37. Boykin and Toms, "Black Child Socialization," 41.

38. A. G. Hilliard III, "Behavioral Style, Culture, and Teaching and Learning," *Journal of Negro Education, 61,* no. 3 (Summer 1992): 370–371.

39. Ibid., 370.

40. Ibid.

41. Ibid., 371.

42. Ibid.

43. Ibid.

44. Ibid., 373.

45. B. J. Shade, "Afro-American Cognitive Style: A Variable in School Success?" *Review of Educational Research, 52,* no. 2 (Summer 1982): 220.

46. J. E. Hale-Benson, *Black Children: Their Roots, Culture, and Learning Styles,* rev. ed. (Baltimore: Johns Hopkins University Press, 1986).

47. R. Cohen, "Conceptual Styles, Culture Conflict and Nonverbal Tests of Intelligence," *American Anthropologist, 71*: 828–856.

48. A. Hilliard, "Alternatives to IQ Testing: An Approach to the Identification of Gifted Minority Children" (Final report to the California State Department of Education, 1976).

49. G. Gay, "Culturally Diverse Students and Social Studies," in *Handbook of Research on Social Studies Teaching and Learning,* ed. J. P. Shaver (New York: Macmillan, 1991).

50. K. Swisher and D. Deyhle, "Styles of Learning and Learning Styles: Educational Conflicts for American Indian/Alaskan Native Youth," *Journal of Multilingual and Multicultural Development 8,* no. 4 (1987): 350.

51. Ibid.

52. J. C. Phillips, "College of, by and for Navajo Indians," *Chronicle of Higher Education,* 15 (January 16, 1978): 10–12.

53. Swisher and Deyhle, "Styles of Learning and Learning Styles," 348.

54. Worthley, "Learning Style Factor," 18.

55. F. M. Yoshiwara, "Shattering Myths: Japanese American Educational Issues," in *Education of Asian and Pacific Americans: Historical Perspectives and Prescriptions for the Future,* eds. Don T. Nakanski and Marsha Hirano-Nakanski (Phoenix, AZ: Oryx Press, 1983), 23.

56. B. H. Suzuki, "The Education of Asian and Pacific Americans: An Introductory Overview," in *Education of Asian and Pacific Americans: Historical Perspectives and Prescriptions for the Future,* eds. Don T. Nakanishi and Marsha Hirano-Nakanishi (Phoenix, AZ: Oryx Press, 1983), 9.

57. Worthley, "Learning Style Factor."

58. A. F. Gregorc, "Learning/Teaching Styles," in *Student Learning Styles: Diagnosing and Prescribing Programs* (Reston, VA: National Association of Secondary School Principals, 1979), 24.

59. Ibid.

60. Ibid.

61. B. Bree Fischer and L. Fischer, "Styles in Teaching and Learning," *Educational Leadership, 36* (January 1979): 245–254; see also Gregorc, "Learning/Teaching Styles."

62. Dunn and Dunn, *Teaching Secondary Students Through Their Individual Learning Styles*, 142.

63. Ibid.

64. Ibid., 145.

65. Witkin, Moore, and McDonald, "Cognitive Style."

66. B. J. R. Shade (Ed.), *Culture, Style and the Educative Process* (Springfield, IL: Charles C Thomas, 1989), 33.

67. Ibid., 337.

68. Ibid.

69. K. M. Teel, "A White Educator's Ongoing Journey," in *Building Racial and Cultural Competence in the Classroom: Strategies from Urban Educators*, eds. K. M. Teel and J. E. Obidah (New York: Teachers College Press), 149.

70. G. Gay, *Culturally Relevant Teaching: Theory, Research, and Practice* (New York: Teachers College Press, 2000), 1.

71. Ibid., 29.

72. G. Ladson-Billings, "But That's Just Good Teaching! The Case for Culturally Relevant Pedagogy," *Theory into Practice, 34*, no. 3 (Summer 1995): 161–165; Ladson-Billings, *The Dream Keepers* (San Francisco: Jossey-Bass, 1994); Ladson-Billings, "Liberatory Consequences of Literacy: A Case of Culturally Relevant Instruction for African-American Students," *Journal of Negro Education, 61*, 378–391.

73. Ladson-Billings, *Theory into Practice*, 162.

74. Gay, *Culturally Relevant Teaching*, 29–35.

75. Ladson-Billings, "Liberatory Consequences," 383.

76. L. Delpit, *Other People's Children: Cultural Conflict in the Classroom* (New York: The New Press, 1995), 41.

77. Ibid.

78. Ibid., 42.

79. J. Chlebo, "There Is No Rose Garden: A Second Generation Rural Head Start Program," Indiana University (Ph.D. diss., 1990).

80. Ibid., 169.

81. Ibid., 171.

82. C. Velez-Ibanez and J. Greenberg, "Formation and Transformation of Funds of Knowledge," in *Funds of Knowledge: Theorizing Practices in Households, Communities, and Classrooms*, eds. N. Gonzales, L. Moll, and C. Amanti (Mahwah, NJ: Lawrence Earlbaum), 47.

83. L. C. Moll, C. Amanti, D. Neff, and N. Gonzalez, "Funds of Knowledge for Teaching: Using a Qualitative Approach to Connect Homes and Classrooms," *Theory into Practice, 31*, no. 2 (1992): 132–140.

84. N. Gonzalez, "Funds of Knowledge for Teaching in Latino Households," in N. Gonzalez, L. Moll, and C. Amanti, Eds., *Funds of Knowledge: Theorizing Practices in Households, Communities, and Classrooms* (Mahwah, NJ: Lawrence Erlbaum Associates, 2005), 91.

85. Moll et al. "Funds of Knowledge," 133.

86. Ibid., 238.

87. Ibid., 133.

88. Ibid., 139.

89. N. Gonzalez, "Processual Approaches to Multicultural Education," *Journal of Applied Behavioral Science, 31*, no. 2 (1995): 234.

90. J. V. Diller and J. Moule, *Cultural Competence: A Primer for Educators* (Belmont, CA: Thompson Wadsworth), 13; and K. N. Robins, R. B. Lindsey, D. B. Lindsey, and R. D. Terrell, *Culturally Proficient Instruction: A Guide for People Who Teach*, 2nd ed. (Thousand Oaks, CA: Corwin), 2.

91. Robins et al., *Culturally Proficient Instruction*, 2.

92. T. L. Cross, B. J. Bazron, K. W. Dennis, and M. R. Isaacs, *Toward a Culturally Competent System of Care* (Washington, DC: Georgetown University Development Center), 22–24.

Chapter 9

1. In addition to Chapters 8 and 10, see G. Q. Conchas, *The Color of Success: Race and High-Achieving Urban Youth* (NY: Teachers College Press, 2006), G. Gay, *Culturally Responsive Teaching*, 2nd ed. (NY: Teachers College Press, in press), J. L. McBrien, "Educational Needs and Barriers for Refugee

Students in the United States: A Review of the Literature," *Review of Educational Research, 75*, no. 3 (Fall 2005): 329–364; C. Suarez-Orozco, M. M. Suarez-Orozco, and I. Todorova, *Learning in a New Land: Immigrant Students in American Society* (Cambridge, MA: Harvard University Press, 2008).

2. http://nces.ed.gov/nationsreportcard.

3. G. Orfield, D. Losen, J. Wald, and C. Swanson, *Losing Our Future: How Minority Youth Are Being Left Behind by the Graduation Rate Crisis* (Cambridge, MA: The Civil Rights Project at Harvard University, 2004), 1.

4. Ibid., 2–3.

5. L. M. Covington Clarkson, "Demographic Data and Immigrant Student Achievement," *Theory Into Practice, 47* (2008): 20–26.

6. *Preparing English Language Learners for Academic Success* (Alexandria, VA: Center for Public Education, 2007), 2–3.

7. Ibid., 4.

8. Ibid., 6.

9. See McBrien, "Educational Needs and Barriers for Refugee Students in the United States"; Suarez-Orozco, Suarez-Orozco, Todorova, *Learning in a New Land.*

10. Suarez-Orozco, Suarez-Orozco, Todorova, *Learning in a New Land*, 40.

11. Ibid.

12. S. R. Katz, "Teaching in Tensions: Latino Immigrant Youth, Their Teachers, and the Structures of Schooling," *Teachers College Record, 100*, no. 4 (1999): 802, 32 pages.

13. Ibid., 811.

14. Ibid.

15. Ibid., 823.

16. Ibid., 828.

17. Ibid., 837.

18. B. Francis and C. Skelton, Introduction in *Investigating Gender: Contemporary Perspectives in Education*, Becky Francis and Christine Skelton, eds. (Buckingham, England: Open University Press, 2002), i.

19. M. Conroy, "Sexism in Our Schools: Training Girls for Failure?" *Better Homes and Gardens* (1988), 44.

20. Ibid., 2.

21. J. Dillabough, "Gender Theory and Research in Education: Modernist Traditions and Emerging Contemporary Themes," in *Investigating Gender: Contemporary Perspectives in Education*, Becky Francis and Christine Skelton, eds. (Buckingham, England: Open University Press, 2002), 11.

22. C. Skelton, "Typical Boys?" in *Investigating Gender: Contemporary Perspectives in Education*, Becky Francis and Christine Skelton, eds. (Buckingham, England: Open University Press, 2002), 169.

23. Ibid.

24. Skelton, "Typical Boys?" 171.

25. Ibid.

26. J. Kenway and L. Fitzclarence, "Masculinity, Violence, and Schooling: Challenging 'Poisonous Pedagogies,'" *Gender and Education, 9*, no. 1 (1997): 117–133.

27. Skelton, "Typical Boys?" 172.

28. Ibid.

29. Ibid.

30. M. J. Kehily, "Issues of Gender and Sexuality in Schools," in *Investigating Gender: Contemporary Perspectives in Education*, Becky Francis and Christine Skelton, eds. (Buckingham, England: Open University Press, 2002), 117.

31. C. Gilligan, *In a Different Voice* (Cambridge, MA: Harvard University Press, 1982).

32. M. F. Belenky, B. McVicker Clinchy, N. Rule Goldberger, and J. Martuch Tarule, *Women's Ways of Knowing: The Development of Self, Voice, and Mind* (New York: Basic Books, 1986).

33. Ibid., 23.

34. M. Brown Parlee, "Conversational Politics," in *Feminist Frontiers: Rethinking Sex, Gender, and Society*, L. Richardson and V. Taylor, eds. (New York: Random House, 1983), 8.

35. Ibid.

36. Conroy, "Sexism in Our Schools."

37. M. Sapon-Shevin, "Gender, Introduction to Sexuality, and Social Justice in Education," in *Handbook of Social Justice in Education*, W. Ayers, T. Quinn, and D. Stovall, eds., 279–283 (New York: Routledge, 2009).

38. Ibid., 279.

39. Ibid., 281.

40. J. G. Kosciw, "Gender Equity and Lesbian, Gay, Bisexual, and Transgender Issues in Education," in *Handbook for Achieving Gender Equity Through Education, E2*, S. Klein, ed., 553–571 (Mahwah, NJ: Lawrence Erlbaum, 2007).

41. Ibid., 553.

42. M. Henning-Stout, S. James, and S. Macintosh, "Reducing Harassment of Lesbian, Gay, Bisexual, Transgender, and Questioning Youth in Schools," *School Psychology Review, 29*, no. 2 (2000): 180.

43. Ibid., 191.

44. Ibid., 180.

45. Kehily, "Issues of Gender and Sexuality," 120.

46. Ibid.

47. L. Bennett, "Break the Silence: GLBT Students and Their Allies Confront Ostracism and Isolation at School," *Teaching Tolerance*, no. 26 (Fall 2004): 36.

48. F. Skelton and C. Francis, "Endnotes: Gender, School Policies, and Practices," in *Investigating Gender: Contemporary Perspectives in Education*, Becky Francis and Christine Skelton, eds. (Buckingham, England: Open University Press, 2002), 193.

49. Skelton, "Typical Boys?" 175.

50. Ibid.

51. K. Cosier, "Creating Safe Schools for Queer Youth," in *Handbook of Social Justice in Education*, W. Ayers, T. Quinn, and D. Stovall, eds., 285–303 (New York: Routledge, 2009).

52. Refer to sources at the end of the chapter.

53. Kosciw, "Gender Equity and Lesbian, Gay, Bisexual, and Transgender Issues in Education," 563.

54. Sapon-Shevin, "Gender, Introduction to Sexuality, and Social Justice in Education," 282.

55. J. Scott and D. Leonhardt, "Shadowy Lines That Still Divide," *New York Times*, May 15, 2005. See series of nine articles at www.nytimes.com.

56. Ibid.

57. Ibid.

58. D. I. Levine, an economist and mobility researcher at the University of California, Berkeley, quoted in Scott and Leonhardt, "Shadowy Lines That Still Divide," 4.

59. S. Fass and N. K. Cauthen, "Child Poverty in States Hit by Hurricane Katrina," National Center for Children in Poverty, Mailman School of Public Health, Columbia University, New York, 2005, 4 pages.

60. Except as otherwise noted, all information in this section is taken from, "Basic Facts about Low-Income Children in the United States," National Center for Children in Poverty, Mailman School of Public Health, Columbia University, New York, February 2005, 4 pages. These figures can be updated at www.nccp.org.

61. E. Gershoff, "Living at the Edge: Low Income and Development of America's Kindergartners," *Research Brief* no. 4, National Center for Children in Poverty, Mailman School of Public Health, Columbia University, New York, November 2003, p. 2.

62. "Basic Facts about Low-Income Children in the United States," National Center for Children in Poverty.

63. C. N. Lee, "Socioeconomic Statistics and Demographics," *Asian-Nation: The Landscape of Asian America*. Available at www.asian-nation.org/demographics.shtml. (accessed February 4, 2009).

64. O. Patterson, op. cit., 392.

65. Ibid., 3.

66. M. Harrington, *Who Are the Poor?* (Washington, DC: Justice for All, 1987), 18.

67. Ibid., 13.

68. "Exceptional and Homeless," *Today*. Council for Exceptional Children, 9, no. 6 (March 2003): 1.

69. Ibid.

70. "Basic Facts about Low-Income Children in the United States," National Center for Children in Poverty.

71. Ibid.

72. D. Land and N. Legters, "The Extent and Consequences of Risk in U.S. Education," *Educating At-Risk Students, NSSE Yearbook* (Chicago: University of Chicago Press, 2002), 1–28.

73. B. Nye, L. V. Hedges, and S. Konstantopoulos, "The Long-Term Effects of Small Classes: A Five-Year Follow-Up of the Tennessee Class Size Experiment," *Educational Evaluation and Policy Analysis, 21*, no. 2 (1999): 127–142.

74. Land and Legters, "Extent and Consequences of Risk."

75. U.S. Department of Education, Office of Special Education and Rehabilitation Series, Annual Report to Congress on the Implementation of The Individuals with Disabilities Education Act, and National Center of Educational Statistics, Common Core Data Survey, from Table prepared June 2000.

76. Ibid.

77. N. St. John, "School Integration, Classroom Climate, and Achievement," ERIC ED 052 269 (January 1971); St. John, *School Desegregation: Outcomes for Children* (New York: John Wiley & Sons, 1975).

78. C. Bennett, "A Study of Classroom Climate in Desegregated Schools," *Urban Review, 13* (Winter 1981); Bennett, "Student Initiated Interaction as an Indicator of Interracial Acceptance," *Journal of Classroom Interaction, 15* (Summer 1980).

79. M. A. Gibson, P. Gandara, and J. P. Koyama (eds.), *School Connections: U.S. Mexican Youth, Peers, and School Achievement* (New York: Teachers College Press, 2004), 5–6.

80. Ibid., 7.

81. Ibid., 8.

82. Ibid.

83. Ibid., 10.

84. Ibid.

85. J. D. Vigil, "Gangs and Group Membership: Implications for Schooling," in *School Connections: U.S. Mexican Youth, Peers, and School Achievement* (New York: Teachers College Press, 2004), 87–106.

86. Ibid.

87. S. Fordham and J. Ogbu, "Black Students' School Success: Coping with the " 'Burden of Acting White,' " *Urban Review*, 18, no. 3 (1986): 176–206.

88. Ibid., 177.

89. Ibid.

90. Ibid.

91. L. Delpit, *Teaching Other People's Children: Cultural Conflicts in the Classroom* (New York: New Press, 1995).

92. W. Cross, "Oppositional Identity and African American Youth: Issues and Prospects," Chapter 7 in *Toward a Common Destiny*, W. D. Hawley and A. W. Jackson, eds. (San Francisco: Jossey-Bass, 1995), 190.

93. Fordham and Ogbu, "Black Students' School Success," 203.

94. E. Sargent, "Freeing Myself: Discoveries That Unshackle the Mind," *Washington Post*, February 10, 1985. (Quoted in Fordham and Ogbu, "Black Students' School Success," 198–199.)

95. D. Losen and G. Orfield, Introduction in *Racial Inequity in Special Education* (Boston: Harvard Education Press, 2002), xv.

96. Ibid.

97. See the Council for Exceptional Children website for legislation updates and special-education teaching strategies, at www.ce.sped.org.

98. National Center for Education Statistics, Elementary and Secondary: Programs for the Disabled, Table 52, p. 72.

99. Losen and Orfield, Introduction.

100. R. Slavin, *Educational Psychology*, 4th ed. (Boston: Allyn and Bacon, 1994), 453.

101. Assessment of Diversity in America's Teaching Force: A Call to Action. National Collaborative on Diversity in the Teaching Force (Washington, DC, October 2004), 4.

102. E. G. Fierros and J. W. Conroy, "Double Jeopardy: An Exploration of Restrictiveness and Race in Special Education," in *Racial Inequity in Special Education*, D. Losen and G. Orfield, eds. (Boston: Harvard Education Press, 2002), 50.

103. Losen and Orfield, *Racial Inequity in Special Education*, xviii.

104. D. Oswald, M. Coutinho, and A. Best, "Community and School Predictors of Overrepresentation of Minority Children in Special Education," in *Racial Inequity in Special Education*, D. Losen and G. Orfield, eds. (Boston: Harvard Education Press, 2002), 6.

105. Ibid.

106. B. A. Boyd and V. I. Correa, "Developing a Framework for Reducing the Cultural Clash between African American Parents and the Special Education System," *Multicultural Perspectives,* 7, no. 2 (2005): 3–11.

107. Ibid., 4.

108. Ibid., 7.

109. D. Osher, D. Woodruff, and A. E. Sims, "Schools Make a Difference: Overrepresentation of African American Youth in Special Education and the Juvenile Justice System," in *Racial Inequity in Special Education*, D. Losen and G. Orfield, eds. (Boston: Harvard Education Press, 2002), 105.

110. R. Slavin, D. DeVries, and K. Edwards, *Co-operative Learning* (New York: Longman, 1983); E. G. Cohen and M. B. Arias, "Accelerating the Education of Language Minority At-risk Students" (paper presented at Conference on Accelerating the Education of At-risk Students, Stanford University, November 17–18, 1988).

111. Ibid.

112. Ibid., 61.

113. Ibid., 62.

114. Ibid.

115. R. Slavin, *Using Student Team Learning*, rev. ed. (Baltimore: Center for Social Organization of Schools, Johns Hopkins University, 1980), 2–3. Reprinted by permission of the author.

116. R. Slavin, *Teacher Manual for Student Team Learning* (Baltimore: Center for Social Organization of Schools, Johns Hopkins University, 1978), 6–7. Reprinted by permission of the author.

117. Slavin et al., *Cooperative Learning*, 27.

118. Ibid., 32–33.

119. Ibid., 52–53.

120. E. G. Cohen, "Restructuring the Classroom: Conditions for Productive Small Groups," *Review of Educational Research,* 64 (Spring 1994): 1–35.

121. Cohen and Arias. "Acceleration Education."

122. E. G. Cohen, R. Lotan, and L. Catanzarite, "Treating Status Problems in the Cooperative Classroom," in *Cooperative Learning: Theory and Research*, S. Sharon, ed. (New York: Praeger, 1990).

123. E. Cohen, *Designing Groupwork: Strategies for Heterogeneous Classrooms* (New York: Teachers College Press, 1986).

124. M. Fantini and G. Weinstein, *The Disadvantaged: Challenge to Education* (New York: Harper & Row, 1968).

125. M. Benitez, "A Blueprint for the Education of the Mexican American," ERIC ED 076 294 (March 1973).

Chapter 10

1. M. Suàrez-Orozco, "Everything You Ever Wanted to Know About Assimilation but Were Afraid to Ask," in *The New Immigration: An Interdisciplinary Reader*, ed. M. M. Suàrez-Orozco, C. Suàrez-Orozco, and D. Baolian Qin, 67–83 (New York: Routledge, 2005).

2. L. Hoffman and J. Sable, *Public Elementary and Secondary Students, Staff, and School Districts: School Year 2003–2004* (Washington, DC: National Center for Educational Statistics, 2006).

3. National Council of Teachers of English, *English Language Learners: A Policy Research Brief* (Urbana, IL: NCTE).

4. International Reading Association, "English language learners: An Overview." http://www.reading.org/Resources/ResourcesByTopic/EnglishLearners/Overview.aspx

5. P. Hopstock and T. Stephenson, *Native Languages and Limited English Proficient Students* (Washington, DC: U.S. Department of Eduction, 2003).

6. S. Peregoy and O. Boyle. *Reading, Writing, and Learning in ESL: A Resource Book for Teaching K–12 English Learners*, 5th ed. (Boston: Pearson, 2008).

7. National Council of Teachers of English, *English Language Learners.*

8. Peregoy and Boyle, *Reading, Writing, and Learning in ESL.*

9. National Council of Teachers of English, *English Language Learners.*

10. Ibid.

11. C. G. Spinelli. "Addressing the Issue of Cultural and Linguistic Diversity and Assessment: Informal Evaluation Measures for English Language Learners," *Reading & Writing Quarterly*, 24, no. 1 (2008): 101–118.

12. O. J. Garcia, J. Kleifgen, and L. Falchi, *From English Language Learners to Emergent Bilinguals* (New York: Teachers College Press, 2008); G. Valdès, *Learning and Not Learning English: Latino Students in American Schools* (New York: Teachers College Press, 2001).

13. G. Gay, *Culturally Responsive Teaching: Theory, Research, and Practice* (New York: Teachers College Press, 2000).

14. R. Garcia, *Learning in Two Languages* (Bloomington, IN: Phi Delta Kappa Educational Foundation, 1976).

15. J. Crawford, *Bilingual Education: History, Politics, Theory and Practice*, 4th ed. (Trenton, NJ: Crane Publishing, 1999).

16. J. Feder, "English as the Official Language of the United States—Legal Background and Analysis of Legislation in the 110th Congress." ILW.COM (Congressional Research Service).

17. J. Crawford, "Language Politics in the United States: The Paradox of Bilingual Education," In *The Politics of Multiculturalism and Bilingual Education: Students and Teachers Caught in the Cross Fire*, ed. C. Ovando and P. McLaren (Boston: McGraw-Hill, 2000).

18. Ibid., 123.

19. J. Crawford, "Obituary: The Bilingual Education Act, 1968–2002." Available online at http://www.rethinkingschools.org/archive/16_04/Bil164.shtml.

20. B. Perez and M. E. Torres-Guzmàn, *Learning in Two Worlds: An Integrated Spanish/English Biliteracy Approach* (New York: Longman, 1992), xxiii.

21. Peregoy and Boyle, *Reading, Writing, and Learning in ESL*, 25.

22. Crawford, *Bilingual Education.*

23. Ibid.

24. R. C. Troike, "Synthesis of Research on Bilingual Education," *Educational Leadership*, 38 (March 1981): 498–504.

25. Peregoy and Boyle, *Reading, Writing, and Learning in ESL*, 25.

26. S. Krashen, *Principles and Practice in Second Language Acquisition* (London: Prentice-Hall International (UK) Ltd., 1981).

27. S. Watts-Taffe and D. M. Truscott, "Using What We Know About Language and Literacy Development for ESL Students in the Mainstream Classroom," *Language Arts*, 77, no. 3 (2000): 258–264.

28. This example is based on Karen Shuster Webb's section on bilingual education that appeared in previous editions of this book.

29. K. Au, "Social Constructivism and the School Literacy Learning of Students of Diverse Backgrounds," *Journal of Literacy Research*, 30 (1998): 297–319.

30. G. Wells, *The Meaning Makers: Children Learning Language and Using Language to Learn* (Portsmouth, NH: Heinemann, 1986).

31. Watts-Taffe and Truscott, "Using What We Know About Language and Literacy Development for ESL Students in the Mainstream Classroom."

32. Peregoy and Boyle, *Reading, Writing, and Learning in ESL*, 64.

33. Ibid., 64.

34. J. Cummins, "The Acquisition of English as a Second Language," in *Reading Instruction for ESL Students*, ed. K. Spangenberg-Urbschat and R. Pritchard (Delaware: International Reading Association, 1994).

35. Peregoy and Boyle, *Reading, Writing, and Learning in ESL.*

36. J. Echevarria and A. Graves, *Sheltered Content Instruction: Teaching English Language Learners with Diverse Abilities* (Boston: Pearson, 2007).

37. J. Baugh and G. Smitherman, "Linguistic Emancipation in Global Perspective," in *Talkin Black Talk*, eds. H. Samy Alim and J. Baugh (New York: Teachers College Press, 2007).

38. C. Kynard, "The Blues Playingest Dog You Ever Heard of: (Re)positioning Literacy Through African American Blues Rhetoric," *Reading Research Quarterly, 43*, no. 4 (2008): 356–373; T. Redd and K. S. Webb, *A Teacher's Guide to African American Language: What a Writing Teacher Should Know* (Urbana, IL: National Council of Teachers of English, 2005); E. Richardson, *Hiphop Literacies* (New York: Routledge, 2006); G. Smitherman, *Talkin and Tesifyin: The language of Black America* (Detroit, MI: Wayne State University Press, 1977).

39. J. Baugh, *Out of the Mouths of Slaves: African American Language and Educational Malpractice* (Austin: University of Texas Press, 1999).

40. C. Lee, "A Culturally Based Cognitive Apprenticeship: Teaching African American High School Students Skills in Literary Interpretation," *Reading Research Quarterly, 30,* no. 4 (1995): 608–630; C. Lee, *Culture, Literacy, and Learning: Taking Bloom in the Midst of the Whirlwind* (New York: Teachers College Press).

41. Gay, *Culturally Responsive Teaching,* 29.

42. Gay, *Culturally Responsive Teaching*; G. Ladson-Billings, *The Dreamkeepers* (San Francisco: Jossey-Bass, 1994); S. Nieto, *Language, Culture, and Teaching: Critical Perspectives for a New Century* (Mahwah, NJ: Lawrence Erlbaum, 2002).

43. Gay, *Culturally Responsive Teaching.*

44. M. R. Hawkins, *Language Learning and Teacher Education: A Sociocultural Approach* (Clevedon: Multilingual Matters, 2004).

45. C. Snow, M. S. Burns, and P. Griffin, *Preventing Reading Difficulties in Young Children* (Washington, DC: National Academies Press, 1998).

46. International Reading Association, *Second-Language Literacy Instruction: A Position Statement* (Newark DE: IRA).

47. C. Espinosa, "Finding Memorable Moments: Images and Identities in Autobiographical Writing," *Language Arts, 84,* no. 2 (2006): 136–144.

48. Ibid., 139.

49. Ibid.

50. G. Campano, *Immigrant Students and Literacy: Reading, Writing, and Remembering* (New York: Teachers College Press, 2007), 60.

51. Campano, personal communication, April 24, 2009.

52. Campano, *Immigrant Students and Literacy,* 68.

53. Ibid.

54. C. Medina, "The Construction of Drama Worlds as Literary Interpretation of Latina Feminist Literature," *Research in Drama Education, 9,* no. 2 (2004): 145–160.

55. J. Dworin, "The Family Stories Project: Using Funds of Knowledge for Writing," *The Reading Teacher, 59,* no. 6 (2006): 510–520.

56. L. Moll, "Literacy Research in Community and Classroom: A Sociocultural Approach," in *Theoretical Models and Processes of Reading,* ed. R. Ruddell, M. R. Ruddell, and H. Singer, 179–207 (Newark, DE: International Reading Association, 1994).

57. J. Dworin, "The Family Stories Project," 519.

58. Gay, *Culturally Responsive Teaching*; Ladson-Billings, *The Dreamkeepers*; Y. Freeman and D. Freeman, *Academic Language for English Language Learners and Struggling Readers* (Portsmouth, NH: Heinemann, 2009).

59. Kynard, "The Blues Playingest Dog You Ever Heard of."

60. Smitherman, *Talkin and Testifyin.*

61. Kynard, "The Blues Playingest Dog You Ever Heard of," 366.

62. Smitherman, *Talkin and Testifyin.*

63. Kynard, "The Blues Playingest Dog You Ever Heard of," 367.

64. L. Christensen, "The Politics of Correction," *Rethinking Schools, 18*, no. 1. Available at http://www.rethinkingschools.org/archive/18_01/corr181.shtml.

65. Los Angeles Unified School District, Academic Language Mastery Program. Available at http://www.learnmedia.com/aemp/index.html.

66. Smitherman, *Talkin and Testifyin*; J. R. Rickford and R. J. Rickford, *Spoken Soul: The Story of Black English* (New York: John Wiley & Sons, 2000).

67. Freeman and Freeman, *Academic Language for English Language Learners and Struggling Readers*.

68. G. Wiggins and J. McTighe, *Understanding by Design* (Alexandria, VA: Association for Supervision and Curriculum Development, 2005).

69. Freeman and Freeman, *Academic Language for English Language Learners and Struggling Readers*, 178.

70. Ibid., 180.

71. L. Christensen, "Putting out the Linguistic Welcome Mat: Honoring Students' Home Languages Builds an Inclusive Classroom," *Rethinking Schools, 23*, no. 1 (2008): 20.

72. Alim and Baugh, *Talking Black Talk*.

73. Ibid., 11.

74. N. Hornberger and S. M. Coronel-Molina, "Quechua Language Shift, Maintenance and Revitalization in the Andes: The Case for Language Planning," *International Journal of the Sociology of Language* (2004), 167, 9–68.

75. S. Greymorning, *A Will to Survive: Indigenous Essays on the Politics of Culture, Language, and Identity* (Boston: McGraw Hill, 2004).

76. Ibid., xxii.

77. International Reading Association, *English Language Learners: An Overview*, National Council of Teachers of English, *English Language Learners: A Policy Research Brief*.

78. Spinelli, "Addressing the Issue of Cultural and Linguistic Diversity and Assessment."

Chapter 11

1. The original model was developed by the author for presentation at a curriculum institute sponsored by the Association for Supervision and Curriculum Development, Boston, October 17–18, 1975. A later version was included in M. C. Mills (comp. and ed.), *Multi-Cultural Education* (Charleston: West Virginia Department of Education, 1976.) The revised model integrated into the original model dimensions from R. Hanvey, *An Attainable Global Perspective* (New York: Center for War/Peace Studies, 1975).

2. R. Takaki, *Strangers from a Different Shore: A History of Asian Americans* (New York: Penguin, 1989).

3. Ibid., 13.

4. King, J. E., "Diaspora Literacy and Consciousness in the Struggle against Mis-Edu-cation," in the Black Community. *Journal of Negro Education, 61*, no. 3 (1992): 317–340.

5. Ibid., 326.

6. Ibid., 327.

7. G. J. Posner and A. N. Rudnitsky, *Course Design: A Guide to Curriculum Development for Teachers*, rev. ed. (New York: Longman, 1982), 50.

8. Ibid., 45.

9. R. Paul, *Critical Thinking: What Every Person Needs to Survive in a Rapidly Changing World* (Santa Rosa, CA: Foundation for Critical Thinking, 1993).

10. Ibid., 139.

11. Ibid., 136.

12. E. W. Cassidy and D. G. Kurfman, "Decision Making as Purpose and Process," in *Developing Decision-Making Skills*, 47th Yearbook, 1977. National Council for the Social Studies, 1–28.

13. K. Y. Chun-Hoon, "Teaching the Asian-American Experience" in *Teaching Ethnic Studies: Concepts and Strategies*, ed. J. A. Banks, (Washington, DC: National Council for the Social Studies, 1973), 139. Quotations from this source, the NCSS 43rd Yearbook, are reprinted by permission of the publisher.

14. Ibid., 122.

15. L. Tiedt and I. M. Tiedt, *Multicultural Teaching: A Handbook of Activities, Information, and Resources* (Boston: Allyn & Bacon, 1979), 84–88.

16. F. Berry and J. W. Blassingame, *Long Memory: The Black Experience in America* (New York: Oxford University Press, 1982). Quotations from this source are reprinted with permission.

17. Ibid.

18. Ibid., 31.

19. C. V. Hamilton, "Race and Education: A Search for Legitimacy." in *Issues in Race and Ethnic Relations*, ed. J. Rothman 101–115 (Itasca, IL: F. E. Peacock, 1977). Originally published in *Harvard Educational Review, 38*, no. 4: 669–684. Copyright © by President and Fellows of Harvard College. Reprinted by permission.

20. J. O. Killens, *Black Man's Burden* (New York: Trident Press, 1965), 14–15.

21. Ibid., 17.

22. L. Bennett, "Was Abe Lincoln a White Supremacist?" *Ebony, 23*, no. 4 (February (1968), 35.

23. *More Than Bows and Arrows* (Seattle, WA: Cinema Associates, 1978); A. Hirschfelder, *Happily May I Walk: American Indians and Alaska Natives Today* (New York: Scribner, 1986), and J. Weatherford, *Indian Givers: How The Indians of the Americas Transformed the World* (New York: Fawcett Columbine, 1988).

24. Adapted from J. D. Forbes, "Teaching Native American Values and Cultures," in *Teaching Ethnic Studies: Concepts and Strategies* ed. J. A. Banks (Washington, DC: National Council for the Social Studies, 1973), 218–219. Reprinted by permission of the author and publisher.

25. D. Johnson, "The Contribution of the Humanities to a Global Perspective in Teacher Education," ERIC ED 265 114, 1987.

26. D. Levering Lewis, *When Harlem Was in Vogue* (New York: Knopf, 1981), 15.

27. *Chinese Americans, Realities and Myths*, multimedia kit, The Association of Chinese Teachers (TACT) Curriculum Materials, 74–6A Ninth Avenue, San Francisco, CA 94118; and S. Steiner, *Fusang: The Chinese Who Built America* (New York: Harper & Row, 1979).

28. L. W. Levine, *Black Culture and Black Consciousness* (Oxford, England: Oxford University Press, 1977), 397.

29. C. E. Cortez, "Teaching the Chicano Experience," in *Teaching Ethnic Studies: Concepts and Strategies* ed. J. A. Banks (Washington, DC: National Council for the Social Studies, 1973), 191.

30. Denis Wood, "The Power of Maps," *Scientific American*, May 1990, 90.

31. R. Hanvey, *An Attainable Global Perspective* (New York: Center for War/Peace Studies, 1975), 4.

32. Ibid., 8.

33. Ibid., 10.

34. Ibid., 11.

35. Ibid.

36. S. P. Huntington, "The Clash of Civilizations?" in *Foreign Affairs* (Summer 1993): 26.

37. Ibid., 31.

38. Ibid.

39. Ibid., 40.

40. Copyright 1926 by Alfred A. Knopf, Inc., and renewed by Langston Hughes. Reprinted from *Selected Poems of Langston Hughes*, by permission of Alfred A. Knopf, Inc.

41. A. J. Kraemer, "A Cultural Self-Awareness Approach to Improving Intercultural Communication Skills," ERIC ED 079 213 (April 1975): 2.

42. Hanvey, *An Attainable Global Perspective*, 12.

43. W. B. Gudykunst and Y. Y. Kim, *Communicating with Strangers: An Approach to Intercultural Communication* (Reading, MA: Addison-Wesley, 1984), 230.

44. Ibid., 231.

45. Ibid.

46. D. Dufty, S. Sawkins, N. Pickard, J. Power, and A. Bowe, *Seeing It Their Way: Ideas, Activities, and Resources for Intercultural Studies* (London, England: Reed Education, 1976).

47. Ibid.

48. Wolsk, "An Experience Centered Curriculum: Exercises in Personal and Social Reality," UNESCO (Paris), ERIC ED 099 269, 1974; and see also D. Casteel, *Cross-Cultural Models of Teaching: Latin American Example* (Gainesville, FL: University of Florida Press, 1976).

49. H. C. Triandis, "Culture Training, Cognitive Complexity and Interpersonal Attitudes," in *Cross-Cultural Perspectives on Learning*, eds. R. W. Brislin, S. Bochner, and W. J. Lonner (New York: John Wiley & Sons, 1975), 70–71.

50. F. Rivera, "The Teaching of Chicano History," in *The Chicanos: Mexican American Voices*, eds. E. W. Ludwig and J. Santibanez (New York: Penguin, 1971), 200.

51. M. Miles, *Annie and the Old One*, illustr. Peter Parnall (Boston: Little, Brown, 1971).

52. B. Dodds Stanford and K. Amin, *Black Literature for High School Students* (Urbana, IL: National Council of Teachers of English, 1978), 10.

53. Ibid., 11–12.

54. See R. M. Young, "Racist Society, Racist Science," *Multicultural Teaching*, 5, no. 3 (Summer 1987): 43–50. See also D. Bell, *And We Are Not Yet Saved: The Elusive Quest for Racial Justice* (New York: Basic Books, 1987).

55. L. Anderson, *Schooling and Citizenship in a Global Age: An Exploration of the Meaning and Significance of Global Education* (Bloomington, IN: Social Studies Development Center, 1979).

56. Ibid., 438–439.

57. Ibid., 447.

58. Ibid., 464.

59. This list is based in part on Dufty et al., *Seeing It Their Way*, 149.

60. This lesson plan has been field tested in two classes of eleventh-grade American Literature students at a large suburban high school in Indiana.

61. Hanvey, *An Attainable Global Perspective*, 6.

62. L. Anderson, "Some Propositions about the Nature of Global Studies," Northwestern University, u.d. ms., 6.

63. Ibid.

64. D. Lasswell "Multiple Loyalties in a Shrinking World" (paper presented at the National Council of the Social Studies conference, Washington, DC, November 29, 1968). Also see G. Allport, *The Nature of Prejudice* (Reading, MA: Addison-Wesley, 1979).

65. Hanvey, *An Attainable Global Perspective*, 7.

66. Ibid., 13.

67. Ibid.

68. Anderson, "Some Propositions," 6.

69. Hanvey, *An Attainable Global Perspective*, 22.

70. R. Joyce and A. M. Nicholson, "Imperatives for Global Education," in *Schooling for a Global Age*, ed. J. A. Becker (New York: McGraw-Hill, 1979).

71. Ballard, *Monsoon: A Novel to End World Hunger* (Marina Del Rey, CA: New Horizons, 1986).

72. B. A. Reardon (ed.), *Teaching for Global Responsibility* (New York: Teachers College Press, 1988).

73. Ibid., 24.

74. Ibid., 81–82.

75. See, for example, "Education for Racial Equality under Attack," *Multicultural Teaching*, 5, no. 3 (Summer 1987): 4–7; and C. Grant and C. Sleeter, "The Literature on Multicultural Education: Review and Analysis," *Educational Review*, 37, no. 2 (1985): 97–118.

76. See, for example, R. D. Hess and F. M. Newman, "Political Socialization in the Schools," *Harvard Education Review*, 38 (Summer 1968): 528–545; B. Seasholes, "Political Socialization of Blacks: Implications for Self and Society," in *Black Self-Concept*, eds. J. A. Banks and J. D. Grambs (New York: McGraw-Hill, 1972); L. H. Ehman, "Political Socialization and the High School Social Studies Curriculum" (Ph.D. diss., University of Michigan, 1970); and C. Bennett Button, "Political Education and Minority Youth," in *New Views of Children and Politics*, ed. R. G. Niemi (San Francisco: Jossey-Bass, 1974). See also R. Muller, *New Genesis, Shaping a Global Spirituality* (Garden City, NY: Doubleday, 1982) and N. van Oudenhoven, "Act Locally, Think Globally: Some Comments on Prosocial Behavior, Information Processing and Development Education" (New York: UNICEF, Information Division, "Development Education Paper No. 24," September 1982).

77. B. Seasholes, "Political Socialization of Blacks: Implications for Self and Society," in *Black Self-Concept*, Banks and Grambs, eds.

78. J. A. Banks, *An Introduction to Multicultural Education*, 2nd ed. (Boston: Allyn & Bacon, 1999), 31.

Index

Photo Credits

p.1, Jim Cummins/Getty Images-Taxi; p. 16, 32, 80, 87, 126, 219, 242, 287, 306 Christine I. Bennett; p. 24, Mark Richards/PhotoEdit; p. 47, Courtesy of Deborah S. Hutton; p. 107, Jeff Greenberg/PhotoEdit; p. 131 Richard Lord/PhotoEdit, Inc.; p. 159 Jeff Greenberg/PhotoEdit Inc.; 166 Kayte M. Deioma/PhotoEdit, Inc.; p. 190, Lindfors Photography; p. 209, EyeWire Collection/PhotoDisk/Getty Images; p. 221 Laimate Druskis/Pearson Education/PH College; p. 250, 390 David Young-Wolff/PhotoEdit; p. 261, courtesy of M. Daub; p. 263, E. Zuckerman/PhotoEdit; p. 278, Brian Smith Photography; 315, Karen Mancinelli/Pearson Learning Photo Studio; p. 370 Silver Burdett Ginn; p.372, Bob Daemmrich Photography, Inc.